THE BUTTERFLIES OF INDIA, BURMAH AND CEYLON

THE BUTTERFLIES OF INDIA, BURMAH AND CEYLON

G. F. L. MARSHALL, LIONEL DE NICEVILLE

GYAN

Published by

Gyan Publishing House
5, Ansari Road
Daryaganj, New Delhi-110002
Phone: 011-47034999, 9811692060
E-mail: books@gyanbooks.com

Distribution Network
gyanbooks.com
India, USA, Canada, UK, Australia

ISBN: 978-93-7097-013-7 (PB)

First Published, 1882

2nd Impression 2025

Printed at: Gyan Press, Delhi.

THE BUTTERFLIES OF INDIA, BURMAH AND CEYLON

Author G. F. L. MARSHALL, LIONEL DE NICEVILLE

FRONTISPIECE.

1 & 1 a. PAPILIO LAESTRYGONUM. 2 & 2 a. ÆMONA AMATHUSIA. 3 & 3a. ÆMONA PEALII.

Behari Lal Das del. J. W. M. direx.t West, Newman & Co. chr. lith.

THE BUTTERFLIES OF INDIA, BURMAH AND CEYLON.

A DESCRIPTIVE HANDBOOK OF ALL THE KNOWN SPECIES OF RHOPALOCEROUS LEPIDOPTERA INHABITING THAT REGION, WITH NOTICES OF ALLIED SPECIES OCCURRING IN THE NEIGHBOURING COUNTRIES ALONG THE BORDER; WITH NUMEROUS ILLUSTRATIONS.

BY

MAJOR G. F. L. MARSHALL, ROYAL ENGINEERS,

Fellow of the Zoological Society of London; and Member of the Asiatic Society of Bengal and of the British Ornithologists' Union:

AND

LIONEL DE NICÉVILLE,

Assistant in the Entomological Department, Indian Museum, Calcutta; and Member of the Entomological Society, London; and of the Asiatic Society, Bengal.

The Illustrations

DRAWN BY BABU GRIS CHUNDER CHUCKERBUTTY AND BABU BEHARI LALL DASS.

THE WOOD ENGRAVINGS BY GEORGE PEARSON.

THE AUTOTYPE PLATES BY THE AUTOTYPE COMPANY OF LONDON.

THE CHROMO-LITHOGRAPHS BY MESSRS. WEST, NEWMAN & CO.

Calcutta:

PRINTED AND PUBLISHED BY THE CALCUTTA CENTRAL PRESS CO., LD.,

5, COUNCIL HOUSE STREET.

1882.

"HOW MUCH KNOWLEDGE IS LOST BY THE SCATTERED FORMS IN WHICH IT IS USHERED INTO THE WORLD! HOW MANY SOLITARY STUDENTS SPEND HALF THEIR LIVES IN MAKING DISCOVERIES WHICH HAD BEEN PERFECTED A CENTURY BEFORE THEIR TIME, FOR WANT OF A CONDENSED EXHIBITION OF WHAT IS KNOWN!"

TO

HIS EXCELLENCY

The Most Honourable The Marquess of Ripon,

K.G., G.M.S.I., G.M.I.E., &c., &c.,

VICEROY AND GOVERNOR-GENERAL OF INDIA,

WHO HAS DEIGNED TO TAKE A KINDLY

INTEREST IN THE PROSECUTION OF THE WORK,

THIS BOOK

IS

BY PERMISSION

MOST RESPECTFULLY DEDICATED.

VOL. I.—Part I.

TABLE OF CONTENTS.

VOL. I.

NYMPHALIDÆ.

DANAINÆ, SATYRINÆ, ELYMNIINÆ, MORPHINÆ, ACRÆINÆ.

LIST OF ILLUSTRATIONS.

Part I.—DANAINÆ.

Part II.—SATYRINÆ; ELYMNIINÆ; MORPHINÆ; ACRÆINÆ.

GLOSSARY OF TECHNICAL TERMS.

Abdomen, the section of the body behind the thorax. See p. 10.

Abdominal Margin, the inner edge of the hindwing next the body. See p. 11.

Acuminate, angled or angular, in contradistinction to rounded. See Pl. XIII, *f.* 30, ♀, apex of forewing of *Cyllogenes suradeva.*

Acute, pointed, less than a right angle.

Adpressed. See "Appressed."

Aenescent, bronzed, (*ăēnĕus*, of bronze).

Anal, near or pertaining to the hinder end of the abdomen, (*ānus*, the fundament).

Anal Angle, the angle formed by the inner (or abdominal) with the outer margin in the hindwing. See p. 11 and Pl. I.

Anastomosing, the opening of one vessel or channel into another, (*αναστομουν*, to furnish with a mouth or opening).

Annular, in the form of a ring.

Annulations, rings, (*annŭlātus*, furnished with a ring).

Annulated, ringed.

Antennæ, long, slender appendages of the head. See p. 10 and Pl. I.

Anterior Margin, the fore margin of either wing. See p. 11 and Pl. I.

Apex, the tip or summit of either wing, where the anterior and outer margins meet. See p. 11 and Pl. I.

Apical, at or pertaining to the apex.

Appressed, pressed close, (*apprĭmĕre*, to press to).

Areolets, an obsolete term for the spaces between the nervules in the wings.

Articulation, connection by joints; one of the sections of a jointed series, (*artĭcŭlāre*, to divide into joints; *artĭcŭlus*, a little joint, a knuckle).

Atrophied, died away, withered, (*ἀτροφέω*, to have no food, to pine away).

Band, a broad, even stripe.

Basal, at or pertaining to the base.

Base, of the wings, the part at or near junction with the body.

Bifid, cleft in two; opening with a cleft, (*bĭfindĕre*, to cleave in two).

Bifurcate, having two prongs like a fork.

Bipupilled, with reference to an ocellus, having two central spots or pupils.

Blind Ocellus, an eye-like mark on the wing with the central spot wanting.

Blotch, a large, irregular marking.

Carinate, keeled, (*cărīna*, a keel).

Cartilaginous, tough, of the nature of gristle.

Caudal, at or pertaining to the tail, (*cauda*, a tail).

Caudate, tailed; furnished with an appendage like a tail.

Cell. See "Discoidal Cell;" also p. 11 and Pl. I. Also occasionally used with reference to the space between any two nervules or nervures.

Chalybeate, steely, (*chălybs*, steel).

Chrysalis. See p. 9.

Cilia, fine hair-like fringes, chiefly on outer margin of wing, (*cĭlia*, eyelashes).

Cinereous, ashy grey, (*cĭnis*, ashes).

Clavate, club-shaped, (*clāva*, a club).

Club, the knob at the tip of an antenna.

Cocoon, the case formed by many caterpillars in which to change into pupæ.

Common, when applied to markings as bands, fasciæ, &c., means that they extend to both wings.

Compressed, flattened from side to side, as if by lateral pressure, in contradistinction to depressed or flattened downwards.

Concave, curved inwards, as in the outer margin of forewing of *Cœlites epiminthia*, Pl. XIII, *f.* 31; or the scallops in the margin of hindwing of *Papilio læstrygonum*, *see* Frontispiece.

Confluent, running together, (*conflŭens*, flowing into).

Congeneric, belonging to the same genus.

Constricted, drawn together, or contracted so as to be narrower or smaller at certain points like a string of beads at the intervals between the beads, (*constrĭngĕre*, to draw tight, to strain).

Contiguous, touching joining, (*con*, with, *tangĕre*, to touch).

Convex, curved outwards, as in the inner margin of forewing of *Euplœa elisa*, ♂, Pl. VIII, *f.* 14.

Convergent, directed towards one point, (*con*, with; *vergĕre*, to incline).

Cordate, heart-shaped, (*cor*, the heart).

Coriaceous, leathery, (*cŏrĭum*, leather).

Corneous, horny, hard, (*cornū*, a horn).

Costa, the anterior or costal margin, (*costa*, a rib). See p. 11.

Costal, at or pertaining to the costa.

Coxa, the hip, the first joint (see Joint) of the leg from the body, projected downward. See p. 10 and Pl. I.

Crenated, having the edge regularly notched whether leaving rounded or angular projections, (*crena*, a notch).

Crenulated, diminutive of crenated, (*crenula*, a little notch).

Crepuscular, affecting the twilight, (*crĕpuscŭlum*, little night, dim, twilight).

Cretaceous, chalky, (*creta*, chalk).

Cupreous, coppery, (*cuprum*, copper).

Dentate, toothed; used to express the outline of a wing or marking when furnished with projections.

Denticulate, small-toothed, (*dentĭcŭlatus*, furnished with small teeth or prongs).

Diaphanous, transparent, pellucid, (διαφαίνειν, to let (*a thing*) be seen through).

Digoneutic, having two broods in the years, (δίς twice; γόνος, a begetting).

Dimorphism, presenting two different forms or appearances, (δίς, twice; μορφή, shape, form, appearance); thus when the sexes differ it is sexual dimorphism, and when the spring and autumn broods differ it is seasonal dimorphism.

Disc, a somewhat indefinite expression for a portion of the surface of the wing. See p. 12.

Discal, at or pertaining to the disc.

Discal Spaces, the spaces between the nervules on the disc.

Disco-cellular Nervules, the nervules closing the discoidal cell of the wing. See p. 11 and Pl. I.

Discoidal Cell, the part of the wing enclosed between the subcostal and median nervures and disco-cellular nervules. See p. 11.

Discoidal Interspaces, the spaces above the discoidal nervules. See p. 12.

Discoidal Nervules, the nervules extending from the disco-cellulars to the outer margin. See p. 11 and Pl. I.

Discoidal Streak, a streak within the discoidal cell.

Diurnal, pertaining to the day time, as opposed to nocturnal, (*dĭes*, a day).

Divaricated, spread asunder, (*divarĭcāre*, to stretch apart).

Dorsal, pertaining to the back; in butterflies, the upper surface of the thorax and abdomen, (*dorsum*, the back).

Duplex, two-fold; double, divided.

Emarginate, having the margin interrupted by a notch or segment apparently cut out. See inner margin of hindwing of *Epinephele davendra*, Pl. XV, *f.* 39, (*ē*, from or out of; *margo*, a margin).

Emitted, sent out, (*ēmitto*, I send forth).

Entire, used with reference to the wings, to signify that the outline is even and regular.

Erectile, capable of being erected or raised.

Exarticulate, having no joints.

Excised, cut out, (*ex*, out; *cædo*, I cut).

Exserted, protruded, (*exsĕro*, I put forth, or thrust out).

Exterior Margin, the margin of the wing furthest from the body. See p. 11 and Pl. I.

Falcate, hooked or bent like a sickle. See Pl. XII, *f.* 29; forewing of *Melanitis zitenius*, (*falx*, a sickle).

Family, an aggregate of allied genera.

Fascia, a band.

Fasciated, banded.

Femora, plural of femur.

Femur, the thigh; the apparent second joint (see Joint) of the leg of a butterfly, directed upwards. See p. 10 and Pl. I.

Ferruginous, dusky red, like iron rust, (*ferrūgo*, iron rust).

Filament, a thin thread-like appendage, (*fīlum*, a thread).

Filamentous, thread-like.

Filiform, thread-shaped, long, slender, and of equal thickness throughout.

Fimbriate, fringed, (*fimbrĭātus*, separated into shreds or filaments).

Flexuous, bending, winding, or tortuous, (*flexus*, a bending).

Folliculate, provided with glands, foldings or cavities, (*follĭcŭlus*, a small bag or sac).

Fuliginous, sooty, (*fūlīgo*, soot or lamp-black).

Fulgid, glittering, shining.

Fulvous, tawny, reddish yellow, the colour of a lion, (*fulvus*, tawny).

Furcate, forked, (*furca*, a fork).

Fuscescent, inclining to swarthy.

Fuscous, swarthy, dusky.

Fusiform, spindle-shaped; thick in the middle and fining down at each end, (*fūsus*, a spindle).

Geminated, double; united; used for expressing a pair of coalescing spots or ocelli. See Pl. XVII, *f.* 64, *Ypthima hyagriva*, underside, the ocelli of the hindwing are geminated; that on the forewing is bipupilled.

Genus, an aggregate of allied species.

Glabrous, smooth, (*glăber*, without hair).

Glaucous, silvery, bluish grey or pale bluish green, but always with a sheen, (γλαυκος, gleaming, bright, glancing).

Globose, spherical or nearly so, (*glŏbōsus*, rounded).

Granulated, with a rough surface; consisting of or resembling grains, (*grānum*, a small particle).

Hatched, closely marked with numerous thin transverse lines.

Haustellate, suctorial, living by suction, furnished with a haustellum or proboscis, (*haurio*, I draw up).

Haustellum, the proboscis. See p. 9 and Pl. I, (*haurio*, I draw up).

Heterocera, moths. See p. 7.

Hinder Margin, the outer margin. See p. 11.

Hirsute, coarsely hairy, (*hirsūtus*, rough, shaggy, bristly).

Hyaline, glassy, clear like glass, (ὑαλος, glass).

Imago, a butterfly, the perfect or last stage of the insect.

Imbricate, overlapping, (*imbrex*, a hollow tile) used in connection with the wing-scales.

Incised, cut into, clipped, (*incīdo*, I cut into).

Incrassate, thickened, becoming thicker, (*incrassāre*, to thicken).

Inner Margin. See p. 11 and Pl. I.

Inosculate, to join in mouth to mouth, (*osculor*, to kiss).

Interrupted, separated or abruptly broken through.

Interspace, the space between any two adjacent nervures or nervules in the wings.

Internal Area, the space between the submedian nervure and inner margin of forewing. See p. 12.

Internal Nervure, a small nervure at base of forewing, wanting in many butterflies. See p. 12.

Interno-median Area, the space between the median and submedian nervures. See p. 12.

Irides, plural of iris.

Iridescent, reflecting rainbow colours, (*īris*, a rainbow).

Iris, the ring in an ocellus or eye-like spot on the wings, usually bright-coloured, (*īris*, a rainbow).

Irrorated, specked, sprinkled with minute dots or marks, (*irrōrāre*, to bedew).

Joint, used in describing the leg or any jointed appendage to express the parts joined together, such as the "femur," "tibia," &c.

Labial, at or pertaining to the under lip, (*labium*, a lip).

Labial Palpi. See p. 9 and Pl. I.

Labium, the under lip. See p. 9.

Labral, at or pertaining to the upper lip, (*labrum*, a lip).

Labrum, the upper lip. See p. 9.

Lacinia, one of the divisions which form a fringe, (*lăcĭnĭa*, a lappet or flap).

Laciniate, fringed.

Laminæ, thin sheets or leaves.

Laminated, composed of a series of thin sheets one on another.

Lanceolate, gradually tapering towards one extremity, (*lancĕŏla*, a little lance).

Lateral, on or along the sides.

Larva, a caterpillar in Lepidoptera; the second stage of development in an insect.

Lepidoptera, the order to which both butterflies and moths belong; literally "scale-wings." See p. 7.

Limaciform, slug-shaped, (*līmax*, a slug).

Lobe, a rounded protuberance in form or outline.

Lobular, consisting of or furnished with lobes.

Lobulate, lobe-shaped.

Longitudinal, lengthwise, from head to tail of body, or from base to outer margin of wing.

Lunular, composed of lunules.

Lunule, a crescent-shaped spot, (*lūna*, the moon).

Luteous, yellowish, or saffron-yellow, (*lūteus*, dyed with the herb *lūtum*).

Macula, spot, stain, blot, blotch.

Macular, consisting of spots more or less coalescing. See p. 12.

Maculated, spotted.

Mandibulæ, the upper jaws, rudimentary and inconspicuous in butterflies.

Margaritaceous, pearly, (*margărīta*, a pearl).

Marginal, when applied to markings on the wings; at the *outer* edge.

Maxillæ, the under jaws; in butterflies developed into a long tube.

Maxillary, pertaining to the under jaws.

Maxillary Palpi, the palpi of the lower jaws.

Median Nervure, the central rib of the wing-frame, below the discoidal cell. See p. 11 and Pl. I.

Median Interspaces, the spaces between the branches of the median nervure.

Membranaceous, resembling a membrane, a thin expanded tissue, (*membrāna*, the skin that covers the vital parts of the body).

Membranous. See "Membranaceous."

Mesothorax, middle section of the thorax. See p. 10.

Metamorphōsis, change of form, or outward appearance, transformation; (μετά, implying change of condition, (μορφή, shape).

Metathorax, hindermost section of the thorax. See p. 10.

Mimetic, imitative, apt to imitate, (μιμεῖσθαι, to imitate). See p. 2.

Monogoneutic, having a single brood each year, (μονος, alone; γόνος, a begetting).

Nervule, a branch rib or veinlet of the framework of the wings. See p. 11.

Nervure, a main rib or vein of the framework of the wings. See p. 11.

Neuration, the arrangement of the nervures and nervules of the wings.

Obconic, inversely conical, the narrow end downwards.

Oblique, with reference to bands of colour on the wing, not perpendicular to the costa or axis of length.

Obovate, inversely ovate, the narrow end downwards.

Obsolete, almost disappeared, (*obsŏlētūs*, worn out, old, thrown off).

Obtuse, blunt at the extremity.

Ocellus, an eye-like spot on the wing consisting of one or more rings of different colours with a central spot.

Ochreous or **Ochraceous**, a pale dull yellow, (ὠχρός, pale yellow).

Olivaceous, olive coloured, or dark brownish green, (*ŏlīva*, an olive).

Oral, at or pertaining to the mouth (*ōs, ōris*, the mouth).

Osmeteria, scent-glands, (ὀσμή, a smell, a scent).

Ovate, shaped like an egg, with one end broader than the other, (*ōvum*, an egg).

Oviparous, egg bearing, (*ōvum*, an egg; *părĭo*, I bring forth).

Pagina, the surface of a wing; upper or under, (*pāgĭna*, a page).

Palpi, appendages of the maxillæ and labium; those of the latter or "labial palpi" are largely developed in butterflies. See p. 9 and Pl. I.

Papillæ, applied to the minute leaf-like projections at the end of the proboscis, (*păpilla*, a nipple).

Parenchyma, soft cellular tissue, (παρα, beside; ἐγκεῖν, to pour in).

Paronychia, appendages to the claw found in certain genera of butterflies; more or less triangular in form, membranaceous, hairy, sometimes so broad as almost to conceal the claw, sometimes narrow and almost linear, (παρα, beside; ὄνυξ, the nail).

Patagia, shoulder-plates, attached to the thorax just above the base of the fore-wings, (*pătăgium*, the edging on a Roman lady's tunic). See p. 10.

Patch, a large marking or extent of any colour.

Pectoral Legs, the forelegs of a caterpillar. See p. 8, (*pectus*, the breast).

Peduncle, a stem or stalk, (*pĕduncŭlus*, diminutive of *pes*, a foot).

Pellucid, transparent.

Piceous, pitchy, pitch-black, (*pĭcĕus*, made of pitch).

Pilose, hairy, (*pĭlus*, a hair).

Plumose, softly feathery, (*plūma*, a small soft feather; the downy part of a feather).

Polygoneutic, having several broods in the course of a year, (πολύς, many; γόνος, a begetting).

Porrect, projected forwards, as opposed to erect, (*porrectus*, stretched out, extended).

Posterior Angle, the hinder angle of the forewing. See p. 11 and Pl. I.

Posterior Margin, the outer margin of the wing, or that furthest from the body. See p. 11.

Prædiscoidal Cell, a small space at base of hindwing, closed by a slender nervule connecting the costal and subcostal nervures. See p. 11.

Precostal Nervure, a short nervure at the base of the hindwing. See p. 11.

Primary, or **Primaries**, a term used by some authors to express the forewing.

Proboscis, a trunk or snout. See Pl. I.

Process, a protuberance, or projecting part.

Produced, lengthened out, elongated.

Prolegs, the fleshy hindlegs of caterpillars See p. 8.

Prothoracic, at or pertaining to the prothorax.

Prothorax, the front segment of the thorax nearest the head. See p. 10.

Pterygodes. See "Tegulæ," and p. 10, (πτέρυξ, a wing; εἶδος, shape).

Pubescent, downy, finely hairy.

Pulvillus, an appendage to the base of the claws, sometimes elongate and jointed, sometimes minute, and often wanting altogether, (*Pulvillus*, a little cushion).

Pupa, a chrysalis.

Pupil, a spot in the central part of an ocellus.

Pyriform, pear-shaped, (*pyrum* or *pĭrum*, a pear).

Quadrate, squared, shaped like a square, (*quadrum*, a square).

Radial, a term applied to the discoidal nervules. See p. 11 and Pl. I.

Recumbent, reclining, settled down.

RECURVED, bent backwards, turned back, or curved in two directions like an S.

RÈTRACTILE, capable of being drawn back, (*re*, back ; *trăhĕre*, to draw).

RHOPALOCERA, butterflies or "club-horns." See p. 7.

SAC, a small bag or pouch.

SAGITTATE, arrow-shaped, (*săgitta*, an arrow).

SCALLOPED, having the margin cut out with concave segments of circles.

SCENT POUCH, an organ attached to the wing or other part of the body of the males of some genera, secreting odours.

SCUTELLUM, a small triangular portion of the mesothorax, (*scūtum*, a shield).

SEASONAL DIMORPHISM, having the autumn or summer broods differing from the spring brood. See p. 2.

SECONDARY or SECONDARIES, a term used by some authors to express the hindwing.

SEGMENT, a division of the body, (*sĕco*, I cut).

SEMIHYALINE, somewhat glassy. See "Hyaline."

SERICEOUS, silky, (*sērĭcus*, silken).

SERIES, a line or row; generally of spots on the wings.

SERPENTINE, obscure green, or rich oil-green of various shades ; like the mineral serpentine.

SERRATED, notched, (*serra*, a saw).

SETÆ, bristles, (*sēta*, a bristle).

SETOSE, bristly.

SHOT, glossed with a surface colour visible only in certain lights.

SINUATE, wavy, (*sīnus*, a curve).

SINUOUS, wavy. See "Sinuate."

SPACE, the area between two nervures or nervules or a nervure or nervule and the margin.

SPATULAR, shaped like a spattle, a roundish end with a narrow linear base, (*spatula*, a spattle).

SPATULATE, See "Spatular."

SPECIES, a group of individuals presumably descended from the same parental stock.

SPINOUS, furnished with spines.

SPINNERET, a small perforated organ through which a caterpillar emits its silk.

SPIRACLE, an aperture, a round or narrow opening on the surface of the body used for breathing, (*spīrăcŭlum*, an air-hole).

SQUAMOSE, full of scales, (*squāma*, a scale).

SQUAMOUS, scaly.

STEMMATIC, a term applied to the simple eyes of an insect, which are placed on the crown of the head, and are scarcely visible ; not to be confounded with the compound eyes, which are large and protruding, and which are referred to when the eyes are mentioned, unless the stemmatic eyes are specially indicated, (*stemma*, a wreath ; anything to crown with).

STREAK, a narrow stripe.

STRIA. See "Striga."

STRIATED, marked with striæ, or fine very short lines.

STRIDULATION, with insects the noise produced in some species by friction of the external organs, (*strīdeo*, I creak, buzz, rattle).

STRIGA, a streak, (*strĭngere*, to scrape). Generally a very short streak.

SUB, as a prefix in composition used to denote near to or approaching to, or somewhat, (implying diminution), but *not* under.

SUBANAL, near the anal region ; usually applied to that of the hindwing.

SUBAPICAL, near the apical region. See "Apical."

SUBCORIACEOUS, somewhat leathery. See "Coriaceous."

SUBCOSTAL AREA, the space between the costal and subcostal nervures. See p. 12.

SUBCOSTAL NERVURE, the rib of the framework of the wing bounding the discoidal cell on the upper side. See p. 11.

SUBCOSTAL NERVULES, the branches of the subcostal nervure. See p. 11.

SUBDIAPHANOUS, somewhat transparent. See "Diaphanous."

SUFFUSED, clouded or obscured, tinged, (*suffundĕre*, to pour through ; to overspread).

SUBFOLLICULATE, somewhat glandular. See "Folliculate."

SUBMARGINAL, near to the margin, usually the outer margin.

SUBMEDIAN NURVURE. See p. 12 and Pl. I.

SUBULATE, awl-shaped, narrow, narrowing to a point from a broadish base, (*sūbŭla*, an awl).

SUTURAL AREA, the posterior or inner-marginal area where the wings overlap, (*sūtūra*, a seam).

SYNONYM, a name that has fallen into disuse from any cause.

TARSUS, the fourth apparent joint (see JOINT) of the leg in the perfect insect. See p. 10 and Pl. I.

TAIL, a long projection from the outer margin of the hindwing; also applied to the anal extremity of the body.

TEGULÆ, shoulder-plates on the thorax at the bases of the forewings, (*tēgŭla*, a tile). See "Patagia" and p. 10.

TENTACULA, a thread-like or filiform appendage.

TESTACEOUS, shell-like, (*testa*, a shell).

TETRAPOD, four-footed, applied to butterflies having the forelegs imperfect, (τέσσαρες, four; πους, a foot).

THORAX, the middle section of the body to which all the limbs are attached. See p. 10.

TIBIA, the apparent third joint (see JOINT) of the leg in the perfect insect. See p. 10 and Pl. I.

TIPPETS. See "Tegulæ" and "Patagia;" also p. 10.

TRACHEÆ, the respiratory organs or system of tubes for the admission of air to the viscera.

TRANSVERSE, as applied, to markings on the wing means in the direction of the breadth of the wing. See p. 12.

TRIARTICULATE, three-jointed (*trēs*, three; *artĭcŭlus*, a little joint).

TRIFID, three-cleft, split into three points, (*trēs*, three; *findĕre*, to cleave).

TRIFURCATE, three-forked, branching into three directions, (*trēs*, three; *furca*, a fork).

TROCHANTER, the joint between the coxa and the femur. See p. 10.

TRUNCATE, cut off, or appearing as if cut off at the top, (*truncus*, maimed, cut short).

TRUNK. See "Proboscis."

TUBERCLE, a small warty projection or knob, (*tūber*, a hump or knob).

TUBERCULATE, furnished with tubercles.

UNGUES, claws, (*unguis*, a nail or claw).

UNDERSIDE, the surface exposed when the butterfly's wings are closed.

UNDULATE, wavy, (*unda*, a wave).

UNICOLOROUS, of one uniform colour.

UPPERSIDE, the surfaces in contact when the butterfly's wings are closed.

VEINS, the main ribs of the frame-work of the wings. See "Nervures."

VEINLETS. See "Nervules."

VILLOSE, very shaggy with soft hairs, covered with fine hairs, (*villus*, shaggy hair).

VILLOUS, hairy.

VIOLACEOUS, inclining to violet; pale violet.

VITTA, used to signify a short streak, (*vitta*, a ribbon, fillet).

VITTIFORM, shaped like a Vitta.

PREFACE.

—o—

INDIA, the land of sunshine, is a land of Butterflies; for, though in the arid plains of the north insect-life languishes during the dry months, it revives marvellously when the periodic rains set in; and in the moister parts of the country, especially to the east and south, and in the warm valleys of the hilly regions, the amazing numbers of Butterflies and other beautiful insects cannot but strike the most unobservant. In one of his charming essays on tropical nature, Professor A. R. Wallace has remarked that, although in tropical countries individual flowers attain to a size and brilliancy of colouring unknown in temperate climates, it is merely in the individual flower, and not in general effect, that the products of tropical climes excel. There is nothing in tropical landscapes, for instance, that can compare with the heather and gorse of our own country, or with the gorgeous carpeting of the alpine valleys, ever moist with the melting snows. But in insect-life it is otherwise; both in size and beauty of individuals, and in prolific luxuriance of numbers, the tropics easily bear off the palm; the largest and most beautiful of European Butterflies sink into insignificance beside the *Ornithoptera*, *Morpho*, and *Thaumantis* of the tropics; while, perhaps, few sights in nature are more strangely beautiful to the traveller in these Eastern valleys than the patches of damp sand which may be found in torrent-beds in the forests literally carpeted with Butterflies of every hue, closely packed together, busily inbibing the moisture from the sand, and, again, as startled by the approach of an intruder, they rise expanding into a cloud of gorgeous colours of every hue. The difficulty in securing rare species is, in such localities, literally the difficulty of singling them out of a crowd.

The large size, the quaint shapes, and the dazzling brilliancy of the colouring of many of the Indian Butterflies have made them favourite objects of observation and often of collection; but, though collections are frequently made or purchased, comparatively little has been done here towards investigating the life-history of these beautiful creatures, or towards improving the opportunities offered by such a study of gaining light on the scientific questions and problems of zoology.

The study of Entomolgy is not merely an interesting recreation for those who can find leisure and opportunity to pursue it, but, even when restricted to Butterflies only, it offers a field for scientific enquiry of the highest importance, in connection especially with the origin of species and other cognate questions. Putting aside the various stages of egg, caterpillar, and chrysalis, through which all Butterflies pass, and in which opportunities for study are ample, the perfect insect, as it emerges from the chrysalis, exhibits variations at least as numerous and important as those of other classes of living organisms, while the short duration of its life, and the quickly succeeding generations, offer facilities for tracing the course of such variations, and thus deducing the causes which govern them, perhaps unrivalled in the whole field of nature. These variations, though possibly traceable ultimately to the same causes, may be grouped under several heads. It must not be forgotten that variety is in a certain sense universal, for no two individuals are really absolutely alike; but numerous individuals are to be found so closely resembling each other that, to the naked eye, no difference is traceable; or, if traceable, the differences are so slight as to leave no room for doubt, even if other evidence were wanting, that the individuals are derived from the same parental stock; or, in other words, belong to the same pecies. It this close similarity of individuals were constant in each species, there would be no difficulty in discriminating and identifying insects, though, at the same time, the scientific value of the study would be largely reduced ; but it is not so. First we find that in some species the sexes are differentiated—the females differing from the males either in colour or style of markings, and even in form and outline of the wings, these differences being constant in each sex. Again, we find that in different climates Butterflies, apparently the same in general character, present constant differences in colour or style of marking of more or less importance, but frequently sufficient to justify the description of each form under a separate name. Again, in different localities, even where the differences of climate are inappreciable, such as notably the various islands of an archipelago, and in a lesser degree disconnected valleys of a mountain range, the Butterflies of each locality often present constant and well marked differences, particularly in the size and extent of markings, thus forming what have been termed "geographical" varieties in contradistinction to "climatic" varieties ; and yet, again, we have the most interesting and important variation of all occurring among Butterflies which have two or more broods in the year ; and in which the summer and autumn broods differ from the spring brood more or less, sometimes so widely in colour and markings that, until the question was conclusively set at rest by breeding Butterflies of the one type from the eggs of Butterflies of the other, the two forms were described and universally accepted as representing two distinct species.

Thus we have "sexual," "climatic," "geographic," and "seasonal" variations, each of which can be referred more or less confidently to known external causes ; but, in addition to these, the study of the subject is complicated by individual variations, which appear to be quite irrespective of external conditions ; such variations are exhibited in different species in different degrees, or possibly the tendency to vary may pass through more or less active or dormant stages at different epochs of the history of each group. At the present time some species, notably among the *Junonias*, are wonderfully constant to the type ; others, again, differ so universally among themselves that scarcely any two specimens, even from the same locality, are alike. Of such variations the under-surfaces of the wings in *Melanitis leda* and *M. ismene*, and in the great "oak-leaf" Butterflies of the genus *Kallima*, are noteworthy instances ; also the numbers and size of the ocelli in many genera of the *Satyrinæ* : and, again, instead of a single typical form, with minor differences in each individual, we sometimes find, as in the case of *Papilio polytes* or *P. memnon*, that there are several distinct types, described by the earlier authors as distinct species, but which in reality spring promiscuously from the same stock—a single batch of the eggs laid by a single female having been found to produce two or more of the different forms. And, lastly, we find that specimens aberrant from the type occur singly and casually here and there from time to time, and coexisting in the same localities with specimens of the normal form. It may easily be conceived that among insects with such manifold tendencies to variation and such brief periods of existence, the clue to the laws which govern such developments may most readily be found.

The phenomenon of "mimicry," too, is deserving of the closest scientific observation. One of the earliest puzzles met with by the observer of Butterflies lies in finding males and females in company, apparently belonging not only to different species, but different genera, and even families ; but closer examination reveals that the female in reality belongs to the same species as the male, although its coloration and markings are excellent imitations of a totally different Butterfly, generally of a much commoner Butterfly, and almost always of a Butterfly less subject than its own species to destruction by birds and reptiles. The subject is too extensive to enter on here, but it is one that should never be lost sight of in investigating the life-history of insects.

The field for observation offered by the British Indian Empire is as varied as it is vast. We have every climate, from the eternal snows to the tropics—and all the most interesting phenomena of Entomology may here be studied in life—yet little has been done beyond attaching a name to each different form or species; and even in this preliminary ground-work the greater portion of the labour has been carried on, not by Englishmen, but by foreigners. The larger number of our Indian species have been named by French, German or Russian naturalists, while not one per cent. have been named by English naturalists in this country. The few among our countrymen out here who have taken up the study have worked under difficulties sufficient to dishearten the most ardent student; and the usual result has been that their laboriously collected observations and notes have either been lost altogether, or rendered comparatively useless owing to difficulties in identification of the species observed, or to omission of some detail, the importance of which could only be known to skilled zoologists.

The reason for this state of affairs is obvious. No attempt has hitherto been made to bring the study of the science within the reach of the public in this country. The published information regarding Indian Butterflies is scattered over numerous works, many of which are out of print, and are either not to be bought at all, or else only at prices beyond the means of private individuals. The older books deal with Butterflies from all parts of the world, and the more recent papers regarding the Butterflies of particular localities, such as the "Butterflies of Malacca," by Butler, the "Butterflies of Tenasserim," of the "Andamans and Nicobars," of "Bengal," of the "North-West Himalayas," &c., by Moore, consist of bare and incomplete lists of names, with descriptions of a few new species; and, while amply fulfilling the special object with which they were published, are of no use whatever to the general public, except to the few who, having access to good museums and libraries, have at hand the means of supplementing for themselves the information given.

It has been well nigh impossible under such circumstances for collectors of Butterflies in this country to name their own specimens, and our knowledge of Indian Butterflies has been limited to the contents of such of the more important collections as have been from time to time sent to the Museums of Europe for study and description; but the contents of the smaller collections have, for the most part, been left unrecorded. It is probable that there are, comparatively, few species in this country still unnamed; but that something in this direction still remains to be done is proved by the fact that, since it became known about a year and a half ago that this book was under preparation, nearly fifty new species have been discovered by naturalists in this country—a number far exceeding that of all the species hitherto named by working naturalists in India.

But in the matter of scientific observation of habits and life-history we repeat that very little has been done. To get this we must be mainly independent of foreign help—we must depend on our own exertions. No one collector, however zealous, and no single observer, however accurate and persevering, can exhaust the subject even in a single locality. It is by the combined efforts of the many that progress will be secured. The study in this country has hitherto, as we have shown, lacked the stimulus and interest that a knowledge of the nomenclature, and a record of what had previously been discovered, would have supplied; and it is to supply this want, and to secure the co-operation of all those who take an interest in the matter, that a descriptive handbook is required. It has been no small encouragement to us to find that, in the comparatively short time that has elapsed since this work was commenced, we have received hearty sympathy and help from naturalists all over the country, who have not only redoubled their exertions in collecting and observing, but have generously assisted us with specimens, notes, and valuable advice, while several gentlemen, not previously interested in the subject, have undertaken to collect in various localities. Professor J. Wood-Mason, Deputy Superintendent of the Indian Museum, Calcutta, has also in view of this publication thoroughly re-arranged and investigated the national collection, and published numerous papers and local lists of the greatest value, besides assisting us most kindly in discriminating the species. Owing to his exertions the national collection has been more than doubled since this book was begun.

From Burma we have received specimens of almost every species hitherto recorded; also of numerous species new to the country, and of several new to science, through the kindness of Captains C. T. Bingham and C. H. E. Adamson, and Messrs. Eugene Oates and T. C. Hill. To Captain Bingham's exertions the discovery of *Zophoëssa dura*, *Neope bhima*, *Penthima binghami*, *Papilio claræ*, the male of *Zeuxidia masoni*, the female of *Thaumantis louisa*, and many other new and interesting forms is due. From the Andamans and Nicobars, Colonel T. Cadell, V.C., and Mr. A. R. de Roepstorff have kindly sent numerous specimens, including many species new to science. We have also been aided from Eastern Manipur by Mr. A. O. Hume; from Assam by Mr. C. Donovan and Surgeon-Major G. R. Johnson; from Sikkim by Messrs. Otto Möller and W. Davison; from Western Bengal by Messrs. W. E. Brooks and C. J. Marshall; from Naini Tal by Mr. E. T. Atkinson; from the North-West Himalayas by Lieutenant-Colonel A. M. Lang, R.E.; Mrs. Deane, General Macintyre, Mr. Robert Ellis in Pangi; Mr. A. Grahame Young in Kulu; Major C. H. T. Marshall in Chumba; the Rev. A. W. Heyde in Ladak; and Major J. Biddulph in Gilgit; from Agra by Mr. C. A. R. Crommelin; from Sind by Major C. Swinhoe; from Bombay by Mr. E. H. Aitken; from Poona and Ratnagiri by Mr. G. Vidal; from the Wynaad by Mr. Rhodes Morgan; from Travancore by Messrs. Ferguson and Bourdillon. To Mr. Ferguson, especially, we owe the discovery of *Mycalesis oculus*, and of that remarkable insect *Parantirrhœa marshalli*; and from Ceylon we have been assisted by the Hon'ble F. Mackwood;—to all these gentlemen our thanks are due for the welcome aid afforded us in this laborious task, but most of all we are indebted to Captain C. T. Bingham, who not only is a most skilful collector, but most generously has placed at our disposal the whole results of his labours.

This book does not attempt a life-history of each or any of the insects. The time has not arrived for such a work; the details required for a life-history cannot be gathered until a knowledge of the nomenclature is far more widely diffused. It is simply designed as a handbook of reference, as complete as possible in itself, for the convenience of naturalists in the field who have no access to libraries. Where necessary full extracts from other works, not usually available, are given; and where possible and advisable, the description of species are given in the words of the original describers, supplemented by any further details needed to complete them. For the genera the admirable descriptions by Westwood (in the Genera of Diurnal Lepidoptera) have been followed as closely as possible.

The book will comprise detailed descriptions of every genus and species known to occur within the limits of India, British Burma and Ceylon; and short descriptions will be added in smaller type of species from neighbouring countries on the border, such as Malacca, Siam, Yunan, Thibet, South Turkestan, Afghanistan and Beluchistan, which, though not yet recorded from within Indian limits, may very probably subsequently be found to occur within our border.

The absence of coloured illustrations is a great drawback, especially to beginners; but coloured illustrations are expensive; and, as the great object in issuing the book at all is to give it as wide a circulation as possible, it has been thought expedient to confine the illustrations for the most part to uncoloured engravings, and to restrict the number to what will be sufficient to indicate the more typical forms and to supplement the written descriptions. At least one illustration of each genus, and generally of each sub-genus, will be given, as mere description fails to convey to any, except to the practised Entomologist, a sufficiently clear conception of the forms, especially in outline; and a glance at the plates will usually be sufficient to guide the beginner as to the place where the description of any particular species may be found.

After the book is published, and if the circulation it attains appears to warrant it, coloured illustrations will be published in continuation.

No pains have been spared to render this hand-book as complete as possible: and, in judging of the result, we trust that the public will remember the difficulties under which works of this nature are necessarily undertaken in this country: and that the compilation has been carried on, not in the quiet and leisure of a studio, but in the intervals of a busy official life.

INTRODUCTION.

DANAIS *(Salatura)* GENUTIA, Cramer.

Class.—INSECTA.
Order.—LEPIDOPTERA.
Sub-order.—RHOPALOCERA.

THE insects of this order are distinguished from other insects by their having the wings more or less densely covered with minute scales of various colours, whence the name LEPIDOPTERA, (λεπις, a scale ; πτερόν, a wing).

The order, which comprises an enormous number of different species, is divided into two sub-orders—HETEROCERA, or Moths, and RHOPALOCERA, or Butterflies : the insects of the latter sub-order are alone treated of in this book. The distinction between the sub-orders is primarily based on the structure of the antennæ as expressed in the terms Rhopalocera (ῥόπαλον, a club ; κέρας, a horn), and Heterocera (ἕτερος, different ; κέρας, a horn), the antennæ of Butterflies being more or less uniform in structure and clubbed at the tip, while those of Moths exhibit great variations of structure among different genera and species, and even in the different sexes of the same species.

But there are several other characteristics by which Butterflies can generally be distinguished from Moths. Butterflies are never nocturnal in their habits. Some few species fly at twilight, but with very few exceptions they fly only in the day-time, and, as a rule, are active on the wing only during sunshine ; the eyes of Butterflies too are larger as a rule and more prominent than those of Moths : again the antennæ of Butterflies, which are straight, filamentous and more or less clubbed at the tip, are always held erect or extended in front of the head, and are never either twisted or folded away by the insect. On the other hand the antennæ of Moths are highly flexible, and during repose are almost invariably folded backwards along the body and concealed under the wings. Again, the division between the thorax and the abdomen is strongly defined in Butterflies, while in most Moths the division is inconspicuous ; and, lastly, Butterflies may be distinguished by the position of the wings in repose being, among them, more or less erect over the back and never folded close along the body ; or, in other words, Butterflies when in repose usually exhibit the under-surface of the wing ; Moths in repose have only the upper surface visible.

None of these distinctive features taken singly will always suffice to distinguish a Butterfly from a Moth ; perhaps the surest test of all is the erect posture or otherwise of the antennæ. If the antennæ are folded under the wings in repose it may be at once safely concluded that the insect is not a Butterfly, even though it may fly by day, or hold its wings partially erect. In some genera of Butterflies the club at the end of the antenna is almost obsolete, but still the antennæ are straight, erect and never folded back or concealed. On the other hand, many of the Moths are day-fliers, many have slender bodies, and in many the shape of the wings and general appearance present great similarities to the appearance of Butterflies, but in such cases the structure of the antennæ will serve to determine the affinities.*

Butterflies, as well as Moths, are oviparous, and pass through four stages of development—the egg, the caterpillar, the chrysalis, and the imago, or perfect insect. The usual extreme period of existence extends to one year, during which all four stages are accomplished ; but in numerous instances, especially in warm climates, where the winter is short and the summer long, one or more intermediate broods occur, in fact in some cases there is a continuous succession of broods throughout the year, while occasionally, under unfavourable circumstances, the egg or the chrysalis may lie dormant through more than one season.

The EGGS of Butterflies are deposited either singly on in groups, on the leaves or bark of trees as a rule ; sometimes on the calyx of a flower, as in some of the *Lycænidæ*, but always on or near to the food-plant of the caterpillar. In form and pattern the eggs are strangely diversified, far more so than among birds ; but for each species the eggs are uniform in shape, colour, and structure, so that the species to which any particular egg belongs can easily be identified : at the same time the eggs of closely allied species often differ widely, so that among Butterflies the eggs afford little or no indication of the affinities of the perfect insect. The laying season varies according to the habits of the species—some kinds passing the winter or "hybernating" in the egg state, some as caterpillars, some as chrysalises, and some, again, in the perfect state.

The CATERPILLARS of Butterflies are usually elongate, and more or less cylindrical in shape, (see Plate II). They consist of thirteen segments, the first of which forms the head and is furnished with twelve microscopic eyes, situated near the mouth, six on each side, and generally arranged in a circle. These eyes are highly convex, only enabling the caterpillar to see objects when close against its mouth ; the head varies in shape very much, and is generally furnished with two short, sometimes retractile, antennæ, and two feelers, which usually emerge one on each side from the apex of the underlip, and appear to correspond with the labial palpi of the perfect insect ; and occasionally with other protuberances of various kinds. The mouth is furnished with a pair of strong, horny, toothed jaws or *mandibulæ*, working sideways, and a lower pair of jaws of a softer consistency termed *maxillæ* ; these latter are furnished with a pair of small jointed organs corresponding to the palpi. Near the summit of the labium or underlip, is a small orifice through which issues the silken thread which caterpillars produce. The legs are sixteen in number, arranged in pairs on the second, third, fourth, seventh, eighth, ninth, tenth, and thirteenth segments ; the front three pairs, or the true legs, which correspond to the legs in the perfect insect, are horny, jointed, and terminate in a strong claw ; the last five pairs are very different in structure, being wide, fleshy and broadened at the base, and are termed "prolegs" or "claspers" ; the last pair of claspers are termed the "anal" claspers, and the remaining four pairs the "abdominal" claspers. The true legs in front are also sometimes called the "pectoral" legs. Caterpillars are also provided with eighteen "spiracles" or breathing holes arranged in rows along their sides—one row on each side of nine spiracles, one to each segment, except the first, third, fourth, and thirteenth, on which they are wanting. These spiracles are the mouths of air-tubes which constitute the respiratory system. Besides these regular structural features, they are often furnished with remarkable appendages, (see Plate II). The caterpillars of *Athyma* and some other genera are provided with erect processes, more or less spiny towards the tip. Some caterpillars, such as those of *Adolias*, have lengthened procumbent appendages on each side, fringed with long hairs ;

* In some aberrant genera of American Moths the antennæ are clubbed. But no Indian Moths, so far as we know, exhibit this feature.

those of *Elymnias* and *Melanitis* have two lengthened appendages on the hinder segment and two short ones on the head; those of *Charaxes* have four projections on the head and two short ones on the hinder segment; in the *Hesperidæ* the head is usually large and the neck narrow, while in the *Pierinæ* the head is small. The outline, though typically cylindrical, varies from fusiform among the slug-like caterpillars of the *Lycænidæ*, to an almost uniform lengthened cylinder among the *Pierinæ*. Caterpillars are often nocturnal feeders, and escape observation by lying concealed during the day-time.

The CHRYSALISES too vary much in shape, colour and ornamentation, (see Plate II); the colour usually being adapted to that of the surface to which the chrysalis is attached. The only peculiarities on which it is necessary to touch in this short introductory notice, are in the matter of positions selected for transformation, and the methods of securing the chrysalis from disturbance during the state of torpor. There are five typical methods adopted for this purpose: first, the suspension of the chrysalis by the tail only from the underside of a leaf or twig or other object; this is the usual practice with the *Nymphalidæ*, (see Plate II, *Athyma leucothoë* and *Adolias lubentina*); second, the suspension of the chrysalis in a horizontal position, or with the head inclined upwards, attached by the tail and also by a thread passed round the middle of the body and secured at both ends: this position is adopted by many of the *Lycænidæ*, (see Plate II, *Amblypodia timoleon*); third, the suspension of the chrysalis by the tail vertically, head downwards, but girt in addition by a thread round the middle of the body: this method is of frequent occurrence among the *Pierinæ*, (see Plate II, *Hebomoia glaucippe*); fourth, the attachment of the chrysalis by the tail, but in an erect position with the head upwards, and further secured by threads, either passing round the middle of the body, or attached on either side: this is the usual posture among the *Papilionidæ*, (see Plate II, *Papilio polytes**); fifth, with the chrysalis free, but enclosed either in the rolled-up edge of a leaf, or between two or more small leaves drawn together by silky threads. This method is typical among the *Hesperidæ*, (see Plate II, *Ismene œdipodea*). In the genus *Parnassius* (*Papilionidæ*) the chrysalis is enclosed in a loose silky web on a leaf; the chrysalis of the "Grayling" (*Hipparchia semale*) is described by Newman as being placed beneath the surface of the soil, and there are doubtless many other exceptions; but the five postures and methods described above are typical of the five great divisions of Butterflies.

The IMAGO or perfect state is the most highly developed, and a knowledge of the structure of its various organs is essential to the comprehension of the divisions into families and genera. Plate I. shows the principal features, and explains the names, which have been used to describe the different parts. A careful study of this plate will render the descriptions of the species intelligible to the reader. The perfect insect has always four wings and six legs, the latter sometimes not all fully developed; the body is in three sections—the head, the thorax, and the abdomen; and the head is furnished with antennæ, eyes, and oral appendages. Butterflies derive their nourishment from liquid substances, and the structure of the mouth is adapted to this end. The under jaws are developed into a long flexible tube called the "proboscis" or "haustellum," which, when not in use, is curled up closely under the face; the under lip (or *labium*) is furnished with two processes, called the "labial palpi" or "palpi" (see Plate I.) projected forwards, or upwards, one on each side of the mouth; the upper jaws and upper lip (or *labrum*) are rudimentary and scarcely discernible.

The PALPI consist of three joints, the middle one usually the longest, the basal and terminal joints being often very short. They are covered with scales or hairs, varying much in length and texture. The very long hairs of the palpi are distinctive of the family *Satyrinæ*; they also vary much in size and form, and occasionally, as in *Libythea*, and in some of the *Lycænidæ*, are very largely developed; in some cases the palpi are separated throughout their length; in others they meet at the tip, forming a sort of beak in front of the head.

* The position shown in the figure of the chrysalis of *Papilio polytes* in Plate II, is not typical. The abdominal half of the chrysalis and the stem to which it is attached should be at least vertical, if not leaning slightly over; the upper half of the chrysalis extending outwards nearly horizontally.

The EYES of Butterflies are large, immovable, compound and convex ; sometimes smooth, sometimes hairy, and consist of a great number of separate lenses. Butterflies also are said to possess two extremely minute simple or "stemmatic" eyes, placed on the crown of the head and scarcely visible, but the existence of these latter has been disputed.

The ANTENNÆ, which project from the forehead between the eyes, are of moderate length, being from one-half to seven-eighths, usually about two-thirds, the length of the body, and consist of a great number of segments, which increase in diameter more or less gradually towards the tip ; the knob thus formed at the tip varies considerably in shape in different families, and affords useful distinctive characters. Typically the antennæ are straight, but in some genera they are hooked at the tip ; they are always erect and never concealed during repose.

The THORAX forms the middle part of the body between the head and the abdomen ; to it all the wings and legs are united, and it contains the muscles by which all the limbs are actuated. It is shorter than the abdomen, and consists of three segments, so closely united as to appear to form a single piece. The first nearest the head is called the *prothorax*, and bears the fore pair of legs ; the middle one, the *mesothorax*, which bears the middle pair of legs and the forewings ; and that nearest the abdomen, the *metathorax*, which bears the hindlegs and hindwings.

To the mesothorax, just above the wing joints, are attached a pair of triangular scales, like epaulets, which have been called "*tegulæ*" or "*patagia*" or "*pterygodes*" or "*tippets.*" The surface of the thorax is covered with hairs of greater or less density and length.

The ABDOMEN is united to the thorax by a narrow link. It consists of nine segments, and is of a softer consistency than the thorax : the only appendages to the abdomen which require notice at present are the large anal valves, which are found in the males of some species of *Papilionidæ.*

The LEGS are six in number, but in a large number of species the fore pair of legs is imperfect, unfitted for walking, and held drawn up close to the sides of the thorax, and partially concealed by its hairs, the Butterfly appearing as if it had only four legs. The characters of the legs are of great importance, and on the extent of development of the forelegs the primary divisions of Butterflies into families usually rests. The perfect leg consists of the following parts :—(1), the *coxa*, which is attached to the body, corresponds with the hip, and is directed vertically downwards ; (2), the short joint connecting the femur with the coxa, called the *trochanter*, is counted as the second section of the leg ; (3), the *femur*, which is jointed to the coxa, corresponds with the thigh, and is directed upwards ; (4), the *tibia* or shank, which is jointed to the femur, and directed downwards ; the joint between the tibia and femur being the most elevated point of the leg in repose ; (5), the *tarsus*, which is jointed to and directed in prolongation of the tibia ; the tarsus in all perfect legs consisting of five joints. The coxa and femur are often hairy, and in imperfect forelegs the tibia and tarsus are likewise often more or less densely fringed with hairs ; the tibia of the foreleg in *Papilionidæ* and *Hesperidæ* has a spur about the middle, which is present in no other family of Butterflies. The tibia of the hindleg has also one pair of moveable spines in most of the *Papilionidæ*, and two pairs in many of the *Hesperidæ*. The tarsus in the perfect leg is terminated by two claws, which are sometimes entire or simple, and sometimes bifid ; at the base of the claws the tarsus is also furnished in some families with other appendages, called *paronychia* and *pulvilli* (see Glossary of Terms) ; the development of these appendages when present varies a good deal in the different genera.

The WINGS are larger among Lepidoptera in proportion to the body than in any other order of insects, and among Butterflies form the most conspicuous parts of the whole insect. The usual shape of the forewing is triangular, and that of the hindwing rounded, but the outline, though usually similar in allied species and often affording specific and even generic characters, is subject to great variations. These variations often mark sexual distinctions, but occasionally individuals of the same species and sex differ widely in outline, as in the case of the females of

P. memnon, some of which have a large spatulate tail to the hindwing, while in others no sign of a tail is visible. The wings consist of a fine translucent membrane, permeated by a number of ribs, like the veins of a leaf or the rays of a fish's fin, and the whole covered more or less densely, both above and beneath, with tiny scales in which the colours of the wing lie. These ribs have been styled by various authors as "nervures" and "nervules," or "veins" and "venlets," or "rays." In this book the former terms are adopted, the *nervures* signifying the main ribs, and the *nervules*, the branches which they throw off. In describing the wing of a Butterfly (see Pl. I.), the junction of the wing with the body is called the *base* (A); the margin nearest the head from the base outwards is called the *costal margin*, or *costa*, or the *anterior margin* (A B); at the end of the costal margin, furthest from the body, is the *apex* (B); the margin furthest from the head from the base outwards is called the *inner* or *interior margin* (A C), and in the hindwing the *abdominal margin* (A D); at the end of the inner margin furthest from the body is the *hinder* or *posterior angle* (C), and in the hindwing the *anal angle* (D); and, lastly, the margin between the apex and the hinder angle is called in this book the *outer* or *exterior margin* (A C and C D); this latter margin has been termed also by some authors the *apical margin*. The term *hinder* (or *posterior*) *margin* has been used by authors with reference both to the outer and inner margins. In accordance with these terms the adjacent parts of the wing are referred to severally as the basal or sub-basal, costal or sub-costal, apical or sub-apical, anal or sub-anal, &c.—the prefix "sub" being used to denote "near to," as basal, at the base—sub-basal, near the base. When *the margin* alone is mentioned, as in describing marginal lines or rows of spots, the outer margin alone is signified. The wings are said to be *entire* when the margin is not serrated or incised in any way.

The *neuration*, or arrangement of the nervures and nervules, follows the same general plan in all Butterflies, though the diversities in detail are numerous and of great value in discriminating families and genera (see Pl. I.); the *costal nervure* (*a*) starts from the base nearest the head and extends just below the costal margin, ending in that margin usually at some distance short of the apex. The costal nervure of the forewing is always simple, but in some of the *Morphinæ* it appears to throw off one or more branches towards the costal margin; in the hindwing there is also usually a small nervure called the *precostal nervure* (*j*), close to the base and between the costal nervure and the costal margin, it is short, recurved and sometimes bifid; immediately below the costal nervure is found the *subcostal nervure* (*b*), which is continued to the outer margin a little below the apex; this nervure throws off two branches or nervules in the hindwing and three, four or five in the forewing (*b1*, *b2*, *b3*). All the branches of this nervure are invariably thrown off on the upper side towards the costa, and either end in the margin near the apex, or coalesce with the costal nervure. They are numbered in order as thrown off from the base—that nearest the base being the *first subcostal nervule*, the next the second, and so on. In the *Elymniinæ* and some others there is a short slender nervule connecting the subcostal with the costal nervure near the base; the space thus enclosed is called the *prædiscoidal cell*. Below the subcostal nervure is a wide space (*h*) owing to the discoidal nervure which should follow, being either wholly or partially wanting. This space, which is usually closed by short transverse nervules, is called the *cell* or *discoidal cell*; the short transverse nervules (*g g*) closing the cell are termed the *disco-cellular nervules*, and are three in number (upper, middle, and lower) in the forewing, and two in number (upper and lower) in the hindwing, the "upper" being the one nearest to the subcostal nervure. From the points of junction of these disco-cellular nervules with each other, the *discoidal nervules* (*c1*, *c2*), two in the forewing and one in the hindwing, extend to the outer margin, these discoidal nervules being considered as branches of a discoidal nervure, which, as noted above, is either partially or wholly wanting; the discoidal cell on its lower edge is bounded by a strong nervure (*d*), termed the *median nervure*. This nervure has three branches, both in the fore and hindwings (*d1*, *d2*, *d3*), called the *median nervules*, which in this case are all invariably thrown off on the underside towards the outer margin, and being numbered in order as they are thrown off from the base, they reach the outer margin in inverse order, the first ending nearest the hinder angle, and the third nearest the apex. The lower disco-cellular nervule (when present) closes the cell by junction with the median nervure; below the median nervure is another nervure extending from the base of the wing to near the hinder angle, and without branches, called the *submedian nervure* (*c*). This nervure is occasionally (especially in the *Papilionidæ* and *Morphinæ*) joined to the median nervure near the base, by a short connecting nervule, termed the *interno-median nervule* (not shown in the plate). Lastly, between the submedian nervure and the inner margin is occasionally found a short nervure from the base, often not extending to the inner margin, and called the *internal nervure* (*f*).

This net-work of branches greatly facilitates exact description of the distribution of the colours and position of the markings, and of the various sexual appendages which are found on the wings of Butterflies, the latter chiefly in the males. When the names attached to the various margins, nervures, and nervules are impressed on the memory, the terms denoting the various areas will be readily understood. Broadly speaking the wing is divided, for purposes of description, into the following areas:—(1), the *costal area*, between the costal nervure and costal margin; (2), the *subcostal area* between the subcostal and costal nervures; (3), the *discoidal cell*; (4), the *interno-median area* between the median and submedian nervules; (5), the *internal area* between the submedian nervure and the inner margin; (6), the *basal area* comprising the portion of all the above areas nearest to the base; (7), the *apical area* near the apex; and (8), the marginal area along the outer margin. The remaining portion of the wing between the discoidal cell and the marginal area is often loosely called the *disc* or *discal area*; but for greater accuracy it is usual to define the interspaces between each pair of nervules. Thus, the space between the first and second median nervules is termed the *first median interspace*; that between the second and third, the *second median interspace*; that between the third median and lower discoidal nervules, the *third median interspace*; that between the lower and upper discoidal nervules, the *lower discoidal interspace*; and that between the upper discoidal and last subcostal nervules, the *upper discoidal interspace*, and so on.

The following expression used in describing also require some explanation. When the term *both wings* is used it refers to the fore and hindwings of one side, not both forewings or both hindwings. The *length* of a wing is measured from the base to the apex; the *breadth* from the hinder angle to the costa; the *expanse* is usually taken as twice the length of the forewing plus the breadth of the body. A band or stripe of colour is said to be *longitudinal* when it is in the direction of the length of the wing, and *transverse* when it is in the direction of the breadth of the wing, whether fore or hind: thus a transverse band on the hindwing can be nearly parallel sometimes to a longitudinal band on the forewing: a *macular* band is a band evidently composed of coalescing spots, and a *lunular* band is one evidently composed of coalescing lunules.

The classification of Butterflies is not of course based on the features of the perfect insect only. The egg, as has been noted above, affords no indication of the affinities of the perfect insect, though, judging from analogy, it is possible that further investigation may remove this apparent anomaly; but the other stages of caterpillar and chrysalis furnish important, and perhaps even more critical, tests of actual affinity than the last or final stage does. In a handbook of this sort the distinctive characters of the perfect insect are more prominently put forward in any case, on account of the perfect insect being more accessible to beginners in the study; and in this particular instance the characters of the earlier stages of Indian Butterflies, being so little known comparatively, it would be premature to attempt to give them the first place, but it is essential to note that the classification, though based nominally on the perfect insect, must be considered as open to revision, when it is found that it entails anomalous grouping of the earlier stages. Generally speaking it will be found that this is not the case, and that the genera, as now defined, group together caterpillars and chrysalises of the same general types and habits.

The sexes of Butterflies differ frequently in colouring, and almost always in outline of wings and size; the female being usually the larger, and having the wings, especially the forewing, broader and more rounded than in the males. But independently of colouring and outline, and also of internal structure, which can only be investigated by dissection under a microscope, there are in most instances external structural features by which the sexes can, with certainty and without much difficulty, be discriminated. Throughout the families in which the forelegs are more or less imperfectly developed, including the *Danainæ*, *Satyrinæ*, *Elymniinæ*, *Morphinæ*, *Acræinæ*, *Nymphalinæ*, *Libythæinæ*, *Nemeobiinæ*, and *Lycænidæ*, the structure of the tarsus of the imperfect foreleg differs in the male and female. These differences vary in the different genera, (see Pl. I, dissections of *Junonia asterie*, *Elymnias undularis* and *Melanitis leda*, figs. *e.* and *f.*) and are detailed in the generic descriptions. In addition to the "foreleg" test the sexes of many species belonging to the above families may be recognised by marks on the wings, which occur in the male sex only. Such are the pouches on the hindwing of many species of *Danais*, the patches of silky appressed scales on the forewing of many species of *Euplœa*, the erectile tufts of hair on the hindwings of *Mycalesis* and of the *Morphinæ*, the raised stripes along the median nervules of the forewing in some species of *Argynnis*. In the *Pierinæ* the sexes almost invariably differ in colour, and the outer margin is more rounded in the females than in the males; but, with few exceptions, as for instance, the eretile tufts on the hindwings of *Catopsilias*, there are few prominent external features to distinguish the sexes. In the *Papilioninæ* the sexual distinctions, irrespective of colour and outline, are very various. *P. polyctor*, and some of its allies, have raised stripes along the median nervules of the males, as in *Argynnis*; in *Leptocircus* and in many species of *Papilio*, such as *P. zaleucus*, *P. nox*, and its allies, the abdominal margin of the hindwing is broadly folded back on to the upper surface in the males. In *Ornithoptera*, and in some *Papilios* males have a pair of conspicuous corneous valves on the last segment of the abdomen; while in *Parnassius* the *females* are furnished with a corneous pouch on this segment. In *Teinopalpus* the male has one tail on the hindwing and the female has three. Among the *Hesperidæ*, the only remaining family, the discrimination of the sexes is often a difficult matter. According to Westwood in some groups* the fore-margin (costa) of the forewing is recurved in the males, the enclosed space being thickly clothed with pale coloured down; in others the males have a large velvety patch near the base of the forewing; in others the males have a thickened oblique ridge in the middle of the forewing; and in others the form of the club of the antennæ differs in the sexes. In life the females are as a rule less active than the males, and less frequently seen on the wing. It often happens that, when males are common in collections, females are rare or even unknown, as from their more sedentary habits they are more likely to escape observation.

The powers and style of flight vary much in the different genera, so much so that a practised observer will generally readily distinguish the different genera on the wing.

The genera in many cases contain a large number of species which can be grouped under several types. Some of the largest of these genera, such as *Danais*, *Euplœa*, *Lethe*, and *Mycalesis* have in recent years been divided up into numerous groups, based chiefly, if not entirely, on the characters of the male insect. The generic value of these sub-divisions is doubtful, but their usefulness as aids to correct arrangement and identification of the species is unquestionable. In order to retain the names of these sub-divisions, many of which will probably be adopted as generic divisions in future works, but which at present we do not feel justified in using to the exclusion of the name of the larger and more completely defined group, of which they form sections, we have usually added in brackets after the generic name, the name of the minor group where it has been separately characterised.

With regard to species and varieties, we have found it convenient to describe, where there is any room for doubt, under its own distinctive name, every form that has been separately characterised. The question whether any particular form represents a species or a variety of a species can at present be decided in most instances in this country only as a matter of conjecture, for a knowledge of the life-history in all its stages is essential to the authoritative settlement of such questions; at the same time the evidently, or apparently allied species, are carefully grouped together, and the nature of the variety is indicated as closely as our present knowledge will allow.

---

* Exclusively American.

Thus a species, say *margarita* of *Euplœa*, belonging to the group which has been discriminated as *Salpinx*, is entered as *Euplœa* (*Salpinx*) *margarita*, and such species as *exprompta*, *nicobarica*, and *vulgaris*, which are all conjectured on very fair grounds to be merely local or geographical varieties of *Danais similis* (of China) are entered as *Danais exprompta*, *Danais nicobarica*, &c., but grouped together in consecutive order with their apparent affinities indicated.

The great importance of a correct record of exact localities cannot be too strongly insisted on. The vague localities used by the earlier writers, such as "East Indies," which may mean any portion of India, Malayana or the Malay Archipelago; or "North India," which may mean anything from the snows of Kashmir to the hot, moist, forests of Assam and Eastern Bengal, are useless for scientific purposes, and should be scrupulously avoided. Such localities have necessarily often been quoted in this book, for in some cases the Butterflies have not been captured since the original description was published, so that the exact localities of capture are still unknown. It is difficult to record on labels any full details, but in addition to the actual locality, the name of the province, and, if in a mountainous district, the approximate elevation above the sea, should invariably be noted. The date of capture too is a most valuable record, not only for information of future collectors in quest of the insect, but as a clue to whether the insect belongs to a spring, summer, or autumn brood. Doubtful localities, such as "Darjeeling," for a butterfly *purchased* at Darjeeling, should be always carefully distinguished from the accurate records of places of capture. The necessity for care in this matter will be understood when it is considered how the Indian Empire is situated. There is a fairly typical "Indian" fauna, as represented by the central portions of Continental India andthe Peninsula, but on the West Coast, stragglers from the African and South Palæarctic fauna may be found. In the North West, and also in the higher ranges of the Himalayas, the Eastern Palæarctic forms occur; on the east the Indo-Malayan fauna is largely represented, and many of the typical Malayan forms occur; and it is of great importance to ascertain, as accurately as possible, the extreme ranges to which the various types extend.

COLLECTING AND PRESERVING.

To start with, a net is the first essential required. In England apparatus for collecting is to be obtained at any of the established Naturalist's shops; in India one has to depend a good deal on one's own ingenuity to supply one's wants in this respect. The main point to aim at is lightness, so far as is compatible with rigidity, of the frame and handle, on which the handiness of the net largely depends. Probably, the simplest form of net is somewhat oval in shape, and made of three joints, which can be riveted together or not at the discretion of the user. For this kind of net all that is required is to have made by any bazar blacksmith a brass Y and two ferules. The Y should be made of three tubes, the lower one somewhat larger and longer than the other two that form the branches. In the lower one a strong, *rigid*. stick is fitted, and for general collecting the stick should not be less than five or six feet in length, though for collecting small "Blues," &c., a shorter stick will be found much more handy. Again, for taking insects that fly high and settle on the upper branches of trees, a pole, 20 or 30 feet in length, may be required. The framework of the net should be in three pieces; the two side pieces (fitting at their bottom ends into the two upper branches of the Y) should be of very tough rigid wood. On their further ends the two ferules are fixed, one end of each being fastened with a rivet, so precluding any chance of the ferule falling off and getting lost. The top of the net may be made of a piece of rattan cane. The circumference of the net when fitted together should again depend upon circumtances. One fifty inches round is a good sized general net, but will be found much too small, unless very skilfully used, to catch the large, fast-flying *Papilios*, &c. Probably a net 70 to 80 inches round will be found the most generally useful, particularly in rich localities, where the larger insects abound. Nothing is more annoying than to lose a large, fine insect, which may be very rare, because one's net is an inch or so too narrow! For a small pocket net one made with the joints folding like the old fashioned parasol, the handle of which doubles up in the middle, will be found very useful.

The framework should be made of four pieces of rattan cane, each piece bent by steaming into a quarter circle, the two end ones fitting, as in the larger net, into a Y-piece. This is a capital net for small insects, and has the great advantage of being easily put together and being "carriable" in an inside pocket. The net itself is a simple bag; a broad hem made of very coarse cotton cloth is made for the framework to run in, the bag being made of any length thought advisable. For the larger net four feet is not too long; about three feet will suffice for the smaller net, the framework of which should not exceed a yard in circumference. Common mosquito netting is a good material for the net; green gauze is better, but is more difficult to obtain; the flimsier the material used, the less is the risk incurred of injuring the insects.

A collecting box is the next essential. It should be made of zinc, and have pieces of sheet cork fixed to the lid and bottom inside by clamps. The box should be made to fit an outside pocket. When starting on a day's collecting, the cork should be well wetted, so that the specimens pinned into it remain limp till they are ready to be set. If the cork is not damped, specimens will get as dry as a chip in an hour or two under the hot sun of India, and require to be relaxed to be set. During a journey, when specimens cannot be set the same day, or when specimens are required to be sent long distances, either for custody or exchange, it is best to put them at once into paper cases. For this purpose a supply of paper should be kept ready, cut into oblongs of various sizes, a little longer than they are broad. Thin Serampore paper, or the thinnest printing paper, answers best; each paper should be folded diagonally once, with the two ends projecting, so that by folding over the right hand edge to the right, and the left hand edge to the left, a closed triangular pocket is formed, in which the Butterfly can be placed. Great care should be taken that the ends fold over the reverse ways, for then the pocket can be easily opened without damage to the Butterfly inside. Only one Butterfly should be put in each paper, and when putting it in the wings should be folded together over the back, and the antennæ put back carefully against the wings. Care should always be taken to prevent injury to the legs and antennæ if the species are to be of any value for scientific purposes. On each paper should be roughly noted the date and place of capture. Specimens thus packed can be safely kept and transported, and can be relaxed at any time. For relaxing two methods are available—first, a zinc box lined with cork well damped inside; second, an unglazed earthen *ghurra* fitted with a top, and containing about two inches of well damped sand. The mouth of the *ghurra* should be wide. The insects to be relaxed should be laid on the damp cork or sand and then closed up, the *ghurra*, if one is used, being wrapped with damp cloths. In a few hours the specimens will be found ready for setting.

Pins are next required. By sending a Post Office Money Order to Messrs. D. F. Taylor & Co., New Hall Works, Birmingham, England, for a sovereign, and specifying the sizes of pins required, a supply will be sent by overland parcel post which will last an ordinary collector for five years. Nos. 11, (large, for *Papilios*, &c.), 12 (medium sized, the pin most wanted), and 6 (small size for "Blues," &c.), will be found a good selection.

Setting boards are required to spread out the insects on when caught and before placing in the collection. They can be easily made out of *Semul* or other soft wood, and should have a groove for the body, regulated in size according to the size of the bodies of the Butterflies intended to be set on them, and a smaller groove in the centre of the larger one for the reception of the pin. In making these boards great care should be exercised in making the pin groove in all the boards of equal depth, which should be one-third of an inch from the bottom of the body-groove. If this is not attended to it will be found that, when the insects are taken off the boards and placed side by side in the store-box or cabinet, being at different heights on the pin, they present a very irregular appearance, all up and down, no two insects at the same level. Uniformity in setting adds greatly to the beauty of a collection. Boards should be made of all sizes—from half-an-inch broad for the tiniest "Blues" to eight inches for the gigantic *Ornithopteras*. The boards should also gently slope downwards on each side from the centre groove, not too much, say about 10°, and the slope in all the boards should be the same.

Lastly, places in which to store the insects, when caught and set, are required. The best are English-made mahogany cabinets, the drawers eighteen inches square, and about two inches deep, with a glass cover to each drawer, and a camphor cell round each. Such cabinets cost from £1 to £1-5 a drawer in England, so are very expensive; but there is nothing like them for preserving the specimens. The next best things are cork-lined store boxes with a single camphor cell, and fitting very closely. Any good native carpenter can turn out such boxes, and instead of cork, *sola* pith can be used; cut into strips and pasted on the top and bottom of the box, with a double layer of moderately thick paper over it, it answers all purposes. The most useful size for store boxes is eighteen inches long, twelve broad, and three deep. If the boxes are all made of the same size, they can be packed very easily into a larger outer box, which is an additional security against mites and mould, the two great enemies to the collector in India. Such store boxes do not require glass covers. The supply of camphor in each box should be kept up most carefully, or else mites will destroy in a very short time the results of one's labors, and as an additional protection, if the insides of the boxes are occasionally painted over with a few drops of oil of aniseed, lemon, grass oil, or any "essential" oil to be obtained at a chemist's, mites will never shew themselves. Should they do so, a few drops of benzine or benzine collas dropped on the specimens affected, will destroy every mite without injuring the specimens in the least if the benzine is pure, but the benzine should first be tried on a *commom specimen* to ascertain its purity, or rare specimens may be injured. Very often an insect will go greasy. To remedy this one has only to immerse the specimen bodily, pin and all, in a bath of benzine; take it out after a few minutes and leave the benzine to evaporate, and it will be found that, not only has the specimen not been injured at all, but that the grease has entirely disappeared, and the specimen is restored to all its original beauty. While the benzine is evaporating, and until the colours return, the specimen should be kept in a separate box in which the air can circulate.

Each specimen, when caught, should have a small label with the exact locality where caught, and date when captured, placed, face downwards, on the pin beneath it. A collection should be arranged in rows, one specimen behind another; the males at the head of each row, the females following, and the name of the species ending each row. When a collection embraces specimens from various localities, it is an advantage to place a label at the side of and below each specimen, shewing where it was taken. This does away with the necessity of taking up each specimen to read the label beneath it, when its place of capture is required to be known, but under no circumstances should the label beneath the specimen be dispensed with, since from every point of view, a collection of insects with the specimens all properly 'localized' is worth far more than one in which the localities of the specimens have not been retained.

For further useful information on these, and on all other matters connected with the collection of insects, including the collecting and management of eggs, caterpillars, and chrysalises for breeding, we would recommend collectors to obtain Dr. H. Guard Knaggs' "Lepidopterists' Guide for the use of the young collector," published by John Van Voorst, 1, Paternoster Row, London, E.C., the new illustrated edition of which can be bought for one shilling.

SYNOPSIS OF THE FAMILIES AND SUBFAMILIES.

RHOPALOCERA.

FAMILIES.

I.—NYMPHALIDÆ, with the FORELEGS very feebly developed in both sexes, short, imperfect, and unfitted for walking. FOREWING with the subcostal nervure emitting four branches exclusive of terminal portion.

I.—DANAINÆ: BODY, long, slender; ANTENNÆ, not half the length of forewing, gradually clavate; PALPI, *short, divergent, erect, very slightly compressed, clothed with dense short porrect hairs*; WINGS, entire, rather lengthened, never dentate or caudate; CELL, closed in both wings; FOREWING, nervures never dilated at base, upper disco-cellular minute or wanting, internal nervure slender, running into the submedian near its base; HINDWING, discoidal nervure appearing as a third subcostal nervule, no prædiscoidal cell.

II.—SATYRINÆ: BODY, short, weak; ANTENNÆ, short, slender, club usually slender but variable in shape; PALPI, *moderately long, divergent, erect, very much compressed, and clothed in front with long porrect hairs;* WINGS, broad, sometimes rounded, often dentate, occasionally falcate in forewing and slightly caudate in hindwing; CELL, closed in both wings; FOREWING, with the nervures generally dilated at base; HINDWING, with no prædiscoidal cell.

III.—ELYMNIINÆ: BODY, rather robust; ANTENNÆ, short, slender, with long, slender, gradually formed club; PALPI, *long, divergent, porrect, nearly straight, only slightly compressed, clothed with short appressed hairs longer on the back edge*; WINGS, dentate, or angled; CELL, broad, generally closed in both wings by long, slender, much curved nervules; FOREWING, with the costal nervure only slightly dilated at base; HINDWING, *furnished with a prædiscoidal cell.*

IV.—MORPHINÆ: BODY, robust, seldom elongate; ANTENNÆ, long, slender, with a slender club; PALPI, *small, wide apart, erect* (elongate and porrect in *Amathusia* and *Zeuxidia*), *front edge narrowed and sharp, clothed with scales or scaly appressed hairs, the back edge often hairy*; WINGS large, broad, ample, sometimes rounded, sometimes with a short broad tail; CELL, in forewing broad, closed—in hindwing open; FOREWING, with the nervures not dilated at base (except in *Cleromé*), the costal nervure sometimes appearing as if branched; HINDWING, with no prædiscoidal cell.

V.—ACRÆINÆ: BODY, long, rather stout; ANTENNÆ, short, abruptly clavate, the club obtuse at tip; PALPI, *long, divergent, erect, hairy, the second joint somewhat swollen*; WINGS, long, narrow, entire, never dentate or caudate; CELL, closed in both wings; FOREWING, nervures not dilated at base; HINDWING, with no prædiscoidal cell, *not channelled* to receive abdomen; NEURATION as in *Danainæ*.

VI.—NYMPHALINÆ: BODY, robust; ANTENNÆ, long, with a broad elongate distinct club; PALPI, *large, protruding, wide apart, scaly, the front edge broadly dilated;* WINGS, large, triangular, but varying much in outline; CELL, sometimes closed in both wings, often open in hindwing, and sometimes open in forewing also; FOREWING, nervures not dilated at base, (except in a few genera, *Ergolis*, *Eurytela*, &c., in which the costal nervure only is dilated), the second subcostal nervule emitted before end of cell; HINDWING, *channelled* to receive abdomen, no prædiscoidal cell.

II.—LEMONIIDÆ, with the FORELEGS small, slender, imperfect, but more developed than in the *Nymphalidæ*; those of the *males* brush-like and clothed with long hairs, the tarsus without joints or claws; of the *females,* longer, slender, scaly, tarsus with the joints longer and more distinct than in the *Nymphalidæ*. FOREWING, subcostal nervure generally with only three branches, the disco-cellulars very slender. All of small size.

I.—LIBYTHÆINÆ: BODY, robust; ANTENNÆ, short, stout, incrassate, or gradually clavate; PALPI, *very long, protruding, united at tip, forming a long conical beak*; CELL, in both wings, closed; FOREWING, very falcate, upper disco-cellular minute.

II.—NEMEOBIINÆ: BODY, slender, or somewhat robust; ANTENNÆ, moderately long, slender, and abruptly clubbed; PALPI, *very small and slender, scarcely advanced in front of the face, the last joint nearly naked*; CELL, in both wings, closed; FOREWING, with the upper disco-cellular obliterated; HINDWING, very variable in shape, *slightly channelled* to receive the abdomen.

III.—LYCÆNIDÆ, with the FORELEGS slender and evidently smaller than the rest, but nearly alike in the sexes, used for walking, scaly; tarsus of the *male* long, exarticulate, that of the *female* jointed like in the hindlegs. FOREWING, with the subcostal nervure emitting only two, or three, branches; the discoidal cell generally narrow owing to the distance between the costal and subcostal nervures. All but one or two of small size. BODY, rather slender; ANTENNÆ, short, often ringed with white, with an elongate distinct club; PALPI, *elongate, terminal joint, slender, horizontal, and nearly naked.* HINDWING, scarcely channelled to receive the abdomen, often with one or more slender tails; precostal nervure apparently wanting.

IV.—PAPILIONIDÆ, with ALL SIX LEGS perfect. WINGS, with the discoidal cells always completely closed; some of the subcostal nervules of the forewing emitted beyond the end of the cell.

I.—PIERINÆ: BODY, slender, or moderately robust; ANTENNÆ, elongate, with an ovate club, or short, incrassate and truncate; PALPI, rather long, porrect, often hairy; FOREWING, *with lower discoidal nervule manifestly distinct from the median nervure*; HINDWING, *channelled to receive the abdomen*; TIBIA of foreleg without any spur in the middle.

II.—PAPILIONINÆ: BODY, short, somewhat robust; ANTENNÆ, gradually clavate, club elongate, sometimes tapering; PALPI, short (except in *Teinopalpus*), pressed close to the face, densely clothed with scales and hairs; FOREWING, *with the lower discoidal nervule united to the third median, and appearing like a fourth median nervule*; HINDWING, never channelled to receive the abdomen; TIBIA of foreleg, with a stout spur about the middle.

V.—HESPERIDÆ, with ALL SIX LEGS perfect. WINGS, with the discoidal cell of hindwing slenderly, and often incompletely closed, subcostal nervure of forewing always with four branches, all four emitted before end of cell. Of small size, very robust build and rapid flight. BODY of all but a few very robust; ANTENNÆ, wide apart at base, with a thick club, or strong curved hook at tip; PALPI, short, very broad, closely pressed against the face, densely squamose. HINDLEGS, generally with a pair of moveable spines at the tip of the tibiæ, and another pair in the middle; MIDDLE LEGS with a pair of moveable spines at the tip of the tibiæ.

The foregoing table is drawn up in accordance with the arrangement adopted in Kirby's "Synonymic Catalogue of Diurnal Lepidoptera," that being the only complete catalogue of the suborder yet published; but there are many points on which the arrangement is open to revision, and possibly improvement, when the life-history of exotic Butterflies becomes more fully known. The position of a few genera has already been altered.

The primary divisions into families are based, as regards the perfect insect, mainly on the structure of the legs, and especially on the extent of development of the forelegs.

The secondary divisions into subfamilies are far less clearly marked, and it is difficult to find distinctive characters of sufficient importance to maintain some of these divisions. The characters given in the table are merely a few of the more important, the remaining characters being detailed in the body of the work.

In the subfamilies of the *Nymphalidæ* the most important test is the structure and clothing of the labial palpi, but even the palpi are not uniform throughout the genera of each subfamily; each division naturally may be expected to embrace, in addition to the more typical genera, aberrant forms showing approaches to other types, and with these there is sometimes considerable difficulty in determining their affinities. The characters given in the table, taken as a whole, will usually be sufficient for identification.

The *Danainæ* form a well-marked group, and, as far as the Indian genera are concerned, no doubt has ever been raised as to the propriety of retaining each and all of them in their present places; their nearest allies are the American subfamily *Heliconinæ*, which latter have no representatives in Asia.

The *Satyrinæ*, too, form a well-marked group, mainly distinguished structurally by the long hairs of the palpi. This character is not fully developed in all the genera, but no genera are included among the Indian *Satyrinæ*, the position of which in the present subfamily has been considered doubtful. One or more of the nervures of the forewing are often, if not always, much dilated at the base; the dilation of the costal nervure occurs also in *Elymnias* and in some genera of *Nymphalinæ*, but the dilation of the subcostal and median nervures is, where it occurs, characteristic of the *Satyrinæ*. The *Satyrinæ* are found in all parts of the world, but are most numerous proportionally in temperate climates.

The *Elymniinæ* in this arrangement are restricted to two very closely allied genera, which, with the exception of a very few east African species, are entirely Asiatic, and the bulk inhabit the Malay Archipelago. They are very closely affined to the *Satyrinæ*, but differ in the clothing of the palpi, and in the presence of a prædiscoidal cell in the hindwing. Westwood included them with *Eurytela*, *Ergolis* and *Hypanis*, (which also have the costal nervure dilated at base) as a separate subfamily under the name of *Eurytelidæ*, and there is a good deal to be said in support of this arrangement; the latter genera are now included among the *Nymphalinæ*, and they form a link between that subfamily and the *Satyrinæ* and *Elymniinæ*.

The *Morphinæ* include several genera (*Amathusia*, *Zeuxidia*, *Enispe*, and *Discophora*) which were included by Westwood among the *Nymphalinæ*, and also one genus, *Xanthotænia*, which Kirby even now includes among the *Nymphalinæ*. The genera which should compose this subfamily, and even the right of this to the rank of a subfamily at all, have been frequently disputed. Horsfield and Swainson grouped it with the *Satyrinæ*; some of the American group have a prædiscoidal cell, showing affinity for the *Elymniinæ*, and some American genera have the discoidal cell in the hindwing closed. These American forms are included in a separate subfamily, *Brassolinæ*, which has no representatives in India. But the characters given in the table will define the Indian genera, and, though numerous divergencies in structural detail exist even among these, the group is clearly a natural one.

The *Acræinæ* contain only two Indian species, which were formerly considered to represent different genera, but now are included in a single genus. About fifty species are found in Africa, one in the Malay Archipelago, one in Australia, and between twenty and thirty in America. So far as the Indian species are concerned, this group is abundantly distinct. The American *Heliconinæ* are closely related to this group.

The *Nymphalinæ* embrace the widest differences of form, outline, and even structure, the long and distinctly clubbed antennæ and the protruding dilated palpi being the most constant features. As arranged in this work they exclude, as stated above, certain genera now included among the *Morphinæ*, and they include other genera which are equally closely allied to the *Elymniinæ*. The minor structural differences to be found within this group will be detailed further on.

The remaining groups, *Libythæinæ*, *Nemeobiinæ* (or *Erycininæ* of Westwood), *Lycænidæ*, *Pierinæ*, *Papilioninæ*, and *Hesperidæ* need no remark; the characters are well defined, and the allocation of the genera composing the groups is undisputed.

FAMILY 1.—NYMPHALIDÆ.

This family includes the whole of the great division of Butterflies in which the forelegs of the perfect insect are undeveloped, having the tarsus rudimentary in *both* sexes. As thus defined it includes all genera in which the chrysalis is simply suspended by the tail and not girt about the body by a thread, (see Plate II, *Athyma leucothoë* and *Adolias lubentina*), with the single exception of the genus *Libythea*, which forms the link between the *Nymphalidæ* and the next family, *Lemoniidæ*. *Libythea* is a very distinct form; it was placed as a separate family by Westwood, and is still retained as a separate subfamily by Kirby; it is classed with *Lemoniidæ* rather than with *Nymphalidæ*, on account of the structure of the forelegs.

It also includes two distinct types of caterpillar:—the "Scolopendriform" (see Plate II, *Athyma leucothoë*), and the "Thysanuriform" (see Plate II, *Adolias garuda*), sections of Horsfield's classification of 1857.

In the aspect of the perfect insect, the *Nymphalidæ* vary greatly; in shape from the long wing of *Hestia* to the short deep wing of *Kallima*; in colour from the sombre *Satyrinæ* to the brilliant *Euplœa* and *Apatura*; in size from the tiny *Ypthima* to the gigantic *Thaumantis*; in structure from the weak *Erebia* and the delicately formed *Cyrestis* to the strong and rapid *Charaxes*; in habit too there is an equally wide divergence, from the shade-loving, sometimes crepuscular *Melanitis* to the *Vanessa*, which basks in the hottest sunshine; but throughout the family the small undeveloped foreleg folded closely against the thorax is a constant and well-marked feature.

SUBFAMILY I.—DANAINÆ,* Bates. (PLATES III TO IX INCLUSIVE.)

Danainæ, Bates, Journ. Ent., vol. ii, p. 176 (1864); *Danaidæ*, Felder, Wien. Ent. Mon., vol. vi, p. 74 (1862); *Danaidæ*, Doubl., Gen. D. L., p. 84 (1847).

HEAD, round. *Eyes*, oval, prominent. *Labial palpi*, divergent, ascending, scarcely rising above the forehead, distinctly triarticulate; the basal joint short, stout, curved; second double the length of the first, subcylindric, slightly curved, rounded at each extremity; third minute, about one-fifth the length of the second, obovate, slightly pointed. *Antennæ*, gradually clavate. *Thorax*, moderately stout. FOREWING, elongate, the *cell* closed; the subcostal nervure always with four branches exclusive of the terminal portion; the first nervule thrown off before the end of the cell, generally distant, at its origin, about one-fourth the length of the cell from the disco-cellular nervule, the second thrown off at the end of the cell or very little before it, the third rather more distant from the second than from the fourth, the fourth about midway between the third and the apex. *Upper disco-cellular nervule* very short, or altogether wanting; *middle* and *lower*, about equal in length; *internal nervure* slender, running into the submedian, causing the latter to appear as if double at its

* In his recently published "Lepidoptera of Ceylon," Mr. F. Moore alters the name of this subfamily to *Euplœinæ* with the following remark: "Linnæus's name of *Danaus* having been adopted in a generic sense by Esper in 1777, and also by Panzer in 1801, for species of *Pierinæ*, its use—as applied by Latreille in 1809, cannot be retained in this group of Butterflies." Possibly this may be strictly correct; but as the name of *Danais* has been in general, if not universal, use in connection with the present subfamily for upwards of seventy years, and as its use in this sense cannot possibly be misunderstood, we have deemed it advisable to retain it here. It is so interwoven withthis sense in all entomological literature that it seems a pity to have disturbed its claim to acceptation on account of an objection founded solely on works which are practically obsolete.

base. HINDWING obovate, the cell closed; the *discoidal nervure* always appearing to be a third subcostal nervule; *abdominal fold* mostly ample. LEGS, (except the forelegs) rather stout and long; *forelegs* imperfect, varying in the sexes; *middle* and *hindlegs* with the *tibiæ* spiny; the *spines* not strikingly developed; the *tarsi* with the basal joint long; second, third, and fourth progressively shorter; fifth longer than the second; all spiny at the sides below; *claws* simple. ABDOMEN, rather slender, nearly as long as the abdominal margin of the hindwing.

CATERPILLAR.—Stout, cylindrical, smaller towards the head, furnished on one or more of the anterior segments with a pair of long, slender, flexible, fleshy tentacula, not retractile; and with a similar, but often shorter, pair on the penultimate segment (*Westwood*). The anterior pair of these processes in all *Danais*, and almost certainly in all *Hestia*, are articulated and freely moveable at the base and function as antennæ (*J. Wood-Mason*).

CHRYSALIS.—Suspended, short, smooth, somewhat ovate, contracted near the middle (*Doubleday*), often with brilliant metallic colouring.

The *Danainæ* are insects of large or moderate size, of slow flapping flight when undisturbed, and of fearless demeanour. They include some of the very commonest of Indian Butterflies, and the commoner species are not only wide-spread, but they occur in most parts in very great numbers. Their fearlessness is evidently the result of the freedom that they enjoy from the attacks of insectivorous birds and reptiles, which they owe to the presence of a pungent semi-aromatic odour pervading the juices of their bodies; these juices, when exuded by pressure, stain the skin yellow and leave a distinct odour; their bodies are moreover very tough and leathery, and they have great tenacity of life, so that any individual which might be accidentally seized and afterwards dropped by a bird, has a good chance of escaping with immunity when more delicately framed insects would be killed or hopelessly maimed. The males often bear curious sexual marks on the wings, and have besides the power of extruding and expanding two long brushes of yellow hairs from their anal extremity which have been thought to disseminate the odour with which the insects are furnished. In connection with the immunity from persecution which these insects enjoy, it is worthy of note that many species belonging to widely different genera, such as *Elymnias*, *Hypolimnas*, some of the *Pierinæ*, *Papilioninæ*, &c., which altogether lack this kind of protection, are found to closely resemble in outward appearance and style of colouration certain species of *Danainæ* which frequent the same localities at the same periods; such genera are termed "mimetic," with reference to this habit of mimicry, which is a subject of great interest and importance for investigation. Regarding the gregarious habits of these insects, Dr. Thwaites* writes from Ceylon: "On a fine sunny day, when calm or nearly so, amazing numbers of one or more species of *Euplœa* may often be observed wending their way in one direction, as if floating upon the air a few feet from the ground, with an apparently sluggish movement of their wings, though really making rapid progress." Captain C. H. E. Adamson also writes that, on one occasion near Moulmein, on the 12th June, he found hundreds of *Euplœæ* of numerous species, all congregated round a single flowering tree in the jungle, at a time when scarcely a single *Euplœa* was to be found elsewhere in the neighbourhood. Mr. Harold Fergusson has observed much the same habit in *Hestia lynceus*, and every one who has paid attention to the subject in this country must have observed the swarms of the common *Danais chrysippus*, *D. genutia*, and *Euplœa core* to be found from time to time in various localities. All the *Danainæ* have the costal and subcostal nervures of the forewing rather widely separated; also the peculiar structure of the internal nervure noted above. They are found in all the four continents and in Australia, though as a rule confined to tropical and sub-tropical regions. The Indo-Malayan region, where the species are very numerous, appears to be the head-quarters of the subfamily. The distinctive characters of the Indian genera are shown in the following table:—

* "Lepidoptera of Ceylon," by F. Moore, F.Z.S.

Key to the Genera of DANAINÆ.

A. Antennæ almost filiform, scarcely perceptibly clavate. Of large size; wings elongate, diaphanous, white with black or blackish spots and marks; no sexual pouch on hindwing of male. *Claws furnished with paronychia and pulvilli.*

I.—HESTIA.

B. Antennæ distinctly clavate.

a. Claws without paronychia or pulvilli.

a[1]. With *no sexual spot on hindwing* of male. Smaller than *Hestia*, but similar in form and colouration.

II.—IDEOPSIS.

b[1]. Generally with *sexual spot or pouch on hindwing* of male. Wings yellowish brown, or bluish or greenish white, bordered and more or less streaked with black.

III.—DANAIS.

b. Claws furnished with paronychia and pulvilli. The sexual marks, usually on forewing of male; wings various shades of velvety-brown or black, often brilliantly glossed and spotted with blue, and often with white spots near the outer margin.

IV.—EUPLŒA.

The genera of *Danais* and *Euplœa* have been further subdivided into minor groups, based mainly on the form and position of the sexual marks in the males; these subdivisions are indicated under each generic head, but the generic names, as defined above, are retained, as they alone appear to have full generic value.

Genus 1.—HESTIA, Hübner. (PLATES III & IV).

Hestia, Hübner, Verz. bek. Schmett., p. 14 (1816); Double., Gen. D. L., p. 94 (1847); Butler, Trans. Ent. Soc. Lond., series iii, vol. v, p. 467 (1867) *Monograph*; *Idea*, Fabricius, Ill. Mag., vol. vi, p. 283 (1808); Latr., Enc. Méth., vol. ix, p. 10 (1819); *Nom. Spec.* Horsfield, Cat. Lep. E. I. C., pl. iii, n. 28 a, b, c, d (1828).

ANTENNÆ, more than half the length of the body, slender, almost filiform, scarcely thickened at the apex. FOREWING, ample, elongate, somewhat oval; the outer margin sometimes sinuate, especially in the males. *Costal nervure* and first subcostal nervule anastomosing; *upper disco-cellular nervule* short but distinct. HINDWING, elongate, obovate; the abdominal fold almost wanting in the MALES, distinct in the FEMALES. FORELEGS, clothed with scales; the *femur* and *tibia* of about equal length; the *tarsus* of the MALES about one-third the length of the tibia, cylindrical, tapering towards the apex, sometimes showing indications of being four-jointed, sometimes constricted near the base, without any signs of articulations. *Tarsus* of the FEMALES clavate, four-jointed, each joint, except the fourth, armed at the apex with a spine on each side. MIDDLE and HINDLEGS, of moderate length; *tarsi*, long, with the last joint dilated. CLAWS, curved, rather short. PARONYCHIA with the outer lacinia strap-shaped, longer than the claw; inner lanceolate, more than half as long as the claw. PULVILLUS jointed, nearly as long as the claw, the second joint broad and corneous.

CATERPILLAR.—Unknown. CHRYSALIS.—Typical as in the subfamily. A chrysalis of *Hestia belia*, Westwood, is figured in Horsfield and Moore's Cat. Lep. E. I. C., vol. i, pl. iv, fig. 12 (1857), from Java.

The *Hestias* are remarkable Butterflies, of large size and with elongate wings; they are essentially tropical insects. About fifteen species are known, all from the Indian or Indo-Malayan regions. Within our limits they seem to be confined to Ceylon, the south of the peninsula and along the western Ghâts to the south Concan, reappearing on the east in Burma and the Andaman Islands. The texture of the wings is delicate, and the colour throughout the group is semi-transparent white or greyish white, sometimes pure, sometimes powdered with blackish scales, with the nervures and numerous spots and marks black. They fly slowly over the tops of bushes and trees, often at considerable height from the ground, but when within reach are not difficult to capture. They are essentially forest-loving insects, and frequent the neighbourhood of pools and streams. Locally they are known by various trivial names, often very appropriate, such as "floater," or "silver paper fly," or "Sylph," in Ceylon; "spectre" or "ghost" in south India; "widow" in Province Wellesley, &c.

The Ceylon species, *H. jasonia*, has been placed by Moore in his recent work on the Lepidoptera of that island under the genus *Nectaria*, of Dalmann, which embraces a section of the genus *Hestia* of Hübner. The characters of this genus, as extracted below from Moore's work,* accord well with those of the Indian species, except that these latter have the disco-cellulars of the hindwing bent inwards, not outwards, but the two form an outward angle at their junction.

Key to the Indian species of HESTIA.

A. With the white ground-colour reaching the margin of the wings between the marginal spots and markings.

- *a.* With the black band across the forewing consisting of a patch above and a distinct patch in the cell; the subapical spots small and separate.
  - *a*¹. Of large size (Exp. 5·5 to 6·5 inches); ground-colour typically grey.
    - 1. H. LYNCEUS, Travancore to Mysore.
    - H. IDEA, Malayana.
  - *b*¹. Of smaller size (Exp. 4·5 to 5·5 inches); ground-colour pure diaphanous white.
    - 2. H. MALABARICA, Western Ghâts, Concan.
    - H. LINTBATA, Malacca.
- *b.* With the patch in the cell large and confluent with the black costal patch above; the subapical spots elongate and coalescing.
  - *a*¹. With the inner margin white below the submedian nervure.
    - 3. H. JASONIA, Ceylon.
  - *b*¹. With the inner margin entirely black below the submedian nervure.
    - 4. H. AGAMARSCHANA, Andamans, Mergui.

B. With the black marginal spots coalescing on the border, the white ground-colour especially on the hindwing not reaching the margin.

- *a.* With the border spots only partially coalesced; the ground-colour white irrorated with black scales.
  - 5. H. CADELLI, South Andamans.
- *b.* The border spots all completely coalesced; the ground-colour pure fleckless white.
  - 6. H. HADENI, Bassein, British Burma.

Many of the species are very closely allied, and the specific differences require further study, especially with regard to geographical distribution. The Mergui specimens of *H. agamarschana* approximate to *H. jasonia* in the presence of the second interno-median spot on the hindwing. The coalescing of the spots on the apical half of the forewing and along the margin of both wings in *H. cadelli* show an approach to *H. hadeni* of Burma rather than to *H. jasonia* of Ceylon. *H. jasonia*, too, appears to be distinct; but between *H. lynceus* and *H. malabarica* there appears to be no constant difference except size, unless the white specimens from Travancore, as large as *H. lynceus*, are really *H. malabarica*, in which case the sole difference is in tone of ground-colour, as the markings are absolutely identical. Out of a large series of *Hestias* from the south Concan sent by Mr. G. Vidal, C. S., there is not a single large or grey specimen, all belonged to the small and white type; and again out of six or seven specimens sent by Mr. Harold Fergusson from the Ashamboo range in Travancore, there were none of the small kind, all were very large; but while none were as grey as the typical *H. lynceus*, some were almost as white as typical *H. malabarica*. The most typical specimens of

---

* *Nectaria*, Dalm., in Billb. Enum. Ins., p. 76 (1820). "Wings semi-diaphanous, large; forewing lengthened, triangular; costa slightly arched; apex quite convex; exterior margin very oblique, waved; posterior margin short, slightly concave in middle; costal nervure extending to half the length of the wing; subcostal with first branch emitted at some distance before end of the cell, and anastomosed to the costal near its end; second branch from near end of the cell; third and fourth at equal distances beyond; the fourth terminating above and the fifth below the apex; cell long; upper disco-cellular inwardly oblique and slightly angled near subcostal, lower outwardly convex; first radial from angle of the upper, and second from near upper end of lower disco-cellular; three median branches wide apart; submedian very recurved. Hindwing lengthened, oval; costal margin curved; apex convex and more or less prolonged; exterior margin slightly waved, anal angle convex; costal nervure short, with a basal forked spur; subcostal branches wide apart, first very short; disco-cellulars bent outward at their middle, the radial emitted from the angle; median branches wide apart; submedian and internal nervures slightly recurved. Body long, slender; palpi porrect, pilose above and beneath; tip pointed; legs long, slender; antennæ slender." (*Moore*, l. c.)

H. lynceus are from the Wynaad, from whence they were sent by Mr. Rhodes Morgan, although numerous specimens in the Indian Museum, Calcutta, from the Kadur District, Mysore, are equally typical as regards the dark-grey ground-colour, though somewhat smaller in expanse. The large Travancore race has been retained for the present as *H. lynceus*, but the point requires further investigation. *H. hadeni* with its very broad pure black border is the most distinct of all the species.

1. Hestia lynceus, Drury.

Papilio lynceus, Drury, Ins., vol. ii, p. 12, pl. vii, fig. i (1773); *Hestia lynceus*, Doubl. and Hew., Gen. D. L., p. 95 (1847), Horsfield and Moore, Cat. Lep. E. I. C., vol. i, p. 134 (1857).

HABITAT: South-west peninsular India; and Malayana.

EXPANSE: 5·3 to 6·3 inches.

DESCRIPTION: "UPPERSIDE, all the wings appear almost transparent and of a glassy hue, having a great number of black spots like velvet on them, of different shapes and sizes, some being round, some oblong, and others like streaks, there being on each *forewing* twenty-eight distinct ones, besides those placed near the anterior edges, which are not easily ascertained from their running into one another; the *hindwing* has thirty-three distinct spots like those on the forewing, whereof some appear double. UNDERSIDE, exactly similar to the upperside. The edges of both wings plain and even." (*Drury*, l. c.)

The above somewhat quaint description is taken from the original by Drury; it is not very definite, but an examination of the plate, though the colouring is overdone, leaves no doubt that the large *Hestias* from the Wynaad are identical with *H. lynceus*, Drury, the expanse of which is 6·3 inches.

The following is a detailed description of the Wynaad species. *Forewing*, with the space between the costal nervure and the margin black for about one-third the length of the wing from the base, then merging into a black spot extending from the margin to the subcostal nervure; beyond this the costal margin is alternately striped white and black. In the cell are three black streaks, the upper one starting from the subcostal nervure, the two lower united towards the base which they do not quite reach; beyond the middle of them is an irregular black patch usually not reaching the nervure on either side; at the end of the cell the disco-cellular nervules are broadly defined with black; a discal series of seven black spots, of which the three nearest the costa are parallel to the end of the cell, and the next four parallel to the outer margin; within this row is an irregular black patch on a black stripe between the median and submedian nervures, and a round black spot between the first and second median nervules; beyond the discal series is a submarginal row consisting of pairs of conical spots placed by the nervules, one on each side of each, and coalescing, and a marginal series, consisting of a conical spot on each nervule with the base outwards and the apex coalescing with the submarginal row, and between each pair of nervules an elongated spot; a narrow black marginal line extends completely round both wings. On the *hindwing*, the markings correspond with those on the forewing; the marginal, submarginal and discal series are similar in style and arrangement, but within the cell there are only two black streaks, the upper one with a short branch near the end. The ground-colour of both wings is semi-transparent white, covered with minute black irrorations giving it a greyish tone. The FEMALE differs from the male in being somewhat larger, the forewing broader and less emarginate. The Tranvancore specimens correspond entirely with the above in markings, but the ground-colour is purer and more opaque white, the black irrorations being confined to the outer half of the wing, or in some cases entirely wanting.

Hestia lynceus appears to be fairly common in the hilly districts of Travancore, but is rather local. Mr. Harold Fergusson writes: "On one occasion, on the 16th February, in a patch of heavy forest at about 3,500 feet elevation, I saw numbers of this *Hestia*. There must have been at least a hundred floating about the trees some twenty feet from the ground. I had seen none before this in any of the other forests, so I should think that they must be local." * * * "Later on during April they were not uncommon, but seldom numerous * * * and throughout May they were common in the hills in suitable localities." They seem to occur only on the hills, not lower than 1,000 feet elevation, and to frequent forests. In the Kadur District, Mysore, at about 2,500 feet elevation, it has been found common in August, October, and November, by Mr. G. H. Kearney, a correspondent of the Indian Museum.

In Malacca, and possibly extending up into Tenasserim, is found a variety of this species figured by Doubleday in the Gen. D. L. (plate xiii, fig. i) as *H. lynceus* var. *idea*; it is smaller than the typical specimens, of equally grey ground-colour, the wings narrower and more elongated, and all the markings smaller, and with no tendency to confluence at the apex of the forewing. Expanse, 5·6 inches.

2. Hestia malabarica, Moore.

H. malabarica, Moore, Ann. and Mag. Nat. Hist., fourth series, vol. xx, p. 46 (1877).

HABITAT: South Concan, Malabar, South India.

EXPANSE: 5 to 5·5 inches (*Moore*); 4·3 to 5·0 inches (*Marshall*).

DESCRIPTION: "Allied to *H. belia*"* [from Java] "but differs on the *forewing* in the costa being black-streaked, the cell-spot more compact, there being also a contiguous but distinct spot situated outside the cell nearer the base, and between the costal and subcostal nervures; the discal series of spots turns to the costa more abruptly and nearer to the end of the cell; these spots are more conical, and have no contiguous patches on the veins. The marginal series of vein-marks are on long peduncles. On the *hindwing* the spots are somewhat smaller. *Abdomen* above with a broad dorsal black band." (*Moore*, l. c.) The FEMALE differs from the male in being rather larger, the *forewing* less emarginate outwardly, broader and more rounded; the *hindwing* is also rounder. All the markings are larger and a deeper black, and the ground-colour not quite such a pure clear white. As the markings of this species are precisely similar in every detail to those of *H. lynceus*, there is no occasion to repeat them.

"'Found in woody places on the western coast, especially on the thick-wooded mountain passes up the Western Ghâts and Nilgiris.'" (*Moore*, l. c.) The *Hestia* found in the northern portions of the Western Ghâts in the south Concan, and on the Goanese frontier, is much smaller than the dimensions given by Moore. Of nine specimens captured by Mr. G. Vidal, none reached 5 inches in expanse, and the smallest was only 4·3 inches; but there can be no doubt that they belong to the species described by Moore. Whether or not it is distinct from *H. lynceus* appears still open to doubt; but if the two species are distinct, the name *H. malabarica* would apply to the smaller northern race. It appears to be common towards the end of March on the wooded passes in the south Concan; a number of them were found on the Onomed and Coessi passes at about 1,600 to 1,700 feet above the sea, in that month.

Another species of this group, *Hestia linteata*,† Butler, has been recorded from Malacca.

**Hestia belia*, Westwood, Cab. Or. Ent., p. 75, pl. xxxvii, fig. 2 (1848). *Habitat*: Java. *Expanse*: 5·5 inches. *Description*: "Wings oval, snow-white, with the veins and spots black; the rather small spot of the discoidal cell scarcely extending into the subcostal area, and with a row of black oval spots beyond the middle of the wings, parallel with the apical margin, which is alternately marked with oblong-oval spots between the nervules, and clavate ones placed on the nervules; the inner false vein in the discoidal cell of the *hindwing* is marked in the middle of its outer edge with a black spot; the apical margin of the wings is rather irregular." (*Westwood*, l. c.)

H. belia differs from all the Indian species by the purer and more opaque ground-colour of the wings, the more rounded outline, the neatly, sharply-defined and rounded character of the spots, and lastly by the discal series on the *forewing* being parallel to the outer margin throughout its length, giving a neater and more regular appearance to the style of the markings. The chrysalis is suspended freely by the tail from the back of a leaf as figured in Horsfield and Moore's Cat. Lep. E. I. C., vol. i, pl. iv, fig. 12 (1857).

† *Hestia linteata*, Butler, Trans. Linn. Soc. Lond., second series, vol. i, Zoology, p. 536, pl. lxix, fig. 6. *Habitat*: Malacca. *Expanse*: 5·5 to 6·7 inches. *Description*: "Nearly allied to *H. belia*, Westwood, but much larger, the veins less broadly black-bordered; spots larger, excepting towards the costa of the *forewing* at apex; discoidal spot of *hindwing* very large; clavate markings terminating the nervules much longer, more slender in the middle." (*Butler*, l. c.)

This species seems to be the Continental representative of *H. belia*, which as yet has only been recorded from Java.

3. Hestia jasonia, Westwood. (PLATE III, FIG. 1 ♂).

H. jasonia, Westwood, Cab. Or. Ent., p. 87, pl. xlii, fig. i (1848), *male*; Butler, Trans. Ent. Soc. Lond. third series, vol. v, p. 470 (1867); *Nectaria jasonia*, Moore, Lep. Cey., p. 3, pl. i, fig. i (1880).

HABITAT: Ceylon.

EXPANSE: 4·75 to 6 inches.

DESCRIPTION: "MALE and FEMALE.—*Wings* semi-hyaline, fuliginous-white; nervures black. UPPERSIDE.—*Forewing* with a black basal costal border, an oblique irregular broad band across the middle of the cell, a short streak on the middle of the costa, a streak through the disco-cellular nervules, a large spot between the base of the two lower median nervules, a crutch-shaped mark extending to the base above the submedian nervure, a discal series of seven angulated-oval spots, a submarginal series of duplex spots terminating in a thickened streak at the end of each nervule, and a marginal row of spots. *Hindwing* with a black, round spot in the middle of the cell, two small spots below it, a discal series of eight angulated-oval spots, two of which are between the costal and subcostal nervures, a submarginal series of duplex spots terminating in a thickened streak at end of each nervule, and a marginal row of spots. *Head* and *thorax* spotted with white; thorax above, palpi and femora beneath, streaked with white. *Abdomen* black above, white beneath. UNDERSIDE of both fore- and hindwings marked as above. Some specimens are darker coloured than that above described, being blackish fuliginous; others, again, have a slight ferruginous tint pervading the wings." (*Moore*, l. c.)

Horsfield and Moore, in the Catalogue of the Lepidoptera in the Indian Museum, p. 135 (1857), record a specimen of this species from Canara (South India), but all the *Hestias* we have yet seen from peninsular India belong either to *H. lynceus* or to *H. malabarica*, and with the solitary exception noted above the present species appears to be confined to Ceylon. A variety, also from Ceylon, has been discriminated by Butler, as having "the wings smaller, fuscescent, especially towards the apex, with the spots more approximating to the external margin." "*Hestia jasonia* affects the glades of woods, and is notable for its graceful flight, rising and descending almost like a gossamer in the air, and well deserving the name of 'the Sylph' which is commonly given to it." (*Dr. Thwaites.*) "It is found only in the deep shade of the damp forest, usually frequenting the vicinity of pools of water and cascades, about which it sails heedless of the spray, the moisture of which may even be beneficial in preserving the elasticity of its thin and delicate wings that bend and undulate in the act of flight." (*Tennent.*) "In the forests, and especially about waterfalls in the western, central, and southern provinces, this Butterfly may be found all the year. It has a very slow floating flight, often poising nearly motionless, and is very easily caught." (*Hutchison*).

The plate is taken from a male specimen from Ceylon, in the Indian Museum, Calcutta; the upperside only is shown; the underside is similar to the upper. In the FEMALE the wings are broader in proportion to their length, but the markings are similar.

4. Hestia agamarschana,* Felder.

H. agamarschana, Felder, Reise Nov., Lep., p. 351, pl. xliii, fig. 7 (1867); Wood-Mason and de Nicéville, Journ. A. S. B., vol. l, pl. ii, p. 244 (1881); *H. jasonia*, var. a, Kirby, Syn. Cat. D. L., p. 2, n. 9 (1871).

HABITAT: Andaman islands, Mergui.

EXPANSE: 4·6 to 5·1 inches.

DESCRIPTION: "MALE.—*Wings* pellucid white, with the nervures black, the cellular folds, coniform spots on the nervures along the margin, with two confluent spots above and oval ones between, an interrupted costal band on the *forewing*, a large confluent spot in the cell, three large spots below the cell, a small subapical band, a disco-cellular series of spots elongated and confluent towards the costa forming an irregular black band, and the internal margin, also on the *hindwing* the cellular spot and eight other round ones besides the marginal series, dusky black; on the UNDERSIDE the spots are paler and smaller." (*Felder*, l. c.)

---

* "? 'Agamarsena' from ἄγαμος 'unmarried,' and, ἄρσην, ἄρσενος 'male,' in allusion to the fact that the describer was ignorant of the opposite (female) sex."

According to Dr. Felder's figure the markings on this species are very similar in style to those of the south Indian *Hestias*, but far more boldly developed. The discal series of spots are much elongated towards the costa, where they are almost completely confluent, forming a wide subapical black band. It has been considered by some authors as a small local variety of *H. jasonia*, but "it obviously differs from *H. jasonia*, Westwood, by the wings being shorter in the inner and longer in the outer margin, by the more concave outer margin of the forewing, and by the longer and narrower discoidal cells." (*Felder*, l. c.). It is further distinguished from that and from all the other Continental types by the conspicuous subapical black band, and the wide black inner margin to the forewing. Quite recently (December, 1881, and January, 1882) three males and a female, which evidently belong to this species, have been taken for the Indian Museum in the Mergui Archipelago; these differ from the type in being a little larger, and in having the black spot near the middle of the streak in the interno-median area of the hindwing. The FEMALE differs from the male in the *forewing* being wider and less emarginate externally; and in all the black markings of both wings being smaller, leaving a greater extent of the pure white ground-colour. See remarks on the following species, *H. cadelli*.

5. **Hestia cadelli**, W.-M. & de N. (PLATE IV, FIG. 2 ♂).

Hestia cadelli, Wood-Mason and de Nicéville, Journ. A. S. B., vol. xlix, part ii, p. 225, pl. xiii, fig. i (1880), *male*; id., vol. l, part ii, p. 244 (1881), *female*.

HABITAT: Port Blair, South Andamans.

EXPANSE: 5 inches; length of forewing, 2·45 inches.

DESCRIPTION: "MALE: Allied to *H. agamarschana*, Felder. *Wings* above pure subpellucid white, clouded, especially on the outer halves, with minute black scales, and marked and veined with intense black; all the markings larger, more or less coalescent, and blurred or paler at the margins; the nervures more broadly black-bordered, and the marginal spots completely run together, so that the wings are all, especially the hindwings, distinctly bordered externally with black. *Forewing* relatively narrower and longer, being more than twice as long as broad, with the discoidal cell equal in length to the submedian nervure, that is to say, to the inner margin, and all but as long as the outer margin measured in a straight line from the extremity of the submedian nervure to that of the subcostal; with the anterior discal spots more elongated and more completely coalesced, the spot between the first and second median nervules alone constantly free, and the large rounded one internal to it in the same interspace coalescent with the enlarged extremity of the cellular mark (which fills the cell nearly to the level of the origin of the second median nervule, and is divided at the base of the wing by three indistinct longitudinal clouded white streaks), and the large mark in front of the submedian nervure larger, triangular, and united by a black streak to the discal black spot beyond it. *Hindwing* shorter and broader, with the outer margin more broadly rounded off, the cell and the interspaces beyond it broader, the spot in it larger, and all those around it free, though exhibiting a tendency to coalesce with the black margins of the nervules. UNDERSIDE, dirty-white, of a dull opalescent tinge, with fuscous-black markings and nervures. FEMALE: Both wings broader, with the markings of the same shape, situation, size, and shade as in the male, from which, in fact, the female differs in the proportions of the organs of flight just in the same manner as does *H. hadeni*, ♀ from *H. cadelli*, ♂" (*vide* Pl. IV).

In describing this species Professor Wood-Mason and Mr. de Nicéville recorded the following note: "This specimen does not agree with Felder's figure and description of *H. agamarschana*, the only species of the genus hitherto recorded from these islands, either in the extent and relations of the black markings or in the shape and proportions of the wings: the former being larger, more or less coalescent generally, and completely run together at the outer margin so as to form a distinct black border to each wing, the hindwing being broadly rounded off at the extremity, and consequently not presenting the peculiar egg-shaped outline so characteristic of these organs in all the hitherto described Indian *Hestias*, *e.g.*, *H. lynceus*, *H. jasonia*, &c., with the latter of which Felder compares his species; the specimen apparently also differs from *H. agamarschana* in having the white of both wings everywhere more or less clouded with minute black scales. *H. agamarschana*, it is true, to judge from Felder's figure of it, has the hindwing a little less pointed, the anterior discal spots on the forewing obviously more elongated, with more black in the cell and behind it, and the markings generally larger than in *H. jasonia*, and it is, as might have been expected, more closely related to the present specimen than to any other species; but, large series of specimens having shown us how extremely constant the different species or local races of *Hestia* are, we cannot unite the two, and we think that the differences they present are in all probability due to a difference of station, and that Helfer may have obtained the specimen that formed the type of Felder's species on a different island. All the Lepidoptera received of late years from the Andamans have been obtained in the immediate vicinity of the settlement at Port Blair, in an area therefore which is a very small fractional part indeed of the Andaman group of Islands, which extends through nearly four degrees of latitude. * * * The specimens of *Hestia* which Hewitson, in his list of Butterflies from the Andamans (Ann. and Mag. Nat. Hist., fourth series, vol. xiv, 1874, p. 356) considers to be specimens of *H. agamarschana* remarkable for their dark colour, doubtless belong to the species now described."

The type specimen, which was obtained by Colonel T. Cadell, V.C., is in the Indian Museum, Calcutta. Another specimen, taken subsequently by Mr. A. R. de Roëpstorff, also in the vicinity of Port Blair, on the 16th April, is in Major Marshall's collection. There are also a large series of both sexes of this species, collected by Mr. de Roëpstorff, in the Indian Museum; they shew no variation whatever from the type, except in one or two specimens having an additional spot on the black streak in the interno-median area of the hindwing. The plate shews the upperside only of a male specimen in the Indian Museum, Calcutta.

6. **Hestia hadeni**, W.-M. & de N. (PLATE IV, FIG. 3 ♀).

H. hadeni, Wood-Mason and de Nicéville, Journ. A. S. B., vol. xlix, part ii, p. 242, pl. xiii, fig. 2 (1880), *female*.

HABITAT: Bassein, British Burma.

EXPANSE: 5·18 inches; length of forewing, 2·54.

DESCRIPTION: "FEMALE: Closely allied to *H. cadelli*. *Wings*, above pure fleckless white, marked and veined with black of a fuscous tint, with the marginal, submarginal, and all but the two posterior (which are subcoalescent with the marginal band) of the discal series of spots in the forewing, but with the marginal and submarginal series only in the hindwing completely run together, so that only the inner portions of the outlines of the innermost series of the coalesced spots are in either case still discernible, and so as to form a very broad outer border of black to both the wings. *Forewing*, broader and shorter, being less than twice as long as broad, the extreme length of the cell bearing the same relation to the submedian nervure and to the less deeply emarginate outer margin; with the spot at the base of the second median nervule smaller and free of the nervules, as also is the discoidal cellular spot at its posterior extremity; the curved club-shaped mark in the interno-median area much as in *H. agamarschana*, but not connected by a black streak with the subcoalescent marginal spot beyond it; the outer black border with a clouded white spot in the first median interspace more or less distinctly separating the second discal black spot off from the band; and the black inner marginal space longitudinally streaked with clouded white. *Hindwing* broader, with its undulated outer margin still more broadly rounded; the spot in the discoidal cell smaller, and the spots around it also rather smaller and free of the black outer border, though exhibiting a tendency to coalesce with it in front of the second median nervule. UNDERSIDE of a less pure white than above, marked and veined with fuscous. *Thorax* more conspicuously marked with greyish-white than in *H. cadelli*, in which these marks are almost effaced, but this character, as also the differences in the proportions, and the less obvious emargination of the outer margin of the wings, may be sexual." The MALE is as yet unknown.

Two specimens, both females, agreeing in every respect with one another, were obtained by Mr. Algernon Haden at Bassein; no other instance of its capture is on record. The type specimen is in the Indian Museum at Calcutta; the figure of it shews the upperside only. For the use of this well-executed plate, on which the two preceding species are represented, we are indebted to Mr. J. Wood-Mason, Natural History Secretary of the Asiatic Society of Bengal, in whose Journal it first appeared.

Genus 2.—IDEOPSIS, Horsfield. (PLATE V).

Ideopsis, Horsfield and Moore, Cat. Lep. E. I. C., vol. i, p. 133 (1857); *Danais*, sect. 4, Doubl., Gen. D. L., p. 90 (1847).

"Closely resembles *Hestia* in form, colouring, and texture of the wings, and to which it has another resemblance in the absence of the sexual spot on the *hindwing*. Like some species of *Danais*, and like the genus *Hestia*, it has the first subcostal nervule anastomosing with the costal nervure. Like most species of *Hestia* the genus *Ideopsis* has the wings somewhat diaphanous, white; the outer margin, nervures, nervules, two or more vittæ in the cell, and a series of dots between the nervules, sometimes coalescing, all fuscous; but notwithstanding these points of resemblance, it may always be known from *Hestia* at first sight by its distinctly clavate antennæ, and on closer examination by its claws devoid of paronychia and pulvilli." (*Doubleday*, l. c.)

The Butterflies belonging to this genus were for a long time included under *Danais*, and form section iv of that genus in Westwood's Genera of Diurnal Lepidoptera. They are a fairly well-marked group, and are distinguished from all species of *Danais* by the *Hestia*-like style of their markings and colouring, and from all except the first group *Radena* by the absence in the males of the sexual spot or pouch on the hindwing. Six species are known, all from the Indo-Malayan region, only one species extending into the Indian limits in Tenasserim; the same species occurs also in China, the other five are insular and local.

7. Ideopsis daos, Boisduval. (PLATE V, FIG. 4 ♂).

Idea daos, Boisd., Sp. Gén., vol. i, pl. xxiv, fig. 3 (1836); *Hestia eudora*, Gray, Lep. Ins. of Nepal, p. 10, pl. ix, fig. 3 (1846); *Idea diardi*, Voll., Tijd. Ent., vol. iii, p. 44, pl. ii, fig. 4 (1860); *Hestia daos*, Doubl., List. Lep. Brit. Mus., pt. i, p. 52; *Ideopsis daos*, Horsfield and Moore, Cat. Lep. E. I. C., vol. i, p. 134 (1857).

HABITAT: Tenasserim, Malay Peninsula, China.

EXPANSE: 4·0 to 4·4 inches.

DESCRIPTION: MALE: Both wings white, thickly irrorated with grey scales, semitransparent, markings black, and also the nervures, which are more or less broadly bordered with the same colour. A narrow black line extends round both wings; *cilia* very short, black, white at the interspaces. *Forewing* with the whole of the costa black, and containing a basal streak about one-third the length of the wing, and three spots gradually decreasing towards the apex and equidistant from each other, white. Three black streaks in the discoidal cell, the anterior onei mmediately behind the subcostal nervure; the other two in the middle of the cell, joined about midway and not quite reaching the base of the cell. A large irregularly-shaped spot occupies the outer end of the cell and extends a little beyond it. A discal series of six spots parallel with the outer margin between the nervules, the apical three small and conical, the point inwards, the lower three larger and circular. A marginal series of large spots placed on the nervules, between each pair of which on the folds are a pair of small marginal spots. A streak between the median and submedian nervures. *Hindwing* with a large spot occupying the outer extremity of the cell, from which issue two streaks united towards the base of the cell and which they do not reach. A discal series of six oval spots, the third and sixth from the apex the smallest, placed between the nervules. A marginal series of spots on the nervules, and between them a series of more or less pear-shaped spots, their points resting on the margin. The submedian nervure is widely bordered with black; between it and the first median nervule is a black streak (Penang specimen). The FEMALE differs from the male in the wings being shorter and broader, and the *forewing* not being emarginate. The ground-colour is also pure diaphanous white, all the markings smaller and clearer. It has also an additional spot on the forewing between the discoidal nervules (Singapore specimen). UNDERSIDE in both sexes, as above.

The caterpillar and chrysalis of *Ideopsis daos* were discovered by Captain Hamilton on the Tenasserim coast; and are figured by Horsfield and Moore (Cat. Lep., E. I. C., vol. i, plate iv, figs. 11, 11 a). The CATERPILLAR is about two inches in length, furnished with four pairs of long fleshy tentacula upwards of half an inch in length, the first pair on the second segment projected horizontally forward over the head, the other three on the third, fifth, and twelfth segments projected upwards and backwards. It is dark ringed between the segments, and has a row of six large oval red spots in the spiracular region on the fifth to tenth segments, both inclusive. The CHRYSALIS is 1·1 inch in length; it is simply suspended by the tail. In general outline it closely resembles the chrysalis of *Hestia belia*, but the tail is more pointed.

The figure is taken from a specimen from Penang in the Indian Museum, Calcutta; the upperside only is shown, the underside being similar in markings to the upperside.

Genus 3.—DANAIS, Latreille. (PLATES V to VII).

Danais, Latreille, Enc. Méth., vol. ix, p. 10 (1819); Boisd. and Lec., Lép. Am. Sept., p. 133 (1833); Doubl., Gen. D. L., p. 89 (1847); Butl., Proc. Zool. Soc. Lond., 1866, pp. 43, 171, *Monograph*; *Danaida*, Latr., Hist. Nat. Crust. Ins., vol. xiv, p. 108 (1805); *Danaus*, Latr., Gen. Crust. Ins., vol. iv, p. 201 (1809).

"ANTENNÆ, about one half the length of the body, gradually but distinctly clavate. FORELEGS, with the femora and tibiæ about equal in length; the tarsi shorter. *Tarsi* of the MALES sometimes obscurely two-jointed, the basal joint subcylindric, rather stoutest at the apex; the second joint about one-fourth the length of the first, more or less pointed; sometimes without any indication of joints, subcylindric, tapering towards the base and apex. *Tarsi* of the FEMALES four-jointed, the last joint often indistinct, all, except the last, with a stout spine on each side at the apex. MIDDLE and HINDLEGS with the tarsi very spiny; the claws long, slightly curved; the pulvilli and paronychia obsolete."

"CATERPILLAR.—Subcylindrical, tapering towards the head; furnished with a few long fleshy tentacula, not retractile, placed in pairs, usually on the third and last segments. They are mostly white, tinged with green or purple, marked with tranverse bands or narrow rings of black, the space between them often marked with yellow dots. They feed chiefly on ASCLEPIADEÆ."

"CHRYSALIS.—Suspended by the tail, ovate, contracted about the middle; the abdomen very short. They are commonly of a beautiful transparent green, spotted with black, and banded and spotted with gold, sometimes altogether of the most brilliant golden colour." (*Westwood.*)

Danais is distinguished from *Euplœa* by the want of paronychia and pulvilli, as well as by the style of the sexual mark in the males, when present. This genus comprises several well-marked groups, and has a very wide range; some species are to be found in the warm latitudes of every part of the globe. The perfect insects generally appear within fifteen days after the chrysalis form has been assumed. They are of slow flapping flight, but often sailing high in the air with their wings expanded; most of the species are numerous and abundant where found.

The Indian species of *Danais* come under the following groups:—

A. The males having the anterior tibiæ and tarsi covered with short scales and fringed with thinly scattered long hairs; colours fuscous, with whitish or hyaline markings.

a. Males with no scent-pouch on the hindwing.

I. RADENA, Moore.

b. Males with two scent-pouches on the hindwing, marked on the underside by dilatation of the *first median* nervule and submedian nervure.

II. PARANTICA, Moore.

c. Males with two scent-pouches on the hindwing, marked on the underside by dilatation of the submedian and *internal* nervures.

III. CHITTIRA,* Moore.

d. Males with one scent-pouch between the first median nervule and submedian nervure protruding on the underside as a prominent sac.

IV. TIRUMALA, Moore.

B. The males having the anterior tibiæ and tarsi covered with long, hair-like, not appressed scales, colours tawny brown with black and white markings.

a. Males with one scent-pouch placed as in *Tirumala*, but with the sac not nearly so prominent.

V. SALATURA, Moore.

---

* This group contains two types, very distinct in form and style of markings; the first has the wings elongate narrow, and with the hyaline markings greatly predominating (type *D. tytia*). This is probably the type separated as CADUGA by Moore, but we have been unable to obtain any diagnosis of *Caduga*, and therefore cannot assign the name with certainty; the second has the wings shorter and broader, and the hyaline markings much reduced and narrow. This latter is the true *Chittira* of Moore (type, *D. taprobana*).

First Group.—RADENA. "*Forewing* moderately long, triangular; first subcostal nervule emitted at about one-third before end of the cell, and anastomosed to the costal in the middle; second nervule emitted before end of the cell. *Hindwing* broad, somewhat triangular; costal margin long, nearly straight; abdominal margin long; costal nervure very convex from the base, and then extending straight along the edge of the margin; cell broad, long; subcostal and median nervules very wide apart. No scent-pouch in the male. *Antennæ* longer than in allied genera, and with a more gradually thickened and blunt club. *Larva* (*R. juventa*) with two pairs of fleshy filaments. Type, *R. similis*, Linnæus, from China." (*Moore*, Lep. Ceylon, p. 3, 1880).

Only three species of this group occur within Indian limits; another occurs in Siam (*D. persimilis*), and another in Java (*D. juventa*), and it is possible that these may one and all be merely fixed geographical varieties of the type *D. similis.* The absence of the sexual spot in the male is a very distinctive feature found in no other group of Indian *Danais,* and linking this group with the foregoing genera. In the absence of the sexual spot the males can be distinguished by the pointed tip of the tarsus of the imperfect foreleg, which in the females terminates in a brush; and by the narrower and less rounded wings.

Key to the Indian species of Radena.

A. *a.* Males with no scent-pouch on the hindwing; both wings blackish, with subhyaline markings.

- *a*[1]. The white streaks from the base narrow; no defined black border to the wings.
  - 8. D. (*Radena*) VULGARIS, Burma.
- *b*[1]. The whitish spaces on the basal area greatly predominating, leaving a well-defined dark border beyond.
  - *a*[2]. The cell in the hindwing with two broad black streaks.
    - 9. D. (*Radena*) EXPROMPTA, Ceylon.
    - D. (*Radena*) PERSIMILIS, Siam.
  - *b*[2]. The cell in the hindwing almost entirely hyaline.
    - 10. D. (*Radena*) NICOBARICA, Nicobars.

8. Danais vulgaris, Butler.

D. melissa, Doubleday (*nec* Cramer), List Lep. Brit. Mus., vol. i, p. 49 (1844); Gen. D. L., p. 92, n. 28 (1847); *D. vulgaris*, Butler, Ent. Month. Mag., vol. xi, p. 164 (1874); Moore, Proc. Zool. Soc. Lond., 1878, p. 822.

HABITAT: Burma, Mergui, Singapore, Borneo.

EXPANSE: 3·3 to 3·7 inches.

DESCRIPTION: "Allied to *D. similis*, altogether smaller, with all the spots paler and smaller, and all the streaks narrower; the second and third spots of the postcellular series smaller." (*Butler*, l. c.)

This is the original description, but in the absence of description or specimens of *D. similis* which does not occur in India, and which has been but lately correctly discriminated, somewhat more is necessary to render it intelligible.

MALE. *Forewing* black; a streak in the discoidal cell from the base, followed by an irregular outwardly indented blotch near the end; a subcostal streak, followed by three decreasing subcostal spots, one between each pair of the nervules; an inwardly pointed streak above the first discoidal nervule; an oval spot touching the cell and an outwardly dentate spot some way beyond it between the first and second discoidal nervules; a similar pair of spots, but closer together between the second discoidal and third median nervules; a single large spot in each of the median interspaces near the base; two lengthened streaks starting from the base between the median and submedian nervures; a submarginal row of seven increasing spots, one between each pair of nervules, the apical one minute; an incomplete marginal row from the hinder angle of minute spots, two between each pair of nervules, and a short streak from the base below the submedian nervure—all subhyaline bluish-white. *Hindwing* brown, darker towards the apex; a spot at the base, a short streak above the costal nervure, and a longer one below it; two lengthened streaks in the cell joined at the base, with a short streak between them from the end; five streaks outside the cell, one in each interspace; two lengthened streaks from the base below the cell, (the inner one tinged ochreous,) and one on each side of the internal nervure (also tinged ochreous); an irregular submarginal row of small elongate spots, coalescing with the streaks at the anal angle; and an incomplete marginal row of minute round spots evanescent at the apex—subhyaline bluish-white. UNDERSIDE: *Forewing* cupreous brown, blacker on the middle of the wing. *Hindwing* of a paler and uniform tint; all the subhyaline markings in both wings as on upperside.

Danais vulgaris is recorded by Butler from Nepal, Assam, Bengal, Moulmein, Singapore, Borneo, and Java; but if it really does occur anywhere west of Burma it is extremely rare. Limborg met with it at Ahsown, Moulmein to Meetan, and the Houngduran source in Upper Tenasserim; Mr. A. Haden has taken it at Bassein; Captain C. H. E. Adamson has taken specimens in the neighbourhood of Moulmein in March, June, October and December; Captain Bingham took it in the Thoungyeen forests in May. It is common at Rangoon; Dr. J. Anderson has taken it at Mergui in December; and there are two specimens in the Indian Museum, Calcutta—one from Malacca, the other from Borneo. It is apparently not uncommon in Upper Tenasserim throughout the year, and is probably frequently overlooked; but we know of no instance of its occurrence as yet even in Pegu or Arakan. The true *D. similis*, which is a native of Formosa and China, only really differs from *D. vulgaris* in being somewhat larger. The figure is taken from a male specimen from Malacca, in the Indian Museum, Calcutta, and shews the upper and underside.

9. **Danais exprompta**, Butler.

D. exprompta, Butler, Ent. Month. Mag., vol. xi, p. 164 (1874); *Radena exprompta*, Moore, Lep. Ceylon, p. 4, pl. ii, fig. i. (1880), *female*.

HABITAT: Ceylon.

EXPANSE: 3·25 inches (*Butler*); 2·75 to 3 inches (*Moore*).

DESCRIPTION: "Allied to *D. similis*, much smaller, the pale spots and streaks broader at base of wings, and in the series bounding the cell of *hindwing*; the second and third spots of the postcellular series in *forewing* considerably smaller; the long cuneiform spot of the outer discal series nearer to apical margin. UNDERSIDE, altogether paler and less coppery in tint." (*Butler*, l. c.)

The above is the original description; the following more detailed description is taken from Moore's "Lepidoptera of Ceylon":—

"MALE and FEMALE: UPPERSIDE blackish-brown; abdominal margin pale brown. *Forewing* with a pale blue narrow discoidal streak, and a large sinuous quadrate spot beyond it; a slender costal streak; two streaks below the cell, and a slender basal streak on inner margin; two large discal spots, three small upper spots, and five subapical spots, the upper three of which are slender; a submarginal regular series of seven small spots, and a marginal row of minute spots. *Hindwing* with pale blue, broad, basal streaks, large discal spots, an irregular submarginal and marginal row of small spots. *Head, thorax,* and *palpi* white spotted. *Femora* beneath streaked with white. *Abdomen,* brown above, paler beneath. UNDERSIDE : *Forewing* dark brown ; *hindwing* umber-brown ; markings as above, but paler."

"Common in Kottawa forest, but have not seen it elsewhere." (*Wade*). It appears to be confined to the island of Ceylon ; no record of its occurrence elsewhere has been made.

A closely allied species belonging to this group has lately been described from Siam under the name of *D. persimilis.**

10. Danais nicobarica, W.-M. & de N.

D. similis, var. *nicobarica*, Wood-Mason and de Nicéville, Journ. A. S. B., vol. 1, pt. ii, p. 225 (1881).

HABITAT : Great Nicobar.

EXPANSE : *Male,* 3·1 inches ; *female,* 3·2 inches.

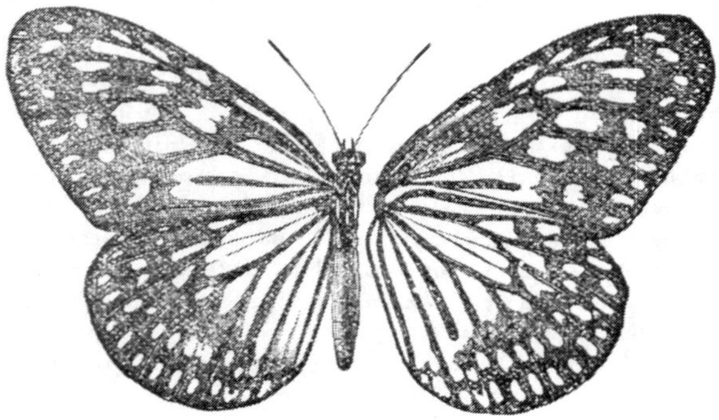

DESCRIPTION : " MALE and FEMALE : Nearest to *D. exprompta,* Butler from Ceylon, from the figure † of which species (probably that of a female, though the sex is not stated) it differs, in the *forewing* in having the streak in the base of the interno-median area broader, occupying all but the entire breadth of the space, shorter, and marked along the middle by a linear streak (instead of being divided into two long and narrow streaks connected at the base only) ; and, in the *hindwing,* in having the cell entirely subdiaphanous greenish or bluish white, except for two excessively fine and faint longitudinal and apically-divergent dusky lines much as in *D. juventa* (instead of being divided by two very broad and black ones into two streaks, the posterior of which is strongly recurved at its free end) ; the discal series of bluish streaks immediately beyond the cell much narrower and shorter ; and the ground-colour around them consequently of greater extent and giving to this portion of the wing a much darker appearance, again much as in *D. juventa.* The MALE differs from the female in the bluish markings of both wings being of a much deeper shade, and, with the exceptions to be stated, larger ; in the *forewing* being narrower and externally slightly emarginate (instead of well rounded), with its outer submarginal series of spots reduced to small specks, and the three posterior ones of its inner series externally distinctly tridentate ; and in the *hindwing* being also apparently somewhat narrower and less rounded externally, with both series of submarginal spots much smaller,—with its two posterior veins margined on both sides with fuscous of a far lighter and duller tint than the rest of the ground,—and with the submedian one of them more prominent, with the wing membrane on each side of it raised into a slight fold, and the two light streaks that bound it dirty whitey-brown : the male of this species is, in fact, provided with a distinct, though little-specialized, sexual mark or scent-gland."

---

* *Danais persimilis,* Moore, Proc. Zool. Soc. Lond., 1879, p. 136. HABITAT : Petchaburree, Bankok District, Siam (April 12th, 1875). EXPANSE : 2·37 inches. DESCRIPTION : " Nearest allied to *D. exprompta,* Butler (the Ceylon form of *D. juventa),* but is much smaller in size. The markings are similar ; but those from the base of the wings are very much more attenuated and shorter, and the discal spots also smaller, the markings on the *hindwing* being more attenuated than those in *D. grammica.*" (*Moore,* l. c.). *D. agleoides* is probably referred to here.

† Moore, 'Lep. Ceylon,' pl. ii. fig. 2, 1880, *female.*

"One male and three females, the latter agreeing exactly with one another, from Great Nicobar." No notice of its occurrence elsewhere has been recorded. The figure shews the upper and underside of a female in the Indian Museum, Calcutta.

Second Group.—PARANTICA. "*Forewing* long, narrow; inner margin lengthened; first subcostal nervule emitted at one-fourth before end of the cell and touching the costal nervure near its end; the second emitted immediately before the end of the cell; cell long, narrow. *Hindwing* somewhat elongated; exterior margin very convex; abdominal margin short; costal nervure arched from base and thence extending along edge of the margin; cell very long and narrow. MALE with two spatular-shaped scent-pouches, one (the largest) being on the first median nervule, the other (about one-fourth its size) on the submedian nervure, near their end, each being visible on the underside by the slender swelling of these nervures at that part. *Antennæ* with lengthened slender tip. *Larva* with two pair of fleshy filaments. Type, *D. aglea*, Cramer." (*Moore*, 'Lep. Ceylon,' p. 7.)

This group is further divisible into two sections, the first of which has for its type *D. cleona*, Cramer; the Butterflies of this section comprise the smallest species of the genus, and are distinguished from all other species of *Danais* by having beautiful pure yellow tints on the hyaline markings of the wings; they are Malayan Butterflies, and within Indian limits are extremely rare. Four species are included in the Indian list, but the claims of two of them for inclusion rest on somewhat obscure data, especially those of *D. aspasia*, which is recorded from south India. The Butterflies of the second section, type *D. aglea*, are rather larger in size, and have no trace of the pure yellow tints; their head-quarters too are in Malayana, but they extend over the greater part of India, and some of the species are common where they occur. Of the five Indian species, one is found in Ceylon only; another, which is doubtfully distinct from the Ceylon species, occurs throughout peninsular India; another in north India extending into Burma; another in Burma extending to the Nicobars; and the last is confined to the Andaman Islands. They are all comparatively delicately-formed Butterflies, with rather elongate wings, and having the hyaline markings usually preponderating over the blackish ground-colour.

Key to the Indian species of Parantica.

A. *b*. Males with two scent-pouches on the hindwing, visible on the underside by dilatation of the *first median nervule* and submedian nervure. Wings blackish, with hyaline markings.

- *a*¹. Of small size; some of the hyaline markings tinged with pure yellow.
  - *a*². With yellowish tints on both wings.
    - *a*³. With only one, or two, very small discal spots between the third and second median nervules.
      - 11. D. *(Parantica)* CLEONA, N. India (?), Java.
    - *b*³. With two spots, the inner one filling the base of the interspace.
      - *a*⁴. Outer margin of forewing convex and scarcely emarginate; the streaks between the discoidal nervules short and broad.
        - 12. D. *(Parantica)* PHILOMELA, Nepal (?), Java.
      - *b*⁴. Outer margin of forewing highly emarginate; the streaks between the discoidal nervules long and narrow.
        - 13. D. *(Parantica)* CROCEA, Burma, Java.
  - *b*². With yellowish tints on hindwing only.
    - 14. D. *(Parantica)* ASPASIA, Tranquebar (?).
- *b*¹. Of rather larger size; no pure yellow tints.
  - *a*². Deep black, with pure hyaline white markings; hindwing with the black streaks very fine and white spaces wide.
    - 15. D. *(Parantica)* MELANOLEUCA, Andamans.
  - *b*². Fuscous, with dull hyaline bluish-white markings.
    - *a*³. Forewing with the hyaline streak between the discoidal nervules almost touching the disco-cellular nervule.
      - 16. D. *(Parantica)* AGLEA, N. India, Burma,
    - *b*³. Forewing with the streak between the discoidal nervules not nearly reaching the disco-cellular nervule.
      - *a*⁴. Forewing lengthened and emarginate on outer margin, hyaline markings large, prominent.
        - 17. D. *(Parantica)* CEYLANICA, Ceylon.
        - 18. D. *(Parantica)* GRAMMICA, S. India.
      - *b*⁴. Wings comparatively short and rounded; all the hyaline spots small, and the streaks narrow.
        - 19. D. *(Parantica)* AGLEOIDES, Burma, Nicobars.

D. ceylanica is precisely similar to *D. grammica*, except that its tone of colouration is somewhat darker, and the hyaline markings are rather less prominent; they are very doubtfully distinct as species.

11. **Danais cleona**, Cramer.

Papilio cleona, Cramer, Pap. Ex., vol. iv, pl. ccclxxvii, fig. F (1781); Herbst, Pap., pl. cxxvi, fig. i (1793); *Danais cleona*, Godt., Enc. Méth., vol. ix, p. 190, n. 47 (1819); Blanc., Voy. au Pôle Sud, vol. iv, p. 386, pl. ii, fig. 3 (1853); *Danais lutescens*, Butler, Proc. Zool. Soc. Lond., 1866, p. 172, n. 5, p. 173, fig. 3, *female*.

HABITAT: North India (apud *Westwood* and *Butler*), Java, Borneo.

EXPANSE: 3·0 to 3·5 inches.

DESCRIPTION: The following description is taken from Cramer's plate:—MALE: UPPERSIDE: *Forewing* black, with a short basal streak and beyond it an oval spot, both in the cell; three submarginal spots along the costa, below which are a short and broad streak below the subcostal nervure, a longer one between the discoidal nervules; a large spot above and a small one below the third median nervule; two spots below the second median nervule, the inner one large and completely filling the base of the interspace; and the space between the median and submedian nervules from the base to rather more than half the length of the wing—all hyaline tinted with pure yellow. A submarginal series of spots one between each pair of nervules, and a marginal row of smaller spots not reaching the apex, two between each pair of nervules—both series white. *Hindwing* also black; the entire discoidal cell, a series of spots round it between the nervules, a double streak joined at the base below the median nervure, a single streak below the submedian (and probably another near the abdominal margin) hyaline, tinted with pure yellow. A submarginal and marginal row of white spots as on forewing, except that in the hindwing there are two spots between each pair of nervules in both series. The usual black sexual marks. The FEMALE from Ceram and Borneo has been described by Butler as a separate species under the name of *D. lutescens*, and is stated to be "closely allied to *D. cleona* of Cramer, from which it differs chiefly in its pale colouring, more rounded and shorter wings, and larger spots." (*Butler*, l. c.) His figure agrees exactly with Cramer's, except in the outline of the wings being more rounded, and in the discoidal cell of the *forewing* being entirely hyaline. Blanchard's figure of a *female* (apparently) from Ceram in the "Voyage au Pôle Sud" shows a second very small spot inwardly between the third and second median nervules, which is absent from both Cramer's figure of a ♂, and Butler's of a ♀, thus showing an approach to *D. philomela* and *D. crocea*.

Atkinson (Ent. Month Mag., vol. iv, p. 60, 1867) records having taken *D. cleona* at Jounpur, North-Western Provinces, in July. This record at any rate goes to prove that at least one species of this group of *Danais* still occurs in Continental India, but as far as we know there is no specimen of *D. cleona* now in any collection in this country.

12. **Danais philomela**, Zinken-Sommer.

Euplœa philomela, Zinken-Sommer, Nava Acta Ac. Nat. Cur., vol. xv, p. 184, pl. xvi, fig. 17 (1831).

HABITAT: Nepal (apud *Butler* and *Kirby*), Java.

EXPANSE: ♂, 2·5; ♀, 2·9 inches.

DESCRIPTION: MALE UPPERSIDE: *Forewing* black: with the discoidal cell; two spots between the third and second median nervules; two larger spots between the second and first, the inner one of each pair entirely filling the base of the interspace; the entire space between the median nervure, first median nervule and the submedian nervure to within a fourth of the length of the wing from the outer margin—pure hyaline yellow. Three subcostal oval spots, one between each pair of the subcostal nervules; two streaks below these, the lower the longest; an outwardly indented spot between the second discoidal and third median nervules; a submarginal series of increasing spots, one between each pair of nervules; a very incomplete series of smaller marginal spots, two between each pair of nervules—white. The discoidal cell has near its middle a dusky streak, and the median nervure is widely bordered on both sides with black. *Hindwing* also black; with two small spots at the base; a very short streak above the costal nervure; a long one below it; the entire cell; a streak below the first subcostal nervule; a longer and broader one below this; a spot between the discoidal and the third median nervules; another between the third and second, with a small round spot beyond it; a broad streak between the second and first, filling the base of the interspace, also with a small round spot beyond it; two broad streaks connected at the base, between the median and submedian nervures; a streak between the submedian and internal nervures—pure hyaline yellow. A small spot at the end of the streak below the costal nervure; a spot beyond the streak between the first and second subcostal nervules; an irregular, submarginal row of small spots interrupted at the black sexual mark; a regular marginal series; both series with two spots between each pair of nervules—white. The streak between the internal nervure and the abdominal margin almost white, but faintly tinged with yellow. UNDERSIDE as above. Described from a Javan specimen in the Indian Museum, Calcutta. The figure of a FEMALE given in the "Nova Acta" differs from the male in the *forewing* being broader, rounder, and but slightly emarginate; in having only the broad space below the median nervure tinged with yellow; and the submarginal series of spots on the *hindwing* complete from the absence necessarily of the male sexual spot.

Butler writes (Proc. Zool. Soc. Lond., 1866, p. 456):—"*Euplœa philomela* of Zinken-Sommer, hitherto placed as a synonym of *D. cleona* of Cramer, must be kept separate from it. This species, excepting in form, bears a more general appearance to my *D. crocea*; it is intermediate between the two species; and the male, two specimens of which I have discovered in the [British] Museum collection, is of the same form as my *D. gloriola*, ♂. It may be easily distinguished from *D. crocea*, not only by its different form, but by the male having the entire basal portion of the *forewing* yellow, and the subapical streaks much broader and shorter. HABITAT: Java, Nepal." It is included in the Indian list on the strength of the above quotation. If it does really occur in North India, it is rare; it was not met with in Tenasserim either by Limborg or Captain Bingham.

13. **Danais crocea**, Butler. (PLATE V, FIG. 6 ♂).

D. crocea, Butler, Proc. Zool. Soc. Lond., 1866, p. 57, pl. iv, figs. 5, 6.

HABITAT: Nepal?, Assam?, Burma, Penang, Malacca, Singapur, Java, Borneo.

EXPANSE: ♂, 2·5 to 3·12; ♀, 2·62 to 3·19 inches.

DESCRIPTION: "Allied to *D. cleona*, Cramer, from which it differs in having the cell of *fore-* and the costa of *hindwings* unclouded; the subapical and submarginal spots more numerous, and white, not yellow; an additional yellow spot below the base of the third median nervule, the nervures not so broadly margined with brown, and the wings more transparent. UNDERSIDE the same as above. *Note.*—In some specimens the whole transparent portion of the *forewing* is clear white, with a slight tinge of yellow at the base." (*Butler*, l. c.)

"Occurs at Penang in August and September." (*W. L. Distant.*)

The figure is taken from a male specimen in the Indian Museum, Calcutta, from Kyouk Phyoo, Burma, and shows both upper and underside. This specimen differs from Butler's description as given above, in that the cell of the *forewing* is decidedly clouded, but it corresponds exactly with his figure No. 5—the real point of diference between this species and *D. cleona* being the absence in the latter, or very minute size if present, of the inner spot between the second and third median nervules of the forewing. Dr. Anderson took two male specimens of this species at Mergui in December, and one in March.

14. **Danais aspasia**, Fabricius.

Papilio aspasius, Fabricius, Mant. Ins., vol. ii, p. 15, n. 145 (1787).

HABITAT: Tranquebar.

EXPANSE: (not given.)

DESCRIPTION: "Wings oblong, entire, black with hyaline streaks and spots. *Hindwing* yellow at the base; *head* and *thorax* black, spotted with white; *abdomen* fuscous. *Forewing*, black, the base streaked and the apex spotted with hyaline. *Hindwing*, yellow at the base, with the veins black, the margin black, with hyaline spots."

The above is the original description by Fabricius; there does not appear to be any recent record of the occurrence of this species, but the description is sufficient to admit of identification if the Butterfly should again be found.

15. **Danais melanoleuca**, Moore.

D. melanoleuca, Moore, Proc. Zool. Soc. Lond., 1877, p. 581, pl. lviii, fig. 3.

HABITAT: South Andamans (Port Blair).

EXPANSE: ♂, 2·3 to 2·8; ♀, 2·6 to 3·3 inches.

DESCRIPTION: "MALE and FEMALE: Black. *Forewing*, with white space within the cell, two-thirds of space between first median nervule and submedian nervure; four discal spots, an indistinct costal basal streak, three costal spots before the apex, two lower elongated streaks, followed by a dentate spot, and three smaller rounded submarginal spots; some marginal white dots near the posterior angle, and a small spot below the apex, the space within the cell with short, narrow, dusky streaks from its end, and a median dusky line within the space below the median nervure. [In the numerous specimens in the Indian Museum, Calcutta, the submarginal spots are five to seven in number]. *Hindwing*, with white space within the cell and between the nervures to one-third from the outer margin, the upper spaces concave, and the lower conical externally; an indistinct dusky lunule crossing the end of the two lower median spaces, a prominent black bifid streak within the cell, and a line between first median nervule and submedian nervure; a submarginal series of small white spots, two between each pair of nervules (two being obsolete in the male on the sexual mark), and a marginal series of seven smaller spots from anal angle. *Head* and *thorax* with white spots and streaks. *Abdomen*, cinereous brown above, white beneath. *Femora* and *tibiæ*, white streaked." (*Moore*, l. c.) On the UNDERSIDE the markings are similar, but the marginal and submarginal series of spots are larger and complete on both wings. In the *forewing* the white space in the cell is sullied; and the two streaks beyond the cell and the spots below them are extended towards the submarginal spots, and very concave externally. In the *hindwing* the lower median white spaces, and the subcostal space are shortened, while the discal white spaces are lengthened, making the black border much more irregular in width than on the upperside.

D. melanoleuca is only as yet known from the Andamans, and is probably a local, insular, though very well marked, species, nearly allied to *D. vitrina*, Felder. It appears to be common at Port Blair, where it is on the wing throughout the year.

16. **Danais aglea**, Cramer. (PLATE VI, FIG. 7 ♂ ♀).

Papilio aglea, Cramer, Pap. Ex., vol. iv, pl. ccclxxvii, fig. E (1781), *male*; Herbst, Pap., pl. cxxv, fig. 5 (1793); *Danais similis*, Godart, Enc. Méth., vol. ix, p. 190, n. 46 (1819); *Danais aglea*, Moore, Proc. Zool. Soc. Lond., 1878, p. 822.

HABITAT: Sub-Himalayas, Assam, Burma, Tenasserim.

EXPANSE: 3·0 to 3·8 inches.

DESCRIPTION: MALE. *Forewing*, swarthy black; the discoidal cell, a narrow subcostal streak from the base nearly to the first subcostal branch, beyond this three decreasing spots between the subcostal branches, behind these spots a streak in front of the first discoidal nervule, and a longer one between the discoidal nervules; one spot above the third median nervule outwardly concave; two between the third and second, and two between the second and first, the inner of each of these pairs filling the base of the interspace; the entire space between the median and submedian nervures to within one-fourth of the length of the wing from the outer margin; a submarginal row of seven increasing spots, one between each pair of nervules; and a marginal row of two smaller spots between each pair of nervules disappearing towards the apex—bluish subhyaline white; two dusky streaks from the end of the cell uniting towards the middle and not reaching the base, and a dusky streak in the middle of the hyaline space below the median nervure. *Hindwing* also swarthy black; the discoidal cell subhyaline, with a bifid blackish streak not reaching the base; two spots at the base; a streak above the costal nervure; an elongated streak below the costal nervure; five broad streaks round the end of the cell completely filling the interspaces at the base; the two in the median interspaces crossed near the end by a black bar not always complete; two broad streaks connected at the base, between the median and submedian nervures; and a single broad streak on each side of the internal nervure; a marginal and a submarginal row of spots two between each pair of nervules in each row—hyaline bluish-white. The submarginal row interrupted at the sexual mark. UNDERSIDE lighter, the bluish white markings similar but more prominent; none of the submarginal or marginal series of spots obsolete. The sexual spot on the first median nervule of the *hindwing* is deep intense black, and divided by a very narrow white streak on each side of the black nervule, which is slenderly dilated. The submedian nervure also is white and slenderly dilated in that portion adjoining the sexual spot. On the *forewing* the lower white streak between the discoidal nervules and the discal spot below it are extended in a crescent shape, half encircling the submarginal spots beyond. On the *hindwing* the white interspaces on either side of the discoidal nervule extend to and coalesce with the submarginal spots beyond, forming a prominent white patch on the border. FEMALE: Similar to the male, except that the wings are somewhat broader and the *forewing* less falcate. The sexual mark on the *hindwing* is of course absent. so the submarginal row of spots on that wing is complete and uninterrupted. *Cilia* black, spotted with white at the interspaces. *Head* and *thorax* spotted and streaked with white. *Abdomen* swarthy above, chalky white beneath.

D. aglea inhabits the region of heavy rainfall in north-east India, extending along the submontane tarais to the Sutlej, but common only towards the east. There is only one record of its occurrence so far west as Simla. A single specimen was taken by Mr. de Nicéville in a garden about 1,000 feet below Simla in July. Three specimens were taken in November, 1880, at Naiashahr in the Saharanpore district by Mrs. Deane; and there is a specimen from Mussoorie in the Indian Museum, Calcutta, but in the north-west Himalayas it is decidedly a rare insect. In Kumaon there is no record as yet of its occurrence; in Sikkim it was taken in November by Mr. Otto Möller in the Great Runjit Valley at 1,200 to 3,500 feet elevation; and in the Darjeeling tarai and up to 6,000 feet elevation in the hills Mr. de Nicéville found it plentiful in October. In the Khasi hills it occurs in November; in Tenasserim Limborg took it in the winter at 3,000 to 6,000 feet elevation; and Captain C. T. Bingham found it there commonly in February up to 1,500 feet elevation, and again in August to November. Dr. J. Anderson took it at Mergui in December.

The figure shows the upperside of male and female from specimens from Sibsagar, Assam, in the Indian Museum, Calcutta.

17. **Danais ceylanica,** Felder.

D. ceylanica, Felder, Verh. zool.-bot. Gesellsch. Wien, vol. xii, p. 479, n. 90 (1862); *Parantica ceylonica*, Moore, Lep. Cey., p. 8, pl. ii, figs. 2, 2 a, larva and pupa (1880).

HABITAT: Ceylon.

EXPANSE: 3 to 3·25 inches.

DESCRIPTION: "MALE and FEMALE. UPPERSIDE, dark fuliginous-brown. *Forewing* with a bluish-white narrow discoidal streak, above which are two parallel contiguous slender lines, two lengthened streaks below the cell, five discal spots, two upper slender streaks, and three costal spots, a submarginal row of small mostly cordate spots, and a marginal row of more or less indistinct smaller spots. *Hindwing* with broad bluish-white basal streaks, regular series of discal quadrate spots, the two lower of which have a contiguous or continuous outer spot, an irregular submarginal and marginal row of small spots. The two scent-pouches [as usual] in the male. *Head, thorax*, and *palpi*, white-spotted, a dorsal streak on the thorax, and the femora beneath, white. *Abdomen* brown above, white beneath. UNDERSIDE brown, markings clearer. *Forewing* with the discoidal streaks more distinct; above the cell is a slender line, and the upper discal spot and the streak are concave externally. *Hindwing* with a black pouch area [as usual] in the male."

"LARVA. cylindrical, reddish-purple, two black fleshy filaments on third and two on twelfth segment; two dorsal rows of round chrome-yellow spots, and a lateral row of broken chrome-yellow spots, with intervening white dots on each segment. *Head* and *legs* black, white spotted. PUPA green, much constricted below the thorax, with blue and golden scattered dots and black raised dots on upper segments. Feeds on *Cryptolepis*, &c." (*Moore*, l. c.)

In his original short description of this species Felder remarks: "A local variety of *D. aglea* from north India ntermediate between it and *D. agleoides*; the Ceylon form differs from both by its less sharply defined white markings and from *D. agleoides* also by its much broader streaks." It appears that both Felder and also Moore in his more recent works must have overlooked *D. grammica*, which was figured by Boisduval so long ago as 1836. *D. ceylanica* is really a local form of *D. grammica*, which is the common south Indian species, and only differs from it by its generally darker colour, owing to the greater preponderance of the swarthy ground-colour; some specimens from Trevandrum are indistinguishable from *D. ceylanica*, although those from the Western Ghâts are notably paler as they extend northwards, and it is doubtful whether the name *ceylanica* should not be suppressed and the Ceylon species be included under the name *grammica*.

"Found everywhere all the year in open or partially cultivated places, but not often in forest. Flight slow and heavy. Perhaps the commonest Butterfly in Ceylon." (*Hutchison*).

18. **Danais grammica**, Boisduval.

D. grammica, Boisd., Sp. Gén., Lép., vol. i, pl. vi, fig. 10 (1836).

HABITAT: South India.

EXPANSE: 2·7 to 3·4 inches.

DESCRIPTION: Boisduval's original figure, which unfortunately shows only the underside, and the costal margin of the forewing of the upperside, is the only authority for indentifying this species, neither locality nor description being given. The figure corresponds exactly in markings with *D. ceylanica*, except that the outer of the three subcostal spots on the upperside of the forewing is wanting in *D. grammica*. The south Indian *Danais* of this type also corresponds in markings with *D. ceylanica*, but in a specimen from Belgaum the third subcostal spot is wanting, and the similarity with Boisduval's figure is complete. We have, therefore, even though this character is utterly inconstant, retained Boisduval's name for the south Indian species. The only points by which it can be distinguished from *D. ceylanica* are that it is slightly less black in general colouration, and on the upperside the marginal series of spots on the forewing is almost always complete to the apex in *D. grammica*, whereas in *D. ceylanica* it is seldom, if ever, complete; but if the localities were unknown it would be hardly possible to distinguish accurately between the species. There is little doubt that the Ceylon and south Indian species will eventually have to be united under the name *D. grammica*.

Moore records this species from Java and the Nicobars, and Butler records it from Moulmein, Malacca, and Java; but it is probable that *D. agleoides* is the species referred to in both cases, for out of the numerous collections we have received from Burma and the Nicobars, we have not found a single specimen approaching to *D. grammica*, while numerous specimens of *D. agleoides* have been sent. (*See* Journ. A. S. B., vol. l, part ii, p. 224, 1881).

D. grammica has been taken in Travancore by Messrs. Bourdillon and Fergusson; in August in the hills near Trevandrum; and in the Ashamboo range in May. In Calicut it has been taken in September; at Bangalore in August and November. A number of specimens were taken by Mr. G. Vidal, C. S., in the south Concan; on the Ghâts and on the Goanese frontier at 1,500 to 1,700 feet above the sea at the latter end of March; and in Belgaum it is common in October. A single specimen was also taken at Mahableshwar at

Christmas by Mr. E. H. Aitken, and there is a specimen from Poona in the Indian Museum. Calcutta; but there is no record of its occurrence further north. This species is well distinguished from *D. aglea* so far as our present knowledge goes, and the geographical ranges of the two species seem to be widely separated; no species of this group occurs north of the Bombay Presidency, where *D. grammica* occurs, till *D. aglea* is met with in the N.-W. sub-Himalayas on the West. Our knowledge of the East Coast fauna is very limited at present, but as yet *D. aglea* has not been recorded from any place south of Assam in India proper, while *D. grammica* is not known to extend further north than Madras. If specimens should ultimately be found extending northwards along the East Coast, as is not improbable, it will be interesting to discover what approach, if any, they make to *D. aglea.*

19. **Danais agleoides,** Felder.

D. agleoides, Felder, Wien. Ent. Mon., vol. iv, p. 398, n. 17 (1860).

HABITAT: Burma, Malayana, Nicobars, Java.

EXPANSE: 2·7 to 3·2 inches.

DESCRIPTION: "MALE: Wings swarthy. *Forewing* with a costal streak and another internal one narrow, four wider discal ones, three costal spots, below the second of which a pair of elongated spots, then five in the disc and others external and marginal arranged in series, subhyaline; the apex above fuscous. *Hindwing* with seven streaks from the base, eight diversely formed discal streaks, and others placed irregularly in a double external row, subhyaline. Approximates very closely to *Danais aglea,* Cramer, but the wings are shorter and broader." (*Felder*, l. c.)

The above is a translation of Felder's short original description. The subhyaline markings on the upperside of the *forewing* are similar to those in *Danais aglea,* except being smaller, and the cell being divided along almost its whole length into three bluish-white streaks, which are joined at the base, the upper one being exceedingly narrow; and the internomedian area being occupied by two basally-joined streaks, the upper one much angled where the first median nervule is given off, the lower one straight. The *hindwing* has in the cell three hyaline streaks, the upper and lower ones joined at the base, the middle one short and lying outwardly between them. UNDERSIDE marked as above, but paler, wherein it differs much from *D. aglea.* As compared with *D. aglea, D. agleoides* is a much more compact and blacker insect, all the hyaline streaks being very narrow and the spots small. It is a very constant and well-marked species. The FEMALE only differs from the male in the absence of the sexual mark and the broader and more rounded outline of the wings.

It occurs commonly at Rangoon in January, July and September, and probably at other seasons also. On Nancowry Island, Nicobars, Mr. A. de Roëpstorff took many specimens in August and September, and on Great Nicobar Island in October. It also occurs at Sambelong, Nicobars (*Moore*). Dr. J. Anderson took it very commonly in the Mergui Archipelago in the cold weather. There is a specimen in the Indian Museum, Calcutta, labelled "Dukhun," "Sykes;" but the locality is probably erroneous, as *D. agleoides* appears to be confined to the east of the Bay of Bengal.

Third Group.—CHITTIRA: "Male with two scent-pouches, one spatular-shaped on the submedian nervure, accompanied by the dilated or swollen nervure, the other being the internal nervure dilated, but without any adjacent spatular patch." (*Moore,* Lep. Ceylon, p. 8). This includes two distinct types as regards style of markings and outline of the wings; the first group is represented by two species only in India, which are confined to the Himalayas, Assam and Burma; they have the wings elongate, especially the forewing, and the hyaline markings greatly predominating at the base of the wings; the second group also contains only two Indian species, one peculiar to Ceylon, and the other to the hills of south India; they have the wings comparatively short and broad, and the hyaline markings narrow and much reduced, the colours generally being far more opaque.

Key to the Indian species of Chittira.

A. *c* Males with two scent-pouches on hindwing, marked by dilatation of the submedian and internal nervures. Colours black or brown, with hyaline markings.

a[1]. Forewing, elongate; hyaline markings broad and extensive, occupying almost all the basal area of the wing. Of large size.

a[2]. With the margin of hindwing broadly ferruginous.

20. D. TYTIA, Himalayas, Burma.

b[2]. With the margin of hindwing broadly swarthy, always with whitish minute marginal spots.

21. D. MELANEUS, E. Himalayas, Burma.

b[1]. "Forewing somewhat short and broad; costal margin much arched, inner margin long; hindwing broadly oval, very convex externally. Antennæ with a tolerably thick club." (*Chittira* as restricted by Moore). Hyaline markings reduced, narrow.

a[2]. With white basal streaks on hindwing below the cell; and a brown streak in the whitish space on forewing below the cell.

22. D. (*Chittira*) NILGIRIENSIS, South India.

b[2]. With no white basal streaks on hindwing below the cell; and with no brown streak in the whitish space below the cell in forewing.

23. D. (*Chittira*) TAPROBANA, Ceylon.

20. Danais tytia, Gray.

D. tytia, Gray, Lep. Ins. Nepal, p. 9, pl. ix, fig. 2 (1846); Doubl. Hew., Gen. D. L., pl. xii, fig. 4 (1847); Moore, Proc. Zool. Soc. Lond., 1878, p. 822; *Danais sita*, Koll., Hüg. Kasch., vol. iv, p. 424, pl. vi (1848).

HABITAT: Himalayas, extending into Tenasserim.

EXPANSE: 3·5 to 4·4 inches.

DESCRIPTION: "*Forewing* black, with white semi-transparent spots between the nervures. *Hindwing* brownish-red, with the centre of the nervures near the base, and spots semi-transparent white, also a black spot at the anal angle." (*Gray*, l. c.) MALE: *Forewing* with the discoidal cell; three elongated decreasing spots along the costa; two streaks below these, the lower the longer; a spot below the end of the latter; two large spots between the second and third median nervules; two larger ones between the first and second, the inner one completely filling the angle made by the junction of the median nervure and first median nervule; the entire space between the median and submedian nervures to within one-fourth of the length of the wing from the outer margin; a narrow streak below the submedian nervure extending from the base half the length of the wing; a submarginal row of seven increasing spots, one between each pair of nervules; and an incomplete row of very small marginal spots not reaching the apex, two between each pair of nervules—hyaline bluish-white. *Hindwing* bright ferruginous; the disco-cellular and first and second median nervules black towards the margin; the discoidal cell hyaline, generally with a bifid streak within, not reaching the base; a small streak above the costal nervure at the base; an elongated streak below the costal; five spots around the end of the cell, one between each pair of nervules; two broad streaks connected at the base between the median and submedian nervures; and a single broad streak on either side of the internal nervure—hyaline bluish-white. A few submarginal bluish-white spots from the apex and faint traces of a marginal series. The usual sexual marks near the anal angle blackish. *Cilia* black, spotted with white at the interspaces. *Head* and *thorax* black, spotted with white. *Abdomen* ferruginous, streaked with white below. UNDERSIDE with the markings generally similar to the upperside; the apex of *forewing* ferruginous; the marginal series of spots complete to the apex; and also complete, large and conspicuous on the *hindwing*. FEMALE: Similar to the male, except that the marginal and submarginal rows of spots on the upperside of the *hindwing* are more apparent, and the sexual mark is absent.

D. tytia is one of the largest and most striking species of the genus, the wings are much elongated, and the forewing is somewhat falcate, especially in the male. It is found throughout the Himalayas from Kashmir eastwards extending into Tenasserim; to the west it is comparatively rare, getting commoner towards the east. According to Col. Lang it is a forest-loving insect, frequenting in the Western Himalayas, wooded glens, at 6,000 to 7,000 feet altitude, with a high and soaring flight. In Kulu "it is not uncommon ; it has four broods—the first brood appearing in April at the lower altitudes ; the second brood appears in June at about 6,000 feet elevation ; a third brood appears in August and the first week in September ; and the fourth, which is much the smallest in numbers, appears late in October. It is strong on the wing and a high flier ; the long pendant flowers of the hill *toon* (*Cedrela serrata*) are much affected by it." (*A. Grahame Young*). Near Simla it appears to be rare. Mr. de Nicéville, who has carefully explored the surrounding hills himself, only found *D. tytia* on the wing once, in a wooded glen near Theog on the Hindustan and Thibet road ; and though it is said actually to swarm in the Simla hills in some years, it has not done so to his knowledge since 1876. From Mussoorie specimens were brought by Herr von Hügel. In Kumaon, according to Mr. E. T. Atkinson, it is common about Naini Tal and Almorah from September to November. It has been reported also from Nepal and Bhutan. In Sikkim it is common ; in the Khasi hills it is found in the autumn, and in the hilly districts of Burma it is common during the cold weather. It has also been found in Western Yunan.

21. **Danais melaneus,** Cramer. (PLATE V, FIG. 5 ♂ ♀).

Papilio melaneus, Cram., Pap. Ex., vol. i, pl. xxx, fig. D (1775) ; Herbst, Pap., pl. cxxiii, fig. 5 (1793) ; *Hestia ephyre*, Hübner, Verz. bek. Schmett., p. 15, n. 74 (1816) ; *Danais melane*, Godart, Enc. Méth., vol. ix, p. 192, n. 53 (1819) ; *Danais melaneus*, Moore, Proc. Zool. Soc. Lond., 1878, p. 822.

HABITAT : The Eastern Himalayas, extending through Burma to Malayana and Java.

EXPANSE : 3·1 to 4·4 inches.

DESCRIPTION : *Forewing* marked spot for spot as in *D. tytia*, but differs from that species in being less elongate and falcate ; the *hindwing* also is shorter and rounder. The ground-colour of the *hindwing* is swarthy instead of bright ferruginous, and the bifid streak in the cell, which is generally present in *D. tytia*, is never seen in this species ; the marginal and submarginal series of small spots are, however, more distinct. The UNDERSIDE agrees exactly in markings with *D. tytia*, but the ground-colour of the *hindwing* differs in the same way as it does on the upperside.

D. melaneus is found in Sikkim, Sylhet, and the Khasi hills in November. In October also Mr. de Nicéville found it in profusion in the Sikkim tarai and as high as 6,000 feet in the Darjiling hills. In Tenasserim it was taken by Limborg in the cold weather at Ahsown, Moulmein, and Meetan. Captain Bingham took it in the Thoungyeen forests in the Tenasserim interior in the spring months ; and it has been found in Penang, Malacca, and Java. It is apparently a forest-loving insect, similar in habits and in general appearance to *D. tytia*.

The figure is taken from specimens from Sibsagar in the Indian Museum, Calcutta, and shows the upperside of both sexes ; the female on the left, and the male on the right.

22. **Danais nilgiriensis,** Moore. (PLATE VI, FIG. 9 ♂).

D. nilgiriensis, Moore, Ann. and Mag. Nat. Hist., fourth series, vol. xx, p. 44 (1877).

HABITAT : Conoor, Nilgiris ; Ashamboo Hills.

EXPANSE : 3·0 to 3·8 inches.

DESCRIPTION : " Fuliginous black, with bluish-white markings. *Forewing*, with a bluish-white, black-streaked stripe within the cell ; three subapical costal spots, below which are two narrow streaks, the lower elongated ; five spots within the disc ; an elongated, black-centered, triangular streak between median and submedian nervures ; a submarginal series of seven spots, the lower, second, and third with a dentate point outward ; a short marginal row of small dots from posterior angle. *Hindwing*, with a bluish-white, narrow, fusiform streak within the cell ; five contiguous small narrow spots outside the cell ; three long narrow abdominal streaks ; a submarginal series of spots, the upper two largest, the third denate, the others small ; a marginal row of smaller spots. *Head, thorax,* and *legs* black, spotted and streaked with white. *Abdomen,* blackish above, grey beneath. UNDERSIDE paler, markings as above." (*Moore.* l. c.) In the above description Moore omits to mention the presence on the upperside of the *forewing* of a narrow streak from the base half along the length of the wing below the submedian nervure ; and on the *hindwing* there are four abdominal streaks, two joined at the base, between the first median nervule and the submedian nervure, and one on either side of the internal nervure. On the UNDERSIDE the *forewing* is darker in the middle of the disc, the *hindwing* irrorated with grey, except a discal band beyond the cell from the costa to the anal angle, which is brown, like the disc of the forewing. The FEMALE differs from the male in the absence in the *hindwing* of the sexual marks which are presen in the male ; the submarginal row of spots therefore consists of nine instead of six spots.

"Not common in the winter in Travancore ; it occurs on the hills from 2,000 feet upwards ; throughout February it is tolerably common. In April and May it was fairly common above 3,000 feet, and some specimens have been taken in June." (*Harold Fergusson*). Common at Conoor in July. It appears to be a local though very well-marked species, peculiar to the hills in the south of the peninsula.

The figure shows the upper and undersides of a male from Conoor in the Indian Museum, Calcutta.

23. **Danais taprobana,** Felder.

D. taprobana, Felder, Reise Nov., Lep., vol. ii, p. 349, pl. xlii, fig. 4 (1865), *male* ; *Danais fumata,* Butler, Proc. Zool. Soc. Lond., 1866, p. 53 ; *Chittira fumata,* Moore, Lep. Cey., p. 9, pl. iv, figs. 1, 1*a* (1880).

HABITAT : Ceylon.

EXPANSE : 2·75 to 3·8 inches.

DESCRIPTION : "UPPERSIDE : *Forewing* rich brown, with a long discoidal streak ; a large patch below the median nervure, extending from the base to the middle of the first median branch ; two spots between the first and second median branches, one in the middle, and one at the base of the nervules ; three submarginal spots, one below each of the median branches, and often a fourth below the lower discoidal nervule ; an oblique band from beyond the middle of the costa to the middle of the third median branch, divided into five spots by the nervules ; one or two minute spots near the end of the cell, below the third median branch, and two small obliquely placed subapical spots in, and nearly completing the submarginal series—pale-greenish white, semi-transparent. *Hindwing* rich brown ; interior margin paler ; the cell a short streak above near its termination, a minute streak near the costa beyond the middle (often wanting), a minute spot beyond the end of the cell, a submarginal row of three small spots near the apex, and an incomplete marginal row of four or five minute dots (generally absent in the male)—pale greenish white, semi-transparent. *Cilia* brown with whitish interspaces. *Body* brown. UNDERSIDE : *Wings* golden brown, a patch of darker colour below the end of the cell in the *hindwing,* markings nearly as above, but the basal hyaline marks much suffused with brown ; only one subapical spot on *forewing* ; and in the *hindwing,* the marginal dots are larger and present in both sexes. BODY : *Thorax* black, spotted with yellow. *Abdomen* pale ochreous." (*Butler,* l. c.) The FEMALE differs from the male only in the absence of the sexual marks, and in the presence of the marginal dots on upperside of hindwing.

This exceedingly well-marked species seems confined to the Island of Ceylon. There is no record of its capture on the Indian Continent. In Ceylon, according to Hutchison, it is "found all the year round, scarce in February and March ; in the hills at from 3,000 to 6,000 feet elevation ; in forest and often in coffee plantations. Common at Newera Eliya, and several miles round. Flight slow and heavy."

Fourth Group:—TIRUMALA: "*Forewing* broad, triangular; first branch of the subcostal nervure emitted at one-fifth before the end of the cell and free from the costal, the second emitted from the end of the cell. *Hindwing* broadly oval; exterior margin very convex; costal nervure slightly curved; cell short, anteriorly oblique; second subcostal branch starting from nearer the first, and third median branch nearer the second than in *Radena.* Male, with an open scent-pouch between the first median nervule and submedian nervure, the pendent sac of which is prominent on the underside. *Antennæ* shorter than in *Radena,* the club shorter and tip more pointed. *Larva* with two pair of fleshy filaments. Type *D. limniacæ,* Cramer." (*Moore,* Lep. Ceylon, p. 4, 1880).

This group is represented by three species in the Indian region, and a fourth is included on somewhat doubtful grounds. They appear to be more variable in their markings than the species of other allied groups of *Danais,* so much so that specimens are often found which it is difficult to identify with certainty. Their colouration is a beautiful indigo black with subhyaline bluish-white spots and streaks; all the species are of rather large size, and two of them are very common.

Key to the Indian species of Tirumala.

A. *♂* Males with one scent-pouch on hindwing, prominent on underside as a pendent sac. Colours blue black, with subhyaline markings.

- *a²*. With two hyaline streaks from the base in the cell of forewing.
  - 24. D. (*Tirumala*) GAUTAMA, Burma.
- *b²* With only a single streak from the base in the cell of forewing.
  - *a³*. Hyaline markings large, prominent and very pale.
    - *a⁴*. Wings broad and short, marginal spots on hindwing brown, basal area of hindwing almost entirely hyaline, with no dark streak between median and submedian nervures.
      - 25. D. (*Tirumala*) MELISSA, India (?), Java.
    - *b⁴*. Wings somewhat elongate, no brown spots on hindwing; marginal spots prominent; the hyaline mark between median and submedian nervures of hindwing cleft outwardly by a dark streak.
      - 26. D. (*Tirumala*) LIMNIACE, India.
  - *b³*. Hyaline markings small, dark, and distinct, with no tendency to coalesce.
    - 27. D. (*Tirumala*) SEPTENTRIONIS, India.

24. Danais guatama, Moore.

D. gautama, Moore, Ann. and Mag. Nat. Hist., fouth series, vol. xx, p. 43 (1877).

HABITAT: Arakan, Meplay Valley, Henzadah, Burma.

EXPANSE: 3·4 to 4·0 inches.

DESCRIPTION: "FEMALE: Black with bluish-white markings. *Forewing* with two long streaks within base of cell and three short streaks at its end; a series of five narrow streaks beyond end of the cell; six discal spots; two lengthened narrow streaks starting from base between the median and submedian nervures, and a spot beyond, the upper streak broken near its end; three small spots before the apex, and a marginal row of spots; a short streak at base of hind margin. *Hindwing* with three streaks within the cell, an elongated discal series of streaks, and two outer marginal rows of small spots." (*Moore,* l. c.) The MALE differs only from the female in having the black sexual spot, which is situated between the first median nervule and submedian nervure, and is produced into a pouch below with the opening on the upperside. UNDERSIDE like the upperside, except that the apical region of the *forewing* and the whole of the *hindwing* is ochreous brown.

"Most nearly allied to *D. septentrionis,* Butler, but differs in the shape of the *forewing* (that of *D. gautama* being shorter), the two basal streaks within base of the cell, the wider interspaces between the discal and marginal spots, and in the form of the streaks below the cell. On the *hindwing* it has an additional streak within the cell, and the discal streaks between the veins are broad." (*Moore,* l. c.)

D. gautama, to judge from the recorded instances of its capture, seems to be very local. It has hitherto only been reported from a limited portion of British Burma. Captain C. T. Bingham took a single specimen in the Meplay Valley in February, and Captain C. H. E. Adamson has sent a single male specimen from Moulmein, where it was captured on the 12th June, and Dr. Anderson took it commonly in the Mergui Archipelago in December. It is probably not uncommon, but overlooked owing to its great superficial resemblance to the common *D. septentrionis*, though when once recognised it is a well-marked and easily distinguished species.

25. **Danais melissa**, Cramer.

Papilio melissa, Cramer, Pap. Ex., vol. iv, pl. ccclxxvii, figs. C, D (1781); Herbst, Pap., pl. cxxv, figs. 3, 4 (1793); *Danais melissa*, Godart, Enc. Méth., vol. ix, p. 192, n. 50 (1819).

HABITAT : (N. India ?, Singapore ?) ; Java.

EXPANSE : ♂, 3·0 to 3·5 inches.

DESCRIPTION : MALE : *Forewing* black ; a narrow streak in the cell from the base, and an irregular spot beyond it ; one subcostal spot beyond the end of the cell, immediately below which are three elongate spots between the nervules ; a round spot touching the cell below the third median nervule ; a larger, somewhat elongate, spot below the second ; and a large spot above an elongate basal streak with a small separate rounded spot beyond them, below the third median nervule ; a sinuate submarginal series of nine spots, the apical four, one between each pair of nervules, the next four in pairs in the median interspaces ; and a marginal series of smaller spots—subhyaline bluish-white. *Hindwing* with the entire cell ; a spot at the base of the wing ; a slightly larger on eabove the costal nervure at its base ; a streak below it with a spot beyond ; a spot between the subcostal branches touching the cell ; two streaks filling the base of the interspaces on either side of the discoidal nervule ; two short narrow streaks joined at the base in each of the two median interspaces, the outer pair much the smaller ; the whole space between the median and submedian nervures from the base to the sexual mark ; and three lengthened abdominal streaks, the two below the submedian nervure joined at the base ; a very irregular submarginal series of small somewhat elongate spots—subhyaline bluish-white. A marginal row, equally irregular, of very small spots, white at the apex and anal angle, those between them brown. UNDERSIDE : *Forewing* black ; *hindwing* somewhat cupreous ; the markings identical with those of the upperside, except that the marginal and submarginal spots are much more prominent, especially on the hindwing ; both series are complete and all the spots are whitish with no brown tint. *Cilia* black, spotted with white. Described from Cramer's figures.

D. melissa is quoted by Westwood, Moore, and Butler as occurring in India, and on the strength of these authorities it is retained in the Indian list ; but we have never seen a specimen taken in India, and we have great doubts as to whether it really does occur here. It is a Javan insect, and differs from the common *D. limniace* of India, which also occurs in Java, notably in having the basal area of the hindwing almost entirely hyaline leaving a prominent dark outer border,—in other words in *D. melissa* the hyaline spots on the outer half of the wing are reduced, and towards the margin evanescent, while those towards the base are enlarged greatly. Both these species vary much, and some specimens of the Indian *D. limniace* show an approach to *D. melissa* in the style of their markings, but none that we have seen could be separated from the Indian species or united with the Javan. The specimens of *D. melissa* from Java in the Indian Museum, Calcutta, differ from Cramer's figures on the forewing in having the three markings below the median nervure entirely coalescing, and on the hindwing in having a small dark streak in the cell, the hyaline streaks below it coalescing, making the abdominal area much paler, and the marginal spots bluish-white not brown, thus showing that this species is as liable to variation as is *D. limniace*.

26. Danais limniace, Cramer.

Papilio limniace, Cramer, Pap. Ex., vol. i, pl. lix, figs. D, E (1775); Herbst, Pap., pl. cxxiii, figs. 3, 4 (1793); *Danais leopardus*, Butler, Proc. Zool. Soc. Lond., 1866, p 52, n. 36; *D. limniace*, G. Semper, Journ. des Mus. God., heft xiv, p. 139, pl. viii, fig. 6 (1879); *Tirumala limniacæ*, Moore, Lep. Cey., p. 4, pl. i, fig. 3 (1880).

HABITAT: Throughout the Indian region.

EXPANSE: 2·6 to 4·2; usually about 3·5 inches.

DESCRIPTION: MALE: *Forewing* deep blue-black; a streak from the base, with an outwardly indented spot beyond in the cell; two short subcostal streaks (the outer sometimes evanescent) just beyond the cell, with three streaks immediately below them, one between each pair of the nervules, the first narrow, the second and third broader, the third short and oval; a spot touching the cell below the third median nervule, a larger and longer spot below the second, and in the space between the first median nervule and submedian nervure are an elongate streak from the base, above it a shorter and broader streak, and beyond them a rounded spot—subhyaline bluish-white; these three latter markings are very variable. In some specimens all three are distinct; in others the two streaks coalesce; in others again the upper streak coalesces with the spot leaving the lower streak free, and, lastly, all three sometimes are almost completely confluent. A sinuous submarginal row of nine unequal-sized, rounded, rather prominent spots, and a marginal row of ten to twelve smaller spots—also hyaline bluish-white. *Hindwing* also deep blue-black, with a spot at the base, a short streak above the costal nervure, another with a rounded spot beyond it below the costal nervure; a small spot near the cell between the subcostal nervules, a wide streak on each side of the discoidal nervule touching the cell; two short streaks united at the base in each median interspace, the outer pair much the smaller; a similar pair, but much wider, between the median and submedian nervures from the base to the sexual mark; a similar, but much longer, pair below the submedian, and a lengthened abdominal streak—subhyaline bluish-white. The discoidal cell in some specimens is entirely subhyaline; in others there is a single black streak near the end, and in others again this streak is bind and very prominent. An irregular prominent submarginal row of spots; all those above the second median nervule are rounded; those below it somewhat elongate; the rounded spots are in pairs between the nervules with the outer of each pair large and the inner small; a more regular marginal row of smaller spots also hyaline bluish-white. UNDERSIDE agrees in markings with the upperside, but on the apical area of the *forewing* and the whole of the *hindwing* the ground-colour is cupreous. The *head* and *thorax* are blue-black, spotted and streaked with white. *Abdomen* swarthy above, and fulvous, with whitish spots below. FEMALE: Differs only from the male in the pair of subhyaline streaks below the median nervure being lengthened across the space occupied in the male by the sexual organ, which latter is of course absent in the female.

"*Larva* yellowish-white or yellowish-green, with a pair of long fleshy filaments on third, and a short pair on twelfth segment; the filaments black and greenish-white, longitudinally lined with black points; each segment with transverse black bars, one on each, thicker, which bifurcates near the lateral line; a narrower bar at anterior edge, and two, also narrower, at posterior part of the segment; lateral band yellow; head and feet ringed with black. *Pupa* green, somewhat cylindrical, constricted below the thorax, with golden scattered dots and beaded ring. Feeds on *Asclepias*." (*Moore*, Lep. Ceylon, p. 5). Figured in Horsfield and Moore's Cat. Lep. E. I. C., pl. iv, figs. 3,3a (1857).

The range of this species is very wide. It is found in the driest as well in the dampest localities, and extends into the Himalayas up to at least 6,000 feet. In Travancore, according to Mr. Harold Fergusson, it is common from the foot of the hills to the summits, most abundant in November and December, common throughout February, only a few seen in March, but again fairly common at the higher elevations in April and May. It is common throughout the Deccan, extending into Sind, and throughout the plains of north India it is on the wing nearly all the year round; and in the outer Himalayas from Kashmir to Nepal. In Kulu Mr. A. Grahame Young writes that it is common in some years, rare in others, and occurs in May, August, and October. Mr. S. E. Peal has taken it at Sibsagar in Upper Assam. It is not uncommon in Rangoon, and in the Nicobar Islands. In Calcutta it is plentiful all through the year, and to be met with everywhere, particularly in gardens, where it is almost the commonest insect seen. Like the rest of the genus it has a slow flapping flight, and settles frequently often at the very end of a dead stick.

27. **Danais septentrionis,** Butler. (PLATE VI, FIG. 8 ♂ ♀).

Danais septentrionis, Butler, Ent. Month. Mag., vol. xi, p. 163 (1874); *D. septentrionis*, G. Semper, Journ. des Mus. God., heft xiv, p. 140, pl. viii, fig 7 (1879); *Tirumala septentrionis*, Moore, Lep. Cey., p. 5, pl. i, fig. 2 (1880).

HABITAT: India.

EXPANSE: 3·4 to 4·4 inches.

DESCRIPTION: "Allied to *D. hamata*,* of McLeay, but constantly much larger. UPPERSIDE: *Forewing* with the spots on the disc smaller. *Hindwing* olive-brown (instead of chocolate-brown); the streaks beyond the cell, between the subcostal and radial nervures, narrower, longer, and not notched externally; the brown patch in the cell broader (frequently reaching to the radial nervure without a notch); submarginal spots more elongated. UNDERSIDE: *Forewing* paler than in *D. hamata*: *hindwing* more cupreous in tint." (*Butler*, l. c.)

D. septentrionis is the common dark form of blue *Danais* that has frequently passed as *D. similis*† in collections in this country. It differs from *D. limniace* in its usually larger size and in the deeper blue tone of the subhyaline markings, which are also smaller and more distinct throughout. On the *forewing* the streaks on either side of the lower discoidal nervule are narrow and pointed externally, the lower one always the shorter, whereas in *D. limniace* they are broad and truncate; the basal streak below the median nervure is short, narrow and widely separated from the spot above and the one beyond it, except in some specimens from S. India. On the *hindwing* the subhyaline markings in the cell are reduced to two streaks, with sometimes a minute spot between them at the outer end of the cell. On the UNDERSIDE the marking are similar to those of the upperside, and the cupreous tints of the fore- and hindwings are much darker than in *D. limniace.*

This Butterfly seems to be less generally distributed than *D. limniace.* It has not been recorded from the Andamans or Nicobars, but is common in Tenasserim, in Assam, and in the Eastern Himalayas and tarais; it is rare in the Western Himalayas; and appears again in south India and Ceylon, but from the sub-Himalayan tracts on the north to Bangalore on the south we have as yet no record of its occurrence. The south Indian and Ceylon form is much smaller than that from north-east India. Specimens from south India (Bangalore, Kadur district, and Calicut) show an approximation to *D. limniace* in their much lighter generalt one of colouration and the more or less complete coalescing of the spots and streaks behind the median nervure in the forewing; but the streaks on either side of the lower discoidal nervule are decidedly proportionally longer, narrower, and externally more pointed, showing that these aberrant specimens really belong to the present species *D. septentrionis.* In the Simla district Mr. de Nicéville has taken itrather sparingly from August to October, and only in beds of streams with richly wooded sides; in one such locality near Kotgarh, elevation about 6,000 feet, it was fairly plentiful in August, 1879. Mr. A. Grahame Young writes that "it very seldom occurs in Kulu, generally in July." In Chumba at 3,000 feet elevation there is a spring brood in April; and Mr. E. T. Atkinson, C.S., reports having found it common in the lower hills and plains below Kumaon; and Mr. F. Bourdillon has taken it in Travancore in May.

The figure shows the upperside of both male and female from specimens from Sibsagar in the Indian Museum, Calcutta.

Fifth Group.—SALATURA: "*Forewing* lengthened, triangular; costa slightly arched; apex more or less rounded; exterior margin waved, oblique, slightly convex in the middle;

---

* From Australia.

† See No. 8, *D. vulgaris*.

inner margin slightly recurved; costal nervure extending to two-thirds the length, first subcostal branch emitted before end of the cell, second at end of the cell, third and fourth at equal distances from its end; cell long; upper disco-cellular bent inwards, and angled at its upper and lower end, lower outwardly oblique; radials from angles of upper disco-cellular; median branches widely separated, submedian slightly recurved. *Hindwing* broadly oval; exterior margin rounded, slightly sinuous; costal nervure short, curved upward, and emitting a short basal spur; first subcostal emitted before end of the cell, and curving upward before the apex, second slightly bent at end of the cell; disco-cellulars very oblique, upper shortest and slightly concave, radial from their middle; second median branch near end of the cell; lower bent near its base, submedian nearly straight, internal recurved. MALE with an open scent-pouch between first median nervule and submedian nervure. Body long; palpi pilose; middle and hindlegs slender. *Larva* with three pairs of fleshy filaments. Type, *D. genutia*, Cramer." (*Moore*, Lep. Ceylon, p. 5, 1880).

This group includes all the species of what are known as "tawny" *Danais*, and is represented within Indian limits by eight species, some of which probably are insular or local, and may eventually prove to be merely geographical varieties; some of them are exceedingly common, and two of them are found everywhere throughout the country, often in immense numbers. The group has a very wide range, extending from Eastern Europe throughout Southern and Eastern Asia, to Australia; also to South Europe, North Africa and North America. Out of the eight species included as Indian, the claim of one, *D. philene*, to admission is extremely doubtful; it is included on the authority of Butler's identification.

Key to the Indian species of Salatura.

B. *a*. Males with a scent-pouch on hindwing, situated as in *Tirumala*, but with the sac not so prominent on underside. Wings opaque; prevailing colour tawny yellowish-brown, with black and white markings.

- *a*[1]. The nervures of the wings not defined with black; the outer margin of both wings black, with white spots.
  - *a*[2]. Apex of forewing black with a white subapical macular band.
    - *a*[3]. Hindwing uniform tawny.
      28. D. *(Salatura)* CHRYSIPPUS, India.
    - *b*[3]. Hindwing suffused with pure white.
      29. D. *(Salatura)* ALCIPPUS, N. W. India, Rangoon.
  - *b*[2]. Apex of forewing tawny, the white subapical band obsolete.
    30. D. *(Salatura)* DORIPPUS, Sind.
- *b*[1]. The nervures more or less broadly defined with black.
  - *a*[2]. Hindwing bright ferruginous.
    - *a*[3]. With white marginal and submarginal spots.
      31. D. *(Salatura)* GENUTIA,* India.
    - *b*[3]. Without white marginal and submarginal spots.
      32. D. *(Salatura)* NIPALENSIS, Nepal.
  - *b*[2]. Hindwing dull dark ferruginous, with fine bifid white spots on the disc on underside; nervures of forewing only partially defined with black on upperside.
    33. D. *(Salatura)* PHILENE, Punjab (?), Java.
  - *c*[2]. Hindwing very dark brown with pure white streaks.
    - *a*[3]. With two oblique rows of white spots from costa of forewing; white streaks on hindwing large.
      34. D. *(Salatura)* HEGESIPPUS, N. E. India, Orissa, Burma.
    - *b*[3]. With the inner row of white spots on forewing evanescent or wanting; white streaks on hindwing narrow.
      35. D. *(Salatura)* NESIPPUS, Nicobars.
  - *d*[2]. Hindwing dark brown with sullied white streaks.
    36. D. *(Salatura)* MELANIPPUS, N. E. India.

* *D. genutia* is the name under which the Butterfly, commonly known as *D. plexippus*, must stand; see detailed description of this species.

28. **Danais chrysippus**, Linnæus. (PLATE VI, FIG. 10 ♂ ♀.)

Papilio chrysippus, Linnæus, Mus. Ulr., p 263 (1764); Syst. Nat., vol. i, pt. ii, p. 767, n. 119 (1767); Cramer, Pap. Ex., vol. ii, pl. cxviii, figs. B, C (1777); *Papilio ægyptius*, Schreber, Nov. Sp. Ins., p. 9, figs. 11, 12 (1759); Herbst, Pap., pl. clv, figs. 1, 2 (1794); *Danais chrysippe*, Godt., Enc. Méth, vol. ix, p. 187, n. 38 (1819); *Danais chrysippus*, Horsfield and Moore, Cat. Lep. E. I. C., vol. i, pl. iv, figs. 7, caterpillar, 7a, chrysalis; *Salatura chrysippus*, Moore, Lep. Cey., p. 7, pl. iii, figs. 1, male; 1a, female; 1b, caterpillar and chrysalis (1880).

HABITAT: Throughout India and Burma up to 7,000 feet elevation.

EXPANSE: 2·25 to 3·4 inches.

DESCRIPTION: MALE and FEMALE. UPPERSIDE: *Forewing*, with the costa narrowly, the whole apical area, including a small portion of the extremity of the cell, and decreasingly to the inner angle fuscous black; the rest of the wing bright ferruginous, darker in the cell and sometimes a little below and beyond it. A small quadrate spot on the costa, about one-third the length of the wing from the base; a larger one beyond it; an oblique band of five spots from the costa to the third median nervule, divided by the black nervules; a small spot between the discoidal and third median nervules touching the cell, and sometimes a smaller one above it; a round spot, variable in size, on the inner margin of the black apical area between the first and second median nervules; a submarginal and marginal series of small spots, the former always with two increasing spots at the apex, the series sometimes extending from the apex to the third median nervule, but generally with only the two spots below the macular band present, the upper one of the two always the largest, as are also the spots below them in the marginal series, white. In some specimens the apical area beyond the macular band is suffused between the veins with ferruginous. *Hindwing* bright ferruginous, narrowly bordered with a black band, irregular towards the apex, inwardly scalloped towards the anal angle. Three white spots at the apical angle; the upper disco-cellular nervule bordered with a black spot below the point where the second subcostal nervule is given off; another black spot where the discoidal nervure is given off; and a third filling the outer angle of the cell, where the third median nervule is given off. In some specimens the nervules on the disc are narrowly bordered with white. A marginal series of small somewhat squarish spots placed on the marginal black band, frequently evanescent towards the apex. The MALE has in addition a black sexual spot placed against the first median nervule, and extending into the space between it and the submedian nervure. UNDERSIDE: *Forewing* as above, except that the macular subapical band of white spots is only inwardly margined with black, the apical area from that band almost up to the marginal black band being ochreous. There is also an additional spot along the costa of the submarginal series. *Hindwing* ochreous, all the veins and the spots on the disco-cellular nervules more or less bordered with white; the sexual mark in the *male* centred with a white spot, the marginal black band inwardly irregularly defined with white, and the marginal white series of spots always complete, lunular, and much larger than on the upperside.

D. chrysippus is the commonest and most widely spread of all the Indian Butterflies. It is found throughout Eastern and Southern Asia, and even extends into Europe and North Africa. No locality seems to be unsuited to it. Up to a level of 7,000 feet above the sea, it may be found anywhere in the Indian Empire, but perhaps the dry hot plains of Northern India are on the whole the most congenial to it. At all events there it is the most conspicuous as it is almost the one solitary species that can thrive in the dust and glare. It seems moreover to be as indifferent to season as it is to locality, and in the plains of north India at all events it is to be found throughout the year, though most abundant in the winter months. It is hardly necessary to quote localities or dates in this case, for wherever the temperature is high enough, *D. chrysippus* may be found throughout the year. It has however not been recorded from the Andaman isles, though it occurs at the Nicobars. Only in the hills does its appearance seem to be governed by season. Mr. de Nicéville has only met with it in the Simla district in the autumn. Mr. A. Grahame Young, writing from Kulu, gives, with reference to this species, the following note which is of interest as relating to its occurrence out of India:—

"Common in Kulu; the first brood appears in June, then a succession of broods from August throughout the autumn. I found a great number of the larvæ of this insect whilst marching through the Sialkot District in May. They were on that species of *Euphorbium*, so common on sandy ground in the Punjab. I bred a lot, but all that I can now remember is that they emerge from the pupa on the average in about twelve days. I first saw this insect while travelling through South Persia many years ago. I met with a few at Khaneh Zeenon, 32 miles south of Shiraz, early in April, and at Dasht-i-arjun, a grassy plain surrounded by mountains a few miles further on, elevation nearly 6,000 feet, they were out on the banks of a small river in swarms during six hours that I halted there. I must have seen some thousands; they were all fresh from the chrysalis, and the surrounding herbage was covered with these pupæ, and with newly emerged insects."

The following description of the caterpillar and chrysalis of *D. chrysippus* is taken from a paper by Mrs. T. Vernon Wollaston in the Ann. and Mag. Nat. Hist., fifth series, vol. iii, p. 221 (1879).

"The caterpillar of this *Danais* is rather more than an inch and a half in length, and of a delicate French grey, each segment being ornamented with five black transverse lines, the second and third ones of which are somewhat broader, and enclose too large yellow transverse patches. There is a yellow spiracle-line very much interrupted, the skin being puckered, and the spiracles themselves scarcely visible. The head has three broad, transverse, arched, black lines, the anterior one of which encloses a yellow space, bordered in front by a straight basal line. The third, sixth, and last segments are each furnished with a pair of conspicuous dark retractile [?] horns, the anterior pair of which are almost twice the length of the others. When fully fed, it suspends itself by its tail, and turns into an obtuse semi-transparent chrysalis, beautifully marked with small golden spots, placed elliptically round the head, and with a black, raised, semi-circular line near the tail, the posterior edge of which is of a brilliant gold; there is also a minute golden spot about the position of the centre of the enclosed wings. These golden markings, however, disappear by the absorption of the fluids, as the enclosed insect approaches maturity."

The caterpillar feeds in India on *Calotropis gigantea* (Lang); *Asclepias curasavica* (Moore). The chrysalides in *Danais chrysippus* are dichroic, some being bright green, and others pale pinkish, wax-white, but Mr. Wood-Mason has ascertained that this difference in colour is not sexual, males and females being produced indifferently from green and pink chrysalides, and he considers that we here have to do with an instance of the same animal at the same stage of its development being protected by its resemblance to twc different parts of the vegetable organism on which it feeds and resides, namely, the leaves and the blossoms, the green chrysalises matching green leaves, and the pink ones being of a colour likely to be mistaken by birds, reptiles, and predaceous insects for a blossom.

The figures, taken from Calcutta specimens in the Indian Musuem, Calcutta, shows the upperside of a male on the left and female on the right.

29. **Danais alcippus,** Cramer.

Papilio alcippus, Cramer, Pap. Ex, vol. ii, pl. cxxvii, figs. E, F (1777); Fabricius, Ent. Syst., vol. iii, pt. i, p. 50, n. 155 (1793); Herbst, Pap., pl. clv, figs. 5, 6 (1794); *Euplœa alcippe*, Hübner, Verz. bek. Schmett., p. 15 (1816); Ochsenh., pl. iv, p. 120; *Danais alcippe*, Godart, Enc. Méth., vol. ix, p. 188, n. 39 (1819).

HABITAT: Plains of North-West India, and Rangoon.

EXPANSE: 2·9 to 3·5 inches.

DESCRIPTION: This species differs from *D. chrysippus* in the *hindwing* on both the upper and undersides being more or less, particularly in the middle of the wing, suffused with pure white. This character is very varied in different specimens, both in uniformity and extent; in some, it covers the whole of the middle of the wing: in others it is confined to the area below the cell only, and again in others, it is streaked and sullied with fulvous.

Its appearance is so erratic over a large extent of country that in distribution as well as in inconstancy of the extent of white, the idea of its being only a casual variety of *D. chrysippus* is suggested; but the variety, if such it should prove to be, is so well marked that it is worthy of retention as a distinct species, until the discovery of the caterpillar, which is as yet unknown, sets the question at rest.

D. alcippus is found occasionally throughout the plains of Northern India. According to Major C. Swinhoe it is scarce in Sind, appearing in November and December. Mr. de Nicéville took two specimens at Nurpur in the Punjab in May. In the N.-W. Provinces it is still more scarce, the only place where it is known to have occurred being Lucknow, where two specimens were taken by Col. Lang; towards the East it is certainly nowhere common. There is a single specimen from Rangoon in the Indian Museum, Calcutta.

30. **Danais dorippus,** Klug.

Euplœa dorippus, Klug, Symb. Phys., pl. xlviii, figs 1—5 (1845); *Danais chrysippus*, var. c, Kirby, Syst. Cat. D. L., p. 7 (1871); *D. dorippus*, Oberthür, Etudes d' Entom., 3 me, livr., p. 24, pl. i, fig. 5, (1878) *male*, from Zanzibar.

HABITAT: Sind, extending to South-Eastern Europe and Africa.

EXPANSE: 2·3 to 3·6 inches.

DESCRIPTION: This species may at once be distinguished from *D. chrysippus* by the absence on the UPPERSIDE of the *forewing* of the black apical patch, and the white subapical band the spot outside the cell and the one on the inner margin of the black apical patch between the first and second median nervules. The submarginal row of spots in *D. dorippus* is generally entirely wanting; if present at all it consists of two or three spots between the first and third median nervules. The marginal series is also very abbreviated, three spots at the apex, and a few between the first and third median nervules being generally alone present, though sometimes the series is nearly complete, but the spots are always smaller than in *D. chrysippus*. *Hindwing* as in *D. chrysippus*, except that the marginal series of white dots is almost obsolete. UNDERSIDE bright fulvous; deep ferruginous colour nearly filling the cell; light ochreous at the apex. Two spots, one on each side of the discoidal nervule, just beyond and touching the cell, a subapical oblique band of five spots from the costa to the third median nervule, divided by the veins, (these spots are faintly seen on the upperside through transparency)—white. Otherwise as in *D. chrysippus*. The hindwing is in all respects like that of *D. chrysippus*.

A single male specimen from Karachi has the whole cell of forewing and base of both wings, suffused with deep ferruginous on the *upperside*, and on the *underside* the whole cell and base of forewing only. Another female specimen from Mulleer, Sind, has the subapical band of white spots entirely absent.

The only notice of the occurrence of *D. dorippus* within Indian limits (it is common in Africa) that has been received is from Major C. Swinhoe, who writes from Karachi that he has observed it in Sind in January, June, August, September, November, and December, but never commonly.

31. **Danais genutia,*** Cramer.

Papilio genutia, Cramer, Pap. Ex., vol. iii, pl. ccvi, figs. C, D (1779); *Papilio genutius*, Herbst, Pap., pl. cliv, figs. 1, 2 (1794); *Salatura genutia*, Moore, Lep. Ceylon, p. 6, pl. iv, figs. 2 male, 2*a* female (1880); *Danais plexippus*, auctorum, *nec* Linnæus.

HABITAT: Throughout India and Burma up to 7,000 feet elevation.

EXPANSE: 2·6 to 4·0 inches.

---

* For figure, see page 7.

DESCRIPTION: UPPERSIDE: *Forewing* bright rich fulvous, with the costa, the whole apical area to the inner angle, including the upper end of the cell, and decreasingly to the base along the inner margin—black. The median nervure and the first and second median nervules, which alone cross the fulvous ground, broadly bordered with black. On the costa there is first a small spot about one-third the length of the wing from the base, then two spots at the end of the cell divided by the first subcostal branch—white. A white spot touching, but outside the cell, between the discoidal nervules; an irregular band of six white spots from the costa to the second median nervule; this band increases to the fifth spot, which is the largest; the sixth is much smaller and rounded. There is generally one, sometimes two, round white spots on the inner edge of the black apical area between the second median nervule and the submedian nervure, one in each interspace; a submarginal and marginal series of white spots, more or less obsolete, especially towards the apex, but always present and large between the second and third median nervules. *Hindwing* lighter fulvous, margined with black, on which are placed two rows of rounded dots, the inner one evanescent, especially towards the apex. All the nervures broadly bordered with black. UNDERSIDE as above in the *forewing*, except that the area between the subapical band of white spots and the apex is suffused with ochreous. The submarginal and marginal series of spots are larger, as are also the spots on either side of the first median nervule when present. *Hindwing* only differs from the upperside in having all the nervures bordered with white outside their black margins; the two series of dots much larger. *Cilia* black, spotted with white at the interspaces. *Head* and *thorax* black, spotted and streaked with white. *Abdomen* ferruginous, spotted with white. In some specimens on the upperside of the *hindwing*, the abdominal margin and the fulvous spaces are more or less streaked or suffused with violet-white, showing an approach to *D. melanippus*. The FEMALE differs from the male only in the absence of the sexual mark, which in that sex is placed against the first median nervule and lies between it and the submedian nervure. On the upperside this mark is entirely black; on the underside black, centred with a short white streak.

"LARVA, cylindrical, black, with a pair of black fleshy filaments on the third, sixth, and twelfth segments, the first pair longest; each segment with one interrupted white streak along its anterior edge, succeeded by three white transverse spots, followed by two transversely elongated yellow spots, the posterior edge of the segment having two parallel interrupted white streaks; lateral band yellow, crossed at the middle of each segment by a black line; abdominal line black; head and feet black, ringed with white. PUPA somewhat cylindrical, posterior end hemispherical, anterior ending in two slight prominences; bright green, with a dorsal ring of silvery dots, and a few scattered golden dots." (*Moore*, Lep. Ceylon, p. 6.)

This species has hitherto passed as *D. plexippus*, Linnæus, but Messrs. Salvin and Godman have recently shown conclusively in their "Biologia Centrali-Americana," that Linnæus' name applies to an American species of this type, which is distinct from the Asiatic species. The error appears to have originated with Fabricius, and has till quite recently passed undetected. The Indian species must, therefore, stand as *D. genutia* of Cramer, by whom it has been correctly figured.

D. genutia is as widely spread and only less common than *D. chrysippus*. In Tenasserim it was found by Limborg throughout the cold weather up to 5,000 feet; in the Nicobars it is common; Captain C. T. Bingham found it in Tenasserim in March and April; it is common in the Malay Peninsula in August and September. In the plains of north India it is common throughout the winter; while in the Himalayas and Khasi hills it is most common in the autumn. In Kulu, according to Mr. Grahame Young, a few appear in June, and from the middle of August, a succession of broods come out till late in the autumn; in Chumba a few are on the wing in April. On the West Coast it does not appear to be common, at all events in the spring, but in Travancore, according to Messrs. Fergusson and Bourdillon, it is very common in March, and fairly common in April.

32. Danais nipalensis, Moore.

D. nipalensis, Moore, Ann. and Mag. Nat. Hist., fourth series, vol. xx, p. 43 (1877).

HABITAT : Katmandu, Nepal.

EXPANSE : 3·9 inches.

DESCRIPTION : " MALE : UPPERSIDE dull ferruginous black. *Forewing* with the basal internal half bright ferruginous, intersected by the black veins ; an oblique subapical narrow series of five white spots, the second, third, and fourth elongated, the fourth longest, the fifth subconical ; a series of two median submarginal, and four marginal small white spots. *Hindwing*, with the spaces between the veins to beyond the disc ferruginous, intersected by broad black-margined veins. *Cilia* alternate black and white. *Head, thorax*, and *legs* black, spotted and streaked with white. *Abdomen* ferruginous. UNDERSIDE, paler ferruginous black, marked as above. Nearest to *D. chrysippus*, from which it may be distinguished by the absence of all white markings, except the narrow oblique subapical series on the forewing." (*Moore*, l. c.)

This is apparently a local species ; no record of its occurrence elsewhere can be traced. It seems to be more nearly related to *D. genutia* than to *D. chrysippus*, but the description is given as originally recorded. We have never seen a specimen.

33. Danais philene, Cramer.

Papilio philene, Cramer, Pap. Ex., vol. iv, pl. ccclxxv, figs. A, B (1781) ; Herbst, Pap., pl. cliv, figs. 3, 4 (1794) ; *Danais philene*, Godt., Enc. Méth., vol. ix, p. 187, n. 37 (1819) ; *Euplœa philene*, Hübn., Verz. bek. Schmett., p. 15 (1816).

HABITAT : North India (?), Java, Amboyna.

EXPANSE : 3·6 inches, (from Cramer's plate).

DESCRIPTION : " Wings slightly sinuous, dark ferruginous, with here and there some nervures and the hinder margin of a blackish-brown, the latter dotted whith wite ; the *forewing* blackish at the apex, with a very white maculated band ; the *underside* of the *hindwing* with some bifid white spots on the disc ; size about the same as *D. plexippus* [*D. genutia*]. *Forewing*, blackish brown, with a large lengthened patch of dark ferruginous red at the base, divided by a blackish nervure ; a subapical white band of five spots, of which the four nearest the costa are oblong and joined, the fifth almost round and separated from the others ; this band is preceded interiorly by a longitudinal white line on the costa, and the hind [outer] margin has two rows of equally white spots, of which the inner line is shorter. *Hindwing*, dark ferruginous with blackish nervures, the outer border smoky brown, with a double or single row of white dots. The UNDERSIDE of the *forewing* is, with a slight difference in shade, almost the same as the upperside. In the *hindwing* it differs in that the disc has five white bifid spots, and the pocket in the male is marked with a small longitudinal line of the same colour ; also that the spots on the border are brighter, a little larger, and the two rows are both complete. The thorax is black with white dots ; the abdomen is brownish above, yellow below ; the antennæ are black."

The above is Godart's description of this species, which is included in the Indian list on the strength of a notice by Mr. Butler* of a small collection of Butterflies made in the North-West Punjab, containing the following entry :—" *D. philene*, Cheta, about twenty miles from Murree ; found in lime and orange gardens." No other record of its occurrence has been traced, nor is it known whether any specimen exists in Indian collections ; and it seems likely that a mistake was made in the identification, for the insect belongs to the Indo-Malayan region, and wide-spread as many of the species of *Danainæ* are, it would be a singular occurrence if a Malayan species were found in the North-West Himalayas and not in the vast

* Proc. Zool. Soc., Lond., 1870, p. 725, n. 2.

intermediate region. It appears to differ from *D. genutia* chiefly in the nervures of the forewing being without the black borders on upperside, in the presence of the five bifid white spots in the disc of the hindwing on the underside, and in the tone of the ferruginous basal area of the wings.

The caterpillar and chrysalis were discovered by Horsfield in Java, and are figured in the Cat. Lep. E. I. C., plate iv., figs. 5, 5a (1857). The caterpillar has only four tentacula, two long ones on the third segment, and two short ones on the last segment but one; it feeds in Java "on a species of *cissus*, bearing the native name of *Galing*." (*Horsfield*.) It was found in December. The chrysalis is short and very obtuse. These figures are almost identical with those given at pl. iii, figs. 8, 8a, of Horsfield's Catalogue (1829), of *D. plexippus* (= *D. genutia*), and gives rise to the suspicion that the metamorphoses shown belong to one and the same insect, most probably of *D. philene*.

34. **Danais hegesippus,** Cramer.

Papilio hegesippus, Cramer, Pap. Ex., vol. ii, pl. clxxx, fig. A (1777); Fabricius, Ent. Syst., vol. iii, pt. i, p. 52, n. 160 (1793); *Euplœa hegesippe*, Hübner, Verz. bek. Schmett., p. 15 (1816); *Danais hegesippe*, Godart, Enc. Méth., vol. ix, p. 189, n. 42 (1819); *Danais melanippe*, G. R. Gray, Lep. Ins. Nepal, p. 10, pl. ix, fig. 1 (1846); *Danais chirona*, G. R. Gray, l. c., p. 10 (1833).

HABITAT: Eastern Bengal, Orissa, Burma.

EXPANSE: 2·7 to 3·6 inches.

DESCRIPTION: UPPERSIDE: *Forewing* as in *D. genutia*, except that the fulvous streak below the submedian nervure is never present in *D. hegesippus*, the macular band of white spots across the apex is less prominent, and the sixth spot of this band is placed much nearer the base of the wing; the spot below it between the second and first median nervules is also usually much more prominent. In Cramer's figure the narrow fulvous streak below the submedian nervure is shown, but in a long series of Indian specimens before us it is invariably wanting. *Hindwing* fuscous brown in Cramer's plate, and also in some Rangoon specimens, but usually almost black. All the fulvous ground-colour of this wing in *D. genutia* is replaced in *D. hegesippus* with pure white, the streaks in the interspaces beyond the cell being much more restricted, in some specimens being much reduced and sullied with fulvous at the edges; the marginal and submarginal series of round spots always complete, and more prominent than in *D. genutia*. UNDERSIDE similar to the upperside, but all the white markings on the *hindwing* are more prominent, and except the two long abdominal streaks are outwardly suffused with fulvous, increasing in extent towards the costa, the spaces above the subcostal nervure being almost entirely fulvous. The FEMALE only differs from the male in the absence of the sexual mark on the hindwing.

D. hegesippus does not seem to be very common anywhere. Mr. de Nicéville, who has carefully collected in the neighbourhood of Calcutta, notes: "On November 15th and December 18th, 1878, in a garden on the outskirts of Calcutta, I took two specimens of this insect on each occasion and have never seen it since. It seems to have a lower, and, if possible, lazier flight than *D. genutia*, from which species, by reason of its white striped lower wings, it is easily distinguished even on the wing." Specimens may not unfrequently be found in the collections made by soldiers for sale in the neighbourhood of Rangoon, but neither Limborg nor Captain Bingham met with it in Tenasserim, in the winter and early summer months. There is one specimen in the Indian Museum, Calcutta, from Orissa; and another from the old East India Company's Museum, labelled "Dukhun, Colonel Sykes," but we know of no other specimen taken in that part of India, the locality is probably erroneous.

35. **Danais nesippus,** Felder.

D. nesippus, Felder, Verh. zool.-bot. Gesellsch. Wien, vol. xii, p. 486, n. 123 (1862); Reise Nov., Lep., vol. ii, p. 347, n. 484 (1867).

HABITAT: Nancowry, Sambelong, Nicobars.

EXPANSE: 2·8 to 3·2 inches.

DESCRIPTION : " MALE : Wings above fuscous. *Forewing*, with the triangular basal area, rufescent fulvous ; a three-fold subcostal spot (the cellular part and interior rather narrow) two small cellular spots, a small subapical band of five increasingly elongated spots, two spots between the median branches, and a double submarginal series of unequal spots (the inner row shorter), white. *Hindwing* paler, with the cellular area, and increasing subulate spots between the second subcostal branch, and the internal margin and somewhat large spots in two series before the margin, white. UNDERSIDE : *Forewing* paler, of a slightly violet tinge, the [fulvous] patch broader, with the white spots [of the upperside] but larger. *Hindwing* suffused with violet-hoary, with a serpentine gloss in certain positions, with basal spots, two subcostal (the first at the base emitting a line), and others on the border larger than those of the upperside, white ; with the costa fulvous from the base, the radiating spots much more ample, with the upper ones exteriorly stained with ochraceous-fulvous, and with the two subcostal ones also of the same colour. FEMALE : Wings wider, more deeply coloured than in the male. A local form of *D. melanippus*, Cramer." (*Felder*, l. c. in Reise Novara).

Felder also remarks* that *D. nesippus* is " a local variety of *D. hegesippus*, Cramer, which as well as this and *D. melanippus*, Cramer, is again a local subspecies of *D. lotis.*† The Nicobar form differs from all the numerous specimens of *D. hegesippus*, which I received from Java and Malacca in the narrow, rust-red coloured streaks of the forewing, and the much narrower white radial spots of the hindwing. Regarding the latter difference it is nearer allied to *D. melanippus*, but the above mentioned streaks in this species are coloured ochre-brown."

We have a large series of this insect in our collection ; it is an insular form of *D. hegesippus*, from which it differs in the almost complete absence of the first band of white spots outside the cell of the forewing, which in *D. hegesippus* are prominent, and the white streaks in *D. nesippus* are somewhat narrower. Mr. de Roëpstorff took numbers of the species at Nancowry in August ; and it is recorded by Felder from Great Nicobar.

36. **Danais melanippus,** Cramer.

Papilio melanippus, Cramer, Pap. Ex., vol. ii, pl. cxxvii, figs. A, B (1777) ; *Papilio hegesippus*, Herbst, Pap., pl. clv, figs. 7, 8 (1794).

HABITAT : Nepal, Assam, Penang, Malacca, Java.

EXPANSE : 3 inches.

DESCRIPTION : Differs from *D. genutia* in the *forewing* in not having any fulvous between the second and third median nervules, or below the submedian nervure ; the macular subapical white band is less prominent, and the series between it and the cell is reduced to a spot on the costa. On the *hindwing* the fulvous patch in the cell pales almost to white inwardly, and all the streaks beyond the cell are very narrow and short, the abdominal streaks are also narrow. The marginal and submarginal series of white spots are very small and obsolete, especially the inner series, about the region of the third median nervule. The UNDERSIDE differs from that side of *D. genutia* in the same way as the uppersides of the two species differ one from the other.

D. melanippus is a native of Java ; the above description is taken from Cramer's figure of a male specimen from that island. It is certainly very rare in India, if indeed the records of its occurrence are not cases of mistaken identity, though Butler, in his paper on the Malacca Butterflies, gives the above-quoted Indian localities for it.

---

* Verh. zool.-bot. Gessellsch. Wien, vol. xii, p. 486 (1862).

† From Java.

Genus 4.—EUPLŒA, Fabricius. (PLATES VII—IX).

Fabricius, Illiger's Mag., vol. vi, p. 280 (1807); Doubleday, Gen. D. L., p. 86 (1847); Butler, Proc. Zool. Soc. Lond., 1866, p. 268, *Monograph*; id., Journ. Linn. Soc., Zoology, vol. xiv, p. 290 (1878), *Monograph*: *Trepsichrois*, *Crastia*, *Salpinx*, Hübner, Verz. bek. Schmett., pp. 16, 17 (1816).

"ANTENNÆ, rather more than half as long as the whole length of the body, gradually clavate. FORELEGS, with the femur and tibia about equal in length; the tarsus shorter; of the MALE cylindric, rather tapering to a point at the extremity, indistinctly biarticulate; second joint about one-third the length of the first, both clothed with scales and hairs; of the FEMALE, clavate, quadriarticulate; the first joint longer than the rest combined, much broadest at the apex, where it has a stout spine on each side; second and third short, furnished with a tuft of hair on each side near the base, and a spine at the apex; the fourth joint minute, furnished with a tuft of hairs. MIDDLE and HINDLEGS strong, the claws rather stout, curved. The PARONYCHIA divided into two laciniæ; the outer elongate, lanceolate, hairy, as long as the claw; the inner not quite equal in length to the outer, more hairy, elongate, lanceolate, the apex curving inward over the base of the pulvillus. PULVILLUS not so long as the claws, jointed; the second joint broad, corneous." (*Doubleday*).

LARVA, with several pairs of elongate fleshy tentacula, usually on the penultimate, and on two or more of the anterior segments. PUPA, short, obtuse, with the abdomen much rounded.

The *Eupløas* are of rather large size; usually of a swarthy brown or black colour, sometimes rufescent, generally with a veivety appearance, and often with brilliant blue or purple reflections, especially in the forewing; more or less spotted with white or violet; sometimes streaked with white on the hindwing; typically the spots are arranged in a double marginal series on both wings, sometimes with a third discal row, but the extent to which these markings are developed varies greatly, and in many species some or most of them are entirely wanting. The thorax and head are spotted with white, especially below. In the *forewing* the inner margin is in the MALE, usually much rounded outwardly, with a convex outline often covering a large portion of the hindwing even when the wings are extended for flight; in the FEMALE it is usually straight or very slightly convex towards the base, sometimes even emarginate or slightly concave towards the exterior angle. In some of the groups the males have one or two impressed silky streaks on the interno-median area of the forewing, composed of scales differently formed from those on the rest of the wing. These streaks, together with a patch of differently formed and paler scales present in some groups on the anterior portion of the upperside of the hindwing, and covered by the forewing, are probably scent-producing organs. The sexes in a few species also differ materially in the colour of the hindwing, the males having the wing nearly uniform dark colour, and the females having it streaked with white; but as a rule the differences in colour are slight, and the sexes are only to be distinguished by their structure and outline, and by the presence or absence of the sexual marks on the wings.

About 160 species of *Euplœa* have been described; it is an eastern-Asiatic genus, most highly developed in the Malay Archipelago, and extending into Australia. Species also are recorded from the islands of Mauritius, Bourbon, and Madagascar. Upwards of forty species are included in the Indian list, but owing to the variations in individuals and the indefiniteness of many of the original descriptions, their identification is often very difficult; many of the species inhabiting the same locality are so similar in appearance on the wing that some are apt to be overlooked. They affect patches of scrub in cultivation, and the edges of forests, and fly rather slowly and heavily; they are most abundant in warm, damp, tropical climates, and seem to shun dry places, whether cold or hot. Only a single species, *E. core*, is found commonly in India proper; no less than twenty-two species occur in Burma, of which some extend to north-east India; seventeen species are found in north-east India including those extending from Burma; seven species are found in the Andamans and Nicobars, all but two of which appear to be confined to those islands; three only are found in south India, but in Ceylon there are six species, all but one of which occur nowhere else within Indian limits. The foregoing remarks include as species all that have been separately described, although, as in the case of the allies of *E. core*,—*E. asela*, *E. vermiculata*, and *E. subdita*, the different forms are almost certainly only geographical varieties.

This genus was divided by Hübner into three or four groups, each with a well-marked general outline; and more recently Butler has extended this division into seven groups; more recently still Moore has discriminated two other groups, which will be noted further on, and is about to monograph the whole genus; but the characters of the new groups he has given seem to agree with those already discriminated by Butler, whose definitions are used in this book.

Key to the Groups of EUPLŒA.

A. With a large patch of whitish or pale yellow scales on the anterior portion of the hindwing in the male.

a. Forewing in the male, with the inner margin strongly arched, and having an elongated silky or blue spot depressed on the interno-median area; of medium size.

I. SALPINX* (Hübner, as restricted by Butler).

b. With no silky or blue depressed spot on interno-median area; of very large size.

II. MACROPLŒA (Butler).

c. With no silky or blue depressed spot on interno-median area; of small size.

III. CALLIPLŒA (Butler).

B. With a small yellow patch within the cell of hindwing at origin of first subcostal nervule; no brand on forewing in the male.

IV. TREPSICHROIS (Hübner).

C. With no yellowish patch on hindwing in the male.

a. With no trace of a brand on the interno-median area of forewing of male.

V. CRASTIA (Hübner).

b. With a single more or less strongly defined brand on interno-median area of forewing of male.

VI. EUPLŒA (Fabricius, as restricted by Butler).

c. With two well-defined brands on interno-median area of forewing in male.

VII. STICTOPLŒA† (Butler).

There is something very remarkable about these groups; they are based almost entirely on the sexual marks of the male insect, but in many cases these distinctions are accompanied by differences of outline that cannot be mistaken; the most curious point is that frequently the same style of colouration runs through two or more of the groups; thus *Salpinx sinhala* and *Stictoplœa coreoïdes* so closely resemble each other and *E. core* in colour and markings that until quite recently the distinctions were unrecognised. In like manner *Stictoplœa grotei* closely resembles *E. limborgii* in colour and markings; some specimens of the female of *Macroplœa castelnaui* are a very good likeness on a large scale of *E. godartii*. *Salpinx margarita* bears a similar resemblance to *Crastia cupreipennis* which occurs with it in the Mergui Archipelago and Upper Tenasserim, and *Crastia camaralzeman* from Siam. *Crastia simulatrix* closely resembles *Euplœa camorta*, &c., &c. The difficulty of distinguishing the species on the wing is a great hindrance to observation of the insects in life. The claim of the groups to generic rank appears still to be doubtful, and there is much to be learned in connection with them.

First Group.—SALPINX (Hübner, as restricted by Butler): "For the most part large insects, the males of which invariably have a strongly arched inner margin to the *forewing*, which is frequently ornamented with an elongated depressed silky or blue spot; the *hindwing* invariably with a large patch of whitish or pale yellow, cut by the subcostal nervure."—(*Butler*, Journ. Linn. Soc., Zoology, vol. xiv, p. 295, 1878). The wings are generally ample, and more or less rounded externally. The habitat of this group is extreme north-east India and Burma, extending down the Malay peninsula. Of the Indian species only one is found in the Nicobar islands, and one species is found in the neighbourhood of Calcutta, in Sikkim, and again in southern India and Ceylon; the whole of the remainder are found only to the north and east of the Bay of Bengal. One species of this group, *E. superba*, is taken by Moore in the Lepidoptera of Ceylon, p. 10 (1880), as the type of a new genus which, under the name of *Isamia*, he characterises as follows:—"Wings large, broad; *forewing* in male elongated, somewhat quadrate; apex slightly acuminate; exterior margin oblique, waved; posterior margin convex, with a large sericeous streak between the first median nervule and submedian nervure; *hindwing* triangular, costa long, convex; exterior margin convex, waved; a moderate-sized pale upper discoidal patch."

---

* Includes *Isamia*, Moore.
† Includes *Narmada*, Moore.

No explanation of any kind is given as to how this differs from *Salpinx* of Hübner, or from *Salpinx* as restricted by Butler, or why the older name has been dropped. *E. superba* and its allies certainly differ from other species of *Salpinx* in the form of the sexual brand of the forewing, but it is more probable that they are really different forms of a single species than a group of species forming a distinct genus.

Key to the Indian species of SALPINX.

A. Forewing comparatively narrow and elongated, the apex acute. Males with a prominent elongate sericeous streak on the forewing, somewhat as in true *Euplœa*, scarcely visible on the underside. All more or less shot with brilliant blue; and with a prominent lilac spot in the cell of the forewing on the underside.

- *a.* Forewing with numerous violet or white spots in three series.
  - *a.*[1] The brilliant blue shot reaching the submarginal row of spots on the forewing; the border spots of the hindwing white and prominent.
    - 37. E. *(Salpinx)* SUPERBA (North India?), China.
  - *b.*[1] The brilliant blue shot reaching the marginal row of spots on the forewing.
    - *a.*[2] The border spots on the hindwing very indistinct or obsolete.
      - 38. E. *(Salpinx)* ROGENHOFERI, N.-E. India, Burma.
    - *b.*[2] The border spots on the hindwing pale, but distinct.
      - 39. E. *(Salpinx)* IRAWADA, Burma.
- *b.* Forewing with few and indistinct spots, no series complete; the border spots of the hindwing white and prominent.
  - *a.*[1] The brilliant blue shot variable in extent, but usually covering the basal two-thirds only of the forewing.
    - 40. E. *(Salpinx)* MARGARITA, Tenasserim.

B. Forewing shorter and very broad. Males with a broad short oval sericeous brand, not prominent, generally concolorous with, but paler than, the ground-colour, visible on the underside as a raised dark spot. The blue shot less brilliant and often wanting; no spot as a rule in the cell of the forewing on the underside.

- *a.* Forewing very broad, with a *decreasing* row of submarginal spots, the third largest; border spots of the hindwing small but prominent.
  - *a.*[1] Forewing brown, sometimes faintly glossed with blue at the base.
    - 41. E. *(Salpinx)* CRASSA, Burma.
    - 42. E. *(Salpinx)* ERICHSONII, Burma.
  - *b.*[1] The basal area of the forewing brilliant blue.
    - 43. E. *(Salpinx)* MASONI, Burma.
- *b.* Forewing less broad, with the row of submarginal spots all nearly equal-sized.
  - *a.*[1] The blue shot usually suffusing the entire forewing, but very variable in intensity.
    - 44. E. *(Salpinx)* KLUGII, N.-E. India.
    - 45. E. *(Salpinx)* GRANTII, Cachar.
  - *b.*[1] The blue shot brilliant, but not reaching the outer margin of the forewing; the discal series of spots abbreviated, the third considerably the largest.
    - 46. E. *(Salpinx)* ILLUSTRIS, N.-E. India.
    - E. *(Salpinx)* CHLOE, Malayana.
    - E. *(Salpinx)* ÆGYPTUS, Malayana.
  - *c.*[1] The blue shot usually entirely wanting, faintly present in some specimens; the forewing brown, with border spots as in *E. core*.
    - 47. E. *(Salpinx)* SINHALA, Sikkim, Calcutta, S. India, Ceylon.

C. Forewing shaped much as in the preceding group. Male with a broad *violet* streak on the internomedian area; visible on the underside as a dark raised spot.

- *a.* Forewing with no large white patch from middle of costa; the hindwing without white basal streaks on the upperside.
  - *a.*[1] Forewing shot throughout with deep blue; with prominent violet spots.
    - *a.*[2] The marginal series of spots partially present near the hinder angle of both wings.
      - 48. E. *(Salpinx)* VESTIGIATA, Malayana.
    - *b.*[2] The marginal series of spots absent from both wings.
      - 49. E. *(Salpinx)* NOVARÆ, Nicobars.
  - *b.*[1] Forewing blackish-swarthy; the hindwing with the anal angle white.
    - 50. E. *(Salpinx)* LEUCOGONYS, (N.-E. India?), Malacca.
- *b.* Forewing with a large white patch from middle of the costa; the hindwing with white basa streaks on both sides; of smaller size.
  - *a.*[1] Wings shot with deep violet-blue.
    - 51. E. *(Salpinx)* RHADAMANTHUS, N.-E. India, Burma.
  - *b.*[1] Wings not shot with violet-blue.
    - 52. E *(Salpinx)* DIOCLETIANUS, (N.-E. India?), Burma.

The first four species, *E. superba*, *E. rogenhoferi*, *E. irawada*, and *E. margarita* are very closely allied, and may possibly be only different forms of the same species; the type of the group is *E. superba*, which has the forewing with three series of violet and white spots and shot with brilliant blue as far as the submarginal series, while the hindwing has two rows of white and prominent border spots; *E. margarita* only appears to differ from it in the almost entire absence of spots on the forewing; and in that it has the blue shot variable in extent, never reaching beyond the submarginal series of spots, and frequently confined to the basal two-thirds of the forewing; the extent to which the spots on the forewing are present varies greatly in this species, and some examples approach very closely indeed to *E. superba*. *E. rogenhoferi* and *E. irawada*, on the other hand, differ chiefly in having the blue shot of the forewing extending to the outer margin, and the border spots of the hindwing either pale or obsolete; *E. irawada*, the Burmese form, has the spots of the hindwing distinct, while *E. rogenhoferi*, the Assamese form, has, as is the case in several parallel instances, the border spots almost, if not quite, obsolete. Typical specimens can easily be distinguished, but none of the distinctive characters seem to be altogether permanent.

The FEMALES in this group are usually coloured and marked like the males, but lack the sexual brand on the forewing and the yellowish patch on the hindwing, and have the inner margin of the forewing nearly straight. *E. rhadamanthus* and *E. diocletianus* are the only species of this group in which the sexes differ at all widely in colour and markings.

37. **Euplœa superba**, Herbst.

Papilio superbus, Herbst, Pap., vol v, pl. cxix, fig. 3, *female*, pl. cxx, figs. 1, 2, *male* (1792); *Papilio midamus*, Fabricius (*nec* Linnæus), Syst. Ent., p. 479, n. 161 (1775), *female*; *Linnas mutabilis midamis*, Hübner, Samml. Ex. Schmett., p. 16 (1816); *Danais alopia*, Godart, Enc. Méth., vol. ix, p. 177, n. 4 (1819); *Euplœa superba*, Horsfield and Moore, Cat. Lep. E. I. C., p. 131, n. 263 (1857); *Isamia superba*, Moore, Lep. Cey., p. 10 (1880).

HABITAT: (Darjiling *apud* Moore ?, North India *apud* Butler ?); China.

EXPANSE: 4·2 inches.

DESCRIPTION: MALE: UPPERSIDE.—*Forewing* deep brown, lighter towards the outer margin, suffused with brilliant blue up to the submarginal series of spots. A subcostal spot above the extremity of the cell, bluish-white. A spot in the cell, and a series of six spots, the third and fourth the largest, exterior to it, violet. A long dark impressed sexual mark in the interno-median area. A submarginal sinuous series of seven white spots, the second from the apex the largest, the seventh minute, sometimes geminate. A marginal series of small round white dots, obsolete towards the apex. *Hindwing* cupreous-brown, darkest about the median nervure, very pale on the costal area. A white patch across the subcostal nervure extending into, below, and beyond the cell. A submarginal row of spots, the two upper ones rounded, the third geminated, the remainder elongated; a marginal series of small round spots, all chalky-white. UNDERSIDE bronzy-brown, darkest on the disc. On the *forewing* the discal series of spots are reduced to two, one in each space between the median nervules, the lower elongated, violet-white. The marginal and submarginal series of spots as on upperside, white. The inner margin broadly white. The *hindwing* has several white spots at the base; a small spot in the cell, and beyond it six small streaks, all violet-white. The submarginal and marginal series of spots on both wings as above, except that they are larger and clearer white. The FEMALE differs from the male in the absence of the sexual brand, and the inner margin of the *forewing* being straight, not outwardly lobed, as in the male. No patch of chalky-white scales on the anterior portion of the *hindwing*. Described from specimens from China in the Indian Museum, Calcutta.

We have never seen a specimen taken in India. It is entered in the list of species occurring within our limits on the strength of Horsfield and Moore's and Butler's identifications, but we doubt its occurrence there.

38. **Euplœa rogenhoferi**, Felder.

E. rogenhoferi, Felder, Reise Nov., Lep., vol. ii, p. 325, n. 446 (1865), *male*; *E. splendens*, Butler, Proc. Zool. Soc. Lond., 1866, p. 272, n. 9, *male*.

HABITAT: Eastern Himalayas, Upper Assam, Cachar, Khasi Hills, Bassein.

EXPANSE: 3·4 to 4·4 inches.

DESCRIPTION: "MALE: UPPERSIDE.—*Forewing* blackish swarthy, shot throughout with greenish blue; the outer margin with two series of white spots, the marginal series not reaching the apex, the submarginal series with the forepart arched from the costa, but not reaching the inner margin; with a short angulated series of seven oblong violet spots placed beyond the cell, and extending from the costa above the cell to the lower median interspace; one spot near the end of the cell; and a pale streak placed below the first median nervule. *Hindwing* paler, slightly bluish, the costal area pale; a rather large ochreous spot placed on the subcostal nervure, and two series of very indistinct spots on the outer margin. The *body* swarthy, dotted with white anteriorly. UNDERSIDE: *Forewing* coppery-fuscous, the inner margin pale, with the series of submarginal spots as on upperside, but the inner series with smaller spots; a spot below the middle of the costa, one near the end of the cell, one below the end of the cell, and one large oblong spot between the median nervules—white. *Hindwing* coppery-fuscous, with two series of white submarginal spots; the inner series being of minute dots; with an angulate series of violet-white spots beyond the end of the cell, and one spot in the cell, and some white dots at the base. *Body* swarthy, the thorax dotted with white."

"Allied to *E. superba*, Herbst [from North India (?) and China], but more brilliantly shot with variable blue-green; the outer margin of the forewing more arched; the costa of the hindwing not so angular; the discoidal spots of the forewing much larger and oblong, and the submarginal spots smaller; the submarginal spots of the hindwing nearly obsolete. Below, the discoidal spots are much more distinct and larger, the submarginal spots of the forewing more numerous, and the inner submarginal series of the hindwing very small, especially towards the apex and anal angle." (*Butler*, l. c.) The FEMALE differs from the male in the absence of the sexual mark on the upperside of the *forewing*, but it has a long pale violet streak on the underside in the position occupied by this mark in the male; the inner margin is also straight, not lobed, as in the male. No anterior creamy-white patch of scales on the *hindwing*. UNDERSIDE somewhat lighter in both wings.

E. rogenhoferi is found, but not very commonly, in Assam, extending through the Eastern Himalayas as far as the valley of the Sardah, which separates Kumaon from Nepal. To the westward of this range it is much rarer than to the eastward. Mr. Wood-Mason took three males and a female in Cachar from April to June. The specimens from Bassein of this group which we have identified as *E. rogenhoferi* agree with the description of *E. irawada*, the next species, and may possibly be referable to it. At any rate the two are closely allied, and only appear to differ in the comparative prominence of the spots on the hindwing and possibly also in the tone of the blue shot.

39. **Euplœa irawada**, Moore.

E. irawada, Moore, Ann. and Mag. Nat. Hist., fourth series, vol. xx, p. 45 (1877).

HABITAT: Henzada, Rangoon District, Burma.

EXPANSE: 3·5 inches.

DESCRIPTION: "MALE: UPPERSIDE, dark blackish brown. *Forewing* glossed with brilliant steel-blue; a lilac-blue spot at lower end of the cell, and a contiguous discal series of six similar spots; a marginal upper series of six small white spots, and a marginal lower row of white dots; an elongated, silky, impressed streak between first median nervule and submedian nervure. *Hindwing* with a flesh-coloured patch extending over upper part of the cell, anterior margin broadly cinereous; a submarginal row of pale oval spots, and a marginal row of small round spots. UNDERSIDE brown. *Forewing* suffused in the disc with black; hind margin broadly and an elongated lower discal spot cinereous white; second discal spot and cell spot blue, upper spots minute, marginal rows of white spots distinct. *Hindwing* with marginal row of distinct white spots, submarginal row partly obsolete; a small blue spot at end of, and a contiguous series outside the cell." (*Moore*, l. c.)

E. irawada appears to be very rare ; we know of no specimens in collections in India, unless those of *E. rogenhoferi* from Bassein referred to above really belong to this species. These specimens answer exactly to the description of *E. irawada*, but they are inseparable from the Assam examples of *E. rogenhoferi*.

40. **Euplœa margarita,** Butler.

E. margarita, Butler, Proc. Zool. Soc. Lond., 1866, p. 279, n. 34 ; *Salpinx margarita*, Moore, d., 1878, p. 823 ; *E. adamsoni*, Marshall, Journ. A. S. B., vol. xlix, part ii, p. 245 (1880).

HABITAT : Upper Tenasserim, Penang, Malacca.

EXPANSE : ♂, 3·6 to 4·2 ; ♂, 4·1 to 4·5 inches.

DESCRIPTION : UPPERSIDE, olivaceous-fuscous ; *forewing* fuscescent, shot with blue and green, with one white costal spot ; in the MALE with two blue discal spots, one subapical dot, one anal, and one submarginal, ochreous ; in the FEMALE with one white discal spot. *Hindwing* of the MALE with the costal margin ochreous-white, a rather large ochreous subcostal spot, and two submarginal rows of ochreous-white spots on the outer margin ; of the FEMALE with two rows of spots, those at the anal angle coalescing ; the inner row elongate. *Body* swarthy, blackish in front with white spots. UNDERSIDE paler ; *forewing* with some scattered submarginal white dots, and one costal, two discal spots, the lower large and elongate, and a lunule in the cell, iridescent ; the inner margin pale. Of the FEMALE with an elongate ochreous discal streak placed near the margin. *Hindwing* of the MALE with five dots, of the FEMALE with six discal, and two in the cell, white, iridescent ; the submarginal spots as on the upperside ; and the base dotted with white. *Body* blackish swarthy, dotted with white. *Antennæ* black." (*Butler*, l. c.)

The brilliant blue shot does not, as would be gathered from the original description above, cover the entire forewing ; it never extends beyond the submarginal series of spots, and in many specimens it does not cover more than two-thirds of the distance from the base, the whole of the outer portion of the wing being paler bright brown with no trace of blue. In typical *E. margarita*, where the blue shot extends to the position of the submarginal series, the costa is comparatively short, the apex somewhat acuminate, and the outer margin distinctly convex ; on the other hand, where the blue shot is confined to the basal two-thirds, the costa is lower, the apex rounded, and the exterior margin straighter, sometimes even somewhat emarginate ; this latter form was, owing to the wording of the original description, redescribed as *E. adamsoni*,* Marshall, (Journ. A. S. B., vol. xlix, part ii, p. 245, 1880). It is possible that the two forms may still be distinct, but numerous intermediate varieties occur, and we are unable to separate them.

Euplœa margarita has as yet been found only in Tenasserim and the Mergui Archipelago, where Dr. J. Anderson took it somewhat commonly in the cold weather. Captain C. H. E. Adamson took a single male at Moulmein in the autumn ; another male was subsequently taken at the Mayla Choung in September ; numerous specimens were taken by Captain C. T. Bingham in the Thoungyeen forests in December ; and again in June by Captain Adamson near Moulmein. The FEMALE differs from the male in the absence of the usual sexual marks, namely the silky stripe on the forewing and the yellowish-white patch on the hindwing ; the sexual mark on the forewing is however replaced on the underside by a lengthened violet streak in the position of the mark in the male ; also in having the inner margin of the forewing straight, not convex, and the submarginal series of spots on the hindwing considerably larger and more elongate, the spots in and around the cell are also more prominent.

The next three species, *E. crassa*, *E. erichsonii*, and *E. masoni*, are also very closely allied ; typical specimens of each are easily separable, but numerous intermediate forms occur, and all three are found in the same localities. It is probable that they are all merely varieties of one species, *E. erichsonii* ; the extent to which the submarginal series is continued towards the

* *Euplœa adamsoni*, Marshall. HABITAT : Moulmein. EXPANSE : 3·6 to 4 inches. DESCRIPTION : MALE ; Allied to *E. superba*, Herbst, but differing on the UPPERSIDE of the *forewing* in that the brilliant blue gloss is confined to the basal two-thirds not reaching to the costa or the inner margin, and that the spots are reduced to four in number, all very small, one subcostal above the end of the cell, and one at the end of the cell, both lilac ; and two near anal angle, one marginal, the other submarginal, white. *Hindwing* as in *E. superba*.

hinder angle, the spots when present of the discal series, and the intensity of the blue shot when present, are all extremely variable. In all three the great breadth of the wings, the comparative shortness of the forewing, and the extremely convex inner margin of that wing in the males distinguishes them from other species of *Salpinx*, and the enlargement of the third and adjacent spots in the submarginal series is also a very distinctive feature which is found in no other species of *Euplœa* in this country, except in *E. (Crastia) bremeri* and *E. vermiculata* to a lesser degree; the enlargement of the third spot in the discal series of *E. (Salpinx) illustris* indicates an affinity with this group.

41. **Euplœa crassa,** Butler.

E. crassa, Butler, Proc. Zool. Soc. Lond., 1866, p. 278, n. 31; *Salpinx crassa*, Moore, id., 1878, p. 822.

HABITAT: Burma, Siam.

EXPANSE: ♂, 3·6 to 4·0; ♀, 3·5 to 4·1 inches.

DESCRIPTION: "UPPERSIDE coppery-olivaceous, slightly swarthy, and shot with blue at the base; *forewing* with the apex very acute, with two rows of white submarginal spots, the inner row rather large towards the apex, and violet-white; with three discal dots behind the extremity of the cell, and one costal spot, violet-white. *Hindwing*, with the costa white, two series of white spots, the inner row towards the apex a little the larger. The *body* swarthy, *abdomen* bluish, and the *head* spotted with ochreous. UNDERSIDE, paler; *forewing* with two series of spots, the inner apical, the outer continued; one large internal spot, one costal, and often two behind the end of the cell, roseate-white. *Hindwing* with two submarginal rows of spots, and dotted with white at the base; *abdomen* ashy, spotted with white in the middle." (*Butler*, l. c.)

E. crassa, as we identify it, occurs in Rangoon in June; and a number of specimens were taken by Limborg in Upper Tenasserim in the cold weather. Three of these latter specimens, now in the Indian Museum, Calcutta, have the submarginal row of spots on the upperside of the forewing complete, but one of them shows indistinct traces of a discal series. Of five males and four females taken by Dr. J. Anderson in the Mergui Archipelago in the cold weather, three males and one female shew traces of a discal series of spots. See remarks on the following species, *E. erichsonii*.

42. **Euplœa erichsonii,** Felder.

E. erichsonii, Felder, Reise Nov., Lep., vol. ii, p. 324, n. 444 (1865).

HABITAT: Eastern Himalayas, Cachar, Burma.

EXPANSE: 3·6 to 4·2 inches.

DESCRIPTION: "MALE:—The *cilia* striolated with white. UPPERSIDE, dilute bronzed or rufescent-swarthy, the basal half deeper coloured and slightly tinted with violet in certain lights. *Forewing* with a short interior silky streak; eight submarginal spots in a row slightly bent towards the costa, opalescent-white, dotted with violet round the edge, enclosing a small white spot; the three upper ones larger than the others, increasing in size from the costa, and placed very close together; the remainder decreasing in size. A marginal row of small white spots placed in pairs between the nervules; sometimes also two narrow violet-white spots outside the end of the cell. *Hindwing* pale anteriorly, the costal margin pearly-white, with two white spots; also eight small external decreasing spots, and a marginal row of smaller spots, all white. UNDERSIDE, paler, with the submarginal spots as above, but whiter. *Forewing*, with the depressed internal spot, a subcostal spot, another median rather large, sometimes a third above it, and two small ones beyond the cell, lilac-white; the submarginal spots much smaller than on the upperside, dot-shaped, and white. *Hindwing*, with white spots at the base; the two upper of the external spots smaller than on the upperside, and one above these dot-shaped; the remainder larger than on the upperside, and whiter. FEMALE: UPPERSIDE, paler than in the male, the markings similar, often indeed larger (the lower submarginal ones sometimes entirely absent or evanescent), but the marginal spots are sometimes dot-like. *Forewing*, with an obsolete subcostal spot, violet." (*Felder*, l. c.)

This species has been considered and most probably is identical with *E. crassa*; we republish both orginal descriptions, as there are two distinct forms—the one with no discal spots and the submarginal row complete on *forewing*, the other with a discal row, and the submarginal series incomplete; but among the numerous specimens in the Indian Museum, and in our collections, there are no less than eight which have the submarginal series abbreviated, and the discal series wanting; and it is impossible to say to which of the two species, if distinct, these specimens should be referred: probably, they are really all one species which will stand as *E. erichsonii*, Felder. The form we indentify as *E. erichsonii* is common in the neighbourhood of Moulmein in the autumn. Captain C. H. E. Adamson has sent us a specimen taken in June, in that locality, and we have one specimen taken at Rangoon in June, and Captain C. T. Bingham has taken it in the Meplay valley in February, and in the Thoungyeen forests in May. In the Indian Museum, Calcutta, there are four males and two females taken by Limborg in Upper Tenasserim in the cold weather, and one female from Cachar taken by Mr. Wood-Mason in April.

43. **Euplœa masoni**, Moore.

Salpinx masoni, Moore, Proc. Zool. Soc. Lond., 1878, p. 823.

HABITAT: Upper Tenasserim; Taoo, 3,000 to 5,000 feet; above Ahsown.

EXPANSE: 3·25 to 4·2 inches.

DESCRIPTION: "MALE.—Allied to *E. crassa*, Butler, but differing in its darker colour, in the basal area of the *forewing* being bright glossy blue, and the marginal spots on this wing confined more to the apex. *Hindwing*, less convex along the exterior margin; otherwise similarly marked. From *E. klugii*, Moore, this species may be distinguished by the blue gloss being confined to the basal area, whereas in *E. klugii* it is more brilliant, and suffuses the entire wing." (*Moore*, l. c.) The prominence of the two rows of marginal spots on the hindwing in this species, as well as the breadth of the wings, distinguish it from *E. illustris*.

E. masoni has been taken only in Tenasserim, where it is not uncommon, though less so than either of the others. The specimens in our collections, which accord well with this description, are barely if at all separable from *E. erichsonii*.

44. **Euplœa klugii**, Moore.

E. klugii, Moore, Horsfield and Moore, Cat. Lep. E. I. C., vol. i, p. 130, n. 258 (1857).

HABITAT: N. India, Bhutan, Cachar, Sylhet, Upper Burma.

EXPANSE: 3·0 to 4·1 inches.

DESCRIPTION: "MALE: UPPERSIDE deep brown, having on the *forewing* a brilliant blue gloss, a submarginal row of small bluish-white spots, and an inner parallel row of larger spots, also a bluish spot on costal margin; one within discoidal cell; two linear bluish marks, one between each discoidal nervule; and a rather indistinct bluish mark between the submedian and median nervures. *Hindwing* paler brown, darkest and glossed with blue in the middle; a submarginal row of white spots and a short inner row from anterior margin; also a patch of creamy-white near middle of the wing. UNDERSIDE brown. *Forewing* with the two rows of *white* spots smaller; one spot on costal margin, one small narrow spot between second discoidal and first [? third] median nervules, and a larger spot between second and third [? first] median nervules; a creamy-white patch on posterior base of the wing. *Hindwing*, with two rows of white spots. FEMALE: UPPERSIDE nearly as in male. *Forewing*, with the submarginal row of spots obsolete. *Hindwing*, pale brown, darkest and slightly glossed with blue in the middle; two white spots only of inner row distinct, the rest of two rows indistinct; without the creamy-white patch. UNDERSIDE, nearly as in male, but not having the creamy-white patch. Shape of wings as in *Euplœa superba*, Herbst." (*Moore*, l. c.)

This is a very variable species. The blue gloss is much deeper and more brilliant in some specimens than in others, and in one male and three females from Cachar, and one female from Sylhet, it only reaches to midway between the disco-cellular nervules and the submarginal series of spots, and moreover the gloss is not at all vivid even where present. In some examples, taken by the Yunan Expedition, probably in Upper Burma, the marginal series of dots on the forewing is entirely wanting ; in Cachar and Sylhet specimens this series is sometimes confined to six or seven spots towards the hinder angle, in others it is complete to the apex ; the submarginal series is also equally inconstant ; in some specimens there are only five spots, in others the series is complete. These spots also differ in size and colour—some are small, equal-sized, round and white, others are large, elongated, unequal-sized and violet ; some specimens have a very prominent cell spot and a discal series of four spots, others again are without all these spots. The two marginal series of spots on the hindwing are also very inconstant ; in some examples they are quite obsolete, in others as prominent as in *E. superba.* The underside is also as diversely marked as the upperside, but it seems clear, even from the specimens in the Museum, that all these are but casual variations of the same species.

Mr. Wood-Mason met with this species commonly in Cachar from April to June ; and Mr. A. O. Hume took it in the eastern hills of Manipur in May.

45. **Euplœa grantii,** Butler.

Salpinx grantii, Butler, Trans. Ent. Soc. Lond., 1879, p. 2.

HABITAT : Cachar.

EXPANSE : 3·92 inches.

DESCRIPTION : " FEMALE : *Forewing* above rich piceous brown, shot with purple, darkest in the centre, and palest at external angle, a small white subcostal spot just above the end of the cell, a crescent-shaped lilac spot in the cell, a circular spot on the first median interspace, two fusiform spots beyond the cell, and a series of seven spots, the sixth pyriform, parallel to the outer margin : all these spots lilac with white centres ; an ill-defined lilac spot on the second median interspace, a submarginal series of eight white dots between the lower radial and the external angle. *Hindwing* piceous brown, faintly shot with purple, the costal and external areas broadly paler, two series of pale brown spots parallel to the outer margin, the first of the inner series white-centred, costal border whitish. UNDERSIDE olive-brown. *Forewing* with the median area suffused with piceous, inner border whitish, a pinky-white subcostal spot, and three in an increasing oblique series above each of the median nervules ; three or four scattered white dots in an interrupted discal series parallel to the outer margin, and six rather larger white dots in a submarginal series between the lower radial and the external angle. *Hindwing* with several white dots at the base, a discal series of ten white spots, the upper three rounded, in an oblique subapical series, the remainder rather elongated and parallel to the outer margin ; nine white submarginal dots between the radial and the anal angle."

" This species may readily be distinguished from *E. splendens*, ♀ [=*E. rogenhoferi*] by the greater width, and less brilliant purple (not blue) shot of the forewing ; also in the more numerous submarginal spots of the forewing, the inner series being, moreover, larger and lilac, whereas in *S. splendens* [=*E. rogenhoferi*] they are pure white, with pale violet borders ; the discoidal spot not present on the underside, but an additional spot beyond the cell, the outer spots smaller ; no lilac dots beyond the cell of hindwing." (*Butler*, l. c.)

From the description this species seems nearest allied to *E. klugii.* Out of a very long series of this latter species in the Indian Museum, Calcutta, we are able to pick out individual specimens that agree with the description of *E. grantii*, but we are unable to separate these specimens from *E. klugii*, which is one of the most variable of *Euplœas.* It appears to us that *E. grantii* is only one of the numerous varieties of *E. klugii*, but we have retained the original description of it as a reference to the type alone can settle the question whether it is a distinct species or not.

46. **Euplœa illustris,** Butler.

Salpinx illustris, Butler, Journ. Linn. Soc., Zoology, vol. xiv, p. 294, n. 36 (1878).

HABITAT: Sylhet.

EXPANSE: 3·9 inches.

DESCRIPTION: "MALE: Nearly allied to *E. klugii*, Moore, but the outer border of the *forewing* deep chocolate-brown, not covered by the blue shot, and with the white shots upon it smaller; the discal series of spots abbreviated, not extending below the inferior discoidal interspace; the third spot in the series considerably larger." (*Butler*, l. c.)

This appears to be a very distinct species from either of the two foregoing, though it may ultimately prove to be only a variety of *E. klugii*; and it seems to be rare. The Indian Museum, Calcutta, possesses a single male specimen; the female is as yet unknown.

Two allied species, *Euplœa chloë*,* Guérin, and *Euplœa ægyptus*† Butler, occur in the Malay peninsula, &c.

47. **Euplœa sinhala,** Moore. (PLATE VII, FIG. 12 ♂ ♀).

E sinhala, Moore, Ann. and Mag. Nat. Hist., fourth series, vol. xx, p. 45 (1877); *Isamia sinhala*, Moore, Lep. Cey., p. 10, pl. v, fig. 1 (1880), *male*.

HABITAT: Sikkim, Calcutta, South India, Ceylon.

EXPANSE: 3·3 to 4·3 inches.

DESCRIPTION: "MALE: UPPERSIDE dark velvety olive-brown, external margins paler. *Forewing* with a short broad oval sericeous streak between the lower median and submedian veins, a submarginal row of small ochreous-white spots, and marginal lower row of minute spots. *Hindwing* with a broad flesh-coloured discoidal patch; costal border broadly cinereous, a submarginal series of oval ochreous-white spots, and marginal series of small round spots. UNDERSIDE paler olive-brown throughout. *Forewing* with hind margin broadly cinereous; the sexual mark dusky; a curved discal series of whitish spots near the cell; both wings with a submarginal and marginal series of spots as above. *Body* black; thorax, head, palpi and forelegs white spotted." (*Moore*, Lep. Ceylon, p. 10.) The FEMALE differs from the male in the absence of the sexual brand, and the inner margin of the forewing being straight, not

---

* *Euplœa chloë*, Guérin. HABITAT: Penang, Malacca, Johore, Sumatra. EXPANSE: Male, 3·8 inches. DESCRIPTION: "Wings entire, swarthy. *Forewing* shining violet at the base (in certain positions); both wings on both sides with white marginal spots arranged in a double series. UNDERSIDE with discal spots white and tinted with violet."

"Intermediate between *E. alcathoë* and *E. coreta* of Godart. UPPERSIDE, both wings blackish-brown, with a beautiful vivid violet-blue reflection, occupying the greater part of the forewing from the base to just beyond the middle (in the male, the only sex that we have seen). The *forewing* has on the UPPERSIDE near the costa and beyond the middle two small scarcely visible bluish streaks, and near the apex four white spots. Also on the external border a row of white dots starting from the internal angle and not reaching the apex. *Hindwing* on both sides with two rows of white spots on the hinder border, of which the interior are rather oblong; on the upperside it has also at the middle and near the costal margin a large triangular well defined patch of dingy-white. UNDERSIDE of both wings of a glistening brown. *Forewing* with the same marks and spots as on the upperside, but a little larger; the two little streaks near the costa are much more prominent and whiter. Beyond the four spots near the apex there are three others very small, linear, forming a parallel band in the line of the margin; two white spots encircled with violet in the middle, below which is a rather large oblong white spot. UNDERSIDE of the *hindwing* has besides the two rows of white spots on the border seven small violet-white marks, and some small white dots at the base. *Cilia* alternately black and white. *Body* and *head* black, spotted with white." (Guérin in Delessert Souv. Voy. d. l'Inde, pt. ii, p. 71, 1843).

† *Euplœa ægyptus*, Butler. HABITAT: Singapore, Sumatra, Borneo. EXPANSE: Male, 4 inches. DESCRIPTION: "MALE: Wings elongate, swarthy on upperside. *Forewing* with a short shining discal streak, five white subapical spots, and one indistinct rosy subcostal spot, two minute costal streaks. *Hindwing* with two submarginal rows of white, sometimes indistinct dots, the costal margin white. *Body* swarthy, forepart blackish and spotted with white; *antennæ* black. UNDERSIDE, olivaceous-fuscous. *Forewing* with the inner margin white, with the costal streak and white subapical spots as on upperside, with a series of much interrupted marginal dots, and one submarginal spot at the anal angle; one discal spot, one in the cell, and a discal band with an oily appearance. *Hindwing* with two submarginal series of white spots, the inner series short; an arched discal series of violet dots, and one dot in the cell. *Body* with the thorax black, spotted with white; *antennæ* black; *abdomen* swarthy, banded with white." (Butler, Proc. Zool. Soc Lond., 1866, p. 277, n. 26.) Distant remarks (Rhop. Malay, p. 22):—"Butler gives another species, *E. ægyptus*, as having been received from Singapore. That Singapore specimen, however, no longer remains in the National collection under that name, and was probably so recorded in error."

lobed; also in the absence of the flesh-coloured patch on the hindwing. The ochreous-white markings are also more prominent.

In Indian specimens on the *forewing* the spots of the submarginal row increase from the costa to the first median nervule, and the next interspace below contains two small adjoining spots; the marginal series is also complete in many specimens to the apex. A male specimen taken by Mr. Otto Möller in the Sikkim tarai in August has the upperside of the forewing very perceptibly shot with blue; the marginal rows of spots on both wings smaller, especially the submarginal series on the forewing, the spot below the third median nervule in that series being obsolete.

This species on the upperside bears a very close resemblance to *E. core*, except in outline of the forewing, and the flesh-coloured patch on the hindwing, which latter is concealed by the inner margin of the forewing. On the underside it may be readily distinguished by the absence of the spot in the cell of both wings, which are invariably present in *E. core*. The apex of the forewing is more acuminate, and the inner margin much more convex; both wings are wider and more ample than in *E. core*.

Our collections contain specimens taken at Trevandrum in July by Mr. H. S. Fergusson, at Calicut in September, in the Wynaad by Mr. Rhodes Morgan, and from Bhadrachullum taken by Mr. W. T. Blanford. In the neighbourhood of Calcutta Mr. de Nicéville has found it common throughout the year. In Ceylon it has been "taken at Galle and Kandy by Captain Wade."

The figure shows the upperside of both sexes—the male on the left, the female on the right, from specimens in the Indian Museum, taken near Calcutta.

The next three species, *E. vestigiata*, *E. novaræ*, and *E. leucogonys*, and also *E. eunice* from Java, are closely allied. The true *E. eunice* inhabits Java, and, according to the original description, has only a submarginal row of violet spots, one subcostal, and one interno-median spot on the forewing; the Continental race from Burma and Malacca, which is referred to as *E. vestigiata*, further differs from the Javan species in having, in addition, numerous spots on the disc of the forewing, and an incomplete marginal series from the hinder angles of both wings; but the extent to which these markings are developed differs so greatly in individuals, even from the same locality, that the Continental race can hardly be separated with propriety. The Nicobar race agrees with the true *E. eunice* from Java in the absence of the marginal series from both wings, but it has the spots on the disc even more largely developed than in the Continental race. It is as yet a rare insect, and we have never seen a specimen, and it is possible that when more specimens have been observed, this race may also be found to vary as much as the Continental race does, in fact "Felder clearly defines this variability in his description;" in the meantime, as the Nicobar form may be peculiar, we have retained it as distinct under the name *E. novaræ* given to it by Felder. All these races have the wings shot with brilliant blue in *both* sexes.

48. **Euplœa vestigiata,** Butler.

E. vestigiata, Butler, Proc. Zool. Soc. Lond., 1866, p. 288, n. 58, fig. i, *female*; *Calliplœa vestigiata*, Butler. Trans. Linn. Soc., Zoology, second series, vol. i, p. 535, n. 2 (1876); *Euplœa vestigiata*, Distant, Rhop. Malay., p. 26, pl. iii, figs. 6 *male*, 7 *female* (1882).

HABITAT: Upper Tenasserim, Penang, Malacca, Sumatra and Java.

EXPANSE: 3·5 to 3·9 inches.

DESCRIPTION: MALE: UPPERSIDE.—*Forewing* uniform velvety blackish-brown (scarcely perceptibly paler at hinder angle), shot throughout with deep but brilliant blue; with a submarginal series of prominent violet spots, a subcostal spot above end of the cell, and a broad short streak of violet below the first median nervule. In one specimen the submarginal row is incomplete, only four spots being present on the apical half, but in all the other specimens examined the row is complete, and prominent as far as the first median nervule; in addition to these markings some specimens show a few small round marginal dots towards the hinder angle, some have two short discal streaks below the discoidal nervules, some have a short streak above the interno-median streak, and others have a short streak below it; all these spots and streaks being violet. *Hindwing* paler brown, suffused darker and slightly tinted with blue on and about the median nervule; the costal area hoary, a large ochreous patch about the subcostal nervure covering the upper half of the cell, and extending above it; a submarginal decreasing row of three or four violet spots from the costa (almost obsolete in one specimen), and a few marginal dots from anal angle; in one specimen the submarginal row is complete to anal angle. UNDERSIDE paler brown, with the spots paler violet, almost white. *Forewing* with the interno-median area cinereous, the streak of the upperside visible as a raised concolorous mark; a conspicuous broad oval whitish patch above the first median nervule, two discal streaks sometimes prominent, sometimes obsolete, a subcostal violet spot; the submarginal row much smaller than on upperside and partially obsolete in one specimen; and a marginal row of small prominent dots, usually complete, but partially obsolete, in one specimen. *Hindwing* with a decreasing submarginal row of round whitish spots from the costa to anal angle; and a corresponding row of rounded marginal dots from anal angle not quite reaching the apex. The usual basal white dots, but no spots on the disc of the hindwing, and none in the cell of either wing, on upper or underside. The FEMALE differs from the male on the UPPERSIDE in having the submarginal spots of the *forewing* prominently centered with white; also in having the inner margin straight, not bowed out as in the male, and on the *hindwing* in the absence of the subcostal ochreous patch. On the UNDERSIDE the *forewing* is similar, except that the internal cinereous area does not nearly reach the median nervule, and the raised sexual streak is absent; on the *hindwing* the marginal and submarginal spots are rather more prominent. One female, evidently aberrant, has a conspicuous geminate violet spot at end of the cell in the forewing.

Notwithstanding that Butler in his original description of this species* omits all mention of the brilliant blue shot, it is clear from Distant's description in his "Rhopalocera Malayana," written after examination of the type, that the species here described is *E. vestigiata*, Butler. Neither Butler nor Distant refer in their descriptions to *E. eunice*, Godart, from Java, of which the present species appears to us to be only the continental form. Distant remarks that *E. vestigiata* "appears to be a variable species [of this there can be no doubt], and is probably a race of the *E. novaræ*, Felder. Felder clearly defines this variability in his description; in fact, with the qualifications he there admits in the markings of several varieties, the Province Wellesley specimens might almost be considered as agreeing with some of his Nicobar types. This Malay form somewhat differs from Javan specimens of *E. vestigiata*, which Mr. Kirby was probably correct in considering a variety of Felder's species."

Numerous specimens of this species were taken by Captain C. H. E. Adamson, near Moulmein, on 12th June; and a single male was taken at the Maylachoung, by Captain C. T. Bingham, on the 24th September; but it is a rare Butterfly, and has not hitherto been recorded as occurring within Indian limits.

49. Euplœa novaræ, Felder.

E. novaræ, Felder, Verh. zool.-bot. Gesellsch. Wien, vol. xii, p. 482, n. 108 (1862); Reise Nov., Lep., vol. ii, p. 317, n. 430, pl. xxxix, fig. 7 (1865), *male*.

HABITAT: Kar Nicobar.

EXPANSE: 4·1 inches.

---

* *Euplœa vestigiata*, Butler. HABITAT: Malacca, Sumatra, Java. EXPANSE: Male, 3·55; female 3·4 inches. DESCRIPTION: "*Forewing* above blackish-swarthy, the margin slightly rufous, with eight or nine submarginal spots, one costal spot, and a short internal discal streak, violet. *Hindwing* olivaceous-swarthy, deeper in the middle; with the costal margin whitish, with three subapical white spots; the MALE with a rather large subtriangular ochreous spot placed near the costa. *Body* blackish-swarthy, spotted with white in front; the *antennæ* black. UNDERSIDE olivaceous, with the interior margin ochreous-white; in the MALE with six submarginal dots, nine marginal, and one rather large oval discal spot, white; one oval discal internal spot ashy; one small costal spot and two discal placed behind the cell, violet-white. *Forewing* of the FEMALE with nine submarginal spots, four subanal dots, two minute subapical dots, and one large oval discal spot, white; one costal spot violet-white. *Hindwing* with ten submarginal spots, and nine or ten anal marginal spots, white; two elongated discal dots between the subcostal nervules, violet-white. *Body*, with the thorax black, spotted with white, the abdomen ashy-fuscous; the *antennæ* black." (*Butler*, Proc. Zool. Soc. Lond., 1866, p. 288, n. 58, fig. 1, *female*).

DESCRIPTION : " MALE, with the *cilia* marked with white. *Forewing* above blackish chestnut, deeply suffused with violet blue in certain lights, with a subcostal spot, two behind the cell (sometimes entirely wanting), three median elongated (the first sometimes wanting, the third minute, and the middle one large and powdered with white), and seven to nine others submarginal of different shapes, pale violet blue. *Hindwing* pale silky fuscous, towards the base almost as in the forewing, the anterior margin silky white, with two white spots, the surface with the usual shelly appearance; two or three decreasing spots, violet encircled with swarthy. UNDERSIDE, pale rufescent fuscous, with white basal spots. *Forewing*, with a subcostal spot, two beyond the cell, four large interior, a bent submarginal dot-shaped series often interrupted, and a marginal series of minute spots. *Hindwing*, with some very small external spots, and others before the hinder margin violet blue, more or less powdered with white, and ringed with swarthy. *Forewing*, with the internal area as usual. A beautiful local form of the Javan *E. eunice*." (*Felder*, l. c.)

This is a very rare insect and we have never seen a specimen.

50. **Euplœa leucogonys,** Butler.

Salpinx leucogonys, Butler, Trans. Linn. Soc. Lond., Zoology, second series, vol. i, p. 536, pl. lxviii, fig. 5 (1876), *female*.

HABITAT : Nepal (?) Assam (?) Malacca.

EXPANSE : 3·2 inches.

DESCRIPTION : FEMALE. "Nearly allied to *E. vestigiata*, Butler, but smaller; the costa of *forewing* not so strongly arched, the outer margin slightly inarched in the centre; the submarginal spot on second median nervule wanting; the subcostal spot above the end of the cell much smaller, the spot on interno-median area widened into a notched blotch, all the spots lilac. *Hindwing*, paler, only three lilacine whitish spots placed obliquely near apex; no submarginal spots; anal angle white. UNDERSIDE : *Forewing*, with only two or three submarginal and three or four marginal white dots. *Hindwing*, with no white blotches beyond the cell." (*Butler*, l. c.) The figure shews on the *hindwing* three white submarginal spots one in each interspace above the discoidal nervule; and five large violet-white spots on the margin at the anal angle. Distant remarks (Rhop. Malay., p. 27, *note*) :—" Butler's figure is somewhat misleading, the marginal spots to hindwing having been enlarged and exaggerated by the artist compared with those on the type specimen in the British Museum which I have examined." Mr. Distant considers *E. leucogonys* as merely a small variety of *E. vestigiata*.

This also appears to be a rare insect, and we have never seen a specimen; its occurrence in "Nepal and Assam" must be considered doubtful pending further evidence; it belongs to a Malayan group.

51. **Euplœa rhadamanthus,** Fabricius. (PLATE VII, FIG. 11, ♂ ♀).

Papilio rhadamanthus, Fabricius, Ent. Syst., vol. iii, pt. i, p. 42, n. 127 (1793); *Trepsichrois thoösa*, Hübner, Samml. Ex. Schmett. (1806-1824); *Danais alcidice* et *rhadamia*, Godart, Enc. Méth., vol. ix, p. 180, nn. 13, 14 (1819); *Salpinx rhadamanthus*, Moore, Proc. Zool. Soc. Lond., 1878, p. 822.

HABITAT : Eastern Himalayas and Burma.

EXPANSE : 3·0 to 3·8 inches.

DESCRIPTION : MALE : *Forewing* black, tinged with brown at the base, and shot throughout with deep violet blue, brightest towards the exterior margin; a broad bar of white from the costa almost to the median nervure, cut into four irregular parts by the black costal and subcostal nervures; below this and outside the cell is a white spot of variable size between the second and third branches of the median nervure; this spot is sometimes altogether wanting, and in some cases a second white spot appears between the first and second median nervules.

Below the first median nervule is an oval longitudinal violet spot; four submarginal spots near the apex, and a larger one between the first and second median nervules, violet, often white centred; a few minute marginal dots near the anal angle, also violet. *Hindwing* with four white streaks from the base below the cell, followed by a short white dash tipped with violet, a whitish patch near the base cut by the subcostal nervure; the rest of the costal area rather pale silky brown; the exterior half black, shot with deep violet blue. Two small violet spots just beyond the end of the cell, two submarginal spots beyond these, and two more near the anal angle, and a few minute marginal dots (sometimes entirely wanting) from anal angle, also violet. UNDERSIDE brown, markings similar to those of the upperside, but whiter. In the *forewing* the second spot below the white patch, which is usually wanting on the upperside, is large and conspicuous on the underside; the submarginal spots are white, and the marginal series, which are violet, are more complete than on the upperside, especially towards the apex. In the *hindwing*, the whitish subcostal patch is wanting, and in addition to the white streaks below the cell, there are three white streaks in the cell, the upper one short, sometimes divided, the middle one longer and narrow, the lower the broadest and longest; a series of five streaks outside the cell.

The above description is taken from a large series of specimens collected in Upper Tenasserim, by Captain C. T. Bingham, and from a few collected in the Khasi hills by Mr. J. P. Cock. In specimens from Sikkim, in Colonel Lang's collection, the white markings are altogether larger and more prominent than in Burmese specimens. The Sikkim specimens also average a good deal larger; they are paler and browner, especially at the base of the forewing; the white spot outside the cell of forewing, between the second and third median nervules, which is small or wanting in Burman specimens, is large and prominent in those from Sikkim, giving a different character to the white band. The marginal blue spots at anal angle of *forewing* are more numerous, often as many as seven being present, while in Burman specimens usually only two are visible, and apparently four is the maximum. On the *hindwing* all the spots are larger, the submarginal series shows usually six from the anal angle instead of two, and the marginal series has eight or ten, while in Burman specimens these latter are often entirely wanting, always minute, and seldom if ever exceeding six in number.

The FEMALE is paler and brown, not black, and shot with blue only on the outer half; all the markings are larger, whiter, and more prominent. In the *hindwing* the cell has also three large white streaks in it, occupying almost the entire area; they are confluent in the specimen figured, leaving only interrupted black streaks between. On the UPPERSIDE the costal margin of the *hindwing* is broadly white; the marginal and submarginal spots on both wings are circled with violet, and on the UNDERSIDE some are white, some are violet. The sexual spot is of course wanting, though it is replaced in the Sikkim specimen figured by a pale streak of grey scales. A single female sent by Captain Bingham from the Thoungyeen forests in Tenasserim differs from Sikkim females precisely as in the males as far as the white markings are concerned, but in it the blue gloss is scarcely perceptible at all, instead of being brighter as from analogy it should have been.

E. rhadamanthus is very common in North-Eastern India, from Sikkim to Tenasserim, in hilly tracts at elevations of from 1,000 to 4,000 feet above the sea. In the Khasi hills it is on the wing in the late autumn. In Upper Tenasserim, Captain C. T. Bingham found it common between Meeawuddy and Kankarit in February, in the Thoungyeen forests in March and April, and in the Donat range in April. The single female specimen referred to above was taken in the Thoungyeen forests in the autumn. Mr. Wood-Mason took numerous males and three females in Cachar from April to August; and Dr. J. Anderson took males only in the Mergui Archipelago in the cold weather.

The figure shows the upperside of the male and female from Sikkim specimens in the Indian Museum, Calcutta.

52. Euplœa diocletianus, Fabricius.

Papilio diocletianus, Fabricius, Ent. Syst., vol. iii, pt. i, p. 40, n. 118 (1793); *Danais diocletia*, Godart, Enc. Méth., vol. ix, p. 181, n. 16 (1819); *Calliplœa diocletianus*, Butler, Trans. Linn. Soc., Zoology, second series, vol. i, p. 535 (1876); *Euplœa diocletianus*, Distant, Rhop. Malay., p. 28, pl. iv, figs. 4 *male*, 5 *female* (1882).

HABITAT: (Nepal, Assam ?), Penang, Malacca, Singapore, Siam, Java.

EXPANSE: ♂, 3·4; ♀, 3·1 inches (from Distant's figures).

DESCRIPTION: "Wings entire, black. *Forewing* with a white interrupted band. *Hindwing* with some white lines at the base, and a double row of spots of this colour on the margin. Of the size of *D. claudia* [= *Euplœa midamus*], to which it is closely allied; the underside of both wings resemble the upperside. *Forewing* black, with a white band formed of four large spots, one transverse line of four dots of this colour, and some dots equally white along the margin. *Hindwing* blackish-brown, with some white longitudinal lines towards the base, and two rows of white spots along the margin. The head and thorax are of a deep black, with some white spots; the upperside of the abdomen is blackish, the underside ashy with some very black bands." (*Godart*, l. c.)

E. diocletianus has usually been considered as indentical with *E. rhadamanthus*, but the absence of all mention of the conspicuous violet blue shot, the pure white character of the markings, and the black colour of the wings, seem to indicate its distinctness from that species in both sexes. We have never seen a specimen, and if it occurs at all in "Nepal and Assam" (which we doubt), it must be extremely rare. It is included in Butler's paper on the Butterflies of Malacca* as *Calliplœa diocletianus*. It is probably a local form of *E. rhadamanthus* developed in the Malay Peninsula. The Tenasserim female of *E. rhadamanthus* shows a decided approach to this species in colouration, but it is small, far smaller than average specimens of *E. midamus*. Distant remarks: "This is evidently a Malay race of *E. rhadamanthus*, a species which I follow Moore and Butler in considering as typically represented in Northern India. It possesses also another and very distinct Bornean race, described as *E. lowii*. The principal difference between these three species or races is that of a gradually increasing melanism, which is least in the North Indian *E. rhadamanthus*, and greatest in the Bornean form *E. lowii*." According to Distant's description, the wings in this species are dark indigo-blue, not black.

Second group.—MACROPLŒA, *Butler.*—Mr. Butler has separated this group from the foregoing in the following terms:—"This genus [*Salpinx*, Hübner], is not altogether a satisfactory one; it contains two groups, the one being much like an enormous form of *Calliplœa* (I refer to the *S. phænareta* group), the other having a blue or sericeous brand upon the interno-median area; in other respects the species seem nearly allied. I propose to give the first of these groups the subgeneric title of *Macroplœa*." (*Butler*, Journ. Linn. Soc., Zoology, vol. xiv, p. 292 (1878).

This subgroup is only represented by two species within Indian limits, of which one is found is Ceylon; the other, a native of the Malay Peninsula, extends into Burma, and has been found in the Nicobar Isles. The *Euplœas* of this type are large insects, without the brilliant purple or blue gloss, and usually with three more or less complete rows of marginal and submarginal spots. They differ from the *Salpinx* group only in having ***no brand*** on the interno-median area of the forewing of the male, and in their *large size*; the outer margin of the hindwing in the male too appears as if it had been oiled.

Key to the Indian species of Macroplœa.

A. Upperside golden-fuscous; forewing with three rows of violet-white spots.
- *a.* With the violet-white markings prominent; the three rows on forewing complete.
  - 53. E (*Macroplœa*) CASTLENAUI, Burma, Nicobars.
- *b.* With the violet-white markings small; the discal series incomplete.
  - 54. E. (*Macroplœa*) ELISA, Ceylon.

---

* Trans. Linn. Soc., Zoology, second series, vol. i, p. 535 (1876).

53. **Euplœa castelnaui,** Felder.

E. castelnaui, Felder, Reise Nov., Lep., vol. ii, p. 315, n. 427 (1865), *female*; *E. phœbus*, Butler Proc Zool. Soc. Lond., 1866, p. 270, n 3; *Macroplœa phœbus*, Butler, Journ. Linn. Soc., Zoology, vol. xiv p 292 (1878); *E. castelnaui*, Distant, Rhop. Malay., p. 24, pl. ii, fig. 6 (1882), *female*.

HABITAT: Tenasserim, Penang, Nicobars, Java.

EXPANSE: ♂, 4·5 to 5·3; ♀, 4·9 to 5·3 inches.

DESCRIPTION: "*Forewing* elongate. UPPERSIDE golden-fuscous, the costa fuscous, and the internal area fuscescent; the outer margin with three rows of white submarginal spots, and one spot near the end of the cell; the external row composed of small oblong spots; the middle row with spots increasing in size near the costa, and arranged in a curved line; the inner row angulate, with oblong spots increasing in size near the costa. *Hindwing*, purpurascent, the costal area ochreous-white, and the middle of the cell ochreous [in the MALE], the external and internal areas rufous-swarthy. Of the FEMALE with three continuous rows of rufescent-white submarginal spots on the outer margin: of the MALE with three interrupted rows not reaching the anal angle, and the anal angle appears as if oiled. UNDERSIDE, *forewing*, fuscescent at base, purpurascent in the middle in certain positions; the inner margin pale, with a rather large white subanal spot; the outer margin with rows of spots as on the upperside, the two external rows, however, with smaller spots, and the inner row beyond the end of the cell sometimes obsolete, and of larger spots. *Hindwing*, coppery-fuscous, the outer margin in the MALE fuscescent, with a marginal row of white dots, and three subapical, and an arched series of five violet dots beyond the end of the cell; in the FEMALE with two rows of dots, an inner arched series of seven violet dots, and one near end of the cell. *Body* with the thorax black, spotted with ochreous; *abdomen* ashy; *antennæ* black. This species is quite distinct from *E. prothoë*, Godart, being much smaller, of a more golden-colour, and quite differently spotted." (*Butler*, l. c.)

A female, taken by Captain C. H. E. Adamson at Nyounting, near Moulmein, in September, has the whole apical area of the forewing powdered with violescent-white, the two inner rows of spots above the third median nervule being almost lost in the ground-colour, which in that part is almost pure white; the spots on both wings are also larger, and more diffused. The inner margin of the forewing is straight, while in the male it is enormously lobed to cover the ochreous patch of scales on the hindwing, which is present in that sex though absent in the female. The female is altogether a much paler insect, especially on the underside, where all the markings are larger than in the male. The spots outside the cell on the underside of many males are eight in number, there being two short parallel streaks between the first median nervule and submedian nervure.

Mr. de Roepstorff has taken two male specimens in the Nicobars. Dr. J. Anderson took one male and seven females in January, also two females in March, in the Mergui Archipelago. These female examples are darker than the Moulmein specimen; the three series of spots on the forewing are also distinct, though exhibiting a tendency to coalesce.

54. **Euplœa elisa,** Butler, (PLATE VIII, FIG. 14, ♂).

E. elisa, Butler, Proc. Zool. Soc. Lond., 1866, p. 270, n. 4; *Macroplœa elisa*, id., Journ. Linn. Soc, Zoology, vol. xiv, p. 292 (1878); id., Moore, Lep. Ceylon, p. 9, pl. v, figs. 2 *male*, 2a *female* (1880).

HABITAT: Ceylon.

EXPANSE: ♂, 4·25 to 4·80; ♀, 4·1 to 4·7 inches.

DESCRIPTION: "*Forewing* above golden-fuscous, the inner margin fuscescent, with three rows of white spots, the inner row short with three spots placed between the median nervules, the outer row not reaching the apex; the middle row in the MALE much interrupted, in the FEMALE continuous, curved near the costa; one spot near the end of the cell. *Hindwing* of the MALE coppery-fuscous, the costal area ochreous-white, and the middle of the cell ochreous; with three discal spots placed beyond the cell; the outer margin fuscous; the anal margin as if oiled. Of the FEMALE the *hindwing* is golden-fuscous, with the costal margin pale; the outer margin with two submarginal series of white dots, indistinct at the anal angle; and a series of three spots placed beyond the cell. *Body* swarthy, darker and white-spotted in front; the *antennæ* black. UNDERSIDE: *Forewing* as on upperside, but the spots are larger, and the external submarginal row is continuous in the MALE. *Hindwing*, of the MALE, paler; on the outer margin with a row of five marginal dots in the middle, and an angulate row of violet dots beyond the end of the cell; some minute white spots at the base. *Hindwing*, of the FEMALE, as on upperside, but the internal series beyond the end of the cell has six dots, and one near the end of the cell. *Body* with the thorax black, spotted with white; *abdomen* fuscous; *antennæ* black." (*Butler*, l. c.)

"LARVA* purple-brown, with two black-tipped red fleshy filaments on second, two on third, and two on twelfth segments; each segment with transverse black streaks; lateral line purple; head and legs black. PUPA thick, broad, purple-grey, fasciated with golden-yellow; abdominal segments black-beaded." (*Moore*, Lep. Ceylon, p. 10, 1880.)

"Taken on low ground at Colombo among hedges round native gardens at any time, but not very common. Of slow heavy flight; settles on leaves, and is easily caught" (*Hutchison*). "Commonly found at Galle among cocoanut trees and low bushes" (*Wade*). There is as yet no record of its occurrence except in Ceylon.

The figure is taken from a male specimen from Ceylon in the collection of the Hon'ble F. Mackwood.

Third group.—CALLIPLŒA, *Butler*.—"The species of *Callіplœa* are all of small size; they have the inner border of the *forewing* in the *males*, strongly developed, and covering a large subcostal yellowish patch upon the *hindwing*; but *without any trace of a brand on the interno-median area* of the *forewing*." (*Butler*, Journ. Linn. Soc., Zoology, vol. xiv, p. 296, 1878.)

Only one species of this group has been recorded from India; the exact locality is not stated, but probably it is from the north-eastern corner into which the Malayan fauna extends. It appears to be rare.

Key to the Indian species of Calliplœa.

A. Costal margin and apical half of *forewing* deep chestnut, shot with violet or blue.
  a. With the spots on *forewing* violet-silvery speckled with white; two cellular spots sometimes confluent.
    55. E. (*Calliplœa*) LEDERERI, Eastern India.

55. Euplœa ledereri, Felder.

E. ledereri, Felder, Wien. Ent. Monatsch., vol. iv, p. 397, n. 14 (1860); id., Reise Nov., Lep., vol. ii, p. 317, n. 431, pl. xl, figs. 5, 6 (1865), *male*; *Euplœa inquinata*, Butler, Proc. Zool. Soc. Lond., 1866, p. 288, fig. 2, *male*, p. 291, n. 65; *E. ledereri*, Distant, Rhop. Malay., p. 26, pl. ii, fig. 10 (1882), *male*.

HABITAT: Eastern India, Malacca interior.

EXPANSE: 2·75 to 3 inches.

DESCRIPTION: "MALE.—With the *cilia* marked with white. UPPERSIDE dilute chestnut-swarthy. *Forewing* with the costal margin and anterior half spread with deep chestnut, and in certain positions shot with violet; with two cellular spots sometimes confluent, two subcostal, a third below the second discoidal nervule sometimes rather larger, a fourth rather large, subapical and trifid, and four submarginal, silvery violet more or less powdered with white. *Hindwing* with the border beyond the cell much paler, the costal area silky-hoary with two white spots; the usual discal patch shortened, and well separated from the origin of the discoidal nervure. UNDERSIDE, pale shining fuscous. *Forewing* with a subcostal spot, three discal, others external small, and marginal dots. *Hindwing* with external decreasing spots, and rather larger marginal dots, white." (*Felder*, l. c.)

---

* Figured on pl. iv, fig. 8; chrysalis, 8a, of Horsfield and Moore's Cat. Lep. E. I. C., vol. i (1857), from drawings of E. L. Layard, as the larva of *E. prothoë*.

This species, if it really does occur with Indian limits, is very rare; we have never seen a specimen. Distant remarks that "it appears to be almost confined to the Malay Peninsula, especially if there should be any error in the locality of Assam, as given by Mr. Warwick to the British Museum." It is nearly allied to, and probably is only the continental form of, *Euplœa mazares*, Moore, from Java, of which a figure of the upper and underside of a male in the Indian Museum, Calcutta, is given below:—

EUPLŒA MAZARES, Moore.

Fourth Group.—TREPSICHROIS, *Hübner.*—"Forewing elongated, the outer margin subangulated and slightly inarched below the apex; the inner margin of the male very slightly convex, without trace of a brand, but the hindwing with a small yellowish patch in the cell at the origin of the first subcostal branch." (*Butler*, Journ. Linn. Soc., Zoology, vol. xiv, p. 296, 1878).

The elongated forewing distinguishes this group and the two following from the three which precede. Only a single species of this group is found within Indian limits, and only three others are known which represent the group in the Malay Archipelago. The females differ greatly from the males in having the hindwing profusely striped with white. The Indian species extends from Burma through the Himalayas to Kulu, and is the widest spread and commonest of all the *Euplœas* of Northern India, except *E. core*.

Key to the Indian species of Trepsichrois.

A. Forewing velvety-brown, shot with bright blue, and with bluish-white spots on the outer half.
56. E. (*Trepsichrois*) MIDAMUS, N. India, Burma.

56. **Euplœa midamus**, Linnæus. (PLATE VIII, FIG. 13, ♂ ♀.)

Papilio midamus, Linnæus, Mus. Ulr., p. 251, n. 70 (1764); id., Syst. Nat., vol. i, part 2, p. 765, n. 108 (1767); *Papilio claudia*, Fabricius, Gen. Ins., p. 263 (1777), *female*; *Danais midama*, Godart, Enc. Méth., vol. ix, p. 179, n. 12 (1819); *Trepsichrois midamus*, Hübner, Verz. bek. Schmett., p. 16, n. 92 (1816); *Papilio basilissa*, Cramer, Pap. Ex., vol. iii, pl. cclxvi, fig. C (1780), *female*; *Euplœa midamus*, Distant Rhop. Malay., p. 24, pl. ii, figs. 8 *male*, 9 *female* (1882).

HABITAT: N.-W. Himalayas to Burma.

EXPANSE: ♂, 3·0 to 4·2; ♀, 3·5 to 4·6 inches.

DESCRIPTION: MALE: UPPERSIDE, *forewing* deep velvety blackish-brown, glossed with brilliant blue, brightest on the apical half, where it forms in some lights a large patch of this colour. The basal half spotless, the outer half with numerous pale blue spots, powdered and often centred with white, and arranged as follows:—A marginal row of small spots, regular, two between each pair of nervules, decreasing towards and seldom reaching the apex; a submarginal row of larger spots, irregular, one between each pair of nervules; a discal row, very irregular, of seven spots, and angled at two points, commencing with a small costal spot, and ending with an oblong interno-median spot; and one spot in the cell near the end. *Hindwing* velvety brown, the costal area ashy testaceous, with a small yellowish patch within the cell at origin of first subcostal nervule, otherwise entirely unspotted, though occasionally a faint trace of an obsolete marginal row is visible. There is also a large patch of lengthened, plush-like, modified scales somewhat lighter coloured than the ground, filling the upper and outer two-thirds of the cell, and extending beyond it almost to the outer margin, bounded posteriorly by the third median nervule and extending to above the first subscostal branch. This patch of scales, together with the small yellowish patch also within and nearer the base of the cell, is peculiar to this group of *Euplœas*. UNDERSIDE, paler brown. *Forewing*, with the interno-marginal area broadly tinged with ashy, and showing a broad whitish streak near base, almost covered by the hindwing. Spots as on upperside, but violet-white, smaller, and the oblong interno-median spot which terminates the discal row is wanting on the underside. *Hindwing* with a marginal row of two spots between each pair of nervules, from anal angle not usually reaching the apex ; a submarginal similar row from apex, incomplete towards the anal angle ; a spot in the cell at the end, and three or four small streaks arranged outside it on the disc, violet-white ; the *cilia* spotted with white on both wings.

The above description is from specimens from Shillong, which are of large size ; the specimens from Upper Tenasserim are much smaller, and on the underside the spots are all smaller ; many of them, especially on the hindwing, are completely wanting, and where present are very minute. In some Sikkim specimens also the spots are similarly small, and more or less wanting on the underside. On the underside of the *abdomen* there are six transverse bands of lilac-white in Shillong and Sikkim specimens, while in the Tenasserim specimens there are seldom more than three. FEMALE : Brown, darkest towards the apex of forewing, and much streaked with white, especially on the hindwing. *Forewing* with a large patch on outer half shot with bright blue ; the spots as in the male, but except on the blue-shot patch the spots are pure white ; from the base of the wing a faint brownish-white streak in the cell, and a longer and whiter streak (sometimes double) in the interno-median area, coalescing with the last spot of the discal series. *Hindwing* with a row of rounded marginal spots, a submarginal row of white streaks, two between each pair of nervules, short at the apex, but towards the anal angle extended right up to the base of the wing ; a discal series longest at the costa, and three or four streaks in the cell, all white. UNDERSIDE as on upperside, but the streaks from base of *forewing* broader, more prominent and purer white ; some of the spots and streaks on the outer half of both wings tinted faintly with blue. The specimens from Tenasserim, as do the males, average smaller in size than those from Shillong.

LARVA.—Ground-colour testaceous, marked with crimson and black perpendicular lines on the segments, a spiracular row of black spots and some yellow blotches just above the legs. The face is also marked with crimson and black ; legs red ; the third, fourth, fifth, and twelfth segments have each a pair of very long tentacula springing from the subdorsal region, and standing almost upright over the body ; the lower portion of these processes is crimson, the upper black. Figure 10 of Plate IV, of Horsfield and Moore's Cat. Lep. E. I. C. (1857), from Java, where it "feeds on a species of *Ficus*, December." Also Plate III, figs. 10, caterpillar, and 10a, chrysalis, of Horsfield's Cat. Lep E. I. C. (1829). PUPA, Figure 10a.—Castaneous, beautifully marked with gold.

E. midamus is, with the exception of *E. core*, the commonest and most widely spread of all the *Euplœas* of North India, but, except in the far east, it is only found in the warm valleys of mountainous regions. It extends from Tenasserim as far west as Kulu, where Mr. A. Grahame Young has taken a single specimen. Mr. de Nicéville also took a single worn female at Kalka, Punjab, in October. A single specimen was taken by Colonel Lang, at Sitapur, in Oudh, but its occurrence in the plains of Oudh must be very exceptional. In Kumaon it is found, but rarely, in the warm valleys in the rains. In Nepal it seems to be common near Khatmandu, as Dr. Scully brought down numerous specimens. Mr. de Nicéville has taken it commonly in the Sikkim tarai, and below Darjiling in the autumn. In the Khasi hills it is common in the autumn and cold weather. Mr. Wood-Mason found it abundant in Cachar throughout the hot weather. Dr. J. Anderson also took numerous specimens in the Mergui Archipelago throughout the cold months; and in Upper Tenasserim Captain Bingham found it common in the Thoungyeen forests in March and April.

Butler records *E. mulciber* as a distinct species, occurring with *E. midamus* at Malacca. Cramer's figure of *E. mulciber*, however, is almost identical with the common *E. midamus* of North-East India. *E. mulciber* is figured by Distant (Rhop. Malay., pl. iii, figs. 1 *male*, 2 *female* 1882), who never met with it in the Malay Peninsula, and remarks (page 26) that "it has been considered as the constant Bornean race or form of *E. midamus*, and peculiar to that island."

The figure shows the upperside of a male from the Khasi hills, and of a female from Sibsagar, Assam, both in the Indian Museum, Calcutta.

Fifth group.—CRASTIA, *Hübner.*—"Males with more acuminate forewing than in *Trepsichrois* the inner margin much more convex; no brand on the forewing, and no yellowish spot in the cell of the hindwing. Females similar to *Trepsichrois* in form." (*Butler*, Journ. Linn. Soc., Zoology, vol. xiv, p. 297, 1878).

This is a Malayan group; four species are recorded as occurring within Indian limits, one in the Nicobars, the others all in the extreme east on the borders of Malayana. All the species are comparatively rare within Indian limits, and we have no specific record of any being taken, except in Tenasserim and the Nicobars.

Key to the Indian species of Crastia.

A. With the wings above spotless black-fuscous, suffused with the deepest violet-blue, bordered externally with paler unglossed fuscous.

57. E. *(Crastia)* SIMULATRIX, Nicobars.

B. Basal three-fourths of forewing glossed with blue; hindwing with two series of small whitish spots.

a. Rufescent swarthy; hindwing not blue glossed; spots small.

58. E. *(Crastia)* MODESTA, Burma.

E. *(Crastia)* CAMARALZEMAN, Siam.

b. Cupreous brown; hindwing blue glossed; spots larger.

59. E. *(Crastia)* CUPREIPENNIS, Burma.

C. Wings blackish-swarthy, unglossed with blue; forewing with three more or less complete series of white spots.

60. E. *(Crastia)* BREMERI, Mergui.

E. *(Crastia)* MALAVICA, Malayana.

57. Euplœa simulatrix, W.-M. and de N.

E. (Crastia) simulatrix, Wood-Mason and de Nicéville, Journn. A. S. B., vol. l, part ii, p. 229 (1881), *male*; idem, id., vol. li, p. 15, pl. iii, fig. 1 *male*, 2 *female* (1882).

HABITAT: Great Nicobar.

EXPANSE: ♂, 3·7; ♀, 3·18 to 3·86 inches.

DESCRIPTION: "MALE. UPPERSIDE spotless black-fuscous, suffused with the deepest violet-blue, externally tolerably broadly bordered with paler unglossed fuscous. *Hindwing* with an oval patch of iridescent lighter modified scales, occupying about the second and third fifths of the length of the organ, extending from the middle of the discoidal cell to the middle of the interspace between the costal and subcostal nervures at its widest part, and bounded in front by an indistinct streak of cretaceous white; and with the space in front of this oval patch, and of the apical portion of the first subcostal branch, cinereous. UNDERSIDE lighter and less sombrely coloured, their dark basal portions being distinctly glossed with purple-violet, more broadly bordered with paler fuscous, and marked with prominent spots and streaks. *Forewing* with eight spots, *viz.*, a subapical series of three dots, the posterior of which is equal to the other two taken together, a somewhat elongated large spot between the first and second median nervules, nearly pure white; a reversed comma-shaped spot near the end of the cell, a rounded one and a short linear streak beyond it, the former between the second and third median nervules, and the latter between the third median nervule and the discoidal nervure, and a subcostal spot on a level with the end of the cell, bluish or violet-white, with a streak pointed at both ends in the meddle of the interno-median area, and, posterior to this, a similarly shaped and placed patch divided by the submedian nervure, cretaceous-white; and with the sutural cell behind the whitey-brown patch cinereous and satiny. *Hindwing* with a submarginal series of minute violet-white dots, a cellular spot and a curvilinear series of six just outside it bluish white, in addition to the usual basal dots. FEMALE: Wings above and below all lighter and more broadly bordered externally with paler colour of much the same tint as in *E. camorta*. *Forewing* above with an increasing series of three subapical spots, an elongated subcostal spot, a minute dot near the end of the cell, and a larger one just beyond it near the base of the interspace between the second and third median nervules, and white. *Hindwing* above spotless. UNDERSIDE with the discal spots of *both wings*, and the subapical ones of the *forewing* larger and more prominent, but with the submarginal series of the *hindwing* incomplete and less distinct, there being only two speck-like representatives of them on one hindwing and three in the other, and with a short linear dash between the submedian nervure and the first median nervule, forming a seventh circumcellular mark; the spots all coloured as in the male. The second and smaller specimen approaches the male in the colour of the upperside, and in the breadth of the pale outer borders; it lacks the seventh circumcellular mark, and has only one indistinct representative of the submarginal series of dots on the underside of the hindwing."

"Appears to be very closely allied to the Javan *E. sepulchralis*, Butler."

"A single male and two female specimens from Great Nicobar. On the upperside, it very closely resembles *E. camorta*, of which it is in all probability a mimic, differing from that species, however, in its rather darker and more sombre hue, and in being devoid of a silky sexual streak, and on the underside in the presence of a submarginal series of dots in the posterior wing." (*Wood-Mason* and *de Nicéville*, l. c.)

58. **Euplœa modesta**, Butler.

E. modesta, Butler, Proc. Zool. Soc. Lond., 1866, p. 273, n. 13.

HABITAT: Tenasserim (?), Siam.

EXPANSE: 3·2 inches.

DESCRIPTION: "MALE: UPPERSIDE rufescent swarthy. *Forewing* with the basal area bluish. *Hindwing* with the costal area paler; a rather large fuscous subcostal spot, the outer margin with two rows of ochreous-white submarginal spots, the inner row with elongate spots not reaching the apex. *Body* rufous-swarthy, the head spotted with white. *Antennæ* black. UNDERSIDE paler. *Forewing* with the outer portion of the internal area ochreous, and the margin broadly ashy; one discal spot, and two dots, one costal, and a spot at the end of the cell, bluish-white. *Hindwing* with submarginal spots as above, seven discal spots in an arched series, and a spot at the end of the cell, violet-white; some white dots at the base. *Body* with the thorax ashy, spotted with white; the abdomen swarthy with elongated ochreous median spots. *Antennæ* black." (*Butler*, l. c.) FEMALE undescribed. See remarks on the following species, *E. cupreipennis*.

An allied species, *E. camaralzeman*,* Butler, is recorded from Siam.

59. **Euplœa cupreipennis**, Moore.

Crastia cupreipennis, Moore, Proc. Zool. Soc. Lond., 1878, p. 823.

HABITAT: Mergui, Upper Tenasserim.

EXPANSE: 3·13 to 3·60 inches.

DESCRIPTION: "Allied to *E. modesta* from Siam. UPPERSIDE cupreous-brown, the outer borders broadly paler. *Forewing* with the basal area blue-glossed. *Hindwing* with

---

**E. camaralzeman*, Butler. HABITAT: Siam. EXPANSE: 4·1 inches. DESCRIPTION: "MALE: UPPERSIDE blackish-swarthy. *Forewing* with the basal area shot with greenish-blue, one indistinct white spot below the end of the cell. *Hindwing*, with the costal margin paler, in the middle greenish-blue; with twelve ochreous-white marginal spots, and a submarginal anal series. *Body* blackish swarthy, anteriorly spotted with white; the *antennæ* black. UNDERSIDE olivaceous. *Forewing* with the basal area fuscescent and shot with greenish-blue; the internal area paler, and one dot at the end of the cell, and three minute anal spots white. *Hindwing* with submarginal spots as on upperside, five discal spots, and one at the end of cell, ochreous-white. *Body* with the thorax black, spotted with white; the abdomen swarthy, with blue median spots." (*Butler*, Proc. Zool. Soc. Lond., 1866, p. 271, n. 6, pl. xxix, fig. 1, *male*).

the cell and contiguous area also blue-glossed. The two marginal series of spots larger." (*Moore,* l. c.) The FEMALE differs from the male in having the inner margin of the forewing straight, the apex more rounded, and the outer margin slightly concave; also in lacking on the hindwing the large pale fuscous subcostal patch, which, in the males, covers the anterior half of the cell.

Seven males and a single female have been sent to us by Captain C. T. Bingham from the Thoungyeen forests in Upper Tenasserim, the locality from which the type specimen of the species was taken by Limborg in 1876-77. Of these specimens one only has the forewing swarthy and scarcely perceptibly paler externally; all the others have the *forewing* rufescent-brown rather than "cupreous-brown," and with the outer margin broadly paler, and the basal three-fourths shot with bright blue; in all the cell and contiguous area of the *hindwing* is blue glossed; the two marginal series of spots on this wing are prominent and somewhat variable in size, and there can be little doubt that they all belong to the species separated as *E. cupreipennis* by Moore. No mention is made in the original descriptions of either this species or *E. modesta* of any spots on the upperside of the forewing; but in nearly all the specimens we have seen there are traces of white dots—in some a few marginal dots near the hinder angle, in others a more or less incomplete submarginal series, in others one or two on the disc outside the cell, or one in the cell, or one subcostal, but in all cases these dots, even when conspicuous, are small and so variable that no two specimens appear to exhibit them to precisely the same extent.

Dr. J. Anderson also took numerous specimens for the Indian Museum during the cold weather in the Mergui Archipelago. They present precisely the same differences as are shown in the specimens taken by Captain Bingham. One pair have no spots whatever on the upperside of the forewing. The females of *E. cupreipennis* can be distinguished from the same sex of *E. margarita* by their smaller size, and the discal spots on the upperside of the forewing, when present, being pure white instead of violet. We have seen no specimens precisely answering to the description of *E. modesta*; but *E. cupreipennis,* if distinct, is evidently very closely allied to it, and it seems probable that both forms represent only a single species, which should stand as *E. modesta.*

60. **Euplœa bremeri,** Felder.

E. bremeri, Felder, Wein. Ent. Monatsch., vol. iv, p. 398, n. 16 (1860); id., Distant, Rhop. Malay., p. 23, pl. ii, fig. 4 (1882), *male.*

HABITAT: Mergui, Penang, Malacca, Singapore, Borneo, Sumatra.

EXPANSE: 2·9 to 3·9 inches.

DESCRIPTION: "MALE: UPPERSIDE blackish-swarthy, with a marginal series of white spots on both wings. *Forewing* with two or four discal spots, and eight outer spots (the fourth and fifth much larger), white. *Hindwing* with an outer row of white dots more or less obsolete. UNDERSIDE, both wings swarthy, with the outer and marginal spots, as on upperside. *Forewing* whitish inwardly, with a costal spot, and four others discal (one in the cell). *Hindwing* with six or seven discal spots (one in the cell), white. Very nearly allied to *E. crameri** (*Lucas, Moore*), but differing in the presence of the marginal spots of the forewing, and the outer spots of the hindwing." (*Felder,* l. c.)

Dr. J. Anderson met with this species very commonly in the Mergui Archipelago throughout the cold weather. The males on the upperside of the forewing have usually four discal spots, one subcostal just above the extremity of the cell, one in the cell, and one in each of

---

* *E. crameri,* Lucas, Rev. Zool., 1853, p. 318. (Plate viii, fig. 15, *male*). HABITAT: Borneo. EXPANSE: 3·65 inches. DESCRIPTION: MALE: "UPPERSIDE wholly velvety blackish-brown, having a bluish tint, and slightly paler on exterior margins. *Forewing* with a short transverse row of six white spots from anterior margin, close to apex, the first two small, the third large and longest, the fourth the same size as the first, fifth and sixth very small; also a small spot near discoidal cell, between first and second median nervules. *Hindwing* with two small white spots near anterior angle. UNDERSIDE, clear deep brown. *Forewing* with white spots as on upperside, also with three spots along costal margin, and some on the disc. *Hindwing,* with a submarginal row of small white spots, and some on the disc." (*Moore, Horsfield* and *Moore,* Cat. Lep. E. I. C., p. 129, n. 256 (1857).

The figure is taken from a male specimen from Borneo in the Indian Museum, Calcutta, and shows the upper and undersides.

the median interspaces ; the spot in the cell and the spot in the lower median interspace are however sometimes wanting. The two marginal series of spots on the hindwing occasionally do not reach the anal angle. On the underside there are either two or three discal spots on the forewing, besides invariably one in the cell. The FEMALES are a little more variable ; some have a spot in the cell of the forewing on the upperside, and two spots in the median interspaces ; others have a complete series of five spots, one in each interspace, outside the cell, and two subcostal spots. The marginal series of dots are sometimes obsolescent towards the apex.

An allied species, *E. malayica*,* is recorded from Penang, &c.

Sixth Group.—EUPLŒA, *Fabricius* (Restricted).—"The species of this group are for the most part similar in form to those of the *Crastia* group ; but the male has a more or less strongly defined longitudinal brand on the interno-median area of the *forewing*." (*Butler*, Journ. Linn. Soc., Zoology, vol. xiv, p. 299, 1878). The true *Euplœas* are the most widely spread of all the groups, and present the greatest variation in colour. There are fourteen species in the Indian region, and one or other species is found commonly in almost every part of India.

Key to the Indian species of Euplœa.

A. With the sexual brand short (under ·20 of an inch, except in *E. subdita* ·25), narrow, inconspicuous.

a. Velvety brown, with a more or less complete and conspicuous double row of whitish spots on the outer border of both wings.

*a*¹. Forewing with the spots of inner row at apex rounded.

61. E. CORE, India.

*b*¹. Forewing with the inner spots at apex large and elongate.

62. E. VERMICULATA, N. India.

*c*¹. Forewing with the outer spots at apex obsolescent.

63. E. ASELA, Ceylon.

E. LAYARDI, Siam.

*d*¹. As in *E. core*, but with the basal area shot with blue, the spots smaller.

64. E. SUBDITA, Burma.

b. Deep swarthy, with border spots small and rounded.

*a*¹. *Hindwing* with inner row usually conspicuous.

65. E. ESPERI, Nicobars.

*b*¹. Hindwing with the inner row wanting.

66. E. FRAUENFELDII, Ceylon.

---

* *Crastia malayica*, Butler, Journ. Linn. Soc., Zoology, vol. xiv, p. 297 (1878); *Euplœa malayica*, Distant, Rhop. Malay., p. 22, pl. ii, fig. 7 (1882), *male*. HABITAT : Malacca, Penang, Singapore. EXPANSE : 4·6 inches. DESCRIPTION : "Closely allied to *Crastia ochsenheimeri*, Moore, † but larger, considerably darker, and with the white spots much larger, both the submarginal series in the *hindwing* of the MALE complete ; the FEMALE with a spot in the cell, followed by three complete series." (*Butler*, l. c.) "This is but a constant local race of *E. ochsenheimeri*, Moore, a species which Butler considers is probably the *E. gyllenhalii*, Lucas, and is apparently confined to Java. The Bornean form has also been separated, under the name *E. scudderi*. *E. malayica* is in itself variable, as in a second male specimen which I possess, the spots on the upper surface are much smaller, and the submarginal spots to the hindwing are very faint and obscure towards the anal angle." (*Distant*, l. c.)

† *Euplœa ochsenheimeri*, Moore, Horsfield and Moore, Cat. Lep. E. I. C., vol. i, p. 132, n. 264 (1857). HABITAT : Java. EXPANSE : 3·75 inches. DESCRIPTION : MALE : UPPERSIDE silky brown, darkest on the *hindwing*, and having a golden-greenish metallic lustre in some lights. *Forewing* with a submarginal row of small white spots (two between each nervule) ; two other parallel rows of somewhat larger spots (one between each nervule in each row) ; also one spot between first and second branches of subcostal vein, and one within the discoidal cell ; narrow *cilia* between indentations spotted with white. *Hindwing* with two short rows of four very small white spots near anterior angle ; narrow *cilia* spotted with white. UNDERSIDE as above, but the *hindwing* having the submarginal row of white spots continued along the whole margin ; also a row outside discoidal cell ; some white spots also at the base of the wings. FEMALE paler, the rows of white spots on UPPERSIDE of *forewing* disposed exactly the same, but are larger, those on the *hindwing* more straggling, and but few being distinct. UNDERSIDE as above, the *forewing* having also a longitudinal club-shaped streak between submedian and median nervures. *Hindwing* with three rows of white spots, also one spot within discoidal cell, and some spots disposed at base of the wings. Shape of wings as in *Euplœa midamus*." (*Moore*, l. c.)

B. With the sexual brand short ('20 to '30 in *E. andamanensis*, '25 to '35 in *E. godartii* and *E. camorta*), but conspicuous and rather broad.

a. Upperside with spots on the border.

a¹. Pale brown, darkest on external border.

67. E. ANDAMANENSIS, Andamans.

b¹. Rufescent brown; apex of forewing broadly suffused with violet-white.

68. E. GODARTII, Burma.

b. Upperside with few or no spots on either wing, none on the outer margin.

a¹. Underside with two subapical spots on *forewing*, and five on the disc on *hindwing*.

69. E. SCHERZERI, Ceylon.

b¹ Underside with no subapical spots on *forewing*, and six to seven on the disc on *hindwing*.

70. E. CAMORTA, Nicobars.

C. With the sexual brand long ('45 in *E. alcathoë*), and conspicuous; the inner row of spots on *hindwing* narrow and very elongate.

a. *Forewing* velvety black, scarcely perceptibly glossed with violet; both rows of spots on *hindwing* prominent.

71. E. ALCATHOË, N.-E. India, Burma.

b. *Forewing* shot with violet; outer row of spots on *hindwing* obsolete.

72. E. MENETRIESII, N.-E. India ? Burma.

D. With the sexual brand long ('55 in *E. deione*, '65 to '75 in *E. limborgii*), very broad and conspicuous. Forewing splendidly shot with blue.

a. *Hindwing* with border spots obsolescent.

73. E. DEIONE, N.-E. India.

b. *Hindwing* with border spots prominent.

74. E. LIMBORGII Burma.

E. PINWILLI, Malacca.

The first four species—*E. core*, *E. vermiculata*, *E. asela*, and *E. subdita*—are probably merely local races or subspecies of *E. core*. *E. subdita*, which represents the Burman form, is the most distinct of all, with its perceptible blue shot, and comparatively large sexual brand. *E. asela*, the Ceylon form, is distinct too as far as typical specimens from that Island are concerned; but the *E. core* of South India shows a very close approach to it, some specimens being indistinguishable from the Ceylon form. *E. vermiculata* of Northern India is more variable still, typical specimens are easily recognised, but the gradations between it and the typical *E. core* are so numerous that it is impossible to separate the two.

61. **Euplœa core,** Cramer. (PLATE IX, FIG. 16, ♂ ♀).

Papilio core, Cramer, Pap. Ex., vol. iii, pl. CCLXVI, figs. E, F (1780); *Danais coreta*, Godart. Enc. Méith., vol. ix, p. 178, n. 6 (1819).

HABITAT: India generally.

EXPANSE: ♂, 3'0 to 4'0; ♂, 3'4 to 3'8 inches.

DESCRIPTION: UPPERSIDE rich dark velvety-brown, rather paler on the *hindwing*, and much paler on the margin, narrowly on *forewing*, more broadly on *hindwing*; a double continuous series of white spots on the margin of *both wings*, those on the *hindwing* largest. The inner series is on the *forewing* continued prominently right up to the costa, one spot between each pair of nervules, rounded; on the *hindwing* the spots above the third median nervule are as on the forewing; below that nervule they are somewhat elongate-oval, and two between each pair of nervules. The outer series consists of two spots between each pair of nervules on *both wings*, decreasirg towards the apex of *forewing*, where the uppermost are obsolete. A small internal silky streak on the forewing in the MALE. The FEMALE is paler than the male, is without the silky streak, has a straight inner margin to the *forewing*, and usually a white subcostal dot near upper end of cell in that wing, and one outside the cell between the first and second median branches in addition to the two series of marginal spots, which latter are larger and more cloudy at the edges on the *forewing*. UNDERSIDE paler, darkest on the disc of the *forewing*, the marginal spots as above but more prominent and whiter. *Forewing* in both sexes, with a subcostal spot, three or four on the disc (one in the cell), and an internal streak, violet-white. *Hindwing* with a spot in the cell, and five on the disc round the end of the cell, violet-white; in the *male* the second of these spots is sometimes wanting: the usual basal spots.

Papilio corus (Fabricius, Ent. Syst., vol. iii, pt. i, p. 41, n. 122 (1793), is usually identified with this species, but according to the original description "*Danais cora* appears to differ from *D. coreta* (= *E. core*) only in having on the upperside four white dots on the middle of the *forewing*, and two similar ones in the middle of the *hindwing*." (*Godart*, Enc. Méth., vol. ix, p. 178, n. 7, 1819).

LARVA.—Above lilac, with three transverse darker lines on each segment, the spiracular region being ochreous, the abdominal region deep brown; with two tentacula on the second segment springing from the spiracular region one on each side and pointing forwards in front of the head; and two curled ones each on the third, sixth, and twelfth segments, springing from the subdorsal region. The spiracles have each a dark brown border. "Reared on *Nerium odorum*." (*Lang*). PUPA.—Smooth, rounded and fulvous, beautifully marked with silvery or golden dots and streaks. Figured on plate iv, figs. 9, 9*a*, of Horsfield and Moore's Cat. Lep., E. I. C. (1857).

E. core is by far the commonest and most widely spread of all the *Euplœas*, being found in suitable localities throughout the continent. It does not appear to extend into Tenasserim, where it is replaced by the closely allied *E. subdita*. In the N.-W. Himalayas it occurs up to an elevation of about 8,000 feet, but is never common at this altitude.

The figure shows the upperside of a male and female from Calcutta specimens in the Indian Museum, Calcutta.

62. **Euplœa vermiculata**, Butler.

E. vermiculata, Butler, Proc. Zool. Soc. Lond., 1866, p. 276, n. 24.

HABITAT: Northern India.

EXPANSE: 3·25 to 4·1 inches.

DESCRIPTION: "UPPERSIDE: *Forewing* swarthy, the outer margin paler; with nine submarginal spots, rather large at the apex, and marginal spots much smaller, white. *Hindwing* paler, fuscescent at base, with two submarginal rows of white spots, the inner row of large elongate spots. *Body* swarthy. *Head* black, dotted with white. *Antennæ* black. UNDERSIDE, paler. *Forewing* with one costal spot, two discal, and one near end of cell, white; submarginal rows as on upperside, but larger. *Hindwing* with submarginal spots near apex and anal angle coalescent; otherwise as on upperside; five discal spots in an angulate row beyond the cell, and one near end of cell. This species appears to be allied to *E. core*, of which it may possibly be the northern form; it differs from it chiefly in having the submarginal spots exceedingly large and distinct, especially near the apex." (*Butler*, l. c.)

We retain this species on Butler's authority, but it does not seem a satisfactory one. The *E. core* of north India approaches the *E. vermiculata* type in precisely the same way as the *E. core* of extreme south India approaches the *E. asela* type. A few picked specimens of *E. vermiculata* taken separately, appear very distinct, but the type is not constant even in the same locality. In a large series collected at Naiashahr in the Saharanpur district, by Mrs. Deane, there were several specimens of typical *E. vermiculata*, male and female, several of typical *E. core*, and numerous intermediate forms.

63. **Euplœa asela**, Moore.

E. asela, Moore, Ann. and Mag. Nat. Hist., fourth series, vol. xx, p. 45 (1877); id., Lep. Ceylon, p. 11, pl. vi, figs. 2, *imago*, 2a, *caterpillar* and *chrysalis* (1880).

HABITAT: Ceylon.

EXPANSE: 3·25 to 3·80 inches.

DESCRIPTION: "MALE and FEMALE. UPPERSIDE dark velvety olive-brown, broadly paler externally. *Forewing* with a submarginal and less distinct lower marginal row of small brownish-white spots, the former series curving to the costa before the apex. MALE with a single short slender sericeous streak between the first median nervule and submedian nervure. *Hindwing* with a submarginal row of brownish-white oval spots, and a marginal row of smaller round spots. UNDERSIDE paler, both rows of marginal spots clearer; both wings with a small spot at end of the cell, and a contiguous discal curved series of spots. *Body* blackish; thorax, head, palpi, forelegs and abdomen beneath white spotted; middle and hindlegs beneath white streaked."

"LARVA cylindrical, purple-white or dove-colour, with a pair of curled red fleshy filaments on three of the anterior segments, and a pair on the twelfth segment; each segment transversely barred with narrow white lines, lateral band pinkish-white with black and red dots; abdominal line black; head and legs black, streaked with white. Feeds on *Nerium oleander*, &c. PUPA golden yellow, constricted below the thorax, streaked and banded with brown; dorsal segments black spotted." (*Moore*, Lep Cey.)

In Ceylon "found everywhere, in the plains and up to 6,000 feet, in forest or open ground. At Colombo it occurs from October to January; elsewhere all the year. Flight slow, heavy. Often comes into the house in numbers, sometimes settling on one's clothes." (*Hutchison*). The typical form is found in the island of Ceylon, but specimens from south India approach this form very closely, just as in the parallel case of *Danais grammica* and *D. ceylanica*. *E. asela* is apparently only a geographical variety of the Indian *E. core*.

In Siam another species, *E. layardi*,* occurs, which appears to be closely allied to this group: it seems to differ only from *E. asela* in having a subcostal spot above the upper end of the cell, and another spot below the lower end of the cell in the second median interspace.

64. **Euplœa subdita**, Moore.

E. subdita, Moore, Proc. Zool. Soc. Lond., 1878, p. 823.

HABITAT: Akyab, Upper Tenasserim.

EXPANSE: ♂, 3·13 to 3·90; ♀, 3·70 inches.

DESCRIPTION: "Allied to *E. core*. MALE: UPPERSIDE paler, markings similar, smaller and paler. *Forewing*, shorter, broader, and the posterior margin more convex; basal area slightly blue-glossed; markings indistinct." (*Moore*, l. c.) The FEMALE differs from the same sex of *E. core* in being paler, the submarginal row of spots on the *forewing* reduced to two at the apex, and three at the posterior angle, these spots all very small; the marginal series reduced to five, which are confined towards the posterior angle of the wing. Both series of spots on the *hindwing* are also smaller.

The male of this species can at once be distinguished from *E. core* by the perceptible blue gloss of the forewing, and the female by the two series of spots on the forewing being compared with *E. core*, almost obsolete.

The Indian Museum has two specimens, male and female, taken by Mr. Wood-Mason, at Akyab, in September.

The next two species, *E. esperi* and *E. frauenfeldii*, are closely allied, but as in the parallel cases of *E. comorta* and *E. scherzeri*, and of *Danais nicobarica* and *D. exprompta*, the local races are separable; the Ceylon species *E. frauenfeldii* differing from the Nicobar form chiefly in the almost complete absence of the inner marginal row of spots on the hindwing, and the fainter development of the outer row. *E. frauenfeldii* is very rare, and the female is

* *E. layardi*, Druce. HABITAT: Chentaboom, Siam. EXPANSE: 4 inches. "DESCRIPTION: UPPERSIDE, brown, paler round the outer margin. *Forewing*, with two whitish spots at the end of [outside] the cell, and a double row of white spots round the outer margin. *Hindwing* with a band of oval-shaped white spots crossing it from the anal angle to the anterior margin, and a submarginal row of small white spots. UNDERSIDE as above, except that all the white spots are plainer." (Druce, Proc. Zool. Soc. Lond., 1874, p. 103, n. 9, pl. xvi, fig. 1.)

still unknown. *E. esperi* has recently been discovered to be far from uncommon in the Nicobar isles, and as might be expected the extent to which the spots of both wings are developed is found to be very variable. In one male specimen from Pulo Kondol in the Indian Museum, Calcutta, the hindwing has only a single marginal series of dots. Both species differ from the *E. core* type in the much darker colour of the surface, and the small size of the white spots, also in the presence of discal spots on the upper surface, which are absent from all the races of *E. core* except *E. layardi*.

65. **Euplœa esperi,** Felder.

E. esperi, Felder, Verh. zool.-bot. Gesellsch. Wien, vol. xii, p. 482, n. 109 (1862), *female*; *E. frauenfeldii*, id., Reise Nov., Lep., vol. ii, p. 342, n. 474 (1865), *female*; *E. esperi*, Moore, Proc. Zool. Soc. Lond., 1877, p. 582; id., Wood-Mason and de Nicéville, Journ. A. S. B., vol. l, pt. ii, p. 227 (1881).

HABITAT: Nicobars.

EXPANSE: 3·4 to 3·8 inches.

DESCRIPTION: "FEMALE.—Wings paler [than in *E. frauenfeldii*], with the discal spots of the underside shewing through above. *Forewing* with a subcostal spot, three discal (one in the cell), seven others external in a bent series, the two uppermost excepted, rather large (the third larger), and dots before the margin (the uppermost evanescent.) *Hindwing* with the external spots small and elongate, and rather large dots before the margin swarthy, powdered with white. UNDERSIDE with the marginal spots of the upperside whiter. *Forewing* with two subcostal spots, below the second beyond the disco-cellular nervule a pair of elongate spots, narrow, a cellular spot, sinuate within, a pair median, a prolonged interior spot and a streak below that. *Hindwing* with a spot in the cell often geminate, and six around it (the second larger), violet-white." (*Felder*, l. c. in Reise Nov.)

MALE swarthy black, markings on the UPPERSIDE similar to those of the female, but with the usual sexual mark, and the inner margin of *forewing* convex. On the UNDERSIDE the markings are also similar, but several of the discal spots of the *forewing* are obsolete or wanting.

This species has as yet only been taken in the Nicobars, where it is one of the commonest Butterflies.

66. **Euplœa frauenfeldii,** Felder.

E. frauenfeldii, Felder, Verh. zool.-bot. Gesellsch. Wien, vol. xii, p. 479, n. 87 (1862), *male*, from Ceylon; Reise Nov. Lep., vol. ii, p. 342, n. 474, *male*, *female*, pl. xli, fig. 4, *male* (1865); *E. frauenfeldii*, Moore, Lep. Cey., p. 12 (1880).

HABITAT: Ceylon.

EXPANSE: ♂, 3·6 inches (Felder's plate), 4 inches (*Moore*).

DESCRIPTION: "MALE: UPPERSIDE deep rufescent swarthy. *Hindwing* a little paler on the margin, the anterior area powdery, and with a somewhat pearly streak as usual. *Forewing* with a subcostal spot, another discal, five on the outer margin near apex (the second elongate), and dots before the lower outer margin. *Hindwing* with white dots before the margin in a bent series. *Forewing* with a cellular spot, and a pair of median spots showing through from the underside, powdered with white. UNDERSIDE paler, the usual basal dots, the spots of the upperside but whiter. *Forewing* with a geminate spot in the cell in addition, another short sublinear, and beyond that a third median somewhat large. *Hindwing* with a small spot in the cell, and five others in an angulate series around it decreasing, unequal, violet-white. *Forewing* with an interior raised spot powdered with hoary, and an internal streak somewhat pearly. *Hindwing* with a minute geminate white spot above the middle of the outer margin." (*Felder*, l. c. in Reise Nov.)

FEMALE unknown. In the "Reise Novara" Felder unites his *E. esperi* with this species describing *E. esperi*, ♀, as the female of *E. frauenfeldii*, and giving Ceylon as the sole habitat for the species; but numerous specimens of the male of *E. esperi* from the Nicobars, hitherto undescribed, are in the Indian Museum, Calcutta. *E. frauenfeldii* is known only from Ceylon, where it is evidently very rare; we have never seen a specimen.

Moore, in the Lepidoptera of Ceylon (p. 12), gives the following description of the male of this rare species, which differs somewhat from the original description by Felder quoted above :—" UPPERSIDE blackish purple-brown. *Forewing* blue glossed, a very small white costal spot above end of the cell, a spot between third and second median nervules, a submarginal series of spots curving from apex, and a lower marginal series of smaller spots, a slender short sericeous streak below the first median nervule. *Hindwing* unmarked, except that it indistinctly shows a submarginal and marginal series of pale brown spots. UNDERSIDE dark olive-brown. *Forewing* with a bluish costal spot, a spot at lower end of the cell, a spot between the third and second median nervules, and a larger elongated white spot below it, the sexual streak and posterior [inner ?] margin being brownish white ; submarginal and marginal spots as above. *Hindwing* with a minute bluish spot at end of the cell, and a contiguous discal series of spots, a marginal series of small white spots, and a submarginal anal series of three or four spots. *Body* black ; head, thorax, palpi and abdomen beneath white spotted ; legs black. Expanse, 4 inches. Taken at Trincomalee on the north-east side of the isand."

67. **Euplœa andamanensis,** Atkinson.

E. andamanensis, Atkinson, Proc. Zool. Soc. Lond., 1873, p. 736, n. 2, pl. lxiii, fig. 2, *male*.

HABITAT : Port Blair, Andaman Isles.

EXPANSE : 3·12 to 4 inches.

DESCRIPTION : " Pale fuliginous with white spots. *Forewing* with a white spot between the extremity of the cell and the costa ; another within the cell near its extremity ; two others below the cell, one between the first and second, the other between the second and third median nervules ; beyond these a curved series of nine white spots from the anterior margin to below the exterior angle, of which the three last are the largest ; followed by a submarginal series of smaller elongated spots, extending from the first discoidal nervule to the exterior angle. The interior margin much rounded in the MALE, in which sex there is a single vitta of dark adpressed scales between the first median nervule and the submedian nervure. In the FEMALE the vitta is replaced by a white streak. *Hindwing* with two somewhat irregular series of elongated white spots, corresponding to the two series in the forewing." (*Atkinson*, l. c.) UNDERSIDE as on upperside, but on the *forewing* the inner discal series of spots is often complete right up to the costa, the lowest spot argest and rou nd, the second also round, but smaller, the four upper ones linear and small. In many specimens some or all of these four latter spots are wanting. On the *hindwing* there is a large, sometimes geminate, spot in the cell, and six irregular discal spots round the end of it in addition to the border rows as on upperside. The discal spots occasionally show faintly by transparency on the upperside also. FEMALE as in the male, except that on the UPPERSIDE in the *forewing*, the sexual streak is replaced by a white rather elongated spot, and the inner margin is nearly straight, not outwardly lobed. On the *hindwing*, the spot in the cell and the six discal spots are faintly present on the upperside, as well as the border rows of spots. UNDERSIDE as in male.

E. andamanensis is a very distinct species ; it is common at Port Blair from March to August, and possibly at other seasons. The original description by Atkinson quoted above has been supplemented and completed from a large series collected by Colonel T. Cadell, V. C., Chief Commissioner of the Andamans, and by Mr. F. A. de Roepstorff, Deputy Commissioner. A marked feature of this species is that the ground-colour is darkest at the outer border instead of at the base of the wings, as is usual in this group. It has only been found as yet in the Andaman islands.

68. **Euplœa godartii,** Lucas.

E. godartii, Lucas, Rev. Zool., 1853, p. 319 ; *E. siamensis*, Felder, Reise Nov., Lep., vol. ii, p. 341, n. 473, pl. xli, fig. 6 (1865), *male*.

HABITAT : Burma.

EXPANSE : ♂, 3·0 to 4·2 ; ♀, 3·2 to 4·0 inches.

DESCRIPTION : " Wings above fuscous, paling on the outer margin. *Forewing* with the apex widely tinted with rosy violet, and white dots as in *E. alcathoë*. *Hindwing* as in *E. core*. UNDERSIDE as in *E. core*, but with the discal spots larger." (*Lucas*, l. c.)

The above is the original description by Lucas, which is hardly sufficiently full. The UPPERSIDE is more brown than swarthy, dark and velvety on the basal half, the outer border broadly paler, and somewhat rufescent. On the *forewing* the violet apical patch, which is formed by a powdering of the spaces between the nervules, varies much both in extent and intensity; in some it extends from the costal margin to the first median nervule, and almost to the end of the cell; in others it is almost entirely absent. The spots too vary very much; the full complement is one subcostal spot, one at end of cell, two on the disc, a few marginal, a few submarginal, and three subapical, the latter being circled with dark brown, and sometimes very prominent; but some of these spots are more or less obsolete in every specimen, and in some they are almost entirely wanting. In the MALE also there is a single small interno-median silky streak, and the inner margin is somewhat convex; in the FEMALE the silky streak is wanting, and the inner margin is nearly straight. *Hindwing* marked with two series of spots on the margin, as in *E. core*, but the spots are smaller, especially the inner series, and more or less sullied with brown. The costal margin is whitish, with a white subcostal spot. UNDERSIDE paler brown, darkest on the disc of the forewing. *Forewing* with the internal margin whitish, and an indistinct whitish streak on the interno-median area; a subcostal spot, a spot at end of the cell, one or two on the disc, and an elongate oval median spot below, violet-white; a few marginal spots near anal angle, three subapical, very variable in size, sometimes absent, and a few posterior ones sometimes wanting in a submarginal series pure white. *Hindwing* with spot in the cell, and five or six round the end of it, discal, violet-white; the two marginal series of spots as on upperside but more prominent and pure white. The usual basal spots. In the FEMALE the median spot on *forewing* is rounded, not elongate-oval, otherwise the markings are similar.

In a female specimen, taken by Captain C. H. E. Adamson, at Moulmein, in September, the submarginal series of spots on the *forewing* is complete, those below the third median nervule being large, pure white and very prominent.

E. godartii is a very distinct species, with its violet powdered apical patch. It appears to be common in Burma from February to July. It was found by Captain Bingham in the Meplay valley in February, and in the Upper Thoungyeen forests in April. By Limborg it was found in Upper Tenasserim, also at Ahsown, Moulmein to Meetan, Hatsiega, Houngduran, and Naththoung to Paboga. In Rangoon it is common in June, July, and September, probably throughout the year. Dr. J. Anderson found it abundantly in the Mergui Archipelago during the winter.

69. **Euplœa scherzeri**, Felder.

E. scherzeri, Felder, Verh. zool.-bot. Gesellsch. Wien, vol. xii, p. 479, n. 88 (1862); id., Reise Nov., Lep., vol. ii, p. 335, n. 463 (1865); id. Moore, Lep. Cey., p. 12 (1880).

HABITAT : Ceylon, Java.

EXPANSE : 3·5 inches (*Moore*).

DESCRIPTION : "MALE : UPPERSIDE deep swarthy, much paler and brownish on the outer margin. *Forewing* with a single short velvety streak in the interior. UNDERSIDE : both wings concolorous, but a little paler. *Forewing* with two internal whitish streaks (the upper one narrow, linear); a spot and two dots discal, a spot below the middle of the costa, and two subapical, bluish-white. *Hindwing* with five very small discal spots (one in the cell), bluish-white." (*Felder*, l. c. in Verh. zool.-bot. Gesellsch. Wien.)

This species is unknown to us. It seems to be closely allied to *E. camorta* from the Nicobars. It has never been figured, but Moore gives the following detailed description in his Lepidoptera of Ceylon:—"MALE : UPPERSIDE purplish olive-brown, darkest on basal area. *Forewing* with a minute white subapical spot, and a lengthened sericeous streak between first median nervule and submedian nervure. *Hindwing* with a subapical series of three small very indistinct pale brown spots. UNDERSIDE paler. *Forewing* with a bluish-white small costal spot, one at lower end of the cell, two beyond, and an elongated lower spot, three or four submarginal spots below the apex. *Hindwing* with a small bluish-white spot at lower end of the cell, a contiguous discal series, three upper submarginal spots and a marginal lower series of spots. *Body* black; head, thorax, palpi and abdomen beneath white spotted; legs black. Expanse, 3·5 inches." The female has never been described.

70. **Euplœa camorta**, Moore.

E. camorta, Moore, Proc. Zool. Soc. Lond., 1877, p. 582: id., Wood-Mason and de Nicéville, Journ. A. S. B., vol. l, pt. ii, p. 228 (1881).

HABITAT: Nicobars.

EXPANSE: ♂, 3·5 to 4·2; ♀, 3·6 to 4·1 inches.

DESCRIPTION: "MALE: UPPERSIDE: Both wings dark blackish olive-brown, paler on the outer margins. *Forewing* with a short straight narrow silky streak beween the first median nervule and submedian nervure. *Hindwing* with the anterior border broadly cinereous, the upper part of the cell being slightly greyish-brown. UNDERSIDE paler. *Forewing* with four bluish-white spots, one being on the costa above the end of the cell, another at its lower end, the other two outside; the sexual streak long, narrow, and patch on hind margin pale flesh-colour. *Hindwing* with seven median bluish-white spots." (*Moore* l. c.) The FEMALE differs from the male in the outer margin of *both wings* being paler, the inner margin of the *forewing* is straight instead of convex, and in the absence of the sexual mark. In addition there is usually a conspicuous violet-white subcostal spot above the end of the cell, and one outside the cell below the third median nervule.

E. camorta, with its conspicuous broad pale margin to both wings, is a very distinct form, having no Indian allies, except apparently *E. scherzeri* from Ceylon. Some specimens show a few spots on the disc on the upperside. It has only been found as yet in the Nicobars, where it is very commonly met with, occurring probably all the year round.

The next two species, *E. alcathoë* and *E. menetriesii*, may be distinguished by the very elongate submarginal spots on the hindwing, which gradually lengthen from the apex to the inner margin, at which point they extend nearly to the base of the wing. They are found only in north-east India and Malayana. In these and in the two remaining species, *E. deione* and *E. limborgii*, the forewing is of a more elongate-ovate form than in any of the preceding species.

71. **Euplœa alcathoë**, Godart. (PLATE IX, FIG. 17 ♂ ♀).

Danais alcathoë, Godart, Enc. Méth., vol. ix, p. 178, n. 5 (1819); *E. doubledayi*, Felder, Reise Nov., Lep., vol. ii, p. 337, n. 467 (1865).

HABITAT: Sikkim, Sylhet, Assam, Naga Hills, Cachar, Mergui, Upper Tenasserim.

EXPANSE: 3·2 to 4·2 inches.

DESCRIPTION: "UPPERSIDE: *Forewing* deep chestnut swarthy, in certain positions slightly suffused with violet, paler at the inner margin: with an internal short and narrow silky streak, and minute white dots before the outer margin. *Hindwing* less intense in colour, much paler towards the margin, with a pearly costal dot, and the anterior area concealed with raised scales, giving the usual powdery appearance; a row of external greatly increasing spots radiate on the inner margin: and others before the margin, slightly elongate, increasing, white, powdered with brown; the lowest of the inner row confluent with the corresponding marginal ones. UNDERSIDE, much paler; the usual basal dots. *Forewing*, darker in the disc, a subcostal spot, and two in the disc (one in the cell), violet-white; an elongate median spot, three subapical, two posterior minute, and a few small dots before the outer margin, white; the internal margin hoary, with an elevated spot and pearly streak, as usual, concealed. *Hindwing* with a spot in the cell, and others very minute around it, violet-white; the marginal spots as on upperside, but longer and whiter. FEMALE, wings much paler. UPPERSIDE: *Forewing* with a subcostal spot, and three discal (one in the cell), violet-white; two or three posterior spots, a few dots before the outer margin, and often with two minute subapical spots, white. *Hindwing* with the costal margin hoary-white, the spots as in the male, but the interior ones longer. UNDERSIDE almost as in the male, but the discal spots, and the posterior spots of the *forewing*, much larger. *Forewing* with an interior much elongated spot, violet-white" (*Felder*, l. c.)

The above description is taken from Felder's description of *E. doubledayi*, which was redescribed as distinct on account of Godart's original description of *E. alcathoë* purporting to be from an Amboyna specimen; but there is no doubt that Godart's locality was incorrect, and the name *E. alcathoë* will stand for this species. The male of *E. alcathoë* is a very black insect, the violet suffusion being scarcely perceptible; and, in the female especially, the very elongated narrow submarginal streaks form a conspicuous distinctive character. On the underside of the forewing of the male the three subapical spots, two minute posterior ones, and the few small dots before the outer margin referred to in the description above, are entirely absent in some specimens, and more or less so in others.

E. alcathoë was found by Limborg in Upper Tenasserim at Ahsown, at 2,000 feet elevation, and Captain C. H. E. Adamson has sent a single male specimen from Moulmein; it has also been taken by Captain Bingham, who has been collecting over the same ground. In Sikkim and Sylhet it appears to be not uncommon. At Shillong a single female specimen was taken in May by the late Mr. J. P. Cock. In this specimen the marginal dots of the forewing are almost obsolete, and the submarginal series is nearly complete, the lowest spot being much the larger. Mr. Wood-Mason found it in profusion in Cachar during the summer. Dr. J. Anderson sent numerous specimens to the Indian Museum, Calcutta, collected during the winter, in the Mergui Archipelago.

The figure shews the upperside of a male and female from Sylhet specimens in the Indian Museum, Calcutta.

72. **Euplœa menetriesii**, Felder.

E. menetriesii, Felder, Wein. Ent. Monatsch., vol. iv, p. 398, n. 15 (1860).

HABITAT: Nepal, Assam (*Butler*), Malacca (*Felder*), Siam, Borneo.

EXPANSE: (Not stated.)

DESCRIPTION: "Wings elongate. *Forewing* of the MALE with the inner margin rather convex. UPPERSIDE deep blackish swarthy, in certain positions shining with violet, with a rather broad velvety internal streak. *Forewing* of the FEMALE obscure brown. *Hindwing* in both sexes brown; on the UPPERSIDE with elongate external spots, and obsolete marginal spots, white; on the UNDERSIDE with the spots of the upperside white, distinct; and seven others discal (one in the cell), violet-tinted. Approaches *E. alcathoë*, but the wings are elongate, the form of the velvety stripe in the male, and the markings in the female, are different." (*Felder*, l. c.)

This species is unknown to us. In all probability the localities "Nepal, Assam" are erroneous, and if found within Indian limits it is most likely to occur in Tenasserim. The description of the male of this species accords closely with that of *E. limborgii*, but it is stated that it is allied to *E. alcathoë*, and the female is, as in *E. alcathoë*, obscure brown, whereas in *E. limborgii* the female is coloured similarly to the male and equally shot with splendid blue.

The next two species are distinguished from all other true *Euplœas* by the almost (generally quite) spotless velvety blackish forewing, splendidly shot with blue, except perhaps from the foregoing, *E. menetriesii*, which is said to have the forewing equally spotless and shining with violet. In *E. deione* from Assam the hindwing is spotless also, or nearly so; in *E. limborgii* from Tenasserim the hindwing has a conspicuous double row of white border spots, the inner somewhat elongate; and in *E. menetriesii*, which also has these border spots, the inner row is said to be elongate, "approaching *E. alcathoë*," which *E. limborgii* can hardly be said to do.

73. Euplœa deione, Westwood.

E. deione, Westwood, Cab. Or. Ent., p. 76, pl. xxxvii, fig. 3 (1848), *male*; *E. poeyi*, Felder, Reise Nov., Lep., vol. ii, p. 340, n. 471 (1867), *female*.

HABITAT: Sikkim, Naga Hills, Assam.

EXPANSE: 3·6 to 4·4 inches.

DESCRIPTION: UPPERSIDE: MALE, black (or deep swarthy, with a slight rufous tinge on forewing, highly rufescent on hindwing). *Forewing*, in certain positions splendidly glossed with blue, having two small white spots, one near the middle of the wing, below the third median nervule, and the other near the middle of the costa above the end of the cell; a large and conspicuous silky brown streak runs parallel to the inner margin near the first branch of the median nervure. *Hindwing* unspotted (but in some specimens an obsolete marginal and submarginal row of small spots is distinctly traceable). UNDERSIDE, both wings brown, outwardly paler. *Forewing* with a few minute white spots at the base. A subcostal spot just above the end of the cell, a spot near the lower end of the cell, a series of spots outside the cell, one between each pair of the nervules, the lowest the largest and oblong, the second less than half the size and round, the third small and linear, all lilac-white. *Hindwing* with a spot in the cell and a series of four or five spots outside it, all lilac-white; sometimes a row of minute submarginal white dots, almost obliterated in the *forewing*.

In a series of the MALES in Colonel Lang's collection, all from Sikkim, the subcostal spot on the upperside of the *forewing* is wanting in some specimens; in others there is a faint cell spot, and in two or three specimens there is a fourth spot between the first and second median nervules. The *hindwing* in all is strongly tinged rufescent, the base and middle darker and faintly shot with blue, the *forewing* alone being black. In one specimen the apical portion of the forewing is distinctly powdered with pale blue in broad streaks between the nervules.

FEMALE (separately described as *E. poyei* by Felder). "UPPERSIDE: *Forewing* deep rufescent swarthy, a little paler on the apical area and margin, in certain positions splendid violet blue almost to the margin; with a subcostal dot, another in the cell, and two median spots (the lower powdery, evanescent) white, margined with violet. *Hindwing* less intense and paler on the margin, with the costal margin paling and powdered with hoary; with small obsolete external spots in a subangulate series, and others before the outer margin dot-shaped, powdered with white, a little more distinct, on a paler ground. UNDERSIDE much paler, the usual spots at the base. *Forewing* with a subcostal spot, another in the cell, two beyond it (the upper narrow, minute—the lower small), two lower, small; and others, before the outer margin, white, more or less powdered with blue, and circled with swarthy; a rather large median spot, and two long internal ones (the upper almost linear), violet-white. *Hindwing* with a spot in the cell, and five beyond it in an angulate series, small, violet-white and circled with swarthy; the external spots, and others before the margin as on the upperside, but whitish and larger." (*Felder*, l. c.)

There can be little doubt but that this is the female of *E. deione* which is found more commonly in the same localities, and the female of which is otherwise unknown. A pair of FEMALES in Colonel Lang's collection agree with this description, except that the UPPERSIDE of the *forewing* has, in one specimen, a fifth spot, shaped like a very small streak, below the first median nervule. On the UNDERSIDE, in the *forewing*, the spot in the cell is double, the inner margin is whitish, a long whitish streak below the median nervure, a large oval spot above it, a prominent round spot above that, a minute streak above again at end of cell, and a subcostal spot, are all the markings. There is no trace of any spots beyond the discal row. On the UNDERSIDE of the *hindwing* there are the following markings: a spot in the cell, a series of six round the end of the cell, that nearest the costa smallest, and the next to it the largest; four small submarginal spots near the anal angle, and nine small marginal spots from the anal angle (two between each pair of nervules in each row); the *cilia* prominently white-spotted.

74. Euplœa limborgii, Moore.

E. limborgii, Moore, Proc. Zool. Soc. Lond., 1878, p. 823, pl. li, fig. 2, *male*.

HABITAT: Upper Tenasserim, Mergui.

EXPANSE: 3·75 to 4·40 inches.

DESCRIPTION: "Allied to *E. deione* from northern India. UPPERSIDE differs in the *forewing* having some very indistinct submarginal white spots, and the *hindwing* having two marginal rows of prominent white spots, similar to, but smaller than, those in *E. margarita*." (*Moore*, l. c.)

MALE: UPPERSIDE: *Forewing* bordered with dark rufous, the rest of the wing velvety black, with a rufous tinge in some positions, in others, splendid shining blue. A broad and very long silky impressed streak on the interno-median area; and a few indistinct marginal dots near anal angle, sometimes entirely wanting. The inner margin slightly convex. *Hindwing* brown, along the median nervure it is suffused darker, and faintly shot with blue on the darkest part; a submarginal row of increasing spots, round at apex, and elongate towards anal angle, and a marginal row of increasing spots, smaller and rounded throughout: in some specimens both rows are complete, prominent, and pure white; in others the spots are smaller, powdered with brown, and obsolescent at apex. UNDERSIDE brown, darkest along median nervure of *forewing*. *Forewing*, with the inner margin pale and whitish, a subcostal spot above the end of the cell, one in the cell, and two discal (the upper one a very small streak), violet-white, a prominent oval white spot between the first and second median nervules, and a few small white marginal and submarginal spots, sometimes entirely wanting. *Hindwing*, with the border rows of spots as on upperside, white; and a spot in the cell, and five small ones round the end of the cell, pale violet: the usual white basal dots. FEMALE: UPPERSIDE, as in the male, but the sexual streak is absent; the inner margin of *forewing* is straight, and a single minute white spec is apparent on the disc between the first and second median nervules. *Hindwing* identical, except that the border spots are as a rule more prominent, the inner row rather more elongated. UNDERSIDE exactly as in male, except that there is a conspicuous lengthened violet-white streak on the interno-median area of *forewing*.

E. limborgii is common in Upper Tenasserim from February till April, and perhaps at other seasons. It was found by Limborg at Ahsown, 2,000 feet above the sea, above Ahsown, at Hatsiega, and at the Houngduran source. Captain C. T. Bingham found it in the Meplay valley in February, between Meeawady and Kankarit, and in the Thoungyeen forests in March, and in the Donat range and the Thoungyeen forests in April. Dr. J. Anderson took three males and a female in December, and one male in March in the Mergui archipelago. It flies lazily in open cultivation and scrub jungle.

E. pinwilli, described by Butler from Malacca, appears to be identical with this species, and, if so, Butler's name would have the priority; but in the absence of specimens of *E. pinwilli* the point cannot be determined; the original description of *E. pinwilli** is appended.

Seventh Group.—STICTOPLŒA, *Butler*. "MALES for the most part with straight inner margins like the females; always with two well-defined sericeous brands on the interno-median area, and placed one above the other." (*Butler*, Journ. Linn. Soc., Zoology, vol. xiv, p. 301, 1878.)

The males of the Indian species have the inner margin of *forewing* bowed and quite distinguishable from those of the females; but the double sericeous brand is a well-marked character.

* *E. pinwilli*, Butler. HABITAT: Malacca. EXPANSE: 4 inches. DESCRIPTION: "*Forewing* brownish piceous, purple-shot, slightly paler along the external border: a long sericeous interno-median streak. *Hindwing* paler brown, deepest at base; two marginal series of whitish spots, clear at anal angle, obsolescent and decreasing towards apex; costal area greyish. UNDERSIDE: *Forewing*, paler than above, with a subcostal spot, and an elliptical interno-median spot, pinky white; a spot in the cell, and two beyond it, bluish-white, two or three white dots at external angle. *Hindwing*, with the submarginal spots clear whitish; a spot in the cell and seven in an arched series beyond it, lilacine whitish; base and pectus white spotted. *E. pinwilli* is allied to *E. menetriesii*, but larger, darker, and shot with purple." (*Butler*, Trans. Linn. Soc., Zoology, second series, vol. i., p. 535, pl. lxix, fig. 9, 1876, where the name is spelt *E. pinwillii*.)

None of the species are common; one species occurs in Burma; three closely allied and doubtfully distinct species are described from N.-E. India; one is found in south India, and another distinct species is found only in Ceylon. The Burman species is very distinct, with the *forewing* splendidly shot with blue, no spots on the disc, and a double marginal series of white spots on the hindwing. The N.-E. Indian species has the forewing with numerous paler blue spots on the disc, and but few marginal spots on the hindwing; the Ceylon species lacks the splendid blue shot; but both these have the two sericeous bands large and well defined as in the *Euplœas* of the *alcathoë* and *deione* types. *E. coreoïdes*, the south Indian form, has almost exactly the colouration of *E. core* and *E. asela*, and strangely enough, like them, has the sexual brands small and inconspicuous.

Key to the Indian species of Stictoplœa.

C. *c.* Males with two well-defined brands on the interno-median area of the forewing.

- *a.*[1] Upperside dark velvety olive-brown, palest externally, with a double row of whitish spots along the border of both wings as in *E. core.*
  - 75. E. (*Stictoplœa*) COREOIDES, S. India.
- *b.*[1] Upperside deep rufescent swarthy, tinged with violet on basal area; border spots of forewing evanescent or wanting.
  - 76. E. (*Stictoplœa*) MONTANA, Ceylon.
- *c.*[1] Upperside forewing shot with vivid blue.
  - *a.*[2] With no discal spots on forewing.
    - 77. E. (*Stictoplœa*) GROTEI, Tenasserim.
  - *b.*[2] With numerous discal spots on forewing.
    - 78. E. (*Stictoplœa*) HOPEI, N.-E. India.
    - 79. E. (*Stictoplœa*) BINOTATA, N.-E. India.
    - 80. E. (*Stictoplœa*) MICROSTICTA, N.-E. India.

In the Lepidoptera of Ceylon, p. 13, Moore has taken *E. coreoïdes* as the type of yet another genus, which, under the name of *Narmada*, he characterises as follows:—" Forewing elongated, triangular; costa slightly arched; apex somewhat acute; exterior margin oblique; posterior [inner ?] margin in male slightly convex, with two sericeous streaks between the median and submedian nervures: hindwing triangular." In what way this is supposed to differ from *Stictoplœa* of Butler, or why Butler's name for this section has been dropped, there is apparently nothing to show. The one single definite expression in the description, namely, the presence of two sericeous brands in the male, is precisely the point on which Butler's prior designation is founded.

75. Euplœa coreoïdes, Moore.

E. coreoïdes, Moore, Ann. and Mag. Nat. Hist., fourth series, vol. xx, p. 44 (1877).

HABITAT: Malabar, Nilgiris, Wynaad, Trevandrum.

EXPANSE: ♂, 3·25 to 3·60; ♀, 3·50 inches.

DESCRIPTION: "Allied to *E. core* (which is also found in the same locality), but distinguished by the two elongated silky impressed marks in the male, the male of *E. core* having but a single short narrow mark. MALE and FEMALE, dark velvety olive-brown, palest externally. MALE: UPPERSIDE: *Forewing*, with a prominent submarginal and marginal series of small white spots; two elongated silky impressed marks between first median nervule and submedian nervure. *Hindwing*, with broader series of white oval and rounded submarginal and smaller rounded marginal spots. UNDERSIDE paler; marginal spots as above; both wings with a small white spot at the end of the cell, and contiguous series beyond. FEMALE, with marginal spots as in male, the submarginal series on *both wings* above, and the discal series on *forewing* beneath being larger." (*Moore*, l. c.)

The female of this species is so slightly different from the same sex of *E. core* that it is only by the following points they can be distinguished: First, by the outline of the forewing being more entire; in *E. core* it is slightly but perceptibly scalloped. Second, on the underside of the forewing having a complete series of six spots, one between each pair of nervules outside the cell; in *E. core* two of these spots, those above the discoidal nervules, are always wanting.

Third, the two brands on the interno-median area of the upperside of the forewing in the male are faintly, but still quite perceptibly, to be traced in the female in the same position. These three points of difference are constant in the three female specimens before us—one from Bangalore, one from Ootacamund, and the third from Trevandrum. It is just possible that with a larger series of females some might be found with one or more of the discal spots wanting, but the outline of the forewing is probably an unvarying character of this species, as it is very perceptible in all the males we have seen.

E. coreoïdes appears to be confined to south India, and is not common. Mr. H. S. Ferguson has sent us two specimens taken near Trevandrum on the 2nd May; and the Indian Museum has two specimens taken at Conoor in August, also specimens taken at Bangalore and Ootacamund. A Trevandrum female shews an approach to the Ceylon *E. montana* in the marginal series of spots on the *forewing* becoming obsolescent.

76. Euplœa montana, Felder.

E. consimilis var. *montana*, Felder, Reise Nov., Lep., vol. iii, p. 330, n. 454 (1865); *Euplœa lankana*, Moore, Ann. and Mag. Nat. Hist., fourth series, vol. xx, p. 44 (1877); *Stictoplœa lankana*, Butler, Journ. Linn. Soc., Zoology, vol. xiv, p. 302 (1878); *Narmada montana*, Moore, Lep. Cey., p. 13, pl. vi, fig. i (1880), *male*.

HABITAT: Ceylon.

EXPANSE: 3·0 to 3·95 inches.

DESCRIPTION: MALE: "Allied to *E. consimilis** from Java, but larger, wings broader, and spots smaller, those before the margin of the *forewing* evanescent. FEMALE: UPPERSIDE: *Forewing*, with the pale border broader, two subcostal violet spots, the interior depressed spots much narrower, more obsolete. *Hindwing* with larger spots. UNDERSIDE: Both wings almost as in the male, but the *forewing* with the spot as on upperside before the middle of the costa, and another beyond the lowest disco-cellular nervule, minute." (*Felder*, l. c.)

The following more detailed description of this species is given by Moore in the "Lepidoptera of Ceylon:—"

"MALE and FEMALE: UPPERSIDE dark velvety olive-brown, paler externally. *Forewing* with a submarginal and marginal row of very small indistinct ochreous-white spots. MALE with two elongated sericeous streaks between the first median nervule and submedian nervure. *Hindwing* with a submarginal and marginal row of ochreous-white spots, the former oval from the anal angle and duplex anteriorly, the latter smaller and round. UNDERSIDE paler, marginal white spots as above, those on forewing more prominent, both wings with a small white spot at end of the cell, and a contiguous discal curved series beyond. *Body* blackish; thorax, head, palpi, and abdomen beneath, white-spotted; forelegs white streaked beneath."

"Captured at Rambodde, Galle, and Kandy." A single specimen, the only one we have seen, sent to us by the Hon'ble F. Mackwood from Ceylon, has the spots of the forewing almost entirely obsolete on the upperside; the shape of the forewing, and its dark velvety almost entirely unspotted appearance, distinguish this species from the south Indian *E. coreoïdes* at a glance.

77. Euplœa grotei, Felder.

E. grotei, Felder, Reise Nov., Lep., vol. ii, p. 339, n. 470, pl. xli, fig. 7 (1865), *female*; *Euplœa grotei*, Butler, Trans. Linn. Soc., Zoology, second series, vol. i, p. 535 (1876); *Stictoplœa grotei*, id., Journ. Linn. Soc., Zoology, vol. xiv, p. 302 (1878).

HABITAT: Cochin, Mergui, Upper Tenasserim, Malacca.

EXPANSE: 3·2 to 4·2 inches.

DESCRIPTION: "MALE: UPPERSIDE: *Forewing* blackish-chestnut and, except on outer margin which is paler, vivid violet-blue in certain positions; a [two ?] rather long interior silky

* *E. consimilis*, Felder. HABITAT: Java. EXPANSE: not given. DESCRIPTION: "MALE: UPPERSIDE. *Forewing* deep rufescent swarthy, and, except on the external border, which is widely and increasingly much paler, faintly tinted with violet in certain positions; the two usual silky internal spots; submarginal spots in a bent series, and dots before the margin, increasing, white. *Hindwing* paler, paling beyond the cell, the anterior area with the usual powdery appearance; and with a costal vitta somewhat pearly white; submarginal spots rather large, increasing, and others before the margin smaller, white, powdered with brown. UNDERSIDE, much paler, the basal dots white, the marginal spots of the upperside but whiter and a little larger. *Forewing* darker about the median nervure, with two elevated interior spots as usual; the internal margin pearly-hoary; with a subcostal spot, two beyond it, and three in the disc, violet-white. *Hindwing* with a spot in the cell, and seven others small around the end of the cell, violet-white." (*Felder*, Reise Nov., Lep., vol. ii, p. 329, n. 454, 1865.)

spot [s ?] and some small chalky-white dots before the outer margin. *Hindwing* paler, in certain positions suffused with violet; the external margin broadly and increasingly much paler; the anterior area powdery, with the usual somewhat pearly costal band; external spots irregularly elongate-oval, and others before the margin smaller, increasing, chalky-white; the uppermost, except where obsolete, best defined, the lowest and last but one of the external row blending with the lowest and last but one of the marginal spots. UNDERSIDE much paler, with the usual basal dots. *Forewing* a little darker in the disc; a subcostal spot, and two discal (one in the cell) small, violet-white; an elongate median spot; and others before the lower outer margin, chalky-white; the usual interior elevated spot, and internal band somewhat pearly, pale at base. *Hindwing* with a spot in the cell, and six outside unequal (the second small), violet-white, encircled with swarthy; the marginal spots as on the upperside but larger, and all best defined on the underside. FEMALE: UPPERSIDE: *Forewing* almost to the margin in certain positions vivid violet-blue; small submarginal spots and dots before the margin pale violet-blue, powdered with white. *Hindwing* darker, and in certain positions more suffused with violet than in the male, the costal margin much paler, with a concealed somewhat pearly band; the submarginal spots rather large, and others before the margin smaller, white, purer than in the male. UNDERSIDE much paler, basal dots white. *Forewing* with a subcostal spot, two beyond it (the lower narrow, minute), and three rather large, discal (one in the cell) on a darker base, bluish-white, circled with blackish; small increasing submarginal dots, and others small before the margin, circled with swarthy, and a rather long violet-white interior linear spot; the inner margin pearly-hoary. *Hindwing* with a rounded spot in the cell, and six others in an angulated row beyond it, violet-white, small; the marginal spots as on upperside." (*Felder*, l. c.)

A single specimen of a *Stictoplœa*, which apparently belongs to this species, was sent by Captain C. H. E. Adamson, from Upper Tenasserim, where it was taken on the 11th February, 1881. It is a male, and differs somewhat from Felder's original description. The *forewing* is shining violet-purple over the whole area to the extreme outer margin, and bears a complete submarginal series of rather small, but prominent violet spots, with a series of smaller marginal spots of the same colour obsolete near the apex; in the *hindwing* the outer border is scarcely perceptibly paler, and the double series of white spots is complete, the outer being rounded or slightly angulate, the inner larger, oval. On the UNDERSIDE the markings correspond exactly with the description, but there is in addition a violet spot on the *forewing* beyond the cell, and above the upper discoidal nervule. It differs from *E. hopei* on the *forewing* in the entire absence of discal spots, and on the *hindwing* in the presence of the double complete series of white spots. Another specimen (male) was subsequently taken at Moulmein by Captain Adamson, feeding at a flowering tree in company with numerous other *Euplœas*, including *E. godartii*, *E. crassa*, *E. masoni*, *E. alcathoë*, and *E. margarita*; and subsequently numerous specimens were taken in the autumn in the Thoungyeen forests, by Captain C. T. Bingham, including one female. These specimens vary much in size, but all agree with the first specimen taken by Captain Adamson, and there can be no doubt that they are the *E. grotei* of Felder. Dr. J. Anderson took one male in January, and two in March in the Mergui archipelago.

The FEMALE only differs from the male in the absence of the sexual marks, and the straight inner margin of the forewing.

78. **Euplœa hopei**, Felder. (PLATE IX, FIG. 18 ♂ ♀).

E. hopei, Felder, Reise Nov., Lep., vol. ii, p. 328, n. 452 (1865); *Stictoplœa hopei*, Butler, Journ. Linn. Soc., Zoology, vol. xiv, p. 302 (1878).

HABITAT: N.-E. India, Sikkim, Naga Hills, Cachar.

EXPANSE: 3·8 to 4·3 inches.

DESCRIPTION: "MALE: UPPERSIDE: *Forewing* chestnut-swarthy, and in certain positions vivid violet-blue; the two usual silky interior spots, a spot within the cell, two median, one subcostal, three beyond the cell, and seven or eight others, larger, submarginal, in a bent series, and from two to six dots before the outer margin, violet-bluish. *Hindwing* deep swarthy, and, except on the paler border, suffused with violet in certain positions; the anterior area with a paler ground, and a concealed pearly whitish costal vitta; submarginal spots white, small, often evanescent, and others before the outer margin obsolete, most frequently entirely absent. UNDERSIDE pale swarthy. *Forewing* with an internal hoary streak, and the two usual internal elevated spots; the subcostal spots, and three discal of the upperside on a darker ground (the lower median one much larger), small submarginal spots in a bent series, and dots before the outer margin, violet-white, circled with blackish swarthy. *Hindwing*, with white basal dots, a spot within the cell, and five or six beyond around it, minute, violet-white, circled with swarthy; the submarginal spots, and dots more or less large before the lower outer margin, white." (*Felder*, l. c.)

Specimens from Sikkim in Colonel Lang's collection have the *forewing* on the upperside deep rufescent swarthy, shot throughout with bright violet-blue; a spot in the cell at end, a small subcostal spot, sometimes absent, an angulate row of four or five discal spots round end of cell, a submarginal row of seven spots, and a few marginal spots from hinder angle, pale violet-blue. The discal and submarginal spots large, especially the latter. *Hindwing* rufescent fuscous, paler than *forewing*, paling towards the margin, faintly shot with violet-blue at the base; the costal margin broadly whitish; a faint indication from the apex of an obsolete submarginal series of white dots. In some specimens this series of spots is very conspicuous, pure white, and not quite reaching the anal angle.

The male only differs from the female in having two long impressed silky streaks on the *forewing*, and the inner margin convex instead of straight; in the *hindwing* of the MALE the submarginal series of spots is almost altogether obsolete; in that of the FEMALE it is rather more prominent. UNDERSIDE paler, rufescent fuscous, darker in the middle of the forewing. *Forewing* with the inner margin broadly white; all the spots of the upperside are represented but smaller, especially in the submarginal row; in the discal series the second from the costa is minute, the third scarcely visible, the fourth large and square, the fifth large and oval. *Hindwing*, with small violet-white dots, a few at the base, one in the cell at end, five discal round the end of the cell smallest towards the costa, three or four submarginal from costal end, one between each pair of nervules, and nine marginal from anal angle, two between each pair of nervules. These two latter series of spots are very variable, in some specimens they are almost complete right round the outer margin of the wing. The female has a bluish-white streak on the interno-median area. In a female specimen from Cachar the submarginal row of spots is very large and white-centred, the discal series is also complete from costa to internal nervure. Mr. Wood-Mason took two pairs in Cachar in June.

The figure is taken from a male and female, showing the upperside, from Sikkim. The specimens are in the Indian Museum, Calcutta.

The two following species have recently been separated by Butler, but the characters on which he bases his distinctions are so excessively variable that it is doubtful whether the separation can ultimately be maintained.

79. **Euplœa binotata**, Butler.

Stictoplœa binotata, Butler, Journ. Linn. Soc., Zoology, vol. xiv, p. 302, n. 7 (1878); *Euplœa callithoë*, Butler (*nec* Boisduval), Proc. Zool. Soc., Lond., 1866, p. 272, n. 10.

HABITAT: Sikkim, Sylhet, N. and E. India, Borneo.

EXPANSE: 4·2 inches.

DESCRIPTION: "MALE and FEMALE: *Forewing* quite as in [*E.*] *S. hopei*, Felder. *Hindwing* with only two white subapical points, all the other spots obsolete. This is the *E. callithoë* of my Monograph, but not of Boisduval." (*Butler*, l. c.)

This is recorded here on Butler's authority as a distinct species, but the single character given in his description as distinguishing it from *E. hopei* is one so variable in the latter species that a distinction based on it should only be accepted with caution, especially when, as in this case, both species occur in the same localities. These remarks apply equally to the following species, *E. microsticta*.

80. **Euplœa microsticta,** Butler.

Stictoplæa microsticta, Butler, Journ. Linn. Soc., Lond., Zoology, vol. xiv, p. 302, n. 6 (1878); id., Trans. Ent. Soc., Lond., 1879, p. 7.

HABITAT : Cachar.

EXPANSE : 4·2 inches.

DESCRIPTION : "UPPERSIDE : *Forewing* like [*E.*] *S. hopei*, except that it is larger, all the spots are considerably smaller, and the purple shot is less vivid. *Hindwing* with only the three first of the discal series of white spots." (*Butler*, l. c.)

A species of *Euplœa*, *E. magnifica*,* has been described from Thibet. It is not clear to which group it should be referred, and Butler makes no mention of it in his revision of the genus *Euplœa*, subsequently published. The description is subjoined for reference.

* *E. magnifica*, Butler. HABITAT : Thibet. EXPANSE : 4 inches. DESCRIPTION : "Female? Wings above bright sepia brown. *Forewing* shot with vivid blue; subapical area densely irrorated with lilacine; a conspicuous subcostal white spot, a second within discoidal cell, and a third on second median interspace, forming together a triangle; a minute whitish point on lower discoidal interspace, and another on first median interspace. *Hindwing*, with a double series of ill-defined, disco-submarginal, pale-ochraceous spots from third median nervule to anal angle. *Body* black, white spotted in front. UNDERSIDE, rich chocolate-brown. *Forewing* with three white spots as above, a fourth oval spot on first median interspace; a small point between lower discoidal, and third median nervules, a subapical point, one submarginal on second median interspace, five nearly marginal points from the third median nervule to the external angle, and some anal-marginal dots on the fringe, whitish. *Hindwing*, with a spot near end of cell, and five unequal spots in a semicircle round extremity of cell, pearly-white; a double submarginal series of yellowish-white spots; fringe dotted with whitish. *Body* black, thorax white-spotted." (*Butler*, Trans. Ent. Soc., Lond., 1874, p. 423.)

NOTE.—Part I, containing the title page, dedication, list of illustrations of Vol. I, glossary of technical terms, preface, introduction, and pp. 21—94, with frontispiece and plates I—IX, reprinted April, 1890.

VOL. I.—Part II.

TABLE OF CONTENTS.

(FAMILY NYMPHALIDÆ—*Continued.*) *Page.*

SUBFAMILY II.—SATYRINÆ, Bates. (PLATES X TO XVII INCLUSIVE.)

Satyrinæ, Bates, Journ. Ent., vol. ii, p. 176 (1864); *Satyridæ*, Swainson, Cab. Cycl., pp. 86, 93 (1840); id., Westwood, Gen. D. L., p. 352 (1850-52).

"BODY, generally small and weak. HEAD, small. *Eyes*, naked, or hairy. *Antennæ* generally short and slender, variable in the form of the club. *Labial palpi* very much compressed, more or less elongated and erect, and clothed in front [in the typical genera] with long porrected hairs. WINGS comparatively large, weak in structure, and generally ocellated on the underside. FOREWING, often with the nervures at the base swollen; the subcostal nervure with its branches free; the first and second emitted [except in *Ypthima* and *Ragadia*] before the anterior extremity of the discoidal cell, which is generally long and always closed. HINDWING with the discoidal cell closed, and not preceded by a prædiscoidal cell; the anal margin forming a gutter for the reception of the abdomen. FORELEGS, very small, those of the MALE brush-shaped, with exarticulate tarsi; and those of the FEMALE rather longer, more scaly, and with the tarsi articulated; claws of the HINDLEGS often bifid."

"LARVA, attenuated at the extremity of the body, and almost pisciform,* tomentose,† terminated by two more or less prominent anal points; the head rounded, sometimes emarginate or bifid, or sometimes surmounted by two spines. Generally graminivorous. PUPA, short, cylindric, not (or scarcely) angulated, and not gilt; suspended by the tail." (*Westwood*, l. c.)

"The *Satyrinæ* are found almost all over the globe, being very numerous in temperate climates; they are usually dull brown or blackish in colouration, occasionally with yellowish or white patches, and on the underside often ocellated and beautifully variegated. Their flight is usually weak and irregular, and they frequent low herbage; many species affect meadows and open grassy slopes, and a large number are found in woods and shady dells, often settling upon dead leaves, and in accordance with their sombre colouring seem less dependent on sunshine than the gaudy Butterflies are, being often seen on the wing on cloudy and even rainy days when no other Butterflies venture forth. They are distinguished typically by their elongate and very hairy palpi, but this feature is not constant throughout all the genera, as shown in the key which follows, and also by the want of a prædiscoidal cell in the hindwing; while the base of one or more of the nervures of the forewing is, in many genera, dilated. The caterpillars live almost entirely on grasses, and feed only during the night.

The *Satyrinæ* are connected on the one hand with *Euplœa* through *Zethera*, a very aberrant form; and on the other hand with *Elymnias* through *Melanitis* and *Parantirrhœa*. The arrangement of the genera here adopted differs from that in Kirby's Synonymic Catalogue, which appears to be founded on Horsfield's system published in 1857. It also differs from that of Butler's Catalogue of the *Satyridæ* in the British Museum, published in 1868, and from that of his "Essay towards an arrangement of the genera" published the same year in the *Entomologist's Monthly Magazine*, (vol. iv, p. 193). The primary characters on which the arrangement should be based are not easy to determine; the clothing of the palpi is probably the most important; on it the present arrangement is based, and to meet it genera are grouped together which exhibit divergencies in other characters; but after careful study of all the Indian genera, the grouping adopted appears to be the best approximation to the natural order.

---

* PISCIFORM, fish-shaped. † TOMENTOSE, woolly.

*

Key to the Indian Genera of SATYRINÆ.

A. With the apex of the cell of the *hindwing* at, or close to, the origin of the second median branch, usually appearing as if the latter were a continuation of the lower disco-cellular nervule.*

a. With the palpi clothed in front with short dense *appressed* hairs.

*a*¹. With the costal nervure only of forewing scarcely perceptibly swollen at base; the eyes naked.

*a*². The hindwing short; rounded, without ocelli.

V.—ZETHERA.

*b*². The hindwing rather elongate, rounded, with ocelli on both sides.

VI.—ANADEBIS.

*b*¹. With the costal nervure of forewing perceptibly, the subcostal and median scarcely perceptibly swollen at the base; the eyes naked.

VII.—CŒLITES.

b. With the palpi clothed in front with moderate or rather short *porrect* hairs.

*a*¹. With the median and submedian nervures usually much swollen at base in addition to the costal nervure, but variable; eyes of *Orsotriæna* naked, of all others hairy: males with one or more scent-pouches on the wings.

VIII.—MYCALESIS.*

*b*¹. With the costal nervure of forewing perceptibly, the subcostal and median scarcely perceptibly swollen at base.

*a*². The eyes naked; the hindwing caudate; of large size.

IX.—NEORINA.

*b*². The eyes hairy.

*a*³. The hindwing usually angulate, often caudate; the underside much variegated.

X.—LETHE. *
XI.—ZOPHOESSA.
XII.—NEOPE.

*b*³. The hindwing rounded or slightly quadrate; the markings of the underside much the same as on the upperside.

XIII.—ORINOMA.
XIV.—RHAPHICERA.

*c*¹. With the costal nervure of forewing greatly, and the median slightly swollen at base. The eyes hairy.

XV.—PARARGE.
XVI.—AMECERA. †

B. With the apex of the cell of the *hindwing* considerably beyond the origin of the second median branch, except in *Ragadia*; the eyes in all naked.

a. With the palpi clothed in front with long porrect hairs.

*a*¹. With the *costal* and *median* nervures of the forewing swollen at the base, except in *Aulocera*, and in many species of *Ypthima*, in which the swelling is scarcely perceptible in the median nervure.

*a*². With the abdominal margin of hindwing not incised, the outer margin scalloped.

XVII.—HIPPARCHIA.

*b*². With the nervures scarcely swollen at base; otherwise as in *Hipparchia*.

XVIII.—AULOCERA.

*c*². With the abdominal margin of hindwing incised; the outer margin scalloped near anal angle.

XIX.—EPINEPHELE.

*d*². With the abdominal margin slightly incised; the outer margin even. The second subcostal branch in the *forewing originating beyond the cell*.

XX.—YPTHIMA.

*b*¹. With only the costal nervure swollen at the base.

*a*². With the wings rather elongate, somewhat denuded of scales.

---

* See separate keys to the subgenera of *Mycalesis and Lethe*, in which the variations which occur in the position of the apex of the cell in the hindwing are pointed out.

† The form of the cell in the hindwing of *Amecera* is almost identical with that of *Nissanga*, a subgenus of *Mycalesis*; in both the origin of the second median nervule is *beyond* the apex of the cell.

a^3. With the lower disco-cellular nervule in the hindwing close to the base of the wing; the second subcostal branch in the forewing *originating beyond the cell.*

XXI.—RAGADIA.

b^3. Outer margin of *forewing* concave, of *hindwing* dentate and slightly caudate.

XXII.—ERITES.

c^3. Outer margin even or but slightly scalloped: discoidal cell narrow and elongate in both wings.

XXIII.—ŒNEIS.

b^2. With the wings broad and rounded; outer margin even or very slightly sinuate in hindwing.

a^3. The costa of forewing much arched from the base.

XXIV.—EREBIA.

XXV.—CALLEREBIA.

b^3. With no ocelli visible on the upperside, except by transparency; those of the underside prominent; inner margin of forewing shorter than in *Erebia*.

XXVI.—ZIPŒTES.

b. With the palpi clothed in front with short dense appressed scaly hairs, and perceptibly tufted behind; the hindwing caudate; the nervures of forewing not swollen at base.

a^1. With the submedian nervure of forewing reaching the hinder angle, and the first median branch reaching the outer margin considerably above it.

XXVII.—MELANITIS.

XXVIII.—HIPIO.

XXIX.—CYLLOGENES.

b^1. With the submedian nervure of forewing short and curved, the first median branch terminating at the hinder angle.

XXX.—PARANTIRRHŒA.

The genera of the *Satyrinæ* are structurally very closely related to each other; but in addition to the structural distinctions noted above each genus exhibits a distinctive style of colouration and markings, which, though sometimes difficult to define, is generally unmistakable to the experienced eye; thus in *Mycalesis* the underside almost invariably has a straight transverse band across the middle of both wings, with a more or less prominent series of ocelli beyond it; in *Lethe* the basal area on the underside is usually either irregularly or not at all variegated; while in *Zophoessa* it is usually ornamented with straighter transverse lines; in *Hipparchia* and the allied groups the upper surface is usually brown, variegated with yellowish brown; in *Aulocera* the upper surface is black with a white transverse common stripe; in *Erebia* the upperside is dark brown, sometimes with ferruginous patches and an ocellus at apex of forewing; in *Ypthima* the upper surface is more uniform lighter brown, and the ocellus at the apex in it and in *Callerebia* is always bipupilled; and so on. Many of the genera comprise but a single species, such as *Anadebis*, *Orinoma*, *Cyllogenes* and *Parantirrhœa*; others again have only one representative within Indian limits, such as *Zethera*, *Pararge*, *Erites*, *Œneis* and *Ragadia*, or only two or three, such as *Cœlites*, *Neorina*, *Rhaphicera* and *Zipœtes*; the genera which contain the greatest number of species, such as *Mycalesis*, *Lethe*, and *Melanitis*, have been recently divided off into several groups, some of which depend, as in the case of the divisions of *Danais* and *Euplœa*, on the presence and position of scent-pouches and tufts of hair on the wings of the male insect. Some few of the genera are purely Indian; others are Asiatic and Malayan; and again others belong only to the Palæarctic region, and occur within our limits only in the mountains on the north and west.

Genus 5.—ZETHERA, Felder. (PLATE XIV.)

Zethera, Felder, Neues Lep., p. 26, n. 61 (June, 1861); *Amechania*, Hewitson, Ex. Butt., vol. ii, pl. i (July, 1861).

"BODY rather large, quadrate; abdomen small and slender. *Eyes* small, smooth. *Palpi* long, densely clothed with scales throughout, pressed closely to the head, where they are clothed with long white hair. ANTENNÆ of moderate length, slender, very slightly thickened towards the point, the articulations distinctly seen. FOREWING large; the costal margin arched, apex rounded, outer margin sinuated at the middle. *Costal nervure* reaching to beyond the middle of the wing; *subcostal nervure* with four branches, the first and second near together before the end of the discoidal cell, the third and fourth at a distance from the other two, equidistant from each other and the apex; *discoidal cell* short; *upper disco-cellular nervule* very short, inclining outwards; *middle disco-cellular* also short, somewhat longer than the upper, forming an obtuse angle with it; *lower disco-cellular* long, curved inwardly [in Z. *diademoides* it is nearly straight], four times the length of the other two together, united to the third branch of the median nervure at a distance from its base. HINDWING oblong circular; *præcostal nervure* curved inwardly; *costal nervure* joining the costal margin at half its length; *subcostal nervure* with its first branch arising at less than a third of the length of the wing; the *discoidal cell* short and broad; the *upper disco-cellular nervule* arising a little below the first branch from the subcostal nervure, short, inclining outwards, the lower three times its length, curved, joining the third median nervule [at or] a very little beyond its base. FORELEGS, short, robust; the *tibiæ* and *tarsi* equally thick, clothed with bristles. HINDLEGS long and slender; the *tibiæ* and *tarsi* slightly spined." (*Hewitson*, l. c.)

Zethera is a Malayan genus; only six species are known, of which four inhabit the Philippine islands, one the Celebes group, and one only is found within Indian limits, where it appears to be a local insect occurring only in Tenasserim, for it is not included in Butler's List of the Butterflies of Malacca (Trans. Linn. Soc., Zoology, second series, vol. i, p. 533, 1876), nor in Distant's "Rhopalocera Malayana." The species from the Celebes, *Z. incerta*, Hewitson, seems to mimic a *Danais*, but the Indian species, which is of a blackish-brown colour with white border spots, appears to mimic some *Euplœa;* it is distinguished by the large and very sharply defined character of the inner row of oval spots on the hindwing; and by having a double marginal series of spots as in many *Danais*. The genus is a very aberrant one, and though clearly belonging to the *Satyrinæ,* it lacks most of the prominent characteristics of that subfamily; none of the nervures are perceptibly swollen at the base, the palpi are not clothed with long porrect hairs, and there is no trace of ocellation on the under surface.

81. **Zethera diademoides**, Moore. (PLATE XIV, FIG. 33 ♂).

Z. diademoides, Moore, Proc. Zool. Soc. Lond., 1878, p. 824, pl. li, fig. 3.

HABITAT: Upper Tenasserim; Taoo, 3,000 to 5,000 feet; Moulai, 3,000 to 6,000 feet; Thoungyeen Forests.

EXPANSE: ♂, 3·0 to 3·2; ♀, 3·25 inches.

DESCRIPTION: "MALE and FEMALE: UPPERSIDE dark brown. *Forewing*, with a submarginal series of seven small bluish-white spots, which decrease in size to the costa; a marginal series of smaller less distinct spots, two between each nervule. *Hindwing*, with a series of six large broad oval spots, [that nearest the costa small, round, the next three rapidly increasing to the fourth, which is largest, the fifth and sixth decreasingly smaller, but still very large]; a submarginal series of small reversely triangular spots, and a marginal series of smaller narrow spots, the two latter series with two of these spots disposed between the nervules. UNDERSIDE, as above." (*Moore*, l. c.)

The type was described from a specimen taken by Limborg in the Expedition of 1876-77. Since then numerous specimens have been taken by Captain C. T. Bingham in the Thoungyeen forests, upper and lower, in March, April and May, and again in the autumn; the spots in these specimens are of a chalky-white, with no trace of bluish in the *forewing*; and on that wing there is usually a trace, sometimes very distinct, of the inner marginal row of spots completing the three series on both wings. The underside is paler and brighter brown, but the markings are identical. The oval spots on the hindwing vary much in size and shape.

The figure is drawn from a male specimen in Major Marshall's collection taken by Captain C. T. Bingham in April, 1880, in the Upper Thoungymen forests in Upper Tenasserim, and shows both upper and undersides.

Genus 6.—ANADEBIS, Butler. (PLATE XIV).

Theope, Moore, Horsfield and Moore, Cat. Lep E. I. C., vol. i, p. 234 (1857), (name preoccupied); *Anadebis*, Butler, Ann. and Mag. of Nat. Hist, third series, vol. xix, p. 50 (1867).

"BODY, with the *thorax* short, hairy; the *head* hairy; the *antennæ* very slender, with scarcely perceptible club, about half the length of the forewing; the *palpi* elongate, erect; the *eyes* projecting, naked. FOREWING large, subtriangular; *costa* strongly arched; *apical angle* rounded; *outer margin* nearly straight; *anal angle* rounded; *inner margin* nearly straight. HINDWING broadly ovate; *costa* nearly straight; *apical angle* rounded; *outer margin* slightly scalloped; *anal angle* slightly rounded. *Nervures* of wing scarcely swollen at base; neuration almost identical with that of *Lethe*." (*Butler*, l. c.)

Moore, in his Catalogue of the Lepidoptera in the East India Museum, placed the type species as *Mycalesis ?*, stating that it "may be separated under the generic name of *Theope*." Butler, in redescribing the genus, notes as follows: "This genus must be placed next to *Neorina*, Westwood, from which it principally differs in the form of the antennæ and the disco-cellular nervules [p. 51]. Although it has somewhat of the appearance of *Mycalesis*, it is totally distinct from it, and is much more nearly allied to *Debis* [=*Lethe*]; in fact the neuration is almost identical with that of the latter genus; but the great size of the typical species, its clubless antennæ, naked eyes, and erect palpi at once distinguish it. In some respects this form seems to be nearly allied to *Amechania*, Hewitson [=*Zethera*, Felder] which should, I think, be placed between it and the genus *Orinoma*, Doubleday." (*Butler*, l.c., p. 50). There is apparently no structural feature by which it can be separated from *Zethera*, except the form of the wings, and as the clothing of the palpi differs from that of *Mycalesis*, *Neorina* and *Lethe*, being further removed from the typical genera of *Satyrinæ* in this feature, its proper place would be, as we have placed it, next to *Zethera*, and before *Mycalesis*, especially as in style of markings, both it and the following genus *Cœlites* present more of the appearance of *Mycalesis* than do either *Neorina* or *Lethe*.

Only a single species is comprised in this genus, which inhabits the north-east corner of India.

82. Anadebis himachala, Moore. (PLATE XIV, FIG. 35 ♀).

Mycalesis (?) himachala, Moore, Horsfield and Moore, Cat. Lep E. I. C., vol. i, p. 234, n. 503 (1857); *Neorina sita*, Felder, Wien. Ent. Monatsch., vol. iii, p. 403, n. 45 (1859); *Ethope himachala*, Moore, Proc. Zool. Soc Lond., 1865, p. 770; *Anadebis himachala*, Butler, Ann. and Mag. of Nat. Hist., third series, vol. xix, p. 51, pl. ii, fig. 1 (1867).

HABITAT: North-East India.

EXPANSE: 2·75 to 3·6 inches.

DESCRIPTION: "UPPERSIDE deep brown, broadly paler along outer margins. *Forewing* with six, and *hindwing* with five ocelli; marginal line deep brown. UNDERSIDE as above, but the *hindwing* with six ocelli, the anterior ocellus large, and the posterior with two white dots." (*Moore*, l. c.). The ocelli are large and contiguous, black with a prominent white pupil ringed with yellowish, then with dark brown, then with yellowish again; beyond them is a narrow edging of the dark brown ground, and beyond that a dark brown submarginal line, bordered on either side with yellowish, the extreme margin being again dark brown The posterior ocellus of the *hindwing* is bipupilled both on the upper and undersides. On the UNDERSIDE the yellowish exterior lines are replaced by whitish lines, and the anterior ocellus of the hindwing is placed back out of line and is much larger than any of the others. The FEMALE is slightly larger than the male, paler, especially towards the apex of the forewing, where there is, in some specimens, an additional small ocellus between the last subcostal nervule and the termination of the costal nervure; and distinctly shows the anterior ocellus of the hindwing on the upperside.

A. himachala is found in Sikkim, Assam, the Khasi Hills, Sylhet, and Cachar; but we have no record as yet of its capture in Burma. It is common in the autumn, and probably at other seasons. Mr. Wood-Mason took it commonly in Cachar in May, July, and August.

The figure is taken from a female specimen in the Indian Museum, Calcutta, from Sibsagar, and shows both the upper and undersides.

Genus 7.—CŒLITES, Westwood. (PLATE XIII).

Cœlites, Westwood, Gen. D.L., p. 367 (1851); id., Distant, Rhop. Malay., p. 45 (1882).

"BODY slender, finely hairy. WINGS large. FOREWING subconcave. HINDWING regularly oval, ocellated beneath, both wings very slightly scalloped. HEAD moderate-sized, finely hairy; *eyes* naked; *palpi* rather small, very compressed, clothed with short scaly hairs, elevated obliquely, but not reaching the level of the top of the eyes, and porrected to a little distance in front of the face; middle joint without a dorsal tuft; terminal joint minute, oval; *antennæ* scarcely more than one-third of the length of the forewing, slightly curved, very slender; gradually, but very slightly, thickened to the tip, forming a very long club but little thicker than the rest of the antennæ, composed of short, scarcely distinct joints, of nearly equal length throughout; *thorax* oval, finely hairy. FOREWING large, triangular-ovate; *costal margin* moderately curved; *apical angle* rounded; *outer margin* more than two-thirds the length of the costal, slightly emarginate, and very slightly scalloped; *hinder angle* rounded; *inner margin* about equal to the costal, nearly straight; *costal nervure* strongly swollen for some distance at the base, extending to the costa opposite the extremity of the discoidal cell; *subcostal nervure* with its first and second branches arising at some distance before the anterior extremity of the cell; third branch arising at about one-fourth of the distance between the cell and the tip of the wing; fourth branch arising about half way between the cell and the tip, uniting with the costa before the tip, the terminal part of the nervure extending to the tip; *upper disco-cellular* arising rather beyond the middle of the wing, very short, transverse; *middle disco-cellular* much longer, slightly curved, and directed obliquely towards the base of the wing; *lower disco-cellular* longer than the middle one, rather angulated at the base, the lower part slightly oblique and directed to the outer margin, uniting with the third branch of the median nervure at a considerable distance from its origin; this third branch being slightly angulated at the place of junction, beyond which it is regularly curved. First branch of the *median nervure* arising nearer the base of the wing than usual. HINDWING regularly oval; *costal margin* curved; *outer margin* slightly scalloped; *subcostal* nervure branching at a considerable distance from the base; *upper disco-cellular* short, curved, forming the base of the discoidal nervure; *lower disco-cellular* much longer, straight, oblique, terminating the narrow discoidal cell at the middle of the wing in an acute angle by its union with the median nervure exactly at the origin of its third branch, which is slightly curved. FORELEGS of the MALE very minute, feathered; *coxa* elongated; *femur* shorter than the coxa, rather thickened at the tip; *tibia* much shorter than the femur, very hairy; *tarsus* extremely short, almost continuous with the tibia, apparently two-jointed; the terminal joint being scarcely visible under a lens."

"The elongate form, the somewhat concave outer margin of the forewing, and the very slightly scalloped margins of both wings are the most evident distinctions of this genus." (*Westwood*, l. c.)

Cœlites is an Indo-Malayan genus, of which only four species and one local subspecies have been described—one is supposed to be confined to north-east India, but the locality is doubtful; another inhabits Burma, extending to Sumatra and Borneo; a third is found in Borneo, with a local subspecies in Malacca; and the fourth in the Celebes group. The two Indian species are very rare, and are both distinguished by a brilliant purple gloss on the basal area of the upperside of both wings.

Key to the Indian species of Cœlites.

A. Both wings elongate, with the basal area of the upperside glossed with brilliant shining purple.

- *a.* Forewing with the outer margin slightly concave; hindwing with the outer margin almost even.
  - 83. C. NOTHIS, N.-E. India.
- *b.* Forewing with the apex more falcate, the outer margin more concave; hindwing angulated at the middle of the outer margin.
  - 84. C. EPIMINTHIA, Burma.

The arrangement of the ocelli in this genus is analogous to that in *Mycalesis*, but the elongate wings and the brilliant purple gloss on the upperside distinguish the species from all other Indian *Satyrinæ* at a glance; the only approach to this colouration being in the male of *Lethe scanda*. Some of the species of *Lethe*, including *L. scanda*, have in the males a tuft of hairs on the upperside of the hindwing below the median nervure at the origin of the second median nervule; a similar tuft is also present in the male of *Cœlites epiminthia*, but it is placed on the submedian nervure; thus showing a further analogy between these genera.

83. **Cœlites nothis**, Doubleday and Hewitson.

C. nothis, Doubleday and Hewitson, Gen. D. L., p. 368, pl. lxvi, fig. 2 (1851).

HABITAT: East India.

EXPANSE: 3 inches.

DESCRIPTION: UPPERSIDE: *Both wings* rich brown, the costa of *forewing* and the outer margins of *both wings* paler; the basal two-thirds brilliantly shot with purple. *Forewing* with two marginal dark brown lines; *hindwing* with two similar lines, but wider apart, and enclosing a band of a lighter colour than the ground. (Described from the figure in the Gen. D. L.) "On the UNDERSIDE the basal half of the wings is dark brown, the apical [outer] half paler, with a pinkish gloss, with several slender brown streaks, parallel with the apical [outer] margin. The *hindwing* is much darker brown than the forewing, and is marked with five ocelli varying in size, the second and the outer one being the largest; they are black, with a minute white pupil, and a fulvous iris surrounded by a narrow brown circle." (*Westwood*, l. c.)

Westwood founded the genus *Cœlites* upon "a single male, not in the best condition." In his figure, however, and also in the description no mention is made of the very conspicuous patch of black hairs and scales on the abdominal margin of the upperside of the hindwing which is present in the male specimen of *C. epiminthia* we possess, and which is probably a male sexual character of insects of this genus; if this be the case the specimen of *C. nothis*, figured and described by him, is a female and not a male as stated. We have never seen a specimen of this rare Butterfly; and it is possible that it may not be Indian after all. "East India," the locality given in the original description, embraces a very large area, and might possibly have included Malayana and the Malay archipelago.

84. **Cœlites epiminthia**, Westwood. (PLATE XIII, FIG. 31 ♂).

C. epiminthia, Westwood, Gen. D. L., p. 368, n. 2 (1851).

HABITAT: Moulmein, Meplay Valley, Upper Tenasserim; Sumatra; Borneo.

EXPANSE: 3 inches.

DESCRIPTION: "Coloured similarly to the preceding [*C. nothis*], *forewing* more falcate; *hindwing* angulated in the middle of the outer margin." (*Westwood*, l. c.)

The male and female specimens of *C. epiminthia* which we have seen differ from the description and figure of *C. nothis* in the *forewing* being less broad, the apex more produced and falcate, and the outer margin more concave; the *hindwing* is also produced into a very short tail at the third median nervule. There is only one marginal line on the UPPERSIDE of *both wings* (in *C. nothis* there are two), which is nearer the margin than in the latter species, and on the *hindwing* it is not bordered on both sides with dull ferruginous. The *hindwing* also bears on the submedian nervure a conspicuous elongate patch of deep black hairs and scales. UNDERSIDE dark brown; *both wings* crossed by a pale violet band, commencing near the costa on the forewing, and crossing the wing beyond the cell; on the hindwing it passes through the outer extremity of the cell, and does not reach the abdominal margin. The outer margin of both wings is defined by a dark fine line, within which are two similar equidistant lines. On the *forewing* within the marginal lines there is a broad band of pale violet. *Hindwing* with five equal-sized submarginal ocelli placed on a pale violet band. The ocelli are black, with white oblique linear pupils surrounded with a ferruginous, and then a brown ring. FEMALE: UPPERSIDE similar to the male, but having a conspicuous subapical lavender band on the *forewing* curving from the costa to the outer margin, along which it is continued till it gradually disappears on the outer margin of the hindwing.

The patch of black hairs on the upperside of the forewing near the abdominal margin in the male is of course absent. UNDERSIDE similar to the male, but the outer violet band extends to the margin beyond the marginal lines, and the third ocellus on the hindwing is decidedly smaller than the others.

Butler in the Cat. Lep. B. M., *Satyridæ*, p. 111 (1868), referring to *C. vicinus*, Felder, from the Celebes, says: "In *C. epiminthia* there are five ocelli in the *forewing*, the second and fifth largest, the third smallest; in the *hindwing* there are also five, the first and last larger. None of the ocelli could, strictly speaking, be described as black; they are olivaceous, with a yellow iris, edged outwardly with dark brown, and they have a diagonal white pupil irrorated with black atoms; these ocelli, moreover, all stand upon a pale violet ground." In making these remarks Butler has evidently misapplied the name *C. epiminthia*, for, as described by Westwood, neither that species nor *C. nothis* have any trace of ocelli on the underside of the forewing; and we have specimens of *C. epiminthia* agreeing with the original description.

Several males of this rare Butterfly were taken by Captain C. H. E. Adamson in the neighbourhood of Moulmein in October, one of which has been sent to us, and Captain C. T. Bingham took a single female in the Meplay valley, also in Upper Tenasserim, in October. Besides these we have no other records of its capture.

The figure is taken from a male specimen from Moulmein, in the collection of Major Marshall, and shows both the upper and undersides.

An allied species, which is considered to be a local subspecies of *C. euptychioides*, Felder (from Borneo), has been described from Malacca by Butler under the name of *C. humilis*;* it differs from both the Indian species in the absence of the purple shot on the upperside, and in the presence of an ocellus on the forewing on the underside.

Genus 8.—MYCALESIS, Hübner. (PLATE XVI).

Mycalesis, Hübner, Verz. bek. Schmett., p. 54 (1816); id., Westwood, Gen. D. L., p. 392 (1851).

"BODY slender, finely hairy. WINGS rather large, plainly and uniformly coloured, those of the MALE generally with a tuft of hairs on the upperside. HEAD rather small; with a small conical tuft of hairs in front. *Eyes* naked [or hairy†] prominent. *Antennæ* scarcely half the length of the forewing, very slender; joints scarcely distinct, terminated by a long but very slender club. *Palpi* porrected obliquely; the tip elevated rather above the level of the top of the eyes, and advanced in front rather farther than the length of the head, very slender; the first and middle joints sparingly clothed beneath with long, porrect, delicate bristles; the middle of the second joint also clothed on the back with a tuft of short hairs; terminal joint very slender, acute at the tip, short, and scarcely setose. *Thorax* rather small, rather compressed, and very convex. *Abdomen* slender. FOREWING with the *costal margin* strongly arched; *apex* rounded; *outer margin* varying from slightly convex to slightly concave, entire, about three-fifths of the length of the costal; *inner margin* about one-fourth longer than the outer, rather dilated in the MALE. *Costal* nervure strongly dilated at the base; *subcostal* nervure with the first and second branches arising before the anterior extremity of the discoidal cell, which extends to the middle of the wing; *upper disco-cellular* very minute; *middle* one longer, curved, rather obliquely directed towards the base of the wing; *outer disco-cellular* much longer, strongly arched, united with the third branch of the median nervure at a short distance from its origin. In the species in which the base of the median nervure is not swollen, the space between its first and second branches is much longer than usual, the

* *Cœlites humilis*, Butler, Ann. and Mag. of Nat. Hist., third series, vol. xx, p. 403, pl. viii, fig. 8, and pl. ix, fig. 2 (1867), *female*; *C. euptychioides*, var. *humilis*, Distant, Rhop. Malay., p. 45, fig. 15 (1882), *female*. HABITAT: Ayerpanas, Malacca. EXPANSE: 3·06 inches. DESCRIPTION: "FEMALE: UPPERSIDE swarthy, the external area of the *forewing* a little darker, of the *hindwing* paler, with an obscure marginal line; *hindwing* with a very indistinct subanal blind ocellus, circled with pale ochreous; the inner margin paler. *Body* swarthy; *Antennæ* ferruginous. UNDERSIDE paler ochraceous, with a wide median band, and another submarginal bearing ocelli, violet; a cloudy discal band swarthy; two distinct irregular marginal lines, swarthy; *forewing* with a small subapical ocellus; *hindwing* with five, the third and fourth small, the fifth large, all black, banded with yellow and beyond that with swarthy and minutely pupilled with white; *body* ochraceous." (*Butler*, l.c.)

† The eyes of the typical African species of *Mycalesis* are naked, but they are hairy in most of the Indian species: see key to the groups.

space between the base of the wing and the first branch being proportionately shortened; in others the base of this nervure is swollen, and the space between the first and second branches as short as usual; *submedian* nervure simple, and curved at the base in some species, which have a slit enclosing a tuft of hairs opposite the origin of the first median nervule; but greatly swollen at the base in other species which have not this slit,* the tuft of hairs in these being placed on the upper surface of the hindwing. HINDWING with the costal nervure extending about two-thirds of the length of the costa; *subcostal* nervure arising opposite the origin of the precostal, its branch arising at a considerable distance from its base; the *disco-cellular* nervules forming a nearly continuous, rather obliquely transverse, termination to the discoidal cell, uniting with the median nervure exactly at, or a little beyond, the origin of its third branch; the *discoidal cell* in some species bears along its outer edge a tuft of long pale hairs, whilst in others it is more generally clothed with numerous shorter hairs; *outer margin* slightly scalloped. FORELEGS of the MALE small; *femur* clothed with scaly hairs, slender, as long as the tibia and tarsus, which are thickly clothed with short hairs. FORELEGS of the FEMALE much longer, slender; *tibia* rather shorter than the femur or tarsus, which latter is articulated, the articulations armed with short spines beneath; the tips destitute of claws. *Four hindlegs* rather long and slender, scaly, destitute of hairs, and with only a few very small spines on the sides of the tibiæ beneath; the tarsi almost destitute of spines, and thickly squamose; the scales hiding the terminal claws."

"The species of *Mycalesis* are distinguished by their uniform dull colours, being generally either black or brown, occasionally varied by a single large eye-like spot on the forewing, with a few ocelli near the outer margin of the hindwing. On the underside they are often marked with a pale slender oblique bar running across both wings, with the ocelli larger, and often elegantly tinged with silver." (*Doubleday*, l. c.)

LARVA and PUPA unknown.

The species present numerous structural differences though maintaining the same general type and style of markings. The African species appear to form a distinct group; and recently Mr. F. Moore (Trans. Ent. Soc. Lond., 1880, p. 155), has divided the Asiatic species into no less than twenty-three distinct genera, of which twelve are represented in India; these divisions, if accepted, must be carried still further as will be seen further on; but as some of the structural features common to both sexes on which reliance is placed in separating the groups, vary in aspect in the sexes of the same species, it is clear that they can only be accepted as generic differences with reservation. The divisions as usual rest chiefly on the structure of the male insect, and especially on the presence and position of the sexual scent-pouches or glands, and the tufts of hair which usually accompany them, and so far as these features go the divisions are more satisfactory. The Indian species of *Mycalesis* come under the following groups:—

Key to the Indian Groups of Mycalesis.

A. Males with a glandular pouch and tuft on both wings.

- *a.* Males with the pouch and tuft on *hindwing* near to the subcostal nervure, and overlapped by the forewing. The eyes hairy. The costal, median, and submedian nervures of forewing much swollen at base.
  - *a*¹. With a glandular patch of raised scales on the middle of the submedian nervure of the *forewing* partly covered by a tuft of long fine hairs.
    - *a*². With the first subcostal nervule of *hindwing* of male much curved upwards at base, then straight; the second very concave from base of first to end of cell.
      I. VIRAPA.
    - *b*². With the first subcostal nervule of hindwing of male swollen at base, and covered on upperside by a tuft of hairs.
      II. GARERIS.
  - *b*¹. With a slight tuft, but no perceptible patch of raised scales on the submedian nervure of *forewing* beyond the swollen base. The first subcostal nervule of hindwing in male not curved at base; the second concave at base and much swollen beneath between base of first and end of cell.
    III. SADARGA.

* And in some also which have it; see VIRAPA, GARERIS and SADARGA.

b. Males with no erectile tuft on *hindwing* near subcostal nervure; but with two recumbent tufts along median nervure on either side. Eyes naked. The costal nervure only swollen at base in forewing.

IV. ORSOTRIÆNA.

B. Males with a glandular pouch and tuft on hindwing only, near to the subcostal nervure and overlapped by the forewing.

a. With the first subcostal nervule in hindwing emitted some distance before end of the cell.

*a*¹. With the second median nervule in hindwing emitted at end of the cell.

*a*². The disco-cellular nervules of forewing very concave; forewing with a tuft of hairs at base of costa overlaying the swollen costa nervure.

V. CALYSISME.

*b*². The disco-cellular nervules of forewing straight; with the hairs at base of costa short, and not overlaying the swollen costal nervure.

VI. TELINGA.

*c*². The forewing broad and short; the outer margin convex.

VII. PACHAMA.

*b*¹. With the second median nervule in hindwing emitted some distance before end of the cell.

*a*¹. The forewing elongate; the outer margin concave.

VIII. CULAPA.

b. With the first subcostal nervule in hindwing emitted immediately before the end of the cell; the second median from *before* the end of the cell.

IX. KABANDA.

c. With the first subcostal nervule in hindwing emitted at the end of the cell.

*a*¹. With the second median nervuie in hindwing emitted *at* the end of the cell.

X. SAMANTA.

*b*¹. With the second median nervule emitted from some distance *beyond* the end of the cell.

XI. NISSANGA.

C. Males with two glandular patches and tufts on the hindwing, placed one near the subcostal nervure and overlapped by the forewing, the other on the submedian nervure.

XII. LOESA.

The foregoing table represents the structural features which define the groups. *Orsotriæna* is very distinct and perhaps worthy of separate generic rank, so also to a lesser degree are *Virapa, Nissanga,* and *Loesa;* but the structural distinctions among the others are comparatively unimportant. In addition to the structural features there are also in many cases different types of colouration which run through the groups, and which are detailed further on.

These are in their habits perhaps the most sedentary of all the diurnal Lepidoptera. They frequent thick herbage in shady places, and rest frequently on the undersides of leaves, seldom taking flight unless disturbed except towards evening, so much so that to secure specimens it is often necessary to beat the bushes to discover them. Upwards of a hundred species have been described, of which some are African and the remainder are spread through Eastern Asia and the Malay Archipelago, extending to Japan, New Guinea, and Australia; a few are found in the valleys of the North-West Himalaya, extending into the mountains of Kashmir and throughout peninsular India and Ceylon in suitable localities, but to the westward of Kashmir they are unknown or unrecorded as yet, in Asia or Europe.

First Group.—VIRAPA: "*Forewing*, with costa arched in the middle, apex convex, exterior margin oblique and even, posterior angle acute; costal, subcostal, and median nervures swollen at the base, first subcostal branch emitted immediately before end of the cell, discocellulars bent inward at their middle, radials from upper near the cell. MALE with a glandular patch of raised scales on the middle of submedian nervure, the patch being partially covered by a tuft of long fine hairs exserted outward from each side of the nervure. *Hindwing* oval, exterior margin convex; first subcostal in MALE much curved upward at the base and thence straight to apex, emitted at more than half distance before end of the cell, second very concave from base of first to end of the cell, upper disco-cellular outwardly convex, lower straight and oblique, radial from their middle; two upper median branches emitted at some distance beyond end of the cell. MALE with a tuft of fine long hairs exserted over a glandular patch at end of subcostal nervure. Antennæ with a well-formed slender club. Palpi uniformly pilose beneath to tip. Eyes very slightly hairy." (*Moore*, Trans. Ent. Soc. Lond., 1880, p. 155).

This group contains only two species, both Indian—the one confined to the Andaman islands, the other inhabiting south India and re-appearing in a somewhat modified form in north-east India and Burma. Both species are dark brown above, with a conspicuous white subapical bar on the forewing; this latter character distinguishes them at once from the other groups.

Key to the Species of Virapa.

A. Males with a glandular pouch and tuft on both wings.

a. *a*¹. *a*². With a white subapical bar on the forewing.

*a*³. With a large ocellus on the upperside of the forewing

85. M. *(Virapa)* RADZA, South Andamans.

*b*³. With no ocelli on the upperside, except faint indications in some specimens of the ocelli of the underside showing through.

86. M. *(Virapa)* ANAXIAS, South and North-East India, Burma.

In describing *M. anaxias*, Hewitson noted as follows: "I have retained this species in the genus *Mycalesis*, although the first disco-cellular nervule of the *hindwing* is very singularly placed, taking its rise from the subcostal nervure near the base of the wing, and, instead of crossing the wing transversely or obliquely, running down longitudinally, until it meets the second disco-cellular nervule at the usual place." The type specimen was from the Nilgiris, but no specimen that we have examined from that or any other locality presents this feature, nor does Moore in the description of his genus *Virapa* notice it; the nearest approach to it is in the species described further on as *M. anaxioides*, though even in this the first disco-cellular nervule takes its rise, not from near the base of the wing, but from immediately beyond the first subcostal branch. It is the subcostal nervure in the male only of *M. anaxias* which, immediately after giving off its first branch, suddenly bows inwards, and then runs "down longitudinally until it meets the" first, not "second disco-cellular nervule."

85. Mycalesis radza, Moore.

M. radza, Moore, Proc. Zool. Soc. Lond., 1877, p. 583, pl. lviii, fig. 2, *male*; *Virapa radza*, id., Trans. Ent. Soc. Lond., 1880, p. 156.

HABITAT: South Andamans (Port Blair).

EXPANSE: ♂, 1·9; ♀, 2·1 inches.

DESCRIPTION: "MALE: UPPERSIDE dark brown. *Forewing* with a narrow, oblique, subapical white band, below which is a large black ocellus with ochreous outer ring and a white central spot. *Hindwing* with a smaller and less distinct ocellus near middle of outer margin. UNDERSIDE brown. *Forewing* with a more prominent white oblique band and lower ocellus, two small geminate ocelli between the white band and apex. *Hindwing* with an outer series of seven prominent ocelli, enclosed within a narrow purple wavy line, the three upper and seventh ocelli small, fourth and sixth larger, the fifth largest. Nearest allied to *M. anaxias*." (*Moore*, l. c.) FEMALE: Larger, and lighter coloured above and below. The subapical band of the *forewing* twice as wide and a purer white, with the posterior subapical ocellus of the *forewing* and the fifth ocellus from the apex of the *hindwing* showing through indistinctly by transparency. UNDERSIDE with a prominent white continuous irregular band commencing at the seventh minute anal ocellus of the hindwing, and joining the subapical band on the forewing, this band being placed behind the series of ocelli on both wings, its inner margin sharply defined, its outer much diffused, widest above the third median nervule of the hindwing, very narrow on the forewing. There is a slight indication of this band in the male.

This species has only as yet been taken in the vicinity of Port Blair in the South Andamans in May, July and August. Though closely allied to *M. anaxias*, it appears to be a distinct species, differing in its smaller size and in the narrower, better defined character of the white subapical band, especially on the underside, where in *M. anaxias* the band extends towards the apex by suffusion with the brown ground.

86. **Mycalesis anaxias**, Hewitson. (PLATE XVI, FIG. 54 ♂).

M. anaxias, Hewitson, Ex. Butt., vol. iii, *Mycalesis* pl. iv, figs. 25, 26 (1862), *male; Virapa anaxias*, Moore, Trans. Ent. Soc. Lond., 1880, p. 156.

HABITAT: Nilgiris, Trevandrum, Travancore, Sikkim, Assam, Naga Hills, Khasi Hills, Upper Tenasserim.

EXPANSE: ♂, 2·1; ♀, 2·4 inches.

DESCRIPTION: "MALE: UPPERSIDE brown. *Forewing* crossed near the apex by an oblique band of white. UNDERSIDE, dark brown from the base to beyond the middle (its border on the forewing angular), followed by a broad margin clouded with lilac and grey, and rufous brown; traversed by three lines of dark brown: the *cilia* lilac. *Forewing* with the white band as above, and three small ocelli, two above, one below the band. *Hindwing* with five ocelli, all black, with white pupils, the iris rufous and indistinct." (*Hewitson*, l. c.). The FEMALE differs from the male in its larger size, broader and more rounded forewing and paler colouration, in consequence of which the ocelli of the underside not unfrequently show through on the upperside. The ocellation of the underside varies greatly in this species, being most developed in Nilgiri specimens, in some of which the hindwing bears seven ocelli, as in *M. radza*, the fifth ocellus is considerably the largest, the first and sixth about half the size, the rest smaller; the fourth ocellus has the largest white pupil, which remains as a white dot in specimens where some of the ocelli are obsolete. In specimens from Tenasserim the white subapical band is as narrow on the upperside as in *M. radza*, but on the underside only appearing as a cloudy white border to the sharply defined deep brown ground; the ocelli too are almost entirely obsolete in the male, the first, fifth, sixth and seventh being visible on the *hindwing* as minute ocelli; the rest including those on the forewing only as very small whitish dots. In the female the ocelli are prominent, but differ somewhat in their proportions from those of Nilgiri specimens, those on the hindwing increasing regularly from the second to the fifth and decreasing to the seventh.

M. anaxias was taken by Limborg in Upper Tenasserim at 3,000 to 6,000 feet elevation. Captain C. T. Bingham took it in the Donat Range in the same locality in January and October, and Mr. Harold Fergusson has taken it in the Ashamboo Hills, Travancore, not uncommonly in March and May at 3,000 to 4,000 feet elevation. It is apparently found only in hilly country.

The figure shows the upper and undersides of a male specimen from Sikkim taken by Mr. de Nicéville in October at 2,000 feet elevation, and now in the Indian Museum, Calcutta.

The next species should, if these groups are to be recognised as generically separate, form the type of a new genus; in colouring it is almost identical with Tenasserim specimens of *M. anaxias*, but the wings are altogether broader and more rounded; in the forewing the costa is comparatively shorter and much more arched, the apex is much more obtuse with a tendency to become acuminate, the exterior margin is convex and nearly erect instead of being straight and oblique, the tuft of hairs over the glandular pouch on the upperside of the forewing is light brown and placed above the submedian nervure, whereas in *M. anaxias* it is black and placed on the nervure lying along it. Further the neuration of the hindwing is widely different; in *M. anaxias* the upper disco-cellular nervule is short, connecting the radial at once with the subcostal at a considerable distance beyond the origin of the first subcostal branch, while in *M. anaxioides* the upper disco-cellular is projected backwards from the base of the radial for some distance, then curving sharply round upwards it joins the subcostal just in advance of the origin of the first branch.

87. **Mycalesis anaxioides,** Marshall, n. sp.

HABITAT : Upper Tenasserim.

EXPANSE : ♂, 2·1 to 2·4 ; ♀, 2·5 inches.

DESCRIPTION : MALE almost identical in colour and markings with Tenasserim specimens of *M. anaxias,* but with the border on the UNDERSIDE duller, lacking the decided lilac and yellowish tints. The seven ocelli of the *hindwing* present, but all minute ; a single, very small, ocellus on the *forewing* above the second median nervule, and above that a series of three or four equally small black dots representing obsolete ocelli ; in *M. anaxias* these dots are white, not black. The FEMALE differs from the male in being paler coloured above and below, and the subapical band on the upperside of the *forewing* twice as wide. UNDERSIDE with the ocelli of the *hindwing* twice as large as in the male, though they are still small, those on the forewing also are more numerous and larger.

Captain C. T. Bingham took two males of this new species in the lower Thoungyeen forests in Upper Tenasserim in May, and one male and a female in March. It appears to affect lower elevations than does *M. anaxias,* but nothing beyond the record of these captures is known of it.

Second Group.—GARERIS : " *Wings* broader than in *Virapa. Forewing* more angular at apex, the costa much more arched, venation of MALE and the glandular patch of raised scales and tuft similar. *Hindwing* with the first subcostal branch in the MALE swollen beneath at its base above the cell, and covered on the upperside by a tuft of hair ; the two upper median branches emitted from end of the cell. Eyes hairy." (*Moore,* Trans. Ent. Soc. Lond., 1880, p. 156).

Key to the Indian Species of Gareris.

A. *a. a*¹. *b*². Upperside of forewing with a large lower, and one or three smaller upper ocelli.

*a*². Underside of both wings with complete series of perfect submarginal ocelli.

88. M. *(Gareris)* GOPA, Sikkim.

*b*². Underside of both wings with incomplete series of rudimentary ocelli.

89. M. *(Gareris)* SANATANA, Kulu, Sikkim, Upper Burma, Tenasserim.

This group contains four species only ; one *(M. francisca,* Cramer) occurs in China, another *(M. perdicias,* Hewitson) is found in Shanghai and Japan. In both the Indian species the median band on the underside is outwardly bordered with pale violet.

88. **Mycalesis gopa,** Felder.

M. gopa, Felder, Reise. Nov., Lep., vol. iii, p. 501, n. 869 (1867) ; Butler, Cat. Lep. B. M., *Satyridæ,* p. 140, n. 57 (1868) ; *Gareris gopa,* Moore, Trans. Ent. Soc. Lond., 1880, p. 157.

HABITAT : Sikkim.

EXPANSE : 2·2 inches.

DESCRIPTION : " MALE : UPPERSIDE fuscous. *Forewing* with a tuft of fuscous hairs above an internal black tuft ; a small subapical ocellus [sometimes with a smaller one above and below it and touching], and another rather large between the first median branches, black, pupilled with white, obsoletely encircled more palely than the ground-colour. *Hindwing* with the external margin paler and divided by a [two] wavy fuscous streak [s]. UNDERSIDE paler, powdered with ochraceous, especially on the paler external margin, which is divided by two fuscous streaks (the inner of which in the forewing is well drawn back), a fuscous basal streak twice bent in the *hindwing,* a streak beyond the middle slender, deeply fuscous, margined outwardly with lilac. *Forewing* with five [or six] black white-pupilled ocelli, circled with ochraceous brown and widely bordered with fuscous, the uppermost, third and fourth minute, the second larger, the lowest large. *Hindwing* with seven ocelli of the same colour in a series nearly parallel to the margin, the second and third smallest of all, the uppermost, fourth and sixth medium sized, the fifth rather large." (*Felder,* l. c.). The female is coloured and marked like the male, differing only in the presence occasionally (not always) of a subanal ocellus on the upperside of the hindwing ; and also in lacking the glandular pouches and tufts.

M. gopa is a rare Butterfly ; it has only hitherto been found in Sikkim. Col. Lang's collection contains several specimens of both sexes taken by Dr. Jerdon, Mr. de Nicéville took a single male specimen at about 3,000 feet elevation in October, and Mr. Otto Möller has recently taken several specimens in the neighbourhood of Darjiling in the same month.

89. **Mycalesis sanatana**, Moore.

M. sanatana, Moore, Horsfield and Moore, Cat. Lep. E. I. C., vol. i, p. 231, n. 489 (1857); *Gareris sanatana*, Moore, Trans. Ent. Soc. Lond., 1880, p. 156.

HABITAT: Kulu, Sikkim, Khasi Hills, Upper Burma, Tenasserim.

EXPANSE: 2 to 2·3 inches.

DESCRIPTION: "UPPERSIDE brown. *Forewing* with a large lower and a smaller upper eye-spot, the latter with a minute one above and below it. UNDERSIDE ochreous-brown; the series of spots white." (*Moore*, l. c.)

In the Indian Museum, Calcutta, are numerous specimens of a *Mycalesis* of this group from Kulu, Sikkim, Upper Burma (Yunan Expedition), and Tenasserim, which agree as far as it goes with the meagre description above. DESCRIPTION: UPPERSIDE brown, with the outer margin of *both wings* paler and slightly greenish: *Forewing* with one, and *hindwing* with two, darker anteciliary lines. *Forewing* with a large black ocellus filling the first median interspace, white-pupilled and with a fulvous iris. A smaller similar ocellus filling the interspace between the subcostal nervure and upper discoidal nervule, in some specimens with two slightly smaller contiguous ocelli in the interspaces immediately above and below it. *Hindwing* unspotted. UNDERSIDE: *Both wings* of an obscure greenish-brown colour, crossed beyond their middle by a common dark brown band, not quite reaching the costa in the forewing, and in which wing it is slightly bent inwards near the costa, nor the abdominal margin in the hindwing. This band is outwardly margined with pale violet. A dark anteciliary line to both wings, within which and rather less than midway between the margin and the median band is a very wavy narrow dark line. *Forewing* with two pairs of dark lines crossing the cell, one near its base the other at its middle. A more or less complete submarginal series of white dots, being the pupils of rudimentary ocelli. *Hindwing* with a similar series of white dots, but the series complete, one between each pair of nervules. A subbasal sinuous dark line. The male differs from the female only in having the sexual characters detailed in the generic diagnosis of *Gareris*.

Mr. A. Graham Young took several specimens in the Kulu valley at the end of May and in June, Mr. Otto Möller has taken it in Sikkim at about 3,000 feet elevation in October, and Captain C. T. Bingham took one female in the Donat range in January; we have no other precise records of its capture. It seems a constant, well-marked species; all the specimens we have seen shew hardly any variation, except in the colour of the median fascia, which varies from almost white to pale violet. The female from the Donat range has moreover the lower ocellus of the upperside very large, and the general colour is paler, especially on the underside, where it has a decided ochraceous tinge.

A species of *Mycalesis* occurs in the Malay peninsula and Borneo, which has been separated by Moore as the type of a distinct genus characterised as follows under the name of *Satoa*, and placed between *Gareris* and *Sadarga*. Genus SATOA. "*Male.*—Wings short; *forewing* more arched than in *Virapa*, apex more rounded; exterior margin less oblique; second subcostal branch emitted before end of the cell; a tuft of fine hair covering a glandular patch below submedian nervure; *hindwing* subconical, exterior margin oblique, anal angle convex, abdominal margin short; a tuft of fine hair covering a glandular subcostal patch; cell short, broad at its end; subcostal deeply recurved at its end, first branch emitted near end of the cell, the second bent downward; disco-cellulars straight, slightly oblique; middle median emitted before end of the cell. *Antennæ* with a slender club; *palpi* somewhat stout; *eyes* hairy." (*Moore*, Trans. Ent. Soc. Lond., 1880, p. 157). This genus or subgenus contains but a single species, *Mycalesis maianeas*, Hewitson.*

---

* *Mycalesis maianeas*, Hewitson. HABITAT: Malacca, Sumatra, Borneo. EXPANSE: Male, 1·9; female, 2·2 inches. DESCRIPTION: "MALE: UPPERSIDE dark brown; the outer half nearly of the *forewing*, and the outer margin of the *hindwing*, rufous brown. *Forewing* with a tuft of hair near the inner margin; the margins of both wings where they meet silvery white. UNDERSIDE dark brown to the middle, rufous brown beyond; the outer margin and two submarginal lines dark brown. *Forewing* with three ocelli, two near the apex minute and touching, the third below the middle, large. *Hindwing* with seven, the first (touching the costal margin), the fourth and fifth, large, the rest smaller, all black, with white pupil and rufous orange iris. FEMALE, like the male, except that it has an orange band on both sides of the *forewing*, and has but one ocellus near the apex. on the underside of the *forewing*." (*Hewitson*, Ex. Butt., vol. iii, p. 87, *Mycalesis* pl. v, figs. 27, 28, (1864), *female*; id., Distant, Rhop. Malay., p. 48, pl. vii, fig. 4 (1882), *female*; *Satoa maianeas*, Moore, Trans. Ent. Soc. Lond., 1880, p. 157).

Third Group.—SADARGA: "*Forewing* shorter, with more rounded and less oblique exterior margin than in *Virapa*, venation similar, but the veins more curved. MALE with a slight tuft (but no perceptible glandular patch of raised scales) on submedian nervure before the swollen base. *Hindwing* very convex externally, first subcostal in MALE not curved at the base; second concave at base and much swollen beneath between first and end of the cell, and with a slight tuft of hairs above; two upper median branches emitted from angle before end of the cell. *Eyes* hairy." (*Moore*, Trans. Ent. Soc. Lond., 1880, p. 157).

Only four species of this group are known, of which two are found in India; both of them inhabit Sylhet in N.-E. Bengal.

Key to the Indian Species of Sadarga.

A. *a.* b^1. Forewing with a very large lower and large upper ocellus on the upperside.

b^2. With the ocelli of the underside of both wings small.

90. M. *(Sadarga)* CHARAKA, Sylhet.

b^3. With the ocelli of the underside of both wings large.

91. M. *(Sadarga)* OCULATA, Sylhet.

90. Mycalesis charaka, Moore.

M. charaka, Moore, Proc. Zool. Soc. Lond., 1874, p. 566; *Sadarga charaka*, id., Trans. Ent. Soc. Lond., 1880, p. 158.

HABITAT: Sylhet, N.-E. Bengal.

EXPANSE: 1·75 inches.

DESCRIPTION: "MALE and FEMALE: UPPERSIDE yellowish olive-brown, outer margins paler. *Forewing* with two very prominent bright-coloured ocelli, the upper one the smaller; and sometimes with two white pupils; the lower ocellus fully a quarter of an inch in diameter. UNDERSIDE pale olive-brown basally, greyish brown externally, divided by a nearly straight transverse discal brown line; two subbasal short zig-gag brown lines on forewing, and one on hindwing. Both wings with a narrow black submarginal line, and a brown fascia or cloud passing through the ocelli. *Forewing* with a linear series of four minute subapical ocelli, and a small, though larger, lower ocellus, the white pupil of which is a half-circle, and occupies nearly the whole of the black portion. *Hindwing* with seven ocelli, the first three subapical, minute, and disposed in a linear oblique series; fourth very minute; fifth the largest (though small); sixth and seventh minute."

"This species is very similar in appearance to *M. gotama* [from China], but may be distinguished by the very considerable difference in the size of the ocelli beneath."

"*Note.*—The specimens of this species in the British Museum collection stand as the representatives of Hübner's *M. otrea* (Zuträge, figs. 79, 80), which name Professor Westwood altered in the 'Genera of Diurnal Lepidoptera' (p. 394) to *ostrea*, believing Hübner's figure to represent a species distinct from Cramer's *otrea;* but I find, after a careful examination of a lengthened series of specimens in the British Museum and others in my own collection, that Hübner's figure well represents a *male* of Cramer's species *(otrea)*, whose figures (pl. cccxiv, figs. A, B) are those of a female. The name *ostrea*, therefore, cannot be retained, as it was applied to Hübner's figure, and *not* to the specimens which Professor Westwood erroneously determined as representing it." (*Moore*, l. c.)

91. Mycalesis oculata, Moore.

Sadarga oculata, Moore, Trans. Ent. Soc. Lond., 1880, p. 158.

HABITAT: Sylhet.

EXPANSE: ♂, 1·8; ♀, 2·1 inches.

DESCRIPTION: "MALE and FEMALE. Similar on the UPPERSIDE to *S. charaka*, the ocelli of the same large size, but the lower somewhat laterally bulged. On the UNDERSIDE the basal area is paler, being of a pale purplish ochreous, the discal transverse line having a much broader yellowish border; the ocelli on both wings are very prominent, and slightly larger than those in *S. gotama*." (*Moore*, l. c.)

There are four males and three females of this species in the Indian Museum, Calcutta, and a single female specimen of the preceding species, *M. charaka*. They were all received at the same time in the same box from Sylhet. The specimens of *M. oculata* shew considerable variation in the size of the ocelli on the underside, and it seems probable that the two species, which occur in exactly the same locality, are really only one variable species.

Between *Sadarga* and the next subgenus *Orsotriæna* are placed two species, *M. sudra*, Felder, from Java and Sumatra, and *M. orseis*, Hewitson, from the Malay Peninsula, Sumatra and Borneo, each of which has been taken by Moore as the type of a new subgenus, of which in each case it is the sole representative. The subgenera are charactérised as follows: DALAPA. "Type, *D. sudra*.* *Forewing* more triangular than in *Gareris*, costa less arched, the exterior margin oblique. MALE with a similar glandular patch of raised scales and tuft on the submedian nervure, but less prominent. *Hindwing* not so broad, somewhat quadrate in form; exterior margin and anal angle more convex, and waved; first subcostal slightly swollen at the base beneath, tufted above; second branch with a slightly raised fold on the upperside extending from first branch to near the end. Club of *antennæ* thicker. *Eyes* hairy." SURALAYA. "Type, *S. orseis*.§ *Forewing* comparatively long and narrow; costa slightly arched; exterior margin oblique, almost straight and even. MALE with a very slight glandular patch (more distinct beneath) sparsely covered with delicate short hairs. *Hindwing* small, oval; exterior margin convex, waved; first subcostal branch slightly swollen at its base, second very concave at its base; cell narrow; disco-cellulars very oblique. MALE with a long tuft of hair covering a glandular patch above base of first subcostal branch. Club of *antennæ* slender. *Eyes* almost naked." (*Moore*, Trans. Ent. Soc. Lond., 1880, pp. 158, 159).

---

* *Mycalesis sudra*, Felder, Reise Nov., Lep., vol. iii, p. 500, n. 868, pl. lxvii, fig. 10 (1867), *female; Dalapa sudra*, Moore, Trans. Ent. Soc. Lond., 1880, p. 159. HABITAT: Java, Buitenzorg, Sumatra. EXPANSE: 2·3 inches. DESCRIPTION: "FEMALE: UPPERSIDE almost as in *M. nala*, but darker as far as the line seen through from the underside, beyond that the two ocelli of the *forewing* very distinct, the submarginal line drawn back but conspicuous. *Hindwing* with two posterior, very distinct, ocelli, the two lines on the margin more wavy, wider, on the paler ground, the inner one broadly palely defined within. UNDERSIDE darker than in *M. nala*, much darker on the disc within the line, which is more distant from the cell than in that species, outwardly defined with diffused whitish, almost straight in the *hindwing*, the ochraceous border broader than in *M. nala*, the submarginal line more drawn back. *Forewing* with two almost similar ocelli; *hindwing* with the upper ones smaller than in *M. nala*." (*Felder*, l. c.)

† *Mycalesis nala*, Felder, Wien. Ent. Monatsch., vol. iii, p. 403, n. 46 (1859). HABITAT: Java. EXPANSE: Not given. DESCRIPTION: "Wings subpellucid. UPPERSIDE (darker in the MALE), with an exterior curved line, and three obscure marginal wavy lines. *Forewing* with two exterior fuscous ocelli (in the MALE tinted more distinctly with yellow) included in a white patch; in the FEMALE with two others between them obsolete. *Hindwing* with a posterior ocellus circled with blackish yellow, marked with a white drop, and some others minute, obsolete. UNDERSIDE brownish fuscous (darker in the MALE), with a swarthy flexuous basal streak (obsolete in the FEMALE), the outer border pale yellowish brown, sprinkled with fuscous dots towards the margin, the exterior fuscous line of the upperside; another adjacent angulate obsolete, a third very angulate beyond, and two others marginal undulate, fuscous. *Forewing* of the MALE with the two ocelli of the upperside smaller and more distinct; of the FEMALE with six unequal exterior black ocelli, pupilled with white and circled with yellow and brown (the first, third and fourth obsolete, the fifth larger). *Hindwing* in both sexes with seven exterior black ocelli, circled with yellow and brown (the fifth largest, the first three and the sixth obsolete in the MALE." (*Felder*, l. c.)

It is not clear to what group *M. nala* belongs in the absence of specimens for examination.

§ *Mycalesis orseis*, Hewitson, Ex. Butt., vol. iii, p. 89, *Mycalesis* pl. vi, figs. 36, 37 (1864), *male*; id., Distant, Rhop. Malay., p. 49, pl. v, fig. 4 (1882), *male; Suralaya orseis*, Moore, Trans. Ent. Soc. Lond., 1880, p. 159. HABITAT: Singapore, Sumatra, Borneo. EXPANSE: 2·1 inches. DESCRIPTION: "MALE: Upperside rufous brown, tinted with lilac. *Both wings* crossed beyond the middle by an indistinct band of lilac (scarcely seen on the *hindwing*), and with two submarginal lines of rufous brown. *Forewing* with two or three very indistinct ocelli. UNDERSIDE: *Both wings* with the basal half rufous, crossed by a line of darker brown, also crossed at the middle by a broad common band of lilac-white, beyond the band yellow (lilac near the apex), with the outer margin and two submarginal lines (the inner line zig-zag) brown. *Forewing* with six ocelli, the first four of equal size, the fifth large, the sixth minute, blind. *Hindwing* with seven ocelli, the fourth and sixth [? fifth] largest; the irides bright orange." (*Hewitson*, l. c)

Distant remarks:—"This species appears to possess the usual variation in macular markings, and is included among the Butterflies of the Malay Peninsula on the authority of the Singapore specimen in the Hewitsonian collection. I have not seen it myself in any other collection from the Malay Peninsula, nor have I been able to examine a female specimen." (*Distant*, l.c.)

Fourth Group.—ORSOTRIÆNA, Wallengren, Kongl. Vet.-Akad. Förh., vol. xv, p. 79 (1858); Moore, Trans. Ent. Soc. Lond., 1880, p. 159. "*Forewing* comparatively shorter, exterior margin less oblique, apex and posterior angle convex; costal nervure only, in both sexes, swollen at the base. MALE with a tuft of fine hairs covering a glandular patch above the base of submedian nervure. *Hindwing* less arched at the base, anal angle convex; first subcostal branch emitted immediately before end of the cell, middle median also emitted before lower end of the cell. MALE with no erectile tuft at the base of subcostal, being replaced by a slight tuft of more delicate and recumbent hairs above and below the median nervure. *Eyes* naked." (*Moore*, l. c.)

The species of this group may be easily identified by several features, in them alone of all the species of *Mycalesis*, the costal nervure only of the forewing is swollen at the base, the median and submedian nervures being simple; in the MALES the tufts of hair on the hindwing are placed by the median nervure instead of by the subcostal, and in both sexes the white band of the underside is on an uniform ground, while in most of the other species the ground-colour is darkest along the inner edge of the line. In this group alone of all the Indian *Mycalesis* the eyes are naked, and the tuft of hairs on the hindwing of the males overlapped by the inner margin of the forewing is absent. It is apparently well worthy of generic separation. Six species are known, and the group extends through the Malay Archipelago to the New Hebrides, New Ireland, and also to Hainan.

Key to the Indian species of Orsotriæna.

A. Males, with a glandular pouch and tuft on both wings.

- *b, a*[1] With the white band of the underside narrow and nearly uniform in width throughout.
  - *a*[2] With the ocelli very large, prominent.
    - 92. M. *(Orsotriæna)* MEDUS, North-India, Burma, Orissa, Nicobars.
  - *b*[2] With the ocelli small, obsolescent.
    - 93. M. *(Orsotriæna)* RUNEKA, North-India, Burma.
- *b*[1] With the white band very wide, widest at the middle.
  - *a*[2] With all the ocelli large, prominent.
    - 94. M. *(Orsotriæna)* MANDATA, South-India, Ceylon.
  - *b*[2] With the ocelli smaller, those of the *forewing* obsolescent.
    - 95. M. *(Orsotriæna)* MANDOSA, South-India.

92. **Mycalesis medus,** Fabricius.

Papilio medus, Fabricius, Syst. Ent., p. 488, n. 198 (1775); *P. hesione*, Cramer, Pap. Ex., vol. 1, pl. xi, figs. C, D (1775); *id.*, Herbst, Pap., pl. cxciii, figs. 4, 5 (1796); *Mycalesis hesione*, Hübner, Verz. bek. Schmett., p. 55, n. 525 (1816); *id.*, Butler, Cat. Fab. Lep. B. M., p. 34, n. 11 (1868); *Orsotriæna hesione*, Wallengren, Kongl. Vet.-Akad. Förh., vol. xv, p. 80 (1858); *Papilio doris*, Cramer, Pap. Ex., vol. iv, pl. ccclxii, fig. C (1781); *P. hamilcar*, Herbst, Pap., pl. cxciii, fig. 3 (1796); *Orsotriæna medus*, Moore, Trans. Ent. Soc. Lond., 1880, p. 160; *Mycalesis medus*, Distant, Rhop. Malay., p. 49, pl. iv, fig. 8 (1882), *male*.

HABITAT: Plains of North-India, Sikkim, Assam, Cachar, Sylhet, Burma, Upper Tenasserim, Orissa, Nicobars, Malayana.

EXPANSE: 1·8 to 2·3 inches.

DESCRIPTION: "UPPERSIDE, *both wings* fuscous, unmarked. UNDERSIDE fuscous, with a common white streak which reaches neither to the costa of the forewing nor to the inner margin of the hindwing. *Forewing* with two black ocelli, with yellow iris and white pupil. *Hindwing* with three; the third smaller." (*Fabricius*, l. c.)

The above is translated from the original description of *M. medus*. The following is Godart's description of *M. hesione*, Cramer: "UPPERSIDE obscure brown without markings. UNDERSIDE with a common white streak and some ocelli, each surrounded with a plumbeous circle, two on the *forewing*, and three on the *hindwing*, of which one is small." (*Godart*, Enc. Méth., vol. ix, pp. 468 and 510 (1819).

The Indian specimens correspond best with *M. hesione*, as in all the species of this group in India there are indications more or less prominent of a plumbeous band round each ocellus, except perhaps in *M. runeka*; but there can be little doubt that the two descriptions indicate the same species, which stands as *M. medus*, Fabricius.

On the UPPERSIDE the median white bar of the underside is usually faintly visible on both wings, which are otherwise without markings, except two marginal whitish fine lines, the inner one less distinct and more waved than the other. On the UNDERSIDE of the *forewing* there is a subapical ocellus, and a larger one below it placed between the two lower median nervules, and extending beyond them. The *hindwing* has a small ocellus placed between the subcostal branches, a larger contiguous ocellus placed below it, and a third sub-equal with the second, between the two lower median nervules and extending beyond them; all these ocelli are black with a white pupil, rufous iris, then a ring of the brown ground-colour, and lastly surrounded with an outer plumbeous ring. This latter ring does not extend completely round the two upper ocelli of the hindwing, but forms one common margin to both, constricted where the two ocelli join. The median white band does not quite reach the costa on the forewing, nor the abdominal margin in the hindwing, and is widest at the costal margin of the hindwing. The FEMALE is somewhat paler coloured above and below; the ocelli are rather larger, the marginal lines more distinct, and the sexual tufts of hair, &c., are of course absent.

Some specimens from Sibsagar, Assam, have the margin of both wings on the underside, but more especially on the hindwing, thickly irrorated with white scales between the ocelli and the two fine marginal whitish lines.

M. medus is common in the Nicobars from August to November, and probably throughout the year. Mr. Wood-Mason took it in Cachar in May, Mr. Oates at Pegu in the same month, and Dr. Anderson in the Mergui archipelago in December and March. Colonel Lang's collection contains specimens from Oudh and also from Umballa; the latter is probably its most westerly limit of distribution. Mr. Otto Möller has taken it in the Sikkim tarai in August and September, and Mr. Taylor at Khurdah, Orissa, in November.

A closely allied species which appears to be distinct, though placed as a synomym of *M. medus* by Moore and Distant, has been described by Butler under the name of *M. cinerea.** It inhabits the Malay peninsula.

93. **Mycalesis runeka**, Moore. (PLATE XVI, FIG. 56 ♂).

M. runeka, Moore, Horsfield and Moore, Cat. Lep. E. I. C., vol. i, p. 234, n. 501 (1857); *Orsotriæna runeka*, Moore, Trans. Ent. Soc. Lond., 1880, p. 160.

HABITAT: Plains and hills of N.-E. India, British Burma.

EXPANSE: 2·1 to 2·3 inches.

DESCRIPTION: "UPPERSIDE uniform dark brown. UNDERSIDE dark brown, paler along the exterior margins; a transverse yellowish-white band crossing both wings. *Forewing* with two, *hindwing* with three pale-brown ocelli." (*Moore*, l. c., in Cat. Lep. E. I. C.) The FEMALE is similar in colour and markings, but lacks the sexual pouches and tufts of hair.

M. runeka is similar in colour to *M. medus* on the upperside, but the small obsolescent ocelli of the underside, especially of the forewing, serve to distinguish it from the latter. Some specimens from Sikkim and Sibsagar, Assam, have the outer margin of both wings, and especially the hindwing, between the ocelli and the two fine marginal dark-brown lines, thickly irrorated with greyish scales. There is a male specimen in the Indian Museum, Calcutta, two from Shillong in Mr. de Nicéville's collection, and others from Tenasserim in Major Marshall's collection, in which the median band of the underside has almost entirely disappeared, leaving hardly

* *Mycalesis cinerea*, Butler. HABITAT: Singapore. EXPANSE: 1·94 inches. DESCRIPTION. "MALE: UPPERSIDE obscure brown, marbled with silky whitish all over, but especially on the *forewing*; a very indistinct oblique median band of the same colour. BODY cinereous. UNDERSIDE coloured almost as in *M. hesione*, [=*M. medus*] but ashy-fuscous, the white band shortened, the marginal line cinereous not white; the marginal band wider, dilated at the anal angle; the submarginal line more whitish, the ocelli smaller; the irides brownish and more slender, with all the cinctures more conspicuous and partly snow white."

"Nearly allied to *M. hesione*, [=*M. medus*] but grey, not brown, and with paler marblings above, and different marginal lines below; the ocellus-zones also brighter and varied with white." (*Butler*, Ann. and Mag. of Nat. Hist., third series, vol. xx, p. 401, pl viii, fig. 9 (1867), *male*.

anything but its dark inner margin; the ocelli are also almost rudimentary. In Burma it is not uncommon from January to May, and possibly in other months. Captain C. T. Bingham has taken it in the Donat range, and at Meplay and various places in the Thoungyeen valley; Mr. C. T. Hill tookit at Tavoy in March; Mr. Wood-Mason took it in Cachar in April; and Dr. Anderson in the Mergui Archipelago in December. In the neighbourhood of Calcutta it is not uncommon in November; and it is also recorded from the Khasi hills, Sikkim, where Mr. de Nicéville has taken it in October, and the Dehra Doon, but it appears to be unknown in the south.

The figure shows the upper and undersides of a male specimen in Major Marshall's collection taken in the Barrackpore Park near Calcutta.

94. **Mycalesis mandata,** Moore.

M. mandata, Moore, Horsfield and Moore, Cat. Lep. E. I. C., vol. i, p. 233, n. 499 (1857); *id.*, Butler, Cat. Lep. B. M., *Satyridæ*, p. 139, n. 51 (1868); *M. gamaliba*, Butler, Ann. and Mag. of Nat. Hist., third series, vol. xix, pl. ii, figs. 3, 3*a*, 3*b* (1867); *Orsotriæna mandata*, Moore, Trans. Ent. Soc. Lond., 1880, p. 160; idem, id., Lep. Cey., p. 22, pl. 11, figs. 1, 1*a* (1880).

HABITAT: Malabar, Canara, Wynaad, Travancore, Ceylon.

EXPANSE: 1·5 to 2·1 inches.

DESCRIPTION: "UPPERSIDE brown, with transverse band of underside indistinctly seen through the wing. UNDERSIDE with broad transverse very white band crossing both wings. *Forewing* with two small ocelli, *hindwing* with three ocelli, the anterior being small, and all encircled with a silvery line."

"*Remark.*—Differs from *Mycalesis hesione* [= *M. medus*], on the underside in having the transverse band three times the width that it is in that species." (*Moore*, l.c. in Cat. Lep. E. I. C.) The FEMALE only differs in lacking the sexual pouches and tufts of hair.

The UPPERSIDE has also the two marginal dark lines bordered inwardly with a whitish line as in *M. medus*; and on the UNDERSIDE the same lines but rather more conspicuous, the ocelli are similar in number, size and position, but the yellow iris is narrower and darker, and the external silvery cincture considerably more prominent.

M. mandata is found in Ceylon and in the south of peninsular India. In Ceylon it "frequents open ground at edges of forests. It is found in the plains, and up to about 3,000 feet in the Western and Central Provinces from May to September. Flight slow and for short distances; it settles down among long grass and is easily captured." (*Hutchison*). Mr. Harold Ferguson has taken it in May at Eridge in the Ashamboo hills in Travancore.

95. **Mycalesis mandosa,** Butler.

M. mandosa, Butler, Cat. Lep. B. M., *Satyridæ*, p. 139, pl. iii, fig. 9 (1868); *Orsotriæna mandosa*, Moore, Trans. Ent. Soc. Lond., 1880, p. 160.

HABITAT: South India, Malabar.

EXPANSE: 1·85 to 2·06 inches.

DESCRIPTION: "The largest of the *M. hesione* [= *M. medus*] group. UPPERSIDE coloured as in *M. mandata*. *Forewing* more elongate. *Hindwing* with the margin more sinuate. UNDERSIDE darker brown, the external margin sprinkled with whitish scales; the ocelli placed as in *M. hesione* not as in *M. mandata*; a broad snow-white median band, gradually narrowing towards the costa of the *forewing*, but on the *hindwing* exactly as in *M. mandata*; the ocelli of the *forewing* brown, very indistinct, of the *hindwing* black, banded with fuscous and inwardly bounded with a plumbous lunule." (*Butler*, l.c.) The FEMALE only differs in lacking the sexual pouches and tufts of hair.

A pair, male and female, of this species has been sent to us by Mr. G. Vidal, which were taken at Malwan in the South Concan in March. These are only 1·85 inches in expanse, and though larger than average specimens of *M. mandata* are not so large as *M. runeka*; they have the same marginal lines on the upper and undersides, and the form of the white band is the same, the only distinctions between them and *M. mandata* being in the small size of the ocelli, especially on the forewing, where they are obsolescent; there is no perceptible difference in the position of the ocelli in any of the species of this group.

Fifth Group.—CALYSISME : "Wings short, broad. *Forewing* with the costa arched at base, apex acute in male, less so in female, exterior margin oblique and curved, posterior angle acute ; costal, median, and submedian nervures swollen at the base ; second subcostal branch emitted immediately before end of the cell ; cell broad ; disco-cellulars very concave, radials from two angles in upper near subcostal. *Hindwing* oval ; costa arched at base ; exterior margin convex, dentate ; first subcostal branch emitted and swollen before end of the cell ; disco-cellulars slightly concave, radial from their middle ; two upper median branches from end of the cell. MALE with a tuft of long hairs at base of subcostal covering a glandular patch of scales. *Body* slender ; *palpi* porrect, slender, finely pilose beneath ; *legs* slender. *Antennæ* slender at tip. *Eyes* hairy." (*Moore*, Trans. Ent. Soc. Lond., 1880, p. 161.)

This group comprises about twenty supposed species, some of which are very closely allied if not inseparable ; fourteen have been described from India, but of these we can only admit four as clearly distinct ; and the remainder are found in the Malayan region extending to China on the East and to Australia. There are two distinct types of colouration and markings—first the "*mineus*" type, in which the basal area of the underside is uniformly coloured, many of the ocelli are always prominent, and they are enclosed in groups by fine sinuous lines ; second the "*perseus*" type, in which the basal area of the underside is always more or less speckled or striated ; the ocelli are usually minute, often replaced by white or black dots, and sometimes quite obsolete ; always well separated in all cases ; the transverse band too is less distinct, sometimes barely traceable. Both types present variations in the outline of the forewing, some species having the apex angled, and others having it rounded, with the outer margin more convex.

Key to the Indian species of Calysisme.

B. Males with a glandular pouch and tuft on hindwing only.

- a, a^1, a^2, a^3. With the basal area of the *underside* uniformly coloured ; the single median pale fascia prominent, most of the ocelli prominent, and enclosed in groups by sinuous lines ; five to seven ocelli on the hindwing.
  - a^4. *Forewing* with the ocellus on the *upperside* small, rudimentary, or entirely absent.
    - 96. M. *(Calysisme)* BLASIUS, India, Burma, Ceylon.
    - *M. (Calysisme) samba*, North India, S. Andamans ?.
    - *M. (Calysisme) lalassis*, North India ?, Gilolo.
    - *M. (Calysisme) lurida*, Cachar.
  - b^4. *Forewing* with the ocellus on the *upperside* prominent.
    - a^5. *Forewing* with two prominent ocelli on the *underside*, and often from one to three additional smaller ocelli generally attached to the larger ones above and below.
      - 97. M. *(Calysisme)* MINEUS, India, Burma, Ceylon, S. Andamans and Nicobars.
      - *M. (Calysisme) drusia*, Ceylon, S. Andamans ?
      - *M. (Calysisme) justina*, Malabar.
      - *M. (Calysisme) cepheus*, Penang.
    - b^5. *Forewing* with four small equal-sized distinct ocelli on the *underside*.
      - 98. M. *(Calysisme)* POLYDECTA, S. India ? China.
      - M. *(Calysisme)* NAUTILUS, Malacca.
- b^3. With the basal area of the *underside* more or less speckled or striated ; the ocelli usually minute or obsolete, and all well separated from each other ; the median fascia narrow and often inconspicuous.
  - 99. M. *(Calysisme)* PERSEUS.
  - *M. (Calysisme) visala.*
  - *M. (Calysisme) subfasciata.*
  - *M. (Calysisme) indistans.*

The first species of this group, *M. blasius*, is chiefly to be distinguished from *M. mineus*, which follows, by its usually smaller size and by its having the ocellus on the upperside of the forewing very small, rudimentary, or altogether wanting ; the median fascia on the underside is also narrower and usually tinged with purplish. The ocellation of the forewing on the underside varies in much the same way as in *M. mineus*. We include under the name *blasius* the *M. samba* of Moore, *M. lalassis*, Hewitson, and *M. lurida*, Butler. *M. samba* much more closely resembles the typical *M. blasius* of Fabricius, than do the forms described by Moore in the Lepidoptera of Ceylon and by Distant in the Rhopalocera Malayana under the name of *M. blasius*; in fact these latter forms are indistinguishable from *M. lalassis*, Hewitson. *M. lalassis* is perhaps the most distinct form of all, but Hewitson himself admitted later on that *M. lalassis* was inseparable from *M. samba*, and it is therefore *à fortiori* inseparable from *M. blasius*. The claims of *M. lurida* to specific separation do not seem to have ever been admitted. The various forms do not even appear to be geographical races, *M. lalassis* was described from Gilolo, but that form is the commonest in Burma and Ceylon also, as well as in Northern India. Butler remarks with reference to *Mycalesis blasius* (Proc. Zool. Soc. Lond., 1867, p. 720):—"This seems to be identical with the *M. samba* of Moore; it differs from *M. lalassis*, Hewitson, in having smaller and less distinct ocelli, and not so many in the forewing; it is also rather smaller." He also states (Cat. Lep. B. M., *Satyridæ*, p. 135):—"*M. blasius* is a distinct species closely allied to, if not identical with, *M. samba*, Moore. Westwood, however, makes it a synonym of *M. mineus*."

96. **Mycalesis blasius**, Fabricius. (PLATE XVI, Fig. 55 ♂).

Papilio blasius, Fabricius, Ent. Syst., Suppl., p. 426, nn. 488, 489 (1798); *Mycalesis blasius*, Butler, Proc. Zool. Soc. Lond., 1867, p. 720; p. 718, fig. 4, *male*; idem, id., Cat. Lep. B. M., *Satyridæ*, p. 137, n. 40 (1868); idem, id., Cat. Fabr. Lep., p. 34, n. 10 (1869); idem, Distant, Rhop. Malay., p. 52, pl. vii, fig. 7 (1882), *male*; *Calysisme blasius*, Moore, Trans. Ent. Soc. Lond., 1880, p. 162; idem, id., Lep. Cey., p. 21, pl. xi, figs. 2, 2a (1880), *male*; *Mycalesis samba*, Moore, Horsfield and Moore, Cat. Lep. E. I. C., vol. i, p. 233, n. 498 (1857); *Calysisme samba*, id., Trans. Ent. Soc. Lond., 1880, p. 163; *Mycalesis lalassis*, Hewitson, Ex. Butt., vol. iii, p. 89, *Mycalesis* pl. vi, fig. 35 (1864), *male*; *Calysisme lalassis*, Moore, Trans. Ent. Soc. Lond., 1880, p. 163; *Mycalesis lurida*, Butler, Trans. Ent. Soc. Lond., 1879, p. 3, *male*.

HABITAT: Northern, Eastern and Southern India, Ceylon, Burma, Malayana.

EXPANSE: 1·5 to 1·9 inches.

DESCRIPTION: "Wings entire. UPPERSIDE *spotless fuscous*. UNDERSIDE scarcely paler, with an oblique median white fascia; *forewing* with *three ocelli* beyond the fascia, black, with yellowish iris and white pupil, the middle one minute, the ocelli included in a common kidney-shaped band; marginal line slender. *Hindwing* with seven unequal ocelli enclosed between two wavy ashy marginal lines meeting on both sides, the marginal line slender." (*Fabricius*, l. c. in Ent. Syst.)

Var. *samba*. "UPPERSIDE dark-brown, exterior margins paler; narrow marginal line black. UNDERSIDE with transverse white line; *forewing* with *two ocelli*; *hindwing* with seven ocelli, the anterior second and third very small; exterior margins pale, with narrow marginal lines." (*Moore*, l. c., in Cat. Lep. E. I. C.)

Var. *lalassis*. "MALE: UPPERSIDE rufous brown, paler at the outer margins, which have near them a line of brown. *Forewing* with a minute white spot opposite the lowest ocellus of the underside. UNDERSIDE rufous brown; *both wings* crossed at the middle by a narrow band of lilac-white; both with two submarginal lines, and a very fine line which borders the ocelli (not singly but all together), lilac-white. *Forewing* with *four ocelli*, the first two touching, the fourth the largest. *Hindwing* with seven, the second, third and sixth [? seventh] minute." (*Hewitson*, l. c., in Ex. Butt.)

Var. *lurida*. "MALE allied to *M. lalassis*, but the basal half of the *forewing* both on upper and undersides suffused with lurid ochraceous; the white stripe of the UNDERSIDE reduced to a slender brown-edged squamous white line, the third of the four ocelli of the *forewing* reduced in size, and only the two first united." (*Butler*, l. c., in Trans. Ent. Soc. Lond.)

The commonest form of the species is well described as follows by Moore in the Lep. Ceylon:—

DESCRIPTION: "MALE and FEMALE: UPPERSIDE dark brown glossed with olive-brown. *Forewing* with or without a discal small white-pupilled black spot. UNDERSIDE dark uniform vinous-brown, with a narrow purple-white discal band crossing *both wings*, and two marginal lunular lines. *Forewing* with four ocelli, the three upper ones small, all encircled by a single purple band, some specimens having a small lower fifth ocellus, which is also encompassed within the single purple band. *Hindwing* with seven ocelli, the second and third upper and the seventh the smallest, all being encircled by a single purple band."

The ocellation of the forewing on the underside exhibits in this country in addition to the variations above noted, many of those detailed in the description of *M. mineus*. The form in which the upper ocellus has a smaller one below it, and the lower ocellus a smaller one above it, and either all four enclosed in one band or enclosed in pairs by two bands, is very common in Northern India. There are also sometimes five ocelli, owing to the appearance of a minute ocellus beneath the fourth ocellus. The presence of the small ocellus on the upperside of the forewing does not accompany any particular disposition of the ocelli of the underside, but is common to all, and the gradations from a spotless upper surface, to a distinct though small ocellus on the forewing are regular and complete.

M. blasius has a slightly different geographical distribution from that of *M. mineus*. It is common in Burma and North-East India, but has not been found in the Andamans or Nicobar Islands, though it was included, apparently erroneously, in Moore's list of the Butterflies of the South Andamans under the name of *M. samba*.* On the other hand it has a more westerly range in continental India, being common in Oudh as far as Lucknow at any rate, and we have a single specimen from the Punjab. It is also found in Ceylon and in the extreme south of the peninsula, but we are unable to say yet whether it, like *M. mineus*, is found along the Eastern Coast. Mr. de Nicéville has taken it commonly in Calcutta throughout the warm months, and Mr. Wood-Mason took it in Cachar in May and June. In Ceylon it is "found at all times in the western and central provinces; plains and up to 2,000 feet elevation on grassy land. Flight short and slow, along edges of forest-paths and grass land, settling on tufts of grass."—(*Hutchison.*)

The figure shews the upper and undersides of a male specimen taken at Calcutta, and now in the Indian Museum, Calcutta.

In the next species under the name *M. mineus*, Linnæus, we have included three forms that have been named as distinct species—*M. drusia*, Cramer, *M. justina*, Cramer, and the original *M. mineus*. Regarding the distinctions between these supposed species great differences of opinion have been shown by various writers. In 1851, Westwood, in the Gen. D. L. (vol. ii, p. 393) placed both *drusia* and *justina* as probable varieties of *M. mineus*; in 1857 Horsfield and Moore in the Cat. Lep. Mus. E. I. C. (p. 231) placed *M. drusia* as a distinct species, giving *M. justina* as a variety, and *M. mineus* as a synonym of the latter, with a mark of interrogation; in 1868, Butler in the Cat. Lep. B. M., *Satyridæ* (p. 135) placed *M. justina* as a variety of *M. mineus*, and *M. drusia* as a distinct species with the following remark (p. 134): "It seems improbable that this is a variety of *M. mineus* as the position of the central band and the ocelli of the underside are quite different. It is just possible that Cramer's figure is from a broken specimen, which might account for these differences; but there is still a distinctive character in the dark colour of the ocellus-irides and the different form of the marginal lines. Mr. Moore has considered some specimens of *M. mineus* to represent *M. drusia*." In 1871 Kirby, in his Synonymic Catalogue of Diurnal Lepidoptera (p. 89) also retains *M. drusia* as distinct, giving *M. justina* as a variety of *M. mineus*; and again in 1880 Moore, in his Lepidoptera of Ceylon, keeps *M. mineus* and *M. drusia* as distinct species, and describes and figures both; but as he figures *M. drusia* with a yellow fascia on the underside and only four ocelli on the hindwing, while he describes it as having a greyish-white fascia and the hindwing with seven ocelli; and as he figures *M. mineus* with a narrow bluish-white fascia, and describes it as having a prominent broad yellowish-white transverse discal band, his work only adds to the obscurity in which the point is involved.

---

* Proc. Zool. Soc. Lond., 1877, p. 583.

The description of *M. mineus* which we extract in full from the newly published "*Rhopalocera Malayana*," by Mr. W. L. Distant, is the first detailed description of the species that has been published authoritatively; it was taken after careful comparison of the specimens figured, with the Linnæan typical specimens in the possession of the Linnæan Society of London, and may be accepted as conclusively settling the question as to what *M. mineus* really is.

The only authority for identifying *M. justina* is Cramer's figure, a detailed description taken from which is appended for reference* ; the only point in which this figure appears to differ from typical *M. mineus* is in having the median fascia of the underside ochreous instead of white.

Similarly the only authority for identifying *M. drusia* is Cramer's figure, a description taken from which is also appended for reference†. This figure differs from typical *M. mineus* in having, like that of *M. justina*, the median fascia ochreous, and in the absence of the seventh (anal) ocellus in the hindwing on the underside, but neither of these characters can be here relied on as indicating specific differences. The great variation in the ocellation of the forewing on the underside which is detailed further on is not referred to in any of the three original descriptions or shewn in the figures, and with these variations manifested in a long series of what are all undoubtedly the same species, we are unable to accept the absence of a single ocellus on the hindwing as a specific character; and as the white and ochreous fasciæ occur with the same distribution of the ocelli, and the gradations from white to ochreous and to greyish are numerous, we cannot arrive at any other conclusion than that the three belong to one and the same species which stands as *M. mineus*, Linnæus.

97. **Mycalesis mineus**, Linnæus.

Papilio mineus, Linnæus, Syst. Nat., vol. i, pt. 2, p. 768, n. 126 (1767); id., Fabricius, Syst. Ent., p. 488, n. 197 (1775); *Satyrus mineus*, Godart, Enc. Méth., vol. ix, p. 510, n. 97 (1819); *Mycalesis mineus*, Butler, Cat. Lep. B. M., *Satyridæ*, p. 135, n. 31 (1868); id., Cat. Fabr. Lep., p. 34, n. 8 (1869); id., Distant, Rhop. Malay., p. 50, pl. iv, figs. 13, *male*, 14, *female*; and var., pl. iv, fig. 7, *male* (1882); *Calysisme mineus*, Moore, Trans. Ent. Soc. Lond., 1880, p. 162; idem, id., Lep. Cey., p. 22, pl. xi, figs. 4, 4*b*, *male*; 4*a*, *female* (1880); *Papilio drusia*, Cramer, Pap. Ex., vol. i, pl. lxxxiv, figs. C, D (1775); *Mycalesis drusia*, Butler, Cat. Lep. B. M., *Satyridæ*, p. 133, n. 26 (1868); idem, id., Cat. Fabr. Lep., p. 33, n. 6 (1869); *Calysisme drusia*, Moore, Trans. Ent Soc Lond., 1880, p. 161; idem, id., Lep. Cey., p. 20, pl. xi, figs. 3, 3*a* (1880), *male*; *Papilio justina*, Cramer, Pap. Ex., vol. iv, pl. cccxxvi, fig. C (1780); *Mycalesis justina*, Hübner, Verz. bek. Schmett., p. 55, n. 524 (1816); *Calysisme justina*, Moore, Trans. Ent. Soc. Lond, 1880, p. 161.

HABITAT: Throughout North-East, and South India, Ceylon, Burma, Malay Peninsula, Andaman and Nicobar Isles, Sumatra, Java and China.

EXPANSE: 1·8 to 2·2 inches.

DESCRIPTION: "MALE: UPPERSIDE fuliginous-brown. *Forewing* with a very faint, pale, straight fascia, which passes a little beyond end of cell, and from which to outer margin the colour is slightly paler; a black spot with a white centre and a faint ochraceous margin between first and second median nervules, and two marginal fuscous lines, the innermost of which becomes faint and obsolete towards apex; *cilia* smoky ochraceous. *Hindwing* with a tuft of long pale hairs situated near costal base of the wing. Two distinct marginal

---

* *Mycalesis justina*, Cramer. HABITAT: Coromandel Coast. EXPANSE: 2 inches. DESCRIPTION: UNDERSIDE rich brown. *Both wings* crossed beyond the middle by a narrow pale ochreous fascia, not quite reaching the costa in the forewing, and extending to the abdominal margin near the anal angle in the hindwing. The usual marginal wavy dark lines, the innermost bounded inwardly by a paler fascia than the ground-colour; on the hindwing the space between the dark lines is ochreous. *Forewing* with a subapical and a larger lower ocellus, black, pupilled with white, and surrounded with a rufous iris. *Hindwing* with seven similar ocelli, the second, third and seventh the smallest and equal-sized; the first and sixth also equal-sized and larger; the fourth and fifth the largest of all. (*Cramer*, Pap. Ex., pl cccxxvi, fig. C (1780).

† *Mycalesis drusia*, Cramer. HABITAT: Coromandel Coast and China. EXPANSE: 2·4 inches. DESCRIPTION: UPPERSIDE, reddish brown, with two paler marginal lines. *Forewing* with an ocellus placed between the upper median nervules, black, pupilled with white, and with a deep yellow iris *Hindwing* unmarked. UNDERSIDE paler dull brown *Both wings* crossed beyond the middle by a pale ochreous fascia, reaching the costa of the forewing and the abdominal margin of the hindwing. Two marginal pale lines, broader than on the upperside. *Forewing* with an upper and larger lower ocellus. *Hindwing* with six ocelli, the first and sixth equal-sized, the second and third smaller, the fourth and fifth largest. (*Cramer*, Pap. Ex., pl lxxxiv, figs. C, D (1777).

lines, on each side of which the colour is dull ochraceous (in some specimens a minute white-centred fuscous spot between second and third median nervules). UNDERSIDE with the colour brighter and paler; *both wings* crossed by a narrow fascia [pure white in the figures], on *forewing* passing somewhat beyond, and on *hindwing* about end of cell. *Forewing* with two submarginal ocellated spots, which are black, with white centres and yellow margins, the first and smallest situate on the discoidal nervules, and perfectly surrounded by a pale greyish line; the second and largest placed on the second and third median nervules, with a pale surrounding greyish line, which terminates inwardly on the transverse white fascia (both these spots sometimes throw off a smaller one, the upper one generally posteriorly and the lower one usually anteriorly); two pale greyish marginal lines, the inner one waved, and the *cilia* also pale greyish. *Hindwing* with seven submarginal ocellated spots of a similar pattern and colour to those on forewing, of which the second and third are minute, the whole series being surrounded by a much waved pale greyish fascia, which in some specimens tends to coalesce and perfectly surround the sixth and seventh spots; two pale greyish marginal fasciæ, the inner one most strongly waved, and the marginal *cilia* also pale greyish. *Body* and *legs* concolorous with the wings. FEMALE, larger than male. UPPERSIDE, *forewing* with the ocellated spot larger and brighter: *hindwing* with two more obscure ocellated spots situate on the second and third median nervules (there are sometimes indications of the commencement of a third spot between the third median nervule and submedian nervure). UNDERSIDE as in male, but with all the spots and markings larger and brighter." (*Distant*, l. c.)

Distant also enumerates two varieties of *M. mineus* as follows :—

Var. *a. Mycalesis cepheus,** Butler. "MALE: This variety differs on the UNDERSIDE of the *forewing* in having an additional spot in front of the lower ocellated spot, and enclosed by the same pale greyish line; and on the UNDERSIDE of the *hindwing* in having the second and third submarginal spots a little longer, which renders the series apparently a little more arched, as Butler describes."

" Var. *b.*, Rhop. Malay., pl. iv, fig 7. "MALE: Differs from typical specimens on the UNDERSIDE by the lower ocellated spot of the *forewing* having a smaller one attached or non-attached to it beneath, but which is also enclosed by the same surrounding pale greyish line. Mr. Moore (Lep. Cey., vol. i, p. 22) describes a like varietal form as not uncommon in Ceylon, and which is indicated in his figure, plate xi, fig. 4*b*. *Hindwing* with the second and third small ocellated spots of typical specimens totally absent." (*Distant*, l.c.)

Distant remarks of *M. mineus*: "This is a very variable species, but not more so than we might expect, when we remember analogous cases of Satyrid variation in Europe." This is quite borne out by the numerous specimens we have examined. On the UPPERSIDE it is very constant, there being invariably one median-sized ocellus between the two lower median nervules in the forewing; the hindwing in the female shews occasionally one or two subanal ocelli by transparency. The variations of the UNDERSIDE are as follows :—

(a) In the *forewing* with two ocelli, the upper one small, the lower twice the size, each encircled with an outer complete ring.

(b.) The upper ocellus with a smaller one attached beneath it, both surrounded with a single outer complete ring; the large lower ocellus as in *(a)*.

(c.) The upper ocellus as in *(a)*; the lower with a smaller one attached above it, and both surrounded with a single ring.

---

* *Mycalesis cepheus*, Butler. HABITAT: Penang. EXPANSE: 1·87 inches. DESCRIPTION: "UPPERSIDE fuscous, with the external margin, the median fascia, and the iris of the ocellus of the *forewing* paler. *Forewing* with a discal blind ocellus obscure fuscous; a marginal line of the same colour; the margin itself black. *Body* fuscous. UNDERSIDE almost as in *M. mineus*, but with the median fascia more slender and duller; the series of ocelli on the *hindwing* more arched. Closely allied to *M. mineus*, but paler on the upperside, with a brown blind ocellus in the forewing; below with a narrower and straighter central band, and the row of hindwing ocelli much more arched; the marginal lines also pale ochreous." (*Butler*, Ann. and Mag. of Nat Hist, third series, vol. xx, p. 402, pl. ix, figs. 3, 4 (1867). Kirby has included *M. cepheus* as a variety of *M. blasius*; but Distant confirms Butler's view as to its being closely allied to *M. mineus*.

(d.) As in *(c)*, but with a second small ocellus attached beneath the large one.

(e.) The upper ocellus with a smaller one attached beneath it; and the lower ocellus with a smaller one above it, all four encircled with one outer ring.

(f.) As in *(e)*, but with a small ocellus beneath the lower ocellus, making five in all.

(g.) The median band is also variable in width and distinctness, and varies in colour from pure white to dull ochreous and in some specimens to greyish white.

In the *hindwing* the second and third ocelli are sometimes entirely wanting (usually in Andaman specimens, sometimes also in Nicobar and continental Indian examples); in some specimens they are rudimentary, in others distinct and equal to the seventh anal one in size. Occasionally, but very rarely, the seventh (anal) ocellus is obsolete. The Andaman specimens referred to above are the *M. drusia* of modern writers; some specimens agree fairly well with the figure of that species. They have the fascia always ochreous, and a male specimen sent to Mr. Moore for identification, with the second and third ocelli on the underside of the hindwing absent, has been named *M. justina* by him, but it does not agree with Cramer's figure of that species, as the latter has all the ocelli present.

M. mineus has been taken in Naini Tal and Mussoorie in the North-West Himalayas, and is found throughout India, except in the dry North-West, extending through the Malay Peninsula in the regions of heavy rainfall. We have specimens from Tenasserim, Pegu, Sylhet, Cachar, the Naga Hills, Assam, Sikkim, Calcutta, Bombay, the Godaveri districts, Travancore, Ceylon, the Andaman and Nicobar islands. The specimens from the Andamans are fairly constant having usually two ocelli on the forewing and the median fascia ochreous; the Nicobar specimens are more variable like those from Continental India. Mr. Otto Möller has taken numerous specimens in the Sikhim tarai from July to September, and in the Sikhim Hills in May and August; also Mr. Wood-Mason in Cachar between those months. We have specimens from the Godavari District, Travancore and Ceylon, which have the median fascia on the underside very narrow and pure white; they are also of very small size, 1·8 inches only in expanse. Typical specimens with a white fascia also occur in the Malay peninsula.

98. **Mycalesis polydecta,** Cramer.

Papilio polydecta, Cramer, Pap. Ex., vol. ii, pl. cxliv, figs. E, F (1777); *Mycalesis polydecta*, Butler, Ann. and Mag. of Nat. Hist., third series, vol. xx, p. 402, pl. ix, figs. 5, 6 (1867), *female*; idem, id., Cat. Lep. B. M., *Satyridæ*, p. 135, n. 33 (1868); idem, id., Cat. Fabr. Lep. B. M., p. 34, n. 9 (1869); *Calysisme polydecta*, Moore, Trans. Ent. Soc. Lond., 1880, p. 162.

HABITAT: Tranquebar? (Cramer), Burma, Sumatra, Borneo, Celebes.

EXPANSE: 2·2 inches.

DESCRIPTION: "UPPERSIDE fuscous, with the margins slightly paler; *forewing* with a large ocellus; *hindwing* with two smaller ocelli, the inner the larger of the two. UNDERSIDE paler, with a whitish median fascia, the outer area bearing ocelli, five on the *forewing*, seven on the *hindwing*; the outer margin pale with black lines."

"Cramer gives the locality of this species as Tranquebar; but I have a specimen, exactly agreeing with his figure, from Borneo. In the British Museum we have it from Celebes, and a variety from Sumatra without ocelli on the upperside of the hindwing." (*Butler*, l. c. in Ann. and Mag. of Nat. Hist.)

We have specimens from Burma which have been identified by Mr. Moore as varieties of *M. polydecta*; they agree fairly well with Cramer's figure, but better still with Butler's figure of this species, and they differ only from *M. mineus* in having a separate ocellus between the second and third median nervules on the underside of the forewing; thus showing either four or five ocelli as follows:—a moderate-sized lower ocellus on the first median interspace, a rather smaller one on the second median interspace, and a subapical one the same size with a smaller one attached below it, and sometimes another attached above it.

With reference to the foregoing note by Butler regarding the British Museum specimens, Distant, in his "Rhopalocera Malayana," (p. 51) remarks:—"Mr. Butler has also included *M. polydecta* in his Malaccan species. The form he has figured (Ann. and Mag. of Nat. Hist., third series, vol. xx, pl. ix, figs. 5, 6, 1867), however, does not agree with Cramer's figure of that species, and from an examination of the Malaccan specimens thus identified in the British Museum I certainly incline to the opinion that such are but varieties of *M. mineus*, and that the true *M. polydecta*, Cramer, cannot, as such, be at present included in this fauna." It is doubtful whether this species really occurs in India either. The specimens from Burma noted above appear to us to be varieties of *mineus* rather than of *polydecta*, and they confirm Distant's view.

A description of *M. polydecta* from Cramer's figure of that species is appended for reference.*

An allied species, *M. nautilus*,† occurs in Malacca.

99. **Mycalesis perseus**, Fabricius.

Papilio perseus, Fabricius, Syst. Ent., p. 488, n. 199 (1775), *female*; id., Donovan, Ins. New Holland, pl. xxvi, fig. 3 (1805); *Mycalesis perseus*, Butler, Proc. Zool Soc. Lond., 1867, p. 719, n. 2; p. 718, fig. 2; idem, id., Cat. Lep. B. M., *Satyridæ*, p. 133 (1868); idem, id., Cat. Fabr. Lep. B. M., p. 33, n. 5 (1869); *Papilio otrea*, Cramer, Pap. Ex., vol. iv, pl. cccxiv, figs. A, B (1780), *female*; *Papilio tabitha*, Fabricius, Ent. Syst., vol. iii, pt. i, p. 243, n. 756 (1793); *Satyrus zopyrus*, Kollar, in Hügel's Kashmir, vol. iv, pt. 2, p. 450, n. 8 (1844); *Calysisme perseus*, Moore, Trans. Ent. Soc. Lond., 1880, p. 163; idem, id., Lep. Cey., p. 21, pl. xii, figs. i, 1a (1880), *male*; *Mycalesis visala*, Moore, Horsfield and Moore, Cat. Lep. E. I. C., vol. 1, p. 230, n. 488 (1857); *Calysisme visala*, Moore, Trans. Ent. Soc. Lond., 1880, p. 164; *Calysisme subfasciata*, Moore, Proc. Zool. Soc. Lond., 1882, p. 237, pl. xii, fig. 8; *Calysisme indistans*, Moore, Trans. Ent. Soc. Lond., 1880, p. 164.

HABITAT: India, Burma, Ceylon, Andamans.

EXPANSE: ♂, 1·75 to 2·0; ♀, 2·0 to 2·4 inches.

DESCRIPTION: "*Papilio danai festivi*. Wings most entire, fuscous. UNDERSIDE with ocellular dots; *forewing* with three, *hindwing* with seven. *Body* fuscous immaculate. *Forewing* fuscous, sometimes immaculate, sometimes with a small ocellus with white pupil before the outer margin. *Hindwing* fuscous immaculate. UNDERSIDE. *Both wings* fuscous at the base, paler outwardly. *Forewing* with three dots. *Hindwing* with seven, white, subocellular. HABITAT: In Nova Hollandia. Mus. Banks." (*Fabricius*, l. c. in Syst. Ent.)

M. perseus is the commonest of all the *Mycalesis* in India, and has a wider range than even *M. mineus*, being found in the north from Burma to Kashmir; and with the exception of the hot dry plains of the Punjab, it is found throughout continental and also peninsular India extending to Ceylon. It is even more variable than *M. mineus*, showing great divergencies in form and size, as well as in colour and markings. There are three well-marked varieties, *M. visala*, *M. subfasciata*, and *M. indistans*, which are usually accepted as distinct species, and which, in certain localities, are widely distinct from the typical *M. perseus* as it there co-exists with them; but an examination of large series of specimens from different parts of the empire leads us to the conclusion that these specific separations cannot be maintained, and pending the discovery of the earlier stages of each form, they must all be considered for the present as varieties more or less specialised of *M. perseus*.

Typical *M. perseus* is a small insect, with the apex of the forewing rounded, not sharply angled. The ocellus of the forewing on the upperside is placed between the first and second

---

* *Mycalesis polydecta*, Cramer. HABITAT: Tranquebar. EXPANSE: 2·2 inches. DESCRIPTION: UPPERSIDE deep brown, outwardly somewhat paler; the margins ochreous, with the usual sinuous dark fine lines. *Forewing* with a medium-sized ocellus between the second and third mediam nervules. *Hindwing* with two smaller ocelli between the median nervules the upper the smaller of the two. All these ocelli black, with white pupil and ochreous iris. UNDERSIDE with the basal area as dark as on the upperside, and bounded by a white medium fascia on both wings, the ground-colour much paler beyond. The margin ochreous with two sinuous darker lines. *Forewing* with four equal-sized small ocelli. *Hindwing* with seven ocelli, all but the fourth and fifth, which are a little larger, equal in size to those on the forewing. The ground-colour of the outer border is pale brown, thickly irrorated with darker brown within the row of ocelli, and beyond it whitish, as far as the inner dark line on the forewing, and extending to the outer dark line on the hindwing. (*Cramer*, Pap., Ex. pl cxliv, figs. E, F (1777).

† *Mycalesis nautilus*, Butler. HABITAT: Malacca. EXPANSE: 1·87 to 2·12 inches. DESCRIPTION: "UPPERSIDE dilute fuscous; *forewing* with three blackish ocelli with scarcely perceptible iris, pupilled with white, of which two are small, subapical, and the third discal; *hindwing* with wavy marginal fuscous lines, and a small blackish subanal ocellus with fulvous iris; the *body* ashy fuscous. UNDERSIDE paler, with the margins as in *M. mineus*; a silvery median fascia, defined with fuscous inwardly and diffused outwardly; a fuscous subbasal line almost entire; *forewing* with five distinct ocelli; the fifth much the larger, arranged in a straight series; *hindwing* with seven ocelli, the first and fourth larger, the fifth largest, the seventh smallest, arranged in an arched series; the *body* ochreous-fuscous. The sexes differ only in size. Closely allied to *M. janardana*, but differing in many essential characters." (*Butler*, Ann. and Mag. of Nat. Hist., third series, vol. xx, p. 402, pl. ix, fig. 7 (1867); *Calysisme nautilus*, Moore, Trans. Ent. Soc. Lond., 1880, p. 162).

median nervules; it is small, and lacks the outer yellowish ring, but is prominently white pupilled. The variations of the UPPERSIDE consist on the *forewing* in the occasional presence of a yellow iris to the ocellus, sometimes very prominent, and sometimes placed on a square lighter patch of the ground-colour; the occasional appearance of a minute subapical ocellus, and the presence of a transverse dark line more or less sharply defining the darker basal area; and on the *hindwing*, in the occasional appearance of one or more blackish spots, sometimes faintly pupilled with white, and placed between the median nervules; these spots are more frequent and more numerous in the females than in the males, but occur in both sexes.

On the UNDERSIDE, the variations are far greater. Typically the colour is dusky grey, speckled with dark brown, darkest at the base, and palest near the outer margin; there is scarcely a trace of the subbasal line, and the discal transverse line consists of a series of fine blackish dentate marks, slightly margined outwardly with ochreous; the submarginal dots on the forewing are minute, white, those on the hindwing also minute, but distinctly ocellular, especially the three nearest to the anal angle. In some specimens the ground-colour is paler throughout; the subbasal line is distinct, and the dark colour is distributed in patches on the base of the wings, and in the forewing between the two lines, there being scarcely any trace of the ochreous edging to the discal line. In others, the discal line is complete and prominently bordered with ochreous sharply defining the basal area, which is uniformly dark in strong contrast to the outer area, which is ochreous brown, more or less completely clouded with earth-brown inwardly and grey outwardly; but the variations in this respect are too numerous to define. In others, again, the subbasal line is distinct, and the entire space between the two lines is conspicuously darker than the rest of the wings. Finally in some specimens the ocelli are well-developed, being even large on the hindwing, very black and minutely pupilled with white, but in all cases well-separated, and not enclosed in groups by sinuous lines, as are those of *M. mineus*.

Typical *M. perseus* is common in the neighbourhood of Calcutta, in Orissa, and throughout the plains of Northern and Central India where there is sufficient moisture. It is found almost throughout the year, and there are certainly numerous broods.

In the Andamans *M. perseus* is very rare, the only three specimens as yet received and which are in the Indian Museum, are considerably larger than the typical Indian ones, the ocellus of the upperside is very large, with a narrow iris; the underside is brown with an ochreous tinge, the basal half being slightly, but perceptibly darker, and the fifth ocellus is prominent on the hindwing, and very black.

Specimens from Burma, where it is common, agree pretty closely with the continental Indian specimens, and show much the same variations, but many have the discal line straighter, narrowly, but distinctly bordered with ochreous, the subbasal line being indistinct and very irregular, the tone of the underside paler grey, with a more distinctly ochreous tinge throughout, in some much more ochreous than in others.

In Travancore there is a variety which has been taken by Mr. H. S. Fergusson, with the striæ and subbasal line almost obsolete, the discal line nearly straight, and narrowly edged outwardly with whitish, not ochreous, the outer area being distinctly and abruptly paler than the basal area, but almost equally uniform in colouration. There is also a specimen in the Indian Museum from the Wynaad, which is larger than typical specimens, has the apex of the forewing more pointed, and in which the underside approximates to the variety *indistans* (described further on) more closely than any specimens do which we have seen from North-India.

The FEMALE is similar to the male in colouration, but has the ocelli often more prominent; and the wings more rounded. It of course lacks the sexual pouch and tuft on the hindwing.

Var. *visala*. (PLATE XVI, FIG. 52 ♂).—" With the apex of the forewing sharply angulated; the UNDERSIDE with two transverse lines across both wings, the outer line across the middle, the inner towards the base of the wing; the row of dots minute, white, the third from anal angle being black. Expanse: 2·25 inches." (*Moore*, Horsfield and Moore, Cat. Lep. E. I. C., vol. i, p. 230, n. 488 (1857).

M. visala is typically considerably larger than *M. perseus* (♂, 2·1 to 2·2; ♀, 2·4 inches), and has the ocellus on the upperside of the forewing larger. The apex of the forewing is sharply angulated in the male, but sometimes less prominently so in the female; it also presents considerable variation on the UNDERSIDE, the most distinctly specialised form having the underside uniform pale greyish-brown, scantily and indistinctly irrorated with dark brown scales; the two transverse lines prominent, brown; and all the nervures of both wings dark brown, contrasting strongly with the greyish brown ground-colour: then come specimens in which the discal line is outwardly, and the subbasal line inwardly, margined with suffused ochreous; then in others a clouded brown band appears beyond on the line of the obsolescent ocelli. Again in others the space between the two transverse lines is darker than the rest of the wing, forming a broad transverse bar darkest at its edges. Again, in others, the discal line is broad, dark brown, and suffused, while the subbasal line is evanescent. And lastly in some specimens both the transverse lines are evanescent, and the nervures are concolorous with the rest of the wing. In all these latter forms the tone of the ground-colour is subject to great variation, being suffused in some entirely, in others more or less, with various shades of ochreous; in others clouded here and there with chestnut, and in others again more or less profusely irrorated with grey. The third spot from the anal angle of the hindwing is usually black, but this is by no means universal, nor is it confined to any particular variety. In many specimens the spot between the lower median nervules on the forewing is somewhat large and pure white. *M. visala* is the commonest form in the Sikkim tarai and hills where typical *M. perseus* is comparatively very rare. It is also found in Bhutan and Upper Assam, and specimens inseparable from it have been sent from Burma, Bombay and Travancore. In the neighbourhood of Calcutta it gives place to the variety *indistans*, but the two forms appear to us to be inseparable, except by selecting typical representatives of each.

Mr. de Nicéville took the male specimen figured, and which shows the upper and undersides, in Sikkim in October. It is now in the Indian Museum, Calcutta.

Var. *subfasciata*. "Nearest allied to *visala*. UPPERSIDE of *both sexes* with a greyer marginal border, and the ocellus on the *forewing* only half the size. UNDERSIDE of *both sexes* much greyer, more densely covered with black-speckled strigæ, the two transverse lines comparatively nearer each other, and the outer line bordered by a broad chestnut-brown suffused fascia. EXPANSE: ♂, 1·88; ♀, 2·0 inches."—(*Moore*, Proc. Zool. Soc. Lond., 1882, p. 237, pl. xii, fig. 8).

This variety was described from Dharmsala in the N.-W. Himalayas. We have not seen the types, but we have specimens, fairly answering to the description, from Sikkim. It is evidently intermediate between *visala* and typical *perseus*, both from its size and from the shape of the forewing which, in the plate, is shown as having the apex rounded.

Var. *indistans*. "Differs from *perseus* in having a more distinctly-pointed apex, and straighter exterior margin, resembling in these respects *visala*. The colour is uniformly much paler above. The UNDERSIDE is especially paler, the transverse discal pale-bordered line more even, and that on the *forewing* is slightly curved inward; the marginal spots are less prominent, or only visible as white spaces, and sometimes are quite obsolete. EXPANSE: ♂, 1·75; ♀, 2·0 inches."—(*Moore*, Trans. Ent. Soc. Lond., 1880, p. 164).

This variety is developed in the plains of North-East India, examples of it from Calcutta (from whence the type was described) being most distinctly specialised, and there it is easily separable from the typical *M. perseus* which co-exists commonly with it. The FEMALE has the apex of the forewing almost as angulate as in the male, the most prominent characteristic of this form is the very pale, almost uniform colouration of the underside, the transverse lines being almost entirely obsolete in typical specimens. It is found in Tenasserim, also in the plains of N.-E. India as far north as Upper Assam, and as far south as Orissa; but in these localities it is far less distinct, specimens from Assam being almost if not quite inseparable from *visala*, and one from Orissa in the Indian Museum being almost inseparable from *perseus*, except that the apex of the forewing is pointed not rounded.

Sixth Group.—TELINGA, *Moore.* "*Forewing* comparatively long and narrow, apex slightly convex, exterior margin oblique, nearly straight, posterior margin convex near the base; cell long. *Hindwing* broad, somewhat quadrate; costa arched at base, and thence straight to apex; exterior margin waved, convexly angular in the middle; anal angle convex; cell broad, triangular; disco-cellulars very long and oblique; second subcostal emitted just before end of the cell; upper and middle median branches from lower end of the cell. MALE with a small subcostal tuft and glandular patch. *Palpi* stout at tip. Club of *antenna* well formed. *Eyes* hairy." (*Moore*, Trans. Ent. Soc. Lond., 1880, p. 167).

Telinga differs but little structurally from *Calysisme*; the *forewing* is rather more elongate, and the lower disco-cellular nervule in that wing is straight not concave; the *hindwing* is also more quadrate and more distinctly waved; but the colouration is far richer and darker, or more rufous; the ocelli of the underside are all well separated as in the *perseus* type. Only two species are known, both from the hills of South India.

Key to the species of Telinga.

B. Males with a glandular patch and tuft on the hindwing only.

a, *a*[1], *b*[2], *a*[3]. Upperside rich dark rufous brown, darkest at the apex of the forewing.

a[4]. The medium-sized lower ocellus on the upperside of the forewing not placed on a rufous patch.

100. M. *(Telinga)* ADOLPHEI, Nilgiris.

a[5]. The large lower ocellus on the upperside of the forewing placed on a rufous patch.

101. M. *(Telinga)* OCULUS, Travancore.

100. Mycalesis adolphei, Guérin.

Satyrus adolphei, Guérin, Deless. Souv. Voy. Inde, pt. 2, p. 76 (1843); *Mycalesis adolphei*, Butler, Cat. Lep. B. M., *Satyridæ*, p. 139, n. 54 (1868); *M. onatas*, Hewitson, Ex. Butt., vol. iii, p. 90, *Mycalesis* pl. vi, fig. 40 (1864) *male*; *Telinga adolphei*, Moore, Trans. Ent. Soc. Lond., 1880, p. 168.

HABITAT: Nilgiris, South India.

EXPANSE: 2·2 to 2·3 inches.

DESCRIPTION: "UPPERSIDE blackish brown, darker towards the costa of the *forewing*, which has near the apex, and a little below the middle, near the outer margin, two very small scarcely visible white points. *Hindwing* with two small ocelli, not prominent, of a tawny yellow, pupilled with black, equally near the outer margin. UNDERSIDE, both wings paler brown than the upperside; the *forewing* showing the two small white points of the upperside. The *hindwing* with two oblique transverse brown bands, the first near the base rather sinuous and not reaching the outer margin; the other beyond the middle, starting from the costa at two-thirds the length of the wing, and terminating at the anal angle. This latter band is straight, clearly defined exteriorly, and diffused interiorly. Between this band and the margin is a series of four small white points, of which the second from the anal angle is circled with black." (*Guérin*, l.c.)

Hewitson described *Mycalesis onatas* as a distinct species with the following remarks:—"This species is very near to *Satyrus adolphei*, of which it is probably only a variety, but since his descriptions are always so full and accurate, and he does not mention the undulations of the underside, I have come to the conclusion that it is distinct." Guérin certainly does not mention these, nor the rufous tinge of the upperside, nor the presence of the transverse lines on the underside of the forewing; but as these latter are an unvarying character of all the species in the genus, they can hardly have been absent from *M. adolphei*, but were probably overlooked. We prefer, therefore, to follow Mr. Moore in uniting these two species under the older name. Hewitson's description of *M. onatas* is appended for reference.*

---

* *Mycalesis onatas*, Hewitson. HABITAT: Nilgiris. EXPANSE: 2 inches. DESCRIPTION: "MALE: UPPERSIDE rufous brown. *Forewing* with the apical half dark brown: one ocellus below the middle, the usual apical ocellus represented on both sides by a minute white spot. *Hindwing* with two blind ocelli. UNDERSIDE rufous brown, undulated with darker colour. *Both wings* crossed beyond the middle by a straight rufous brown line. *Forewing* with the ocellus as above, but smaller *Hindwing* with six ocelli, five minute, the sixth [? fifth] the largest." (*Hewitson*, Ex. Butt, vol. iii, *Mycalesis* pl. vi, fig. 40 (1864), *male*.

The Indian Museum, Calcutta, has received male specimens from Conoor, taken in July. The FEMALE is unknown.

101. **Mycalesis oculus,** Marshall. (PLATE XVI, FIG. 53 ♀).

M. oculus, Marshall, Journ. A. S. B., vol. xlix, pt. 2, p. 247 (1880).

HABITAT: Ashamboo Hills, Travancore.

EXPANSE: ♂, 2·1; ♀, 2·4 inches.

DESCRIPTION: MALE: UPPERSIDE rufous brown, darker on the outer half of the forewing. *Forewing* with an indistinct small black subapical ocellus, pupilled with white, and a large lower black ocellus also white pupilled, and broadly surrounded with ferruginous-yellow; this patch almost reaching the inner margin, and almost connected with the costa by a band of the same colour. *Hindwing* with four increasing black ocelli, white pupilled and with yellow rings, the yellow rings sometimes coalescing. In some specimens these ocelli are blind. UNDERSIDE rich rufous, abruptly paler beyond the discal line; the basal area undulated with darker colour; the discal line slightly sinuous, edged outwardly with a yellow band prominent at the costa of forewing, and obsolete on the hindwing. *Forewing* with the ocelli as on upperside, but smaller, and with much more prominent white pupils; occasionally a third minute ocellus is present between them. *Hindwing* with six ocelli, the fifth from the apex largest, but all varying much in size in different specimens. The FEMALE is larger, and has the yellow edging to the discal band on the underside prominent on both wings. All th ocelli larger, and the markings more distinct. It of course lacks the glandular patch and tuft of hairs of the male.

M. oculus occurs only in the extreme south of the peninsula; it was taken in the Ashamboo Hills in Travancore in May, by Mr. Harold Ferguson.

The figure shows the upper and undersides of a female specimen in the Indian Museum, taken by Mr. Harold S. Ferguson at Eridge, Trevandrum, South India.

Seventh Group.—PACHAMA, *Moore.* "Wings large and broad, but comparatively shorter than in *Samanta. Forewing* with costa arched in the middle, apex rounded, exterior margin slightly oblique and convex; *cilia* prominent. *Hindwing* somewhat bluntly conical; exterior [? anterior] margin slightly arched, apex somewhat angled; exterior margin very oblique and scarcely convex; *cilia* prominent; first subcostal emitted at some distance before end of the cell; cell longer, end much pointed; disco-cellulars very oblique, radial from a slight angle near subcostal. MALE with a subcostal tuft and glandular patch, as in *Samanta. Palpi* slender at tip. Club of *antenna* gradually formed. *Eyes* hairy." (*Moore*, Trans. Ent. Soc. Lond., 1880, p. 165).

This group contains only two species, which are distinguished chiefly by the prominence of the white *cilia* to both wings, and by the very much arched costa of the forewing. So far as there is any certain record both these species are confined to North-East India.

Key to the species of Pachama.

B. Males with a glandular patch and tuft on the hindwing only.

a, a^1, c^2, a^3. Underside crossed by a very prominent white band showing through on the upperside.

a^4. Basal two-thirds of underside densely striated with short dark lines.

102. M. (*Pachama*) MESTRA, Deccan ? Khasi Hills.

b^4. Basal two-thirds of underside not striated but uniformly coloured.

103. M. (*Pachama*) SUAVEOLENS, Cachar.

102. **Mycalesis mestra,** Hewitson.

M. mestra, Hewitson, Ex. Butt, vol. iii, p. 79, *Mycalesis* pl. i, figs. 2, 3 (1862), *female*; *Pachama mestra*, Moore, Trans. Ent. Soc. Lond., 1880, p. 165.

HABITAT: Khasi Hills (*Moore*); Deccan (*Hewitson*).

EXPANSE: ♀, 2·8 inches.

DESCRIPTION: "FEMALE: UPPERSIDE dark brown. *Forewing* crossed beyond the middle by a narrow band of white, followed by two ocelli; one near the apex minute, the other larger; two submarginal black lines, the margin white. *Hindwing* crossed beyond the middle by an indistinct band (seen through); followed by two ocelli towards the anal angle, the one nearest the angle minute, oval, and ill-formed: a submarginal line of rufous-white: the margin broadly white, traversed by a very fine black line. UNDERSIDE rufous, the basal half undulated with dark brown; crossed beyond the middle by a continuous band of white, followed by a broad band of purple-brown marked with several ocelli: on the *forewing* by three; the first (which is minute) and second near the apex; the third (larger) beyond the middle: on the *hindwing* by five, three of them near the apex (the third indistinct), two near the anal angle, large, all with white pupils and rufous border; *both wings* with white and rufous submarginal bands; the margins white." (*Hewitson*, l. c.)

In the figure by Hewitson of the upperside, the ocellus of the hindwing between the first and second median branches is the largest of all; in that of the underside the anal ocellus of the hindwing is bipupilled, almost geminate. The large size and pure white marginal lines of this Butterfly distinguish it from all other Indian species of *Mycalesis*, as well as the large size of the anterior subanal ocellus of the hindwing on the upperside. The locality, "Deccan," given by Hewitson is probably erroneous, but it is a very rare Butterfly.

103. **Mycalesis suaveolens**, W.-M. and de N.

HABITAT: Cachar.

EXPANSE: ♂, 2·5 inches.

DESCRIPTION: MALE: Wings above and below dark sepia, tinged with ashy-white. *Forewing* with the costal and outer margins regularly arched. With a narrow and very indistinct light brownish discal band extending parallel to the outer margin from the subcostal nervure to the third median nervule; with two velvety-black, white-pupilled ocelli encircled by a slender iris of ochreous-brown of almost the same shade as, but more distinctly expressed than, the discal band; with the first of these ocelli the smaller, triple (having a minute white-pupilled ocellule run together with it at either end), and so placed that its pupil lies in the fold between the discoidal nervules; with the second ocellus much the larger, circular, and placed in the middle of the first median interspace, whence it extends a short distance into the two adjoining interspaces; and with two obsolete anteciliary pale lines. *Hindwing* above with a single perfect and slightly elongated ocellus in the first median interspace, the bounding nervules of which it does not reach; with a minute rudimentary ocellus on the fold of the third median interspace on one side only; and with the pale anteciliary lines more distinct than in the forewing. UNDERSIDE darker and more richly coloured, but not striated; with a narrow cretaceous-white common discal band extending from the subcostal nervure in the forewing to the submedian nervure in the hindwing, where it runs into the inner of the two pale anteciliary lines, which, equally distinct in both wings, are somewhat coarser in the forewing; and with a third pale line following the outer configuration of the ocelli. *Forewing* ocellated as above. *Hindwing* with seven ocelli arranged in two decreasing series, the first of which consists of four slightly decreasing ocelli, and the second of three more rapidly decreasing ones, of which the first corresponds to the one visible above, but is larger, extending beyond the limits of its interspace on both sides, so as to touch the second, which is united to the third or anal. *Antennæ* above concolourous with the wings and body, below lighter and indistinctly annulated, becoming orange towards the black orange-tipped club.

A single specimen was taken on Nemotha, N. Cachar, at an elevation of 3,300 feet, in September. Mr. Wood-Mason notes: "The scent-glands and fans, which are much as in *M. malsara*, Moore, emitted a powerful and delicious odour resembling that of vanilla for some hours after the death of the insect."

Between *Pachama* and *Samanta* Moore places a Javan species, *M. moorei*, Felder,* as the type of a distinct genus of which it is the sole representative, and which he characterises as

* *Mycalesis moorei*, Felder, Reise Nov., Lep., vol. iii, p. 502, n. 870, pl. lxvii, fig. 9 (1866), *male*. HABITAT: Java. EXPANSE: 2 inches. DESCRIPTION: "MALE: UPPERSIDE fuscous, with an obsolete darker external line, beyond which the margin is paler. *Hindwing* with a very obsolete line before the margin.

follows : Genus INDALASA. "MALE : *Forewing* somewhat narrow ; costa arched at base ; apex convex ; exterior margin oblique, straight. *Hindwing* narrow, conical ; anterior margin arched at base ; apex slightly produced ; exterior margin oblique, slightly convex ; cell long, fusiform ; a tuft of fine hair at base of subcostal ; first subcostal branch half way between the costal and second ; disco-cellulars very oblique ; two upper median branches from end of the cell. *Antennæ* with a moderately formed club. *Palpi* pointed, and hairy to tip. *Eyes* slightly hairy." Type, *I. moorei.* (*Moore,* Trans. Ent. Soc., Lond., 1880, p. 166).

Eighth Group.—CULAPA, *Moore.* "*Forewing* longer than in *Calysisme;* costa very slightly arched ; apex produced ; exterior margin very oblique and slightly convex below the apex ; cell longer and narrower ; third subcostal branch nearer the fourth. *Hindwing* somewhat quadrate, apical angle slightly acute ; exterior margin convex hindward and truncated at anal angle ; abdominal margin long ; cell triangular ; disco-cellulars very oblique ; middle median branch emitted at some distance before lower end of the cell. MALE with a tuft of fine hair exserted from base of cell, and covering a small glandular patch above base of first subcostal branch. *Antennæ* with a well-formed, slightly-stout club. *Palpi* compactly clothed with shorter hair. *Eyes* hairy." (*Moore,* Proc. Zool. Soc. Lond., 1878, p. 825 ; id., Trans. Ent. Soc. Lond., 1880, p. 165).

Only a single species of this group is known, occurring in Sumatra, and reappearing in Upper Tenasserim. Its elongate forewing, and the great size of the lower ocellus on that wing, are its chief distinctive features.

Key to the species of Culapa.

B. Males with a glandular patch and tuft on the hindwing only.

a, b^1, a^1, a^2. Upperside of forewing in female with one very large ocellus occupying the entire space between the third median nervule and submedian nervure, not quite so large in male.

104. M. (*Culapa*) MNASICLES, Upper Tenasserim, Sumatra.

104. Mycalesis mnasicles, Hewitson.

M. mnasicles, Hewitson, Ex. Butt., vol. iii, *Mycalesis* pl. v, figs. 32, 33 (1864), *male ; Culapa mnasicles,* Moore, Proc. Zool. Soc., Lond., 1878, p. 825 ; idem., id., Trans. Ent. Soc. Lond., 1880, p. 165.

HABITAT : Tenasserim, Sumatra.

EXPANSE : ♂, 2·5 ; ♀, 3·0 inches.

DESCRIPTION : "MALE : UPPERSIDE rufous brown ; both wings with a submarginal black line. *Forewing* with two ocelli, one at the apex minute, the other below the middle, very large. *Hindwing* with one indistinct ocellus and a submarginal band of indistinct lunular spots. UNDERSIDE with the basal half rufous ; both wings crossed before the middle, and at the middle by common rufous brown narrow bands ; both with two black lines near the outer margin, and a submarginal zigzag rufous band. *Forewing* with five ocelli, the first four minute, the fifth larger, and marked with a large white pupil. *Hindwing* with seven small ocelli, the first and fifth the largest. The FEMALE does not differ except in size [and of course in lacking the sexual tuft on the *hindwing*]." (*Hewitson,* l. c.)

M. mnasicles is a rare insect and has only as yet been taken in Upper Tenasserim within Indian limits. Limborg took it in April at Ahsown, 2,000 feet elevation, and Meetan, 3,000 feet elevation ; and Captain C. T. Bingham took a single female also in April in the Thoungyeen forests.

The figure shows the upper and undersides of the female specimen taken by Captain Bingham, and now in the Indian Museum, Calcutta.

UNDERSIDE darker, the line of the upperside swarthy, unequally defined with white externally, the margin beyond it very dilute brown ; with five ocelli in the *forewing*, seven in the *hindwing*, coloured as in *M. sudra,*† and surrounded with fuscous dots, beyond them divided by a submarginal line, much drawn back in the *forewing*, another before the margin, and a third before the cilia slender fuscous." (*Felder,* l. c.)

† Described on p. 110.

Ninth Group.—KABANDA, *Moore.* "Wings short, broad. *Forewing* very much arched from the base, apex and exterior margin slightly convex and even; cell short and broad. *Hindwing* bluntly conical, short; exterior margin almost even, anal angle very convex; costal nervure quite short and nearly straight; first subcostal branch emitted immediately before end of the cell; disco-cellulars almost erect; cell very short; middle median branch emitted before lower end of the cell. MALE with a slight subcostal tuft and glandular patch of scales; median branches dilated and grooved at their base on the upperside. *Antennæ* short, slender. *Palpi* slender at tip. *Eyes* hairy." (*Moore*, Trans. Ent. Soc. Lond., 1880, p. 168.)

Only two species of this group are known, from North-East Bengal and the Khasi Hills. The ocelli are very similar to those of the *M. mineus* type in the group *Calysisme*, but the immaculate upper surface and the vinous or rufous tinge of the colouration as well as the arrangement of the subcostal and median nervules of the hindwing serve to distinguish them.

Key to the Species of Kabanda.

B. Males with a glandular patch and tuft on hindwing only.

b. a^1. The upperside without ocelli on either wing.

a^2. The ground-colour rufous-fuscous, the ocelli of the underside prominent.

105. M. (*Kabanda*) MALSARIDA, N.-E. India.

b^2. The ground-colour dark vinous brown, the ocelli of the underside minute.

106. M. (*Kabanda*) KHASIANA, Khasi Hills.

105. Mycalesis malsarida, Butler.

M. malsarida, Butler, Cat Lep. B. M., *Satyridæ*, p. 134, n. 27, pl. iii, fig. 14 (1868); *Kabanda malsarida*, Moore, Trans. Ent. Soc. Lond., 1880, p. 168.

HABITAT: Khasi Hills, Cherra Punji, Sibsagar, Sylhet, Cachar.

EXPANSE: 1·9 to 2·1 inches.

DESCRIPTION: "UPPERSIDE rufous-fuscous, the apical area of the *forewing* slightly paler; a submarginal line and the external margin darker undulate, a marginal line and on the *hindwing* inwardly another ochraceous not very distinct line; the costa of the *hindwing* ochraceous, at the base sericeous. UNDERSIDE very little darker, the basal area smeared with fuscous. A median fascia almost entire, oblique, violet-plumbeous, abbreviated in the *forewing*; another surrounding the ocelli, and a third submarginal, violet; a submarginal line and the margin itself black, a fulvous marginal line, all undulate. *Forewing* with three small subapical obliquely placed ocelli (the middle one a little larger), and one rather large discal. *Hindwing* with seven ocelli, the second, third, sixth and seventh small, the fifth largest, all deep black, with white pupils and fulvous rings." (*Butler*, l. c.)

There is a male and a female from Sibsagar, Assam, in the Indian Museum, Calcutta. The FEMALE differs from the male only in the absence of the tuft of hairs on the costa of the upperside of the hindwing. Mr. Wood-Mason took a single male on Nemotha, Cachar, 3,300 feet, in September. In all these specimens the basal area of the hindwing on the underside is densely striated with darker colour.

106. Mycalesis khasiana, Moore.

M. khasiana, Moore, Proc. Zool. Soc. Lond., 1874, p. 566; *Kabanda khasiana*, Moore, Trans. Ent. Soc. Lond., 1880, p. 168.

HABITAT: Khasi Hills.

EXPANSE: 1·75 inches.

DESCRIPTION: "MALE: UPPERSIDE dark vinous brown, paler at the apex, and along exterior border; marginal lines black. UNDERSIDE bright vinous brown, purplish grey along exterior border; covered with minute black and grey strigæ: *both wings* with a transverse discal narrow purplish grey band, and a distinct yellow narrow marginal black-bordered band. *Forewing* with five, and *hindwing* with seven minute perfect ocelli." (*Moore*, l. c.)

This species is apparently to be distinguished from the only other species in this group, *M. malsarida*, by the tone of the upper surface and the size of the ocelli on the underside.

An allied species, *M. janardana*, has been separated as the type of a distinct genus under the name of *Martanda** ; the type species occurs in Malacca, and also in Java and Sumatra, and two other species belonging to the same group have been described, one from North China, *M. sangaica*, the other from Macassar, Gilolo, &c., *M. megamede.* This group is evidently closely allied to *Samanta* from the position of the subcostal nervules in the *hindwing*, both branches arising from the end of the cell, and it is intermediate between that group and *Kabanda.* Probably *M. nautilus* (p. 120) belongs to this group.

Tenth Group.—SAMANTA, *Moore.* "*Forewing* arched towards the apex, angle convex. *Hindwing* conical; exterior margin waved; first and second subcostal branches emitted together from end of the cell, base of the first straight, disco-cellulars straight and very slightly oblique; cell short. MALE with a small tuft covering a glandular patch of scales above base of subcostal branch. *Eyes* hairy." (*Moore*, Trans. Ent. Soc. Lond., 1880, p. 166.)

All the species of this group are found in Northern India only, most of them in the hills of N.-E. India extending to Burma.

Key to the Species of Samanta.

B. Males with a glandular patch and tuft on hindwing only.

- *c*, *a*¹, *a*². With the ocelli of the underside distinct and prominent.
  - *a*³. With only two ocelli on the underside of forewing.
    - 107. M. (*Samanta*) HERI, Bhutan.
  - *b*³. With five ocelli on the underside of forewing.
    - *a*⁴. With the ocelli of the underside on a lilac ground in the middle of a broad, dark brown band; the ocelli blind on the upperside, more or less so on the underside.
      - 108. M. (*Samanta*) MALSARA, Mussoorie, Sikkim, Khasi Hills, Assam.
    - *b*⁴. With the ocelli of the underside on a dark brown band with lilac-grey beyond; the ocelli distinctly pupilled above and below.
      - 109. M. (*Samanta*) NICOTIA, Sikkim.
- *b*² With the ocelli of the underside minute, indistinct or obsolete.
  - *a*³. With the ocelli of the upperside blind.
    - *a*⁴. The discal band of the underside broad.
      - 110. M. (*Samanta*) RUDIS, Orissa, Manipur, Naga Hills, Tenasserim.
    - *b*⁴. The discal band of the underside narrow.
      - 111. M. (*Samanta*) LEPCHA, Himalayas, Burma.
  - *b*³. With the ocelli of the upperside pupilled.
    - 112. M. (*Samanta*) LANGI, Mussoorie, Sikkim, Naga and Khasi Hills.

107. **Mycalesis heri**, Moore.

M. heri, Moore, Horsfield and Moore, Cat. Lep. E. I. C., vol. i, p. 233, n. 496 (1857); *Samanta heri*, Moore, Trans. Ent. Soc. Lond., 1880, p. 167.

HABITAT: Bhutan.

EXPANSE: 2·37 inches.

DESCRIPTION:—"MALE: UPPERSIDE brown. *Forewing* with large upper and larger lower ocellus. *Hindwing* with two larger and third smaller ocelli. UNDERSIDE paler, the base covered with short brown undulated striæ; transverse line, inner and outer border to the ocelli pale ochreous. *Forewing* with the two ocelli as above. *Hindwing* with six ocelli; marginal lines brown and pale ochreous." (*Moore*, l. c.)

---

* *Martanda*, Moore, Trans. Ent. Soc. Lond., 1880, p 169. "Wings short. *Forewing* somewhat triangular, apex slightly pointed, exterior margin slightly oblique, nearly straight and even. *Hindwing* bluntly oval; costa very broadly convex at the base; exterior margin convex, slightly waved; cell long, very pointed at lower end; first and second subcostal branches from end of the cell; disco-cellulars very oblique; MALE with a double subcostal tuft covering the glandular patch of scales. *Antennæ* short, club stout. *Palpi* slender at tip. *Eyes* hairy." (*Moore*, l. c.)

Mycalesis janardana, Moore, Horsfield and Moore, Cat. Lep. E. I. C., vol. i, p. 234, n. 502 (1857); idem, id., Distant, Rhop. Malay, p. 54, pl. v, fig. 2 (1882); *Martanda janardana*, Moore, Trans. Ent. Soc. Lond., 1880, p. 169. HABITAT: Malacca, Sumatra, Java. EXPANSE: Male, 1·5; female, 1·7 inches. DESCRIPTION: "MALE: UPPERSIDE dusky brown, palest on the *hindwing*, which has two rather indistinct black spots. UNDERSIDE brown, the basal parts being covered with small narrow striæ; two transverse lines, the outer margined exteriorly with white; *forewing* with six, and *hindwing* with seven small ocelli. FEMALE paler on the *upper* and *undersides*, the latter nearly covered with small dark striæ; the transverse lines paler; the ocelli somewhat larger than in the male." (*Moore*, l. c. in Cat. Lep E. I. C.)

We have never seen a specimen of this species. The underside of the forewing bearing two ocelli only is a character not found in any other species of this group.

108. **Mycalesis malsara**, Moore.

M. malsara, Moore, Horsfield and Moore, Cat. Lep. E. I. C., vol. i, p. 231, n. 492 (1857); id., Hewitson, Ex. Butt., vol. iii, p. 80, *Mycalesis* pl. i, figs. 5, 6 (1862); *Samanta malsara*, Moore, Trans. Ent. Soc. Lond., 1880, p. 166.

HABITAT: Mussoorie, Sikkim, Khasi Hills, Sibsagar, Cherra Punji.

EXPANSE: 1·90 to 2·25 inches.

DESCRIPTION: "UPPERSIDE dark brown. *Forewing* with a transverse brownish-white band, and upper and lower ocelli. *Hindwing* with very indistinct transverse brownish-white streak, and two small ocelli. UNDERSIDE with transverse yellowish-white band well defined across both wings. *Forewing* with five ocelli, the first and third minute. *Hindwing* with seven larger ocelli, the third and seventh smallest." (*Moore*, l. c.)

The above is the original description; the following is a more detailed description by Hewitson, who gives excellent figures of both upper and undersides in his "Exotic Butterflies":—

"UPPERSIDE rufous-brown; *forewing* crossed beyond the middle by a band of white, followed by three blind ocelli (the middle one minute); *hindwing* with one ocellus, indistinct; the outer margins of both wings rufous-white, traversed by two black lines. UNDERSIDE rufous, undulated; crossed beyond the middle by a band of yellowish-white, interrupted where the wings meet, followed by a broad band of dark brown with numerous ocelli; on the *forewing* five, the second and fifth largest; on the *hindwing* seven, the first, second and fifth largest, most of them with white pupils and rufous borders, the whole enclosed on each wing by a tortuous line of lilac; the margins broadly white [yellowish-white?] traversed by two dark lines." (*Hewitson*, l. c.)

In some specimens there are only two blind ocelli on the upperside of the forewing; sometimes no ocelli, sometimes two on the hindwing. The width of the discal band on the underside is also very variable; in some Sikkim, and in a Mussoorie specimen in the Indian Museum, Calcutta, it is less than half as wide as in other Sikkim and Sibsagar specimens. The FEMALE differs in being paler, all the markings more distinct, and in the absence of the male sexual secondary characters.

Mr. de Nicéville took it commonly in Sikkim in October, both in the tarai and lower hills.

109. **Mycalesis nicotia**, Hewitson.

M. nicotia, Hewitson, Gen. D. L., p. 394, pl. lxvi, fig. 4 (1851), *female*; id., Ex. Butt., vol. iii, *Mycalesis* pl. i, fig. 1, *male*; *Samanta nicotia*, Moore, Trans. Ent. Soc. Lond., 1880, p. 167.

HABITAT: Sikkim; S. India (*apud* Butler.)

EXPANSE: 2·3 to 2·5 inches.

DESCRIPTION: "UPPERSIDE dark brown; the outer margin paler, traversed by two submarginal lines of dark brown. *Forewing* with two ocelli, one near the apex, small; the other below it, large. *Hindwing* with one ocellus near the middle of the outer margin; all black with white pupils and rufous borders." (*Hewitson*, l. c. in Ex. Butt.) "UNDERSIDE rufous brown, undulated with numerous darker striæ, broadly margined with lilac [grey], on which are three black lines [the margin is rufous between the two marginal lines]; crossed beyond the middle by a narrow common band of yellow, followed by a broader band of dark brown in which are numerous ocelli; on the *forewing* five, the lowest much the largest; on the *hindwing* seven, the first oval, larger than the three following, which are small, the fifth largest, the sixth and seventh small; all deep black, with rufous margins and white pupils." (*Hewitson*, l. c. in Gen. D. L.)

In the Indian Museum, Calcutta, there is a single male specimen of this species from Sikkim, where it was taken in August. On the upperside of the forewing there is an ocellule attached to the upper ocellus posteriorly, and corresponding with the third ocellus of the underside; and on the hindwing there are two small ocelli in the interspaces above and below that which bears the ocellus described above between the second and third median nervules.

110. **Mycalesis rudis**, Moore.

Samanta rudis, Moore, Trans. Ent. Soc. Lond., 1880, p. 166.

HABITAT: N. India, Manipur, Naga Hills, Orissa, Upper Tenasserim.

EXPANSE: 1·75 to 2·10 inches.

DESCRIPTION: "MALE: UPPERSIDE similar to *S. malsara*, the pale band on the *forewing* being narrower. UNDERSIDE ochreous-brown, with darker brown strigæ, somewhat greyish-brown on external borders. *Both wings* with an ochreous-yellow transverse discal band, the inner margin of which is well defined, the outer suffused; a submarginal series of minute indistinct white-speckled spots, the two subanal being ringed with black; an indistinct ochreous-speckled pale streak crossing middle of the cell on both wings." (*Moore*, l. c.)

Captain C. T. Bingham took two males of this species in the Donat range in Upper Tenasserim in January, and a female in the Upper Thoungyeen forests in April. Mr. A. O. Hume took a single male specimen in the eastern hills of Manipur in May. In some specimens the whitish bar on the upperside of the forewing is as narrow and indistinct as in the following species *M. lepcha*; the two are very nearly allied, but the transverse bar of the underside appears to be constantly much broader in this species than in *M. lepcha*. The underside is irrorated with grey at the base and abdominal margin of hindwing, as well as on the outer margin. The ocelli of the upperside appear to vary; in all the Burman specimens there are three on the forewing, and two on the hindwing distinct; in the Manipur specimen those of the hindwing are indistinct and of the forewing almost entirely obsolete. A single male from Kurdah, Orissa, is a little aberrant. It is somewhat smaller; there are no ocelli on the upperside of the hindwing, and the discal band on the underside is yellow, not ochreous-white, and outwardly more diffused. The underside of this specimen closely resembles some varieties of *M. perseus* from the same locality.

The FEMALE differs in its much paler colouration, the transverse band of the underside being almost white, and in lacking the sexual tuft.

111. **Mycalesis lepcha**, Moore.

Samanta lepcha, Moore, Trans. Ent. Soc. Lond., 1880, p. 167.

HABITAT: N.-W. Himalayas, Nepal, Burma.

EXPANSE: 2·0 to 2·1 inches.

DESCRIPTION: "MALE: UPPERSIDE brown. *Forewing* with an indistinct pale transverse discal narrow line, and two or three submarginal indistinct blind ocelli, the upper two minute. *Hindwing* with one or two similar subanal ocelli. UNDERSIDE brighter coloured, greyish externally, covered with numerous darker brown strigæ. *Both wings* with a prominent very narrow ochreous-yellow transverse discal band, and a submarginal series of indistinct minute black and white speckled spots; a pale speckled indistinct streak crossing both cells." (*Moore*, l. c.)

A single male of this species has been sent to us from Moulmein by Capt. C. H. E. Adamson, and another from Chamba in the N.-W. Himalayas by Major C. H. T. Marshall; in both these specimens the lower ocellus of the forewing alone is prominent on the upperside; the upper one and those of the hindwing being almost completely obsolete; the underside of the Moulmein specimen is irrorated with ochreous on the external margin.

Colonel Lang's collection contains four specimens from Mussoorie taken in May at 7,000 feet elevation.

112. **Mycalesis langi**, de N., *n. sp.*

HABITAT: Naga and Khasi Hills, Sikkim, Mussoorie.

EXPANSE: 2·10 to 2·35 inches.

DESCRIPTION: MALE: UPPERSIDE brown, with two marginal lines on both wings, more prominent on the hindwing; both inwardly defined with ochreous. *Forewing* with a median-sized subapical ocellus, often with a smaller ocellule attached to it posteriorly, and a large lower ocellus placed in the first median interspace, and extending beyond it on both sides. *Hindwing* with one subanal ocellus placed in the first median interspace, variable in size, but usually subequal to the anterior ocellus of the forewing; sometimes with a minute ocellule in the next interspace posteriorly, and another in the interspace between the third median and discoidal nervules. All these ocelli black, pupilled with white, and with a yellow iris. UNDERSIDE brown with a greenish tinge. All but the area immediately interior to the median band profusely striated with darker; beyond the band the ground-colour is somewhat lighter than the rest of the wing. A prominent common wide ochreous median band, inwardly sharply defined, outwardly diffused; beyond this a series of more or less obsolete minute ocelli, in the forewing that in the first median interspace, and in the hindwing the three anal ones usually perfect. A submarginal wavy indistinct line, and the marginal lines as above. FEMALE paler above and below, and without the black-centred glandular patches on both wings, and the tuft of hairs to the hindwing present in the male.

Differs from *M. rudis* and *M. lepcha* chiefly in the large size of the posterior ocellus on the upperside of the forewing, and all the ocelli on the upperside of both wings being white pupilled. This is apparently a distinct species, as the eight specimens (six males and two females) from which this description has been made, show but little variation. Two of the specimens, those from Mussoorie, are in Colonel Lang's collection; one male from Sikkim is in Mr. Otto Möller's collection; the others are in the Indian Museum, Calcutta.

Eleventh Group.—NISSANGA, *Moore.* "Wings short. *Forewing* slightly arched at the base; exterior margin long, slightly convex, and nearly erect; second subcostal emitted at end of the cell. *Hindwing* bluntly conical; costa broadly convex at the base, and thence oblique to the apex; exterior margin oblique; cell short, quadrate, broad at its end; subcostal not swollen, its first branch emitted immediately before end of the cell; disco-cellulars erect, equal in length; two upper median branches emitted at some distance beyond the cell. MALE with a tuft of fine hair covering a glandular patch at base of subcostal branches. *Antennæ* gradually thickened to tip. Apical joint of *palpi* long and slender. *Eyes* hairy." (*Moore*, Trans. Ent. Soc. Lond., 1880, p. 169.)

Only two species of this group are known, both of small size, and distinguishable at once by the peculiar nature of the lower ocellus of the forewing which is placed eccentrically at the lower edge of a light-coloured patch, giving it the appearance of a squinting eye. They are confined to South India and Ceylon.

Key to the Species of Nissanga.

B. Males with a glandular patch and tuft of hairs on hindwing only.

- *c*, *b*¹. *a*². With the lower ocellus of forewing at the lower edge of a light coloured patch.
  - *a*³. Upperside ochreous brown; the ocellular patch yellow.
    - 113. M. (*Nissanga*) PATNIA, Ceylon.
  - *b*³. Upperside dull brown, the ocellular patch ochreous-white.
    - 114. M. (*Nissanga*) JUNONIA, South India.

113. **Mycalesis patnia,** Moore.

M. patnia, Moore, Horsfield and Moore, Cat. Lep. E. I. C., vol. i, p. 232, n. 494 (1857), *male*; *Nissanga patnia*, id., Trans. Ent. Soc. Lond., 1880, p. 170; idem, id., Lep. Cey., p. 23, pl. xii, figs 2, 2*a* (1880), *male*.

HABITAT: Ceylon.

EXPANSE: ♂, 1·62; ♀, 1·75 inches.

DESCRIPTION: "MALE and FEMALE: UPPERSIDE blackish ochreous-brown, a marginal double yellow line on both wings. *Forewing* with a subapical longitudinally-narrow white spot, a large lower black spot (or upper half of an ocellus) pupilled with white, and broadly bordered on the upper half with pale ochreous-yellow, a broad medial ochreous streak from thence to base of wing. *Hindwing* with the discal area suffused with ochreous, and in the

MALE with two minute discal ocelli. UNDERSIDE ochreous-yellow, marginal lines bright yellow. *Forewing* with an elongated subapical white spot and large prominent lower ocellus, the lower portion of which is suffused with black; five transverse lines commencing from the base, and circle round the subapical spot and lower ocellus ochreous-red; a silvery band across the middle of the wing, and another round the upper spot and lower ocellus. *Hindwing* with a subapical and two subanal white spots distantly encircled by a black line, and then by a red line, each again enclosed by a silvery band; a subbasal silvery band and two red lines. BODY brown; *palpi* at the side and *legs* beneath greyish." (*Moore*, l.c. in Lep. Cey).

"Very common, and easy to capture. Taken at Galle and Kandy." (*Captain Wade*). It is apparently confined to the island of Ceylon.

114. Mycalesis junonia, Butler. (PLATE XVI, FIG. 57 ♂).

M. junonia, Butler, Cat. Lep. B.M., *Satyridæ*, p. 146, pl. iii, fig. 4 (1868); *Nissanga junonia*, Moore, Trans. Ent. Soc. Lond., 1880, p 170.

HABITAT: Hills of South India.

EXPANSE: 1·6 to 1·8 inches.

DESCRIPTION: "MALE and FEMALE: UPPERSIDE fuscous, with the margin pale, with a [two] black line [s] on it, the *cilia* varied with greyish and fuscous. *Forewing* with two black ocelli pupilled with white, the upper one circled with brown, the lower one much larger, circled above with an irregular whitish lunule. *Hindwing* with one or two minute indistinct discal ocelli [often absent]. UNDERSIDE olivaceous, otherwise marked almost as in *M. patnia*." (*Butler*, l.c.) Th FEMALE is rather larger than the male, and lacks the secondary sexual charactexs.

Mr. Harold Fergusson writes of this species that in Travancore it was not common in April, and only to be found in heavy forest at about 800 feet elevation; and later on in May that it was fairly common in the hills at the end of the month. There are specimens in the Indian Museum, Calcutta, taken at Koppa Anchee, Kadur District, Mysore.

The figure shows the upper and undersides of a male specimen in the Indian Museum, taken at Trevandrum, South India.

The remaining groups of this section are chiefly confined to the Austro-Malayan region; one species only, *M. fuscum*,* Felder, is found as far north as the Malay Peninsula. It belongs to a group separated by Moore as a new genus under the name of *Mydosama*.† The same group was previously characterised by Felder as *Dasyomma*, but that name was rejected owing to its having been previously used in the order *Diptera*.

Twelfth Group.—LOESA, *Moore*. "MALE: *Forewing* somewhat elongate and narrow; costa arched at the base and apex; exterior margin oblique, slightly convex; second subcostal branch emitted at some distance beyond the cell. *Hindwing* bluntly ovate; costa arched at base; apex, exterior margin and anal angle convex; a tuft of fine hair at base of subcostal, and a slender tuft covering a groove on middle of submedian nervure; cell short, broad in the middle; subcostal concave at its base, first branch emitted close to end of the cell,

---

* *Dasyomma fuscum*, Felder, Wien. Ent. Monatsch., vol. iv, p. 401, n. 27 (1860); *Mycalesis diniche*, Hewitson, Ex. Butt, vol. iii, p. 85, *Mycalesis* pl. iv, fig. 23 (1862), *male*; id., Journ. Linn. Soc., Zoology, vol. viii, p. 146 (1865); *M. margites*, id., Ex. Butt., vol. v, *Mycalesis* pl. ix, fig. 59 (1874), *female*; *Mydosama fuscum*, Moore, Trans. Ent. Soc Lond., 1880, p. 170; *Mycalesis fusca*, Distant, Rhop. Malay., p. 53, pl. v, fig 1 (1882), *female*. HABITAT: Malay Peninsula, Singapore, Sumatra, Borneo. EXPANSE: Male, 1·9; female, 2·3 inches (from Hewitson's figures). DESCRIPTION: "MALE: UPPERSIDE fuscous. *Forewing* with a blind ocellus. *Hindwing* with the disc slightly suffused with violet, with two ocelli scarcely distinct. UNDERSIDE. *Both wings* brown, powdered with fulvous, with two ferruginous discal lines. *Forewing* with four ocelli. *Hindwing* with seven on a ferruginous ground." (*Felder*, l. c.)

† Genus *Mydosama*, Moore, Trans. Ent. Soc. Lond., 1880, p. 170. "Wings short. *Forewing* regularly arched along the costa; exterior margin slightly convex and oblique; second subcostal branch emitted immediately before end of the cell; disco-cellulars very slightly concave. *Hindwing* bluntly conical; costa convex; exterior margin and angles convex, slightly waved; cell broadly triangular; first subcostal branch emitted close to end of the cell, and in the MALE swollen at its base; disco-cellulars oblique, slightly concave; two upper median branches emitted from end of the cell. MALE with a tuft of fine hair covering a glandular patch at base of first subcostal branch. Club of *antennæ* moderate. *Palpi* less laxly clothed beneath than in *Nissanga*, and the terminal joint shorter. *Eyes* hairy." (*Moore*, l. c.)

second concave at its base ; disco-cellulars long, oblique, straight ; two upper median branches from end of the cell. *Antennæ* with a well-formed terminal club ; *palpi* pointed at tip. *Eyes* hairy." (*Moore*, Trans. Ent. Soc. Lond., 1880, p. 177.)

Only two species of this group are known : the type species *L. oroatis** inhabits Java ; the other, which is apparently very closely allied, and may be only the continental representative of the Javan species, was discovered in Upper Tenasserim by Captain C. T. Bingham. The bright rufous colouring of these species gradually darkening to the outer margin, distinguish them from all other Asiatic *Mycalesis*.

Key to the Indian Species of Loesa.

C. Males with two glandular pouches and tufts on hindwing.

a. Upperside rich bright rufous, darker towards the costal and outer margins.

115. M. (*Loesa*) SURKHA, Upper Tenasserim.

115. Mycalesis surkha, Marshall.

M. surkha, Marshall, Journ. A. S. B., vol. li, pt. 2, p. , pl. iv, fig. 1 (1882), *male*; *Loesa fervida*, Butler, Ann. and Mag. of Nat. Hist., fifth series, vol. x, p. 372 (1882).

HABITAT : Donat Range, Upper Tenasserim.

EXPANSE : 2·15 inches.

DESCRIPTION : MALE : UPPERSIDE rich bright fulvous ; the costa, the apical area broadly, and thence decreasing to the inner angle of the *forewing*, and the outer margin of the *hindwing* suffused darker. *Forewing* with a minute black dot in the upper discoidal, and a larger spot in the first median interspace, black, surrounded with an indistinct lighter iris than the ground-colour. UNDERSIDE rich brown, with a common narrow discal purple band, beyond which the ground-colour is much lighter. An indistinct dark bar crosses the middle of the cell in the *forewing*, and a similar subbasal line in the *hindwing*. *Forewing* with the spots of the upperside replaced by two small equal-sized ocelli *Hindwing* with a series of seven ocelli, the first three small, subequal, the fourth minute, the fifth the largest, the sixth and seventh in the same interspace equal in size to the three first. Two indistinct waved marginal lines to both wings. The sexual characters consist of a pale glandular patch on the underside of the inner margin of the forewing, and a similar patch on the upperside of the costal margin of the hindwing, with, on the latter, a tuft of hair at the base of the subcostal nervure, which tuft is dark brown at the base, and the tips of the hairs yellow. A similar tuft of hairs occupies a slit in the middle of the submedian nervure of the hindwing, with the opening above.

Differs from *M. oroatis* in the smaller size of all the ocelli. In *M. oroatis* the lower ocellus on the upperside of the forewing is large, perfect, and occupies the entire breadth of the interspace.

A single specimen was taken by Captain C. T. Bingham in the Donat Range in January, which is now in the Indian Museum, Calcutta ; and another taken in the lower Thoungyeen forests has been deposited in the British Museum, where it now stands as *L. fervida*, Butler. The FEMALE is unknown.

Genus 9.—NEORINA, Westwood. (PLATE XIV).

Neorina, Westwood, Gen. D. L., p. 369 (1851).

"BODY robust ; WINGS large, subtriangular. *Forewing* with a broad oblique pale fascia. *Both wings* with a large ocellus near the outer angle on the underside. HEAD large, hairy, not tufted in front. *Eyes* large, smooth. *Antennæ* not more than two-fifths of the length of the forewing, very slender, much curved downwards at the tip ; joints scarcely distinct, terminated by an elongated, very slender, and gradually formed club. *Palpi* broad, much compressed, very hairy in front, and with a small tuft of hairs in the middle of

---

* *Mycalesis oroatis*, Hewitson, Ex. Butt., vol. iii, p. 90, *Mycalesis* pl. vi, figs. 38, 39 (1864) *male* ; *Loesa oroatis*, Moore, Trans. Ent. Soc. Lond., 1880, p. 177. HABITAT : Java. EXPANSE : 2·0 inches DESCRIPTION : "MALE : UPPERSIDE rufous. *Forewing* with the costal margin, and the apical half dark brown, with two ocelli, one near the apex small and indistinct [not shown in the figure], the other large. *Hindwing* with the outer margin broadly brown. UNDERSIDE dark brown, paler beyond the middle. *Both wings* crossed at the middle by a narrow common band of lilac ; both with the outer margin, and two submarginal lines (the inner much curved [highly lunulate] brown. *Forewing* with two large ocelli. *Hindwing* with seven, the first four of equal size (the fourth immature), the fifth large." (*Hewitson*, l. c.)

the back of the middle joint; terminal joint very small, slender, and oval, obliquely porrected, but scarcely reaching to the level of the top of the eyes. *Thorax* robust, oval, hairy. *Abdomen* elongate, rather narrow. *Forewing* large, subtriangular; costal margin much arched, apex slightly rounded; outer margin five-ninths of the length of the costal margin, nearly straight, and very slightly scalloped; inner angle rounded; inner margin nearly straight in both sexes, considerably longer than the outer. *Costal nervure* but slightly swollen at the base, and extending only to the middle of the costa. *Subcostal nervure* with its branches free; the first and second arising close together before the anterior extremity of the discoidal cell, and uniting with the costa far beyond the extremity of the costal nervure; third branch arising half way between the cell and the tip; fourth branch arising at a little distance beyond the third, extending to the tip of the wing; the terminal part of the nervure extending below the tip. *Upper disco-cellular* nervule very short and oblique, arising at about two-fifths of the length of the wing (at the tip of the little dark brown tooth on the inside of the fulvous bar in *N. hilda*, which in fact forms the boundary of the discoidal cell). *Middle disco-cellular* rather longer, transverse. *Lower disco-cellular* much longer, more oblique, and slightly curved, uniting with the third branch of the median nervure; closing the discoidal cell almost in a right angle, this third branch being angulated at the point of junction, which is at the same distance from the origin of the third branch as exists between the first and second branches. *Hindwing* nearly semicircular, the outer angle rounded; costal margin much arched; outer margin slightly scalloped. The nervures arranged as in *Orinoma*, the *discoidal cell* not extending more than two-fifths of the length of the wing, and closed by a slightly curved lower disco-cellular nervule, united to the median nervure at the origin of its third branch. *Forelegs* of the MALE small, moderately feathered; the divisions being of nearly equal length and thickness. *Four hindlegs* long and strong, scaly, with very few hairs; *tibia* nearly as long as the femur, with two rows of small spines beneath; *tibial spurs* long and very acute; *tarsus* with several rows of short spines beneath and at the sides. *Claws* strong, acute, simple, and very much curved. *Paronychia* minute, bifid."

"*N. hilda*, the type of the genus, might easily, from its general appearance and colouring, be mistaken for one of the *Morphinæ*, but its hairy palpi and the arrangement of the nervures of the wings refer it to the present subfamily, from most of which it is distinguished by the slightly swollen base of the nervures of the forewing, its large size, and peculiar style of markings." (*Westwood*, l. c.)

Key to the Indian Species of Neorina.

A. A prominent band crossing the forewing.

a. Of moderate size (under five inches in expanse); the band yellow; hindwing rounded.

116. N. HILDA, Sikkim, Assam.

b. Of large size (over five inches in expanse in Indian specimens); the band almost white; hindwing with a distinct tail.

117. N. CRISHNA, Cachar, Assam, Java.

c. Of smaller size (about three inches in expanse); with a complete series of ocelli on both wings, on upper and undersides.

118. N. MARGARITÆ, Sikkim.

The latter species, *N. margaritæ*, is only tentatively placed here; it was placed by the describer, Mr. H. J. Elwes, as *Lethe (?)*, and it probably is generically distinct from both *Neorina* and *Lethe*, but in the absence of specimens we can give no positive opinion, nor can we assign to it a place among the *Lethes* for the same reason.

Only one other species in the genus has been described, *N. lowii*, from Sumatra and Borneo. This genus contains the largest and perhaps most striking species of the subfamily *Satyrinæ* that occur in India.

116. Neorina hilda, Westwood.

N. hilda, Westwood, Gen. D. L., p. 370, pl. lxv, fig. 2 (1851), *male*.

HABITAT: N.-E. India (Sikkim and Sibsagar).

EXPANSE: 4·6 to 4·8 inches.

DESCRIPTION: MALE: UPPERSIDE, velvety blackish brown. *Forewing* with a transverse yellow macular band from before the middle of the costa to the hinder angle, and passing just at the outer edge of the short discoidal cell; a large black round somewhat obscure subapical spot with a minute white pupil; a white spot on the upper edge of the large black spot (with a smaller one above it), and a smaller one on its lower edge, and two indistinct dark submarginal sinuous lines. *Cilia* dark brown, paler towards the inner angle. *Hindwing* with the apical margin yellow, in continuation of the transverse band of the forewing; the rest of the outer margin irrorated with yellow scales; two indistinct sinuous submarginal lines of a darker brown colour; the nervules and a spot between each pair along the margin brown, owing to the absence of the yellow irrorations. *Cilia* pale yellow. UNDERSIDE paler and brighter brown. *Forewing* with the yellow macular band of the upperside broader and paler; two dark sinuous submarginal lines, and irrorated with lilac within the inner one towards the apex; a prominent black ocellus between the discoidal nervules, minutely pupilled with white, and narrowly ringed with yellow and dark brown, with two prominent white spots above, and two below, sometimes narrowly ringed with dark brown. *Hindwing* with two dark irregular indistinct subbasal lines, a prominent ocellus between the subcostal nervules as on the forewing. The abdominal margin irrorated with yellow extending into and slightly beyond the cell, the irroration more dense at the anal angle; a submarginal band of lilac irrorations most pronounced towards the apex and anal angle, broadest and most diffused in the middle; four small bluish submarginal spots, the fourth developed as an ocellus, and two dark sinuous submarginal lines; the outer angle yellow as on upperside. The FEMALE differs only in the abdomen being shorter, and the forelegs clothed with short hairs. The markings of the wings are identical with those of the male.

Sikkim and Assam are the only localities from which we have received this species.

117. **Neorina crishna**, Westwood. (PLATE XIV, FIG. 34 ♀).

Cylio crishna, Westwood, Gen. D. L., p. 361 (1851), *male*; *Neorina crishna*, Butler, Cat. Lep. B. M., *Satyridæ*, p. 111, n. 2 (1868).

HABITAT: N.-E. India, Java.

EXPANSE: 3·75 *(Westwood)*; 5·3 tc 5·8 inches.

DESCRIPTION: "MALE; *Forewing* scarcely angulate below the apex. *Hindwing* caudate in the middle. UPPERSIDE, both wings fuscous. *Forewing* with a broad oblique yellowish white band from the middle of the costa to the hinder angle, including a black mark at the extremity of the discoidal cell; a large black subapical ocellus with a minute white pupil, and two white spots circled externally with yellowish [above it]. *Hindwing* with the apex whitish; two ocelli towards the anal angle; both wings with a submarginal wavy yellowish streak. UNDERSIDE similar, with the subapical ocellus of the *forewing* minute. *Hindwing* with an ocellus near the apex, and two minute ocelli towards the anal angle." *(Westwood*, l. c.)

The species which we have called *N. crishna* differs from the original description translated above in the following points: On the UPPERSIDE of the *hindwing* there is no trace of an ocellus in some specimens, and in others there is only one towards the anal angle, which shows through by transparency very indistinctly from the underside. On the UNDERSIDE of the *forewing* the subapical ocellus is large not minute, black, pupilled with white, with a yellow and then a narrow black ring. The *hindwing* has a subapical ocellus as in the forewing, but with the yellow iris dilated at that portion of its circumference directed towards the base of the wing; a somewhat smaller but still large subanal ocellus between the two lower median nervules, and between these two ocelli there are three other much smaller ones, one between each pair of the nervules, their violet centres somewhat blurred; these ocelli are sometimes obsolescent, and only represented by suffused violet dots. *Both wings* with two submarginal dark wavy lines, the area within the inner one and along its outer margin irrorated with violescent scales, which in the hindwing extend up the abdominal margin. There is also an irroration of yellowish scales just beyond and below the discoidal cell. The FEMALE is identical with the male in markings, but can be known by its shorter abdomen, and the forelegs clothed with short hairs.

The great difference in size between the species originally described by Westwood and those referred to above, as well as the notable differences in the ocellation, suggest a doubt as to whether the above identification is correct. Westwood's species is described from Java and

North India, but we know of nothing in North India that answers to it. If it should turn out that the *N. crishna* of Westwood is really confined to Java, a new name would have to be given to the Indian species here described.

Mr. Wood-Mason took numerous specimens on Nemotha, 3,300 feet elevation, in Cachar, in September and October; and there are specimens in the Indian Museum, Calcutta, from Cherra Punji, Assam, and in Major Marshall's collection from Shillong. A female specimen from Cherra Punji is figured, and shews the upper and undersides.

118. **Neorina margaritæ,** Elwes.

Lethe (?) margaritæ, Elwes, Proc. Zool. Soc. Lond., 1882, p. 405, pl. xxv, fig. 1, *male*.

HABITAT: Sikkim.

EXPANSE: 3·1 [3·4 in the plate] inches.

DESCRIPTION: "MALE: Colour hair-brown, paler on underside. [*Forewing*] with a transverse pale fawn-coloured band beyond the discoidal cell, well defined on underside and fainter above; a similar band near the margin of the wing at an acute angle to the first, enclosing five white-pupilled ocelli in a straight row, [distinct on underside, indistinct on upperside]; on the exterior margin are two narrow lines of similar colour to the bands [on both wings on both sides]. Pattern of *hindwing* on the underside somewhat similar, but the transverse band is rather curved outwards, and there is a large ocellus between the first and second subcostal nervules. The ocellus at anal angle has a double pupil. The bands on the hindwing do not show on the upperside, and the ocelli are indistinct. *Antennæ* in size and shape like those of *Neorina hilda*, rufous with reddish tip. *Palpi* longer, more pointed, and less hairy than in *N. hilda*. *Abdomen* and *legs* rather shorter." (*Elwes*, l. c.)

UPPERSIDE: *Both wings* hair-brown, with two narrow pale fawn-coloured bands on the outer margin. *Forewing* with a pale fawn-coloured band beyond the cell, and a submarginal row of indistinct ocelli fading into fawn-coloured spots near the costa. *Hindwing* with five submarginal black spots, the two lower pupilled with white and ringed with yellow, brightest on the outer edge, the three upper blind, and the iris disappearing towards the costa. UNDERSIDE paler, the fawn-coloured marginal lines as on upperside. *Forewing* with a submarginal fawn-coloured band bearing five perfect ocelli; and the transverse fawn-coloured band of the upperside but wider and more distinct. *Hindwing* with a similar submarginal band, also bearing five perfect ocelli, the lowest bipupilled; a separate very large ocellus between the subcostal nervules, and a straight fawn-coloured band from the costa crossing the end of the cell, but not passing the submedian nervure or reaching the lowest ocellus. (Described from the figure).

Captain Elwes, in describing this species, writes: "A single male specimen of this fine and distinct species was in the collection [from Sikkim], and appears very distinct from anything which has been described. At first sight it seems most nearly allied to *N. hilda*, but does not quite agree with that species in neuration. Neither does it agree exactly with either *Zophoessa* or *Lethe*, though it somewhat resembles *L. lunaris*, Butler, in markings. Until we know more of the insect, it will be best to leave it in the genus *Lethe*, which requires careful revision, as the species at present comprised in it are very varied."

In the absence of specimens for examination we are unable to assign a place for this insect in the genus *Lethe*, which embraces forms showing several distinctive structural features. We have, therefore, provisionally placed it with *Neorina* immediately preceding *Lethe*.

Genus 10.—LETHE, Hübner. (PLATES X AND XI).

Lethe, Hübner, Verz. bek. Schmett., p. 56 (1816); *Debis*, Westwood, Gen. D. L., p. 358 (1851).

"BODY, rather small; WINGS large; *hindwing* generally angulated in the middle, with a row of large ocelli. HEAD, rather small, scarcely tufted in front. *Eyes* hairy, prominent, especially in the males. *Palpi* rather elongated, elevated obliquely as high as, or higher than, the level of the top of the eyes, and porrected to a short distance in front of the face; the long middle joint without any tuft on the back, clothed in front with moderately short fine hairs, not forming a close mass; terminal joint very short and slender. *Antennæ* not, or scarcely, half the length of the forewing, very slender; terminated by a slender gradually formed club, composed of very short joints. *Thorax* very short, thick, and hairy. *Abdomen* small. FOREWING triangular-ovate; costal margin strongly curved; apex rounded; outer margin straight, or but little emarginate, about three-fifths of the length of the anterior margin; inner margin nearly straight, about as long as the outer margin. *Costal* nervure dilated at the base, extending rather beyond the middle of the costa. *Subcostal* nervure with its first and second branches arising before the anterior extremity of the discoidal cell, the third and fourth beyond it, about the same distance apart as between the origin of the second and third branches, and of the fourth branch and the tip of the wing. *Upper disco-cellular* very minute, oblique; *middle disco-cellular* much longer, curved at the extremity, being directed rather outwards; *lower disco-cellular* longer than the middle one, nearly straight, also directed obliquely outwards, uniting with the third branch of the median nervure at about the same distance from its origin as exists between the first and second branches; the third branch being considerably angulated at the point of junction, whereby the discoidal cell is closed somewhat acutely rather beyond the middle of the wing. HINDWING subovate, more or less scalloped along the outer margin, which is generally deeply angulated, or rather shortly tailed at the extremity of the third branch of the median nervure. *Precostal* nervure curved, the tip directed outwards. *Costal* nervure extending to about two-thirds of the length of the costa. First branch of the subcostal nervure arising at a moderate distance from its base, the extremity extending to the outer angle of the wing. *Upper* and *lower disco-cellular* nervules oblique, curved, of nearly equal length; the upper one arising at a short distance from the origin of the first branch of the subcostal nervure; the lower one uniting with the median nervure close to, or exactly at, the origin of the third branch, closing the discoidal cell in an acute point. FORELEGS very minute, and thickly clothed with long silky hairs. The tarsus slender, as long as the tibia, and destitute of joints or claws. *Forelegs* of the FEMALE rather longer than those of the male, slender, scaly, destitute of hairs, of nearly equal thickness throughout; the tarsal articulations concealed by scales; obliquely truncate at the tip, where are a few short spines, indicating the very short terminal joints. MIDDLE and HINDLEGS rather short, slender, scaly; *tibia* but very slightly furnished with a few short spines; *tibial spurs* rather long; *tarsi* nearly cylindrical; basal joint half the length of the tarsus, with but a few very short spines on the underside. CLAWS very much curved; *paronychia* very slender."

"The hairy eyes, slender elongated palpi, dilated base of the costal nervure of the forewing, the middle and lower disco-cellular nervules of nearly equal length; and the acute termination of the discoidal cell of the hindwing are the chief characters of this genus." (*Westwood*, l.c.)

This is an Indo-Malayan genus. The species are very numerous, and are widely spread, though, except in East and South India, they seem entirely confined to the hilly regions. They are for the most part brown on the upperside, often with a prominent white bar on the forewing; the underside being always ocellated, often richly variegated, though as a rule not so richly as in *Zophoessa;* and are of rather small size, seldom exceeding three inches in expanse. They are chiefly found in forests and shady places amongst the undergrowth, settling on or near the ground, or upon dead leaves.

There are thirty-five species recorded from India. By far the largest number are found in the Eastern Himalayas and Assam. One species only, *L. europa*, seems very widely spread, as it occurs throughout India, Malayana, Java and China. *L. rohria* also has a wide range, as it is found all along the Himalayas and on our eastern frontier, in Burma, Tenasserim and again in Java. The others are local and many of them rare. The genus requires revision, but the material at our command is not yet sufficient for the purpose; of the thirty-five species recorded we have specimens of only twenty-five, and even of these we have in many instances only one or two, representing a single sex.

The genus is divisable into two main groups, in the first of which the male insects possess sexual glands, and tufts of hair on the wings, showing affinity in this point with *Cœlites* and *Mycalesis;* in the second group the male insects lack these characters, showing affinity with *Zophoessa* and *Neope.* The second group is further divisible into two subgroups, by the shape of the discoidal cell in the *hindwing.*

Key to the Groups of Lethe.

A. Males with a long narrow patch of differently formed scales from those of the rest of the wing, placed on the upperside of the forewing below the median nervule.

B. Males without sexual glands and tufts on either wing.

- *a.* The apex of the cell in the hindwing *at* the origin of the second median nervule.
- *b.* The apex of the cell in the hindwing *beyond* the origin of the second median nervule.

C. White with rufous brown markings *

The differentiation of the sexes in this genus, as regards colour and markings, is considerable and varied, but in most cases the general pattern and style of colouration of the underside of the hindwing is identical in both sexes. The usual difference consists in the presence in the female of a conspicuous white bar or series of spots in the forewing, which in the male is absent; but this is not universal; in some the colouration of the upperside also differs, while in three at least, *L. rohria*, *L. verma* and *L. masoni*, the white bar is found in both sexes. In the first species, *L. scanda*, the sexes are of totally different colours on the upperside, the male being indigo-blue, and the female dark brown, neither sex having white markings. In *L. latiaris*, the female has a narrow pale ochreous fascia on the forewing, which is wanting in the male; and in the other four species of the first group, the female has white markings, which are altogether absent in the males.

The first group contains six Indian species, and is further divisible into three subgroups based on the different nature and position of these sexual tufts, and these subgroups correspond exactly with the geographical distribution of the insects; three species from North-East India have a conspicuous tuft of hairs on the hindwing, in addition to the narrow raised patch near the inner margin of the forewing; one species from Burma and Malayana has the conspicuous tuft of hairs on the hindwing, but in a different position; and, lastly, two species from Ceylon lack the tuft on the hindwing altogether. The principal characters of the species of the first group, found within Indian limits, are given in the key below.

Key to the Indian species of Lethe.

First Group.

A. Males with a long narrow patch of differently formed scales from those of the rest of the wing, placed on the upperside of the forewing below the median nervure.

a. The narrow patch of raised scales placed on either side of the middle of the submedian nervure.

*a*¹. Males with a conspicuous tuft of long black hairs placed upon a glandular patch on the upperside of the hindwing immediately below the cell, and on the base of the second median nervule; the apex of the cell beyond the origin of the second median nervule. The ocelli on underside of hindwing not disintegrated, but some of the ocelli bearing several white dots besides the pupil.

*a*². Male, upperside rich deep indigo-blue, paler on the margins. Female dark brown, with only two indistinct yellowish subapical marks on the upperside of the forewing.

119. L. SCANDA, Sikkim.

*b*². Male, upperside rich rufous brown, crossed at the middle of the forewing by a band of darker brown. Female, with the darker brown band outwardly margined by a series of pure white spots.

120. L. BHAIRAVA, Sikkim.

*c*². Male, upperside pale dull brown; forewing without markings. Female, similar in colouration, but the forewing crossed by a transverse oblique ochreous band.

121. L. LATIARIS, N.-E. India, Burma.

*b*¹. Males with the tuft of hairs on the hindwing placed between the first and second median nervules. The apex of the cell at the origin of the second median nervule. Ocelli on underside of hindwing disintegrated.

122. L. MINERVA, Tenasserim, Malayana.

* The proper position of this species cannot be ascertained in the absence of specimens for examination.

b. Males with the tuft of hairs on the forewing placed between the first median nervule and submedian nervure. Ocelli on underside of hindwing not disintegrated.

a[1]. Male, upperside dark brown, with a few indistinct markings. Female also dark brown, with a conspicuous white band across the forewing.

123. L. *(Hanipha)* SIHALA, Ceylon.

b[1]. Male unknown. Female, upperside ferruginous-brown, with markings somewhat as in *L. sihala*

124. L. *(Hanipha)* DYNSATE, Ceylon.

The glandular patch of scales on the forewing of the North-Indian species is not very conspicuous, but can easily be detected by careful examination.

119. Lethe scanda, Moore.

Debis scanda, Moore, Horsfield and Moore, Cat. Lep. E. I. C., vol. i, p. 218, n. 451 (1857), *male; Debis nada*, idem, id., n. 452, *female*.

HABITAT ; Sikkim.

EXPANSE : ♂, 2·5 ; ♀, 2·62 inches.

DESCRIPTION : "MALE : UPPERSIDE blackish, glossed with blue ; along the margins pale purplish-blue. *Hindwing* with indistinct submarginal black spots. [There is a conspicuous tuft of black hairs placed on the second median nervule from its origin at the median nervure.] UNDERSIDE deep ferruginous-brown. *Forewing* with a transverse paler band across the discoidal cell, and another across the disc ; a submarginal row of [four] pale ocelli. *Hindwing* with two transverse darker lines, and a submarginal series of six, and a geminated seventh ocellus ; margins pale, with a narrow darker line." "FEMALE : UPPERSIDE dark brown. *Forewing* with two indistinct yellowish subapical marks. *Hindwing* with a row of four small black submarginal spots. UNDERSIDE deep bright ferruginous. *Forewing* with transverse band across discoidal cell, and another across the disc, yellowish ; a submarginal row of pale ocelli. *Hindwing* with two transverse darker lines and a row of submarginal ocelli ; margins pale, with a darker narrow line. *Cilia* white. *Remark*.—This may possibly be only the female of the preceding species [*L. scanda*]." (*Moore*, l. c.)

L. scanda is a rare insect, and we have never seen the female. The male is at once distinguished from all the other species of the genus known to us by the upperside being most beautifully glossed with indigo-blue. It has as yet only been found in Sikkim.

120. Lethe bhairava, Moore.

Debis bhairava, Moore, Horsfield and Moore, Cat. Lep. E. I. C., vol. i, p. 217, n. 450 (1857), *female; Debis anysis*, Hewitson, Ex. Butt., vol. iii, *Debis* pl. i, fig. 1 (1862), *male*.

HABITAT : Sikkim.

EXPANSE : ♂, 2·62 to 2·80 ; ♀, 2·6 inches.

DESCRIPTION : "MALE : UPPERSIDE rufous-brown. *Forewing* crossed at the middle by a band of darker brown. *Hindwing* with a tuft of long hair in the middle, and half way between it and the outer margin, four ocelli, the lower two only with white pupils, the iris indistinct light brown. UNDERSIDE rufous. *Forewing* crossed by three bands of rufous-brown ; one near the base ; one a little beyond it, crossing the cell only ; the third beyond the middle, followed by four nearly blind ocelli, though pupilled with white, with a rufous border above and below. *Hindwing* crossed by two rufous bands, one near the base, the other near the middle (curved), followed by seven ocelli ; the first near the costal margin (largest), the seventh near the anal angle (minute, united to the sixth), all black with white pupils ; the iris rufous-orange, bordered with black, and again by rufous-yellow and rufous-brown ; the outer margin and a line near it brown." (*Hewitson*, l. c). "FEMALE : UPPERSIDE olive-brown. *Forewing* with a transverse sharply-defined dusky line, bordered with a series of small white spots, disposed obliquely from beyond the middle of anterior to near posterior margin, one-fourth from the angle ; also a subapical row of four small yellow spots, parallel with exterior margin. *Hindwing* with four submarginal round black spots encircled with pale brown, and medially disposed from near anterior to near anal angle. UNDERSIDE luteous-brown. *Forewing* with two transverse ferruginous-brown lines, the inner one bifid across discoidal cell, the outer straight, and bordered by the white spots; a submarginal row of four pale ocelli, also an anterior terminal yellow spot. *Hindwing* with two transverse ferruginous-brown lines, and a submarginal row of six ocelli; a narrow dark marginal line to both wings." (*Moore*, l. c.) "Except in the form of the hindwing, *L. anysis* seems identical with *L. bhairava*. May it not be the male of that insect?" (*Butler*, Cat. Lep. B. M., *Satyridæ*, p. 117, n. 22 (1868).

Both sexes of this species appear to be rare.

The next species has somewhat the aspect of *L. hyrania*, especially on the underside, but is larger, and the male has a tuft of hair on the upperside of the hindwing.

121. Lethe latiaris, Hewitson.

Debis latiaris, Hewitson, Ex. Butt., vol. iii, *Debis* pl. i, fig. 4 (1862), *female; Lethe latiaris*, Butler, Cat. Lep. B.M., *Satyridæ*, p. 117, n. 23 (1868).

HABITAT: Sylhet, Assam, Khasi Hills, Upper Tenasserim.

EXPANSE: 2·0 to 2·7 inches.

DESCRIPTION: "FEMALE: UPPERSIDE yellow-brown. *Forewing* with an indistinct transverse band at the middle, and a small rufous spot near the apex. *Hindwing* with three indistinct blind ocelli [in one specimen all the ocelli of the underside show through indistinctly by transparency on the upperside]; the outer margin and a line near it dark brown, the space between the lines yellow. *Cilia* grey. UNDERSIDE light grey or yellow-brown. *Both wings* with the outer margin and a line near it dark brown, with between them a line of yellow. *Forewing* crossed before the middle by two short rufous bands; at the middle by a band of white (its inner border rufous), forming a triangle with a broad grey band, which runs parallel to the outer margin, and incloses four small indistinct ocelli. *Hindwing* crossed before the middle by a straight rufous band; at the middle by a curved band of the same colour, followed by seven ocelli; the first apart from the rest, the sixth and seventh (at the anal angle) in one; all black with white pupils, the iris yellow, margined with dark brown, and again with lilac-white." (*Hewitson*, l. c.) "MALE, differs in several particulars from the female. *Hindwing* less angulated, with a discal hairy streak above, and the central bands on the UNDERSIDE are placed slightly nearer together." (*Butler*, l. c.) The *forewing* on the UPPERSIDE is unmarked.

Somewhat rare; it has been taken at Shillong in May.

The next species has the same general aspect as *L. mekara*, and the female has a bent macular band of pure white spots, as in the females of *L. mekara* and its allies.

122. Lethe minerva, Fabricius.

Papilio minerva, Fabricius, Syst. Ent., p. 493, n. 216 (1775); *Papilio arcadia*, Cramer, Pap. Ex., vol. ii, pl. cxvi, figs. E, F (1777), *female; Satyrus caumas*, Godart, Enc. Méth., vol. ix., p. 479, n. 7 (1819); *Lethe arcadia*, Butler, Cat. Lep. B. M., *Satyridæ*, p. 118, n. 24 (1868); id., Moore, Proc. Zool. Soc. Lond., 1878, p. 824.

HABITAT: Upper Tenasserim, Sumatra, Java.

EXPANSE: 2·5 inches.

DESCRIPTION: MALE: UPPERSIDE dark brown, with the extreme outer margins of *both wings* and the *cilia* pale brown. *Forewing* with the basal two-thirds thickly clothed with paler brown hairs than the ground-colour, especially on either side of the middle third of the submedian nervure; the ground-colour on either side of this nervure, but especially behind it being black. Two or three subapical pale spots. *Hindwing* with the basal area and the costal margin dark brown; the cell and abdominal margin thickly clothed with long paler hairs. Outer margin and disc bright ferruginous. Three oval small black spots in the median and discoidal interspaces, a larger and outwardly diffused spot in the upper discoidal interspace. A marginal orange line bounded on either side by very fine dark lines. A conspicuous oval patch of black scales placed at the base of the first median interspace, with a tuft of long hairs lying over it. UNDERSIDE ochreous, suffused darker on the disc and at the outer angle of the forewing. A common subbasal brown line commencing before the apex of the cell in the forewing, and ending near the middle of the abdominal margin of the hindwing; the area beyond it paler; a discal very irregular similar line across both wings. *Forewing* with a submarginal series of four inconspicuous rudimentary ocelli placed on a violet ground, which is continued to the apex; a series of three minute dots with paler borders placed transversly in the middle of the cell. *Hindwing* with a submarginal series of seven indistinct yellow ocelli, the two anal ones run together, with black centres broken up into numerous minute dots; marginal lines to *both wings* as on upperside. FEMALE differs on the upperside in having all the ground-colour except the apex and outer margin of the forewing, bright ferruginous. *Forewing*, with the subapical spots pure white, and with a bent macular band of pure white spots across the disc. The anterior spot elongate and somewhat quadrate, reaching from the costa to the lower discoidal nervule; a large rounded spot in the second median interspace; a smaller one in the interspace below, and the last, double the size of the one above it, in the space below the first median nervule. *Hindwing* with a fifth diffused black spot in the space above the subcostal nervure. UNDERSIDE paler than in the male, with a white band across the disc of the *forewing*, outwardly sharply angled, and inwardly clearly defined with a dark brown line.

Godart's description of *Satyrus caumas** is appended for reference. It is not known why Messrs. Moore and Butler have rejected the older Fabrician name for this species.

Captain C. T. Bingham took this species in the Donat Range and Meplay in January, at Meplay in January and February, in the Thoungyeen Forests in March and May, and at Houndraw in November; and Limborg took it at Ahsown probably in the cold weather.

The next two species are closely allied, and have the same general aspect as *L. daretis* and *L. drypetis* of the second group; and having, in the female only, a conspicuous white bar on the forewing. Moore, in his "Lepidoptera of Ceylon," page 18, has placed them in a distinct genus from *Lethe*, which he characterises as follows:—*Genus* HANIPHA. "Wings similar in form and venation to *Lethe*, but the *forewing* comparatively shorter and of less breadth, and the *hindwing* longer. MALE with a conspicuous lengthened tuft of short hairs transversely covering a sericeous patch of compact raised scales between the first median nervule and submedian nervure; first median nervule much curved. Type, *H. sihala*," (*Moore*, l. c.)

123. **Lethe sihala**, Moore.

L. sihala, Moore, Proc. Zool. Soc. Lond., 1872, p. 555; *Hanipha sihala*, id. Lep. Cey., p. 19, pl. viii, figs. 2, 2b, *male*; 2a, *female* (1880).

HABITAT: Ceylon.

EXPANSE: ♂, 2·25; ♀, 2·50 inches.

DESCRIPTION: "MALE: UPPERSIDE dark olive-brown. *Forewing* with two very indistinct or obsolete dusky-white apical spots, and a longitudinal tuft of long blackish-brown hairs between first median nervule and submedian nervure. *Hindwing* with a submarginal series of indistinct black spots. UNDERSIDE, basal area dark brown, apical area pale brown, being divided on the *forewing* by an oblique discal chalybeate-purple streak, and on the *hindwing* by a discal medially-angled dark brown line; a submarginal series of four very indistinct ocelli on *forewing* formed by a central black dot, and two chalybeate rings; a submarginal series of six larger ocelli on *hindwing*, formed by a black spot with a single white central dot and fulvous outer ring, each being encircled by a purple border; *both wings* with a dark brown purple-bordered subbasal transverse line. FEMALE: UPPERSIDE brown, basal area paler. *Forewing* with a broad oblique discal white band and a terminal spot near posterior angle; a small

---

* *Satyrus caumas*, Godart. DESCRIPTION: "MALE; UPPERSIDE dark brown, with a little tuft of black hairs on the disc of *hindwing;* and an ashy spot, elliptic. longitudinal, surrounded with black, towards the middle of the inner margin of the *forewing*. FEMALE: UPPERSIDE dark tawny, terminated on the *forewing* by a blackish space, triangular and very large, on which there is a transverse white macular band bent hindwards, and followed by a white dot which faces the apex. *Hindwing* has parallel to the outer margin a row of four large black eye-like spots. These spots are also present in the male, but of a darker colour. BOTH SEXES: UNDERSIDE reddish-grey, with three transverse ferruginous lines, of which the second and third are more undulate than the anterior one, and enclosing on the *hindwing* six yellowish contiguous ocelli, having the iris of a pearly-grey, the pupil black and sprinkled with dots, which appear as if gilded. On the *forewing* these same lines enclose some indistinct ocellated dots. *Body* brown; *antennæ* reddish." (*Godart*, Enc. Méth, vol. ix, p 479, n. 7 (1819).

white apical spot and two indistinct streaks below it ; an indistinct series of blackish submarginal spots. *Hindwing* with a submarginal series of five black spots, the middle spot very small ; the upper spots with broad irregular whitish-brown borders, the two lower with pale brown rings and a white central dot. UNDERSIDE brown at base ; outer borders paler. *Forewing* with oblique band as above, and five submarginal spots. *Hindwing* as in male ; subbasal transverse line purple-bordered, and the irregular medial line with whitish-brown outer border. The female of this species is much like that of *L. dynsate*, but it differs in having a narrower oblique discal band, and more defined subapical white and black spots on the forewing, and the hindwing has paler interspaces between the outer series of spots. The underside also differs in the forewing having five submarginal ringlet spots instead of four, and the hindwing has all the spots smaller, the costal spot and the second anal being one-third less in size." (*Moore*, l.c. in Lep. Cey.)

"Rare and very local ; observed only in two places in forest land near Newera Eliya. Habits similar to those of *L. drypetis.*" (*Hutchison*). We have never seen this Butterfly.

124. **Lethe dynsate,** Hewitson.

Debis dynsate, Hewitson, Ex. Butt., vol. iii, *Debis* pl. ii, figs. 9, 10 (1863), *female*; *Lethe dynsate*, Butler, Cat. Lep. B. M., *Satyridæ*, p. 115, n. 10 (1868) ; *Hanipha dynsate*, Moore, Lep. Cey., p. 20, pl. ix, figs. 1, 1*a* (1880), *female*.

HABITAT : Ceylon.

EXPANSE : 2·55 inches.

DESCRIPTION : "FEMALE : UPPERSIDE rufous-brown. *Forewing* dark brown, except near the base, crossed at the middle by a broad *equal band* of white, and a solitary white spot ; two indistinct white spots near the apex [the lower one with a rounded dark spot contiguous to it internally]. *Hindwing* with a large bilobed spot near the apex, followed by three black blind ocelli (one [the first] minute). [The apical spot is on a yellowish ground ; internal to it is a yellowish spot; and an indistinct yellowish band crosses the wing from just beyond the extremity of the cell, where the third median nervule is given off, to the first median nervule. The *forewing* has a submarginal black line, and the *hindwing* two similar lines]. UNDERSIDE rufous and grey-brown. *Forewing* with the white band continuous to the anal angle, with, between it and the apex, a band of three blind ocelli [placed on a lilac ground reaching to the apex where it expands and coalesces with a lilac submarginal line, which latter is bordered on both sides with a black line. A violet band from the subcostal nervure crosses the middle of the cell, and is continued across the wing till it meets the band on the hindwing. It is bordered on both sides with a dark brown line]. *Hindwing* with a band of six perfect ocelli, the first and fifth large, the other four small and somewhat misshapen, each with two or three white dots." (*Hewitson*, l. c.) A violet line edged internally only with dark brown, crosses the wing before the middle in continuation of that on the forewing ; beyond the middle of the wing the brown ground-colour deepens and terminates abruptly in an irregular line greatly extended above the third median nervule, succeeded by a grey band above the discoidal nervule, and a yellow band below from the third median nervule ; the usual yellow and violet submarginal lines, separated by and edged with dark brown ; the violet line wide at apex where it extends beyond the brown line up to the ocelli ; the ocelli ringed with yellow, then brown, and then incompletely with grey. MALE unknown.

We have never seen a specimen of this insect ; the additions to the description have been made from Hewitson's figures of the species.

The second group contains a very large number of species, and presents considerable variations in the outline of the wings, but the transition from the elongate forewing and highly caudate hindwing of *L. sinorix* to the short broad forewing and rounded, scarcely caudate, hindwing of *L. sidonis*, is so gradual that the separation into subgroups on this point only would be impossible. The only structural variation in this group of any note is in the position of the apex of the cell in the hindwing. The differentiation of the sexes varies widely.

Key to the Indian species of Lethe.

Second Group.

B. Males without sexual glands and tufts on either wing.

a. The apex of the cell in the hindwing *at* the origin of the second median nervule.

a^1. Males with the forewing narrow and elongate; the outer margin concave. Ocelli on underside of hindwing *not* disintegrated.

a^2. Hindwing with a long narrow tail. Underside ground-colour nearly uniform, with two distinct narrow dark transverse lines, the inner one not outwardly bordered with lilac.

a^3. With the ocelli on the upperside of the hindwing placed on a ferruginous ground.

125. L. SINORIX, Assam.

b^3. With the ocelli on the upperside of the hindwing not on a ferruginous ground.

126. L. KANSA, Sikkim, Assam, Burma.

b^2. Hindwing with the tail shorter and more blunt. Underside with the ground-colour paler externally, and darker on the disc; the inner transverse line distinctly bordered with lilac on its outer edge.

a^3. Upperside of forewing uniform brown.

a^4. Male, upperside, hindwing with the ocelli placed on a ferruginous ground.

127. L. SAMIO, East India.

128. L. PURANA, Habitat unknown.*

b^3. Upperside of forewing with the outer area abruptly paler.

a^4. Male, upperside, hindwing with five blind ocelli; underside, forewing with five ocelli.

129. L. VINDHYA, Assam, Tenasserim.

130. L. DOLOPES,† Sikkim.

b^4. Male, upperside, hindwing with four blind ocelli; underside, forewing with six ocelli.

131. L. ALBERTA, Benares, Tenasserim.

b^1. Males with the forewing somewhat broader and less elongate; the outer margin less concave; tail short and inconspicuous. Ocelli on underside of hindwing disintegrated FEMALE with the white band angulate, macular.

a^2. The dark median fascia on the underside of the hindwing slightly angled outwardly at its middle.

132. L. MEKARA, N.-E. India, Burma.

b^2. The dark median fascia on the underside of the hindwing sharply angled outwardly at its middle, being produced into a conspicuous projection outwards.

a^3. Male with the outer margin of the upperside of the hindwing bright ferruginous. Female with the base of both wings on the upperside bright ferruginous.

133. L. DISTANS, Sikkim.

b^3. Male with the upperside of the hindwing entirely deep brown. Female with the base of both wings on the upperside dull ferruginous.

134. L. CHANDICA, N.-E. India, Burma.

c^1. Forewing short and broad; outer margin slightly concave; hindwing, tail somewhat long; ocelli on underside disintegrated. FEMALE with the white band straight.

a^2. With a prominent single straight violet-white streak crossing the subbasal area of both wings on the underside.

135. L. EUROPA, India, Burma, Andamans.

---

* In the description of this species neither sex nor habitat are given. Butler remarks (Cat. Lep. B. M. *Satyridæ*, p. 118): "Is not this the female of *L. samio*?" The description of *L. purana* is apparently that of a female.

† The specimen described is a female. It seems probable that it is the opposite sex of *L. vindhya*.

b[2]. Male, upperside, forewing unmarked. Female with the discal white band on the upperside of the forewing reaching the first median nervule.

136. L. DRYPETIS, Ceylon.

137. L. TODARA, S. India.

c[2]. Male, upperside, forewing with three small ochreous costal spots, the outer two touching. Female with the discal band on upperside of forewing reaching the submedian nervure; hindwing, upperside, with the blind ocelli having distinct irides.

138. L. DARETIS, Ceylon.

d[2]. Male, upperside, forewing with the spots larger, and an additional subapical spot beyond and below the outer ones. Female, hindwing with a few dark spots on upperside, with no distinct irides.

139. L. DYRTA, Himalayas, Assam, Burma.

e[2]. Male, upperside, forewing with another additional spot near the margin between the lower median nervules. Female with the discal band on upperside of forewing broken up into three large quadrate spots.

140. L. NEELGHERRIENSIS, S. India, Ceylon.

d[1]. Forewing short and broad; outer margin straight or convex, hindwing with the tail short and inconspicuous.

a[2]. Ocelli on underside of hindwing disintegrated.

141. L. SATYAVATI, Assam.

b[2]. Ocelli on underside of hindwing not disintegrated.

a[3]. Male, underside, forewing with two brown lines crossing the cell. Female with a conspicuous straight discal white band across the upperside of the forewing.

a[4]. Underside not tinted with lilac; the ocelli on a pale ground.

142. L. HYRANIA, N.-W. Himalayas.

b[4]. Underside tinted with lilac; the ocelli on a shining lilac ground. Female unknown.

143. L. DINARBAS, Sikkim.

b[3]. Male, underside, forewing with three brown lines crossing the cell. Female unknown.

144. L. SERBONIS, Sikkim.

c[3]. Male and female, upperside, forewing with a conspicuous even curved white band across the disc.

145. L. ROHRIA, Himalayas to Tenasserim.

125. Lethe sinorix, Hewitson.

Debis sinorix, Hewitson, Ex. Butt., vol. iii; *Debis* pl. iii, figs. 19, 20 (1863), *male*.

HABITAT: Cherra Punji and Sibsagar, Assam; Dafla Hills.

EXPANSE: 2·6 to 3·0 inches.

DESCRIPTION: "MALE: UPPERSIDE rufous-brown. *Forewing* with three pale yellow spots near the apex. *Hindwing* with a broad rufous band near the outer margin, encircling four round black spots: the second spot large, the fourth small. [In some specimens there is a fifth spot placed between the third median and discoidal nervules; and a sixth placed in the interspace behind the first median nervule.] UNDERSIDE rufous. *Both wings* crossed by two continuous linear bands of rufous-brown. *Forewing* with the apex lilac-white; the three yellow spots as above, and associated with them two small ocelli. *Hindwing* with a band of six small ocelli, the third out of line [sometimes entirely absent], each with white pupil and rufous iris bordered with brown, and again with silvery white [the anal one is usually bipupilled]: a triangular white spot at the anal angle: a submarginal line of lilac-white; the margin rufous, bordered on both sides with black." (*Hewitson*, l. c.) The FEMALE is unknown.

We have no precise record of the capture of this species. It is closely allied to *L. kansa*, and seems confined to our eastern frontier.

126. Lethe kansa, Moore.

Debis kansa, Moore, Horsfield and Moore, Cat. Lep. E. I. C., vol. i, p. 220, n. 456 (1857).

HABITAT: Sikkim, Manipur, Sibsagar, Upper Tenasserim.

EXPANSE: 2·75 to 3·00 inches.

DESCRIPTION: "MALE: UPPERSIDE glossy olive-brown. *Hindwing* with caudal appendage somewhat long; marginal row of blackish spots indistinct. UNDERSIDE drab, with two transverse dark lines. *Forewing* with four pale ocelli. *Hindwing* with six small black ocelli, encircled by a yellow, brown, and then a lavender-coloured line; the sixth minute and geminated." (*Moore*, l. c.)

Moore's description of the female, which is appended below,* is manifestly erroneous, and appears to have been taken from a specimen of *L. vindhya*, Felder.

The MALE on the UPPERSIDE of the *forewing* frequently has three submarginal ochreous spots, the first placed in the interspace above the termination of the costal nervure, the other two in the interspaces below the second discoidal and third median nervules, one in each. In the *hindwing* the submarginal spots are very distinct, black, rounded, and enclosed each in an ochreous ring; the first and fifth are subequal in size; the second the largest, but only a little larger than the fourth; the third the smallest of all. The usual marginal fine lines. On the UNDERSIDE the ground-colour is usually glossed with violet; the *forewing* in many specimens has a short dark brown transverse bar across the middle of the cell; and the disco-cellular nervules in *both wings* defined with dark brown. The FEMALE differs from the male in the wings being broader and the markings more distinct, especially the ochreous spots on the *forewing*, and it has in addition two or three ochreous subcostal spots as the outer edge of the transverse line which partially shows through from the underside; the outer dark line on the UNDERSIDE of the *hindwing* is more conspicuously dilated into a round spot in the middle of the interspace between the third median and discoidal nervules than in the male.

Messrs. Otto Möller and de Nicéville have taken both sexes of this species in the Sikkim Hills at low elevations in October. Mr. A. O. Hume took it in the eastern hills of Manipur in May, and Captain C. T. Bingham in the Thoungyeen forests in March.

127. Lethe samio, Doubleday, Hewitson.

Debis samio, Doubleday, Hewitson, Gen. D. L., p. 360, n. 8, pl. lxi, fig. 3 (1851), *male*.

HABITAT: East India.

EXPANSE: 2·7 inches.

DESCRIPTION: MALE: UPPERSIDE, *both wings* dark rich brown. *Forewing* narrow, produced; outer margin slightly concave, without spots or markings. *Hindwing* with a broad rufous band near the outer margin, bearing four round black spots, the third very small and out of line, being placed close to the outer margin. A fifth spot between the first and second median nervules is black, oval, and has an outer ferruginous ring. An indistinct submarginal black line. (Described from the figure in the Gen. D. L. The underside is not shown, but some hints regarding it can be gathered from the description of *L. distans*, p. 148.)

On the upperside the forewing agrees exactly with *L. mekara*, but differs from *L. sinorix* in being quite immaculate. The *hindwing* differs from both *L. mekara* and *L. sinorix* in having the rufous band much brighter in colour, more sharply defined, and not extending to the fifth spot, which is separated from it by the ground-colour.

We have not seen a specimen of this species, nor, as far as we are aware, has any record of the capture of a second specimen ever been published. See remarks on the following species; also *L. distans*, p. 148.

---

* *Debis kansa*. "FEMALE: UPPERSIDE dark brown. *Forewing* with darker line across the disc. *Hindwing* with five large black spots, narrowly encircled with red, from anterior angle. UNDERSIDE brown, darkest within the outer transverse line; the inner line within, about the apex of *forewing*, glossed with lavender-colour; ocelli pale. *Hindwing* with the anterior first and fifth ocellus large, that at the anal angle geminated, all encircled with a glossy lavender band." (*Moore*, Cat. Lep. E. I. C., vol. i, p. 220, n. 456 (1857).

128. Lethe purana, Felder.

Debis purana, Felder, Wien. Ent. Monatsch., vol. iii, p. 401, n. 43 (1859); *Lethe purana*, Butler, Cat. Lep. B. M., *Satyridæ*, p. 118, n. 28 (1868).

HABITAT: Not given.

EXPANSE: Not given.

DESCRIPTION: "UPPERSIDE fulvous-brown. *Forewing* subfalcate, with the apex subtruncate, with an external nearly straight macular fascia, diffused outwardly, and an adjacent obsolete spot, white. *Hindwing* extended, subcaudate externally; the *cilia* white at the tips, with an angulate discal striga, and an adjacent obsolete spot, swarthy; an external band pale fulvescent, with four large spots uniform, each spot (the third excepted) large, rounded, marked with swarthy, with a round black ocellus circled with yellow, including a white spot near the anal angle; a marginal fulvescent line. UNDERSIDE pale brown, shining with lilac. *Forewing* paler outwardly, with a subbasal striga, terminated externally with lilac powdering, and another oblique discal, broadly bordered with white externally, ferruginous swarthy; four obsolete exterior ocelli whitish-brown, with a swarthy pupil marked with white, margined with brown, and placed on a white ground tinted with lilac; with two marginal swarthy lines. *Hindwing* with a straight submedian striga, margined externally with lilac; a discal litura and another striga, angulate, corresponding to the upperside, swarthy; six exterior black ocelli arranged in a bent line, broadly circled with yellow, and margined with swarthy, including a white drop (geminate in the anal one), each placed upon a whitish lilac ground; an anal spot of the same colour, and two swarthy marginal lines."

"*D. purana* is allied to *D. samio*, Doubleday, but is sufficiently distinguished from it by the white band of the forewing, the different position and formation of the ocelli, the more angular hindwing and the bands being entirely differently formed." (*Felder*, l. c.) "Is not this the female of *L. samio?*" (*Butler*, l. c.) The description is apparently that of a female, and it is not improbable that Butler's suggestion is a correct one. We have never seen a specimen of this species, nor has any other record of its capture been published to our knowledge.

129. Lethe vindhya, Felder.

Debis vindhya, Felder, Wien. Ent. Monatsch., vol. iii, p. 402, n. 44 (1859).

HABITAT: Assam; Donat Range, Upper Tenasserim.

EXPANSE: ♂, 3·6 to 3·8 inches.

DESCRIPTION: "MALE: UPPERSIDE ferruginous-swarthy, with an exterior obsolete swarthy line. *Forewing* subfalcate, the outer border paler. *Hindwing* subcaudate, with five large exterior obsolete blackish-swarthy spots, the last marked with a white dot. UNDERSIDE brown, with the basal half (especially about the disc) obscure swarthy, terminated outwardly by a swarthy line (in the forewing oblique, continuous; in the hindwing curved, subangulate in the middle); with a submedian striga on both wings, swarthy, margined outwardly with lilac, and two marginal swarthy lines. *Forewing* outwardly and at the apex powdered with lilac; a cellular patch swarthy, circled with white; five exterior ocelli arranged in a line, yellow, circled with swarthy and white, including a black pupil marked with white. *Hindwing* with six unequal ocelli arranged in a bent line, black, narrowly bordered with yellow and fuscous, marked with a white drop, each on a lilac ground, the first and fourth [? fifth] much larger, the sixth geminate. *Thorax* and *abdomen* black above, beneath pale fawn-colour."

"This species reminds one on the upperside of *Debis* [= *Lethe*] *samio*, Doubleday, and differs from *L. purana* in the absence of the white band on the forewing, the different curve of the outer line of the hindwing, and the less projecting angles of the same." (*Felder*, l. c.)

There can be but little doubt that *L. dolopes* which follows is the female of this species, but in the absence of sufficient evidence to decide the point, we retain them for the present as distinct.

This is a very distinct and beautiful species. In the Indian Museum, Calcutta, there are two male specimens, one from Sibsagar, Assam, the other with no precise locality; and in

Major Marshall's collection there is a single male taken by Captain C. T. Bingham in the Donat Range, Upper Tenasserim, in January. (See remarks on *L. alberta*, below.)

130. Lethe dolopes, Hewitson.

Debis dolopes, Hewitson, Ent. Month. Mag., vol. ix, p. 85 (1872).

HABITAT: Sikkim.

EXPANSE: 2·5 inches.

DESCRIPTION: "FEMALE: UPPERSIDE rufous-brown. *Forewing* crossed from the costal margin beyond its middle to a little above the anal angle by a band of paler colour, straight until it reaches the submedian nervure, where it makes an angle inwards. *Hindwing* tailed: crossed by a submarginal band of five blind black ocelli bordered with dull yellow, the middle ocellus much smaller than the rest. UNDERSIDE: *Both wings* rufous-brown to beyond the middle, crossed by a continuous common band of dark brown, bordered outwardly by lilac-white, the margin of the brown sharp and well defined: the wing beyond it rufous-white. *Forewing* with four scarcely visible ocelli. *Hindwing* with seven ocelli, which are small and black, each with a white centre and yellow iris bordered with brown, the first and fifth largest." (*Hewitson*, l. c.)

We have not seem a specimen of *L. dolopes*, but as the description of the underside agrees well with that of *L. vindhya*, we are inclined to believe, as noted above, that *L. dolopes* is only the female of that species.

131. Lethe alberta, Butler.

L. alberta, Butler, Ann. and Mag. of Nat. Hist., fourth series, vol. viii, p. 283 (1871); idem, id., Lep. Ex., p. 87, pl. xxxiii, fig. 5 (1872), *male*.

HABITAT: Benares, Tanasserim.

EXPANSE: 2·92 inches.

DESCRIPTION: "MALE: UPPERSIDE olivaceous-fuscous. *Forewing* with the apical area abruptly paler. *Hindwing* with four large black blind ocelli, circled with ferruginous; the external margin blackish; a very indistinct swarthy submarginal line. UNDERSIDE chestnut-swarthy; the apical area paler; a black median line, margined outwardly with grey; another discal defining the basal area, angulate in the hindwing. *Forewing* with the margin tinted with rosy; a black submarginal line; the discal area rosy towards the inside, swarthy outwardly, with the apex bluish; six discal ocelli black, circled with yellow, and zoned with rosy. *Hindwing* with the external margin greenish; a black submarginal line; the discal area ochraceous-fuscous inwardly, blackish chestnut outwardly; seven ocelli in an irregular series; the fifth the largest, black, circled with yellow, and zoned with pale green. *Body* cinereous-fuscous. Allied to *L. samio, distans, &c.*" (*Butler*, l. c. in Ann. and Mag. of Nat. Hist.)

Butler in his Lep. Ex. states that he has seen a female of this species in Mr. Moore's collection, but it is as yet undescribed. We have never seen *L. alberta*: the habitat given (Benares) is almost certainly incorrect, no *Lethe*, except possibly *L. europa*, is likely to occur in the plains of the North-West Provinces, at all events so far away from the hills.

Among a collection of Butterflies taken to England by Captain Bingham from Tenasserim and presented to the British Museum is a *Lethe* regarding which Butler writes "probably conspecific with *L. alberta*, though differing from the type of that species in having five instead of four large ocelli on the upperside of the hindwing, and lilacine instead of greenish zones to the ocelli on the underside. A nearly allied, though apparently distinct, species found in Darjiling has sericeous pink zones to the ocelli." (*Butler*, Ann. and Mag. of Nat. Hist., fifth series, vol. x, p. 373, 1882). It is probable that Mr. Butler's remarks apply to the Tenasserim *Lethe* we have identified above as *L. vindhya*, and it seems further probable that in describing *L. alberta* Felder's description of *L. vindhya* was overlooked by Mr. Butler, and that the two are inseparable; if the four ocelli of the *hindwing* on the upperside and the green zones on the underside are not constant characters, there is nothing that we can trace to separate the two as distinct species.

132. **Lethe mekara**, Moore. (PLATE XI, FIG. 24 ♂ ♀.)

Debis mekara, Moore, Horsfield and Moore, Cat., Lep. E. I. C., vol. i, p. 219, n. 454 (1857).

HABITAT: N.-E. India and Upper Tenasserim.

EXPANSE: 2·6 to 3·1 inches.

DESCRIPTION: "MALE: UPPERSIDE glossy olive-brown. *Hindwing* with four round spots encircled with red. UNDERSIDE with two transverse lines. *Forewing* with five submarginal pale ocelli. *Hindwing* with six brown ocelli, encircled by a yellow and then a black line, the centre being minutely spangled with white." (*Moore*, l. c.) FEMALE: UPPERSIDE rufescent brown. *Forewing* with the apical area darker, almost black in a fresh specimen from Tenasserim, crossed beyond the cell by an angulate macular white band, consisting of a short oblique bar from the costa to third median nervule, below which are two triangular spots directed inwards, one on each median interspace: a subapical bifid white spot near the costa. *Hindwing* as in the male, but rufescent instead of brown, and having five or six round black spots circled with paler red, the two upper large, the third smallest, except when the sixth is present, in which case the latter is the smallest. UNDERSIDE ochreous. *Both wings* crossed by a continuous brown subbasal line not quite reaching the margin at either end, beyond which the ground-colour is paler; a broad median dark brown band sharply defined externally crosses both wings, straight on the forewing, somewhat angled on the hindwing at the middle. *Forewing* with the white macular band as on the upperside, cutting through the median brown band in its upper half, the white spots below following its exterior margin; five or six obscure ocelli, the first and fourth incomplete; the outer margin brown bearing two ochreous lines finely defined with dark brown. *Hindwing* with six ochreous brown ocelli, complete, of irregular shape spangled with whitish, and circled with yellow and dark brown; outer margin as in forewing, but the marginal lines clearer and brighter. Except in the absence of the white band of the forewing, and the straighter outline of the median band the underside of the male closely resembles that of the female.

The underside of this species very closely resembles that of *L. chandica*, but in the latter species the outer margin of the median brown band on the hindwing is far more sharply angulate extending into a lengthened point beyond the cell. *L. mekara* is found in the same tracts as *L. chandica*, and extends also into Tenasserim, where it has been taken both by Limborg and Captain C. T. Bingham, but not commonly. Captain Bingham has sent a female from the Donat Range, taken in April, and a male in February. The latter of these two specimens differs from North-Indian examples in having the ferruginous outer area of the upperside of the hindwing brighter in shade, and rather more extended. On the underside the ground-colour is more ochreous. The ferruginous ground-colour of the upperside of both wings of the female is also brighter. Mr. Otto Möller has taken it in Sikkim in April, August, and October.

The figure is taken from a male specimen from Sikkim, and a female specimen from Sibsagar, in the Indian Museum, Calcutta, and shows the upperside of both.

133. **Lethe distans**, Butler.

L. distans, Butler, Trans. Ent. Soc. Lond., 1870, p. 488; idem, id., Lep. Exot., p. 87, pl. xxxiii, figs. 4, 6 *male*, 7 *female* (1872).

HABITAT: Darjiling.

EXPANSE: ♂, 2·75; ♀, 3·1 inches.

DESCRIPTION: "MALE, allied to *L. samio*,* differing in the more arched costa, and sinuate outer margin of the *forewing*. *Hindwing* above, with dusky-ferruginous outer area, exhibiting five blackish spots, the second the largest, outer margin dusky, especially towards the anal angle. UNDERSIDE paler than in *L. samio*; the prevailing colour pale ochraceous, the central lines much more irregular and wider apart than in *L. samio*; the ocelli of the *hindwing* irregular, with numerous pupils; the fourth not thrown out of the series as in *L. samio*."

---

* *Lethe samio*, p. 145, *ante*.

(*Butler*, l. c. in Trans. Ent. Soc. Lond.) "FEMALE: UPPERSIDE, with the basal area ferruginous. *Forewing* with a small band beyond the cell, a bifid subapical spot; and three [as in *L. minerva* not two as in *L. mekara*] discal, submedian, in an angulate transverse row, white. *Hindwing* with the ocelli circled widely with yellow; a median angulate line black inwardly, and yellow outwardly; otherwise almost as in the male." (*Butler*, l. c. in Lep. Ex.)

This appears to be a very rare species; we have never seen a specimen. It differs from *L. mekara* in the MALE, in the outer area of the forewing being abruptly paler as shewn in the figure (in *L. samio* it is concolorous throughout), and in having five instead of four black spots in the *hindwing*. On the UNDERSIDE the central lines in *L. distans* are far more irregular than they are in *L. mekara*. The FEMALE differs on the UPPERSIDE of the *hindwing* from *L. mekara* in the basal ferruginous area being produced into a long curved point at the third median nervule, and this area and the spots being outwardly defined with yellow.

134. **Lethe chandica**, Moore.

Debis chandica, Moore, Horsfield and Moore, Cat. Lep. E. I. C., vol. i, p. 219, n 455 (1857).

HABITAT: North-East India; Tenasserim.

EXPANSE: ♂, 2·5 to 3·0; ♀, 2·62 to 3·00 inches.

DESCRIPTION: "MALE: UPPERSIDE dark brown, about the disc blackish. *Hindwing* with indistinct submarginal spots. UNDERSIDE: *Forewing* pale drab-brown, and having a purple tinge; along costal margin, and broadly on exterior margin, yellowish; transverse red line crossing from middle of discoidal cell; and another irregular brown line across the disc; five pale ocelli; straight marginal, and wavy submarginal line. *Hindwing* drab-brown, two irregular zig-zag transverse lines, anteriorly within yellowish, posteriorly ferruginous-brown; six ocelli encircled with a yellow and brown line, the three anterior, and last posterior, black, the other two drab, all minutely spangled with white; exterior margin yellowish; marginal line, and submarginal row of ill-defined lunular marks, ferruginous-brown. FEMALE: UPPERSIDE: *Forewing* with the basal half obliquely brownish-red, anterior half brown, with a band obliquely from middle of costal margin, terminated by two spots, white: also a small white subapical spot. *Hindwing* brownish-red, anterior angle and along exterior margin yellowish, a submarginal row of indistinct spots and marginal line black. UNDERSIDE as in male, excepting that the oblique band of *forewing* is more distinct." (*Moore*, l. c.)

Lethe chandica is not uncommon in the lower valleys in Sikkim, where Mr. Otto Möller has taken it in May, August, and October. It also occurs in the Khasi Hills and Sylhet. Mr. A. O. Hume took it in the Eastern hills of Manipur in May; Captain C. T. Bingham in the Thoungyeen forests in Upper Tenasserim, in September; and the late Mr. Cock took it at Shillong. See remarks on *L. mekara*, p. 148.

135. **Lethe europa**, Fabricius.

Papilio europa, Fabricius, Syst. Ent., p. 500, n. 247 (1775); *Oreas marmorea europa*, Hübner, Samml: Exot. Schmett., vol. i, pl. xc, figs. 1-4 (1805); *Lethe europa*, id., Verz, bek. Schmett., p 56, n. 534 (1816); *Satyrus europa*, Godart, Enc. Méth., vol. ix, p 478, n. 6 (1819); *Papilio beroë*, Cramer, Pap. Ex., vol. i, pl. lxxix, figs. C, D (1775), *female*; *Papilio arete*, Cramer, Pap Ex., vol. iv. pl. cccxiii, figs. E, F (1780), *male*; *Lethe arcuata*, Butler, Cat. Lep. B. M., *Satyridæ*, p. 114, n. 4, pl. ii, fig. 3 (1868), *male*; *Lethe europa*, Distant, Rhop Malay., p. 43, pl. v, fig. 5, *male*, 6 *female* (1882).

HABITAT: The plains of India, Sikkim, Burma, the Andamans, Malayana, and China.

EXPANSE: 2·4 to 3·0 inches.

DESCRIPTION: MALE: UPPERSIDE dull brown. *Forewing* with an incomplete pale band from the costa just beyond the cell, and coincident with the white inner band below, nearly obsolete in some specimens; a trifid whitish spot with a pale ochreous spot below it near the apex; two ochreous marginal interrupted lines edged with dusky, broadly internally. *Hindwing* also with two ochreous marginal lines defined with dusky, broadly bordered with dusky internally; a row of submarginal black spots sometimes obsolete, that near the apex coalescing with the dusky margin. UNDERSIDE with the basal area dark umber brown, crossed by a prominent silvery white subbasal streak on both wings. *Forewing* with a white oblique transverse discal band tinged with yellow, joined at the middle by a pale band from the apex, forming together a Y-shaped figure, and enclosing a dark brown triangular patch; a row of six ocelli on the outer pale band, the sixth geminate, all grey with irregular black pupils, and circled with pale brown and violet; the area beyond the ocelli yellowish, shading into dark brown towards the margin, and grey at the apex; two ochreous marginal lines sharply defined with black lines. *Hindwing* with six very large ocelli, all profusely irrorated with white, and all, except the first, disintegrated, the whole enclosed by a silvery lilac line; an outer ochreous and an inner silvery marginal line both sharply defined with black. *Cilia* ochreous. FEMALE similar to the male, but paler coloured; on the UPPERSIDE the *forewing* is crossed from middle of costa to outer angle by a broad straight pure white band, the subapical spots are pure white; and on the *hindwing* the submarginal black spots are more prominent. UNDERSIDE similar to the male, but having in addition a broad transverse white bar on forewing which more or less obliterates the two lower ocelli.

This is the type corresponding with *L. arete* of Cramer, which is common in Sikkim, Assam, Sylhet, Upper Tenasserim, Calcutta, South India, and the Andaman Islands. There is another form corresponding with *L. beroë* of Cramer, in which the basal portion of the wings on the underside is much paler, and the silvery subbasal streak is broadly bordered externally on the hindwing, and up to the cell of the forewing with pale grey. This form was found commonly in the Barrackpore Park in November, by Major Marshall, and was taken by Captain C. T. Bingham in Upper Tenasserim from December to April. The only specimen from Calicut in the Indian Museum seems to be intermediate between the two forms. The specimens from the Andamans are the largest and darkest of all. It occurs also in Orissa, but has not been recorded from Ceylon; and Mr. de Nicéville has taken it in Sikkim, in October. Its range is exceedingly wide, and it is the only *Lethe* that we know to occur in the plains of India.

Mr. Kirby in his supplement places *L. arete* as a distinct variety.

136. **Lethe drypetis**, Hewitson.

Debis drypetis, Hewitson Ex. Butt., vol. iii, *Debis* pl. ii, figs. 11, 12 (1863), *female; Debis embolina*, Butler, Ent. Month. Mag., vol. iii, p. 77 (1866), *male; Lethe drypetis*, Moore, Lep. Cey., p. 17, pl. viii, figs. 1, 1*b male*, 1*a female* (1882).

HABITAT: Ceylon.

EXPANSE: 2·4 to 2·6 inches.

DESCRIPTION: "MALE: UPPERSIDE dark olive-brown. *Forewing* without markings. *Hindwing* with three submarginal very indistinct small black spots. UNDERSIDE dark brown; *both wings* with a transverse subbasal wavy dark-bordered purple line. *Forewing* with an oblique transverse discal purple band, a submarginal curved row of five small purple-bordered ocelli, the upper one indistinct, a marginal narrow pale wavy line. *Hindwing* with a transverse discal medially-angled purple-bordered dark brown line; a submarginal row of five purple-bordered ocelli, the first or upper one and the fifth only regularly formed; the others oval and numerously white speckled; a marginal distinct lunular purple line. *Cilia* brownish-ochreous. FEMALE: UPPERSIDE ferruginous olive-brown, externally dusky-brown. *Forewing* with two prominent subapical ochreous-white spots, an oblique transverse discal macular band extending to first median nervule, submarginal small indistinct black spots. *Hindwing* with four upper submarginal ochreous-yellow outer bordered black spots, the second spot large, and extending to the pale-bordered marginal line, the first being a minute apical dot with broad yellow outer border. UNDERSIDE paler, markings as in male, except that on the *forewing* the oblique discal band is purplish-white, the lower submarginal ocellus is absent, and the ocelli on *both wings* are bordered with purplish-white. *Body* dark olive-brown; *palpi* at sides, and *legs* beneath grey streaked." (*Moore*, l. c.)

"Taken [in Ceylon] in the hills of the Central Province at 3,000 feet and slightly above at all times. Very local; found in several spots of limited extent." (*Hutchison.*)

137. **Lethe todara**, Moore.

L. todara, Moore, Trans. Ent. Soc. Lond., 1881, p. 305.

HABITAT : Nilgiris.

EXPANSE : ♂, 2·3 ; ♀, 2·6 inches.

DESCRIPTION : "MALE : UPPERSIDE dark olive-brown, both wings without markings. UNDERSIDE dark vinous-brown. *Forewing* with a transverse duplex subbasal and an oblique discal waved purple line, a submarginal row of five indistinct small ocelli encircled by a purple border; a marginal narrow purple line, the extreme outer margin being ochreous. *Hindwing* with a transverse discal waved medially angled purple line, six submarginal ocelli encircled by a purple border, the first and fifth large and regularly formed, the second, third, and fourth, and duplex sixth narrow and minutely white-speckled ; a narrow marginal purple line and ochreous outer border. FEMALE : UPPERSIDE ochreous-brown, dusky externally. *Forewing* with two ochreous-white, small, ill-defined, subapical spots, and an oblique discal irregular band. *Hindwing* with three submarginal apical black spots, the two lower slightly bordered externally with ochreous-white, above them is an ochreous-white apical spot ; marginal line bordered with pale ochreous. UNDERSIDE paler, markings as in male, but more prominent, and all with paler purple borders. *Forewing* with an oblique discal ochreous-white band, which extends to the posterior angle, the lower submarginal ocellus obsolete, extreme outer margin of *both wings* ochreous."

"This species is nearest allied to the Ceylonese *Lethe drypetis*, Hewitson." (*Moore*, l. c.) After a careful examination of a large series of *L. drypetis* from Ceylon, and *L. todara* from South India and Orissa, we have come to the conclusion that there is only one species, which will stand as *L. drypetis*, as we can detect not the slightest difference between the Ceylon and continental examples ; no indication is given of the characters relied on, and the descriptions by Moore of both species apply equally well to the specimens from both localities. We have specimens taken at Mynall 2,000 feet elevation in May, at Trevandrum in June, and at Calicut in September, also examples from the Wynaad, and from Khurdah in Orissa.

138. **Lethe daretis**, Hewitson.

Debis daretis, Hewitson, Ex. Butt., vol. iii, p. 75, *Debis* pl. ii, figs. 7, 8 (1863), *female* ; *Lethe daretis*, Moore, Lep. Cey., p. 18, pl. vii, figs. 2, *2b male*, *2a female* (1880).

HABITAT : Ceylon.

EXPANSE : ♂, 2·1 ; ♀, 2·4 inches.

DESCRIPTION : "MALE : UPPERSIDE dark olive-brown. *Forewing* with a very small ochreous costal spot above end of the cell, and two small less distinct spots before the apex. Hindwing with a submarginal row of five small indistinct black slightly pale-bordered spots. UNDERSIDE dark brown, with a median and subbasal transverse sinuous purple-grey band on *both wings*. *Forewing* with an oblique discal transverse pale ochreous irregular lunular band, five small black purple-bordered submarginal ocelli, and marginal lunular purple line. *Hindwing* with six distinct well-formed purple-bordered submarginal ocelli, and marginal lunular purple line. FEMALE : UPPERSIDE ferruginous olive-brown. *Forewing* with two prominent ochreous-yellow subapical spots, transverse discal macular band extending to the submedian nervure, and four or five small indistinct black submarginal spots. *Hindwing* with a submarginal row of five well-defined oval ochreous-yellow bordered black spots, an upper marginal narrow lunular yellow line. UNDERSIDE as in male, markings more prominent, oblique discal band on *forewing* broader. *Cilia* alternated with white. *Body* dark brown. *Palpi* at sides, and *legs* beneath grey streaked." (*Moore*, l. c.)

"Found [in Ceylon] all the year round, but most plentiful in the spring in the hills of the Central Province at about 5,000 to 6,000 feet elevation, in grass-land or close to forests. Rather shy, flight rapid, often settling down in grass, or on open road." (*Hutchison.*)

139. **Lethe dyrta**, Felder. (PLATE X, FIG. 22 ♂ ♀).

Debis dyrta, Felder, Reise Novara, Lep., vol. iii, p. 497, n. 860 (1867); *Lethe dyrta*, Butler, Cat. Lep. B. M., *Satyridæ*, p. 115, n. 6 (1868).

HABITAT; The Himalayas generally up to 8,000 feet from Murree eastwards; the Khasi Hills; Meplay Valley, Tenasserim.

EXPANSE: ♂, 2·1 to 2·2; ♀, 2·4 to 2·5 inches.

DESCRIPTION: "FEMALE: UPPERSIDE dilute swarthy, the *cilia* broadly intersected with white. *Forewing* with the apical half darker, the band as in *L. drypetis* but a little broader and pure white, more oblique, and more excised within, excised at the lower discoidal fold without; with a whitish spot below the band, and three subapical placed as in *L. drypetis*, but the lowest evanescent. *Hindwing* with a rounded subapical spot, a somewhat diffuse macular band parallel with the margin, a narrow stripe before the margin, and the margin before the cilia, obscure swarthy. UNDERSIDE much paler. *Forewing* with a small fascia extending below the cell, defined externally with hoary; then a bent stripe on a hoary ground within the cell, and the apical two-thirds broadly deep fuscous; the white band as on the upperside, but wider and almost reaching the submedian nervure; three blackish ocelli with white irides, and broadly circled with swarthy and lilac-white, connected with and starting from the white band, with two upper subapical spots merging into the swarthy ground-colour at the outer edge; a lilac-white streak edged with swarthy, much dilated at the apex, and another fulvescent streak immediately beyond it before the margin. *Hindwing* with two swarthy basal streaks, connected, and each bearing a hoary stripe, the outer giving out a process beyond the cell; six large ocelli broadly circled with swarthy and lilac-white; the uppermost largest and retired inwardly with a single white pupil, the last but one blind, and the last geminate, black speckled with white with a yellowish iris; the remaining three yellowish brown, the pupil black, lacerated, and profusely speckled with white; a lilac-white stripe, defined with swarthy, widely on the inside, and another fulvous streak before the margin." (*Felder*, l. c.) MALE similar to the female, but smaller, the UPPERSIDE lacking the white band on the *forewing*, having in its place a whitish spot on the costa, while only the extreme apex is darker. On the UNDERSIDE the white band is indistinct, and a fourth ocellus appears on the line of the band.

Felder also states that "the margin of the wings is more regularly scalloped between the nervures than in the allied *L. drypetis*, and the outer margin of the forewing not concave." But these distinctions do not appear to hold good, as many specimens of *L. dyrta* have the outer margin of the forewing distinctly concave, and the margin is not more regularly scalloped than in *L. drypetis*; the chief distinction in the female appears to lie in the upperside of the *hindwing*, which in *L. drypetis* has an ochreous subapical spot, and all the marginal and submarginal markings more boldly defined. The males can easily be distinguished from one another, as the upperside of the forewing in *L. drypetis* is unmarked, while in *L. dyrta* there are three subapical ochreous spots.

L. dyrta has been found in Tenasserim by Captain C. T. Bingham in February; in the Khasi Hills in May and November; and in the N.-W. Himalayas it is very common throughout the warmer months.

There is a *Lethe* found in the Khasi Hills of this type, which differs from *L. dyrta* by having in both sexes on the upperside of the *hindwing* a distinct submarginal row of five blackish spots largest near the costa, and more or less distinctly bordered with paler brown externally. Moreover in all Shillong specimens the white band of the female is extended by an adjacent large white bifid spot below the first median nervule, whereas in the Western Himalayan specimens there is only a slight suffusion of whitish just below the nervule in continuation of the white band.

The figure is taken from a male specimen from Shillong, and a female from Kulu, and shows the uppersides only.

140. **Lethe neelgherriensis,** Guérin.

Satyrus (Cyllo) neelgheriensis and *neelgherriensis*, Guérin, in Delessert's Voy. dans l'Inde, pt. 2, p. 74, pl. xxi, figs. 1, 1a (1843), *male; Debis neilgherriensis*, Horsfield and Moore, Cat. Lep. E. I. C., vol. i, p. 217, n. 447 (1857); *D. neelgheriensis*, Hewitson, Ex. Butt., vol. iii, *Debis* pl. ii, fig. 6 (1863), *female; Lethe neelgherriensis*, Butler, Cat. Lep. B. M. *Satyridæ*, p. 115, n. 8 (1868); id., Moore, Lep. Cey., p. 16, pl. vii, figs. 1 *male*, 1 *a female* (1880).

HABITAT: South India, Ceylon.

EXPANSE: 2·1 to 2·3 inches.

DESCRIPTION: MALE: "UPPERSIDE blackish smoky-brown. *Forewing* with a yellowish spot beyond the middle at the costal margin, divided into three by the nervules; two square spots near the apex; and another spot near the external margin at one-third the length from the hinder angle. *Hindwing* unspotted, but showing through by transparency some traces of the ocelli of the underside [especially the second ocellus from the apex, at the site of which there is, in some specimens, a round indistinct dark spot]; the marginal lines as on underside, but less distinctly marked. UNDERSIDE with a very irregular sinuous and dented greyish white band across both wings, larger towards the costa of the forewing, not corresponding exactly on the hindwing. [This band is bordered with brown on both sides; on the *forewing* beyond it is a very zigzag greyish white line across the cell; an irregular whitish macular line from the costa beyond the cell to the hinder angle, and a row of five round ocelli concave to the outer margin on a whitish ground; the uppermost obsolete at the apex; the margin is narrowly dark brown, followed by a yellowish line, then a dark brown line, then a grey line bordered on the outside with dusky.] *Hindwing* with another greyish band bordered with brown a little beyond the middle, and strongly angulated towards the outer margin a little before the middle of its length; between this last band and the margin are situated six black ocelli encircled with first yellow, then brown, and then ashy grey; the first, which touches the costa, is the largest, and has in the middle a large white pupil; the three following are oval and elongated, the black portion with a great number of little white dots scattered over it; the fourth [? fifth] is quite round, much retired towards the margin, and well defined, having in the middle only three or four white dots [it is often entirely blind], the ocellus at the anal angle is in a line with the third, fourth and fifth, [? second, third and fourth] and geminate with two black ovals surrounded with and separated by yellow, and sprinkled with numerous white dots. Both wings have the *cilia* whitish; and the *hindwing* has the marginal lines as in the forewing, but more sinuous and irregular."

The above is taken from Guérin's original description, the parts in brackets being added to complete it where deficient.

"FEMALE: UPPERSIDE, light brown. *Forewing* with the outer half dark brown, crossed obliquely beyond the middle of the wing by three white spots, and near the apex by two of the same colour. *Hindwing* with a band of four spots beyond the middle, the outer margin and two submarginal lines black. [The narrow line between the margin and first submarginal black line is yellowish.] UNDERSIDE grey and rufous-brown. *Forewing* with the white spots as above, and between them a band of three ocelli. [The three white spots across the middle tend to become confluent, forming an irregular maculated band across the wing.] *Hindwing* with two perfect ocelli only—one, the largest, at the costal margin, the other towards the anal angle; between these ocelli there is a trifid triangular space minutely dotted with black and white; and at the anal angle an eye-like rufous spot enclosing two oval spots of black, dotted with white." (*Hewitson*, l. c.)

L. neelgherriensis very closely resembles *L. dyrta* on the underside, so much so that, with the exception of the band of the forewing being maculated and irregular in the former, and prominent and continuous in the latter, the differences are very difficult to describe. On the upperside, however, the presence in *L. neelgherriensis* of the whitish spot on the forewing of the male near the hinder angle, and in the female the white band being replaced by three separate square white spots, render it notably distinct from *L. dyrta*.

In Horsfield and Moore's Cat. Lep. E. I. C. (1857) it is recorded from Bhutan, N. India, and Darjiling; but this probably requires confirmation; it was originally described both by

Guérin and Hewitson from the Nilgiri Hills, and is probably to be found in suitable localities throughout the south of the peninsula. Mr. Fergusson has taken it in the Ashamboo Hills in Travancore in May, and again in July at Trevandrum. Mr. E. H. Aitken took it at Khandalla in April. Lieutenant-Colonel Swinhoe has taken it at Mhow in the autumn, and also commonly at Abu; but we have never seen a specimen from further north than this latter place. It also occurs in Ceylon, where it is "found in the neighbourhood of coffee-plantations south of Newera Eliya, at about 3,000 feet elevation. It appears plentifully, except from January to March." *(Hutchison).* "Taken also at Kandy and Dickoya by Captain Wade." (*Moore*, l. c. in Lep. Cey.)

141. **Lethe satyavati**, de N.

L. satyavati, de Nicéville, Journ. A.S.B., vol. xlix, pt. 2, p 246 (1880).

HABITAT: Sibsagar, Assam.

EXPANSE: 2·7 inches.

DESCRIPTION: FEMALE: UPPERSIDE dull brown, paler towards the margins. *Forewing* with an indistinct submarginal darker line. *Hindwing* with a submarginal series of four rounded spots darker than the ground-colour, placed one in each interspace above the first median nervule; two marginal darker lines defined inwardly by paler lines than the ground-colour. UNDERSIDE pale brown, with no ochreous tint, and washed with lilac, especially on the outer half. *Both wings* crossed by a prominent brown nearly straight subbasal line outwardly margined with lilac. *Forewing* with an irregular discal transverse brown line; a bar in the cell within the subbasal line; five indistinct submarginal ocelli circled with lilac and brown on a lilac ground; and a yellowish marginal line edged on both sides with dusky, within which is a brown waved band on the lilac ground between the ocelli and the margin. *Hindwing* with a discal very much angled dark brown line, within which is a very distinct lilac litura above the third median nervule and just beyond the apex of the cell; the submarginal ocelli large, the upper one distinctly pupilled with white, and all of them profusely speckled with white; the usual marginal markings. Similar in outline to *L. latiaris*, ♀, and differing from it on the upperside in markings only in the absence of the transverse oblique ochreous line, and the subcostal spot near the apex of the forewing.

The MALE is unknown. The type specimen, the only one seen, is in the Indian Museum, Calcutta.

142. **Lethe hyrania**, Kollar.

Satyrus hyrania, Kollar in Hügel's Kaschmir, vol. iv, pt. 2, p. 449, n. 7, pl. xvii, figs. 1, 2 (1844), *male*; *Satyrus isana*, idem, id, p. 448, n. 6, pl. xvi, figs. 3, 4 *female*.

HABITAT: N.-W. Himalayas.

EXPANSE: 2·2 inches.

DESCRIPTION: "MALE: UPPERSIDE, swarthy. *Hindwing* obtusely dentate, with four obsolete black ocellate spots. UNDERSIDE: *Forewing* with three obsolete ocelli at the apex, and a pale oblique median streak. *Hindwing* with six black white-pupilled ocelli, the last geminate, and two narrow obscure stripes. FEMALE: Wings swarthy. *Forewing* with an oblique band on both surfaces, and a spot near the apex, white. *Hindwing* obtusely dentate, with four obsolete black ocelli on the upperside. UNDERSIDE with three ocelli at the apex in the *forewing*; six on the *hindwing*, white-pupilled, first, fourth, and fifth larger, the sixth geminate; the streaks angulate, fuscous, the *cilia* paler, marked with black." *(Kollar,* l. c.)

The upper surface in the MALE is, in fresh specimens, a rather glossy and not very dark olive brown; on the *forewing* is a very faint trace from the costa of a paler oblique medial band, and near the apex a yellowish trifid spot, below which is sometimes a small round dark spot. On the *hindwing* are four or five submarginal blackish spots, the second usually largest and oblong; the third the smallest, the last white-pupilled and ringed with yellowish; the third and fourth are also sometimes faintly ringed with yellowish; the margin has three narrow dark lines, narrowly separated by yellowish interspaces. UNDERSIDE paler. *Forewing* with two narrow darker lines across the cell, neither of which extend at all beyond it; a narrow sinuous dark line from the costa towards the hinder angle, and broadly edged outwardly with whitish from the costa narrowing to the middle of the wing; a whitish trifid spot near the apex, below which a greyish submarginal obscure patch, bearing three faint white-pupilled ocelli; the margin paler, with three narrow dark lines. *Hindwing* with a narrow dark streak cutting across the cell from the costa, and not reaching the abdominal margin; the disco-cellulars defined by a dark line, and beyond it a sinuous dark line across the wing; six black ocelli, each with a single white pupil, the sixth geminate; the first and fifth largest, circled with yellowish, then darkish brown, then obscure grey; three dark lines along the margin, the inner one dilated between the median nervules. The FEMALE is somewhat paler, with a greenish tinge at base; the *forewing* crossed by a conspicuous white band from the costa to the hinder angle, beyond and at both edges of which the apical portion is blackish, and with a trifid white spot near the costa. On the UNDERSIDE the *forewing* shows the same white band, broadly edged with bright dark brown on the inside, and a large triangular patch of the same colour on the outside from the costa; the outer border paler, greyish towards the apex, and marked as in the male. *Hindwing*, as in the male. In a single specimen received from Kulu the white band has invaded the cell between the points where the second and third median nervules are given off, thus giving the inner side of the band a very irregular appearance.

The female, which is much rarer in collections than the male, was originally described as a distinct species under the name *isana*, Kollar, and subsequently erroneously identified as the female of *L. rohria*. The male was originally obtained at Simla by Herr von Hügel, and the female at Mussooree. Both sexes have been taken at an elevation of 7,000 feet by Colonel Lang, at Mussooree, in June, and in Lower Kunawar; in May numbers of the males were taken by Major C. H. T. Marshall in Chumba; and both sexes by Mr. A. Graham Young in Kulu from May to July, and the male only by Mrs. Deane in Chini in June. There is no record at present of its having been taken further east than Mussooree.

143. **Lethe dinarbas**, Hewitson.

Debis dinarbas, Hewitson, Ex. Butt., vol. iii, *Debis* pl. iii, fig. 15 (1863), *male*.

HABITAT: North India, Sikkim.

EXPANSE: 2·1 inches.

DESCRIPTION: "UPPERSIDE brown. *Forewing* crossed at the middle by a very indistinct band of brown; a minute bifid white spot and obscure brown spot near the apex. *Hindwing* with four obscure brown spots (one minute) near the outer margin, the spot nearest the anal angle dotted with white. UNDERSIDE brown. *Forewing* paler towards the outer margin, tinted with lilac; the cell crossed by two rufous lines, the transverse band and apical spot as above, but more distinct, with, between them, three minute ocelli (one blind); the outer margin and two submarginal lines rufous-brown. *Hindwing* crossed transversely by two rufous-brown bands; one before the middle straight, the other at the middle curved, followed by a band of six ocelli, each with white pupil, and rufous iris bordered with brown and lilac." (*Hewitson*, l. c.)

We have only seen males of this species from Sikkim; the female is apparently unknown. The anal ocellus on the underside of the hindwing in the specimens we have seen is geminate. Hewitson's figure is much too rufous, and the lilac colouration is much too vivid. This species differs from *L. hyrania* only in the darker colouration of the ground-colour above and below; and on the underside in being washed with lilac. In *L. hyrania* there is no trace whatever of this colour. It is probably only a geographical variety of *L. hyrania*.

144. **Lethe serbonis**, Hewitson.

Debis serbonis, Hewitson, Ent. Month. Mag., vol. xiii, p. 151 (1876); id., Desc. Lep. Coll. Atkinson, p. 2, pl. i, figs. 4, 5 (1879), *male*.

HABITAT: Sikkim.

EXPANSE: 2·9 inches.

DESCRIPTION: MALE: "UPPERSIDE rufous-brown. *Both wings* with two submarginal brown lines. *Forewing* with two indistinct pale spots on the costal margin beyond the middle. *Hindwing* with a series of three black eye-like spots, and an ocellus marked with white near the anal angle. UNDERSIDE rufous. *Forewing* with a zig-zag brown line, and a large pale spot, bordered on both sides with brown within the cell; the disco-cellular nervules brown, crossed beyond the middle by a dark brown band, bounded outwardly, near the costal margin, by a dull white spot; a white spot near the apex, and below two small ocelli, one of which is incomplete, followed by a band of brown, and a submarginal band also brown. *Hindwing* crossed by two brown bands, one before, the other at the middle; a brown line at the end of the cell; a series of six ocelli, the first and fifth larger and more distinct than the rest; the outer margin and a line near it black." (*Hewitson*, l. c. in Desc. Lep. Coll. Atk.)

The FEMALE is unknown; and all the males we have seen are from Sikkim.

145. **Lethe rohria,** Fabricius.

Papilio rohria, Fabricius, Mant. Ins., vol. ii, p. 45, n. 446 (1787); *Satyrus rohria*, Godart, Enc. Méth., vol. ix, p. 479, n. 8 (1819.)

HABITAT: Java, Upper Tenasserim, Khasi Hills, Sikkim, and thence through the Himalayas as far west as Simla.

EXPANSE: 2·0 to 2·25 inches.

DESCRIPTION: MALE. UPPERSIDE dark brown, blackish on the outer half of the forewing. *Forewing* crossed about the middle by a pure white regular curved band extending to the submedian nervure at the anal angle, and two ill-defined white spots near the apex. *Hindwing* with two narrow yellowish lines near the margin, which are continued less distinctly on to the forewing, and with faint traces of the ocelli of the underside showing through; occasionally some of their sites marked by a dark ill-defined spot. UNDERSIDE with the white band as on upperside. *Forewing* with three decreasing submarginal ocelli; a white streak from the costa near apex, which dividing partially encloses the three ocelli from above, two submarginal purplish-white lines, and before the middle a straight pearly grey streak across the wing. *Hindwing* with a pearly grey, straight streak in continuation of that on the forewing, then a sinuous line of the same colour from the inner margin directed towards the pupil of the apical ocellus, and thence following its contour to the costa, and joining with the first streak just before the abdominal margin, and close to the sixth (anal) ocellus; six perfect ocelli beyond, the first very large, the fifth large, all more or less pupilled with white dots, and ringed with yellow, then brown, then grey; two narrow submarginal lines, the outer tinged yellowish, the inner violet-white. The FEMALE is paler on the upperside, the band of the *forewing* rather wider, and the marginal lines of the *hindwing* are yellower and more prominent. On the UNDERSIDE too the colours are paler and less brilliant; otherwise the markings are similar.

In specimens from Sikkim the apical ocellus of the hindwing is very large indeed, and pupilled with a single prominent white spot. In specimens from Tenasserim this ocellus is not so large, and is generally blind; the ground-colour in both sexes is browner, and the grey markings are duller, lacking the pearly tint, and often tinged whitish.

Lethe rohria is not uncommon in Upper Tenasserim; it was found by Limborg at Hatsiega, and on the Taoo plateau at 3,000 to 5,000 feet elevation; and by Captain C. T. Bingham in the Meplay valley in February; and in the Upper Thoungyeen forests in April, September, and October. In the Khasi Hills it is found in the autumn. Mr. Otto Möller has taken it in the Sikkim tarai in July, in the Sikkim Hills, where it appears to be common, at 4,000 feet elevation in April, August, September to November, and also in the valley of the Great Ranjit in November, at 1,200 to 3,500 feet elevation, where Mr. de Nicéville also took it commonly in October. Further to the west it becomes much rarer. Dr. Scully took a pair at Khatmandu in Nepal. It is found in Kumaon at moderate elevations, and Colonel Lang, R.E., possesses a specimen from Gurhwal. Mr. de Nicéville has taken two specimens in the neighbourhood of Simla, but further to the west no record exists of its occurrence. Kashmir has erroneously been stated as a locality for *Lethe rohria*, but this arose from *Debis isana* of Kollar having been mistaken for the female of this species, whereas it really is the female of *L. hyrania.*

L. rohria is very similar in colouration to *L. verma*, but differs in some points, and conspicuously in the outline of the wings (see *L. verma*). Next to *L. europa* it has the widest range of all the species of *Lethe* occurring within Indian limits.

Key to the Indian species of Lethe.

Third group.

B. Males without sexual glands and tufts on either wing.

b. The apex of the cell in the hindwing *beyond* the origin of the second median nervule.

a^1. Male and female, upperside, forewing with a conspicuous almost straight broad white band across the disc; underside, hindwing with the ocelli not disintegrated.

a^2. Upperside, forewing without an apical white spot. Underside, hindwing with two narrow transverse sinuous silvery-lilac lines across the disc.

146. L. *(Tansima)** VERMA, N.-W. Himalayas to Assam.

b^2. Upperside, forewing with an apical white spot. Underside, hindwing with no silvery-lilac lines across the disc.

147. L. *(Tansima)* MASONI, Sikkim.

b^1. Underside with four very irregular more or less interrupted silvery lines across the basal area of the hindwing.

a^2. Underside of forewing with silvery-lilac markings; the ocelli of hindwing perfect.

a^3. Underside of forewing unmarked, except by an incomplete silvery submarginal line near apex, and three minute dots within it; underside of hindwing with the second and third ocelli out of line.

148. L. SIDERIA, Sikkim.

b^3. Underside of forewing with a lilac bar (often obsolete) across the cell defined on both sides with darker brown; a dark brown transverse line beyond the cell, edged outwardly near costa with lilac, and another shorter one beyond defined with lilac-white above the ocelli; three or four minute ocelli on a paler ground; underside of hindwing with all the ocelli in line.

149. L. SIDONIS, Himalayas, Assam, Khasi Hills.

b^2. Underside of forewing with ochreous markings.

a^3. Underside with the ocelli of the hindwing with the irides blurred and indistinct, the black centre generally obsolete. Forewing with an ochreous bar across the cell.

150 L. MAITRYA, Himalayas.

b^3. Underside, with the ocelli of the hindwing perfect, the black centres usually conspicuous, and the irides well marked; no ochreous bar across the cell.

151. L. NICETAS, Himalayas.

c^2. Underside of forewing with pure white markings; a pure white complete submarginal line on both wings; ocelli perfect, those of forewing with white rings, of hindwing on a pure white ground.

152. L. VISRAVA, N.-E. Bengal, Sikkim.

The species of this group differ from the typical species *L. europa* and its allies, and all the species preceding *L. europa*, notably in having the hindwing rounded, the outer margin sinuate, but scarcely perceptibly dentate, and in having the apex of the cell in the *hindwing* considerably less acute, and situated well beyond the origin of the second median nervule; but this feature is not even constant in the same species; a female specimen of *L. nicetas* from Kulu having the second median nervule almost exactly in prolongation of the lower disco-cellular nervule, while in the males from the same locality the distance varies, and is often

* *Genus* TANSIMA, *Moore*. "FEMALE. Wings short, broad. *Forewing* with the costa much arched at the base, apex rounded, exterior margin very slightly oblique and convex; cell broad; first and second subcostal branches emitted near end of the cell, third trifid; disco-cellulars outwardly oblique, upper bent near the subcostal, concave below, lower slightly concave anteriorly; radials emitted from their angles. *Hindwing* broadly oval, exterior margin convex; cell broadly triangular. *Palpi* long, slender, pilose beneath. *Antennæ* slender. *Legs* slender, naked." (*Moore*, Trans. Ent. Soc. Lond., 1881, p 305).

considerable. The group contains two forms, in one of these which has been separated under the generic name of *Tansima*, Moore, with *Lethe verma* as its type the cell in both wings is very broad; the other has the cell of the forewing much as in typical *Lethe*.

146. Lethe verma, Kollar. (PLATE X, FIG. 23 ♂).

Satyrus verma, Kollar, in Hügel's Kaschmir, vol. iv, pt. 2, p. 447, pl. xvi, figs. 1, 2 (1848); *Tansima verma*, Moore, Proc. Zool. Soc. Lond., 1882, p. 235.

HABITAT: Upper Tenasserim, Khasi Hills, Assam, and westward through the Himalayas as far as Chumba, and the borders of Kashmir.

EXPANSE: 2·0 to 2·4 inches.

DESCRIPTION: MALE and FEMALE alike, except that the female is rather paler in colouration. UPPERSIDE swarthy brown, darkest externally. *Forewing* with a conspicuous nearly straight white band from the middle of the costa, passing just beyond the cell to the first median nervule near the outer margin. *Both wings* with two narrow pale submarginal lines, bordered and separated by fine blackish lines. In some specimens the *hindwing* is unspotted, in others the sites of the ocelli on the underside are marked on the upperside by indistinct blackish spots, always most prominent between the median nervules; these spots again are sometimes white-pupilled and are sometimes perfect ocelli, ringed with yellowish. These variations do not seem to be peculiar to any locality; the specimens from Chumba show usually one, two, or three white-pupilled spots. A specimen from Shillong shows no white pupils at all, while another from the Sikkim Himalayas has four perfect ocelli, the two between the median nervules being especially prominent; and lastly in the large series from Simla in Mr. de Nicéville's collection many of the specimens have only faint traces of the white pupils, while in some the spots are hardly perceptible. UNDERSIDE lighter and rather brighter brown. *Forewing* with the white band as on the upperside, but extending a little below the first median nervule; above it two contiguous submarginal ocelli, black, with white pupil and yellow iris; above this an irregular whitish streak near the costa; two greyish submarginal lines widening towards the apex, edged with and separated by fine dark lines. *Hindwing* with submarginal lines as on forewing, but the outer one more decidedly tinged with yellowish; six perfect ocelli, that near the anal angle bipupilled; the first, fourth, and fifth larger than the others, black, with white pupils, and ringed with yellow, then brown, then lilac-grey. Between the ocelli and the base are two narrow lilac-grey lines, that nearest the base nearly straight, the outer one very sinuous, both edged on the side furthest from the other one with darker brown.

Lethe verma is of much the same style of colouration as *L. rohria*, but on the upperside it lacks the subapical whitish spots of the forewing, and the band is broader, more oblique, not reaching the hinder angle, and often tinged with yellowish, and on the underside the grey bands of the hindwing are far less prominent, and the ocelli are more uniformly pupilled with a single white dot. But the most marked difference is in the outline of the wings. The forewing is broader, the inner margin being much longer, and the hindwing is much rounded, dentate, but scarcely perceptibly caudate. It has a very wide range in the hills of Northern India, being much more common in the North-West Himalayas, and extending further in that direction than *L. rohria* does.

According to Colonel Lang this is an autumnal insect in the North-west Himalayas, affecting shady localities, and trees in preference to rocks, pitching on the trunks of rhododendrons and oaks. His specimens were taken in lower Kunawar at an elevation of 7,000 feet, and at Mussoorie. There is, however, a summer brood, as Mr. de Nicéville has taken it then commonly in Simla at about 5,000 feet elevation in forest, settled on the dark rough bark of the deodar, where, till disturbed, it is completely hidden. It was not found in Kashmir either by von Hügel or by Captain Reed. Major C. H. T. Marshall found it extremely commonly in Chumba in May at Kujjiar. In Sikkim Mr. de Nicéville took it in October, and Mr. Otto Möller in November at 4,000 feet elevation. It was taken in the same month at Shillong by Mr. J. P. Cock, and Mr. Ossian Limborg found it at Moolai in Upper

Tenasserim, at an elevation of 3,000 to 6,000 feet. In Sikkim it is far less commonly met with than *L. rohria*; in the North-West Himalayas it is *L. verma* that is most frequently seen.

The figure is taken from a male specimen from Shillong in Major Marshall's collection.

147. Lethe masoni, Elwes.

Debis (Tansima) masoni, Elwes, Proc. Zool. Soc. Lond., 1882, p. 405, pl. xxv, fig. 2.

HABITAT: Sikkim.

EXPANSE: 2·3 inches.

DESCRIPTION: "Resembles *L. verma*, Kollar, in general appearance, size, form, and colour; but is distinguished on the UPPERSIDE by a single white spot near the apex of the *forewing*, which wing is slightly undulate and fringed white. The anterior angle of the *hindwing* is bordered and fringed white. On the UNDERSIDE there is one ocellus close to the white spot near the apex of the *forewing*, and the ground-colour of the *hindwing* is overlaid with greyish scales, and without the transverse steely bands of *L. verma*. The ocelli resemble those of *L. verma* in number, size, and position, but are ringed with hair-brown instead of fulvous. The sexes do not differ." (*Elwes*, l.c.) On the underside of the hindwing there is in the figure a short subbasal dark brown line, a sinuous one beyond crossing the middle of the cell and reaching the costal and abdominal margins, a short one defining the disco-cellular nervules, and a fourth very sinuous one across the disc from the costa to the submedian nervure.

In describing this species Captain Elwes writes: "Of this species, which, though allied to *L. verma*, is very distinct, I received a large number of specimens which do not vary. As this insect has never been taken before, I imagine it to be from the Chumbi valley, on the other side of the Passes, but it is probably not found at extreme elevations."

148. Lethe siderea, Marshall.

L. siderea, Marshall, Journ. A. S. B., vol. xlix, pt. ii, p. 246 (1880).

HABITAT: Sikkim.

EXPANSE: 2·1 inches.

DESCRIPTION: MALE: Differs from *L. sidonis*, ♂, in being smaller, and in the uniform absolutely spotless upper surface, somewhat darker towards the outer margin. UNDERSIDE uniform brown. *Forewing* entirely wanting the discal bands and the whitish spots on the costal margin; the only markings being three minute submarginal white spots beyond the cell, the middle one faintly ringed with black; a single yellowish marginal line edged on both sides with dark brown, and within this a distinct silvery-lilac submarginal line extending from the apex to the second median nervule. *Hindwing* with all the silvery streaks brighter and distinctly lilac; the submarginal silvery line very slightly dilated at the anal angle; the ocelli all blacker, and less prominently pupilled with white. The second and third ocelli much nearer the margin than the others, giving the line of ocelli a strong curve outwards, the silvery band within following this curve, and deeply sinuated outwards beyond the cell; the ground-colour being uniform brown, scarcely at all darkened at the edges of the silvery lines. The *hindwing* less distinctly caudate.

We have only seen two specimens of this species, both from Sikkim, which agree exactly the one with the other. The irregular curve of the series of ocelli on the underside of the *hindwing* at once distinguishes *L. siderea* from all the numerous specimens of *L. sidonis* we have seen.

149. Lethe sidonis, Hewitson.

Debis sidonis, Hewitson, Ex. Butt., vol. iii, *Debis* pl. iii, fig. 16 (1863), *male*.

HABITAT: The Himalayas from Kulu to Sikkim, extending into Sylhet.

EXPANSE: 2·0 to 2·2 inches.

DESCRIPTION: "MALE: Upperside dark [uniform] brown. *Forewing* with an indistinct white spot near the apex. *Hindwing* with two or three indistinct black spots near the outer margin. UNDERSIDE brown. *Forewing* with an indistinct band across the cell, a white spot beyond the middle of the costal margin part of a brown band which crosses the wing, a second white spot near the apex, and below it three black spots dotted with white. *Hindwing* crossed by several lines of silvery white, followed by a band of seven black ocelli; the first (at the costal margin), and the fifth large, two at the anal angle touching, each with a white pupil and rufous iris, bordered with [brown, and then] silvery white; a submarginal line of silvery white; the margin rufous, bordered on both sides with black." (*Hewitson*, l.c.) On the underside of the *hindwing* the silvery white submarginal line is narrow at the apex, and much dilated at the anal angle; and on each side of the series of ocelli is a broad darker and brighter brown edging to the silvery lines which enclose it. The *forewing* has two narrow yellowish submarginal lines. The *cilia* are dotted with whitish. The FEMALE differs from the male on the UPPERSIDE in having the ground-colour immediately within the marginal lines somewhat darker, more especially so on the *hindwing*, where it forms a distinct submarginal band. The ocelli also on that wing are more distinct. The outer margin of *both wings* are also somewhat more deeply scalloped. UNDERSIDE as in the male.

L. sidonis is a somewhat variable insect. Some specimens from Sikkim are smaller than *L. siderea*, the forewing as immaculate on the upperside as in that species, and the hindwing in some of these small specimens shews no sign of the submarginal series of blackish round spots, which are distinct in other specimens quite as small, and in the larger ones. On the underside of the forewing there is every gradation from a spotless cell to one bearing a prominent transverse violet bar at its middle, on both sides margined with darker brown than the ground-colour. Specimens from Mussoorie have the upperside quite immaculate, the silvery undulating lines on the underside of the hindwing are far duller and altogether less prominent than in more eastern examples, while in the Kulu specimens these lines are obsolete; and in all the Western Himalayan specimens the underside of the forewing has no trace of the bar across the cell.

Mr. A. Graham Young took three specimens of *L. sidonis* on the Tihír Pass in Kulu in July; Colonel Lang took a few at Mussoorie in June; in Sikkim, at from 5,000 to 7,000 feet elevation Mr. de Nicéville took it most commonly in roads through forests, in October; and the late Mr. Cock took it at Shillong in July. It is far commoner in the Eastern than in the Western Himalayas.

150. **Lethe maitrya**, de N. (PLATE X, FIG. 20 ♂.)

L. maitrya, de Nicéville, Journ. A. S. B., vol. xlix, pt. ii, p. 245 (1880).

HABITAT: Jalauri Pass, Narkunda, N.-W. Himalayas; Sikkim.

EXPANSE: 2·1 to 2·2 inches.

DESCRIPTION: MALE: UPPERSIDE deep shining brown. *Cilia* marked with ochreous at the interspaces. *Forewing* crossed beyond the cell by a pale ochreous, outwardly curved band, narrowest and most distinct at the costa, almost obsolete on reaching the third median nervule. A subapical trifid spot divided by the subcostal nervules. *Hindwing* with the ocelli below showing through indistinctly in black spots, and a hardly perceptible submarginal series of black lunules. UNDERSIDE. *Forewing* with a prominent outwardly curved bar, extending across the cell just beyond its middle; the band beyond the cell of the upperside, but much more distinct, both ochreous. The trifid subapical spot as above but whitish, below which are four minute white dots, the remains of obsolete ocelli, one on each interspace; some indistinct marginal lines. *Hindwing* crossed by four very irregular lilascent lines, the first pair basal, the second discal, and enclosing the disco-cellular nervules, which are margined on both sides with lilascent. The innermost line of this pair is inwardly narrowly, and the outermost line outwardly broadly margined with a deeper shade of brown than the ground. A submarginal band of six ocelli, the first four from the apex joined, the fifth separate, the sixth small and geminate; these ocelli are all very indistinct, and have lilascent pupils, and are outwardly margined with that colour. An almost obsolete lilascent submarginal line dilated within the first median nervule, and extending up the abdominal margin, outwardly bordered, especially at the anal angle, with a rufous line.

Allied to *L. sidonis*, from fresh Sikkim specimens of which species it differs on the upperside in having a band across the forewing beyond the cell, and on the underside this same band being very prominent, as is also the bar in the cell. The ocelli and submarginal lilascent line are also very indistinct in *L. maitrya*.

Mr. de Nicéville took a single male, from which the figure is taken, on the Jalauri Pass, at about 8,000 feet elevation on July 29th, 1879. In Colonel Lang's collection there is a male from Narkunda on the Hindustan and Thibet Road, taken by himself in July, which is identical with the type specimen; and a male and two females from Sikkim, collected by Dr. T. C. Jerdon, that evidently belong to this species. The latter are somewhat smaller than the type specimen described above, but agree with it in the blurring of the ocelli on the underside of the hindwing, and in having an ochreous bar in the cell of the forewing, which latter feature is absent from all the specimens of *L. sidonis* we have seen, and to which *L. maitrya* is evidently closely allied, as also it is to *L. nicetas*, differing from the latter chiefly in having the ocelli blurred. *L. maitrya* seems to be intermediate between *L. sidonis* and *L. nicetas*.

151. **Lethe nicetas**, Hewitson.

Debis nicetas, Hewitson, Ex. Butt., vol. iii, *Debis* pl. iii, figs. 17, 18 (1863), *female*.

HABITAT: Himalayas, from Sikkim to Kulu.

EXPANSE: 1·8 to 2·25 inches.

DESCRIPTION: "FEMALE: UPPERSIDE light rufous-brown. *Forewing* with the outer half darker brown, crossed beyond the middle by a macular band of pale yellow, and nearer the apex by three spots of the same colour. *Hindwing* with a band of five black spots with rufous border; the outer margin rufous, bordered on both sides with black; some submarginal dark-brown conical spots. UNDERSIDE rufous-yellow. *Forewing* as on upperside, except that the transverse band is continuous, and that two of the three spots near the apex are small ocelli. *Hindwing* from the base to the middle rufous-brown, crossed by several indistinct lilac bands; the outer half rufous-yellow, darker towards the outer margin, crossed by a band of seven black ocelli (two at the anal angle touching), each with a white pupil and rufous iris bordered with lilac; a submarginal band of silvery white; the margin rufous, bordered on both sides with black." (*Hewitson*, l. c.) MALE smaller than the female, the costal margin only of the UPPERSIDE of the *forewing* darker, the yellow maculated band very indistinct, and the two lower of the subapical spots wanting. *Hindwing* with the spots smaller and much less distinctly bordered with rufous. UNDERSIDE as in the female. On the upperside of the *hindwing* in both sexes the row of black blind ocelli are very distinct; in the preceding species, *L. maitrya*, they can hardly be traced. On the underside of the hindwing the rufous brown of the basal half is sharply defined, highly dentate and outwardly more or less margined with pure yellow, while in *L. maitrya* it is less distinct, sinuate rather than dentate, and with scarcely a trace of yellow beyond, and that only in a Sikkim specimen.

L. nicetas is found at from 3,000 to 6,000 feet elevation in suitable localities in the Himalayas, from Sikkim to Kulu; it does not seem to be common anywhere, and is rarer to the west than to the east. In Kulu Mr. A. Graham Young has taken it in May, July and October, but never plentifully. These latter are much smaller than specimens from the Eastern Himalayas.

152. **Lethe visrava**, Moore.

Debis visrava, Moore, Proc. Zool. Soc. Lond., 1865, p. 768, pl. xli, fig. 4, *male*.

HABITAT: Sikkim; N.-E. Bengal.

EXPANSE: 2 inches.

DESCRIPTION: "MALE: UPPERSIDE dull brown. *Forewing* with three small black white-centred ocelli before the apex, and a marginal white line. *Hindwing* with six submarginal blackish spots, the third and last small, bordered outwardly with white; a marginal narrow white lunulated band, and outer dark double line. UNDERSIDE pale dull brown. *Forewing* with each apical dot encircled with white; marginal band white. *Hindwing* with purple-white irregular basal lines, seven ocelli, each composed of a black spot with white centre and yellow outer circle, the two last ocelli geminated, all bordered with white, a marginal narrow white lunulated band, and extreme outer marginal yellowish line." (*Moore*, l. c.) The yellowish marginal line is as usual narrowly edged with blackish on both sides. *Cilia* white. On both sides the white bordering of the ocelli is very broad outwardly, and coalescent forming a white band, and having only a series of brown lunules between it and the white marginal line.

L. visrava appears to be rare. Colonel Lang's collection contains three male specimens from Sikkim. The FEMALE is unknown.

The single remaining species we have been obliged to keep separate; for in the absence of specimens for examination it is impossible to determine its affinities and proper place in the genus.

Key to the Indian species of Lethe.

Fourth Group.

C. White, with rufous brown markings.

153. L. DELIADES, Sikkim.

153. Lethe deliades, Hewitson.

Debis deliades, Hewitson, Ent. Month. Mag., vol. ix, p. 84 (1872).

HABITAT: Sikkim.

EXPANSE: 2·3 inches.

DESCRIPTION: "UPPERSIDE white. *Forewing* with the costal margin from the base to the middle, the whole of the cell and a little beyond it, a triangular spot between the first and second median nervules near their base, the apex (where it is broad, and marked on the costal margin by a small trifid white spot and two small black ocelli, each dotted with white) and the outer margin (where it is deeply sinuated on the inner border), and a round spot near the anal angle, all dark rufous-brown: a submarginal line of dark brown. *Hindwing* crossed beyond the middle by a series of seven blind ocelli: the first, second, third, and fourth large, the others small. A submarginal series of lunular brown spots: the outer margin rufous-yellow, bordered on both sides with black. UNDERSIDE as above, except that the *forewing* is nearly white, the spots on the upperside being scarcely visible; that the *hindwing* has perfect black ocelli, each with a white centre and rufous iris; and that the submarginal lunular spots are also rufous."

"This is a remarkable species, and cannot be compared in colour with any other butterfly." (*Hewitson*, l. c.) We have never seen this species.

Genus 11.—ZOPHOESSA, Westwood. (PLATE X.)

Zophoessa, Westwood, Gen. D. L., vol. ii, p. 362 (1851).

"BODY moderate-sized; eyes hairy; *forewing* elongate-triangular; *hindwing* [usually] tailed. HEAD small, wider in the male than in the female, hairy, not tufted. *Eyes* prominent, hairy. *Antennæ* not half the length of the forewing, very slender, terminated by a distinct elongate, slender club. *Palpi* long, slender, compressed, elevated obliquely considerably higher than the level of the top of the eyes; the long second joint not clothed behind with a tuft of hairs, the front with numerous long hairs; terminal joint minute. *Thorax* short, very convex, finely hairy. *Abdomen* small and slender in the males, elongate-ovate in the females. FOREWING large, elongate-triangular; costal margin but slightly curved; apical angle obtuse; outer margin long, slightly concave, not scalloped; inner angle rounded; inner margin nearly straight. *Costal* nervure rather dilated at the base, extending to the costa a little beyond the middle. *Subcostal* nervure with the first and second branches arising near the middle of the wing; the second close to the anterior extremity of the discoidal cell; the third and fourth arising at equal distances apart beyond the cell. *Upper disco-cellular* extremely short, oblique; *middle disco-cellular* rather longer, less oblique, straight; *lower disco-cellular* very much longer, nearly straight, almost transverse, uniting with the third branch of the median nervure at about the same distance from its base as exists between the first and second branches; the third branch being angulated at the place of junction, beyond which it is slightly curved. HINDWING subovate ; costal margin slightly arched ; outer margin scalloped ; the middle at the extremity of the third branch of the median nervure being [usually] elongated into a tail ; the space within the extremity of the first branch being deeply emarginate. *Precostal* nervure very short, furcate at the tip. *Costal* nervure extending to about two-thirds of the length of the costa. *Subcostal* nervure branching at a considerable distance from the base. *Upper disco-cellular* short, curved, but rather longer than the space between the branches of the subcostal nervure. *Lower disco-cellular* longer than the upper, curved, uniting with the median nervure close to the origin of the third branch, which is slightly curved, and extends to the outside of the tail. FORELEGS of the *male* very minute, the *femur* and *tibia* of equal length, slightly hairy ; the *tarsus* longer than the tibia, very hairy and brush-like. Of the *female* not longer than those of the male, cylindrical ; the *tibia* externally clothed with a few hairs ; the *tarsus* scarcely more than half the length of the tibia, scaly, rather dilated, and obliquely truncate at the tip, with a few very short rather thick spines nearly concealed by the scales. MIDDLE and HINDLEGS rather short, slender ; *tibia* with a few very fine spines on the underside ; *tibial spurs* rather long ; *tarsus* armed on the sides beneath with rows of fine spines, *claws* elongated, curved, very acute, entire." (*Westwood*, l. c.)

The species of *Zophoessa* are confined to the north and east of India, and are unknown beyond Indian limits ; most of them are rare and local, and even those which have the widest range appear to be only found in a few localities wide apart. In the Western Himalayas they are found between 7,000 and 9,000 feet elevation ; but eastwards they inhabit the lower ranges ; and in Tenasserim the only species that has yet been found was taken at scarcely 1.000 feet above the sea. All of them have a submarginal series of blackish spots on the upperside of the hindwing, and a submarginal series of prominent ocelli on the underside.

Key to the species of Zophoessa.

A. Upperside brown, with a row of black spots on the hindwing ; underside much variegated.
- *a*. Hindwing distinctly tailed.
  - *a*¹. Of large size (2·5 inches and above in expanse) ; upperside, forewing unmarked by bands and spots.
    - *a*². Underside, basal area pale brown.
      - *a*³. Upperside, forewing with the outer margin scarcely perceptibly paler.
        - 154. Z. SURA, Eastern Himalayas, Assam.
      - *b*³. Upperside, forewing with the outer margin distinctly paler.
        - 155. Z. DURA, Upper Tenasserim.
    - *b*². Underside, basal area ochreous.
      - 156. Z. GOALPARA, Himalayas, Assam.
  - *b*¹. Of small size (2·5 inches and under in expanse) ; upperside, forewing marked with bands and spots.
    - *a*². Upperside, forewing with the discal band macular.
      - *a*³. Upperside, markings orange-yellow.
        - 157. Z. ATKINSONIA, Eastern Himalayas.
      - *b*³. Upperside, markings ochreous.
        - 158. Z. JALAURIDA, North-West Himalayas.
    - *b*². Upperside, forewing with the discal band straight, continuous.
      - *a*³. Underside, forewing with numerous bands, one only silvery.
        - 159. Z. BALADEVA, Eastern Himalayas.
      - *b*³. Underside, forewing with three bands only, all silvery.
        - 160. Z. ANDERSONI, Upper Burma.
      - *c*³. Underside, forewing with two bands only, not silvery.
        - 161. Z. DIRPHIA, Eastern Himalayas.
- *b*. Hindwing scarcely perceptibly tailed.
  - *a*¹. Underside, forewing with the cell marked with three transverse dark brown bars.
    - 162. Z. YAMA, Himalayas, Khasi Hills.

This genus was not a very satisfactory one even when only the type species *Z. sura* was known; but since the discovery of the other species it has become almost impossible to specify the characters which may be relied on to distinguish it from *Lethe*. Typically *Zophoessa* is of larger size, but *Z. atkinsonia*, *Z. baladeva* and *Z. jalaurida* are smaller than the average *Lethes*. Typically the hindwing is more strongly caudate, but *Z. yama* has the tails almost obsolete; typically again *Zophoessa* has the forewing more triangular with the outer margin concave, but no species of *Zophoessa* has the forewing so concave as it is in *L. sinorix*, and in almost all the outer margin of that wing is straight; typically the character of the markings of the underside is much more variegated and usually with bolder and straighter transverse lines than in *Lethe*, but in *Z. jalaurida* the markings of the underside agree well in general style with those of *L. nicetas*. Typically again in *Zophoessa* the base of the forewing is almost destitute of the dense clothing of short hairs which in many species of *Lethe* overlies the scales on the base of the wing and the entire discoidal cell, but this feature it also lacks in common with the concluding group of small *Lethes* which includes *L. nicetas*. But on the other hand there are no sexual glandular patches or tufts of hairs on the wings in *Zophoessa* such as are found in the first group of *Lethes*; and perhaps the most important difference lies in the small extent to which the sexes, so far as is known, are differentiated in *Zophoessa*; in all cases in which both sexes are known the female differs but little either in colour or markings from the male; and there is no such prominent characteristic of the female as the white band on the forewing so general in *Lethe*. *Z. yama* appears to belong more properly to the second group of the next genus, *Neope*, with which it corresponds in the outline of the wings as well as in the markings of the underside. See remarks on the genus *Neope*.

154. **Zophoessa sura,** Doubleday, Hewitson.

Z. sura, Doubleday, Hewitson, Gen. D. L., vol. ii, p. 362, n. 1, pl. lxi, fig. 1 (1851), *female*.

HABITAT: Bhutan, Sikkim, Sylhet, Assam.

EXPANSE: 2·8 to 3·4 inches.

DESCRIPTION: MALE: UPPERSIDE, velvety chocolate-brown. *Forewing* with the outer margin paler, with a suffused submarginal darker line. A very indistinct blackish bar near the outer end of the cell, an equally indistinct fulvous spot on the costa beyond the cell, and another subapical trifid one somewhat more distinct. *Hindwing* strongly caudate, with a broad outer paler band bordered both inwardly and outwardly with a darker shade of the ground-colour, and bearing five round dark brown spots, the middle one the smallest. Two marginal pale lines, the inner one the more prominent, divided by a line of the ground-colour. UNDERSIDE paler, with dark brown and silvery purplish-white bars and markings. *Forewing* light brown, gradually deepening from the base to beyond the middle of the wing where it forms a dark band across the wing just beyond the cell, sharply defined, and somewhat sinuous outwardly; beyond this is a silvery purplish-white band, broad at the costa, diffused outwardly, and gradually disappearing towards the inner margin, terminated on the costa by a pure white spot. Beyond this band the ground-colour is again light brown, ending before the margin in another dark band sharply defined outwardly. The margin is pale brown, bearing a fine darker brown line; the extreme margin defined with a dark line. Three small decreasing ocelli on the discoidal and upper median interspaces, above which are three small costal purplish-white spots divided by the subcostal nervules. The ocelli are variable in number, some specimens having two, others only one ocellus. Crossing the cell at its middle is a wide deep brown bar, beyond which is a slightly narrower silvery purplish-white bar; then another dark bar inwardly sharply defined, outwardly becoming diffused into the paler ground-colour; the extremity of the cell again irrorated with silvery in an incomplete bar. *Hindwing* light brown, shaded with deeper brown, and crossed by first a short basal streak; second by a pair of narrow irregular lines enclosing a space of a deeper colour than the ground; third by two other lines from the costa to the abdominal margin, somewhat far apart and irregular, the space between them irrorated with silvery bluish-white, which is also the colour of all the lines. The inner of this last pair of lines is inwardly narrowly, and the outer one outwardly widely bordered with deep brown, as are also the disco-cellular nervules. A submarginal series of six large ocelli, the anal one geminate, black, pupilled with white, the black portion being often irrorated with silvery-bluish scales, with a yellow iris surrounded by a brown and then a silvery ring ; the dark brown margin having an irregular purplish-white line, then a narrow dark brown line, a broader ferruginous line, and lastly the extreme margin defined by dark brown. *Cilia* alternately brown and whitish.

FEMALE much lighter above and below. UPPERSIDE, *forewing* with the basal area gradually deepening to beyond the cell, where it ends abruptly, and is followed by a pale brown band across the wing, inwardly sharply defined with its edge very irregular, outwardly diffused, palest at the inner margin. The spots in the *hindwing* placed on a paler ground than in the male. UNDERSIDE, *hindwing* with the area narrowly within and more widely beyond the disco-cellular nervules irrorated with ochreous, otherwise as in the male.

As far as is known, *Z. sura* is confined to the north-east of Bengal, and is rare. Mr. Otto Möller took two male specimens near Darjiling at 6,000 feet, in November.

155. **Zophoessa dura,** Marshall.

Z. dura, Marshall, Journ. A. S. B., vol. li, pt. ii, p. 38, pl. iv, fig. 2 (1882), *male*.

EXPANSE : ♂, 2·8 inches.

HABITAT : Upper Tenasserim.

DESCRIPTION : MALE. UPPERSIDE, *both wings* dark velvet brown, with a faint purple gloss and in some lights a golden sheen, the outer margins abruptly paler, the pale margin widening on the hindwing, where it occupies nearly half the wing. *Forewing* with an indistinct dark brown submarginal line on the pale ground. *Hindwing* with four round blackish spots on the pale ground, and beyond them a dusky marginal line, followed by the usual outer yellowish lines divided by a fine dusky line. UNDERSIDE as in *Z. sura*, Moore, to which this species is closely allied, but the silvery-grey and chestnut markings are less prominent, and the grey zig-zag lines at the base of the *hindwing* are much more convex in outline.

The spots on the upperside of the hindwing are much smaller than in *Z. sura*, the two on the median interspaces are prominent, the other two are obsolescent.

Taken by Captain C. T. Bingham in the lower Thoungyeen forests in Upper Tenasserim in May. The type specimen, which is unique, is now in the Indian Museum, Calcutta.

156. **Zophoessa goalpara,** Moore.

Z. goalpara, Moore, Proc. Zool. Soc. Lond., 1865, p. 768.

HABITAT : Sikkim, Assam.

EXPANSE : ♂, 2·5 to 2·8 ; ♀, 3·0 inches.

DESCRIPTION : "MALE : UPPERSIDE glossy olive-brown, palest on the exterior margin. *Forewing* with a marginal suffused brown line. *Hindwing* with a transverse discal line, a submarginal series of round spots, and marginal lunulated line dark brown. UNDERSIDE pale glossy greyish olive-brown, suffused with darker brown exteriorly. *Forewing* with two short bands within the cell, a transverse discal band, and suffused submarginal line dark brown. *Hindwing* with subbasal transverse bifid line and transverse discal sinuous band dark brown, a submarginal series of seven dark brown ocelli, the last two at anal angle geminated, each with a white central dot and yellowish border, the whole having an outer pale whitish border along each side, a marginal line of pale lunules. FEMALE dark olive-brown, pale greyish-brown exteriorly. *Forewing* with a marginal suffused brown line. *Hindwing* with a submarginal series of brown pale-bordered spots, a marginal narrow lunulated pale line bordered with brown. UNDERSIDE glossy greyish olive-brown, palest exteriorly ; markings as in male, but more suffused ; those of the *hindwing* each with a pale border ; the submarginal ocelli less defined, the three upper partially covered with blue, the two next wholly so, the geminated last jet-black, the whole of them having each a separate pale-white outer circle. *Forewing* with three small indistinct subapical ocelli." (*Moore*, l.c.)

On the UPPERSIDE of the *forewing* in the MALE there are a dark brown transverse discal band and two more or less prominent bands in the cell corresponding to those of the underside; and on the *hindwing* beyond the lunulated line is a fine dark brown submarginal line, and the margin itself is narrowly dark brown, the narrow space between being ferruginous. On the UNDERSIDE in fresh specimens the ground-colour is a pale yellowish olivaceous; on the *forewing* are sometimes two inconspicuous small ocelli, one on each side of the lower discoidal nervule, above which is a group of three small white spots near the costa, and a narrow dark line beyond the suffused submarginal band. On the *hindwing* there is also a broad basal streak, and the marginal lines as on upperside. We have not yet seen the female.

Z. goalpara, though apparently very local, has a wide range. The Indian Museum has a single specimen from Sibsagar in Upper Assam; in the neighbourhood of Darjiling in Sikkim it is found but rarely; and in the neighbourhood of Simla it is not uncommon in some years at Sidhpore and in the Narkunda forests at about 9,000 feet elevation at the end of July and the beginning of August; but there is no record as yet of its occurrence in the vast intermediate area. The specimens from Simla differ from those from Sikkim in having on the UPPERSIDE the spots on the *hindwing* smaller; and on the UNDERSIDE in that the yellowish basal area of the *hindwing* is much more suffused with brown, especially towards the abdominal margin, the pure yellowish tone being confined to the space between the subbasal and discal brown bands above the median nervure, and to narrow diffused edgings to all the brown bands. This suffusion with brown is apparent even in Sikkim specimens, but in them it is far less pronounced and less extended.

157. **Zophoessa atkinsonia**, Hewitson.

Z. atkinsonia, Hewitson, Ent. Month. Mag., vol. xiii, p. 151 (1876); id., Moore, Desc. Lep. Coll. Atkinson, p. 2, pl. i, figs. 2, 3 (1879), *male*.

HABITAT: Sikkim.

EXPANSE: 2·1 to 2·2 inches.

DESCRIPTION: "MALE: UPPERSIDE dark brown, rufous towards the base. *Both wings* with a submarginal black line. *Forewing* marked by several rufous-orange spots; two in the cell, a quadrifid band beyond these, three (one bifid) near the apex, and five below the middle. *Hindwing* with a rufous-orange band near the outer margin, marked by five black spots; a submarginal rufous line. UNDERSIDE rufous-brown; a spot in the cell, which is bordered on both sides with brown, and a continuous band beyond the middle, sinuated and bordered inwardly with dark brown, both yellow; a series of four small white spots near the apex, and two submarginal linear brown bands. *Hindwing* tinted with green near the base, marked by two short bands of yellow, and followed by a broader band of the same colour; the outer half of the wing rufous-brown, marked by five black ocelli, with rufous iris and pupil of blue; a submarginal band of white." (*Hewitson*, l. c. in Desc. Lep. Coll. Atk.) The FEMALE is unknown.

Rare. Colonel Lang's collection contains a single specimen from Sikkim and there is a single specimen in the Indian Museum, Calcutta.

158. **Zophoessa jalaurida**, de N. (PLATE X, FIG. 19♂.)

Z. jalaurida, de Nicéville, Journ. A. S. B., vol. xlix, pt. ii, p. 245, n. 2 (1880.)

HABITAT: N.-W. Himalayas.

EXPANSE: 2·3 inches.

DESCRIPTION: MALE: UPPERSIDE of *both wings* deep brown. *Cilia* brown, ochreous at the interspaces. *Forewing* with a somewhat constricted band across the cell beyond its middle, widely bordered on both sides with a deeper shade of the ground-colour. A transverse discal band extending from the costa to the inner margin, divided anteriorly by the veins into four somewhat square-shaped spots, below the third median nervule consisting of diamond-shaped spots. A subapical spot divided into three portions by the veins, followed by four small round spots, the third from the apex slightly the largest ; all the bands and spots ochreous. An indistinct suffused submarginal dark brown line. *Hindwing* with an indistinct dark bar across the cell near its end, the disco-cellular nervules bordered on both sides with deep brown, and a band beyond the cell across the wing also of a deeper brown than the ground-colour. Six round black spots (the anal one small and indistinct) with pale circumferences placed upon a somewhat lighter coloured band than the rest of the wing. The margin dark brown with two ochreous lines divided by a dark brown line. UNDERSIDE paler brown than above, and without any sheen. *Forewing* with the bands and spots as above, only more distinct and yellower; the first two of the four round subapical spots developed into ocelli with lilascene pupils and placed on a light band. *Hindwing* slightly greenish on the abdominal margin and base ; an irregular streak at the base wide below the cell; parallel to this is a line from the costa to the median nervure; beyond this a W-shaped figure, the first line of the W being in the cell, the last ending near abdominal margin. Outside the cell a transverse streak, somewhat straight from the costa (where it is very broad) to the third median nervule, to which point it gradually decreases, beyond this it is very narrow and sinuous; the first median nervule is inwardly bordered from its origin to the point where it is cut by the last named streak with silvery-white, which is the colour of all the lines and streaks. A band of six black ocelli, pupilled with blue, with yellow irides and narrowly circled with brown and then grey lines ; the fourth from the outer angle with the blue pupil very large, and nearly covering the black portion, the sixth bipupilled. A submarginal lilascent line extending up the abdominal margin, beyond which are two dark fine lines with a broader ferruginous line between them. The FEMALE is unknown.

Z. jalaurida appears to be confined to the Western Himalayas, and occupies the most westerly range of the genus. Mr. de Nicéville took a large number of this species near the top of the Jalauri Pass on July 29th, 1879; none were on the wing, but all were settled on the red flower of a *Persicaria* which grows abundantly in the thick forest between 6,000 and 8,000 feet which clothes the Kulu side of the Pass. Strangely enough this flower was entirely disregarded by all the other butterflies (except the single *Lethe maitrya* taken in the same place) flying about, and he took them settled on nothing else. *Z. jalaurida* is also not uncommon in the Narkunda and Bhagi forests in the neighbourhood of Simla, at about 8,000 to 9,000 feet elevation, at the end of July and the beginning of August. Colonel Lang took several specimens there in 1865 ; and in 1882 Mr. Doherty, an American naturalist, found it commonly there at the same season, but we have no record of its occurrence in any other localities as yet.

The figure is taken from a male now in the Indian Museum, Calcutta, and shows the upper and undersides.

159. **Zophoessa baladeva,** Moore.

Z. baladeva, Moore, Proc. Zool. Soc. Lond., 1865, p. 769, pl. xli, fig. 5, *male*.

HABITAT : Sikkim.

EXPANSE : 2·12 to 2·35 inches.

DESCRIPTION : "MALE : UPPERSIDE greenish olive-brown. *Forewing* with three pale apical bands, the first oblique, each extending from the costa to near the posterior angle, the medial band having a linear series of small dark spots. *Hindwing* with a submarginal series of black, pale-ferruginous-bordered spots, the lower spot with a central white dot ; a narrow marginal double black line. UNDERSIDE yellowish olive-brown. *Forewing* with bands crossing the cell ; the oblique discal and submarginal band and marginal line pale yellow, the medial band composed of six small uniform ocelli, each with a black spot having a white dot and pale ferruginous outer circle, the whole bordered inwardly by a silvery-white band. *Hindwing* with a straight silvery-white band from inner margin extending across the cell, beneath which it terminates with yellow; a basal streak, discal and marginal lines yellow ; the ocelli seven in number, and very prominent, each composed of a jet-black spot with white central dot (the lowest spot with two), and pale ferruginous outer circle ; the upper spot bordered with yellow ; the others with a silvery-white inner band ; space below the last two ocelli ferruginous ; marginal lines black." (*Moore*, l.c.)

On the underside of the *forewing* there is a short streak near the base of the cell, and another at its extremity, both pale yellow, in addition to the streaks mentioned above. On the *hindwing* the upper ocellus is twice the size of any of the others, and well retired; there are also only *six* ocelli, if the anal one is considered to be bipupilled. The dark marginal lines are inwardly bordered with yellowish. The first and third median nervules of the hindwing are produced into two short but distinct tails. The FEMALE is unknown.

Rare. The few specimens in our collections are all from Sikkim.

160. **Zophoessa andersoni**, Atkinson.

Z. andersoni, Atkinson, Proc. Zool. Soc. Lond., 1871, p. 215, n. 2, pl. xii, fig. 3; id., Anderson's Researches, vol. i, p. 922, vol. ii, pl. lxxxi, fig. 3 (1878).

HABITAT: Upper Burma.

EXPANSE: 2·25 inches.

DESCRIPTION: "UPPERSIDE brown. *Forewing* crossed by two pale bands rising from the costa, and directed towards the posterior angle, but not reaching it; the first beyond the extremity of the cell, the second intermediate between the first and exterior margin, [beyond which are a series of five equal-sized obsolete ocelli, with small distinct black pupils]. *Hindwing* with a pale submarginal belt containing a series of incomplete ocelli. The first and third median nervules produced into short tails. UNDERSIDE bright ferruginous. *Forewing* crossed by three silvery-white bands, the first cutting the middle of the cell at right angles, the second and third corresponding to the pale bands on the upperside. Exterior to the third band a series of rudimentary ocelli reduced to four dark points. The exterior marginal lines bordered within by yellow. *Hindwing* crossed by two silvery-white bands, the first cutting the lower part of the cell, and corresponding to the first band of the forewing, the second equidistant between the first and the exterior margin, and corresponding to the second band of the forewing. At either end of the second band and within it are ocelli, the upper with one, and the lower with two white pupils ringed with black. Exterior to the second band a series of four white-pupilled ocelli, their outer edge forming an interrupted yellowish-white band. The exterior margin sharply defined by two fine black lines divided by a yellow line, and bordered within by bright yellow. *Cilia* yellow. *Antennæ* brown, with ferruginous tips." (*Atkinson*, l.c.) It is probable that a male is described, but the sex is not mentioned.

Very rare. There are two male specimens in the Indian Museum,—one brought by the Yunan Expedition from Ponsee, where it was taken in March, 1868, the other without locality.

161. **Zophoessa dirphia**, Druce.

Z. dirphia, Druce, Cist. Ent., vol. i, p. 357 (1875).

HABITAT: Sikkim.

EXPANSE: 2·5 inches.

DESCRIPTION: "UPPERSIDE dark brown. *Forewing* crossed beyond the middle from the costal margin to near the anal angle by a pale brown band almost yellow on the costal margin, a yellow spot beyond near the apex, below which are three minute black spots. *Hindwing* dark brown, with a submarginal row of four incomplete ocelli, the second the largest, the third minute, the *cilia* of both wings white. UNDERSIDE bright chestnut brown. *Forewing* crossed beyond the middle by a cream coloured band, a pale coloured band crossing the middle of the cell, bordered widely within by a wide reddish-brown band which crosses both wings, terminating near the inner margin of the hindwing; a row of four white-pupilled ocelli near the outer margin, which is pale brown with a very fine dark brown submarginal line. *Hindwing* crossed beyond the middle by a reddish-brown band, bordered outwardly by pale yellowish-brown; a submarginal row of six white-pupilled ocelli, the first and fifth the largest; the outer margin pale brown, with a dark submarginal brown line. This species is allied to *Z. andersoni*, Atkinson." (*Druce*, l. c.)

This is the only species of this genus which we have not seen; it must be very rare.

162. Zophoessa yama, Moore. (PLATE X, FIG. 21 ♂.)

Z. yama, Moore, Horsfield and Moore, Cat. Lep. E. I. C., vol. i, p. 221, n. 458 (1857).

HABITAT: Mussoorie, Kumaon, Bhutan, Sikkim, Khasi Hills, Sylhet.

EXPANSE: 2·8 to 3·4 inches.

DESCRIPTION: "Differs from *Z. sura* in having no caudal appendage to the hindwing. UNDERSIDE having on the *forewing* three pale bands crossing the discoidal cell, and four submarginal ocelli; the *hindwing* having the basal portion irrorated with minute pale dots, the transverse streaks more oblique, and the ocelli, seven in number, are black, encircled with a pale and then a dark line, centred with a minute white dot, that at the anal angle being, as it were, geminated. *Cilia* seen from upperside yellowish-white. Sexes alike." (*Moore*, l.c.)

Z. yama, of all the species of *Zophoessa* yet known, has the underside the most profusely variegated; but it lacks the silvery purplish-white markings of *Z. sura*, being only here and there scarcely irrorated with that colour; and on the upperside of the forewing the ochreous spots on the costa are much more prominent than in *Z. sura*, more especially so in specimens from Shillong. In specimens from Sikkim the ocelli on the underside of the forewing show through on the upperside slightly. In specimens from the Khasi Hills, they are even more distinct; while in those from Mussoorie they sometimes do not show at all. It is not uncommon in the Khasi Hills and Sikkim, where its colour is velvety chocolate-brown, the buff cilia being very broad and conspicuous. It extends westwards in the hills as far as Mussoorie, where its general colouration is totally different in tone, though the markings are identical in arrangement. Specimens from Mussoorie are much paler and of a yellowish-brown, smaller in size, and with the buff cilia inconspicuous. On the underside, too, the markings are paler and less conspicuously defined. This is no doubt a local variety, resulting from the drier climate of the western hills; there are analogous variations dependent on comparative humidity of climate in every branch of the animal kingdom. The FEMALE has the wings slightly broader, and is generally paler and duller in colour, the markings of the underside especially being duller and less distinct, but in other respects identical with those of the male.

Z. yama occurs in the Khasi Hills in May, and at Mussoorie, at 7,000 feet elevation, in June; Mr. E. T. Atkinson also records it from the outer ranges of the Himalayas in Kumaon.

The figure shows the upper and undersides of a male specimen from Shillong in Major Marshall's collection.

Genus 12.—NEOPE, Butler. (PLATE XI.)

Neope, Butler, Ann. and Mag. of Nat. Hist., third series, vol. xix, p. 166, pl. iv, fig. 7*a* (1867), *structure*; *Enope*, Moore, Horsfield and Moore, Cat. Lep. E. I. C., vol. i, p. 228 (1857); *Blanaida*, Kirby, Syn. Cat. D. L., Supplement, p. 699 (1877).

"WINGS large: *forewing* elongate, subtriangular; costa rather convex; outer margin denticulate; inner margin somewhat convex, rarely straight; nervures scarcely tumid at the base, arranged as in *Lethe*, with spots and ocelli as in *Lasiommata*. *Forewing* with the shape and neuration of *Lethe*, &c. UNDERSIDE with submarginal ocelli, basal area scrawled with irregular streaks and bands. *Antennæ* with a gradually formed club."

"The species composing this genus seem very closely allied to some of the species of *Lethe*." (*Butler*, l. c.)

Kirby has recently proposed the name of *Blanaida* for this genus, on the ground that *Neope* is preoccupied; but the nearest approach to preoccupation is in the genus *Neopus* of the Raptorial suborder of *Aves*, and as there is a sufficient difference between *Neopus* and *Neope* for all practical purposes, there does not seem to be any justification for suppressing the latter.

This is a small genus; only eight species are known, of which five are found in Indian limits, and the remainder in China and Japan. The Indian species are confined to the Himalayas, extending into Burma, and the genus is unrepresented either in the plains of North India or in the South. The *Neopes* are forest-loving insects, not common anywhere apparently except in Sikkim.

Key to the Indian species of Neope.

A. Upperside dark brown, with numerous ochreous spots and markings throughout ; hindwing distinctly tailed.

a. Of small size : forewing with the median and submedian nervures broadly defined with ochreous.

163. N. PULAHA, Himalayas.

b. Of large size ; none of the nervures defined with ochreous.

164. N. BHADRA, Sikkim ; Assam.

165. N. KHASIANA, Khasi Hills.

B. Upperside ochreous-brown, with a prominent series of submarginal black spots on both wings ; hindwing scarcely perceptibly tailed.

a. Underside with a prominent nearly straight ochreous discal band on both wings ; forewing with five ocelli, four of them pupilled with white.

166. N. BHIMA, Burma.

b. Underside with no ochreous discal band ; forewing with one ocellus and two black spots.

167. N MOOREI, India.

The genus *Neope* includes two groups differing considerably from one another in outline, and from each other and from all allied genera in the character of their markings, both of which are represented in India, and correspond to the *atkinsonia* and *yama* types in *Zophoessa*. The first, which has the forewing rather elongate and the hindwing quadrate and distinctly tailed, is distinguished by numerous ochreous spots irregularly scattered on the upperside on the dark ground and in no regular pattern ; on the underside, moreover, the markings are more irregular, and the bands on the hindwing are perpendicular to the body, instead of being parallel to it, as in all *Zophoessas*. The second which has the wings shorter, broader, and more rounded and similar in outline to *Z. yama* is distinguished by having on the upperside on *both* wings a submarginal row of large oval black spots on a yellowish ground ; on the underside the markings resemble generally those of *Z. yama* in arrangement. Structurally there appears to be nothing to separate *Neope* from *Zophoessa* except the outline of the wings, in the first or typical group ; if this feature were taken as a basis, *N. bhima* and *N. moorei* would form a separate genus, in which *Z. yama* should be included. The male insects possess no glandular patches or tufts of hair on the wings ; and the sexes are scarcely, if at all, differentiated, agreeing in both these respects with *Zophoessa*, but the differences in style of markings pointed out above render it convenient to retain them in a separate genus ; the antennæ are perhaps more gradually and less abruptly clavate than in *Zophoessa*.

The first group contains three species, all inhabiting the hills to the North of India.

163. Neope pulaha, Moore. (PLATE XI, FIG. 25♀.)

Lasiommata ? pulaha and *Enope pulaha*, Moore, Horsfield and Moore, Cat. Lep. E. I. C., vol. i, p. 227, n. 477 (1857).

HABITAT : Throughout the Himalayas to Upper Burma.

EXPANSE : 2·5 to 2·9 inches.

DESCRIPTION : "UPPERSIDE chocolate-brown, dusky about the apex and margins. *Forewing* with the veins at the base, a stripe at extremity of discoidal cell, and two transverse series of spots, ochreous-yellow. *Hindwing* with two rows of ochreous-yellow spots. *Cilia* spotted with yellowish-white. UNDERSIDE dark brown. *Forewing* with three bars across the discoidal cell and subapical spots tinged with white ; lower series of spots and space below the cell yellow. *Hindwing* with a submarginal row of eight ocelli and a single ocellus at abdominal angle ; an irregular dark brown band from middle of anterior to middle of abdominal margin ; markings about anterior margin tinged with white."

"Remark.—This species is somewhat allied in form to *Heteronympha merope*, Fabricius [from Australia]." (*Moore*, l. c.) The sexes in this species are alike. The underside of the hindwing has numerous irregular dark brown zig-zag lines and markings, too irregular to describe in detail, including several ochreous spots outlined with dark brown, and between the markings the ground-colour is irregularly and beautifully irrorated with lilac-white scales throughout, grouped here and there into cloudy bands and lunular lines in Sikkim and Eastern Himalayan specimens. The specimens taken at Kujiar in the Western Himalayas are smaller and paler, with the ochreous spots much larger, and the markings of the underside on the hindwing far less rich and prominent; they are perhaps separable as a local subspecies, but the differences are no greater than the colder and drier climate of the Western Himalayas would account for.

Major C. H. T. Marshall took *N. pulaha* at Kajiar, near Chamba, in April. Colonel Lang took it in lower Kunawar at 7,000 feet elevation, and again at Narkunda near Simla at about 9,000 feet elevation, and the Indian Musuem, Calcutta, has specimens from Mussoorie, and Sikkim, and one taken by the Yunan Expedition.

Regarding its habits, Colonel Lang notes as follows:—"I have only seen two specimens of this species in two localities far apart in the interior of the Himalaya, in dark forests of Oak, Sycamore, and Horse-chestnut, affecting shade and pitching on trunks of trees." (Ent. Month. Mag., vol. i, p. 182 (1864). Mr. A. Graham Young writes of this species as follows:—"I have as yet never seen it but on the Tihir Pass and the Jamere Mountain, Kulu. On the 21st July, 1872, it was *in swarms* round an oak tree on the top of a stony ascent, called Ghora Dik-Wallee."

The figure shows the upper and undersides of a female specimen from Sikkim in the Indian Museum, Calcutta.

164. **Neope bhadra,** Moore.

Lasiommata ? bhadra and *Enope bhadra*, Moore, Horsfield and Moore, Cat. Lep. E. I. C., vol. i, p. 227, n. 478 (1857).

HABITAT: Sikkim, Assam.

EXPANSE: 3·2 to 3·7 inches.

DESCRIPTION: "UPPERSIDE blackish-brown, suffused with chocolate-brown at the base of forewing and along abdominal margin. *Forewing* with two transverse bars within discoidal cell, and two rows of spots across the wing yellowish, the lower inner spot being long. *Hindwing* with two rows of irregular-shaped spots, and small space about extremity of discoidal cell deep ochreous-yellow, the last spot on each row near anal angle encircling a spot of black. UNDERSIDE dark brown, tinged in parts with pink. *Forewing* with markings as above, also with a subapical eye-spot. *Hindwing* with a series of seven ocelli, and a smaller spot at abdominal angle; base of the wing varied with pale ochreous-white and dark brown markings." (*Moore*, l. c.) The FEMALE does not differ from the male in markings.

The underside of the hindwing is beautifully variegated; there is a short greyish white streak along the costa from the base, then a broad dark brown band perpendicular to the body irregularly variegated with ochreous and lilac grey irrorated markings; then a greyish white band from the middle of the body to the costa, followed by a dark brown broad band below, which bears a very irregular band of yellowish irrorations defined by yellowish lines, and the paler ground-colour beyond on which the ocelli are placed, is irregularly irrorated with ochreous and lilac-white; the margin is brown, profusely irrorated with yellowish towards the anal angle, and bears two sinuous dark brown lines, in addition to the extreme marginal line, which is also dark brown.

Mr. de Nicéville found this species in profusion in the Great Runjit Valley, Sikkim, in October. It settles on the road with closed wings, flying off into the jungle when disturbed. The beautifully variegated underside of this species effectually hides it when settled, as is its habit, amongst dead leaves. Mr. Otto Möller has also taken it in the neighbourhood of Darjiling in May and June.

165. **Neope khasiana,** Moore.

N. khasiana, Moore, Trans. Ent. Soc. Lond., 1881, p. 306.

HABITAT: Khasi Hills.

EXPANSE: 3·25 inches.

DESCRIPTION: "MALE. Allied to *N. bhadra.* UPPERSIDE: markings on *forewing* similar, the two streaks within the cell much less distinct, that crossing its middle almost obsolete; the streak between the first median nervule and submedian nervure narrower, and confluent with its terminal spot. *Hindwing* ochreous-yellow, with the costal border and apical end of exterior border brown, the immediate base of the wing ochreous-brown; a large oval dark brown spot beyond lower end of the cell, and a discal curved series of six round spots decreasing in size to a minute spot above anal angle. UNDERSIDE similarly marked to *N. bhadra*, except that there are two subapical ocelli, the lower one situated between the third and second median nervules; the three streaks crossing the cell are zig-zag, and the posterior margin broadly ochreous. *Hindwing* with a regular transverse subbasal ochreous-white fascia, the dark spot at end of the cell smaller and more prominent, the transverse series of ocelli also smaller, the interspace on both sides paler ochreous-brown." (*Moore*, l.c.)

This species appears to differ from *N. bhadra* chiefly on the upperside of the hindwing. In the latter species there is often a distinct ocellus between the third and second median nervules on the underside of the forewing. We have never seen a specimen of *N. khasiana.*

The next group contains only two species in India, the remaining species of the genus being found in China and Japan. Of the two Indian species, one has been found only in Upper Tennasserim, and of the other the precise locality is doubtful; both are evidently very rare.

166. **Neope bhima,** Marshall. (PLATE XI, FIG. 26 ♀.)

N. bhima, Marshall, Journ. A.S.B., vol. xlix, pt. ii, p. 246, n. 6 (1880).

HABITAT: Upper Tenasserim.

EXPANSE: 3·0 inches.

DESCRIPTION: FEMALE. UPPERSIDE ochreous-brown. *Forewing* with a yellowish submarginal macular band narrowed at the costa and inner margin and widest in the middle, bearing three large oval black spots, one between the discoidal nervules, the others between the median nervules, and (in one specimen) a small round black spot below the first median nervule, and above the third median nervule is a small incomplete ocellus; between this band and the cell is another paler yellowish band, narrow, ill-defined, brightest at the costa, and divided by the dark nervules. *Hindwing* with five prominent oval black spots narrowly circled with yellow on a somewhat paler ground, the middle one smallest and rounded; a faint trace of the ocelli of the underside is seen through at the anal angle; the margin itself and two fine marginal lines dusky. UNDERSIDE ochreous-grey, variegated with dark brown and pure ochreous; *both wings* crossed by an almost straight prominent ochreous band (greyish on the hindwing) just beyond the middle. *Forewing* with the ocelli as on upperside, but smaller, and all pupilled with white (except the lowermost); beyond the ocelli is another ochreous band, and two fine marginal lines and the margin itself dusky; in the discoidal cell there are three transverse sinuous brown bands, the first near the base narrow, the second across the middle broader, bearing four ochreous spots and appearing like two figures of 8; the third near the extremity zig-zag, widest at the lower end; the space beyond it irregularly variegated. *Hindwing* with three prominent brown spots near the base, two in the cell, and one above bearing ochreous pupils, the rest of the basal half irrorated with brown and bearing numerous irregular zig-zag brown lines, some bordered and some centred with ochreous. Eight nearly equal black ocelli pupilled with white and banded with pure yellow and dark brown, arranged in a sinuous line, the seventh and eighth confluent; marginal lines as on forewing. *Cilia* prominent, ochreous on both sides, marked with brown at the tips of the nervules.

This species has as yet only been found in Tenasserim, where two females were taken by Captain C. T. Bingham in the Upper Thoungyeen forests in March and April. It is allied to *N. moorei*, Butler.

The figure is taken from a female specimen in the collection of Major Marshall from Upper Tenasserim, and shows the upper and undersides.

167. Neope moorei, Butler.

N. moorei, Butler, Ann. and Mag. of Nat. Hist., third series, vol. xix, p. 166, n. 3, pl. iv, fig. 7 (1867), *male;* idem, id., Cat. Lep. B.M., *Satyridæ*, p. 113, n. 4 (1868); *N. goschkevitschii*, Ménétriés, var. *a*, Kirby, Syn. Cat. D.L., p. 42, n. 3 (1871).

HABITAT: East Indies.

EXPANSE: 3·12 inches.

DESCRIPTION: "MALE. UPPERSIDE yellow-olivaceous, the nervures ochreous. *Forewing* with seven elongate oval ochreous spots, the first and second interrupted with a swarthy fasciole, the third, fifth and sixth including large blackish-swarthy spots, and the seventh a small spot. *Hindwing* with seven submarginal ochreous spots, the first and the seventh minute, from the seventh to the second increasing in length, all including swarthy spots; a marginal line and the margin itself greyish-swarthy beyond the middle. *Body* ochreous. UNDERSIDE pale ochraceous; the cell of the *forewing* and the basal area of the *hindwing* irregularly variegated with lines and streaks; a very irregular continuous median band, two marginal lines and the margin itself swarthy. *Forewing* with the apex fuscescent; four submarginal spots, the first ocellate, black, banded with yellow and pupilled with white, the second ochraceous, the third and fourth black. *Hindwing* with seven black ocelli, white pupilled, banded with yellow and again with swarthy, the seventh geminate, the third and fourth small. *Body* pale ochreous." (*Butler*, l. c. in Ann. and Mag. of Nat. Hist.)

"This is evidently a local representative of *N. goschkevitschii.*" (*Butler*, l. c. in Cat. *Satyridæ.*)

We have not seen a specimen of *N. moorei.* The "East Indies" is a wide term, and it is possible that so far as this species is concerned it may not include India at all.

Genus 13.—ORINOMA, Doubleday. (PLATE XIII.)

Orinoma, Doubleday, in Gen. D.L., p. 368 (1851); id., Butler, Ann. and Mag. of Nat. Hist., third series, vol. xix, p. 50, pl. ii, figs. 4, 4*a* (1867), *structure.*

"BODY moderately robust, clothed, especially at the sides of the thorax, in front and behind, with fine hairs; wings with longitudinal interrupted pale bars between the nervules, and not ocellated. *Head* hairy, especially in front, where the hairs form a small tuft. *Eyes* large, hairy. *Antennæ* about two-fifths of the length of the forewing, very slender, curved downwards at the tip, and terminated by a long, gradually formed, but very slender club, the articulations scarcely distinct, finely carinated beneath on the inside. *Palpi* compressed, large, porrected obliquely, reaching nearly to the level of the top of the eyes, and extending forwards nearly to the length of the head, very hairy in front; terminal joint minute, slender. *Thorax* oval; tippets clothed with fulvous hairs; meta-thorax clothed with longer grey hairs. *Abdomen* elongated, slender. FOREWING elongate, subovate; costal margin arched; apical angle rounded; outer margin entire, about three-fifths of the length of the costal margin, very slightly emarginate in the middle; anal angle rounded; inner margin straight in both sexes, of the same length as the outer margin. *Costal nervure* swollen at the base, united to the costa a little beyond the middle of its length; *subcostal nervure* with its first and second branches free, arising before the extremity of the cell; the third at nearly half-way between the cell and the apex; the fourth half-way between the third and the apex, uniting with the costa before reaching the apex, as does also the terminal part of the subcostal nervure, the upper discoidal nervule being extended to the extremity of the rounded apex. *Upper disco-cellular* very short, oblique, arising a little before the middle of the length of the wing; *middle disco-cellular* scarcely longer than the upper, nearly transverse; *lower disco-cellular* much elongated and curved, the extremity directed outwards, and united with the third branch of the median nervure at about the same distance from its origin as exists between the origin of its first and second branches, thus closing the discoidal cell rather before the middle of the wing; the third branch being angulated at the place of junction, beyond which it is rather curved. *Submedian nervure* nearly straight. HINDWING elongate-ovate; costal margin curved; outer and anal angles rounded; outer margin slightly scalloped, the scallop at the extremity of the third branch of the median nervure being rather more decided than the rest. *Prediscoidal* [*precostal* ?] *nervule* erect, curved outwards at the tip. *Subcostal nervure* arising nearer the body than the prediscoidal [precostal?], branching at a considerable distance from its base. *Upper disco-cellular* arising at a little distance from the base of the branch, curved, oblique; *lower disco-cellular* about equal in length to the upper, straight, rather more transverse, uniting with the median nervure exactly at the origin of its second and third branches, the latter of which is curved; the discoidal cell being thus closed in a rather acute point at some little distance before the middle of the wing. FORELEGS of the *male* very slender, small, and pectoral, densely clothed with delicate hairs; the tibia a little shorter than the femur, and the tarsus than the tibia; the tarsus exarticulate and destitute of claws. *Four hindlegs* moderately long, scaly; femur hairy within; tibia scarcely spined beneath; spurs distinct. Tarsus as long as the tibia, scaly, finely spined beneath and at the sides. *Claws* entire, very curved and acute. *Paronychia* minute, bifid." (*Westwood*, l.c.)

The type and only known species of this genus has very little of the general appearance of the *Satyrinæ*, and more resembles some of the *Danainæ* or *Pierinæ*, but the hairy eyes, and the arrangement of the veins of the wing, almost identical with that of *Neorina*, indicate its affinity with the *Satyrinæ*.

168. **Orinoma damaris**, Gray. (PLATE XIII, FIG. 32 ♂.)

O. damaris, Gray, Lep. Ins. Nepal, p. 14, pl. vii, fig. 2, 2 *a* (1846); id., Gen. D. L., pl. lxiii, fig 3 (1851).

HABITAT: Himalayas, Cachar, Assam, Burma.

EXPANSE: 2·6 to 3·35 inches.

DESCRIPTION: "Wings yellowish white, with the veins and marginal bands brown; the costal nervure [base of the discoidal cell] of the forewing orange, with two black spots in the middle. UNDERSIDE paler." (*Gray*, l. c.)

MALE: UPPERSIDE deep swarthy, almost black, with all the markings pale yellowish-white, except the one occupying the basal half of the cell of the forewing, which is rich orange. *Forewing* with a triangular patch of rich orange colour filling the basal half of the cell, outwardly defined by a line of darker colour than the ground, the orange portion marked with two black spots placed obliquely. The upper part of the outer half of the cell is marked with a diffused black patch, below which is a black streak. The rest of the markings are almost identical in pattern with those of *Danais aglea*, except that the long streak in the interno-median area is divided transversely near its middle by a fine, outwardly-angled black line, instead of longitudinally. *Hindwing* with the markings also bearing a very general resemblance to those of *Danais aglea*, but with the yellow space in the cell divided by a black line parallel with the disco-cellulars. UNDERSIDE with all the markings paler and more clearly defined. On both wings there is a submarginal row of obsolete small black ocelli, those on the *hindwing* pupilled with yellowish; also a marginal line divided by the nervules, within which is a series of elongated rectangular marks. *Cilia* dark brown, ochreous at the interspaces. The collar and anterior portion of the thorax with orange hairs. *Body* dark above, pale yellow at the sides, and beneath marked with fine dark narrow longitudinal lines.

Orinoma damaris is a somewhat local insect nowhere very common; in the Kangra district Mr. Hocking records (Proc. Zool. Soc., Lond., 1882, p. 235) that it has been "taken at Jatingri," but is "very local and rare;" in Kumaon Mr. E. T. Atkinson records it as occurring in wooded lowlands, and Major G. F. L. Marshall has taken it in the neighbourhood of Naini Tal; it occurs in Nepal and Sikkim, and also in the Khasi Hills in the autumn; in Cachar, where Mr. Wood-Mason took it on Nemotha in October; and in Sylhet. Captain C. T. Bingham found it in Upper Tenasserim in the lower Thoungyeen forests from March to May. It apparently only occurs in the mountainous parts of North-East India, and at low elevations.

The figure is taken from a male specimen from Sylhet in the Indian Museum, Calcutta.

Genus 14.—RHAPHICERA, Butler. (Plate XV.)

Rhaphicera, Butler, Ann. and Mag. of Nat. Hist., third series, vol. xix, p. 164, pl. iv, fig. 4*a* (1867), *structure.*

"*Forewing* elongate triangular, the costa subconvex ; outer margin short, convex ; inner margin nearly straight. Neuration as in *Lasiommata ;* nervures scarcely dilated at base ; the *disco-cellulars* oblique. *Hindwing* pyriform ; costa almost straight ; outer margin denticulate ; inner margin almost entire. *Antennæ* reaching to the middle of the forewing, elongate, slender, the club gradually formed. *Palpi* elongate, woolly ; the terminal joint short, distinct. *Eyes* hairy." (*Butler*, l. c.)

The neuration differs somewhat from that of *Lasiommata.* In the *forewing* the first and second disco-cellulars are very short, the two discoidal nervules originating close together, and close to the subcostal nervure ; the third disco-cellular is long, nearly straight and oblique. In the *hindwing* the second median nervule originates slightly before the apex of the cell in the typical species (*R. satricus*), and exactly opposite to it in the only other Indian species, while in *Lasiommata* it originates beyond the apex.

Only three species are known, two of which occur in the Himalayas, and the third at Mou-pin in Thibet. The colouration is dark orange-yellow, much marked with black, and the pattern is the same on both upper and undersides ; the hindwing is also prominently ocellated on the underside. They are forest loving insects, settling on the leaves of trees and bushes, with a quick darting flight, and having nothing protective in their colouring they are prominent objects when settled. Both species are rare and very local. The sexes are only slightly differentiated, the female having the same colour and style of markings as the male.

Key to the Indian Species of Rhaphicera.

A. Wings orange-yellow ; the nervures and some bars across the wings and spots black. Hindwing with a submarginal series of ocelli.

- *a.* The nervures narrowly black.
  - 169. R. SATRICUS, Eastern Himalayas.
- *b.* The nervures broadly black ; the base of both wings irrorated with fuscous.
  - 170. R. MOOREI, Western Himalayas.

169. Rhaphicera satricus, Doubleday, Hewitson.

Lasiommata satricus, Doubleday, Hewitson, Gen. D. L., p 387, n. 14, pl. lxiv, fig. 4 (1851), *female ; Rhaphicera satricus*, Butler, Ann. and Mag. of Nat. Hist., third series, vol. xix, p. 164, pl. iv, fig. 3 (1867), *female.*

Habitat : Eastern Himalayas.

Expanse : 2·5 to 2·7 inches.

Description : Male : Upperside rich dark orange yellow ; all the nervures black. *Forewing* with a narrow black bar across the cell in prolongation of the first median nervule, and another much broader one in prolongation of the second ; a broad irregular band beyond the cell from the costa to the first median nervule, and sharply angled outwardly at its middle on the third median nervule ; a short subapical bar from the costa ending with a round spot between the discoidal nervules, a large round spot on the lower median interspace, and the outer margin irregularly (narrowest on the lower median interspace) and the inner margin extending to the submedian nervure, black. *Hindwing* with a similar angulate band beyond the cell, narrow from the costa, almost obliterated above the discoidal nervule, broad and prominent across the median nervules ; four large round submarginal spots, one on either side of the second subcostal, and one on either side of the second median nervule, and the outer margin, black ; two narrow orange lines on the black margin ; *cilia.* orange. Underside. *Forewing* paler yellow ; markings as on upperside, but the apex and outer margin also yellow, bearing a fine black line on the extreme margin, and another incomplete within it, and an irregular line much wider about the third median nervule and following the outline of the dark border of the upperside ; the lower submarginal spot having a small white pupil and the upper one developed into a perfect ocellus, with a bluish-white pupil, yellow iris and blackish outer ring. *Hindwing* bright golden brown with a broad much paler streak from the base covering the entire cell, and extending almost to the outer margin; a line from middle of costal nervure across the cell, an irregular angulate line from the costa outside the cell to the submedian nervure and two fine marginal lines black, a dusky sinuous submarginal line; six submarginal ocelli, the third (sometimes absent) and sixth smaller, and the sixth geminate, all black with prominent bluish-white pupil, yellow iris, and blackish outer ring. **Female** similar in colour and markings.

Rhaphicera satricus is found in Sikkim, and Mr. E. T. Atkinson records it as occurring in the wooded hills beyond Almorah in Kumaon. This is probably the extreme western range of the species; further to the west it is replaced by the allied *R. moorei.*

170. Rhaphicera moorei, Butler. (Plate XV, Fig. 38♂.)

Lasiommata satricus, Moore, Proc. Zool. Soc. Lond., 1865, p. 499, n. 82; *Rhaphicera moorei*, Butler, Ann. and Mag. of Nat. Hist., third series, vol. xix, p. 164, n. 2, pl. iv, fig. 4 (1867), *female*.

Habitat: North-West Himalayas.

Expanse: 2·1 to 2·25 inches.

Description: Male: Upperside as in *R. satricus*, but all the black lines broader, the nervures being bordered as well as defined with black, giving it more the appearance of a black insect spotted with orange; the base of *both wings*, and the inner margin of the *hindwing* broadly irrorated with fuscous. Underside also similar but paler and less brilliant; the base of both wings, and the inner margin of the hindwing broadly irrorated with fuscous as on the upperside; the third ocellus of the hindwing often obsolete, sometimes entirely wanting, the fourth, fifth, and sixth comparatively larger, and closer together. "Female: Upperside pale yellowish-ferruginous, very similar to *R. satricus*, female, but smaller. *Forewing* with all the nervures fuscous, the base fuscescent, the black bands wider, the discal fascia continued to the inner margin; a minute median discal black dot. *Hindwing* more denticulate, the internal area olivaceous-fuscous, with a series of six ocelli with grey pupils; the outer margin fuscescent. Underside: *Forewing* with the discal fascia more slender, the ocelli smaller, the outer margin slightly fuscescent. *Hindwing* paler, the ocelli closer together, the median lines more irregular, continuous; the submarginal lines more undulate." (*Butler*, l.c.)

R. moorei is generally considered a rare insect, but in 1882 it was found in great profusion by Mr. Doherty in the Bhagi and Narkunda forests and again at Theog, all in the neighbourhood of Simla, in August; flying freely during heavy rain, and alighting on the leaves of bushes and trees; it is conspicuous when settled and appears to have nothing protective in its colouration. Colonel Lang notes, "Observed only late in the autumn, in a forest glade in the Himalayas, near a stream with rich vegetation about its banks." His collection contains five specimens from the neighbourhood of Simla taken at 9,000 feet elevation, and two from lower Kunawar, 7,000 feet elevation; it is evidently a very local insect.

The figure represents a male specimen taken by Mr. de Nicéville at Narkunda near Simla in August, and shows the upper and undersides.

The next two genera *Pararge* and *Amecera* represent in India the "hairy-eyed" division of the genus *Satyrus* as defined by Godart and Boisduval. They are both sections of the genus *Lasiommata* of Westwood (Gen. D. L.), which latter also includes both *Neope* and *Rhaphicera*. They are distinguished from the remaining subdivisions of *Satyrus* defined further on as *Hipparchia*, *Aulocera*, and *Epinephele*, not only by having the eyes hairy, but by the position of the apex of the discoidal cell of the hindwing as defined in the key to the genera (p. 96), and by having a complete series of ocelli on the hindwing on the underside. In a few species of *Hipparchia* and *Epinephele* there are two or three perfect ocelli on the underside of the hindwing, but in none is there a perfect series, and in the greater number of species and in all the *Auloceras* the ocelli are entirely absent. Westwood's definition of *Lasiommata* is republished for reference.

Genus **Lasiommata,** Westwood.

Lasiommata, Westwood, Gen. D. L., p. 385 (1851).

"*Body* slender, hairy; costal and median nervures of the *forewing* swollen at the base. *Head* moderate-sized, very hairy, with a frontal tuft. *Eyes* prominent, hairy. *Palpi* porrected obliquely, the tips raised to the level of the tops of the eyes, extending forwards as far as the length of the head, very slender; the front of the basal and second joints thickly clothed with long divaricating hairs, extending to the tip; the terminal joint being extremely short. *Antennæ* straight, distinctly annulated with white, not quite half the length of the forewing, terminated by a distinct, compressed, pear-shaped club, the tip being bent outwards; the club, however, varies considerably in shape, being elongated and very gradually formed in some exotic species. *Thorax* oval, moderate-sized, hairy. *Abdomen* slender. FOREWING large, elongate-triangular; costal margin moderately arched; apex rounded; outer margin entire, more than two-thirds of the length of the costal; inner margin about as long as the outer. *Costal* and *median* nervures dilated at the base, the latter less so than the former. *Neuration* as in *Erebia;* the *upper disco-cellular* very short, transverse; the *middle* and *lower* forming a continuous curved line, the middle one shorter than the lower one; the *discoidal cell* reaching rather beyond the middle of the wing; a nervule extending into the discoidal cell continuous with the lower discoidal nervule; another nervule extending backwards from near the lower extremity of the lower disco-cellular nervule. HINDWING subovate; outer margin moderately scalloped; anal margin not incised near the extremity. *Upper disco-cellular* nervule arising at a short distance from the origin of the branch of the subcostal, considerably curved, and throwing off a nervule backwards into the discoidal cell; *lower disco-cellular* considerably longer than the upper one, also curved, and united with the median nervure at the origin of its third branch, or sometimes preceding the third branch. FORELEGS small, but distinct, and very hairy in both sexes; those of the *male* very slender, and more thickly hairy, with the tarsus simple, and acute at the tip. Those of the *female* scarcely longer; tibia shorter than the femur; tarsus equal to the tibia, dilated, and compressed at the extremity, where it is articulated, and armed on the inside with short spines. *Four hindlegs* moderately long, very slender, scaly; femur hairy beneath; tibia and tarsus with very few spines beneath. *Claws* curved, acute, simple, dilated into an angulated lobe at the base. *Paronychia* slender, bifid. *Pulvillus* small, rounded."

"LARVA. Elongate, villose, with two short points at the tail. PUPA short, thick, with small angular projections, and two points at the head; suspended by the tail." (*Westwood*, l.c.)

The whole of the Indian species belong to two sections which have been generically separated under the names *Pararge* and *Amecera* on the following characters:—

Genus 15.—PARARGE, Hübner.

Pararge, Hübner, Verz. bek. Schmett., p. 59 (1816).

Differs but slightly from *Lasiommata* in having the *median* nervure of the *forewing* but very slightly swollen at base; the outer margin of the forewing is scarcely sinuate, and the inner margin is longer than the outer. The sexes are identical in markings, but differ somewhat in aspect owing to all the black markings being far more prominent in the female. The MALE has no sexual patches of raised scales or tufts of hairs on the wings.

Only a single species occurs within Indian limits; it is found in the North-West Himalayas. The colour is ochreous yellow with the outer margin and a few spots black, and is quite different in aspect from all other Indian species of this subfamily.

171. **Pararge cashmirensis,** Moore.

P. cashmirensis, Moore, Proc. Zool. Soc. Lond., 1874, p. 265, pl. xliii, fig. 3, *male*.

HABITAT: N.-W. Himalayas.

EXPANSE: ♂, 2·0 to 2·2; ♀, 2·2 to 2·35 inches.

DESCRIPTION: "MALE: UPPERSIDE ochreous yellow, brownish at the base. *Cilia* yellowish white, spotted with black. *Forewing* with a black dentate disco-cellular streak, and a dark ochreous-black exterior border, the inner margin of which commences one-third before the apex and curves half round a subapical white-pupilled black spot, and thence attenuates to posterior angle [with a prominent projection inwards between the second and third median nervules]. *Hindwing* with a broad ochreous brown exterior border with waved inner margin, contiguous to which are three black spots, each with a white pupil, the middle spot being the largest, and the anterior the smallest. The FEMALE differs in having two subapical spots and a broad disco-cellular patch on the *forewing*, and a fourth smaller anterior spot on the *hindwing*. UNDERSIDE. *Forewing* paler ochreous, markings as on upperside, but greyish brown, and with three narrow brown transverse streaks within the cell, and an irregular streak beyond it; two bright white-pupilled subapical spots, the upper one small, beneath which is a white dot, all being encompassed by a brownish line. *Hindwing* with greyish-brown base and exterior border, the disc being whitish grey, the division marked by a dark brown irregular zig-zag inner line and a wavy outer line; within this discal portion is a series of six round bright black spots, each having a white pupil (the basal two), and encircled by a yellow and a narrow brown outer ring, the second and third anterior spots being small, the others of equal size."

"*Note.*—The nearest ally to this species is *P. eversmanni*, Eversmann, from Central Asia, figured in the Moscow Bulletin for 1847, vol. ii, pl. ii, figs. 5, 6." (*Moore*, l.c.)

In some specimens the MALE also has on the upperside two subapical spots on the *forewing* and four submarginal on the hindwing; the base and inner half of the latter is suffused with brown. In the FEMALE the suffusion of brown on the hindwing is darker and more extended, the only yellow left being diffused rings round the spots and a small patch at the end of the cell.

Pararge cashmirensis is a rare and very local butterfly; the first capture of it was by the late Captain Reed at Goolmurg, an elevated plateau about 9,000 feet above the sea in Kashmir. Mr. Robert Ellis has since taken it in Pangi in July and August at considerable elevations; it was also taken by Mr. Atkinson in Kashmir, but no other records of its capture can be traced. It is a well-marked conspicuous butterfly that would not fail to attract attention if met with.

Genus 16.—AMECERA, Butler. (PLATE XV.)

Amecera, Butler, Ann. and Mag. of Nat. Hist., third series, vol. xix, p. 162, pl. iv, figs. 1, 1 *a* (1867), *structure*.

DESCRIPTION: "*Forewing* with the outer margin less wavy, and not angulate at the apex. *Hindwing* more elongate, the outer margin scarcely sinuate; otherwise as in *Lasiommata*. *Neuration* as in *Lasiommata*, but the cell of the hindwing shorter. *Antennæ* more elongate and slenderer, the club pyriform and compressed. *Palpi* with the terminal joint more elongate." (*Butler*, l. c.)

In this section Butler has included *Hipparchia baldiva*, but as its eyes are quite destitute of hairs it belongs to, and is here included in, the genus *Hipparchia* restricted. He also includes *Pararge eversmanni*, which is a true *Pararge*, very closely allied to *P. cashmirensis*.

It is doubtful whether the name *Amecera* will not have to give way to *Lasiommata*, of which also *megæra* was the type. Mr. Butler has restricted *Lasiommata* to the section of which *ægeria* is the type, and this arrangement we retain, as it has been followed by Mr. Moore.

The genus *Amecera* is spread over Europe and Western Asia, extending to England on the one hand, and to the Eastern Himalayas on the other. The typical species is *A. megæra*, an English butterfly, with the wings tawny fulvous, marked with smoky brown. Four species have been described from India, all of them restricted to the mountain ranges on the north and north-west frontiers. One of them, *A. schakra*, is very distinct, and is a dominant species, common over a very large extent of country; the other three are all more or less specialised local forms of *A. mæra* of South Europe, the claim of at least one of them to rank as distinct specifically has been opposed by high authorities, and all three are comparatively rare and local. In this genus the males usually, but not universally, have a broad oblique stripe of raised scales on the forewing from the apex of the cell to the middle of the submedian nervure—a feature which they have in common with some of the *Hipparchias* and *Epinepheles.*

Key to the Indian species of Amecera.

A. With the wings smoky brown, with a prominent subapical ocellus on the forewing, and two or more on the hindwing, ringed with fulvous on the upperside; all with six perfect ocelli on the underside of the hindwing.

a. Males with a broad oblique stripe of densely packed scales on the upperside of the forewing.

*a*¹. With a submarginal series of fulvous streaks diminishing from the costa (much wider in the female) on the upperside of the forewing; the male sexual streak narrow, and outwardly dentate along the nervules. Hindwing with two to five submarginal ocelli.

172. A. SCHAKRA, Himalayas.

*b*¹. Male with two fulvous streaks below the ocellus on the forewing; hindwing with four ocelli.

173. A. MÆRULA, Western Himalayas.

*c*¹. Male with the submarginal streaks on forewing more or less obsolete; the sexual streak very wide, not outwardly dentate; female with a prominent triangular fulvous patch divided by the dark nervules only; hindwing with only two ocelli in both sexes.

174. A. MENAVA, Western Himalayas.

b. Males with no stripe of densely packed scales on the upperside of the forewing.

*a*¹. Forewing with the outer dark zone of the ocellus on the underside of the forewing diffused and incomplete.

175. A. MÆROIDES, Western Himalayas.

172. Amecera schakra, Kollar. (PLATE XV, FIGS. 45 ♂, 46 ♀.)

Satyrus schakra, Kollar in Hugel's Kaschmir, vol. iv, pt. ii, p. 446, n. 4, pl. xv, figs. 3, 4 (1848), *male*; *Lasiommata schakra*, Westwood, Gen. D. L., p. 387, n. 12 (1851); *Amecera schakra*, Butler, Ann. and Mag. of Nat. Hist., third series, vol. xix, p. 163, n. 7 (1867).

HABITAT: The Himalayas.

EXPANSE: 2·0 to 2·5 inches.

DESCRIPTION: MALE: "UPPERSIDE fuscous, with an interrupted marginal fulvous band. *Forewing* with one ocellus. *Hindwing* with three ocelli, black, pupilled with white. UNDERSIDE grey. *Forewing* with a large fulvous patch near the hinder angle, with a large apical ocellus, and a smaller obsolete one adjacent. *Hindwing* with six ocelli, each with two rings, and obscure angulate streaks." (*Kollar*, l. c.) FEMALE paler, with an additional fulvous marginal band beyond the ocellus, and the fulvous streaks merging into a pale yellow band between the ocellus and the cell extending nearly to the costa.

Though fairly constant in the markings of the underside *A. schakra* presents considerable variation on the upperside. Besides the difference in tone of the ground-colour due to climate, the MALE shows in the *forewing* differences in the width and prominence of the fulvous marginal band; and in the *hindwing* in the number and prominence of the ocelli. The commonest form has three ocelli, one or more of which are blind, others have two ocelli with a fulvous spot above. Others again have three ocelli with a fulvous spot above. Others have four ocelli, the uppermost blind, and some have five, the uppermost smallest, and well separated. The FEMALE shows the same variation in the ocelli of the hindwing.

A. schakra is one of the commonest butterflies of the Western Himalayas, extending eastwards as far as Sikkim; in the north-west "to be seen at all seasons flitting about the rocky road-side, and pitching on the rocks or banks; more abundant on the outer ranges on bare grassy slopes." (*Colonel A. M. Lang* in Ent. Month. Mag., vol. i, p. 182, 1865.) Mr. A. Graham Young states that in Kulu it is very common, appearing in July, and again in September and October.

LARVA: "Apple-green with pale yellow lateral lines. Feeds on various grasses." (*Graham Young*.)

The figures show the upper and undersides of both sexes; the male from Simla, the female from Mussoorie.

173. Amecera mærula, Felder.

Lasiommata mærula, Felder, Reise Novara, Lep, vol. iii, p. 496, n. 858 (1865).

HABITAT: Kunawar, Pangi.

EXPANSE: Not given.

DESCRIPTION: "MALE: UPPERSIDE as in *L.* [*A.*] *mæra*,* but with the ocellus of the *forewing* larger, and with the two ferruginous-fulvous spots below it narrower, and more distant from the margin. *Hindwing* with four ocelli (the uppermost blind), also larger and more remote from the margin. UNDERSIDE as in *L.* [*A.*] *schakra*, but the *forewing* with the fulvous patch extending into the cell, the streaks in the cell fuscous, the innermost shortest, the ocellus larger, the streak on the inner side of it short, straight. *Hindwing* with the streaks obscurely fuscous, a little more flexuous, the basal streak not at all faint, the ocelli larger. This fine species stands between *L.* [*A.*] *schakra*, which Dr. Stoliczka collected in large numbers on the Southern Himalayas, and our *L.* [*A.*] *mæra*; the underside is very similar to that of *L.* [*A.*] *schakra*, the shape of the wings, however, together with the upperside reminds one of the latter." (*Felder*, l. c.)

In the absence of the type we are unable to state what differences can be especially relied on to separate the species; many of the varieties of *A. schakra* noted above accord fairly with the description of *A. mærula*, though none of them exactly agree, especially in the outline of the forewing; it seems to us probable that *A. mærula* is only a casual variety of *A. schakra*, but we retain it as distinct for the present pending further investigation, and in deference to Dr. Felder's high authority.

A. mærula is apparently very rare, we have never seen a specimen. The description of *A. mæra* from specimens from Prussia is given below.

174. Amecera menava, Moore.

Lasiommata menava, Moore, Proc. Zool. Soc. Lond., 1865, p. 499, n. 83, pl. xxx, fig. 3, *male*.

HABITAT: Western Himalayas; Beluchistan.

EXPANSE: 1·75 to 2·2 inches.

DESCRIPTION: "MALE: UPPERSIDE fuliginous brown. *Forewing* with a large apical jet-black ocellus, with white pupil and ferruginous iris; also a much smaller ocellus between it and the apex. *Hindwing* with two similar ocelli, placed submarginally midway between the anterior and posterior angles, [the inner one much the smaller]. UNDERSIDE with the discal portion of the *forewing* ferruginous; a series of four transverse discoidal streaks, and a submarginal line dark brown, each bordered with pale grey; the ocelli as above, but with yellow irides. *Hindwing* pale greyish brown, with irregular transverse basal brown lines; a series of six black submarginal ocelli, the first five with each a white pupil, and a double brown-bordered yellow iris, the sixth [geminate] at the anal angle, without the white-pupilled

---

* *Amecera mæra*, Linnæus, Faun. Suec., p. 275, n. 1049 (1761). HABITAT: Europe. Expanse, *male*, 2·0 to 2·1, *female* 2·1 inches. DESCRIPTION: MALE. UPPERSIDE dull smoky brown. *Forewing* with a prominent black, white-pupilled subapical ocellus with a minute similar ocellus attached to it below, and another minute ocellus placed outwardly above it; these ocelli placed on a patch of bright fulvous, widest towards the costa, narrowest at the submedian nervure, which it does not quite reach, and divided by the dark nervules. *Hindwing* with two submarginal black, white-pupilled ocelli, each surrounded by a fulvous iris, and with a small spot of the same colour in the interspace above the anterior ocellus, sometimes bearing a small ocellus. UNDERSIDE light greyish brown. *Forewing* with two transverse brown bars in the cell, and the disco-cellulars defined with brown; the ocelli ringed with pale yellow, and enclosed in a single fine brown line; the disc bright fulvous, the margin bearing an inner rather broad waved dark line and two fine marginal lines. *Hindwing* with six black ocelli, the anal one geminate, each with two rings of fulvous and two of dark brown; a basal, a median and a submarginal dark wavy line, all paralled to the outer margin, two very indistinct waved darker lines on the margin. FEMALE similar, but with the bright fulvous patch wider, and extending into the interspace below the submedian nervure; the disc irrorated with fulvous. UNDERSIDE with the fulvous patch larger and brighter. It lacks the usual sexual streak of the male on the upperside of the forewing. (Described from specimens from Prussia).

black centre; a submarginal series of whitish-grey lunules. Allied to *L.* [*A.*] *schakra*, Kollar." (*Moore*, l. c.)

The FEMALE differs in being paler coloured, in lacking the male sexual streak, and in having on the UPPERSIDE of the *forewing* a large triangular bright fulvous patch occupying nearly the apical half of the wing; the ocellus is included in this patch, and it is cut only by the dark nervules, not divided into streaks as in *A. schakra.*

A. menava "comes from middle Kunawar, the pleasant villages of Pangi and Rarung, where the last showers of rain fall at rare intervals. It does not venture to the drier regions; and its uniformly dark colour remains constant, and seems to distinguish it from the more fulvous *L.* [*A.*] *schakra* so common on every rocky roadside in Lower Kunawar and the Simla hills." (Note by Colonel Lang in Proc. Zool. Soc. Lond., l. c.) It is also found in the Pangi and Chini districts in the months of June and July, but it appears to be local, and nowhere very common. Mr. de Nicéville took a male at Nurla, Ladak, on July 5th, and two females,—one each at Chanagund and Kargil, Ladak, on June 30th and July 1st respectively. These were all the specimens he saw, the extremely scanty vegetation of this dry and barren region not being favourable to an abundant insect fauna. Quite recently a female specimen has been taken by Colonel Lang in the Kawas Valley in Beluchistan at 8,000 feet elevation in the month of September, which shows that this species has a far wider range than was at first believed.

175. Amecera mæroides, Felder.

Lasiommata mæroides, Felder, Reise Novara, Lep., vol. iii, p. 496, n. 859, pl. lxix, fig. 1 (1865), *female.*

HABITAT: Dras, Ladak; Chulichang, at 12,000 feet elevation; Pangi.

EXPANSE: ♂, 2·1 to 2·4; ♀, 2·3 to 2·4 inches.

DESCRIPTION: "MALE: UPPERSIDE as in *L.* [*A*] *menava*, but paler; the streaks more obsolete. *Forewing* with the ocellus distinctly surrounded with fulvous, and with two large spots irrorated with fulvous below it. *Hindwing* with two ocelli coloured as in *L.* [*A.*] *menava*, but more broadly ringed and a little nearer to the margin; a fulvous spot annexed to the upper ocellus. UNDERSIDE as in *L.* [*A.*] *menava*, but the *hindwing* with the streaks of the basal half fuscous, scarcely margined with fulvous; that beyond the cell a little more directed outwards towards the costa. FEMALE. UPPERSIDE. *Forewing* with the ocellus placed on a triangular band of deep fulvous. A local form of *L.* [*A.*] *menava*, Moore, which Dr. Stoliczka collected in numbers on the Southern Himalayas near Pangi in Kunawar. The FEMALE differs from the yet undescribed female of *L. menava* in the fulvous patch of the *forewing* being throughout distinctly defined, lighter and hardly divided by the nervules, and in the two ocelli of the hindwing being separated from each other, smaller, and somewhat nearer to the margin, as well as differing on the underside in the same way as described for the male. The two females of *L. menava* taken by Dr. Stoliczka have on the upperside a third irregular ocellus confluent with the large one placed between the second and third median nervules." (*Felder*, l. c.)

A. mæroides is given by Butler in his Cat. *Satyridæ* B. M., p. 126, as a synonym of *A. menava;* but the presence in the male of the large fulvous spots below the ocellus on the upperside of the forewing distinguish it from that species. No difference, however, can be detected on comparing a female of *A. menava* with Felder's figure of a female of *A. mæroides*, except in the slightly larger extent of the fulvous patch on the forewing.

There are three specimens in Major Marshall's collection of an *Amecera* taken at Pangi in July and one female in August by Mr. Robert Ellis; two of the former are clearly males by the structure of the abdomen and of the forelegs, and the outline of the wings, but they have no trace whatever of the male sexual streak on the forewing. They correspond well with Felder's description of *A. mæroides*, and we refer them to that species, although the third specimen, a female, taken at the same time and place, resembles that of *A. schakra*, and not that of *A. menava*, in style of markings of the upperside. All three are much darker in colour than *A. schakra* usually is, but paler than *A. menava*. They are certainly distinct from *A. schakra*; on the UNDERSIDE all four specimens differ both from *A. schakra* and *A. menava* in that the apical ocellus of the *forewing* lacks the well-defined narrow dark outer ring, having only an incomplete rather diffused ring, the lower portion obsolete; in the *hindwing* the ground-colour is paler than even in *A. schakra*, and, as Felder states, the streaks are fuscous scarcely margined with fulvous; and the one beyond the cell is distinctly more irregular and angled in outline. The males correspond so exactly with Felder's description of *A. mæroides* that we cannot doubt their identity with that species, and we can only surmise that a female of *A. menava* has been accidentally figured by Felder as the female of *A. mæroides.*

Genus 17.—HIPPARCHIA, Fabricius.

Hipparchia, Fabricius, Ill. Mag., vol. vi, p. 281 (1807); *Satyrus (in part)*, Westwood, Gen. D. L., p. 388, (1851.)

"BODY generally rather robust, hairy; *forewing* with the costal and median nervures swollen at the base, and the outer margin somewhat scalloped. HEAD rather small, thickly clothed with rather short hairs. *Eyes* prominent, naked. *Palpi* rather short, porrected obliquely, but not reaching much above the level of the middle of the eyes, and extending forwards about half the length of the head, rather thickly clothed beneath with moderately short hairs; the middle joint with a compressed conical tuft of hairs in the middle of the hinder margin; terminal joint very short and oval. *Antennæ* not near half the length of the forewing, very slender, articulations indistinct, not annulated with white; terminated either by a short, abrupt, broad, concave club, or by a long, slender, fusiform club, with its base gradually formed. *Thorax* oval, clothed especially behind with long soft hairs. *Abdomen* moderately elongate-ovate. FOREWING with the costal and median nervures greatly swollen at the base; costal margin well arched, apex rounded; outer margin more than two-thirds the length of the costal; inner margin not, or scarcely, so long as the outer one, nearly straight. *Neuration* as in *Lasiommata;* the third and fourth branches of the subcostal nervure being, however, more approximate to each other than in *Lasiommata*, leaving a greater space between the extremity of the discoidal cell and the third, and between the fourth and the tip of the wing. The *upper disco-cellular* nervule is extremely short and transverse, and the *middle* and *lower* ones nearly continuous and oblique; the latter united with the third branch of the median nervure at about the same distance from its origin as exists between the first and second branches. The *discoidal cell* extends to the middle of the wing. HINDWING broadly ovate, more or less scalloped along the outer margin; the abdominal margin entire. *Neuration* as in *Lasiommata*, except that the *upper disco-cellular* nervule is longer, and the *lower disco-cellular* is united to the third branch of the median nervure at a rather shorter distance from its origin than exists between the first and second branches of the median nervure. FORELEGS of comparatively moderate length, and distinctly visible in both sexes; those of the *male* being much more densely clothed with hair, and those of the *female* rather larger. Tarsus simple in the *male*, but articulated in the *female;* not armed, however, with minute spines at the tips of the joints. *Four hindlegs* rather short, scaly; *femora* almost entirely destitute of hairs beneath; *tibiæ* armed with several rows of spines, set rather widely apart, at the sides beneath; *tibial spurs* very acute, and rather long; *tarsi* armed beneath and at the sides with several rows of short spines; tips of the joints with longer spines. *Claws* entire, long, very acute, and curved. *Paronychia* very slender."

"LARVA pubescent, elongate-conical; head rounded; tail bifurcate; body marked with dark longitudinal stripes. They conceal themselves and remain inactive during the day, but come forth to feed by night, when they may be found in great numbers with the help of a lamp, feeding indifferently on different kinds of grasses. PUPA short, ovoid, glabrous, with the head obtuse and tail pointed; either suspended by the tail, or enclosed in a cocoon of earth mixed with a little silk."—(*Westwood*, l. c.)

The genus *Hipparchia* as restricted is a Palæarctic form, and extends throughout Europe and North Asia, occurring also in North Africa, North America, and Japan. Within our limits they are only found in the mountainous regions on the North-West and West frontiers; most of them appear to be local, and many of them are very rare in collections, as they occur only far in the interior, and at high elevations where naturalists can seldom get opportunities of collecting. They are found on grass and rocky ground, and, with the exception of the aberrant species *H. parisatis*, beyond the limits of tree vegetation as a rule.

Key to the Indian Species of Hipparchia.

A. Upperside swarthy, with a conspicuous white band on the outer margin; the underside of both wings concolorous, with prominent and perfect ocelli.

176. H. PARISATIS, Western Himalayas, Afghanistan, Persia.

B. Upperside brown, with the cilia pale, but no prominent white border; the underside with the forewing more or less ferruginous or tawny on the disc; the hindwing mottled and marbled, with a single very minute ocellus, or with none at all.

a. Upperside brown, without any broad submarginal fulvous fascia; a single subapical ocellus on forewing.

177. H. PIMPLA, Western Himalayas, Afghanistan, Beluchistan.

b. Upperside brown, with several fulvous submarginal streaks forming a much interrupted band on both wings (obscure in the forewing of the male). Forewing with two equal-sized obscure submarginal ocelli.

178. H. DIFFUSA, Western Himalayas.

c. Upperside brown, with a broad fulvous submarginal band on both wings.

a.[1] The fulvous band angulate on its inner edge in both sexes, and bearing two equal-sized ocelli on the forewing, with two *white* spots between them; and a single minute subanal ocellus on the hindwing.

179. H. THELEPHASSA, Beluchistan.

b.[1] The fulvous band with its inner edge straight on the forewing in the male, angulate in the female; bearing two ocelli (often blind) with or without two *black* spots between them on the forewing, and one (sometimes two) minute subanal ocelli on the hindwing.

180. H. BALDIVA, Western Himalayas.

c.[1] The fulvous band broader, with its inner edge angled on the forewing in both sexes; otherwise as in *H. baldiva*, but paler, and usually without the subanal ocellus on hindwing.

181. H. LEHANA, Western Himalayas.

d.[1] The fulvous band regular and sharply defined on both wings, and bearing a single subapical ocellus on forewing; none on hindwing.

182. H. DIGNA, Western Himalayas.

e.[1] The fulvous band defined with dark lunules, narrow on the hindwing, and further from the margin in both wings than in *H. baldiva* and *H. lehana*; bearing two prominent black spots on the forewing, none on the hindwing.

183. H. HUEBNERI, Western Himalayas.

d. Forewing fulvous with brown margin.

184. H. CADESIA, Western Himalayas.

C. Upperside blackish-brown with creamy-white markings.

a. With a creamy-white patch in the cell of the forewing.

185. H. SHANDURA, Western Himalayas.

b. With no creamy-white patch in the cell of the forewing.

186. H. ANTHE, Afghanistan, Persia.

In this genus the sexual mark in the males presents a good deal of variation; typically it is a streak of thickly set differently formed scales on the forewing as in *Amecera*, but much wider, and extending into the discoidal cell; but we are unable to base the arrangement on this structural feature at present as the males of *H. diffusa*, *H. digna*, *H. huebneri*, *H. cadesia*, and *H. shandura*, are not represented in our collections. The most remarkable deviation from the type in this respect is *H. thelephassa*, in which the sexual streak almost entirely fills the discoidal cell, and bears a deep black patch irrorated and often entirely concealed with greyish-brown scales. The form of the antennæ too varies greatly. In *H. pimpla*, *H. digna*, and *H. cadesia* they are gradually clavate; in *H. thelephassa* and *H. shandura* the club is very short and abruptly formed like a rounded knob, while *H. baldiva* and *H. lehana* have the club as abruptly formed, but much more elongate.

The first species, *H. parisatis*, is the largest of all the Indian *Hipparchias*, and differs so widely in colour and style of markings, more especially in the presence of prominent perfect ocelli on the underside of the hindwing, from all the other species, that it stands quite apart, having no near allies. The remaining species all come under the subgenus *Eumenis*, Hübner, according to Scudder, who accepts *H. semele* as the type of this group.

176. Hipparchia parisatis, Kollar. (PLATE XVI, FIG. 47 ♀.)

Satyrus parisatis, Kollar, Denkschr. Akad. Wien. Math.-Nat. Cl., vol. i., p. 52, n. 7 (1850); *Hipparchia (Satyrus) macropthalmus*, Eversmann, Bull. Mosc., vol. xxiv., pt. i, p. 615, n. 5 (1851).

HABITAT: Western Himalayas, Afghanistan, Persia, Armenia.

EXPANSE: 2·7 to 3·2 inches.

DESCRIPTION: "UPPERSIDE black, broadly margined with white. *Hindwing* dentate. UNDERSIDE: *both wings* marbled with cinereous and white, a common angulate median white fascia, two black ocelli on each wing circled with yellow, and pupilled with white. A most distinct species, widely diverse from all of this genus." (*Kollar*, l.c.)

In Indian specimens the UPPERSIDE is of a blackish brown colour, and when fresh beautifully glossed with blue in certain lights. The white outer margin is broadest on the hindwing, and does not reach the apex of the forewing. In some specimens the outer half of the costal margin is whitish, widening out towards the apex. The *forewing* has two submarginal black spots, the upper minutely white-pupilled, the lower blind. The *hindwing* has one subanal black spot with minute white pupil. The UNDERSIDE is pale French-grey, profusely covered with fine irregular dark striæ on the costal half of the *forewing*, and on the entire *hindwing*, and mottled with whitish. With an angulate median white fascia on both wings, inwardly defined by a blackish line, with two large submarginal ocelli on each wing, with yellow iris and narrow dark brown outer ring, the upper prominently white-pupilled on both wings; the lower blind on the forewing, minutely white-pupilled on the hindwing. A narrow submarginal line, and the extreme margin dark brown; the *cilia* white. In Persian specimens the colour is paler brown, and the white margin is much broader, extending beyond the black subanal spot on the hindwing.

The MALE has the sexual mark on the forewing broadly along the median nervure extending into the cell, of the same colour as the ground, but visible owing to the greater density of the scales, and a slight sheen on them owing to their different structure. It has also a single white spot (sometimes two) on the underside of the forewing between the ocelli. The *female* lacks the sexual streak, and has two white spots between the ocelli of the forewing on both upper and undersides, which are sometimes traceable in the male on the upperside. Major Roberts states (Proc. Zool. Soc. Lond., 1880, p. 405) that "when fresh and in the sun the white border is shot with brilliant blue."

H. parisatis is the commonest and most widely spread of all the Indian *Hipparchias*. We have specimens taken by Mrs. Deane in Chini in June; in Pangi by Mr. R. Ellis in July; and in Gilgit by Major J. Biddulph in August. Regarding its habits Colonel Lang writes:—"Obtained on steep precipices over bare hill-sides above the Sutlej; and these Himalayan precipices are not quite the ground for the entomologist, net in hand, and eye fixed on the soaring insect. The aspect of the insect on the wing is quite Nymphalidian—a soaring flight, swift if frightened, pitching in all sorts of inaccessible spots. Subsequently found very commonly in Upper Kunawar, always on steep cliffs, pitching on rocks." It is found commonly throughout the hilly regions of Afghanistan and Beluchistan. In the neighbourhood of Kandahar it "frequents nullas and shady places, and may be caught by dozens at a time. Abundant but local at the end of May, and in June in shady, moist places among the low, rocky, barren hills." (*Major Roberts*, l. c.) Colonel Swinhoe took it in a small field of potatoes, at Chaman in South Afghanistan on the 21st May, and at Mach in the middle of the Bolan pass in July. Mr. de Nicéville has taken it near Simla, and at Kotgarh in the autumn, in Chumba in May, at Budruwah and Junglewah on the frontiers of Kashmir in June, and late in July near Bajoura, Kulu.

The figure is taken from a female specimen in Mr. de Nicéville's collection taken at Junglewah, Kashmir, and shows both the upper and undersides.

177. **Hipparchia pimpla**, Felder.

Satyrus pimpla, Felder, Reise Novara, Lep., vol. iii, p. 494, n. 856, pl lxix, figs. 10, 11 (1866), *female*.

HABITAT : Western Himalayas ; Afghanistan, Beluchistan.

EXPANSE : 1·9 to 2·2 inches.

DESCRIPTION : MALE. UPPERSIDE uniform, rather dark brown, the *cilia* whitish, marked with brown on the nervules. *Forewing* with a black subapical spot, sometimes minutely pupilled with white, and with obsolete paler iris. UNDERSIDE : *forewing* rather paler brown, with a bright ferruginous discal patch covering almost the entire cell, the costal margin marbled with whitish and irregular dark striæ extending into the cell ; the subapical ocellus larger bordered with yellowish on the inner side, followed by a short dark streak ; an incomplete submarginal dark line. *Hindwing* pale brown, irregularly mottled with whitish and dark brown, all the nervules white ; an indistinct subbasal angulate striga dark brown ; a dark brown angulate median streak inwardly diffused, outwardly sharply defined and bordered with white finely mottled with brown ; a submarginal dentate dark line also inwardly diffused and outwardly sharply defined, beyond which the margin is whitish, more conspicuously mottled with brown ; one or two minute subanal black spots marking the positions of obsolete ocelli. FEMALE rather larger, paler brown, the disc tinted with ferruginous, the subapical ocellus much more prominent and with a distinct fulvous iris, with two or three diffused elongate sordid-ferruginous streaks below it. UNDERSIDE much paler, *forewing* with the costal margin ochreous and very slightly mottled, the mottlings scarcely extending into the cell, and showing no defined streaks ; the subapical ocellus large, with pale ochreous yellow iris, the apical area mottled with white, the submarginal line nearly complete. *Hindwing* pale ochreous mottled with brown ; the subbasal, discal, and marginal dark lines narrow, well defined ; the two latter having the ground-colour whitish outwardly.

The female described and figured by Felder is darker than the specimen described above, and lacks the ochreous tinge of the underside.

H. pimpla is a very rare insect, and though found over a large tract of country, is nowhere common. The type specimen, a female, was taken at Chulichang in Ladak ; another female was taken by Major J. Biddulph on the Shandur plateau in Northern Kashmir ; the male, which has not been previously described, was taken at Sher Darwaza near Kabul by Lieutenant H. Whistler-Smith during the late Afghan war ; and again quite recently by Colonel A. M. Lang, R.E., in the neighbourhood of Quetta at Kawas on a rocky peak 8,500 feet altitude in September. It is not very closely allied to *H. arethusa*, Wiener Verzeichniss,* of Europe, with which Felder's original description appended below, † compares it. It is one of the group of which *H. actæa*, Esper, of Southern Europe, is the type, and is most closely allied to a variety from Astrabad which has been separated and figured under the name of *H. bryce*, Ochsenheimer, var. *parthica*, by Lederer (Hor. Soc. Ent. Ross., vol. vi, p. 83, pl. iv, figs. 12 *male*, 13 *female*, (1869) ; *H. bryce*, Ochsenheimer, being itself a synonym of *H. hippodice*, Hübner ; and *H. hippodice*, Hübner, being a variety of *H. actæa*, Esper. A short description of this variety *parthica* is given below ; the male specimen of *H. pimpla* from

* *Satyrus arethusa*, Wiener Verzeichniss. " Wings dentate, UPPERSIDE fuscous, with a fulvous macular fascia and a blind ocellus. UNDERSIDE : *Hindwing* marbled with cinereous and fuscous, with a recurved whitish fascia. The wings are feebly dentate ; of an obscure brown on the UPPERSIDE, with a yellow macular outer band, bearing near the apex of the *forewing*, and near the anal angle of the *hindwing*, a black blind ocellus. UNDERSIDE : *forewing* of a red more or less vivid, with the margins obscure and cut up with blackish, especially on the costa ; the ocellus of the upperside but pupilled with white. *Hindwing* ashy dotted with brown, with a whitish transverse discal band curved below, slightly sinuous above, and preceded outwardly by a small black ocellus with a white pupil. The scallops of the outer margin are whitish. Inhabits Russia, Hungary, the middle of Germany, and several districts of France." (*Godart*, Enc. Méth., vol. ix, p. 517, n. 113 (1819).

† *Satyrus pimpla*, Felder. HABITAT : Western Himalayas ; Ladak ; Chulichang. EXPANSE : 1·9 to 2·2 inches. DESCRIPTION : " FEMALE. Wings with the *cilia* shorter than in *S.* [*H.*] *arethusa*. UPPERSIDE darker. *Forewing* with the disc tinted with ferruginous, with the black subapical ocellus much larger, sometimes pupilled with white, and with a sordid ferruginous iris, and with two or three diffuse elongate sordid ferruginous spots below it. *Hindwing* with the indistinct submarginal streak darker. UNDERSIDE as in *S. arethusa*, but the *forewing* with the fulvous patch covering almost the whole cell, otherwise restricted, well removed from the submarginal streak, the two streaks across the cell wanting, the subapical ocellus larger. *Hindwing* more widely striated, the discal streak prominently bent, not at all directed downwards, but subparallel to the margin, outwardly narrowly defined with hoary-white, and another submarginal, outwardly defined with hoary-white, broader and darker." (*Felder*, Reise Novara, Lep., vol. iii, p. 494, n. 856, pl. lxix, figs. 10, 11 (1866), *female*.

Kawas is barely separable from it, though the female from the Shandur plateau is very distinct, being much paler, while the undersides of both sexes in *parthica* are almost exactly alike.

Hipparchia arethusa, Wiener Verzeichniss, is also found both in the Caucasus and the Kuldja hills; it differs from *H. pimpla* chiefly in having a submarginal series of elongate spots irrorated with fulvous on both wings on the upperside, which are very prominent in some specimens, obsolete in others; also the nervures of the hindwing on the underside are not white.

Hipparchia actæa, var. *parthica*, has the upperside almost exactly like that of *H. pimpla*; and the underside differs very slightly; on the forewing the dark submarginal line is lost in the dark band which widens out greatly at the inner angle; the dark median line is present in both sexes, and in both sexes the costa is broadly brown with fuscous mottlings extending into the cell, and in addition there are several distinct irregular dark bars across the cell; on the hindwing the basal area is darker, the subbasal line is obsolete, the median and submarginal lines are broad, inwardly diffused and outwardly defined by whitish fasciæ; all the nervules are whitish.

Another variety of *H. actæa*, Esper, recorded as *Hipparchia bryce*, var. *amasina*, Staudinger, by Lederer (Hor. Soc. Ent. Ross., vol. viii, p. 11 (1871), and as *H. cordula*, var. *amasina*, Staudinger, by Kirby in the Syn. Cat. D. L., is found at Astrabad in Persia.

178. **Hipparchia diffusa**, Butler.

H. diffusa, Butler, Proc. Zool. Soc. Lond., 1880, p. 147, n. 2.

HABITAT: Ravee Basin, North-West Himalayas.

EXPANSE: 2·1 inches.

DESCRIPTION: "FEMALE. Closely allied to *H. semele*,* from which it principally differs in the obscured and diffused character of the ochraceous patches enclosing the ocelli on the UPPERSIDE of the *forewing*. On the UNDERSIDE the white belt is well marked, more so than in any specimens of *H. semele* which I have seen." (*Butler*, l. c.)

We have never seen this species, but as there is no other *Hipparchia* recorded from the Himalayas which at all approaches to *H. semele*, there should be no difficulty in recognising it. The true *Hipparchia semele*, Linnæus, is found in the Caucasus, and probably still further to the East.

Hipparchia autonoë, Esper, from South Russia and the Kuldja hills, is allied to *H. semele*, and according to Godart's description (Enc. Méth., vol. ix, p. 518, n. 114 (1819) is "brown, with a yellowish transverse band, the band of the forewing more prominent and bearing two black ocelli with white pupils; the band of the hindwing has one smaller ocellus near the anal angle, and sometimes accompanied by two white dots; the underside of the forewing resembles the upperside, except that the disc is reddish; the hindwing is ashy mottled with brown; the, nervures whitish, and with three transverse whitish bands, the small ocellus of the upperside, the margin dentate, and the cilia white." It is figured in Boisduval's Icones, vol. i, pl. xli, figs. 5, 6 (1832), *female*.

---

* *Hipparchia semele*, Linnæus, Faun. Suec., p. 276, n. 1051 (1761). HABITAT: Europe. EXPANSE: 2·3 to 2·5 inches. DESCRIPTION: FEMALE: UPPERSIDE brown; darker on the outer half, with a submarginal band of the same colour, but defined with darker brown. *Forewing* with a black spot with white pupil between the discoidal nervules placed on a fulvous streak across the band, and another similar one placed between the first and second median nervules, the latter having in addition a narrow fulvous streak above and a broader one below; the outer edge of the band being nearly parallel to the margin, the inner edge much angled. *Hindwing* with three inwardly sagittate ferruginous marks on the outer edge of the band, and a fourth on the lower median interspace rounded, and bearing a small black spot with white pupil. UNDERSIDE: *forewing* with the band complete, fulvous, a diffused fulvous patch in the disc, the two black spots with white pupils as on upperside; and the costal margin broadly mottled with whitish and dark brown. *Hindwing* mottled throughout with whitish and dark brown on a pale brown ground, with three very irregular blackish streaks, one subbasal, one discal, and one submarginal; a minute subanal black spot with white pupil. The MALE has the UPPERSIDE more uniform, the fulvous streaks being obsolescent. UNDERSIDE similar, but with the discal streak on the *hindwing* broadly margined outwardly with whitish. The discal sexual mark on the forewing broad, extending into the discoidal cell. (Described from examples from Germany).

179. Hipparchia thelephassa, Hübner.

Eumenis thelephassa, Hübner, Samml. Ex. Schmett., vol. ii, pl. lxxxv, figs. 1—4 (1816—1824); *Satyrus thelephassa*, Herrich Schaffer, Schmett. Eur., vol. i, figs. 178, 179 (1844); figs. 305, 306 (1846); *Hipparchia thelephassa*, T. Klüg, Symb. Phys., pl. xxix, figs. 1—4 (1832); *Satyrus anthelea*, Boisduval, Icones, vol. i, p. 204, pl. xli, figs. 3, 4 (1832), *female*; idem, id., Doubleday, Hewitson, Gen. D. L., pl. lxv, fig. 3 (1851), *female*.

HABITAT: Afghanistan, Beluchistan, Persia, Syria, Russia.

EXPANSE: ♂, 2·1 to 2·3; ♀, 2·4 to 2·7 inches.

DESCRIPTION: MALE. UPPERSIDE brown, with a broad submarginal fulvous band on both wings. *Forewing* with the inner margin of the band much angled at the third median nervule, the outer edge lunulate and parallel with the margin, bearing an upper and lower black spot with minute white pupil; and two white spots between them. The sexual mark extends into the discoidal cell, black overlayed with brown scales. *Hindwing* with the fulvous band abbreviated, its outer edge lunulate and parallel with the margin, its inner edge irregularly dentate and less sharply defined; bearing a single minute black spot with white pupil on the lower median interspace and sometimes a white dot on the upper median interspace. UNDERSIDE. *Forewing* with the fulvous band, ocelli and white dots as on upperside, but with the middle of the disc also fulvous, extending into the cell, the costal margin broadly pale brown, mottled and streaked with whitish and dark brown. *Hindwing* whitish, clouded with pale brown and mottled with darker brown, the subbasal line scarcely traceable; the median rather more defined and indistinctly margined outwardly with a whitish diffused fascia, the submarginal line most distinct and defined with whitish outwardly; a minute subanal ocellus as on upperside. FEMALE as in the male, but lacking the sexual black patch in the cell; and with the inner margin of the fulvous band much more angulate.

The figure by Westwood shows the middle of the disc on the forewing fulvous on the upperside also, but none of the specimens we have examined correspond with it in this particular.

H. thelephassa has as yet only been found within our limits in the assigned districts of Beluchistan now administered by the British Government. It was taken at Chaman in May, at Gwal in May, and at Quetta in May and September, by Lieutenant-Colonel Swinhoe, and in September and October by Colonel A. M. Lang at Quetta at 5,500 feet elevation, the Hanna Valley 6,500 feet, and the Kawas Valley 8,000 feet elevation, "where it was not uncommon among boulders in the gorges of the high valleys." *(Colonel Lang)*. At Kandahar Major Roberts notes that it is "very common at the beginning and middle of May in the nullas and on the rocky slopes at the foot of the hills, resting under the shade of rocks and stones during the heat of the day, and flying about in the early morning and evening, when it is easily captured. In June scarcely a specimen was to be found." (Proc. Zool. Soc. Lond., 1880, p. 405).

A large *Hipparchia* of this type is found commonly in Persia; it differs from *H. thelephassa* in lacking the white dots on both sides, and more notably in having the submarginal fulvous band on the forewing distinctly macular, the patches about the upper ocellus being widely separated from those about the lower ocellus by the brown ground-colour; it seems to be just intermediate between *H. semele* and *H. thelephassa*.

Hipparchia beroë, Herrich-Schäffer, is like a desert form of *H. thelephassa*, all the colours faded and washed with cinereous; but in a variety figured by Lederer in the Ann. Soc. Ent. Belg., vol. xiii, p. 26, pl. 1, fig. 3 (1869-70), *female*, under the name *H. beroë*, Freyer, the band is fulvous and the white spots on it are present in both wings, and it is only to be distinguished from *H. thelephassa* by the band on the forewing being restricted and not reaching either the costa or the inner margin, and divided at the upper median nervule.

Hipparchia pelopea, Klüg, which is found in Persia, appears to belong to this group. Lederer figures a variety of it named *caucasica* (Wien. Ent. Monatsch., vol. viii, p. 168, pl. iii, fig. 5 (1864), *male*), from the Caucasus, which appears to differ from *H. thelephassa* in having the band on the forewing incomplete and macular, not extending above the lower discoidal nervule except for a single elongate spot, on which the upper ocellus is placed, and which does not extend towards the costa; on the hindwing the band is well defined, widening regularly to the first median nervule where it abruptly ends. The white dots between the ocelli of the forewing are large and prominent.

180. **Hipparchia baldiva,** Moore.

Lasiommata baldiva, Moore, Proc. Zool. Soc. Lond., 1865, p. 499, n. 84, pl. xxx, fig. 4, *male*.

HABITAT: Spiti and Thibet.

EXPANSE: 1·87 to 2·5 inches.

DESCRIPTION: "MALE. UPPERSIDE: *Forewing* fuliginous grey. *Hindwing* ashy grey; *both wings* with a broad, irregularly margined, discal ferruginous band, which has on the *forewing* an upper and a lower blackish spot, on the *hindwing* a small spot at its lower end. FEMALE, paler. The *forewing* with the spots on the discal band larger, there being also a third intermediate smaller spot; the spot on the *hindwing* with a white pupil. UNDERSIDE grey, of the FEMALE greyish white, with numerous short blackish striæ. *Forewing* with the disc pale ferruginous, the margins of the band (as seen from above), defined by irregular black lines; in the MALE with a single, in the FEMALE with two black spots, the apical with white pupil and yellow iris; the black dot on the *hindwing* also with white pupil and yellow iris. *Cilia* silvery grey. Allied to *H. thelephassa*." (*Moore*, l. c.)

The MALE of *H. baldiva* may be readily distinguished from that sex of *H. thelephassa* by the sexual mark, which in *H. baldiva* is concolorous with the wing, extending broadly along the median nervure chiefly outside the cell, but inconspicuous. Further in *H. baldiva* the inner margin of the fulvous band on the *forewing* is almost straight, and the spots between the ocelli are either wanting altogether or, if present, are black, not white; on the UNDERSIDE of the *hindwing*, the transverse irregular lines are far more distinct in *H. baldiva* than in *H. thelephassa;* the FEMALE of *H. baldiva* has the inner margin of the fulvous band almost as angulate as in *H. thelephassa*, but it lacks the white spots on both surfaces, and has the irregular lines of the *hindwing* on the UNDERSIDE far more prominent.

H. baldiva is apparently a very local insect; it has never been taken so far as we know, except by Colonel Lang, from whose specimens the original description was taken; the specimens in Colonel Lang's collection are labelled "Thibet, 10,000 feet, taken between Shipkee and Broopcha in July," and the following note is recorded:—"On the bare, brown, stony mountain-slopes of Spiti, Upper Kunawar, Thibet; this species seems to delight in the hot weather of June and July." In Ladak it appears to be replaced by the closely allied *H. lehana*.

181. **Hipparchia lehana,** Moore. (PLATE XVI, FIG. 48♀.)

H. lehana, Moore, Ann. and Mag. of Nat. Hist., fifth series, vol. i, p. 227 (1878); idem, id., Second Yarkund Mission, Lep., p. i, pl. i, fig. 4 (1879), *male*.

HABITAT: Leh (September 6th, 1873); Khabu (13,000 feet), Ladak.

EXPANSE: ♂, 2·00 inches; ♀, 2·25 inches.

DESCRIPTION: "Allied to *H. baldiva*, Moore, from Upper Kunawar. UPPERSIDE paler in colour, the discal transverse luteous band is broader on *both wings*, and its inner border in the MALE is inwardly oblique. BOTH SEXES above and beneath are without the small ocellus on the band above the anal angle. UNDERSIDE also very much paler, and the transverse sinuous lines wider apart." (*Moore*, l. c., in Ann. and Mag.)

Mr. de Nicéville took one male and two females of this species at Chanagund, Ladak, on June 30th. The male differs from the type male of *H. lehana* in being larger (2·55 as against 2·10 inches), and in having the inner edge of the submarginal fulvous band on the upperside of the forewing more distinctly angled inwardly above the third median nervule. On the hindwing, there is a minute black dot in the lower median interspace as in *H. baldiva*, but smaller. The sexual streak is inconspicuous. The females are also larger, (2·90 as against 2·65 inches), otherwise they agree with the female type specimen. The angulation of the inner margin of the fulvous band on the forewing of the male sufficiently distinguishes it from *H. baldiva*.

The figure shows the upper and undersides of a female in Mr. de Nicéville's collection; taken at Chanagund, Ladak.

182. Hipparchia digna, Marshall.

H. digna, Marshall, Journ. A. S. B., vol. li, pt. ii, p. 67 (1882).

HABITAT: N.-W. Himalayas.

EXPANSE: 2·45 inches.

DESCRIPTION: FEMALE. UPPERSIDE, rather dark brown, with a broad fulvous submarginal band outwardly defined with dark lunules, and bearing on the *forewing* a single apical oval black spot scarcely perceptibly pupilled, on the *hindwing* unmarked. The band is regular and well-defined throughout, slightly angulate on its inner edge on both wings, and parallel to the margin, but inversely scalloped on the outer edge; it is well removed from the margin, leaving a much broader brown border than in any other Indian *Hipparchia*. UNDERSIDE: *Forewing* with the fulvous band as on upperside, but ochreous at the costal and inner margins; the black subapical spot, but distinctly pupilled; the middle area of the basal half also fulvous merging into the submarginal band, a dark submarginal dentate line defining the band outwardly, the inner margin broadly dark brown, except where crossed by the band, the outer and costal margins broadly pale brownish mottled with darker brown; and the latter with numerous irregular dark brown striæ, extending into the cell. *Hindwing* pale brownish white, clouded with a darker shade, and mottled throughout with very dark brown striæ: a dark brown dentate line corresponding to the outer margin of the band of the upperside, another corresponding with the inner edge; the space between them being inwardly broadly whitish, outwardly clouded with brown; a subbasal dark line, between which and the discal line the ground-colour is brown, the base of the wing being rather paler brown with several well-defined strigæ.

Two specimens, both females, were taken by Major J. Biddulph on the Shandur plateau in Northern Kashmir.

183. Hipparchia huebneri, Felder.

Satyrus hübneri, Felder, Reise Novara, Lep., vol. iii, p. 494, n. 855, pl. lxix, figs. 8, 9 (1866), *female*.

HABITAT: Lahoul; Shigri, Spiti; Dishungdeo; Gilgit; N.-W. Himalayas.

EXPANSE: 1·9 to 2·1 inches.

DESCRIPTION: "MALE. UPPERSIDE darker than in *Satyrus agave*, Esper [=*Satyrus alcyone*,* Fabricius, *nec* Wien. Verz.], the fascia much deeper fulvous, outwardly acutely dentate, more distant from the margin; in the *forewing* inwardly rather diffused, not at all divided by fuscous veins, and distinctly marked with blind spots; in the *hindwing* shorter, not extending beyond the second subcostal nervule, without an ocellus. UNDERSIDE also darker than in *S. agave*. *Forewing* with the entire disc fulvescent, darker in the middle, divided by a single swarthy disco-cellular litura, the ocelli smaller, the upper one broadly and diffusely circled with ochraceous, the submarginal striga more drawn back anteriorly than as in *Satyrus geyeri*.† *Hindwing* with all the nervules white, the streaks as in *S. geyeri*, but

---

* *Satyrus alcyone*, Fabricius. HABITAT: Russia. DESCRIPTION: "Wings, dentate; upperside fuscous, with a yellow fascia margined with black, not at all sinuate on the forewing, with two ocelli on both sides. UNDERSIDE: *Hindwing* marbled with cinereous and fuscous, no fascia. *Papilio S. alcyone*. Wings dentate, fuscous, banded with yellow; forewing with two ocelli on both sides. Hindwing marbled on the underside. (*Fabricius*, Mant. Ins. vol. ii, p. 38, n. 399 (1787); idem, id., Ent. Syst., vol. iii, pt. i, p. 231, n. 724 (1793.) Closely allied to *S. semele*, but distinguished from it in that the yellow band of the upperside of the wings is better detached from the ground-colour and is bordered with black; that it is straight, and almost continuous on the forewing; that it has no spot, at least well-defined, on the hindwing; that the underside of the latter is destitute of the angulate white band; that the underside of the former, with the exception of the margins which are brown, is everywhere of a pale yellow, and moreover cut transversely by undulate black lines. It inhabits the very elevated places in the southern parts of Russia. It must not be confounded with that variety of *hermione*, of which several authors have made a separate species under the name of *alcyone*." (*Godart*, Enc. Méth., vol. ix, p. 517, n. 112 (1819).

† *Satyrus geyeri*, Herrich-Schäffer, Schmett. Eur., vol. i, figs. 301, 302 (1846-47). HABITAT: Asia Minor. EXPANSE: 2 inches. DESCRIPTION: MALE. UPPERSIDE brown, with an ill-defined paler submarginal band bearing two faint ocelli, and with the other markings of the underside showing through by transparency. UNDERSIDE: *Forewing* pale ochreous, the outer margin brown, inwardly defined with a series of dark convex lunules, a subapical and a lower black spot, each with a minute white pupil; a prominent but interrupted dark line defining the inner edge of the pale submarginal fascia, a dark streak on the disco-cellulars, and another in the cell, the costa and the cell being mottled with fuscous. *Hindwing* brown; the *cilia* and all the nervules white; a highly dentate submarginal line, another median irregular, outwardly broadly defined with white mottled with brown, another basal less irregular, and one on the disco-cellulars dark brown; the whole wing faintly and sparingly irrorated with dark specks.

much darker and more slender, the basal streak less flexuous forming a right angle, the discal streak not at all sloping hindwards, the submarginal streak more receding from the margin, acutely drawn back, outwardly defined with hoary white; no ocellular dot. FEMALE: UPPERSIDE with the fulvous fascia diffused inwardly in the *forewing*, and in the *hindwing* extending to the first subcostal nervule." (*Felder*, l. c.)

The above description being in comparison with species not occurring in India, is difficult to follow. The following description is taken from the plate :—

FEMALE. UPPERSIDE brown, the fulvous fascia sharply defined both inwardly and outwardly on both wings by dark lunulate lines, and with ochreous patches on it at the costal and inner margins of the forewing, and at the costal margin of the hindwing. The *forewing* with a black subapical spot, and another on the lower median interspace both on the fulvous band; the *hindwing* with no spots. UNDERSIDE. *Forewing* with the outer margin pale brown, and the costal margin narrowly so; the rest of the wing fulvous, the outer dark lunulate line defining the fulvous, and the two black spots as on upperside, two short brown streaks across the cell and two beyond it. *Hindwing* with the basal half pale brown, the outer half greyish; the extreme margin dark brown; a dark brown highly dentate submarginal line inwardly suffused with brown; another almost equally dentate defining the pale brown basal half, a subbasal dark, somewhat dentate line; and an incomplete basal line with a spot beyond it in the cell, dark brown; the nervules white. Two specimens both females, taken by Major J. Biddulph at Gilgit in August, and now in Major Marshall's collection, are the only specimens we have seen; they differ from the plate, but correspond with the description, in that the fulvous fascia is inwardly diffused, much more so in one specimen than in the other, and showing a close approach to the following species *H. cadesia.*

Hipparchia geyeri is found in the Caucasus and in the mountains of Ararat. It is allied to *H. huebneri*, but has the band on the upperside brown not fulvous and almost obsolete; on the underside the forewing is paler and duller ochreous, and all the dark markings are very prominent; the hindwing also differs in having the two dark median well defined lines. *Hipparchia agave*, Esper, is also very similar to *H. huebneri;* the band on the upperside is fulvous margined with dark brown, the underside being almost exactly as in *H. geyeri*, but with less white on the hindwing.

Hipparchia regeli, Alphéraky, has lately been described from Kuldja (Hor. Soc. Ent. Ross., vol. xvi, p. 419, n. 91, pl. xv, fig. 23 (1881). EXPANSE: 1·7 inches. UPPERSIDE: "*Forewing* pale olivaceous-fuscous (or brownish), the fascia smoky-white or yellowish-white, bearing two black ocelli with white pupils (very rarely blind). *Hindwing* with the fascia narrower, outwardly dentate, inwardly inversely dentate and everywhere clearly defined. UNDERSIDE of the *hindwing* with the nervures white, the disc greyish (fuscous covered with obscure markings), irregularly terminated, defined with whitish, and an interrupted series of acutely dentate fuscous marks before the margin. *Cilia* everywhere white alternated with grey." It is very closely allied to *H. huebneri*, but has the fulvous band narrower and everywhere better defined.

184. **Hipparchia cadesia,** Moore.

H. cadesia, Moore, Proc. Zool. Soc. Lond., 1874, p. 565, pl. lxvi, fig. 7, *male*.

HABITAT: Kashmir; Boorzil Valley towards Stakpila Pass, 11,000 feet; Leh, Ladak.

EXPANSE: 1·58 to 2·2 inches.

DESCRIPTION: "MALE. UPPERSIDE bright ferruginous; exterior marginal line blackish. *Cilia* yellowish alternated with brown. *Forewing* with the base, costal, and exterior border pale brown; a subapical pale-bordered black spot with a white central dot; subcostal nervure and its branches blackish, terminating in a transverse sinuous submarginal line. *Hindwing* with the base, abdominal and outer border brown, the nervures being ferruginous; a submarginal series of blackish lunules. UNDERSIDE: *forewing* paler ferruginous, the costal and outer borders being fawn-colour; a few transverse brown strigæ within the cell; nervures below the apex terminating in a pale streak. *Hindwing* ferruginous white, numerously covered with short blackish strigæ, which are thickest at the base; nervures prominently whitish; a broad curved transverse median brown band with irregular black borders, and a broad submarginal brown band with black outer dentate lunules; outer margin and base of wing suffused with brown. *Body* and *legs* brown. *Antennæ* yellow, tip ferruginous. Allied to *H. huebneri*, Felder." (*Moore*, l. c).

We have seen only a single specimen of *H. cadesia*, a female taken at Leh in Ladak by the late Dr. Ferdinand Stoliczka, Ph. D., on the 8th September, 1873, and now in the Indian Museum, Calcutta. In Moore's figure of the species the underside of the hindwing has the transverse fasciæ very slightly dentate, but in the specimen here these lines are as highly dentate as in *H. huebneri*. No sexual mark is shewn in the figure or mentioned in the description.

The FEMALE differs from the male in having a small black spot on the first median interspace on both sides of the forewing; it is very closely allied indeed to the female of *H. huebneri*, the only noteworthy features being the complete suffusion of the basal area of the forewing with fulvous, and the very small size of the black spots in *H. cadesia*. Both these characters are variable in *H. huebneri*; and while so far as the types are concerned, there is no difficulty in separating them; it is probable that when more is known about these rare species, it will be found that the line of separation between them cannot be maintained.

The remaining species are much blacker in tone, with the markings on the upperside typically creamy-white, but varieties of several of the species are found in which the markings are more or less deeply tinged with fulvous.

185. **Hipparchia shandura,** Marshall.

H. shandura, Marshall, Journ. A. S. B, vol. li, pt. ii, p. 38, pl. iv, fig. 3 (1882), *female*.

HABITAT: Northern Kashmir.

EXPANSE: ♀, 2.4 inches.

DESCRIPTION: UPPERSIDE, *both wings* dull black, with creamy-white markings. *Forewing* with the costal margin streaked and mottled with grey and black; a large blotch of creamy-white in the discoidal cell, filling it completely from the base to near the extremity where it ends abruptly, and a discal series of longitudinal creamy-white streaks, consisting of a short streak above the subcostal nervure, a very long one below it bearing a round black spot in the middle, a very short narrow streak between the discoidal nervules, a larger streak below the third median nervule, a larger one still below the second median nervule divided transversely by a large blackish spot, a shorter streak filling the whole width between the first median nervule and submedian nervure, and bearing a blackish spot near its outer upper end, and a short streak below the submedian nervure. *Cilia* long, white, broadly interrupted with black at the ends of the nervules. *Hindwing* with a broad discal transverse band of creamy-white longitudinal streaks completely coalesced, widest at the middle, where it extends half way into the discoidal cell, and narrowest at the margins, especially at the costal margin. *Cilia* long, white, scarcely perceptibly interrupted with black. UNDERSIDE. *Forewing* with the costal margin and apex whitish, finely mottled with brown: the cell white, mottled with brown at its upper edge, and with a blackish bar near the extremity; the discal series of streaks as above, but all larger, completely coalescing, and sharply defined with dark brown internally and externally, except at the apex, where they merge into the mottled ground, the two black spots of the upperside reappearing as black ocelli with white pupils. *Hindwing* white mottled with brown, the mottlings deepening into three irregular dark brown mottled transverse bands darkest at their outer edges, one submarginal, one near the base of the cell, and one between these two.

Allied to *H. briseis*, Linnæus, from Northern and Western Asia, but smaller and notably differing in having a large creamy-white patch in the discoidal cell of the forewing completely filling the cell except at its extremity; and in this feature approximating to the species of *Melanargia* (*galathea*, *lachesis*, *psyche*, *clotho*, &c.,) in colouring.

A single specimen, which is now in the Indian Museum, Calcutta, was taken by Major J. Biddulph on the Shandur plateau in Northern Kashmir.

Hipparchia briseis, Linnæus, is found in the Caucasus and near Kuldja, and also in Turkestan. It is a smaller insect; the upperside is almost as in *H. shandura*, but without the creamy-white patch in the cell of the forewing; on the underside the forewing is very similar in markings, but the dark bar across the cell is much wider; the hindwing has the nervures concolorous with the ground, not white as in *H. shandura*, and is of a yellowish-brown tinge, clouded with darker brown, mottled with deep brown throughout in the female, and with a dark submarginal line and two dark patches near the base in the male. There is a large variety of this species found in Persia which is probably the variety referred to by Alphéraky in his paper on the Lepidoptera of Kuldja and the surrounding mountains (Hor. Soc. Ent. Ross., vol. xvi, p. 418 (1881). At first sight it appears very distinct on the underside, which is pale ochreous-brown, almost devoid of mottlings, and the hindwing without any markings whatever in the female, except traces of a broad nebulous paler median band, but the whole of the markings, so far as they appear at all, are exactly as in typical *H. briseis*, and the pale underside is precisely the variation which would be expected from the arid nature of the country in which this variety is found.

Hipparchia heidenreichii, Lederer (Verh. Zool. Bot. Ges., vol. iii, p. 359, pl. i, fig. 2 (1853), also occurs in Turkestan and in the Altai mountains. It is placed by Kirby and Erschoff between *H. briseis* and *H. anthe*, but neither figure nor description is available in this country.

186. **Hipparchia anthe**, Ochsenheimer.

Papilio anthe, Ochsenheimer, Schmett. Eur., vol. i, p. 169, n. 2 (1807); *Papilio persephone*, Hübner, Eur. Schmett., vol. i, figs. 589, 590 (1800-1807); figs. 710, 711 (1825?); *Satyrus anthe*, Boisduval, Icones, p. 200, pl. xl, figs. 3, 4 (1832), *female*; *Hipparchia persephone*, Butler, Cat. Lep. B. M., *Satyridæ*, p. 55, n. 16 (1868); id., Kirby, Syn. Cat. D. L., p. 85, n. 29 (1871).

HABITAT: South Russia, Persia, Afghanistan.

EXPANSE: ♀, 2·8 inches.

DESCRIPTION: UPPERSIDE blackish brown, slightly greyish towards the base, with a greenish reflection in certain lights; with beyond the middle a whitish band almost as in *H. briseis*. *Forewing* with the band interrupted, formed of elongated unequal quadrangular spots, the one nearest the apex the longest, cut in two by a black spot without a pupil, and recurved towards the costa at its inner extremity, where it is divided by the black nervules; the second irregular, narrow, just above the second median nervule; the third placed in the lower median interspace, and also cut in two by a large rather oval black spot; the fourth and fifth short; all the last four spots only separated by the dark nervules. *Hindwing* with the fascia broad and continuous from near the costa to the lowest median nervule, the edges irregular, the inner sharply defined, the outer diffused; a small black spot just beyond the band in the lower median interspace. UNDERSIDE: *forewing* yellowish, greyish along the costa and outer margin, and striated with dark brown; a dark stripe on the disco-cellular nervules, a dark band across the cell beyond the middle, and two indistinct lines nearer the base, and several scattered dark striæ; the whitish macular band as on the upperside, but more dingy and inwardly sharply defined with dark brown; the black spots as on upperside but larger and oval; the interno-median interspace dark brown throughout except where cut by the whitish band; a sinuous dark brown submarginal line; the *cilia* grey, spotted with black at the tips of the nervules. *Hindwing* paler brown, striated with dark brown; all the nervures white; a highly irregular discal line of dark brown lunules and sagittate marks, beyond which is a greyish fascia gradually shading into brown, which deepens outwardly till it is again defined by a dark irregular line, beyond which is a submarginal grey fascia shading into brown towards the margin; the margin itself dark brown, inwardly edged with grey; a short whitish bar and two dark patches in the cell. *Cilia* as on forewing.

H. anthe, as figured by Boisduval, differs from *H. shandura* on the UPPERSIDE in having no whitish patch in the cell, the black spots on the fascia much larger, especially the upper one, and with no trace of white pupils, the black spot below the lower median nervule, and the whitish streak between the discoidal nervules wanting: on the *hindwing* by the whitish fascia being sharply defined inwardly, and not extending into the cell. On the UNDERSIDE by the *forewing* being tinged with yellow, with no whitish patch in the cell, the black spots larger and blind; and on the *hindwing* by having the discal dark brown line continuous, whereas in *H. shandura* it is interrupted by the greyish white band extending back into the cell.

From *H. briseis* it differs in the style of the whitish macular band on the UPPERSIDE, for in *H. briseis* the upper whitish streak of the *forewing* does not curve up to the costa inwardly, the streak between the discoidal nervules is prominent, and the black spots are small, equal, rounded, and distinctly pupilled; while on the *hindwing* the band is wider, extending into the cell, and diffused inwardly as well as outwardly. On the UNDERSIDE *H. briseis* has the *forewing* less decidedly tinged with yellow, and the black spots are small, round, and distinctly pupilled; the *hindwing* is darker and the markings clouded and indistinct, with in the male large dark brown patches.

In some notes* on a small collection of Lepidoptera from the neighbourhood of Kandahar taken by Colonel Swinhoe, Mr. Butler identifies a specimen as "*Hipparchia anthe* ♀, var.? Boeb. Taken on the 14th May at Chaman. It differs somewhat from European examples on the underside; but it would not be safe to regard it as distinct until more examples have been seen." No description of this specimen is given, and we have no other record of its capture on the confines of India.

According to Boisduval (Icones, vol. i, p. 201 (1832), *Hipparchia anthe*, Ochsenheimer, "was discovered by Bœber, and some entomologists still call it *H. anthe*, Bœber (*anthe bœberi*)." None of the standard catalogues or works on Lepidoptera, so far as we can trace, admit "*anthe*, Bœber," and we are not aware on what grounds Mr. Butler has so recently resuscitated the term. It is indeed doubtful whether the name *anthe* should stand at all. *H. anthe*, Ochsenheimer, is identical with *H. persephone*, Hübner, and Mr. Butler records it as *H. persephone*, and remarks "Ochsenheimer has substituted the name *anthe* for *persephone* on the ground of this name having been previously used by Fabricius; such a name, however, does not seem to exist amongst the *Satyrinæ*" (Cat. Lep. B. M. *Satyridæ*, p. 55 (1868); but as M. Erschoff, in his Lepidoptera of Turkestan, dated 1874, rejects the name *persephone* and retains *anthe*, we have adopted his conclusion.

Hipparchia hanifa (*Satyrus hanifa*, Herrich Schäffer, Schmett. Eur., vol. i, figs. 477, 478 (1850?) is a variety of *H. anthe*, and identical apparently with *H. anthe*, var. *caucasica*, *hanifa* (sic), Nordmann (Bull. Mosc., vol. xxiv, pt. i, p. 405, n. 3, pl. ix, figs. 1—3 (1851); it was described in Nordmann's Fauna Taurico-Caucasica, and is included in Erschoff's Lepidoptera of Turkestan. It differs from *H. anthe*, female, on the UPPERSIDE only in having the black spots rounded, and rather smaller, and the white fascia tinged with fulvous in the male, deep fulvous throughout in the female. On the UNDERSIDE also the *forewing* has the black spots smaller, the whole disc yellow, and the macular fascia merged in the yellow ground, and not at all defined; the *hindwing* has the ground-colour finely mottled with dark brown instead of being striated, the whitish fasciæ are more prominent, and the nervures are not prominently irrorated with white. This variety also occurs in Persia, and according to Butler it is "very like *H. pelopea* on the upperside, but without the white intermacular spots". (Cat. Lep. B. M., *Satyridæ*, p. 55 (1868).

Another variety, *H. anthe*, var. *enervata*, Alphéraky, and an aberration named *analoga*, Alphéraky, have been recently described (Hor. Soc. Ent. Ross., vol. xvi, p 418, n. 89 (1881) with the following remarks:—"*H. anthe*, var. *enervata*. A little smaller; UNDERSIDE with

* Ann. and Mag. of Nat. Hist., fifth series, vol. ix, p. 206 (1882).

the nervures of the hindwing not whitish. *H. anthe,* ab. *analoga*. UPPERSIDE with the fasciæ golden yellow; UNDERSIDE as in var. *enervata*. The variety *enervata* is always a little smaller than the true *H. anthe* of South-Eastern Russia. The fasciæ are never of a pure white as in the latter; if indeed on the upperside the bands are white (which is rare), they are always more or less ochraceous on the underside, so also is always part of the disc of the forewing on the underside. But the variety *enervata* is above all characterised by the hindwing, which is not veined with white or whitish. The aberration *analoga* corresponds absolutely to the variety *hanifa*, Nordmann, by the orange-yellow colour of the bands, and with *enervata*, by the underside of the hindwings. The specimens taken in August appear to me smaller but not otherwise distinct from those taken in May. It occurs between 2,000 and 3,500 feet altitude. The *H. anthe* of the Altai and of Ferganah according to Staudinger, as well as all those of Turkestan according to Erschoff, belong to my variety *enervata*." (*Alphéraky*, l. c.)

Hipparchia kaufmanni, Erschoff, (Lep. Turk., p. 19, n. 60, pl. 1, fig. 14 (1874), *female*) from Turkestan is a very distinct species, to judge from the figure; the upperside is brown, the hindwing unmarked, the forewing bearing a small black subapical spot on a white elongate streak which joins a small whitish streak from the costa; a small black spot on the upper median interspace and a large one on the lower, both narrowly ringed with whitish; the underside almost uniform ochreous, the hindwing with indistinct median and submarginal dusky lines; forewing with the black subapical spot, but no pale streak; and the two median spots ringed as on the upperside, and placed on a diffused dark discal patch.

Hipparchia phædra, Linnæus, with which *H. dryas*, Scopoli, is closely allied, if not identical, is also found over the same area; it is very distinct from all the foregoing, the upperside being uniform brown with no trace of a submarginal band, but with two black spots bearing large bluish-silvery pupils; the underside being also dark brown throughout, with the ocelli of the upperside, a darker submarginal band on both wings, and an indistinct median band on the hindwing.

Hipparchia circe, Fabricius, [= *Hipparchia proserpina*, Wiener Verzeichniss] which most nearly resembles the *Aulocera* genus in colouration, has been found in the Caucasus; it very closely resembles *A. padma*, but on the underside the white band is broader and better defined on the forewing; and there are clouded white patches in the cell of the forewing and a broad irregular white streak from the middle of the costa on the hindwing extending across the cell. A variety, *H. virbius*, is recorded from the Caucasus.

Hipparchia hermione, Linnæus, also found in Syria and the Caucasus, is a browner insect almost equally large, but with no white band on the upperside, it being replaced by an indistinct, but uniform, paler brown band. On the underside the band is pale yellowish brown on the forewing, whitish on the hindwing inwardly, and clouded with brown outwardly; the rest of the wing rather dark brown, mottled and freckled with very dark brown; a lunulate dark submarginal line, a dark median line defining the band, and a very irregular dark subbasal line.

The foregoing descriptions will suffice for the identification of all the *Hipparchias* as yet known to occur within our limits; but as shown above numerous species and varieties of this genus are found in the Caucasus, Turkestan and the neighbourhood of Kuldja, and since our own frontier and the intervening regions have been so little explored, it is difficult to predict which of the numerous forms are likely to occur on further research. We have included brief descriptions of all of these so far as our material is sufficient for this, but unfortunately it is incomplete. The species of this genus are not only numerous but are so variable and withal often so closely allied, that, unless the material is complete, conclusive identification is almost impossible.

The genus *Melanargia*, Meigen, which is closely allied to *Hipparchia*, having the eyes naked, but with the median nervure scarcely perceptibly swollen at the base, and with no secondary sexual characters in the male, does not extend to India so far as is yet known. All the species are white with black markings, and the type is the "marbled white" of England, *M. galathea*, Linnæus. One species at least is found in Persia, and a female in the Indian Museum, Calcutta, only differs from the figure of that sex of *M. herta*, Dalman, in Boisduval's Icones, vol. i, pl. xxviii, fig. 3 (1832) in the area of the cell on the upperside of the forewing beyond the transverse bar being clouded with fuscous; the basal area below the cell also more thickly irrorated with fuscous than in the specimen figured by Boisduval. On the hindwing the cell is whitish for the basal two-thirds. A detailed description of this specimen is appended for reference.* Numerous other species of *Melanargia* are recorded from the Caucasus and the adjoining regions.

Genus 18.—AULOCERA, Butler. (PLATE XVI).

Aulocera, Butler, Ent. Month Mag, vol. iv, p. 121 (1867).

"Very closely allied to *Hipparchia;* wings large, black, with a white band; the *cilia* broad, white, variegated with black. BODY woolly. *Eyes* naked. *Palpi* as in *Hipparchia. Antennæ* with a gradually formed club, with a slightly hollowed median longitudinal streak on the underside. NEURATION of the wings as in *Hipparchia*, but the nervures of the *forewing* less tumid at the base; and in the *hindwing* the discoidal cell is more entire, and the costa more convex. It chiefly differs from *Hipparchia* in the form of the antennæ, the character of the markings, and the longer cilia to the wings; the arrangement of the nervures is very similar in both genera." (*Butler*, l. c.)

This genus is exclusively Indian, and, with one doubtful exception, is confined to the temperate and higher elevations in the Himalayas. The doubtful exception is the variety *scylla* of *A. brahminus*, which is described from "near Sylhet," but this locality cannot be accepted without further evidence. *Aulocera* is very closely allied to *Hipparchia*, but the very slight dilation of the base of the nervures of the forewing, and the style of colouration, mark it as a group sufficiently distinct for generic separation.

The sexual streak on the forewing of the male insect is variable, and owing to the dark colour, and density of the clothing of the wing, is often very difficult to trace. In one species (*A. padma*) the scales of the sexual mark have a slight sheen, which shows the position clearly in certain lights; in other species it is only to be traced by the greater opaqueness of the wing, and it differs in intensity in different specimens; its position is between the median nervure and the white transverse fascia, and it extends from the middle of the interspace below the submedian nervure to the interspace below the upper discoidal nervule.

Key to the species of Aulocera.

A. Upperside nearly black, with a prominent whitish transverse fascia across both wings.

- *a*. Forewing triangular, the outer margin straight; the whitish fascia broad on both wings.
  - *a*[1]. Of large size; the whitish fascia reaching the inner margin of the hindwing. Underside with the basal area black with greyish undulations.

    187. A. PADMA, Himalayas.
  - *b*[1]. Of smaller size; the whitish fascia not reaching the inner margin of the hindwing. Underside with the basal area greenish bronze, irrorated with grey on the abdominal margin of the hindwing.

    188. A. SWAHA, Himalayas.
- *b*. Forewing more rounded, the outer margin convex.
  - *a*[1]. With the median fascia very narrow. Of small size. Underside with the basal area fuscous, irrorated with ochreous.

    189. A. BRAHMIMUS, Himalayas.
    A. weranga, N.-W. Himalayas.
    A. scylla, (?) Sylhet.
  - *b*[1]. The median fascia very broad. Underside ochreous, with narrow dark undulations.

    190. A. SARASWATI, Himalayas.

---

* FEMALE: UPPERSIDE fuscous; a large whitish patch in the cell of each wing, a broad whitish band from the second median nervule of forewing continued across the hindwing, covering the whole abdominal margin, and uniting with the patch in the cell. *Forewing* with an irregular discal macular band, an interrupted subapical band beyond it, and a marginal series of large spots all whitish. *Hindwing* with a similar series of large whitish spots almost coalescent along the margin. UNDERSIDE tinged with ochreous; the fuscous obsolescent, except on the disc of the *forewing*. *Hindwing* with broad irregular very pale and indistinct submarginal band and another submedian; no trace of ocelli. Expanse, 2.55 inches.

The species of *Aulocera* are common where found at all; and they seem more fond of sunshine than is usual in this subfamily; one species frequents the sunny paths and glades in oak and rhododendron forests; another is found everywhere at suitable elevations; the third generally frequents the grassy slopes above the forests; and the fourth the grassy slopes and scrub jungle at lower elevations; all of them are fond of settling on paths or rocks, where they rest with their wings closed over their backs. Seven species have been described by different authors, but we are unable to admit more than four of these as really distinct. Among the older described species some confusion in synonomy has occurred, owing to Blanchard describing and figuring the same sex of two species as the opposite sexes of one species.

187. **Aulocera padma,** Kollar.

Satyrus padma, Kollar in Hügel's Kaschmir, vol. iv, pt. ii, p. 445, n. 3, pl. xv, figs. 1, 2 (1848), *female; Satyrus avatara*, Moore, Horsfield and Moore, Cat. Lep., E. I. C., vol. i, p. 229, n. 481 (1857), *male; Aulocera padma* et *avatara*, Butler, Cat. Lep. B. M., *Satyridæ*, p. 49, n. 3, and p. 50, n. 4 (1868); id. Lang, Ent. Month. Mag., vol. iv, p. 246 (1868).

HABITAT: Himalayas.

EXPANSE: ♂, 3·1 to 3·3; ♀, 3·5 to 3·7 inches.

DESCRIPTION: FEMALE: "UPPERSIDE obscure fuscous, with a common whitish fascia; macular in the *forewing*, and bifurcate at the apex. UNDERSIDE fuscous, marbled with grey and whitish, a black ocellus on the *forewing* pupilled with white; the fascia broader in the *forewing*, narrow in the *hindwing;* the *cilia* spotted with whitish and fuscous." (*Kollar*, l. c.) MALE (*A. avatara*, Moore.) "Differs from *A. padma* [the female] in having the transverse maculated band much narrower, and there being no spots running obliquely to the costal margin. It is less in size than *A. padma* [the female] but larger than *A. swaha* and *A. saraswati.*" (*Moore*, l. c.)

A. padma is the largest species of the genus, and is distinguished, in both sexes, by the very black ground-colour of the underside of the *hindwing*. The MALE is further distinguished by the complete absence of the inner subcostal white spots on the upperside of the forewing, a character which is approached in some specimens of the very distinct *A. saraswati*, but in no other species; also by the sexual mark on the forewing being comparatively prominent. The FEMALE has the outer margin of the white fascia indistinct and often much extended by suffusion into the black ground-colour beyond, especially on the underside. It differs from the male in its larger size; and in having considerably more white on the underside; the whitish undulations covering the whole basal area of the hindwing instead of being prominent only on the abdominal margin; the outer half of the wing also is white, undulated irregularly with various shades of brown, least densely towards the costal margin.

A. avatara has hitherto been accepted as a distinct species, and even now some authorities hold to this view; but notwithstanding that *A. avatara* is common over a wide range all the specimens are males so far as has as yet been ascertained; and not a single male specimen of the *A. padma* type can be found. It is true that Mr. Moore when describing *A. avatara* in the Cat. Lep. E. I. C., recorded the single specimen of *A. padma* which the Museum contained, and by which he wrote his comparative description of *A. avatara*, as a male, but that identical specimen is now in the Indian Museum, Calcutta, and notwithstanding that the abdomen and forelegs are missing, the outline of the wings, the white character of the markings, especially on the underside, and complete absence of the sexual mark leave no room for doubt that the specimen is really a female, and that the original discrimination of its sex was erroneous, and so far as the evidence at present goes, the conclusion that the two are opposite sexes of the same species is irresistible.

In 1868, Colonel Lang wrote, "*A. padma* and *A. avatara* I have always found in company, and they have appeared to me as female and male respectively of the same species. They frequent quite different ground to *A. swaha* and *A. saraswati*, and appear at a different season; flying in May and June on the borders of oak and rhododendron forests at the summits of ranges of from 8,000 feet to 10,000 feet altitude. A second brood appears in July in the same localities. They fly with much bolder Nymphalidian flight than their tamer congeners *A. swaha* and *A. saraswati*, and they do not extend out of the Simla district into Kunawur." (Ent. Month. Mag., vol. iv, p. 246).

On the other hand, Mr. A. Graham Young holds that the two species are distinct; he writes of *A. padma* that "it is fairly common in Kulu, and is double brooded, the first brood appearing in June on the grassy slopes amongst and above the upper forests, at an elevation of 10,000 feet or so; the second brood appears at a much lower elevation, from 3,000 to 4,000 feet. It is very punctual in its appearance, as in the fifteen years that I have observed this insect, it has never appeared earlier than the 1st or later than the 3rd October. It is an extremely powerful insect on the wing, and very difficult to take, it flies down one hill straight across the valley, and up the opposite hill at a great pace, keeping some ten feet from the ground, and very rarely settling;" while of *A. avatara* he writes "confounded with the above by superficial observers and cabinet naturalists, it is smaller in size than *A. padma*, and much weaker in flight, taking but short flights, and is easily captured; a succession of broods appear throughout May, June, and July."

A. padma is found in suitable localities throughout the Himalayas from Kashmir to Sikkim. It is a forest-haunting insect; in Simla the males appear plentifully in May and again in July, but the female is usually very scarce; in 1882, however, it was abundant in October.

188. **Aulocera swaha**, Kollar.

Satyrus swaha, Kollar in Hügel's Kaschmir, vol. iv, pt. ii, p. 444, n 1, pl. xiv, figs. 1, 2 (1844); *Satyrus brahminus*, Blanchard, in Jacquemont's Voy. dans l'Inde, vol. iv, Ins, p. 22, n. 18, pl. ii, figs. 5, 6 (1844), *male* (in part); *Aulocera swaha*, Lang, Ent Month Mag., vol. iv., p. 246 (1868).

HABITAT: Himalayas.

EXPANSE: 2·6 to 2·8 inches.

DESCRIPTION: "UPPERSIDE obscure fuscous, glossed with greenish; with a common yellowish-white fascia, in the *forewing* macular, with one ocellus, the ocellus blind. UNDERSIDE paler, the base and margins marbled with greyish; the median common fascia entire, the ocellus pupilled with white; the *cilia* varied with fuscous and yellow." (*Kollar*, l. c.)

A. swaha is the commonest species of the group; and is easily distinguished from *A. padma* by its smaller size; and by the bright bronzy brown, not black, colour of the underside; the white fascia of the upperside has in both sexes the inner white subcostal spot which is lacking in the male of *A. padma (A. avatara)*, and terminates in the forewing in four white spots ranged round a blackish subapical spot; there is also in many specimens a minute subcostal white spot beyond. On the UNDERSIDE the *hindwing* has a diffused greyish band from the apex, where it is broadest, along the outer and abdominal margins, marked with irregular dark brown undulations most densely along the abdominal margin, but more sparingly at the apex; in many specimens this band consists of greyish undulations on a brown ground, and in some there is an irregular dark brown very sinuous line between it and the fascia. The sexual mark in the male is usually very obscure in this species, but in some old specimens in the Indian Museum, Calcutta, it is very distinct, and extends into the cell. The FEMALE differs only in the more rounded outline of the wings; and in having the pale fascia rather broader and its edges less sharply defined. The colouration throughout is much paler.

Typically *A. swaha* has the median fascia creamy-white on both wings on the upperside, and pale buff on the forewing, almost pure white on the hindwing, on the underside. There is a well-marked variety found at the higher elevations in which the fascia is on the upperside deep yellow on the forewing and buff on the hindwing; and on the underside bright yellow on the forewing and almost white on the hindwing. In these specimens the dark brown line beyond the fascia on the underside is more prominent. This is the form figured by Blanchard as the female of *A. brahminus*, but the specimens he figures are evidently males of this variety of *A. swaha*. Typical specimens of this variety are very distinct, but the gradations in tone of the yellow tint are so gradual in intermediate localities that it is impossible to draw the line of separation.

In the Western Himalayas *A. swaha* "abounds during the rainy season, from July to October, from the outer spurs overlooking the Indian plains, for two hundred miles into the interior of the mountain ranges towards the treeless regions of Spiti and Thibet." (*Colonel Lang*). In Kulu Mr. A. Graham Young writes :—" Not uncommon in its peculiar haunts, grassy hills at 7,000 to 8,000 feet elevation, from June to September." Its range to the eastwards is probably extensive in suitable ground, but we have no certain record of its occurrence in the Eastern Himalayas.

The next two species have a very different outline, the wings being more rounded and feebler in appearance ; the outer margin of the forewing being decidedly convex.

189. **Aulocera brahminus,** Blanchard. (PLATE XVI, FIG. 49 ♂ *).

Satyrus brahminus, Blanchard, in Jacquemont's Voy. dans l' Inde, vol. iv, Ins., p. 22, n. 18, pl. ii, fig. 4 (1844), *male* (in part) ; *Aulocera scylla*, Butler, Ent. Mouth. Mag., vol. iv, p. 122, n. 5 (1867) ; *Aulocera werang*, Lang, Ent. Month Mag., vol. iv, p. 247 (1868).

HABITAT : Himalayas.

EXPANSE : 2·4 to 2·7 inches.

DESCRIPTION : UPPERSIDE blackish brown, paler than in *A. swaha ;* the discal white fascia very narrow and attenuated especially on the hindwing. *Forewing* with an inner white spot, making with the three upper spots of the fascia a group of four surrounding an indistinct oval black spot ; two or three white dashes between the inner spot and the costa, as in *A. padma*, female. *Cilia* white interrupted with black at the end of each nervule. The sexual mark is very obscure. The FEMALE only differs from the male in the shape of the body, and the outline of the wings being more rounded ; the colour and markings are identical. UNDERSIDE paler and brighter brown, irrorated with ochreous scales and with variable grey, ochreous, and dark brown markings ; the white markings as on the upperside, but on the *forewing* the subapical black spot is pupilled with white ; and on the *hindwing* are a few variable whitish suffused spots beyond the discal fascia.

In describing *A. brahminus*, Blanchard erroneously described the yellow variety of *A. swaha* as the female of *A. brahminus ;* he gives a figure of the upperside only of a male *A. brahminus*, and figures of both upper and undersides of males of *A. swaha*, while in his description the two are so mixed up that it is difficult to ascertain what the markings of the true *A. brahminus* on the underside really are. So much of the original description as manifestly applies to this species is appended below for reference,† and it seems to us that the typical form of *A. brahminus* is that which is found at comparatively low elevations about 8,000 feet above the sea, in Kulu and Kashmir. This form is nearly as large as *A. swaha*, and most nearly resembles it on the underside ; but the shape of the wings and the very narrow discal white fascia abundantly distinguish it from that species. The underside is comparatively uniform in colouration, bright brown ; within the discal fascia the whole area of the hindwing is irrorated with ochreous ; and towards the costal margin of both wings are numerous indistinct ochreous and darker brown striæ ; beyond the discal band the ochreous striæ are less indistinct, and appear on the whole of the hindwing and on the apical half of the forewing, some grey striæ also appear in patches at the apex of the forewing, and along the extremity of each nervure of the hindwing, most distinct at the apex and gradually disappearing along the inner margin ; the hindwing also bears two or three suffused whitish spots beyond the fascia, and beyond them again a submarginal series of very indistinct suffused dark brown spots.

---

* Erroneously named *A. weranga* on the plate.

† *Satyrus brahminus*, Blanchard. DESCRIPTION : " UPPERSIDE, *both wings* blackish brown, with a nearly straight oblique transverse white band a little beyond the middle ; on the *forewing* consisting of a series of spots, the first four spots placed in pairs near the costal margin, then two others pyriform pointing outwards, the last quadrangular divided by the black submedian nervure, and reaching the inner margin ; on the *hindwing* the band is almost straight, narrowed towards the anal angle, and interrupted only by the black nervules. UNDERSIDE, *forewing* with a black spot with a white dot in its centre near the apex ; against the white band, along the costal margin and at the apex are some small white and brown striæ. The *hindwing* is similarly striated throughout on each side of the transverse band except that towards the outer margin are some whitish spaces, and the base is also finely powdered with greyish." (*Blanchard*, l. c.)

Var. *weranga*, Lang. "MALE and FEMALE. UPPERSIDE blackish fuscous with a whitish discal fascia; the whitish fascia macular in the *forewing*, bifurcate at the apex, and including an oval black spot; arched on the *hindwing*, slender, obsolescent near the anal angle. *Cilia* white, variegated with black at the end of the nervules. UNDERSIDE scarcely paler, covered with fuscous striæ, *hindwing* greenish at the base, outwardly slightly ochraceous; *forewing* with a subapical spot bearing a minute white dot; *hindwing* with the discal fascia reaching the anal margin, and an exterior series of three subobsolete whitish dots. *Body* black; *antennæ* with the tip obsoletely ochraceous on the underside. HABITAT: Upper Kunawur (Werang Pass). Kashmir (Goolmurg). EXPANSE: 2·6 inches." (*Lang*, Ent. Month. Mag., vol. iv., p. 247 (1868).

A. weranga is a rather smaller insect, and differs from typical *A. brahminus* in the far greater prominence of the ochreous striæ on the underside, so much so that in some specimens it appears as if the ground-colour were ochreous more or less densely striated with brown. Extreme examples are widely distinct from typical *A. brahminus*, but the gradations met with between the two forms renders it impossible to separate them satisfactorily. The extent of the grey striæ too varies greatly; in some specimens the greyish irrorations of the inner margin extend over the whole base of the hindwing. The whitish spots and the submarginal dark brown spots beyond are obsolete in some specimens, and very prominent in others.

Var. *scylla*, Butler. "MALE: UPPERSIDE blackish-fuscous, with a whitish discal fascia, macular on the *forewing*, slender and obsolete near the anal angle on the *hindwing*, bifurcate at the apex of the *forewing*, and including an oval black spot. *Cilia* whitish, variegated with black at the end of the nervules; *body* black; *antennæ* with a yellow club. UNDERSIDE paler, covered with blackish striæ; the subapical spot of the *forewing* ocellated; *hindwing* very slightly yellowish, an outer discal series of whitish spots tinged outwardly with black, the discal fascia distinct at the anal angle. Most nearly allied to *A. brahminus*, but differs in its much smaller size, less sinuated margins, more slender central band, and on the underside in having a row of white spots placed in an arc outside the central band. I have seen three specimens of this species, which all appear to agree in size, pattern and colouration. HABITAT: near Sylhet. EXPANSE: 2·25 inches." (*Butler*, Ent. Month. Mag., vol. iv, p. 122, n. 5 (1867).

Colonel Lang in describing *A. weranga* writes, that "it differs from [the description of] *A. scylla* by its paler colour, larger size, more sinuated margins, and the want of the exterior series of white, black-encircled spots; the whitish dots of *A. weranga* being only two or three in number, very small, and indistinct." Mr. Butler adds, "the two species are nearly allied, but I think quite distinct;" another point of difference being that "the veins on the underside of the hindwing in *A. scylla* are powdered with whitish scales." We are quite unable to separate *A. scylla* from *A. brahminus*; it is described from "near Sylhet," and if that locality could be accepted definitely, there might be some grounds for its separation; but the authority for the habitat rests apparently on a very slender basis, and some specimens of *A. weranga* from the N.-W. Himalayas present every feature that is given as distinctive of *A. scylla*; it is doubtful whether it can even be retained as a distinct variety.

A. brahminus is found so far as we have any certain knowledge only in the N.-W. Himalayas at from 7,000 feet to 13,000 feet elevation; Mr. Graham Young took numerous specimens in 1880 in June on the Ser-ka-joth in North Mundi, two miles south of the Kulu frontier, and forty miles south of the snowy range at barely 8,000 feet elevation; these were all typical *A. brahminus*; Mr. de Nicéville found it very plentifully on the banks of the Chandra Bhaga river, in July, near Koksir on the borders of Lahoul at 7,000 feet elevation, and again at Kailang in Lahoul at about 9,000 feet in the same month; all his specimens being of the *A. weranga* form with the ochreous predominating on the underside, and one, a female from Kailang, has the nervures powdered with white scales and the whitish black-encircled spots of *A. scylla*; the types of *A. weranga* were taken by

Colonel Lang at "12,000 feet elevation, about 1,000 feet below the bleak and bare summit of the Werang pass, amidst the rocky, grassy ground just clear of the forests of *Pinus gerardiana* and *Cedrus deodara*;" in Lahoul, at Patseo, 11,000 feet elevation, specimens were taken in July by the Reverend A. Heydé, which differ from the usual form in the great predominance of the grey irrorations. In Pangi on the Săch pass Mr. R. Ellis took at an elevation of 13,000 feet in August and September some beautifully marked examples in which the prevailing ochreous is beautifully contrasted with the grey markings, and dark brown striæ; the veins in these are powdered with white as in *A. scylla;* and finally a large series taken by Mrs. Bazett at Goolmurg in Kashmir in July at from 9,000 to 10,000 feet elevation, showed every gradation between typical *A. brahminus* and typical *A. weranga.*

The figure (erroneously named *A. weranga* on the plate) shows the upper and undersides of a male in the Indian Museum, Calcutta, taken in the Kulu Valley; of the typical *A. brahminus* form.

190. **Aulocera saraswati,** Kollar.

Satyrus saraswati, Kollar in Hügel's Kaschmir, vol. iv, pt. ii, p. 445, n. 2, pl. xiv, figs. 3, 4 (1844); *Aulocera saraswati*, Butler, Ent. Month. Mag., vol. iv, p. 121, n. 2 (1867); idem, id., Cat. Lep. B. M., *Satyridæ*, p. 49, n. 2 (1868).

HABITAT: Himalayas.

EXPANSE: ♂, 2·7 to 2·85; ♀, 2·9 to 3·5 inches.

DESCRIPTION: "UPPERSIDE obscure fuscous, glossed with greenish, with a common whitish fascia, in the *forewing* macular, with one ocellus, the ocellus blind. UNDERSIDE yellowish, undulated with fuscous, the fascia whitish in the *forewing*, yellowish in the *hindwing;* the ocellus pupilled with white; the *cilia* varied with fuscous and white." (*Kollar*, l. c.)

The white fascia in this species is broader and more regular than in any other. On the UPPERSIDE in the MALE the inner white spot beyond the cell is small and in some specimens evanescent, as in *A. padma*, male; but the narrow white streak below the costa which is often present in *A. padma*, male, is altogether wanting in *A. saraswati.* The sexual mark varies much in prominence, being quite obsolete in some specimens. In the FEMALE the inner white spot is conspicuous, and in some specimens the oval black spot beyond it has a minute white pupil. The UNDERSIDE is very distinct, the basal half is very pale ochreous, fading to greyish white on the inner margin of the hindwing, marked throughout with dark brown striæ, the inner edge of the broad white fascia, which is almost equally whitish on both wings, is defined by a narrow dark brown lunular line, almost straight on the hindwing; beyond the fascia the ground-colour is ochreous marbled with brownish, merging into a diffused dark brown submarginal band, darker and broader on the forewing; the margin is pure grey along the nervules, ochreous in the middle of each interspace, and more or less marked throughout with fine brown striæ. The FEMALE is larger than the male and paler in colour, the markings on the underside similar, but less prominent.

According to Colonel Lang, "*A. saraswati* is not quite so widely spread, appears later, and disappears earlier than *A. swaha;* in August it swarms in the localities affected by it, amongst the luxuriant grass pastures on the less wooded slopes of the hills." In Simla it is not uncommon on the grassy slopes in the neighbourhood in the autumn months. In Pangi Mr. Robert Ellis and Dr. Hutchison took numerous specimens of both sexes in July and August. In Kulu, according to Mr. A. Graham Young, "it appears in July, and remains on the wing until the middle of October: it is common from 4,000 feet and upwards, and greatly affects the thistle flowers, upon which numbers may be captured in their peculiar haunts." There are specimens in the Indian Museum both from Kumaon and Sikkim, so that the range of this species is much wider than was thought when Colonel Lang wrote the note quoted above, fourteen years ago.

Genus 19.—EPINEPHELE, Hübner. (PLATE XV).*

Epinephele, Hübner, Verz. bek. Schmett., p. 59 (1816); *Satyrus* (in part), Westwood, Gen. D. L., vol. ii, p. 388 (1851).

The genus *Epinephele* occupies almost the same range as *Hipparchia*, and is about equally numerously represented here, eleven species having been recorded from within Indian limits. They take the place of the "meadow browns" of England, and in the Himalayas are only found at considerable elevations, and they chiefly frequent grassy uplands. The genus comprises two well-marked groups, first those in which the males have a conspicuous brand on the forewing, composed of silky densely packed scales, and extending along the median nervure below the cell, as in many species of true *Hipparchia;* and second, those in which the males have no trace of a brand on the forewing; this latter group contains the smallest species of the genus, indeed the smallest of the subfamily, with the exception of the still smaller *Ypthimas.* In the first group the shape of the anal angle of the hindwing (see Plate XV, fig. 39, *E. davendra)*, and in the second group the absence of the sexual brand in the male, distinguish them from *Hipparchia*, but the two genera are very closely allied. The antennæ in all the Indian species of *Epinephele* have a gradually-formed club, as also have some of the *Hipparchias.* None of the species of *Epinephele* have a complete series of ocelli on the underside of the hindwing, and in many of them that wing is altogether devoid of ocelli on both sides.

Key to the Indian species of Epinephele.

First group.

A. Males with a well-defined brand on the upperside of the forewing.

a. Males with the forewing fulvous with brown margins; the brand conspicuous, brown, on the fulvous ground; *hindwing* dentate near the anal angle. Underside with an angulate median dark line defined outwardly with whitish; the ocelli generally prominent.

*a*¹. Female with the discal angulate dark line obsolescent on the upperside.

191. E. DAVENDRA, Western Himalayas.

*b*¹. Female with the discal angulate dark line prominent on the upperside.

192. E. ROXANE, Beluchistan, Afghanistan.

b. Male with the upperside as in *a*, but the hindwing quadrate and slightly dentate. Underside with three very irregular dark lines and clouded whitish fasciæ; no ocelli.

193. E. NARICA, Afghanistan.

c. Males with the forewing brown, the brand deeper coloured than the ground; *hindwing* less dentate near anal angle. Underside with the median dark line much more irregular, seldom prominent, and never defined with whitish; the ocelli small or evanescent.

*a*¹. Female with two or three ocelli on the upperside of the forewing, ringed with fulvous and the space between irrorated with fulvous.

194. E. CHEENA, Western Himalayas.

*b*¹. Female with a single subapical black spot on upperside of forewing placed on a fulvous submarginal band.

195. E. INTERPOSITA, Beluchistan, Persia.

191. Epinephele davendra, Moore. (PLATE XV, FIG. 39 ♀).

Epinephile davendra, Moore, Proc. Zool. Soc. Lond., 1865, p 502, n. 94, pl. xxx, fig. 7, *male* and *female.*

HABITAT: Spiti, Pangi, Thibet, Ladak, Kabul.

EXPANSE: 1·75 to 2·0 inches.

DESCRIPTION: "MALE greyish brown. *Forewing* with the space within the discoidal cell to near the apex, and then descending to near the posterior margin ferruginous, this colour being distinctly defined; within it is a single black apical spot. [Or, in other words, the *forewing*

* EPINEPHELE; erroneously spelt EPINEPHILE on the plate.

is fulvous with brown margins, and the brown sexual mark extending from near the inner margin to near the apex of the cell below the median nervure.] UNDERSIDE with the costal and exterior margins of the *forewing* greyish brown, the inner space pale ferruginous, the apical ocellus with a white pupil and brown-bordered yellow iris, which latter, however, does not encircle the spot, being cut off as it were posteriorly; a short streak before the ocellus, and a submarginal line, dark brown. *Hindwing* grey, with delicate minute brown striæ; a discal and a submarginal line dark brown, the former irregularly [even, but angulate] across the disc from middle of anterior to posterior margin, both bordered outwardly with pale white, and having a single anterior and two posterior black ocelli, each with a yellow* brown-bordered iris, and the anterior with a white pupil. FEMALE pale grey, the ferruginous space in the *forewing* ill-defined, and with a second black spot situated near the posterior angle [sometimes evanescent or altogether wanting]. UNDERSIDE as in the male, but with the lower black spot on the *forewing* as above, the anterior ocellus on the *hindwing* being minute or nearly obsolete. Allied to *E. eudora*." (*Moore*, l. c.)

"*Note.*—This is a Thibetian and Spiti insect, affecting the dry hot summer of the rainless region of the Chinese frontier. On a hot June or July day, these sober insects may be seen flitting about the stony hill-sides, 9,000 to 12,000 feet altitude—hill-sides where the *Graminaceæ* are scarce and brown, and grey *Artemisiæ* and *Ephedra* form the principal vegetation. They do not occur in the moister and more wooded regions of the Himalayas; but first appear on the confines of Upper Kunawur, in Spiti, and the Chinese provinces of Gughe and Nâri Khorsum (Thibet)." (*Colonel A. M. Lang, R. E.*, l. c.)

The ocellation on the underside of this species is variable. In the specimens taken by Colonel Lang, who obtained the types, there are three ocelli on the underside of the *hindwing*, one subapical, two subanal; in the male all three are prominent, but never so large as in the next species *E. roxane;* in the female the subapical ocellus is more or less evanescent; in three males taken in Pangi in July by Dr. Hutchison, the subapical ocellus is absent entirely, and the subanal ones are very small, the dark lines too are very faint and less angulate, and their whitish borderings very indistinct, almost obsolete in one specimen. Two males taken by Mr. de Nicéville at Kargil and Nurla in Ladak, early in July, have all the ocelli large, almost as large as in *E. roxane;* one female from Kargil is similarly marked, another female from the same locality has a fourth small ocellus above the subapical one, and another female also from the same locality has only two ocelli, the lower subanal one being entirely wanting. In a male and a female, both taken at Sher Dawaza near Kabul by Lieutenant H. Whistler-Smith, the upper ocellus is entirely wanting; in a second male specimen from the same locality it is present; while in two females from Khistwar, Kashmir, the upper ocellus is obsolete. Moreover the three male specimens from Pangi, that we have referred to above, differ from all the others in the cilia on both wings, both above and below, being pale brown, not more or less white as in the specimens from the other localities; and the scalloping of the hindwing is much less deep.

The figure shows the upper and undersides of a female specimen in the Indian Museum, Calcutta, taken at Kabul by Lieutenant H. Whistler-Smith.

192. Epinephele roxane, Felder.

E. roxane, Felder, Reise Novara, Lep., vol. iii, p. 491, n. 849, pl. lxix, figs. 12, 13 (1866), *female*; id., Butler, Proc. Zool. Soc. Lond., 1880, p. 405.

HABITAT: Western Himalayas, Kunawar, Spiti; Losar, Kargil, Ladak; Beluchistan.

EXPANSE: 2·0 to 2·2 inches.

DESCRIPTION: "FEMALE. UPPERSIDE, hoary-brown; the margin immediately before the cilia fuscous. *Forewing* with the discal area pale fulvous, divided by a streak most often obsolete, and with one black blind ocellus and often another median incomplete, and bordered

* This must be an error: in all the specimens we have seen, including those in Colonel Lang's collection captured with the types of the species, the irides of the ocelli are white or grey, certainly not yellow.

with fuscous. *Hindwing* with a subangulate discal streak, and another submarginal almost obsolete ; the ocelli of the underside more or less visible by transparency. UNDERSIDE paler, with a line before the cilia blackish-fuscous, and another on the cilia white. *Forewing* with the fulvous area paler, a little more extended, more distinctly divided and bordered, the ocellus larger, blacker, with a single white pupil and broad ochraceous iris, circled with fuscous ; the costal and outer margins variegated with fuscous, and here and there irrorated with white. *Hindwing* with fuscous striæ and hoary irrorations, the lines of the upperside much better defined and outwardly bordered with whitish powdery bands ; a subapical ocellus often minute or wanting, and two near anal angle, black, blind, with white iris and circled with fuscous, often with whitish irrorations beyond the subapical ocellus."

"This species, reminding one, by the dentate outline of the *hindwing* and in the markings of the underside, of *H. parisatis*, is a local form of the Thibetan *E. davendra*, Moore. A specimen collected to the east of Pangi in Kunawar is considerably larger than those from Spiti." (*Felder*, l. c.)

E. roxane was for a long time considered identical with *E. davendra*, Moore ; but Mr. Butler has recently recognised its distinctness with the following remark :—"*E. roxane*, although nearly allied to *E. davendra*, differs in its paler colouration, and the more deeply sinuated margin of the hindwing." (*Butler*, l. c.)

No specimen that we have seen from any of the localities quoted in the Western Himalayas can be separated from *E. davendra*, but the form found in the mountains of Beluchistan, which has been identified by Mr. Butler as *E. roxane*, is apparently a distinct geographical variety. It differs from *E. davendra* as stated above, and further by its larger size, and on the UPPERSIDE by the far greater prominence in the female of the discal band, and on the UNDERSIDE by the larger ocelli and the greater prominence of the fuscous striæ and hoary irrorations. The MALE of this race differs from the male of *E. davendra* as in the female on the UNDERSIDE, and in its larger size, but the markings of the upperside appear to be identical The ocellation varies in this species as in *E. davendra*. Dr. Felder figures a female with four ocelli on the underside of the hindwing ; the males have generally three prominent ocelli, but in the females the subapical ocellus is minute or wanting, the two subanal ocelli being large and prominent. The lower ocellus on the forewing of the females is sometimes prominent, sometimes altogether wanting.

In South Afghanistan Captain Roberts found *E. roxane* "commonly at the end of May and in June," and Colonel Lang, R. E., and Colonel Swinhoe have also found it commonly in suitable places in the neighbourhood of Quetta in September and October.

Two other species, *E. comara* and *E. mandane*, which are found in Persia, have the same general style of markings as *E. davendra*, to which they are evidently allied. *E. comara*,* to judge from the figure, is closely allied to the form of *E. roxane* found in Beluchistan. The male chiefly differs on the upperside in having the dark margin of the forewing narrower, and the sexual streak less distinct ; on the underside the forewing is more uniform fulvous ; the basal half not perceptibly darker ; there is no whitish streak from the costa, and the fulvous colour extends much further up within the ocellus. The female has on the upperside only a broad fulvous fascia, and a fulvous spot just beyond the cell ; the basal area not at all irrorated with fulvous ; on the underside the difference is as in the male, but much less pronounced.

---

* *Epinephele comara*, Lederer, Hor. Soc. Ent Ross., vol. viii, p. 12, pl. 1, figs. 9 *male*, 10 *female* (1871). HABITAT : Astrabad, Persia. EXPANSE : *male*, 1·9 ; *female*, 2·1 inches. DESCRIPTION : "*Hindwing* dentate. UPPERSIDE fuscous, the *cilia* whitish. *Forewing* of the MALE rufescent-luteous, margined with fuscous, and with a short transverse fuscous stripe, and a rounded black spot near the apex. FEMALE cinereous-fuscous, with an exterior yellowish fascia bearing a rounded black spot. UNDERSIDE of *both sexes* ochraceous, the black apical spot pupilled. *Hindwing* fuscous-cinereous, a median blackish striga, externally margined with white, and two black ocelli with white irides near the anal angle. The male resembles on the upperside that of *E. narica*, but the wings are less pointed and broader ; the female corresponds more with that of *E. lycaon*." (*Lederer*, l. c.)

*E. mandane** is a very beautiful species, and distinguished especially by the curious elongate shape of the black spot on the forewing, and the very highly dentate outline of the hindwing, the margin of which exhibits at least three distinct tails. From the rest of the *E. davendra* group it is also distinguished by the curved (not angulate) character of the white band on the underside of the hindwing. The female has often one, and sometimes two, round black spots below the spot on the forewing, and the whole of these spots are situated on a more or less prominent fulvous submarginal band defined inwardly, and diffused outwardly; the series of females from Persia in the Indian Museum, Calcutta, show considerable variation.

193. **Epinephele narica,** Hübner.

Papilio narica, Hübner, Eur. Schmett, vol. i, figs 704—707 (1825?); *Satyrus narica*, Boisduval, Icones, p. 212, pl. xlii, figs 3, *male*; 4, 5 *female* (1832.)

HABITAT: South Russia, Western Asia, Afghanistan.

EXPANSE: 1·8 to 2·0 inches.

DESCRIPTION: MALE: UPPERSIDE brown; the *cilia* whitish. *Forewing* with the entire disc fulvous, the margin and the sexual streak alone being brown; colour and markings almost exactly as in *E. davendra*, but the outer margin is straighter in the *forewing*, and less dentate in the *hindwing*. FEMALE: UPPERSIDE very similar in aspect to *E. neoza*, female, but with the *cilia* of both wings white, and the *hindwing* quadrate in outline owing to a prolongation of the discoidal nervule. *Forewing* fulvous, with cinereous-brown margins, the outer margin dusky, a black subapical spot, (and often a second submarginal spot in the lowest median interspace). *Hindwing* cinereous-brown, dusky towards the outer margin. UNDERSIDE also somewhat similar in pattern to that of *E. neoza*, but paler in colouration. *Forewing* pale fulvous; a median indistinct angulate line across the wing, a black subapical ocellus with small white pupil and pale ochreous iris; the ground-colour between the ocellus and median line also pale ochreous merging in the iris; the costa narrowly hoary, mottled with fuscous; the outer margin more broadly cinereous-brown, darkest at inner angle, and a distinct submarginal slightly lunulate dark line. *Hindwing* whitish, a subbasal and a highly irregular median fuscous line, between which the ground-colour is brown, forming a broad irregular sharply defined brown fascia; a brown suffused patch near the costa; then another brown submarginal band inwardly diffused, outwardly sharply defined by a narrow dark lunular line; the margin also clouded with brown, and the whole wing sparingly mottled with fuscous.

Described from Boisduval's figures and from a single female taken by Lieutenant-Colonel C. Swinhoe at Chaman, in South Afghanistan, on the 11th of May, and which is referred to by Mr. A. G. Butler in his Notes on Lieutenant-Colonel Swinhoe's collection as *E. interposita*.† This latter lacks the second submarginal black spot on the forewing, but otherwise corresponds exactly with Boisduval's figure. It has no resemblance to *E. interposita*; and its white cilia and quadrate hindwing at once distinguish it from *E. neoza*, which it most nearly resembles in general aspect.

A closely allied species from the Kirghiz steppes and the Mangyschlak peninsula on the Caspian sea has been separated under the name of *E. naricina*.

Epinephele naricina, Staudinger, (*E. narica*, Hübner, var.?), Berl. Ent. Zeitsch., vol. xiv, p. 100, n. 2 (1870). Smaller than *E. narica*, the smallest male measures 1·3 inches in expanse, and the female 1·5 inches, against a minimum of 1·54 inches in the male of *E. narica*. UPPERSIDE of the *forewing* as in *E. narica*, but the brand of the male is narrower, even

---

* *Epinephele mandane*, Kollar, Denkschr. Akad. Wien Math.-Nat. Cl., vol. i, p. 52, n. 8 (1850). HABITAT: Persia. EXPANSE: 1·7 to 2·1 inches. DESCRIPTION: "*Forewing* entire; *hindwing* acutely dentate. UPPERSIDE cineraceous-fuscous. *Forewing* with an oblong transverse silky black subcostal spot. UNDERSIDE: *Forewing* fulvous in the middle, with an abbreviated white fascia; a black ocellus near the apex, with yellow iris, and white pupil. *Hindwing* cinereous, with a white median arched fascia margined with fuscous; two ocelli near the anal angle black, with white iris. Allied to *E. eudora* [=*E. lycaon*] in size and shape, but the markings of the wings on the underside entirely different. Only two male specimens were brought from the alpine regions of South Persia by Kotschy. This species is also very closely allied to *E. wagneri*, Herrich-Schäffer, (Suppt. ad Lep Eur. Hüb., pl. lxv, figs. 311—313) from which it differs in having the wings on the upperside unicolorous cineraceous-fuscous." (*Kollar*, l. c.) Mr. Kirby gives *E. mandane* as a synomym of *E. wagneri*.

† Ann. and Mag. of Nat. Hist., fifth series, vol. ix, p. 207 (1882).

and the iris far less distinct; and on the underside in having the median dark line very faint on the hindwing, and almost absent from the forewing. The FEMALE differs in having on the underside the median line on the forewing continued straight to the costa and inner margin instead of merging into the rings of the ocelli; and the pale submarginal band on the hindwing is far more prominent. In a large series of this sex in the Indian Museum, Calcutta, obtained from Persia, the upperside has a dark discal fascia well defined externally, diffused inwardly on both wings, and two submarginal black spots, each with a broad pale yellow iris on the forewing.

E. pallescens, *E. amardæa*, *E. dysdora* and *E. cadusia* are also all found in Persia, and belong to this group; of these descriptions are appended below for reference.* The climate of the dry elevated regions in Persia seems peculiarly suited to the development of this genus.

A very distinct species of this group is described by Alphéraky from the neighbourhood of Kuldja under the name of *E. kirghisa*; it has *both wings* fulvous on the upperside, and margined with brown.

Epinephele kirghisa, Alphéraky, Hor. Soc. Ent. Ross., vol. xvi, p. 423, n. 97, pl. xv, figs. 24, ♂; 25, ♀ (1881). EXPANSE: ♂ and ♀, 1·8 inches. DESCRIPTION: "*Forewing* entire, *hindwing* subdentate. UPPERSIDE dilute fulvous, with two rounded black spots (one subapical and the other in the first median interspace), larger in the female, sometimes with white pupils, and the margin of both wings swarthy. MALE with a subcellular greyish-fuscous

---

upperside in lacking the sexual streak; the ocellus is often distinctly white pupilled, and with a second coherent black spot below, and often another lower black spot, each with a distinct though narrow yellowish iris; the submarginal band of fulvous irrorations is much more distinct and often divided into streaks by the fuscous nervules. UNDERSIDE with the ocellus as on upperside; the iris wider; a median dark line on both wings, beyond which is a broad submarginal fascia, fulvous on the forewing, greyish-ochraceous on the hindwing; the basal half of the forewing washed with fulvous, the outer margin of both wings broadly darker than the basal half. (Described from specimens from Prussia.)

* *Epinephele pallescens*, Butler, Cat. Lep. B. M., *Satyridæ*, p. 65, n. 8, pl. iii, fig. 3 (1868), *female*. HABITAT: Persia. EXPANSE: *Male*, 2·0; *female*, 2·1 inches. DESCRIPTION: "UPPERSIDE pale olivaceous-fuscous; the *cilia* whitish. *Forewing* of the MALE with a cinerascent internal basal fascia; the outer margin slightly fuscescent; a black subapical dot; of the FEMALE with a disco-cellular spot, and two elongate and a dot, discal, arranged in a direct series, golden-yellow; a large black subapical ocellus with two pupils placed obliquely (the lower smaller), and irregularly circled with fulvous. *Hindwing* in *both sexes* undulated. UNDERSIDE almost as in *E. ida*." (*Butler*, l. c.) We have no specimens of *E. ida*, but from Godart's description of this and Butler's uncoloured figure of *E. pallescens*, we gather that on the UNDERSIDE the *forewing* is fulvous with a median striga, within which the basal half is somewhat clouded with darker; the ocellus as on upperside, and the costa narrowly, and the outer margin broadly fuscous. *Hindwing* clouded and variegated with greyish, a median very angulate line from costa to inner margin, beyond which the ground-colour is whitish, gradually darkening, and bearing another indistinct submarginal line; no trace of ocelli. It is evidently very close to *E. lycaon*.

Epinephele amardæa, Lederer, Hor. Soc. Ent. Ross, vol. vi, p. 84, pl. v, figs. 3 *male*, 4 *female* (1869). HABITAT: Astrabad, Persia. EXPANSE: *Male*, 1·4; *female*, 1·5 inches. DESCRIPTION: "UPPERSIDE fuscous. *Forewing* with a subapical black spot (on a fulvous disc in the female). UNDERSIDE: *Forewing* fulvous with two brown strigæ, and a subapical spot with white pupil. *Hindwing* greyish, with three serrated fuscous strigæ, washed with hoary outside the second, and two subanal dots adhering to the inner edge of the third striga. The UNDERSIDE is darker, and the markings are more sharply defined than in *E. lycaon*. *Forewing* with the outer margin grey-brown; the costal margin with darker striæ, a dark transverse line across the cell; one median across the wing beyond the cell, and one submarginal—the latter edged paler outwardly." (*Lederer*, l. c.)

Epinephele dysdora, Lederer, Hor. Soc. Ent Ross., vol. vi, p. 85, pl. v, figs. 1 *male*, 2 *female* (1869). HABITAT: Astrabad, Persia. EXPANSE: *Male* and *female*, 1·75 inches. DESCRIPTION: "UPPERSIDE fuscous, with a subapical black spot on a fuscous band (and in the female another smaller below it). UNDERSIDE: *Forewing* fulvous, a fuscous striga before the subapical white-pupilled spot. *Hindwing* cinereous, a sharply defined striga beyond the middle, outwardly washed with whitish; two subanal black dots with yellow irides. Also allied to *E. lycaon*, but the markings of the underside much clearer and more delicate. UPPERSIDE dark brown as in *E. janira*, the hindwing slightly scalloped; the *cilia* brown-grey. *Forewing* in the MALE with a black ocellus at the apex in the fulvous band, which band disappears towards the inner margin, and is somewhat diffused inwardly, and crossed by fuscous veins. The FEMALE has the two black spots surrounded by faint yellowish irides, the fulvous band defined inwardly by a fuscous striga, within which the ground-colour is again suffused with fulvous for a short distance" (*Lederer*, l. c.) In the figure of the UNDERSIDE the forewing is fulvous with brown margins, the spots as on the upperside, a dark median line across the wing, and a dark submarginal line outwardly defined with whitish. *Hindwing* grey-brown, an incomplete subbasal striga; a dark median dentate striga ending just above the anal angle on the inner margin, outwardly defined with whitish, which shades off into the brown beyond, a pale indistinct submarginal fascia, and lunular marginal band; the two subanal ocelli near the inner edge of the pale submarginal fascia.

Epinephele cadusia, Lederer, Hor. Soc Ent. Ross, vol. vi, p. 84, pl. iv, figs. 10 *male*; 11, *female* (1869). HABITAT: Astrabad, Persia. EXPANSE: *Male*, 1·5; *female*, 1·6 inches. DESCRIPTION: "UPPERSIDE fuscous, the *cilia* whitish, the disc fulvous, including a black subapical spot (subgeminate in the female, with another smaller one below). UNDERSIDE. *Forewing* fulvous, with a single brown striga, and a subapical spot with white pupil. *Hindwing* fuscescent-hoary, a median fuscescent striga bent backwards, outwardly washed with whitish. Very close to *E. lycaon*, but smaller, with more rounded wings and whitish cilia; the *forewing* in the male with a fulvous band diffused on the inner side (as in *E. janira*, var. *telmessia*). The UNDERSIDE as in *E. lycaon*, the colouration, however, much lighter, whitish grey, the markings brown-grey. Very common." (*Lederer*, l. c).

diagonal fascia, outwardly dentated [the usual male mark]. UNDERSIDE: *Forewing* paler, bordered with cinereous, the round spots fuscous, pupilled with white (the lower one blind in the male). *Hindwing* cinereous, irrorated with fuscescent, two subanal black dots circled with dilute grey." (*Alphéraky*, l. c.). In the figures the basal area of both wings is clouded darker on the upperside, especially in the female; the *hindwing* on the underside has a distinct dark median line, and an indistinct submarginal and abbreviated basal line. The underside is very similar to that of *E. pulchra*, but the *forewing* has two black spots, and the *hindwing* has the markings prominent.

The next group in which the males lack the sexual mark altogether appears to be confined to the Western Himalayas and Central Asia, and is perhaps worthy of generic separation.

Key to the Indian Species of Epinephele.

Second Group.

B. Males with no perceptible brand on the upperside of the forewing.

a. Underside, hindwing brown, with numerous darker striæ and three irregular transverse more or less conspicuous dark lines.

*a*¹. Upperside with the forewing fulvous, narrowly margined with brown; and with no trace of a discal line.

196. E. PULCHELLA, Western Himalayas.

*b*¹. Upperside, forewing fulvous with broader brown margin and narrow indistinct discal line.

197. E. NEOZA, Kashmir.

*c*¹. Upperside, forewing brown, more or less distinctly irrorated with fulvous except on the margins; the fulvous patch when distinct divided by a broad diffused transverse discal line.

198. E. PULCHRA, Western Himalayas.

b. Underside, hindwing ferruginous brown, with yellowish irregularly disposed spots and blotches.

*a*¹. Male with two ocelli on upperside of forewing; underside of hindwing in both sexes with dark interrupted discal line, and with the basal area darker.

199. E. CŒNONYMPHA, Western Himalayas.

*b*¹. Male with upperside unspotted; or with only a single subapical minute indistinct black spot; underside, hindwing with the ground-colour uniform, no submarginal ocelli.

200. E. MAIZA, Kashmir.

*c*¹. Male unknown; female with an incomplete row of submarginal ocelli on the underside of hindwing.

201. E. GOOLMURGA, Kashmir.

196. **Epinephele pulchella,** Felder. (PLATE XV, FIG. 40 ♂, left hand half.)

E. pulchella, Felder, Reise Novara, Lep., vol. iii, p. 490, n. 847, pl. lxix, fig. 16 (1866), *male*; id., Moore, Proc. Zool. Soc. Lond., 1874, p. 566.

HABITAT: Western Himalayas, Spiti, Ladak.

EXPANSE: 1·6 to 1·9 inches.

DESCRIPTION: "MALE: UPPERSIDE brown. *Forewing* with a large discal patch extending to the base, fulvous; a blackish spot near the apex. *Hindwing* unmarked. UNDERSIDE much paler. *Forewing* with the patch of the upperside but more restricted, deeper coloured, the black spot of the upperside larger, circled with a broad diffuse ochraceous iris, often bearing a white dot; the costal and external margins around the patch irrorated with hoary and variegated with fuscous, a fuscous streak often composed of dentate lunules defining the outer edge of the patch. *Hindwing* variegated with hoary and covered with fuscous striæ; a basal and a discal streak very flexuous, and a third submarginal, macular, blackish-fuscous, more or less conspicuous. FEMALE. *Forewing* with the patch paler. UPPERSIDE with the blackish subapical spot larger, circled with dilute fulvous; sometimes with another smaller spot between the first and second median branches." (*Felder*, l. c.)

"Differs from *E. neoza*, Lang, in being smaller, in the ferruginous [fulvous?] on the forewing being more distinct in the male, and in the absence of the transverse discal sinuous brown line on the forewing." (*Moore*, l. c.)

The localities given for this species by Dr. Felder are Spiti; Losar, Dishungdeo, Kibber, Shalkar, Rupshu, and Rumbog in Ladak; Karnag; Niri Sumdo, 15,000 feet; Padam; Abrang; and Marsmag. Mr. de Nicéville took a large series of males and a single female at Dras and Tashgam in Ladak in June; and according to Moore, Captain Hellard took it in Kashmir, and Major J. Biddulph took a male specimen at Astor at 7,700 feet altitude in September. It appears to affect higher elevations and to occur further in the interior than *E. neoza* does.

The left hand half of the figure shews the upperside of a male in Mr. de Nicéville's collection from Dras, Ladak. The other half of the figure refers to *E. pulchra*, male, not *E. pulchella*, female, as erroneously entered on the plate.

197. **Epinephele neoza,** Lang.

Epinephile neoza, Lang, Ent. Month. Mag., vol. v, p. 35 (1868).

HABITAT: Western Himalayas.

EXPANSE: 1·6 inches (*Lang*); 1·85 actual measurement of the female type specimen.

DESCRIPTION: "MALE: UPPERSIDE greyish-brown. *Forewing* with the discal portion broadly suffused with a satiny brownish-ferruginous; a single apical black spot. UNDERSIDE: *Forewing* with markings as above; but the disc is brightly ferruginous and separated from the grey-brown exterior margin by a narrow, sinuous, darker line; and the apical spot has a minute white pupil and diffused yellowish iris. A transverse, fine, scarcely distinct ferruginous line, strongly angulated outwards below the ocellus, crosses the wing beyond the middle. *Hindwing* greyish-brown, minutely striated and freckled, with three transverse, sinuous and dentated lines darker; the first basal, the second discal, the third simulating a submarginal series of connected lunules. FEMALE: Markings generally as in the male; but the disc of *forewing* on upperside brightly ferruginous, the apical spot larger, and with an indistinct paler ferruginous iris. On the *hindwing* the submarginal lunular line of the underside appears very indistinctly (or not at all) on the upperside." (*Lang*, l. c.)

The type female specimen of *E. neoza* in Colonel Lang's collection differs from the Ladak female of *E. pulchella* in Mr. de Nicéville's collection in being larger, the subapical spot is also larger, the fulvous patch slightly darker, and the outer brown margin rather wider. On the underside the discal angulate line on both wings is rather more distinct in *E. neoza*.

198. **Epinephele pulchra,** Felder. (PLATE XV, FIG. 40 ♂, right hand half.)

E. pulchra, Felder, Reise Novara, Lep., vol. iii, p. 491, n. 848 (1866).

HABITAT: Western Himalayas.

EXPANSE: 1·6 to 2·0 inches.

DESCRIPTION: "MALE. UPPERSIDE as in *E. pulchella*, but the *forewing* with the fulvous patch less bright, divided by the fulvous [fuscous?] nervures, and cut through beyond the middle by an obsolete fuscous angulate streak, within which it is irrorated with fuscous; the margin of the ground-colour beyond wider than in *E. pulchella*, the blackish spot larger; the *hindwing* irrorated with fulvous on the disc. UNDERSIDE as in *E. pulchella*, but the patch of the forewing more restricted and brighter fulvous, divided beyond the middle by the streak of the upperside, but obscure ferruginous and more distinct and the ocellus larger." (*Felder*, l. c.) FEMALE: UPPERSIDE as in the male, but the *forewing* with the fulvous patch brighter, the subapical spot larger, its iris more distinct, and the fuscous angulate discal streak more prominent.

E. pulchra seems to be even more closely allied to *E. neoza* than to *E. pulchella*; typically it is a much darker insect both on the upper and undersides. On the UPPERSIDE the fulvous patch is in some specimens almost altogether obsolete, and in these there is little or no trace of the dark discal line; in others, where the fulvous patch is more prominent, the transverse discal line is prominent also, and the brown margin is wider; but the patch is never so large, so continuous, or so pale as in *E. neoza;* on the underside the markings appear to be identical, but *E. pulchra* is much the darker.

Dr. Felder gives Kunawar; Pangi, Bisahir, and Chini for this species. Mr. de Nicéville took several males at Dras and Tashgam, Ladak, in June; Mr. R. Ellis took it in Pangi in July; Mrs. Bazett took it in Kashmir at Baba Marishi, at 8,400 feet elevation in June, at Katabal at 10,000 feet, and at Goolmurg at 9,400 feet, in July. Major J. Biddulph took a pair, male and female, on the Shandur plateau in northern Kashmir; the female having on the forewing a second black spot placed on the lower median interspace, both spots prominently circled with pale ochraceous, the irides coalescing. Mr. A. Graham Young has sent a single female from the Kulu Valley.

The right hand half of the figure shews the upperside of a male in Mr. de Nicéville's collection from Dras, Ladak, and is not that of a female of *E. pulchella,* as erroneously given on the plate. The other half is correctly named *E. pulchella,* male.

Erschoff in his Lep. Turkestan describes and figures as *E. amardæa,* var. *naubidensis,* a species which seems clearly to belong to this group, and to be closely alied to *E. pulchra.* His description is as follows: "MALE: UPPERSIDE without ocelli. UNDERSIDE: *Hindwing* unicolorous grey, median fascia almost wanting." The figure shows a very small male insect 1 4 inches in expanse, with no sexual brand on the forewing. The UPPERSIDE of *both wings* brown, darkest at the outer margin; the *cilia* paler. UNDERSIDE: *Forewing* fulvous, the outer margin broadly pale brown, with two dark submarginal lines, a subapical small ocellus, and a smaller submedian black spot below; the *hindwing* uniform pale brown, with indistinct dark striæ; and indistinct, but somewhat regular, subbasal, median and marginal dark lines. It is most like *E. pulchra* but smaller, with no trace of the fulvous patch on the upperside, and with two black spots on the underside, and none on the upperside in the forewing. In his paper on the Lepidoptera of Kuldja and the neighbouring mountains (Hor. Soc. Ent. Ross., vol. xvi, p. 425 (1881), Alphéraky also records a species belonging to this group with the following remarks: "*Epinephele* species? Some males of a species probably new, which have also been taken in the Altai by Haberhauer. Dr. Staudinger had determined them as *E. pulchella,* Felder, and truly it is a species closely allied to this latter to judge from the underside especially. I have since received from Dr. Staudinger a male under the name of *E. naubidensis,* Erschoff, which does not appear to me to be distinct from the doubtful *E. pulchella* from the Altai." All these remarks appear to us to apply to one and the same species, which is nearest to *E. pulchra,* not *E. pulchella,* but closely allied to both, and which should stand as *E. naubidensis,* Erschoff.

199. **Epinephele cœnonympha,** Felder.

E. cœnonympha, Felder, Reise Novara, Lep, vol. iii, p. 492, n. 850, pl. lxix, figs. 14, 15 (1866), *female.*

HABITAT: Suroo, Ladak; Western Himalayas.

EXPANSE: ♀, 1·65 inches.

DESCRIPTION: "MALE: UPPERSIDE fuscous, with the forewing below and the hindwing above the internal nervure obscurely and shiningly hoary, [this is not quite clear, and there is no trace of it in the figures which accompany the description]. *Forewing* with an ocellus between the discoidal nervules, and another between the first median nervules, blackish-fuscous, blind, incomplete. UNDERSIDE hoary-fuscous, paler in the exterior region, with a very obsolete submarginal line. *Forewing* with a large fulvous discal patch, ill-defined, divided by a fuscous disco-cellular streak, and a most indistinct small fuscous fascia beyond the cell; the ocelli of the upperside blacker, the upper one with an indistinct ochraceous iris. *Hindwing* densely irrorated with blackish at the base, with a large fulvous patch on the upper base, with a smaller one above coalescing with it, circled with fuscous [the fuscous cincture is not shown in the figure]; the basal region darker, defined by an interrupted flexuous fuscous streak, and margined externally by seven unequal spots, the larger median one excepted, fulvescent, contiguous; with a minute posterior ocellus, obsolete, broadly circled with ochraceous. FEMALE: UPPERSIDE as in the male. *Forewing* beyond the cell shaded with darker, with two blind black ocelli, but broadly circled with ochraceous, (especially the upper smaller one). *Hindwing* showing the markings of the underside. UNDERSIDE as in the male, but darker. *Forewing* with the ocelli larger, more distinct, and with minute white pupils. *Hindwing* with two blind, whitish, subanal spots." (*Felder*, l. c.)

We have never seen *E. cænonympha*, and the type specimens collected by Dr. Stoliczka are apparently unique. It is closely allied to both *E. maiza* and *E. goolmurga*, and approaches the latter most closely by the presence of a subanal ocellus on the underside of the hindwing: the colour is much darker in the figure of the female than that of the females of *E. maiza* and *E. goolmurga* which we have seen, but not darker than fresh males of *E. maiza*. The principal points of distinction appear to be that in *E. cænonympha* the male has two ocelli on the UPPERSIDE of the forewing; and on the UNDERSIDE the fulvous patch on the forewing occupies the entire wing, excepting the narrow brownish margins, and no trace of the discal streak is shown in the figure; whereas this streak is very prominent in *E. maiza*; and on the hindwing the basal area is much darker than the outer area, and edged with an interrupted dark brown lunular line, and the yellowish spots beyond appear to coalesce; whereas in *E. maiza* the colour of the hindwing is uniform, the dark line is absent, and the yellowish spots are well separated; but all these characters are variable, and it is possible that further research will show that *E. maiza* is really inseparable from *E. cænonympha*.

200. **Epinephele maiza**, Lang. (PLATE XV, FIG. 41 ♀).

Epinephile maiza, Lang, Ent. Month, Mag., vol. v, p. 36 (1868); id., Moore, Proc. Zool. Soc. Lond., 1874, p. 265, pl. xliii, fig. 6, *male*.

HABITAT: Goolmurg and Pir Pinjal, Kashmir.

EXPANSE: 1·5 to 1·6 inches.

DESCRIPTION: "MALE: UPPERSIDE dark brown. *Forewing* with a small, scarcely perceptible ocellus [this ocellus is often entirely absent, the upperside being uniform unspotted brown]. *Underside* ferruginous brown. *Forewing* with the discal portion clear ferruginous, traversed by the dark nervures, and crossed by an angular discal band; a small subapical ocellus, distinct, iris yellow, white-pupilled. *Hindwing* with a small subbasal ferruginous patch, and an irregular transverse discal series of yellowish spots." (*Moore*, l. c.) "FEMALE: UPPERSIDE as in *E. goolmurga*, Lang, but with the irides of the ocelli much smaller and darker. UNDERSIDE generally as in *E. goolmurga*; but in the *forewing* the greyish-brown borders and the transverse discal line are much broader and darker. In the *hindwing* the colour is clear, unclouded brown; the basal ferruginous patch is larger, the discal series of cuneiform spots is incomplete and indistinct, formed of smaller, darker spots, and the four submarginal ocelli are entirely wanting. The *forewing* is slightly broader, and has a more rounded apex and more convex exterior margin than in *E. goolmurga*."

"Were this insect and *E. goolmurga* male and female, they would be indubitably set down as sexes of one species, but both appear to be females; these may, however, pertain to one species, which is variable, and of which a larger series must be obtained before its character can be correctly defined." (*Lang*, l. c.)

The FEMALE only appears to differ from the male so far as markings are concerned in having on the *forewing* two blind ocelli on the upperside, and two ocelli with minute white pupils on the underside.

Two specimens of the male from the Pir Pinjal, Kashmir, differ only from a female from the same locality on the upperside of the forewing having but one minute black subapical spot very faintly surrounded with ferruginous, and on the underside in having only one subapical ocellus on the forewing, which is rather smaller than in the female. A large series of the males collected by Mrs. Bazett, at Goolmurg, in July at from 9,000 to 10,000 feet elevation, have no trace of the black subapical spot on the upperside, being of an uniform unspotted dark brown throughout. *E. maiza* appears to be common at Goolmurg, but with the exception of the three specimens from the Pir Punjal in the Indian Museum we have seen it from no other locality.

The figure is taken from the female specimen from the Pir Pinjal, and shows both upper and undersides.

201. **Epinephele goolmurga**, Lang.

Epinephile goolmurga, Lang, Ent. Month. Mag., vol. v, p. 36 (1868).

HABITAT: Goolmurg, Kashmir.

EXPANSE: 1·6 inches.

DESCRIPTION: "FEMALE: UPPERSIDE dark brown. *Forewing* with two rather large black spots, broadly encircled with pale ferruginous; one subapical, the other near posterior angle. UNDERSIDE greyish-brown. *Forewing* with discal portion ferruginous; ocelli as above, but with irides smaller, and with minute white pupils; an indistinct streak closing the cell, and beyond it a transverse discal line, angulated externally beyond the ocelli. *Hindwing* irregularly and indistinctly tinted with fuscous, ferruginous, greenish and glaucous; but a large, medial, ferruginous patch near base; a curved discal series of seven irregular cuneiform spots, pale yellowish ferruginous, and an incomplete submarginal series of small ocelli, black with yellowish irides; two below apical and two above anal, angle. HEAD, thorax, abdomen, palpi and antennæ, brown; eyes ferruginous." (*Lang*, l. c.)

The MALE is unknown. *E. goolmurga* is evidently very closely allied to the preceding species, *E. maiza*, but the type specimen which, so far as we know, is unique, differs from the female of *E. maiza* to an extent which warrants its being kept distinct till more specimens are obtained; the differences are detailed in the description of *E. maiza*, female, which precedes. The type specimen was taken by Dr. Jerdon at Goolmurg at 9,000 feet elevation.

Genus 20.—YPTHIMA, Hübner. (PLATE XVII.)

Ypthima, Hübner, Verz. bek. Schmett., p. 63 (1816); id., Westwood, Gen. D. L., p. 394 (1851); *Yphthima*, Hewitson, Trans. Ent. Soc. Lond., third series, vol. ii, p. 283 (1864), *Monograph*.

"BODY small; wings rather large, entire, uniformly and plainly coloured; the forewing generally with a large ocellus near the apex. HEAD small, clothed with long hairs in front. *Eyes* prominent, naked. *Antennæ* not half the length of the forewing, very slender, ringed with white; terminated by a very slender club, gradually formed, with the joints short, and finely carinated beneath on the innerside. *Palpi* rather long, slender, acute at the tip, porrected obliquely, straight, compressed; the tip elevated to the level of the top of the eyes, and extending forward further than the length of the head; clothed beneath with long, straight, divergent, slender, bristly hairs; the terminal joint being but slightly hairy. *Thorax* small, clothed in front with woolly hairs. *Abdomen* elongated, slender, rather thickened at the tip in the *males*. FOREWING large, elongated, triangularly-ovate; costal margin well arched; apex rounded; outer margin entire, convex, about two-thirds of the length of the costal margin; inner margin nearly straight, three-fourths of the length of the costal one. *Costal* nervure strongly swollen at the base. *Subcostal* nervure with its first branch arising just before the anterior extremity of the cell; the second, third, and fourth branches arising at equal distances apart; the second at a considerable distance beyond the cell. *Upper disco-cellular* nervule nearly obsolete, arising at about half the length of the wing. *Middle disco-cellular* curved towards the base of the wing. *Lower disco-cellular* much longer, nearly continuous with the middle one, and united to the third branch of the median nervure at a short distance beyond its origin. *Median* nervure moderately [sometimes greatly] swollen at the base. *Submedian* nervure simple.

HINDWING triangularly ovate; costal margin rounded, as well as the outer margin, which is entire; inner margin slightly emarginate towards the extremity. *Costal* nervure extending to about two-thirds of the length of the costa. *Subcostal* nervure arising just opposite to the præcostal one; its branch arising at a considerable distance from the base. *Upper disco-cellular* arising at a short distance from the origin of the branch, oblique, slightly curved. *Lower disco-cellular* longer, also oblique, and very slightly curved; uniting with the third branch of the median nervure at a little distance beyond its base. FORELEGS of the MALE extremely minute, hairy, concealed among the hairs of the breast. *Coxa* long; remainder forming a very small oval articulated mass, much shorter than the coxa. *Forelegs* of the FEMALE small, but quite distinct, several times longer than those of the male, scaly, destitute of long hairs; the *tibia* shorter than the femur. *Tarsus* about equal in length to the tibia, rather widened to the tip, articulated; the tips of the joints beneath furnished with short spines. *Claws* wanting. *Four hindlegs* scaly, moderately elongate and slender; the *femur* moderately clothed beneath with hairs; *tibiæ* scaly, scarcely spined beneath; *tibial spurs* long; *tarsi* with longer spines on the sides beneath. *Claws* strong, curved, entire. *Paronychia* minute." (*Westwood*, l. c.)

Ypthima, or as it is sometimes spelt *Hyphthima*, *Yphthima*, and *Ipthima* is chiefly an Indian genus. Of the (about) forty species known, no less than twenty-six are found within our limits, but it has a peculiar distribution. Of the Indian species, eight are found in the Western Himalayas, one of which extends to the Eastern Himalayas, and another is found all over India in plains and hills, in suitable localities; one is found in Beluchistan; nine are found in the Eastern Himalayas and Khasi hills; three are found in the plains of North-east India; six are found in Burma; six are found in Central India; six at least are found in South India, of which three appear to be confined to particular ranges of hills; and three are found in Ceylon; but from the Andamans and Nicobars none have been recorded. Beyond our limits a few species are found in Africa, one in Madagascar, a few in the Malay Archipelago and Australia, and others in Japan and China extending to Amoorland.

The species of *Ypthima* are for the most part small insects, none reaching 2·5 inches in expanse, and some of them are among the smallest of the *Rhopalocera*, the *Lycænidæ* and *Hesperiidæ* alone excepted. They are for the most part brown insects with ocelli on both sides of the wings, the underside being almost always finely reticulated with brown undulations on a paler ground; they have almost invariably a bipupilled ocellus on each side of the forewing, and from three to seven ocelli on the underside of the hindwing; but occasionally the ocelli on this wing are entirely wanting; on the upperside of the hindwing they are very variable even in the same species. In habits they are very similar to *Erebia* and *Callerebia*, occurring almost everywhere both in the hills and plains where there is grass, amongst which they take short weak flights, and continually settle; but they differ in distribution, the two latter being palæarctic forms, and only occurring within our limits in the Himalayas and outlying ranges. They may be distinguished from *Callerebia* by their usually much paler colouration, the prominence of their ocelli and of the undulations of the underside. Structurally they differ in the arrangement of the subcostal nervules of the forewing, having the first branch close to the end of the cell, the other three at equal distances beyond, while in all the other genera of this subfamily, except *Ragadia*, the first and second subcostal nervules both originate before the end of the cell; the median nervure of the forewing is usually only slightly swollen at the base, showing an approach in this feature to *Callerebia*, which feature is particularly noticeable in *Y. nikæa* which occurs on the same ground as the *Callerebias*; in only one species, *Y. bolanica*, is the median nervure highly dilated at the base.

The genus is, as in the case of *Epinephele*, *Amecera* and others, divisible into two groups, one of which has, and the other has not, a patch of densely packed scales on the forewing of the male insect. There has been considerable difficulty in identifying the species of *Ypthima* owing to this fact not having hitherto attracted attention, and to the meagre nature of the original descriptions which based the characters in many instances on the numbers of the ocelli—a very inconstant feature, or on comparison with other species to which they were erroneously supposed to be allied. But though the *number* of the ocelli is an unsafe guide, the *arrangement* of them is distinct in all the various minor groups, and affords at once a clue to the affinities, due regard being always had to the fact that the disappearance of one or more, or the appearance of an additional one may frequently be looked for, it will be found that the incomplete or inflated series always gives sufficient trace of the original arrangement to make the identification easy. The ocelli of the upperside of the hindwing are too variable in many species to afford any guide whatever, while in others they seem fairly constant. The arrangement of the ocelli of the underside of the hindwing is given special prominence in the key.

Key to the Indian species of Ypthima.

First group.

A. Males with a broad patch of more densely packed scales on the upperside of the forewing along both sides of the median nervure with a somewhat silky appearance.

a. UNDERSIDE of the hindwing with three ocelli, placed one near apex, and two near anal angle.

202. Y. MOTSCHULSKII, Khasi hills.

b. UNDERSIDE of the hindwing with six ocelli (very rarely seven).

a[1]. These ocelli placed in pairs in echelon, sometimes prominent, sometimes reduced to minute dots. The striation distinct.

a[2]. Underside with only an indistinct median fascia.

203. Y. METHORA, North India (?), Yunan.

Y. NEWBOLDI, Malacca.

b[2]. Underside with subbasal, median, and submarginal fasciæ more or less distinct.

204. Y. PHILOMELA, India, Himalayas, Burma.

205 Y. MARSHALLII Tennasserim.

b[1]. These ocelli reduced to minute dots, often entirely wanting, but when visible arranged as in *Y. philomela;* the striation indistinct; the fasciæ clouded and often tinged with ochreous.

206. Y. INDECORA, Western Himalayas.

c[1]. These ocelli placed, two near apex, and four in linear order from anal angle, the lower pair often geminated; the striation distinct.

a[2]. Upperside with two subanal ocelli on the hindwing.

207. Y. AVANTA, Western Himalayas, Tenasserim.

b[2]. Upperside with three subanal ocelli on the hindwing.

208. Y. ORDINATA, Bengal.

Of this group *Y. philomela* is the most widely spread as well as the most variable species in the genus, and is the only one that occurs in South India. *Y. motschulskii* is very similar in appearance to *Y. nareda* and its allies in the second group, the ocelli in these appear to be remarkably constant. *Y. avanta* and *Y. ordinata* most nearly resemble *Y. singala* and *Y. thora;* and the nearest approach to *Y. indecora* in the second group appears to be in *Y. inica.*

202. Ypthima motschulskii, Bremer, Grey.

Satyrus motschulskyi, Bremer, Grey, Beitr. zur Schmett.-fauna nördl. china's, p. 8, n. 26 (1853); *S. motschulskiji*, Ménétriés, Enum. Corp Anim, pt i, p. 47, n. 782, pl. vi, fig. 5 (1855); *Yphthima motschulskiji*, Hewitson, Trans. Ent. Soc Lond, third series, vol ii, p. 290, n. 17 (1864).

HABITAT: North India, Khasi Hills, China.

EXPANSE: 1·55 to 2·00 inches.

DESCRIPTION: "UPPERSIDE fuscous; each wing with a single ocellus. UNDERSIDE cineraceous, densely undulated with rufous. *Hindwing* with three ocelli."

"Very near to *Y. pandocus*, but differs from it on the upperside in having the iris of the *forewing* slightly divided; and in having one ocellus only on the *hindwing*. UNDERSIDE undulated throughout, and with the apical ocellus of the *hindwing* larger, and bears a great resemblance to *Y. nareda* except in colour." (*Hewitson*, l.c.)

There is a species of *Ypthima* which occurs in Shillong, and which we for the present identify under this name; chiefly because a variety of *Y. motschulskii* from North India is mentioned by Mr. Butler in the Catalogue of the *Satyridæ* in the British Museum (p. 148); it is at once distinguished from all other species having only three ocelli on the underside of the hindwing, by the presence of a sexual brand on the *forewing* of the male placed along either side of the median nervure, which though concolorous with the rest of the wing, is easily seen on holding up the insect against the light, owing to the much greater density of the clothing of scales; the UPPERSIDE is more uniform in colour than in *Y. nareda* and its allies, with no trace of a dark submarginal line, and the colour is more fuliginous. On the UNDERSIDE too the colour is quite uniform rufous brown, covered throughout very finely and densely with cinerascent-ochreous striæ, with no bands or patches of any kind free from striation; the ocelli are as in *Y. nareda*, but rather smaller. The *forewing* is more triangular and the outer margin less convex than in *Y. nareda*.

Typical *Y. motschulskii*, as figured by Ménétriés from Pekin, has the underside clouded with whitish, especially on the *hindwing* as in *Y. pandocus*, but it, as well as the Indian variety here described, differs from *Y. pandocus* in having only a single ocellus on the upperside of the *hindwing*, and further in having the ocellus on the upperside of the *forewing* geminated rather than bipupilled. The Indian specimens measure 1·55 inches in expanse.

We have only as yet received specimens from Shillong, where it has been taken by Dr. E. R. Johnson in March, April, May and July, who writes that "it flies faster than *Y. newara*, frequents more open spaces, and is rather uncommon;" the FEMALE flies in May, and is somewhat larger, paler, and on the UPPERSIDE with traces of the whitish striation so conspicuous in *Y. newara*; on the underside it is equally uniform in colour and striation as the male, but the striation is coarser and the ocelli are larger.

203. **Ypthima methora**, Hewitson.

Yphthima methora, Hewitson, Trans. Ent. Soc. Lond., third series, vol. ii, p. 291, n. 19, pl. xviii, figs 20, 21 (1864), *female*.

HABITAT: North India, Upper Burma.

EXPANSE: 2 inches.

DESCRIPTION: "FEMALE: UPPERSIDE brown, undulated with grey towards the outer margins; the outer margins and *cilia* rufous-brown, traversed by a grey line. *Forewing* with one very large two-pupilled ocellus on both sides. *Hindwing* with five ocelli, all black, with pupils dull silver, with irides rufous, narrow. UNDERSIDE grey, closely undulated throughout with rufous-brown. *Both wings* crossed at the middle by a curved rufous band. *Hindwing* with six ocelli in pairs; the pupils of bright silver; the irides orange-yellow. Nearest to *Y. sakra*, but of very different aspect." (*Hewitson*, l. c.)

The only distinctive feature in the above description is the single curved rufous band crossing both wings on the underside. There are three males in the Indian Museum, Calcutta, taken by the Yunan Expedition which, allowing for the difference in sex, correspond well with Hewitson's figure of this species. They are over two inches in expanse (2·1 to 2·2), and are distinct from *Y. philomela*, aberrant specimens of which sometimes equal them in size; but they belong to the same group, and have a distinct sexual mark on the *forewing*. They are more rufous in tone than *Y. philomela*; the striation of the underside is much more uniform and bolder; and the subbasal fascia is entirely absent, the submarginal scarcely traceable, and the median one alone distinct, but even that not so distinct as in *Y. philomela*.

Further, although Hewitson in his original description describes the ocelli of the upperside of the *hindwing* as pupilled with dull silver, in his figure, and also in all the three specimens in the Indian Museum, they are entirely blind, though large and prominent, and this seems in reality the most striking feature of the species.

An apparently allied species, of which the female alone is known, has been described from the Malay peninsula.*

204. **Ypthima philomela,** Johanssen.

Papilio philomela, Johanssen, Amœn. Acad., vol. vi, p. 404, n. 60 (1764); *Papilio philomelus*, Linnæus, Syst Nat., vol. i, pt. ii, p. 768, n. 123 (1767); *Papilio baldus*, Fabricius, Syst. Ent., Appendix, p. 829 (1775); id., Donovan's Ins. Ind., pl. xxxvi, fig. 2 (1800); *Satyrus baldus*, Godart, Enc. Méth., vol. ix, p. 551, n. 184 (1819); *Yphthima baldus*, Hewitson, Trans. Ent. Soc. Lond., third series, vol. ii, p. 286, n. 9 (1864); *Papilio lara*, Donovan (*nec.* Linnæus), Nat. Rep., vol. ii, pl. lxxi (1834); *Ypthima laroides*, Westwood, Gen. D. L., vol. ii, p. 395, n. 6 (1851).

HABITAT: India, Burma, Java, Sumatra, China.

EXPANSE: 1·35 to 2·30 inches; usually about 1·6 inches.

DESCRIPTION: MALE: UPPERSIDE brown. *Forewing* with one bipupilled ocellus. A broad streak of darker scales extending widely on both sides of the median nervure. *Hindwing* with from two to six ocelli. UNDERSIDE whitish, undulated throughout with brown, with three brown fasciæ, one submarginal, one discal and one subbasal, the latter sometimes indistinct. *Forewing* with one bipupilled ocellus. *Hindwing* with six placed in pairs in echelon. FEMALE: UPPERSIDE paler, with a broad submarginal nebulous band of whitish striæ on which the ocelli are placed, and which is defined inwardly and outwardly with a dark line, otherwise marked as in the male; the male also has traces of this nebulous band, but it is far less distinct.

Y. philomela has a very wide range, and is perhaps the most variable species of the genus; it has not been recorded from Ceylon, but it is found not uncommonly in the Ashamboo hills in Travancore in the extreme south of the peninsula, and through the Wynaad along the Western Ghâts as far as Khandalla; we have no certain record of its occurrence on the east coast or in the Deccan, though it probably will be found in suitable localities throughout the peninsula and Central India; we have specimens from Manbhoom and Orissa, and in Lower Bengal, Eastern Bengal, and Assam it is one of the commonest species. In the Himalayas also it is found as far west as Chumba, and probably throughout the range eastward; in Sikkim it is not uncommon; it is found in the Khasi and Naga hills, Cachar, and in Arakan, Pegu and Tenasserim, and extends to Java. Mr. Distant does not mention it in his "Rhopalocera Malayana," but he appears to have figured and described it under the name *Y. methora* (p. 56, pl. vi, fig. 9, 1882).

The ocelli of the UNDERSIDE of the *hindwing* vary greatly in size and prominence, being sometimes almost entirely obsolete; when large each pair is coalescent, when small, all are well separated, but wherever they can be discerned the arrangement in pairs in echelon is distinct; occasionally a seventh minute ocellus appears below the lower discoidal nervule. On the UPPERSIDE of the *hindwing* the pair of ocelli on the median interspaces is always present (except in a single specimen from Tenasserim in which the upper one is wanting) and prominent, the upper and lower pairs are extremely variable, in some all four are present, and in these cases the ocellation of the upperside corresponds in arrangement with that of the underside; in others almost every variation is presented, every combination from two to six ocelli being represented. On the upperside of one *forewing* only in a female specimen from

---

* *Ypthima newboldi*, Distant. HABITAT: Province Wellesley. EXPANSE: *female*, 1·65 inches DESCRIPTION: "UPPERSIDE pale brown. *Forewing* with a large subovate paler fascia, placed transversely on apical half, and on which is a large black ocellated spot, with a yellow margin and with two small bluish talc-like eyes; this spot is placed a little beyond end of cell, its upper margin extending a little above first discoidal nervule, and its lower margin reaching the second median nervule. *Hindwing* with a broad pale submarginal fascia, on which are three ocellated black spots, with yellow margins and bluish talc-like eyes, the first and smallest of which is placed between second subcostal and discoidal nervules, and the other two, which are largest and placed close together, are situated nearer to the posterior margin, and between the median nervules. UNDERSIDE pale greyish, mottled with brown; ocellated spots as above, but *hindwing* having two additional smaller ones placed close together near anal angle, between third median nervule and submedian nervure and the small spot, as seen above, much larger beneath. Allied to *Y. methora*, Hewitson, but differs in having five instead of six ocellated spots on the underside of the *hindwing*, which have also a different and more unicolorous hue." (*Distant*, Ann and Mag Nat. Hist., fifth series vol. ix, p. 396 (1882), l. c.; idem, id., Rhop. Malay, p. 57, n. 3, pl. iv, fig. 6 (1882), *female*.)

Shillong, but on both wings on the underside; and in another female from Calcutta, on both wings on both sides, there is a small ocellus in the first median interspace.

Specimens from the Western Himalayas are the smallest and darkest, usually only the median pair of ocelli is present on the UPPERSIDE, which in them closely resembles that of *Y. indecora;* occasionally one of the upper pair is present, making three in all, and sometimes one of the lower pair appears; on the UNDERSIDE the ocelli are usually prominent, large, each pair coalescing; the striation is darker and the subbasal fascia is indistinct. Specimens from Sikkim are usually rather larger and paler; the UPPERSIDE shows greater variation in the ocellation; sometimes the upper pair is present and the lower entirely wanting; sometimes the lower pair is present and the upper wanting. In the plains of Lower and Eastern Bengal, Sylhet and Assam the colouration is paler still; all six ocelli are frequently present on the UPPERSIDE of the *hindwing*, especially in the females, but the most common form has five ocelli, the uppermost of the upper pair alone being obsolete; on the UNDERSIDE the ocelli are smaller, distinct, and all well separated; frequently they are minute and in some barely traceable. In our specimens from Shillong this feature is most developed; in scarcely a single specimen of the spring brood are the ocelli prominent, and in many they are for the most part obsolete on the underside, while on the upperside they are darker and usually with only the median pair of ocelli present on the hindwing; these latter are almost indistinguishable from *Y. indecora;* the July brood closely resembles specimens from Sikkim. These two distinct variations are also shewn in specimens taken by Dr. Anderson in the Mergui archipelago during the cold weather. Specimens from the Western Ghâts and hills of South India are intermediate between the Sikkim and Shillong forms; the ocelli are usually small or minute but distinct; specimens from Akyab correspond with those from Sikkim; but in Tenasserim the greatest variation is found in depth of colouration, in ocellation, and above all in size. A MALE from the Meplay valley measures two inches in expanse; the upperside is silky mouse-brown, the nebulous band distinct on the hindwing, barely discernible on the forewing, the apical pair of ocelli are prominent on the hindwing, while the subanal pair is represented by a single minute blind ocellus; the underside is very pale buff, the striation is pale and fine, and the fasciæ are prominent and dark, especially on the forewing; the ocelli of the hindwing are distinct but minute and well separated; and a FEMALE from the lower Thoungyeen forests is dark brown, the nebulous fasciæ prominent on both wings, the median pair of ocelli on the hindwing very large and prominent, with a single apical and a single subanal ocellus small and less distinct; on the UNDERSIDE the striation is bold and dark, the fasciæ prominent, the ocelli of the hindwing very large, each pair with the irides completely coalesced and encircled by a single dark outer line, the subanal pair being geminated.

Y. philomela is found in the Western Himalayas in July; in Sikkim from July to December; in Shillong in March, April and May, and again in July; in Lower and Eastern Bengal it is very common from May to July, and again in November, and probably throughout the year; in Cachar Mr. Wood-Mason took it in profusion from April to October; from Arakan, Pegu, Tenasserim, and the Mergui archipelago, we have specimens taken in all months from October to March; specimens from Khandalla and the Coessi Ghât in the South Konkan were taken by Mr. G. Vidal at the end of March; and from Travancore by Mr. Harold Fergusson at 2,000 feet elevation in March and April.

205. **Ypthima marshallii**, Butler.

Y. marshallii, Butler, Ann. and Mag. of Nat. Hist., fifth series, vol. x, p. 373 (1882).

HABITAT: Upper Tenasserim.

EXPANSE: 1·65 inches.

DESCRIPTION: "UPPERSIDE brownish grey; basal area more dusky than the external area. *Forewing* with a large oval subapical black ocellus, bipupillated with silver, and with dusky-bordered pale straw-coloured iris; an ill-defined submarginal dusky line. *Hindwing* crossed beyond the middle by an oblique subangulated indistinct dusky line; a small blind ocellus on the second subcostal interspace; two large round unipupillate ocelli on the median interspaces, and two minute blind ocelli placed transversely near the anal angle; a wavy dusky submarginal line; base and an abdominal streak dark grey. *Body* blackish. UNDERSIDE whitish stone-brown, finely reticulated with grey; crossed in the middle by two subparallel dusky stripes, those of the forewing more distinct and tinted with yellowish; disc of forewing whiter than the rest of the surface; ocellus as above. *Hindwing* with all the ocelli very minute; an additional punctiform ocellus on first subcostal interspace."

"Allied to *Y. methora;* similar in shape. It appears to be quite constant." (*Butler*, l. c.)

The type specimen, which was taken by Capt. C. T. Bingham at Meplay in the Thoungyeen valley in March, is in the British Museum.

This species is, of course, distinct from *Y. methora*, but we are unable to detect a single character by which it may be separated from *Y. philomela*, specimens of which from the same locality agree with this in every particular, except perhaps the presence of a dark grey abdominal streak, but a dark grey streak on a dusky brownish-grey ground is not easy to trace. No mention is made of the presence or absence of a male sexual streak on the forewing.

206. **Ypthima indecora,** Moore.

Y. indecora, Moore, Proc. Zool. Soc. Lond., 1882, p. 238, pl. xii, fig. 7.

HABITAT: Western Himalayas.

EXPANSE: ♂, 1·25 to 1·50; ♀, 1·37.

DESCRIPTION: "Nearest to *Y. inica*, Hewitson. UPPERSIDE brown. *Forewing* with a darker subbasal oblique shade; a prominent, bipupilled, subapical ocellus. *Hindwing* with two smaller subanal ocelli. UNDERSIDE covered with very slender grey strigæ; two very faint brown fasciæ crossing middle of *both wings*, those on the *hindwing* waved. *Hindwing* with two subapical and three subanal, extremely minute, and indistinct silver-pupilled ocelli." (*Moore*, l. c).

Y. indecora is really most nearly allied to *Y. philomela;* from *Y. inica* it is distinguished by the presence of the sexual streak in the forewing of the male, and by the invariable presence of two subanal ocelli on the upperside of the hindwing, *Y. inica* having no sexual streak, and only a single ocellus on the upperside of the hindwing. From *Y. avanta*, which is found in the same localities in the Western Himalayas, it differs on the upperside in having the ocellus of the forewing large, bipupilled, with distinct yellow iris, and the two on the hindwing each with a single silvery pupil, in these respects corresponding with *Y. ordinata*, and in two specimens that we possess there is a third anal ocellus on the hindwing, making the resemblance to *Y. ordinata* complete; but on the UNDERSIDE it is widely different from both; the ocelli of the *hindwing* when visible are arranged as in *Y. philomela*, but they are always exceedingly minute, and in a large majority of specimens are totally absent; the striation is much less distinct, and the fasciæ are more diffused and tinged with ochreous. In two male specimens on the upperside of the hindwing there is a moderate-sized ocellus above the discoidal nervule. The FEMALE has the *forewing* broader and more rounded at the apex, the ground-colour above and below paler, and on the upperside is decidedly mottled, and lacks the sexual streak of the male on the forewing.

Typical *Y. indecora* appears to be confined to the Western Himalayas, where it has been taken in Pangi, Kulu and Kangra, in April and July. But some varieties of *Y. philomela* in the east and south, in which the subanal ocelli of the upperside of the hindwing are obsolete, and those of the underside minute or obsolescent, approach it very closely indeed, so much so that it is almost impossible to distinguish to which species these varieties belong.

207. **Ypthima avanta,** Moore. (PLATE XVII,* FIG. 66 ♂).

Yphthima avanta, Moore, Proc. Zool. Soc. Lond., 1874, p. 567.

HABITAT: Western Himalayas; (*var.*) Burma.

EXPANSE: 1·25 to 1·50 inches; *var.* 1·70 inches.

---

* Erroneously named *Y. ordinata* on the plate.

DESCRIPTION : "UPPERSIDE dark brown, with an indistinct bipupilled ocellus on the *forewing*, and two subanal ocelli on the *hindwing*. UNDERSIDE grey, numerously covered with dark brown narrow striæ, and crossed with three brown fasciæ, the subbasal one being indistinct. *Forewing* with a bright oval ocellus bipupilled with silver. *Hindwing* with seven small prominent silver-pupilled ocelli, the upper third minute, the two anal geminated." (*Moore*, l. c.)

Y. avanta closely resembles *Y. singala* on the upperside, but has a sexual patch on the forewing of the male, which *Y. singala* lacks. On the underside the ocellation too is somewhat similar, but *Y. singala* almost always lacks the transverse dark fasciæ, which in *Y. avanta* are conspicuous. From *Y. indecora* it differs on the upperside in having the ocelli of the hindwing blind, and that of the forewing small, very indistinct, sometimes quite obsolete ; and on the underside in having the ocelli distinct (though varying in size in different specimens), and always prominently pupilled with silver. From *Y. philomela* it is distinguished by the four lower ocelli on the underside of the hindwing being arranged in linear order, not in pairs in echelon.

The specimen described originally by Mr. Moore with, on the underside of the hindwing, "seven ocelli, the upper third minute," was evidently an aberrant form, for among all the numerous specimens we have seen, the seven ocelli appear in only a single one ; all the rest have the minute upper third ocellus entirely wanting. Similar aberrations occur in *Y. philomela*, in which specimens with seven ocelli are even less uncommon. The FEMALE differs from the male only in having the wings rather broader ; on the UPPERSIDE no sexual patch on the forewing, and the ocellus of the forewing more prominent and distinctly circled with yellow, and on the UNDERSIDE in the single typical specimen we have seen the ocelli are larger with wider yellow irides, the striation is somewhat coarser, and the subbasal fascia is less distinct. The size of the ocelli in the male also differs widely ; in some they are minute with very narrow irides, in others large, with wide yellow irides.

Y. avanta is found in the Western Himalayas from April to August, being common in Kulu and extending to Kashmir on the west, and to Sikkim on the east.

A variety of this species has been taken in Tenasserim by Captain C. T. Bingham, which is considerably larger, 1·7 inches in expanse ; the MALE is on the upperside slightly more fuliginous in colour, and the ocellus of the forewing is represented by a single indistinct dark spot ; on the UNDERSIDE it is slightly paler, and the ocelli of the *hindwing* are very minute. The FEMALE is paler on the UPPERSIDE, with the ocellus of the forewing prominent, bipupilled, and with distinct yellow iris ; and the two on the hindwing each with a single pupil ; there is also on both wings a distinct indication of the broad nebulous submarginal band defined at both edges with darker lines which is so prominent in females of *Y. philomela*. The UNDERSIDE is as in the male, but still paler. The MALE was taken in the lower Thoungyeen forests in May, and the FEMALE in the Donat Range in January.

The figure (named erroneously *Y. ordinata* on the plate) shows the upper and undersides of a male specimen from Kulu, in the Indian Museum, Calcutta. In it the ocellus of the upperside of the forewing is rather more distinct than is usual, and the pupils of the ocelli of the underside of the hindwing, which are silvery and prominent, have unfortunately not come out in the plate ; these ocelli are also larger in this specimen than in typical ones, though we have other examples with the ocelli twice as large.

208. **Ypthima ordinata,** Butler.

Y. ordinata, Butler, Proc. Zool. Soc. Lond., 1880, p. 148, pl. xv, fig. 3.

HABITAT : Bengal.

EXPANSE : 1·4 inches.

DESCRIPTION : "Nearly allied to *Y. lisandra*, rather darker. UPPERSIDE : *Forewing* with the ocellus less widely zoned. *Hindwing* with three ocelli in an oblique decreasing series from third median branch to anal angle. UNDERSIDE decidedly browner, the transverse stripes less prominent. *Hindwing* with six ocelli, forming a regular but interrupted series, two at apical angle, and two on median interspaces of nearly equal size, and two smaller, unequal and confluent at the anal angle; all these ocelli have a single small plumbageous pupil." (*Butler*, l.c.)

The habitat given for *Y. ordinata*, "Bengal," which may mean anything from Kashmir to Orissa, is too vague to afford any clue as to its affinities. In Butler's figure of *Y. ordinata* the underside is indistinguishable from our figure of *Y. avanta*, Plate XVII, fig. 66 (erroneously named *Y. ordinata* on the plate), except that in Butler's figure the cell of the forewing is shorter, the disco-cellulars less oblique and defined by a brown litura; the figure of the upperside has the ocellus of the forewing much more prominent, with distinct yellow iris, and on the hindwing there is a third anal ocellus in a line with the other two.

The ocelli on the underside of the hindwing are prominent, and arranged precisely as in *Y. avanta*, but on the upperside the presence of the third ocellus on the hindwing is the character which apparently should distinguish it. We have a single specimen taken in the Sikkim tarai in July, in which this third ocellus is minutely present, and which should be *Y. ordinata*, but it is indistinguishable from some specimens of *Y. avanta* in which the ocelli of the underside are large.

Key to the Indian species of Ypthima.

Second Group.

B. Males without the patch of densely packed scales along the median nervure on the upperside of the forewing.

a. UNDERSIDE of the hindwing with three ocelli, placed one near the apex, two near the anal angle.

*a*¹. These ocelli large; ground-colour uniform ochreous, densely striated with brown; forewing with the submarginal brown fascia wide at inner margin.

209. Y. NAREDA, Western Himalayas.

*b*¹. These ocelli larger and brighter; ground-colour whiter on hindwing; the striation bolder; forewing with the submarginal fascia even throughout.

210. Y. NEWARA, Eastern Himalayas, Khasi Hills, Assam.

*c*¹. These ocelli smaller; ground-colour much clouded with white: striation irregular in density; forewing with submarginal and median fasciæ more or less distinct.

211. Y. PANDOCUS, North India, Burma, Java.

Y. CORTICARIA, Malacca.

*d*¹. These ocelli variable in size, ground-colour uniform whitish; striation uniform; no fasciæ on the hindwing.

212. Y. ARIASPA, Central India, Punjab.

*e*¹. These ocelli usually minute; forewing with the ocellus with a dark outer zone, below which is a rufous space devoid of undulations.

213. Y. ASTEROPE, Western Himalayas, Central India, Bombay.

b. UNDERSIDE of the hindwing with no trace of ocelli.

*a*¹. Hindwing with four irregular clouded interrupted bands on the underside, and only a single ocellus on the upperside.

214. Y. INICA, Central India.

*b*¹. Hindwing distinctly striated on the underside, the striation not uniform in density, but with no fasciæ; no ocelli on the upperside. Forewing with dark outer zone to the ocellus, but the rufous space below undulated.

215. Y. NARASINGHA, Sikkim.

c. UNDERSIDE of the hindwing with four ocelli placed in pairs, two near apex and two near anal angle.

216. Y. HYAGRIVA, Himalayas.

d. UNDERSIDE of the hindwing with four ocelli placed one near apex, and three in a line from the anal angle, the anal one bipupilled or geminated, sometimes divided, making five ocelli altogether.

*a*¹. The three lower ocelli not placed on a complete dark fascia, the anal one bipupilled.

*a*². Both wings brown.

217. Y HUEBNERI, India, Burma, Malayana.

*b*². The lower half of the hindwing pure white.

218. Y. CEYLONICA, Ceylon, Madras, Orissa.

*b*¹. The three lower ocelli placed on a complete dark fascia, the subanal one geminated, sometimes divided, making five ocelli altogether.

*a*². The fasciæ of both wings converging towards the hinder angle.

219. Y. CHENUI, Nilgiris.

*b*². The fasciæ subparallel.

*a*³. Hindwing greyish ; the striation not uniform ; the fasciæ prominent.

220. Y. ROBINSONI, Pulni Hills.

*b*³. Dark brown throughout ; the striation very faint ; the fasciæ indistinct ; irides obsolete.

221. Y. YPHTHIMOIDES, Ashamboo hills.

e UNDERSIDE of the hindwing with four to six ocelli, typically six in pairs, but one or two often obsolete.

*a*¹. These ocelli in linear order, the ground-colour greyish white.

*a*². The fasciæ of the underside very indistinct or obsolete.

*a*³. Upperside with the ocellus of the forewing obsolete; underside with the ocelli well formed and distinct.

222. Y. SINGALA, Ceylon, Central Provinces, North-West Himalayas.

*b*³. Upperside with the ocellus of the forewing prominent ; underside with the ocelli minute on the hindwing.

223. Y. THORA, Ceylon.

*b*². The fasciæ of the underside distinct, prominent, the ocelli all very prominently pupilled with silver.

224. Y. BOLANICA, Beluchistan.

*b*¹. These ocelli in irregular order, the apical and anal pair geminated, the median distinct, the ground-colour ochreous, uniformly and densely striated ; the fasciæ indistinct or wanting.

*a*². The apical pair of ocelli completely coalescing, not divided by a yellow iris.

225. Y. SAKRA, Himalayas, Khasi and Naga hills.

*b*². The apical pair of ocelli geminated but divided by the yellow iris.

226. Y NIKÆA, Western Himalayas.

*c*². Of very small size, otherwise closely resembling *Y. sakra*

227. Y. TABELLA, The Wynaad.

209. **Ypthima nareda,** Kollar. (PLATE XVII, FIG. 63 ♂).

Satyrus nareda, Kollar, in Hügel's Kaschmir, vol. iv, pt. ii, p. 451, n. 12 (1844) ; ***Yphthima nareda***, Hewitson, Trans. Ent. Soc. Lond., third series, vol ii, p. 284, n. 6, pl. xvii, fig 6 (1864), ***male***.

HABITAT : Himalayas.

EXPANSE : 1·45 to 1·70 inches.

DESCRIPTION : " Wings entire. UPPERSIDE fuscous, ***both wings*** with a single black ocellus with yellow iris, bipupilled in the ***forewing***. UNDERSIDE undulated with yellowish ; ***hindwing*** with three ocelli." (***Kollar***, l. c.)

This is the common species of the Western Himalayas. The MALE insect has no sexual patch on the wings ; and the FEMALE only differs by its slightly paler colouration, rather larger ocelli, and broader more rounded wings. On the UPPERSIDE the outer margin is slightly paler than the rest of the wings, and bears an indistinct dark submarginal line, less distinct on the hindwing. On the UNDERSIDE there is a rufous brown submarginal band on the *forewing*, narrow at the apex and wide at the inner margin ; all the rest of the wing being rufous brown, closely and delicately undulated with yellowish striæ ; the ocelli are large, black, with bluish-silver pupils, and yellow iris, bordered with a narrow outer ring of brown ; that on the *forewing* is subapical, oblong, and bipupilled, those on the *hindwing* are rounded, one subapical large, and two subanal smaller, the lower of the two latter the smallest, and sometimes bipupilled. Hewitson remarks that the anal ocellus is bipupilled in the *female*, but his figure of the female belongs to the next species, *Y. newara*, and the bipupillation of the anal ocellus in reality occurs casually in both sexes.

Y. nareda, as here restricted, appears to be found only in the Western Himalayas, being replaced in the East by the next species, *Y. newara*. It occurs at from 6,000 to 8,000 feet elevation in suitable localities throughout the Western Himalayas, and is not uncommon. We have specimens from Kashmir taken in June at 8,200 feet elevation ; from Pangi and Kulu taken in May and July ; and from the neighbourhood of Simla in July ; it also occurs at Mussoorie and probably in Kumaon.

The figure shows the upper and undersides of a male specimen from Kulu in the Indian Museum, Calcutta.

210. **Ypthima newara**, Moore.

Yphthima newara, Moore, Proc. Zool. Soc. Lond., 1874, p. 567 ; *Y. nareda*, Hewitson, Trans. Ent. Soc. Lond., third series, vol. ii, pl. xvii, fig. 7 (1864), *female*.

HABITAT : Nepal, Sikkim, Assam, Cachar, Upper Burma.

EXPANSE : 1·6 to 2·0 inches.

DESCRIPTION : " MALE : UPPERSIDE brown. *Forewing* with a single subapical ocellus. *Hindwing* with two subanal ocelli, the former bipupilled, and the latter with a single pupil of bright blue. UNDERSIDE yellowish grey, partly covered with numerous short brown strigæ ; *both wings* with a narrow submarginal brown fascia. *Forewing* with a single bipupilled ocellus as above. *Hindwing* with three ocelli, the apical one very large, the anal bipupilled, the other one with a single bright blue pupil. FEMALE : UPPERSIDE brown, externally with short pale strigæ, *both wings* with a single ocellus. UNDERSIDE as in the male."

" Differs from *Y. nareda*, Kollar, in being somewhat larger, the female striated above, the ocelli of both sexes much larger on the underside, and the position of the ocellus on the forewing being less inwardly oblique." (*Moore*, l. c.)

Specimens of *Y. newara* from Sikkim are very distinct, but the Nepal race on which the species is founded seems to approximate to *Y. nareda* far more than the Sikkim race does ; and it is not improbable that this may be merely a geographical variety of *Y. nareda* which it replaces in the Eastern Himalayas. The whitish striæ on the UPPERSIDE of the *female* which cover the outer half of both wings form a well-marked character, and on the UNDERSIDE the very large and brightly coloured ocelli in both sexes, and the even character of the brown submarginal band not widening out below the ocellus, as well as the much bolder striation of the rest of the wing serve to distinguish it.

The second subanal ocellus on the upperside of the *hindwing* is not constant in the male, and it more frequently occurs in the female, being a casual not a sexual variation. There is no sexual patch in the male.

We have specimens of *Y. newara* from Nepal ; from Sikkim taken by Messrs. Otto Möller and de Nicéville in October at about 3,000 feet elevation ; from Sibsagar in Upper Assam ; from Shillong in the Khasi Hills taken by Dr. E. R. Johnson in May and July ; from Cachar taken by Mr. Wood-Mason in May and July ; and others brought by the Yunan Expedition.

211. Ypthima pandocus, Moore.

Yphthima pandocus, Moore, Horsfield and Moore, Cat. Lep. E. I. C., vol. i, p. 235, n. 506 (1857); id., Hewitson, Trans. Ent. Soc. Lond., third series, vol. ii, p. 290, n. 16, pl. xviii, fig. 12 (1864); *Ypthima pandocus*, Butler, Cat. Lep. B. M., *Satyridæ*, p. 149, n. 5 (1868).

HABITAT: N. India, Mergui, Java.

EXPANSE: ♂, 1·5; ♀, 1·75 inches.

DESCRIPTION: "Wings fuscous. *Forewing* on both sides with one ocellus. *Hindwing* with two on the upperside. UNDERSIDE whitish, clouded and undulated with rufous. *Hindwing* with three ocelli." (*Hewitson*, l. c.) The original description by Moore, which is appended for reference,* is of little use, as it is given in comparison with a species from China with which it has but little affinity; the description, moreover, is certainly meagre and apparently inaccurate, for no *Ypthima* that we are acquainted with has only two ocelli on the underside of the hindwing, unless it be by accidental or varietal obliteration of one or more; and two of the original specimens of *Y. pandocus* from the East India Museum are now in the India Museum, Calcutta, and have three (not two) ocelli, as correctly described by Hewitson.

The types of *Y. pandocus* are from Java; they have on the upperside a submarginal dark line within which is an obsolete paler band on which the ocelli of both wings are placed. The underside differs from that of all others in this group by having the ground-colour partially whitish, and the density of the striation very irregular, so that large patches of whitish almost free from striation are left, especially on the hindwing; they are over one and a half inches in expanse.

We have seen nothing from North India agreeing altogether with the types, but we have several specimens, among them one from the old East India Museum collection, labelled "India" and named *Y. pandocus*, agreeing fairly well in colour and markings though very much smaller, barely over an inch in expanse. *Y. pandocus* may be distinguished from *Y. asterope*, the only other species with similar ocellation of the hindwing with so small an expanse, by the greater prevalence of whitish on the underside of the hindwing; and by the absence of the outer brown ring to the ocellus on the underside of the forewing. Besides the specimen labelled "India" referred to above, we have others taken at Barrackpore in November, and at Mergui in March.

An allied species or variety from Malacca has been described by Butler under the name of *Y. corticaria*†; it is redescribed and figured by Distant, but we are unable to discover in what way it is supposed to differ from *Y. pandocus*. Distant's remarks (Rhop. Malay., p. 56, 1882) show that the ocelli in this species are variable, which is borne out by the North Indian examples of *Y. pandocus*, and other allied species; the second subanal ocellus on the upperside of the hindwing is often found in *Y. newara* and sometimes in *Y. nareda*.

---

* *Ypthima pandocus*, Moore. DESCRIPTION: "UPPERSIDE as in *Yphthima lysandra*, but with only two ocelli on the *hindwing*, the lower ocellus being at the anal angle and very small. UNDERSIDE with the *hindwing* having only two ocelli" (*Moore*, l. c.)

† *Ypthima corticaria*, Butler, Trans. Linn. Soc. Lond., second series. vol. i, Zoology, p. 537 (1876); idem, id., Distant, Rhop. Malay., p. 55, pl. vi, fig 8 (1882). HABITAT: Malacca. EXPANSE: 1·7 inches. DESCRIPTION: "UPPERSIDE. *Both wings* greyish brown, an inner submarginal streak, and an outer submarginal line, blackish, diffused. *Forewing* with a large subapical oval black ocellus, with two plumbaginous pupils, and a testaceous iris surrounded by a dusky line; a similar smaller unipupillated rounded ocellus near anal angle of *hindwing*. UNDERSIDE: *Both wings* white, densely reticulated with brown, two ill-defined, interrupted, central, subparallel lines; a submarginal streak and line as above. *Forewing* with the ocellus brighter and better defined than above, outer border pale brown, bounded by the inner submarginal streak. *Hindwing* with three ocelli, one at apex (below which is sometimes another extremely small ocellus), and two placed obliquely at anal angle, the lower one small and irregular. Allied to *Y. nareda*." (*Butler*, l.c.)

In his Rhopalocera Malayana, Mr. Distant remarks: "This species also exhibits the inconstancy of ocellated macular markings. In the type specimen described by Butler there was only one spot on the upperside of the *hindwing* near the anal angle, whilst on the underside the duplex one of the specimen here described was single. In another Malaccan specimen in the British Museum there is a fourth very small ocellated spot below the one at apex."

212. Yphthima ariaspa, Moore.

Yphthima ariaspa, Moore, Proc. Zool. Soc. Lond., 1874, p. 568.

HABITAT: Punjab, Central India.

EXPANSE: 1·1 to 1·4 inches.

DESCRIPTION: "MALE: UPPERSIDE dark brown. *Forewing* with a subapical bipupilled ocellus. *Hindwing* with a small subanal ocellus. UNDERSIDE whitish grey, with numerous narrow brown uniform prominent strigæ. *Forewing* with the ocellus as above. *Hindwing* with a single large subapical ocellus, and two smaller ocelli from anal angle."

"This species is similar in appearance to *Y. nareda*; the ocelli of the upperside are smaller, the ground-colour of the underside being much paler, more uniformly covered with strigæ, and without transverse brown fasciæ." (*Moore*, l. c.)

We have only seen *Y. ariaspa* at present from Mhow in Central India, where it was taken by Colonel C. Swinhoe in May, and again in November. It differs from *Y. motschulskii*, the only other species in which the underside is uniformly coloured and striated throughout, by having the underside whitish with brown striæ coarser and prominent, instead of rufous brown with very fine yellowish striæ; and more conspicuously by the male being entirely devoid of the sexual streak of the forewing. The tone of the upperside which is equally uniform is fuscous, not fuliginous. The wings are rounded as in *Y. nareda*, but it is a smaller insect.

A small variety of this species has also been taken by Colonel Swinhoe at Mhow in November; it differs not only in size, but in its generally darker tone. On the underside the ground-colour is rufous-grey, rather than whitish-grey, but with the same uniform prominent brown striæ; the ocelli of the underside are much smaller, minute in two, and scarcely visible in one specimen; and in one specimen the ocellus on the upperside of the hindwing is altogether absent.

213. Ypthima asterope, Klüg.

Hipparchia asterope, Klüg, Symb. Phys., pl. xxix, figs 11—14 (1832); *Yphthima asterope*, Hewitson, Trans Ent. Soc. Lond., third series, vol. ii, p. 283, n. 1 (1864).

HABITAT: India, Java, China, Syria, Africa.

EXPANSE: 1·25 to 1·50 inches.

DESCRIPTION: UPPERSIDE: "Wings fuscous. *Forewing* with a single ocellus. UNDERSIDE cineraceous, undulated with rufous. *Hindwing* with three ocelli, pupilled with silvery." (*Hewitson*, l. c.). The ocellus of the *forewing* is of course present on the underside also, and has almost always two silvery pupils. On the upperside the hindwing is sometimes immaculate, often with a single small subanal ocellus, and occasionally with three, the upper and lower very minute. The FEMALE is somewhat larger and paler coloured than the male, but its markings are similar.

"This species may be easily known from all others by the circular band of brown which passes round the ocellus on the underside of the forewing, as well as by a rufous space (sometimes clouded with brown), below the said circular band free from undulations. As will be seen from the localities quoted, it is widely distributed, and differs considerably in size. *Y. norma*, of Westwood, [Gen. D. L., vol. ii, pl. lxvii, fig. 1, 1851], from China, I believe to be only a small variety of this species, darker, and wanting the ocellus on the upperside of the forewing; [*hindwing* is evidently meant; Westwood's figure shews an ocellus on the upperside of the forewing, but none on the hindwing] there are similar varieties from the Holy Land. Specimens from Calabar and Natal do not differ from those of Europe [?], except in having the ring of brown which encircles the ocellus of the forewing more distinctly marked above, as in *Y. norma*, and in having the underside more clouded with rufous striæ." (*Hewitson*, l. c.)

Y. asterope is a wide spread and somewhat variable species; the ocelli of the underside are smaller than in any other species with only three ocelli on the underside of the hindwing, often minute, and sometimes scarcely visible, but the characters given above by Hewitson will always serve to distinguish it. It occurs in India in the Western Himalayas, and probably throughout Continental and Peninsular India in suitable localities. We have specimens from Chumba, Kussowli, Naini Tal, Sind, Khandesh, Nagpur, Mhow and Poona. Specimens from Chumba, taken in March by Major C. H. T. Marshall, are very dark in colour, the subanal ocellus on the upperside of the hindwing is prominent in all, and in one there is a smaller ocellus on each side of it, making three in all; the underside is uniformly striated on the hindwing, except in one specimen, which has a trace of a median rufous fascia. Specimens from Mhow, taken in May by Colonel C. Swinhoe, are paler and more whitish on the underside; and in all of them there is a trace, more or less distinct, of a median rufous fascia on the hindwing; the ocelli are very minute and in many of them scarcely traceable. Specimens from Poona, taken in October by Colonel Swinhoe, are typical, all having the ocelli minute but prominent, and only one or two showing a trace of the median rufous fascia on the underside. A single specimen from Hyderabad in Sind is a typical female; so are also two specimens from Amri and Ghindwara in the Central Provinces taken in October by Mr. J. A. Betham.

214. **Ypthima inica,** Hewitson.

Yphthima inica, Hewitson, Trans. Ent. Soc. Lond., third series, vol. ii, p. 284, n. 5, pl. xvii, fig. 5 (1864).

HABITAT: East India.

EXPANSE: 1·7 inches, *Hewitson* (about 1·4 in his figure), 1·1 to 1·3 inches.

DESCRIPTION: "UPPERSIDE rufous-fuscous, each wing with a single ocellus. UNDERSIDE cineraceous, undulated with rufous. *Forewing* with a single ocellus. FEMALE: UPPERSIDE rufous-brown, with a single ocellus on *both wings*. UNDERSIDE with rufous undulations throughout. *Forewing* with the ocellus as above. *Hindwing* without ocelli, clouded with darker colour."

"Closely allied to *Y. asterope*, but without the circular brown band which surrounds the ocellus on the forewing of that species, and also without the rufous space (devoid of undulations) near the anal angle." (*Hewitson*, l. c.)

The only precise record of the occurrence of *Y. inica* that we have received is from Lieutenant-Colonel C. Swinhoe, who writes that "it was very common at Mhow in Central India from November until March, when it was replaced by *Y. asterope*, which has been just as common ever since, but I have not captured a single *Y. inica* since the 20th March. I have also *Y. inica* from Paras Pani near Mirzapur taken in February." Not one of these specimens that we have seen come anywhere near the dimensions given by Hewitson (1·7 inches in expanse); they are all far smaller, ranging from 1·1 to 1·3 inches only in expanse; but they correspond well with the description, and some examples which were sent to the British Museum were identified by Mr. Butler as *Y. inica*, Hewitson; so that they may be accepted as *Y. inica* pending further research. These are, as Hewitson remarks, very closely allied to *Y. asterope*, and the fact recorded above by Colonel Swinhoe suggests the idea that they may be only the winter brood of that species. They are easily distinguishable from all other species in which the ocelli of the underside of the hindwing are entirely absent by the markings of that wing which on the underside has four irregular, interrupted, generally clouded and indistinct dark bands, the intervening spaces paler, and about the middle of the wing often washed with ochreous. The MALE of *Y. inica* has no trace of the sexual patch on the forewing. *Y. indecora*, which most nearly approaches it in the aspect of the underside, may be distinguished by its larger size, the presence of the sexual patch in the male, and of at least two ocelli on the upperside of the hindwing.

215. **Ypthima narasingha,** Moore.

Yphthima narasinga, Moore, Horsfield and Moore, Cat. Lep. E. I. C., vol. i, p. 236, n. 509 (1857); id., Hewitson, Trans. Ent. Soc. Lond., third series, vol. ii, p. 291, n. 21, pl. xviii, fig. 19 (1864).

HABITAT: Sikkim.

EXPANSE: 2 inches.

DESCRIPTION: "UPPERSIDE with only one ocellus on the *forewing*. UNDERSIDE greenish-grey, covered with short undulated darker striæ, the one ocellus on the *forewing* only, beneath which are two descending dark lines to posterior margin." (*Moore*, l. c.) "UPPERSIDE fuscous. *Forewing* with a single ocellus on both sides. UNDERSIDE cineraceous, undulated with rufous. *Hindwing* with minute white dots. The only species which has no ocelli on either side of the *hindwing*. On the underside some minute white spots occupy the place where in other species the ocelli are placed." (*Hewitson*, l. c.)

We have never seen this rare species, and are at a loss to recognise its affinities; the entire absence of ocelli from the upperside of the hindwing occurs in other species only in aberrant examples here and there, as in *Y. singala*. In Hewitson's figure (uncoloured) of the underside of *Y. narasingha* in the hindwing the striation is less dense at the outer margin, and again across the middle of the wing, giving a somewhat clouded appearance on the submarginal and basal areas; but besides the undulations there is no indication of any other markings whatever. On the forewing the dark line encircling the ocellus is remarkable; it is nearest to that of *Y. asterope*, but lacks the rufous space below devoid of undulations; the line starts from the inner edge of the ocellus to about the lower median nervule, where it is continued parallel to the inner margin, then sharply curving upwards continues parallel to the outer margin, disappearing before it reaches the costa, having a curiously quadrate appearance.

216. **Ypthima hyagriva**, Moore. (PLATE XVII, FIG. 64 ♀.)

Yphthima hyagriva, Moore, Horsfield and Moore, Cat. Lep. E. I. C., vol. i, p. 236, n. 507 (1857); id., Hewitson, Trans. Ent. Soc. Lond., third series, vol. ii, p. 291, n. 20, pl. xviii, fig. 11 (1864).

HABITAT: Himalayas.

EXPANSE: 1·5 to 1·9 inches.

DESCRIPTION: "UPPERSIDE with only two ocelli, one being at apex of the *forewing*, the other on the *hindwing* near the anal angle. UNDERSIDE yellowish. *Hindwing* covered with short narrow undulated striæ, with two anterior and two posterior ocelli; a marginal line and submarginal streak blackish." (*Moore*, l. c.) "Easily known from all the other species by the broad submarginal line of brown on both sides, by the geminated oval ocelli near the apex of the *hindwing*, and the ochreous colour of the underside." (*Hewitson*, l. c.)

The UPPERSIDE is dark brown, slightly paler externally, and with a blackish submarginal line, obsolete in the male, but prominent in the FEMALE; the ocellus of the forewing is variable, sometimes rounded, with a single pupil, sometimes ovate with two pupils; the UNDERSIDE is ochreous brown, the submarginal line prominent in both sexes. The ocelli are large and prominent, black, with a single bluish-white pupil to each on the hindwing, broad yellow iris and dark outer line. The uniform colouring of the forewing on the underside (the hindwing only being striated), and the arrangement of the ocelli of the hindwing, a large geminated pair at the apex, and another large geminated pair at the anal angle, render this species notably distinct; the nearest approach to it being some aberrant examples of *Y. nikæa*. The male has no trace of the sexual patch on the forewing. *Y. hyagriva* was originally described from Darjiling, but we have only as yet received it from the Western Himalayas, where it does not appear to be common. Mr. A. Graham Young took it in the Kulu Valley in August and September.

The figure shows the upper and undersides of a female specimen from Kulu, in the Indian Museum, Calcutta.

217. **Ypthima huebneri**, Kirby. (PLATE XVII, FIG. 65 ♂.)

Y. philomela, Hübner (*nec* Linnæus), Zutr. Ex. Schmett., figs. 83, 84 (1818); *Yphthima philomela*, Hewitson, Trans. Ent Soc. Lond., third series, vol. ii, p. 284, n. 4 (1864); *Ypthima philomela*, Butler, Cat. Lep. B. M., *Satyridæ*, p. 152, n. 18 (1868); *Y. hübneri*, Kirby, Syn. Cat. D. L., p. 95, n. 18 (1871); idem, id., Distant, Rhop. Malay., p. 57, pl. vii, fig. 5 (1882), *female*.

HABITAT: Peninsular and North India, Burma, Malay Peninsula, Sumatra, Java, Celebes.

EXPANSE: 1·2 to 1·5 inches.

DESCRIPTION: "UPPERSIDE fuscous; *forewing* with one ocellus; *hindwing* with two. UNDERSIDE whitish, undulated with rufous; *forewing* with one ocellus, *hindwing* with four, placed one near the apex, and three together towards the anal angle; they are indistinctly pupilled with silver." (*Hewitson*, l. c.)

Y. huebneri is a very variable insect; typically the UPPERSIDE of the MALE is uniform rather pale fuliginous brown, with an indistinct dark submarginal line on both wings, and two ocelli on the *hindwing*, and one large bipupilled ocellus on the *forewing*. The UPPERSIDE of the FEMALE has two indistinct bands of whitish striæ on the forewing, one on either side of the ocellus meeting at the hinder angle, and continued on the hindwing as an indistinct submarginal pale band, and the ocellus of the forewing is larger with prominent yellow iris margined with brown. On the UNDERSIDE in both sexes the ocelli are typically prominent on both wings, the ground-colour is whitish, especially on the hindwing, finely but not very densely striated with rufous-brown; a marginal rufous line on both wings, a short line from the lower edge of the ocellus on the forewing; and a median fascia distinct on the forewing, but disappearing on the hindwing.

The variations of the UPPERSIDE, which are casual and common to both sexes, are as follows:—(*a.*) With the *forewing* immaculate; and again with great diversity in the size and prominence of the ocellus when present. (*b.*) With the *hindwing* immaculate. (*c.*) The *hindwing* with a single ocellus between the lower median nervules. (*d.*) The *hindwing* with a second ocellus between the upper median nervules. (*e.*) The *hindwing* with a third minute (sometimes geminate) ocellus at the anal angle. (*f.*) The *hindwing* with a fourth ocellus at apex, the ocellation in this case being similar to that of the underside.

The variations of the UNDERSIDE are in the ocellation of the *hindwing*, every gradation being found from prominent very black ocelli with minute silvery pupils, and wide pale ochreous irides, to minute dots, and in some cases no trace of ocelli whatever; and also there is a slight variation in the density of the rufous striæ, and in the prominence of the rufous fasciæ; where the ocelli are minute or obsolete, the striation is, as a rule, less dense, giving a paler, more whitish, tone to the whole, and at the same time the narrow rufous bands are more prominent, and on the hindwing the median band is more irregular.

In one very aberrant female specimen from Calcutta the yellow irides of the ocelli on the underside of the hindwing coalesce, forming a distinct yellow submarginal band, defined on both sides with a dark line, and bearing besides the usual four ocelli, a fifth and sixth, minute, placed one on each side of the discoidal nervule. In another female from Sibsagar the subapical ocellus is highly irregular in shape, having apparently two, if not three, other minute ocelli coalescing with it on its margin.

Where the ocelli of the underside are traceable, *Y. huebneri* can be distinguished from all others by their number and position, except from *Y. ceylonica*, *Y. chenui*, and *Y. robinsoni*. *Y. ceylonica* has the lower half of the hindwing pure white on both sides, and *Y. chenui* and *Y. robinsoni* have the rufous bands of the underside very broad and prominent, and the three subanal ocelli of the hindwing placed on the dark submarginal band.

Where the ocelli of the underside are indistinguishable on the hindwing, the species is not so easy to determine; from *Y. philomela* and its allies, *Y. ordinata*, *Y. indecora*, *Y. methora*, *Y. marshallii*, &c., it can be distinguished by the absence of the sexual patch on the forewing of the male; from *Y. narasingha* by its smaller size, and by the presence of the rufous fasciæ on the underside; from *Y. inica* by its larger size, whitish colour of the underside and comparatively uniform striation; and from *Y. asterope* by the absence of the large outer brown band encircling the ocellus on the underside of the forewing.

Y. huebneri is very common in the neighbourhood of Calcutta, throughout the year, and in Assam as far north as Sibsagar at any rate; and in both these localities every variation appears to be represented. We have specimens also from Manbhoom both with and without the ocelli on the upperside of the hindwing; and typical specimens from the Sikkim tarai taken by Mr. Otto Möller from July to September; also from Akyab taken in July; from Pegu taken in May and June, and from Gyne in Burma, taken by Captain C. H. E. Adamson in January. In these latter the male is typical, the female has the ocelli minute, and the rufous median fascia prominent on the underside. Lieutenant-Colonel C. Swinhoe has taken a few specimens at Mahableshwar in May which are typical. Mr. G. Vidal took numerous specimens in March on the Coessi and Onomed Ghâts, in the South Konkan, and in these all the males were typical, with prominent ocelli on the underside of the hindwing, and the median fascia obsolete; while all the females have the ocelli minute or obsolete, and the median fascia prominent. Typical specimens have also been taken in the Upper Godaveri districts, by Mr. C. R. Morris in September; and at Trevandrum and in the Ashamboo Hills, in May, by Mr. Harold Fergusson. The specimens from the South are much darker in tone than those from North-East India. Two male specimens from Chumba notably differ from typical *Y. huebneri* in the uniform colour of the upperside with no dark marginal line, and in the uniformly and densely striated underside, with no trace of fasciæ. These are the only specimens we have seen from North-West India, and are a distinct geographical variety.

The figure shows the upper and undersides of a male specimen from Barrackpore in Major Marshall's collection.

218. **Ypthima ceylonica,** Hewitson.

Yphthima ceylonica, Hewitson, Trans. Ent. Soc. Lond., third series, vol. ii, p. 288, pl. xviii, figs. 14, 15 (1864); *Ypthima ceylonica*, Moore, Lep. Cey., p. 25, pl. xii, figs. 5, *male*; 5 *a*, *female* (1880).

HABITAT: Ceylon, Travancore, Madras, Orissa.

EXPANSE: 1·1 to 1·55 inches.

DESCRIPTION: "UPPERSIDE rufous-brown. *Forewing* with one large ocellus, with two silver pupils. *Hindwing* with the outer half white, the outer margin and a submarginal line of black; one obscure ocellus and a minute black spot. UNDERSIDE white, undulated with rufous-brown. *Forewing* with the ocellus as above, thickly undulated towards the outer margin. *Hindwing* slightly undulated near the margins, with four ocelli, one near the apex, three near the anal angle, the outer ocellus minute, blind, the anal ocellus with two pupils of silver."

"The ocelli on the underside of the hindwing differ much. In one specimen, three are perfect, one blind; in another two only are perfect." (*Hewitson*, l. c.)

This is a very remarkable species; on the UPPERSIDE the lower half of the hindwing is pure snowy white, contrasting strongly with the brown hue of the rest of the wing; the FEMALE is similarly coloured to the male, but both sexes show considerable variation. On the UPPERSIDE of the *hindwing* there is often a subapical black spot, with sometimes a smaller one below it, and three rather large subanal perfect ocelli, sometimes one or more blind; the upper one is often minute and the lower one sometimes wanting altogether. On the UNDERSIDE the *forewing* is undulated throughout, finely and sparingly towards the base, densely on the outer area; the *hindwing* is typically almost entirely pure white, there being only a few delicate undulations near the margins, but in some specimens the basal area is also undulated, and in others again the undulations extend, though sparingly, over the entire wing. The ocellation of the underside is as in *Y. huebneri*, and as in that species is variable.

Till quite recently *Y. ceylonica* was believed to be confined to the island of Ceylon; but it has now been taken in Travancore by Mr. H. Fergusson, and in Orissa by Mr. W. C. Taylor, and Mr. Kirby records it from Madras. In the Orissa specimens the striation of the underside is denser and shows a considerable approximation to *Y. huebneri*, to which it is evidently closely allied. The male has no trace whatever of the brand on the forewing.

In Ceylon *Y. ceylonica* is "very common at Galle and Colombo among grass and weeds by the roadside. Flight short, constantly settling down on leaves or in grass." (*Hutchison*).

219. **Ypthima chenui,** Guérin.

Satyrus chenu, Guérin, in Deless. Souv. Voy. Ind, pt. ii, p. 77, pl. xxi, figs. 2, 2 *a* (1843), *female*; *Yphthima chenu*, Hewitson, Trans. Ent. Soc. Lond., third series, vol. ii, p. 285, n. 7 (1864); *Ypthima chenui*, Kirby, Syn. Cat. D. L., p. 95, n. 15 (1871).

HABITAT: Nilgiri Hills, South India.

EXPANSE: 1·33 to 1·75 inches.

DESCRIPTION: "UPPERSIDE greyish-brown, with some fine nebulous paler striæ towards the outer margin. *Forewing* with, near the apex, a large round black ocellus with wide yellow iris, and two small pupils of shining blue. *Hindwing* with two much smaller ocelli, black, with yellow iris, and a single very small blue pupil, placed submarginally between the median nervules. UNDERSIDE ashy-grey with numerous small undulated tranverse brown striæ. *Forewing* with the ocellus as on upperside. *Hindwing* with three [four in the figure] ocelli, the two of the upperside, and a third near the costa and more distant from the outer margin, [and a fourth towards the anal angle, minute, geminate. This latter ocellus, though omitted from the original description, is clearly shown in Guérin's figure, and is of much importance as showing the affinity of the species with *Y. huebneri* rather than with *Y. motschulskii*]. *Forewing* with the outer margin of a yellowish-brown, and two bands of the same colour starting nearly from the same point on the inner margin near the hinder angle and diverging towards the costa, the one within the other beyond the large subapical ocellus. *Hindwing* with the external margin equally yellowish-brown, and with three bands of the same colour, and the commencement of a fourth band, on which is placed the ocellus near the costa. The band near the base is slightly arched, and does not reach the inner margin; the two others diverge from the anal angle to the costa on either side of the apical ocellus. *Body* and *antennæ* brown, the underside variegated with grey. There are also smaller individual specimens which do not at all differ from this description." (*Guérin*, l. c.)

Y. chenui is a rare species. Guérin's figure is evidently that of a female, and the single female specimen in Mr. de Nicéville's collection, which is the only one that we have seen, corresponds exactly with it; the male is apparently unknown, but it is probable that the smaller specimens referred to above by Guérin were males, and that the sexes do not differ in colouration. Unfortunately the original descriptions of the species in this genus, in no case mention the sexual mark on the wing of the male insect, but it is most probable that in this species the male mark is wanting. It flies in July in the Nilgiri Hills.

220. **Ypthima robinsoni,** Distant.

Y. robinsoni, Distant, Ann. and Mag. of Nat. Hist., fifth series, vol. x, p. 406 (1882).

HABITAT: Pulni, and Rhodi canal, South-India.

EXPANSE: 1·27 inches.

DESCRIPTION: "UPPERSIDE very dark fuliginous. *Forewing* with an ovate ocellated spot (black, with two small bluish centres and an ochraceous margin) placed a little beyond the cell, its upper margin reaching just above the upper discoidal nervule, and its lower margin extending a little beneath the first [third] median nervule. *Hindwing* with two small rounded ocellated spots (black, with a bluish centre and ochraceous margin) placed between the median nervules. UNDERSIDE: *Forewing* slightly paler than on upperside, with the ocellated spot brighter, and crossed by two dark transverse fasciæ, the first near the apex of the cell, and the second somewhat submarginal. *Hindwing* greyish, with numerous dark strigæ, which are very thickly and confluently situate at the basal area, and crossed by three dark fuscous fasciæ, the first and narrowest very slightly curved, passing through the middle of the cell, the middle one very oblique, crossing the apex of the cell, and the third submarginal, broadest near the apex, and narrowing towards the anal angle; between the second and third fasciæ the colour is very pale greyish, and contains a small ocellated spot between the subcostal nervules; on the dark outer fascia are three ocellated spots, placed two between the median nervules and one between the first median nervule and submedian nervure; all these spots are black, with bluish centres and ochraceous margins. *Body* and *legs* more or less concolourous with the wings."

"This species is allied to *Y. chenui*, Guérin, from which it differs, on the underside, by the darker colouration, the different direction of the two dark fasciæ on the forewing. which do not approximate towards each other on the inner margin as in Guérin's species, and also by the second and third dark fasciæ on the hindwing, which in *Y. robinsoni* are subparallel and placed somewhat close together, the ocellated spots much smaller, &c." (*Distant*, l. c.)

We have never seen *Y. robinsoni,* but from the description it appears to approximate very closely to *Y. yphthimoides,* if indeed the two descriptions do not apply to one and the same species.

No indication of difference between the sexes is given, nor is any mention made of the presence or absence of the sexual patch on the forewing of the male ; in all probability this mark is absent as in *Y. huebneri.*

221. Ypthima yphthimoides, Moore.

Callerebia yphthimoides, Moore, Trans. Ent. Soc. Lond., 1881, p. 307.

HABITAT : Hills of Travancore, South-India.

EXPANSE : ♂, 1·5 to 1·9 ; ♀, 1·9 to 2·0 inches.

DESCRIPTION : " MALE and FEMALE : UPPERSIDE dark olive-brown. *Forewing* with a bipupilled ocellus encircled by a narrow indistinct orange-yellow border. *Hindwing* with two small subanal ocelli. UNDERSIDE numerously covered with grey strigæ. *Forewing* with the ocellus as above, and a slight brownish submarginal and a discal fascia. *Hindwing* with three broader and more distinct transverse fasciæ, a small apical ocellus and four lower, smaller, decreasing ocelli." (*Moore,* l.c.)

Originally described as a *Callerebia,* but the arrangement of the subcostal nervules of the forewing is as in *Ypthima* to which it certainly belongs ; the colour approaches that of a *Callerebia,* but the markings are those of an *Ypthima.* The genus *Callerebia* is restricted in India to the Himalayas and outlying ranges.

Mr. Fergusson writes from Trevandrum : " *Ypthima yphthimoides* is to be found on the hills here only on grass land near the tops of the hills. The specimens I got were from two localities—one a small patch of grass about an acre in extent, at an elevation of 3,500 feet, and the other on a grass hill called Pon Mudi (golden hill) about 3,000 feet ; here they were fairly abundant." It also occurs in April at Colathoorpolay Patnas, 4,000 feet, Travancore.

In the nine males which Mr. Fergusson has sent us there is no variation on the upperside, but on the underside of the hindwing in one specimen there are two additional ocelli, placed one on either side of the discoidal nervule, and in one female on the upperside of the hindwing there are two additional small geminate ocelli at the anal angle ; and in another female there are three further additional small ocelli placed above the two large median ocelli, making seven in all. On either side of the outer dark fascia on the underside of the hindwing there are two pale, almost white fasciæ, in fresh specimens.

222. Ypthima singala, Felder.

Yphthima singala, Felder, Vehr. zool.-bot. Gesellsch., vol. xviii, p. 283 (1868) ; *Ypthima singala,* Moore, Lep. Cey., p. 24, pl xii, figs. 3, 3*a* (1880), *male.*

HABITAT : Ceylon, India.

EXPANSE : 1·3 to 1·5 inches.

DESCRIPTION : " MALE : UPPERSIDE brown. *Hindwing* [typically immaculate] with one, sometimes two, small, indistinct, subanal spots encircled with yellow. UNDERSIDE cinereous, numerously covered with short brown strigæ. *Forewing* with transverse indistinct brown discal and marginal band, and a prominent bipupilled ocellus. *Hindwing* with six [five in the figure, the uppermost being absent] small well-formed ocelli disposed in regular linear order, the first upper being very minute. FEMALE : UPPERSIDE : *Forewing* with a subapical bipupilled ocellus. *Hindwing* with three small subanal ocelli. UNDERSIDE as in the male." (*Moore,* l. c.)

Felder's original description* is given in comparison with *Y. lysandra,* Hewitson, *nec*

---

* *Y. singala,* Felder. DESCRIPTION : " MALE a little larger than *Y. lysandra,* Hewitson, *nec* Cramer. *Forewing* with the apex, *hindwing* with the anal angle more produced, the disco-cellular nervules of the forewing more oblique, and, therefore, the upper angle of the cell more drawn back UPPERSIDE, *both wings* (in our specimen) immaculate. UNDERSIDE pale hoary, much more densely and uniformly striated with fuscous. *Forewing* with an ocellus with narrower iris than in that species. *Hindwing* with five small ocelli, three lower in the same line, the second (below the second subcostal branch) and the fourth (between the first and the second median branches) a little larger." (*Felder,* l. c.).

Cramer; it is clear that the species identified by Hewitson with *Y. lysandra*, Cramer, was not that species, but what it really was we cannot ascertain. The true *Y. lysandra* is from China, and is very distinct, the UPPERSIDE being uniform rather dark brown, with one bipupilled ocellus on the *forewing*, and three subanal prominent on the *hindwing*. The UNDERSIDE is ochreous, uniformly striated with brown. *Forewing* with the ocellus as usual, no dark fasciæ, the inner margin broadly white. *Hindwing* with two prominent subapical ocelli on a short dark band, beyond and in continuation of which is a whitish fascia to the inner margin; below this is another short dark band from anal angle bearing three prominent ocelli placed in a line.

Y. singala was originally described from a specimen from Badulla in Ceylon at an elevation of 3,000 feet. In Moore's "Lep. Ceylon" it is stated to be "rare; a few specimens only taken in long grass on borders of coffee-plantations at Buselowe, 3,000 feet elevation." (*Hutchison*). In the Indian Museum, Calcutta, there are five specimens of the male, three of them typical with no ocelli on the upperside on either wing, and two have two subanal ocelli on the hindwing, the upper minute and evanescent. On the underside of the *hindwing* four ocelli are always present, one above the discoidal nervule, and one below each median nervule; sometimes there are six by the appearance of a minute apical and a minute subanal ocellus, and sometimes five by the absence of one or other of these latter: the linear arrangement of these ocelli distinguish *Y. singala* from all other species of this group except *Y. thora*, which is closely allied to it, and *Y. bolanica* which is otherwise widely diverse. The MALE of *Y. singala* has no trace of a sexual patch on the forewing.

Until recently *Y. singala* was believed to be confined to the island of Ceylon, but in October last a pair, male and female, were taken by Mr. J. A. Betham in the Central Provinces near Nagpore, which are inseparable from Ceylon examples. A specimen in Major Marshall's collection, taken at Barrackpore in November, seems to link this species with *Y. huebneri*, the third and fourth ocelli of the hindwing are slightly out of line, the anal pair is geminated, and the first is larger than the second. In Colonel Lang's collection are two typical males from Kussowli; and a very aberrant male from the Rajmahal district, with the fasciæ on the underside of the hindwing very prominent.

223. **Ypthima thora,** Moore.

Y. thora, Moore, Lep. Cey., p. 24, pl. xii, figs. 4, 4*a* (1880), *male*.

HABITAT: Ceylon.

EXPANSE: ♂, 1·4 inches.

DESCRIPTION: "MALE: UPPERSIDE brown. *Forewing* with a prominent subapical bipupilled ocellus. *Hindwing* with a small indistinct subanal ocellus. UNDERSIDE cinereous, numerously covered with short delicate brown strigæ. *Forewing* with a very indistinct discal and marginal band, ocellus prominent. *Hindwing* with five very minute ocelli, disposed in linear order." (*Moore*, l. c.) FEMALE somewhat paler than the male, wings broader, the markings identical.

We have never seen this species; it is evidently very closely allied to *Y. singala*, but appears to be distinct, though the only point of difference is on the upperside of the *forewing*, which has an ocellus which is absent from male *Y. singala*, though present in the female of that species. It is not known whether the MALE has or has not a sexual patch on the forewing; in all probability it is absent, as in *Y. singala*.

224. **Ypthima bolanica,** Marshall, n. sp.

HABITAT: Mach, Bolan Pass, Beluchistan.

EXPANSE: ♂, 1·6 inches.

DESCRIPTION: MALE: UPPERSIDE dark brown, (distinctly glossed with purple in some lights when fresh as in *Callerebia)*. *Forewing* with a prominent black ocellus with two large bluish-silver pupils and narrow yellow iris, ringed with dark brown, then with mottled greyish more broadly, and then again with dark brown. *Hindwing* with one black ocellus very prominently pupilled with bluish-silver between the lower median nervules some distance from the margin, and two bluish-silver specks on the submarginal dark line near the anal angle being the pupils of obsolete geminate ocelli, a submarginal sinuous dark brown line; the margin of both wings narrowly whitish, defined on the inside with dark brown; the *cilia* brown. UNDERSIDE greyish-white, covered more or less with fine reddish-brown striæ. *Forewing* with the ocellus as on upperside. *Hindwing* with six ocelli, the first three in a line from the costa small, the third minute, the fourth between the first and second median branches large, the fifth and sixth geminated at the anal angle, all prominently pupilled with bluish-silver as on the upperside; the *cilia* brown, the margin of both wings narrowly pure white, inwardly defined by a brown line, then a whitish mottled line, broadest at costa of forewing and ending at the fifth ocellus of the *hindwing*; two brown lines one on each side of the ocellus of forewing, and meeting below it, continued on the *hindwing* as a single narrow band on which the first three ocelli are placed, and terminating just beyond the third; a short brown line from the costa of forewing, defined exteriorly with whitish, and again another brown line continued across the hindwing to the abdominal margin, and on the latter wing defined externally with whitish, the basal area more densely striated than the external area; no defined fascia on basal half.

Y. bolanica is unlike any other known species of this genus; it perhaps most nearly approaches *Y. ordinata* in the markings of the underside, but there is no trace of a subbasal fascia; the median and submarginal fasciæ are much more distinct, the ground-colour beyond the median fascia is whiter, and the ocellation is very different, the six ocelli of the hindwing being nearly in a straight line. The median nervure is much swollen at the base, more so than in any other species; and there is no trace of the sexual patch on the forewing of the MALE.

Taken by Lieutenant-Colonel Swinhoe, in whose collection the type specimen is, at Mach in the Bolan Pass in September, 1879.

225. **Ypthima sakra**, Moore. (PLATE XVII, FIG. 67 ♂.)

Yphthima sakra, Moore, Horsfield and Moore, Cat. Lep. E. I. C., vol. i, p. 236, n. 508 (1857); id., Hewitson, Trans. Ent. Soc. Lond., third series, vol. ii, p. 290, n. 18, pl. xviii, fig 18 (1864).

HABITAT: Himalayas, Khasi and Naga Hills, Upper Burma.

EXPANSE: 1·85 to 2·1 inches.

DESCRIPTION: "UPPERSIDE [brown], with five ocelli, one being on the *forewing*, three near anal angle, and one (but indistinct) near anterior angle of the *hindwing*. UNDERSIDE yellow, covered with short narrow dark brown striæ. *Hindwing* with geminated anterior, and three single posterior ocelli." (*Moore*, l. c.)

For remarks see the next species, *Y. nikæa*.

The figure shows the upper and undersides of a male specimen from Shillong in the Indian Museum, Calcutta.

226. **Ypthima nikæa**, Moore.

Yphthima nikæa, Moore, Proc Zool. Soc. Lond., 1874, p. 567.

HABITAT: N.-W. Himalayas.

EXPANSE: 1·7 to 2·1 inches.

DESCRIPTION: "UPPERSIDE dark brown; pupils of ocelli blue. *Forewing* with a subapical bipupilled ocellus (smaller than in *Y. sakra*). *Hindwing* with two subanal ocelli. MALE sometimes with only one subanal ocellus. UNDERSIDE grey, with numerous short brown narrow strigæ. *Forewing* with the ocellus as above, and a distinct brown submarginal transverse fascia. *Hindwing* with five ocelli, the two apical being the largest and joined together, though having a yellow band between them; the other three ocelli in a linear series from anal angle, the anal one bipupilled."

"Differs from *Y. sakra* in its smaller size, darker colour above and greyer below; and may be distinguished by the difference of the apical ocelli on the hindwing, which in *Y. sakra* have no intervening yellow band." (*Moore*, l. c.)

This species seems to us to be but a casual variety of *Y. sakra*. Taking the absence of the yellow intervening band between the apical ocelli of the underside of the *hindwing*, as given by Mr. Moore, as the test character, we have specimens of *Y. sakra* from the Eastern hills of Manipur, Shillong in the Khasi hills, Sikkim, Simla, Pangi, and various localities in the Chumba State which borders on Kashmir: while we have *Y. nikæa* from many localities in the North-West Himalayas, and a typical specimen from the eastern hills of Manipur.

Of the specimens of *Y. sakra*, that from Manipur has only three ocelli on the UPPERSIDE of the hindwing, the apical one being absent; those from Shillong have four ocelli, the one nearest the anal angle being however minute or obsolescent, and one specimen (the one figured) has only two ocelli; the specimens from Sikkim are typical, having all four ocelli prominent; one from Chumba is also typical, with all four ocelli prominent; one from Simla has three ocelli, the one nearest the anal angle being absent; others from Pangi and Chumba have only two ocelli placed between the median nervules (as in the Shillong specimen figured), the upper one sometimes minute. On the UNDERSIDE there is more uniformity, all the specimens having the five ocelli of the *hindwing*—two apical, three subanal—prominent, except in one specimen from Simla, in which the ocellus of the upper median interspace is minute, and another has this ocellus absent altogether, and one from Kujiar in the Chumba State has the anal ocellus quite round with a single pupil. There is considerable variation in the density and coarseness of the striation, in the tone of the ground-colour, and the prominence of the submarginal dark band: the Eastern specimens are as a rule yellower, the striation is coarser, and the submarginal band more prominent; but there are exceptions to every point. The FEMALE has broader wings, and the upperside is less uniform in colour, having frequently a broad nebulous submarginal band of pale striæ, these striæ sometimes extending with more or less density over the entire wing.

The specimens of *Y. nikæa* vary quite as much, but the occurrence of four ocelli on the UPPERSIDE of the hindwing is very rare; usually there are two, and frequently there is only one; the anal ocellus is generally altogether wanting, the ocellus between the lower median nervules is always present; the one between the upper median nervules is also found in both sexes wherever the ocelli are limited to two in number, and occasionally there is a third ocellus above the discoidal nervule. On the UNDERSIDE typically the ocelli are five in number as in *Y. sakra*, but frequently the ocellus of the upper median interspace is absent, leaving two near apex and two near anal angle, presenting very much the appearance of *Y. hyagriva*; the density and coarseness of the striation, the tone of the ground-colour, and the prominence of the submarginal dark band, are all as variable as in *Y. sakra*. The FEMALE differs from the male as in *Y. sakra*.

In both species and in both sexes there is occasionally a second ocellus on the underside of the *forewing* placed in the lower median interspace. The uniform brown of the upperside, and the uniform striation of the underside, together with the large size, serve to distinguish both *Y. sakra* and *Y. nikæa* from other species of the genus.

Y. sakra was taken in the Manipur hills in May by Mr. A. O. Hume; in Shillong it occurs in May and also in September; in Sikkim it has been taken at an elevation of 7,000 feet in September; in the N.-W. Himalayas it has been taken in Chumba at 6,000 feet elevation in April and May by Major C. H. T. Marshall; and throughout the hills at 6,000 to 8,000 feet elevation it is common in the rains on grassy slopes and at the edges of forests.

Y. nikæa was also taken in May in the Manipur hills; and in the N.-W. Himalayas it occurs in April and May, and throughout the rains it is extremely common at 6,000 to 8,000 feet elevation in suitable localities; out of a large series taken by Mr. de Nicéville at Simla there is not a single specimen of *Y. sakra*, and though by no means universal, *Y. nikæa* is evidently the dominant form in the west, as *Y. sakra* is in the east.

227. **Ypthima tabella,** Marshall, n. sp.

HABITAT: Wynaad, South India.

EXPANSE: ♂, 1·15 inches.

DESCRIPTION: MALE: UPPERSIDE brown, uniform in shade. *Forewing* with a not very prominent bipupilled ocellus. *Hindwing* with two submarginal ocelli between the median nervules, the upper one minute. UNDERSIDE paler brown, with greyish undulations most numerous on the hindwing. *Forewing* with the ocellus as usual. *Hindwing* with six ocelli placed in pairs in echelon, the apical pair geminate on the lower subcostal nervule, the upper minute, the median pair complete but touching on the median interspaces, the anal pair geminate, the lower being extremely minute, the outer margin somewhat darker, but no trace otherwise of fasciæ on the underside. No sexual patch on forewing on upperside.

At first sight *Y. tabella* appears to be only a dwarf specimen of *Y. sakra*, but the grayer tone of the striation of the underside, the subanal ocellus being geminated not bipupilled, the very small size, and also the locality from whence it comes, mark it as distinct. It is distinguished from *Y. philomela* and its allies by the absence of the sexual mark in the male. Nothing approaching *Y. sakra* is known to occur south of the Khasi hills in the vast intermediate country between them, and the Wynaad where *Y. tabella* appears.

Genus 21.—RAGADIA, Westwood. (PLATE XV.)

Neonympha, subgenus *Ragadia*, Westwood, Gen. D. L., vol. ii, p. 376 (1851).

"Distinguished from *Neonympha* [an American genus] by the very singular arrangement of the veins of the wings, especially of the hindwing; the lower disco-cellular nervule being placed almost at the base of the wing, and furnished with an elongated pouch in the males. The costal nervure of the forewing is alone swollen at the base." (*Westwood*, l. c.)

BODY slender. HEAD wide, *antennæ* slender, distinctly articulated, with a slender gradually formed club. *Eyes* almost naked. PALPI moderately long, densely clothed in front with rather long bristly hairs, not tufted at the back, terminal joint slender. FOREWING somewhat elongate; *costa* slightly curved; *outer margin* oblique, slightly convex; *costal* nervure alone swollen at the base, the remaining nervures simple; *disco-cellular nervules* concave, the *upper* very short, the *middle* long, the *lower* longer still, and joining the median nervure at an acute angle some distance beyond the origin of its second branch; *subcostal nervure* with its branches free and short, the *second* originating beyond the cell, as in *Ypthima; discoidal* nervules from the junctions of the disco-cellulars, the upper one originating very close to the subcostal nervure. HINDWING rounded; *præcostal* nervure very short, curved outwardly; *costal* nervure curved at base, and joining the costal margin at about one-half its length. *Subcostal* nervure almost straight; *discoidal cell* very short and acute; *discoidal* nervule curved at its base and appearing to originate from the subcostal nervule below; the lower *disco-cellular* appearing to originate from the subcostal at some distance nearer the base, then acutely angled outwardly and joining the median nervure at a very acute angle some distance before the origin of its *first* branch; along its free part closing the cell it is simple in the FEMALE, but in the MALE it is developed along its underside into a narrow glandular pouch, and on the upperside is furnished with a small tuft of fine long hairs which lie along it. FORELEGS of the FEMALE slender, destitute of hairs, the joints of the *tarsus* very short, dilated, distinct, each furnished with a single spine on the lower side, and appearing as a clubbed termination to the slender leg: of the MALE wanting in our only specimen.

Ragadia is a very remarkable and aberrant genus; and its affinities are difficult to determine; according to the characters taken in the key to the genera it should have come in the first group, as the apex of the cell in the hindwing is distinctly *not* beyond the origin of the second median nervule, nor are the eyes entirely destitute of hairs; of the first group it has most affinity with *Mycalesis*, especially in the dilation of the disco-cellular nervule in the hindwing and the tuft of hairs along it in the male, but its nearest ally is evidently *Ypthima*, with which it corresponds in the arrangement of the subcostal nervules of the forewing; in the brilliant silver pupillation of the ocelli; in the shape of the wings and in habits. It differs in style of colouration and structurally in having the median nervure of the forewing simple, though, even in this feature some species of *Ypthima* approach it; but the curious construction of the cell of the hindwing places it apart by itself. Only a single species of this genus is found within our limits, occurring in Burma and North-Eastern Bengal; and only one other species is known which inhabits Java, Borneo, and the Philippine Islands, with varieties in Mindanao and Luzon. The Indian species is a small brown insect with whitish transverse bands crossing both wings, and with a complete discal series of silver-pupilled ocelli on both wings on the underside.

228. **Ragadia crisilda,** Hewitson. (PLATE XV, FIG. 36 ♀.)

R. crisilda, Hewitson, Ex. Butt., vol. iii, *Euptychia* et *Ragadia*, figs. 5, 6 (1862), *female*.

HABITAT: Sylhet, Tenasserim.

EXPANSE: ♂, 1·6; ♀, 1·85 inches.

DESCRIPTION: MALE and FEMALE: "UPPERSIDE brown, *both wings* crossed at the middle by a broad oblique band of white; both with a narrow band of white parallel to the outer margin, obscured towards the apex of the *forewing*, [and both showing the pale basal bands of the underside through by transparency]. UNDERSIDE white; *both wings* with the outer margin and five transverse bands brown, three parallel bands before the middle (crossing the *forewing* obliquely), the fifth band near the outer margin narrow; the fourth beyond the middle [broad], marked with numerous ocelli, on the *forewing* by six of equal size, [in our specimens of both sexes there are eight ocelli, the upper one minute, the two lowest small placed in the interspace below the first median nervule]; on the *hindwing* by seven [six in our male specimen], the third and fifth the largest; the seventh (near the anal angle) minute; all black, with silver pupils, the iris orange; the second, third, and fourth ocelli of the *hindwing* enclosed in one iris." (*Hewitson*, l. c.) The FEMALE is slightly larger than the male, and has the wings broader and more rounded, the white markings all sullied; all the ocelli larger.

R. crisilda is apparently a rare insect. It was originally described from Sylhet, and Colonel Lang's collection contains two males from that locality; Kirby notes it from the Khasi hills, (if this is correct it probably only occurs at the foot of them), and the Indian Museum, Calcutta, has two specimens, believed to have been taken in Cachar. The only recent record of its capture is by Captain C. H. E. Adamson, who took several specimens flying among long grass by the Aploon Choung in the neighbourhood of Moulmein in October, the only occasion on which he ever saw them.

The figure is taken from a female specimen in the Indian Museum, Calcutta, from Cachar, and shows both upper and undersides.

Genus 22.—ERITES, Westwood. (PLATE XVI.)

Satyrus [*Hipparchia*], subgenus *Erites*, Westwood, Gen. D. L., vol. ii, p. 392 (1851); *Erites*, Distant, Rhop. Malay., p. 46 (1882).

"FOREWING somewhat elongate and narrow, with the *costa* arched and slightly convex at its apex, the *apex* rounded [sometimes slightly falcate]; *outer margin* nearly straight, or very slightly waved inwardly about the middle; *inner margin* nearly straight [about equal in length to the outer margin]; *costal nervure* very strongly dilated at the base; *first* and *second subcostal* nervules emitted before the end of the cell; *upper disco-cellular* nervule very short, directed a little outwardly at base, and then somewhat concavely in its greater length to apex; *lower disco-cellular* nearly straight, and very slightly directed either outwardly or inwardly. HINDWING irregularly subovate, with the outer margin waved and produced into an obtuse angle or tail near the first [third] median nervule; nervules well separated at their origin; *disco-cellular* nervules about or almost subequal in length, the upper one concave, the lower one almost straight. [HEAD wide]; *eyes* prominent and naked; *palpi* clothed beneath with fine long semi-erect hairs, somewhat separated and placed in tufts; *antennæ* slender, the apical portion slightly and gradually thickened." [BODY slender]. (*Distant*, l. c.)

This is a very beautiful genus; the wings are delicate and semi-transparent; the forewing has a large ocellus at the hinder angle, and four small ones above it, and the hindwing has a complete submarginal row of ocelli, and both wings are crossed by two median fasciæ, the outer one much angled on the hindwing; the markings of the underside show through by transparency on the upperside. The wings of the FEMALE are slightly broader than in the male, the forelegs are long, slender, destitute of hairs; of the MALE shorter, and very hairy. The male has no sexual glands or tufts of hair.

Erites is an Indo-Malayan genus; only five species are known; the type *E. medura* is found in Java and Sumatra; two species are found within our limits, one in Tenasserim and the other in Cachar; the remaining two are found in Borneo and Labuan. The Indian species both appear to be local and not common even where they occur.

Key to the Indian species of Erites.

A. Wings pale brown, forewing with a large black ocellus at the hinder angle.

a. The forewing not falcate; the large ocellus blind on upperside; and with a large bluish-silver pupil and wide well-defined ochreous iris on underside.

229. E. ANGULARIS, Tenasserim.

b. The forewing somewhat falcate, the large ocellus with prominent pure white pupil and narrow indistinct iris on both upper and undersides.

230. E. FALCIPENNIS, Cachar.

229. Erites angularis, Moore. (PLATE XVI, FIG. 50 ♀.)

E. angularis, Moore, Proc. Zool. Soc. Lond., 1878, p. 825; id., Distant, Rhop. Malay., p. 46, pl. v, fig. 3 (1882), *male*.

HABITAT: Upper Tenasserim, Perak.

EXPANSE: 2·12 to 2·50 inches.

DESCRIPTION: "MALE: Wings longer than in *E. medura*, Horsfield* (from Java); the *forewing* being more produced at the apex and the *hindwing* posteriorly. UNDERSIDE similarly marked, excepting that the yellow-bordered black spot on the *forewing* is more oval, and the spots on the *hindwing* smaller, this wing also having the inner yellow band acutely angled in the middle." (*Moore*, l. c.)

MALE: UPPERSIDE light brown. *Forewing* fuscescent towards the outer margin; all the markings of the underside showing through by transparency. *Hindwing* with five black submarginal spots, with or without small yellowish pupils, the fifth on the lower median interspace the largest, with distinct yellow iris and fuscous outer ring, the rest with the yellow iris and fuscous ring decreasingly fainter; three dark brown lines on the margin following its contour and divided by yellow lines, prominent on the hindwing, obsolescent on the forewing. UNDERSIDE pale brown, pearly on the hindwing. *Forewing* undulated throughout with fuscous striæ, with two fuscous bands across the disc, the inner straight, the outer concave, beyond which is a large oval black ocellus near the hinder angle, with large silvery-bluish eccentric pupil, broad yellow iris, and narrow outer fuscous ring; above which are four small faint submarginal ocelli; three dark lines on the outer margin divided by yellow lines. *Hindwing* also undulated with fuscous striæ; with two yellow bands in continuation of the bands on the forewing, both sharply angulated outwards at the middle; the inner on both edges, and the

* *Erites medura*, Horsfield. HABITAT: Java. EXPANSE: 2·45 inches. DESCRIPTION: UPPERSIDE pale brown, much darker on the margins, the striæ of the underside shewing through on the basal areas. *Forewing* with a brown streak crossing the wing obliquely, and continued on to the hindwing, cutting the lower outer angle of the cell in the forewing, and crossing the middle of the cell on the hindwing; beyond this a much darker brown sinuous streak across the disc, which is also continued on to the hindwing, where however it is ochreous and highly angled, and defined with dark brown on both edges. A large round black ocellus near the hinder angle, with a pale pupil, yellow iris and dark outer ring; two small ocelli above, one on each side of the lower discoidal nervule. Three marginal black lines divided by yellow lines. *Hindwing* with four large submarginal ocelli, with pale pupils and wide yellow irides, all touching. Three marginal fine yellow lines. UNDERSIDE paler, the fasciæ on *both wings* ochreous; the subapical ocelli of the *forewing* more distinct and three in number, the large lower ocellus more oval in shape than on the upperside. *Hindwing* with the submarginal ocelli smaller and the irides less distinct. (Described from Horsfield's figure in the Cat Lep. E I. C., pl. v, figs. 8, 8*a* (1829) Hewitson records (Journ. Linn Soc. Lond., Zoology, vol. viii, p 145 (1865), a variety of *E. medura* from Singapore and Sumatra, and another from Singapore and Sarawak.

outer on its inner edge, defined with fuscous lines ; five small perfect submarginal ocelli, the second and fifth larger, the third fourth and fifth on a clouded ferruginous ground ; the margin as in the forewing, but the lines more prominent. FEMALE : UPPERSIDE as in the male, but on the *forewing* the large blackish spot at the hinder angle is much more prominent ; and on the *hindwing* the ocelli are all larger and without pupils, but with the yellow iris wide and prominent in all ; the outer band is also distinctly outwardly margined with yellow. UNDERSIDE precisely as in the male, but the bands on the forewing are often distinctly yellowish with fuscous margins.

E. angularis has as yet only been found in Tenasserim and in the Malay peninsula. It was originally taken by Limborg on the Taoo plateau at from 3,000 to 5,000 feet elevation : Captain C. T. Bingham took it in the Meplay valley in January, and in the Thoungyeen forests in March ; and Captain C. H. E. Adamson took numerous specimens in the neighbourhood of Moulmein early in October ; these latter were much worn and frayed and probably had been on the wing since early in September.

A female taken in the Thoungyeen forests in March differs from our other female specimens in the ocellus on the upperside of the *forewing* being very nearly round, not oval, with a distinct yellow iris of equal width throughout ; the outer fascia of the *hindwing* much broader and very distinct ; four large black spots beyond twice the size of those in the other specimens, the yellow irides prominent and touching. On the underside of the *hindwing* the two discal fasciæ have almost disappeared, and the five submarginal ocelli are very minute. This specimen differs only in the following particulars from Horsfield's figure of *E. medura :* The outer margin of the forewing is not quite so evenly rounded, being in fact slightly concave ; the large ocellus is not quite so large as in *E. medura*, and the iris is less wide. On the underside the apical ocelli on the forewing are smaller, and on the hindwing the ocelli are minute, and the fasciæ are obsolete. This specimen, however, is much nearer *E. medura* than *E. angularis.*

Mr. W. L. Distant in his Rhopalocera Malayana records the following note : "This species is very distinct, differing from the other three species—[*E. medura*, Java ; *E. elegans*, Borneo ; and *E. argentina*, Labuan]—by the more apically produced *forewing*, and by the inner fascia of the *hindwing* being acutely dentate at its middle ; it also structurally differs in having the lower disco-cellular nervule of the *forewing* slightly directed inwardly." This latter character is not apparent in our Tenasserim specimens, and the two former characters it has in common with the more recently discovered *E. falcipennis.*

The figure is taken from a female specimen in Major Marshall's collection, taken by Captain C. T. Bingham in the Meplay valley ; and shows the upper and undersides.

230. **Erites falcipennis,** W.-M. and de N.

HABITAT : Cachar.

EXPANSE : 2·1 and 2·3 inches.

DESCRIPTION : MALE : Nearest allied to *E. angularis*, Moore, but differs from that species in the colouration of the upperside being dark fuliginous throughout, in the *forewing* being distinctly falcate, the ocellus round and prominently white-pupilled, with a very narrow pale iris. *Hindwing* with the outer fascia and series of blind ocelli hardly defined with ochreous, the outer margin less waved, especially at the third median nervule, where in *E. angularis* the wing is produced into a short tail ; the marginal lines obsolete. UNDERSIDE : All the markings duller and less ochreous. *Forewing* with a small round central pure white pupil to the posterior ocellus, not large, silvery and eccentric as in *E. angularis* ; the iris narrow. On the *hindwing* the ocelli are small, the two discal fasciæ wider and a deeper ochreous ; the striæ on both wings shorter and more thickly disposed, forming on the *hindwing* a submarginal purplish band.

Mr. Wood-Mason took one male in the forests near Silcuri on 6th August, and another male on Nemotha at 3,300 feet elevation on 25th September.

Genus 23.—ŒNEIS, Hübner. (PLATE XV.)

Œneis, Hübner, Verz. bek. Schmett., p. 58 (1816); *Chionobas*, Boisduval, Lép. Amer. Sept., p. 214 (1833); id., Westwood, Gen. D. L., vol. ii, p. 381 (1851); id., Möschler, Wien. Ent. Monatsch., vol. vii, pp. 169, 201 (1863), *Monograph*.

"BODY very hairy; wings but moderately clothed with scales, of a dull brownish buff, or dirty fulvous colour; the hindwing beneath much freckled. HEAD very small, and very hairy. *Eyes* prominent, naked. *Palpi* densely hairy in front, porrected obliquely, scarcely reaching to the level of the top of the eyes, but porrected to the length of the head; terminal joint small, slender-oval, hairy. *Antennæ* short, slender, gradually thickened from the middle into a long but not thick club, obtuse at the tip, concave, finely carinated beneath. *Thorax* very hairy. *Abdomen* small, slender, hairy. FOREWING elongate-triangular; the costal margin scarcely arched; apex rounded; outer margin convex, entire, about two-thirds the length of the costal; inner margin straight, not quite so long as the outer. *Neuration* as in *Erebia*, except that, in consequence of the greater length and narrowness of the wing, the *discoidal cell* is narrowed and elongated to some distance beyond the middle; the *middle* and *lower disco-cellular* nervules (the *upper* being obsolete), forming a nearly continuous, oblique, slightly curved line. HINDWING also elongated, so that it extends considerably beyond the inner angle of the forewing; the costal margin nearly straight; the outer margin rounded, entire, or but slightly scalloped; anal margin entire. *Neuration* as in *Erebia*, except that the discoidal cell is elongated and narrow, extending considerably beyond the middle of the wing; the *upper disco-cellular* nervule is also much elongated, and the *lower* one as long as the space between the base of the third branch of the median nervure and the point of its junction with the lower disco-cellular. FORELEGS of the MALE very small and slender, densely clothed to the tip with long loose hairs; the femur about as long as the tibia, and the tarsus as the tibia. *Four hindlegs* short; femur rather thick, very hairy beneath; tibia clothed all over with long loose hairs; tibial spurs long and acute; tarsi armed beneath and at the sides with rows of spines. *Claws* curved, long, simple, and very acute. *Paronychia* and *pulvillus* small."

"*Œneis* is distinguished from the other genera of *Satyrinæ* partly by the more elongate form of the wings, and shorter inner margin of the *forewing*, which occasions a deeper incision between its hinder angle and the apex of the *hindwing*, partly by the wings being less densely clothed with scales than ordinary, and partly by the pale, livid, or obscure colours of the wings, and the *hindwing* marked with paler nervures beneath. Also by the very hairy condition of the four hindlegs, and the greater elongation of the *discoidal cell* of both wings, and of the *upper disco-cellular* nervule of the *hindwing*." (*Westwood*, l.c.)

The genus is a Palæarctic one extending into the Nearctic region. About twenty species are known, chiefly from the Arctic regions, and from the high mountain ranges in the temperate zone: only a single species occurs within our limits at great elevations in the Himalayas.

231. Œneis pumilus, Felder. (PLATE XV, FIG. 37 ♂).

Chionobas pumilus, Felder, Reise Novara, Lep., vol. iii, p. 490, n. 846, pl. lxix, figs. 6, 7 (1866), *male*; id., Elwes, Proc. Zool. Soc. Lond., 1882, p. 404, pl. xxv, fig. 3.

HABITAT: Ladak, Sikkim, Himalayas.

EXPANSE: 1·9 inches.

DESCRIPTION: "MALE: UPPERSIDE, *both wings* yellowish-brown, with a band beyond the middle ochreous-yellow; the *cilia* whitish spotted with fuscous. *Forewing* with the band edged with fuscous, obsoletely submacular, furcate at apex; in the *hindwing* it is inwardly defined with fuscescent and bisinuated. UNDERSIDE: *Forewing* much paler, hoary on the costal and apical border and irrorated and striated with fuscous, a ferruginous-fuscous cellular streak [on the disco-cellular nervules]; the fascia as on the upperside but edged with ferruginous-fuscous, and including a dot of the same colour between the discoidal nervules; and fuscous irrorations before the cilia. *Hindwing* pale fuscous, closely striated with dark fuscous, chiefly towards the base, with hoary irrorations on the costal margin, the apex and inner margin more or less prominent; the nervules, especially the lower ones, hoary-whitish; an abbreviated dark chestnut-fuscous basal streak inwardly broadly defined with ochraceous, and the fascia as on the upperside, but much paler, edged with deep chestnut-fuscous especially inwardly, outwardly variegated with fuscous." (*Felder*, l.c.)

Œ. pumilus was originally taken by the late Dr. Stoliczka in Ladak on the Lanak pass at about 15,500 feet elevation, at Trantse Sumdo, and at Pangchog, and has never been taken since so far as we know, till quite recently Mr. H. J. Elwes received ten specimens through a native collector in Sikkim which were taken on the borders of Thibet, and probably at a great elevation. The Sikkim race is figured by Mr. Elwes (l. c.), who remarks that the "specimens agree very fairly with Felder's plate, but the markings are more distinct and well defined, especially the outer edge of the band on the hindwing; they are also darker in colour and less yellow in tint."

The figure of the Sikkim race differs considerably from Felder's figure. In the latter, the band on the upperside of the forewing is very broad and continuous, leaving a narrow margin beyond of yellowish brown, which almost disappears at the inner angle; whereas in the figure of the Sikkim race the band is very narrow, distinctly macular, each spot being more or less completely circled with fuscous on both upper and undersides, and the band is well removed from the margin; also on the underside of the hindwing the basal streak is altogether lost in the dark ground-colour. Mr. Elwes' figure represents the markings almost exactly as in *Aulocera brahminus*; the band is identical in formation, and the bifurcated apical portion includes a small dark spot with pale pupil,—in fact it resembles exactly a very small specimen of *A. brahminus* strongly tinted with yellow throughout. Felder's figure on the contrary much resembles in general appearance a small *Hipparchia*, except that on the underside of the hindwing the yellow fascia is in strong contrast with the grey-fuscous ground-colour, and the fascia of the upperside has no trace of the black spots on it which are found in all the Indian *Hipparchias*. It appears to us that the races are separable, and that the Sikkim race should be separately named, but in the absence of specimens it is impossible to decide this.

The figure (which is copied from Felder's figure in the Reise Novara) represents the upper and undersides of a male specimen.

Genus 24.—EREBIA, Dalman. (PLATE XV.)

Erebia, Dalman, Svensk. Handl., p. 58 (1816); id., Boisduval, Gen. Ind. Meth., p. 26 (1840); id., Westwood, Gen. D. L., vol. ii, p. 376 (1851); *Maniola*, Schrank, *apud* Kirby.

"BODY moderately robust, hairy. HEAD moderate-sized, clothed with very long hairs. *Eyes* prominent, lateral, naked, the fore part differently coloured from the hinder part in dried specimens. *Palpi* porrected obliquely, the tips ascending higher than the level of the tops of the eyes, and reaching further in front than the length of the head, very densely clothed with long hairs, extending in front at right angles, and almost concealing the terminal joint, which is slender, short, and villose. *Antennæ* not half the length of the forewing, slender, the joints scarcely distinct; terminated by an oval, rather short, but gradually formed club, (which in some species is short, broad, and spoon-shaped), its basal portion hollowed within, but its extremity curved outward and obtuse. *Thorax* short, oval, very hairy. *Abdomen* moderately short and slender. FOREWING triangularly ovate, entire, and convex along the outer margin; the costal margin but slightly arched; apex rounded; outer margin about three-fourths of the length of the costal; hinder angle rounded; inner margin scarcely as long as the outer, nearly straight. *Costal nervure* extending rather beyond the middle of the costa, slightly swollen at the base, or not thicker than the rest. *Subcostal nervure* slender, its first and second branches arising before the anterior extremity of the discoidal cell, the third and fourth branches free, arising at a greater or less distance apart, beyond the cell; *upper disco-cellular* generally obliterated; *middle disco-cellular* shorter than the outer one, but rather variable in its direction; *lower disco-cellular* considerably longer, nearly straight, but oblique, its extremity being directed towards the outer margin, closing the discoidal cell almost transversely nearly at the middle of the wing, uniting with the third branch of the median nervure at a shorter distance from its base than exists between the first and second branches; the third branch being angulated at the place of junction, beyond which it is nearly straight; the *median* and *submedian* nervures not dilated at the base. HINDWING suboval, entire along the anal margin [it is slightly incised in the Indian species]; the outer margin also entire, or but slightly scalloped; beneath often marked with dark freckles, with a broader dark subcentral fascia. *Subcostal nervure* arising nearer the body than the præcostal, its branch arising at a moderate distance from the base of the wing; the *upper disco-cellular* longer than the space between its base and that of the branch, and sometimes rather arched; the *lower disco-cellular* considerably longer, straight, more oblique, uniting with the third branch of the median nervure at a short distance from its base, closing the discoidal cell rather beyond the middle of the wing. FORELEGS of the MALE extremely minute, concealed among the hairs of the breast, very densely hairy; the tarsus much shorter than the tibia, and very slender. *Forelegs* of the FEMALE much longer, scaly, slender; the outside of the tibia and tarsus with a few rather long setæ; the tarsus nearly as long as the tibia, scaly, not very distinctly articulated, the extremity armed with fine setæ-like spines. *Four hindlegs* moderately long, slender, scaly; femur clothed within with long hairs; tibia armed with a few spines, those on the sides beneath forming rows; tarsus nearly as long as the tibia, more thickly and irregularly spined; *claws* simple; *pulvilli* very minute."

"LARVA rather robust, finely pubescent, longitudinally striated; head small; tail pointed, bifid." (*Westwood*, l. c.)

Erebia is distinguished from the preceding genera by having the wings much rounded in outline, also the costal nervure alone is dilated at the base; and the outer margin is very convex, entire, or scarcely perceptibly sinuate. The colour in the Indian species is velvety blackish-brown on the upperside, with ferruginous or ochreous patches on the disc; and on the underside the hindwing is very thickly clothed with scales and short hairs, dark brown irrorated with greyish throughout, and having a complete discal row of white spots. The structural differences between it and the following genus *Callerebia* are very slight, but there is a well-defined character in the markings so far as our Indian species are concerned; in all the Indian *Erebias* the ferruginous patches are more or less present, the apical ocellus of the forewing is round, and has a single white pupil on the upperside, sometimes very prominent, (occasionally two on the underside in *E. shallada*), and the hindwing is without ocelli of any kind either on upper or underside. In the Indian *Callerebias* the ferruginous patches are never present on the upperside, though the ocelli have often ferruginous irides; the apical ocellus of the forewing is oval and bipupilled on both sides even when least prominent; and the hindwing has almost universally a subanal ocellus on the upperside, and one or more on the underside. The MALE insects have no sexual patches or tufts of hair on the wing. *Erebia* is a Palæarctic genus, of which numerous species occur in Europe and Northern Asia, but only three species occur in India, and these are only found within our limits in the Western Himalayas. In habits they frequent forests and bare grassy slopes at from 6,000 to 14,000 feet elevation, and have a weak flopping flight, with an irregular pitching action.

Key to the Indian species of Erebia.

A. Upperside velvety brown, with ferruginous or ochreous discal patches; the apical ocellus of the forewing round, with a single pupil: no ocelli on the hindwing on upper or undersides.

a. The ferruginous patches of the upperside diffused.

a[1]. The patches large and including the ocellus on the forewing; the ocellus with distinct fulvous iris.

232. E. KALINDA, Western Himalayas.

b[1]. The patches small on both wings and very dark ferruginous, well removed from the ocellus on the forewing; the ocellus with the iris obsolete or indistinct.

233. E. SHALLADA, Western Himalayas.

b. The patch of the forewing paler and ochreous, very large and well-defined; no patch on the hindwing.

234. E. MANI, Ladak.

232. **Erebia kalinda**, Moore.

E. kalinda, Moore, Proc. Zool. Soc. Lond., 1865, p. 501, n. 92, pl. xxx, fig. 5, *female*.

HABITAT: Western Himalayas.

EXPANSE: 1·85 to 2·1 inches.

DESCRIPTION: "FEMALE: UPPERSIDE greenish velvety brown; *both wings* with a ferruginous discal patch, that on the *forewing* being subapical. *Forewing* with an apical black spot, having a white pupil and yellow iris. UNDERSIDE dull brown. *Forewing* as on upperside, but the ferruginous colour extending anteriorly across the discoidal cell; *hindwing* with a submarginal series of white dots; the ferruginous patch obsolete." (*Moore*, l. c.) "The MALE differs from the female in being somewhat smaller, the wings rather narrower, and the exterior margin of the forewing less rounded. The ferruginous patch on the UPPERSIDE of the *hindwing* is obsolete, or nearly so, in some specimens. The *cilia* are long and alternately white and brown (in both sexes)." (*Lang* in epis.) It is also a much darker insect, the ground-colour of the female being pale brown.

The type specimens were taken by Colonel A. M. Lang, R.E., who recorded the following note: "*E. kalinda* is local, and I saw very few, at two places on the hill-sides below the Runang and Werang passes, not at the summit of the pass, but some 2,000 feet lower down. It has a weak low flight among the grass and flowers. The perfect insect appears in June and July at 12,000 to 13,000 feet altitude below the melting snow on the passes in Upper Kunawar." Mr. A. Graham Young has taken it in the Kulu valley in May; Mr. de Nicéville took numerous males and one female at Ulwas in May, and Mr. Robert Ellis and Dr. Hutchison took numerous specimens of both sexes in Pangi in June and July at altitudes of 9,000 feet and upwards. Mr. A. G. Butler, in writing on Dr. Watts' collection (Proc. Zool. Soc. Lond., 1880, p. 147), notes that *E. kalinda* was taken "in pine forests in the Ravi basin up to 12,000 feet."

233. **Erebia shallada**, Lang. (PLATE XV, FIG. 42 ♂).

E. shallada, Lang, Journ. A. S. B., vol. xlix, pt. ii, p. 247 (1880).

HABITAT: Western Himalayas.

EXPANSE: 2·0 to 2·3 inches.

DESCRIPTION: MALE: UPPERSIDE, *both wings* uniform dark velvety brown, with a small diffused dark ferruginous patch within the middle of the exterior margin, and placed between the third and first median nervules in the forewing, but reaching the discoidal nervule in the hindwing. *Cilia* whitish, marked with brown at the ends of the nervules. *Forewing* with a subapical black ocellus having one prominent white pupil, and usually with no iris. UNDERSIDE: *Forewing* dark ferruginous with brown margins, greyish at apex, the subapical ocellus larger than on the upperside, black, with one, sometimes two, pupils, one central, the other when present below it and much smaller; and a narrow yellowish iris. *Hindwing* dark brown, finely mottled with a lighter tint, with a submarginal row of eight white dots. The colour and markings of the underside of the hindwing are almost identical in all the three Indian species of *Erebia*. "FEMALE more rounded in outline than the male, especially the exterior margin of the forewing. UPPERSIDE as in the male, but the brown ground-colour paler, the ferruginous patches lighter and more diffused, the subapical ocellus larger, more distinct, and with two white pupils, one central, the other below it, and smaller. UNDERSIDE as in the male. *Forewing* with the ocellus larger and brighter coloured. *Hindwing* with a narrow sinuous transverse discal band of brighter brown." (*Lang* in epis.)

E. shallada is commoner, and extends to lower elevations than *E. kalinda*; it is rather larger, and the male broader winged; it is darker and less brightly coloured, and approaches the *Callerebias* in appearance, especially in the darker more uniform tone, and in the occasional presence of a second white pupil in the ocellus.

Colonel Lang notes that "it appears to be very local; during three or four years collecting in Kunawar I only twice met with it, taking only five specimens, once at 6,000, and again at

8,000 feet altitude, on grass-covered and rocky slopes above the Sutlej in June." Since then Mr. de Nicéville has taken a large number at Ulwas in company with *E. kalinda* in May; he also found it during that month exceedingly plentifully along all the roads in the station of Dalhousie, and through the thick forest as far as Kujiar. Major C. H. T. Marshall found it commonly at Kujiar near Dalhousie and at other places in the Chumba State in May; and Mr. A. Graham Young took it in Kulu in May and July.

The figure represents a male specimen, taken in Kulu by Mr. A. Graham Young, showing both upper and undersides.

234. **Erebia mani**, de N. (PLATE XV, FIG, 43 ♂).

E. mani, de Nicéville, Journ. A. S. B., vol. xlix, pt. ii, p. 247 (1880.)

HABITAT: Chung Pass and Lingti, Ladak.

EXPANSE: 2·0 to 2·1 inches.

DESCRIPTION: MALE: UPPERSIDE, *both wings* dusky brown. *Cilia* gray at the interspaces. *Forewing* with a somewhat square bright ochreous patch, bounded inwardly above by the disco-cellular nervules, below which it extends in an almost straight line to below the first median nervule, where it becomes merged into the ground-colour; outwardly it almost follows the curve of the wing, but the ground-colour beyond is slightly wider at the apex; anteriorly it is bounded by the subcostal nervure. It bears a large round black spot, with an iris of a slightly lighter colour than the ground, and a minute white pupil. *Hindwing* immaculate. UNDERSIDE: *Forewing* with the discal patch more diffused, extending into the cell, and thickly irrorated with deep ferruginous scales, especially that portion in and just beyond and below the cell. The iris of the black spot is wider and lighter than above. The apex and outer half of the costa thickly irrorated with grey scales, as is also the *hindwing* throughout, which also bears a submarginal series of seven or eight small white dots. FEMALE with both the ground-colour everywhere, and the discal patch on the *forewing* slightly lighter; the grey portions of the *cilia* more prominent.

Mr. de Nicéville took six males and two females on the Chung Pass, on July 10th, and one female at Lingti on the 16th, all at high elevations.

Of the species of *Erebia* occurring in Central and Western Asia beyond our limits, *E. maracandica*,* Erschoff, is the only one which approaches the Indian group. This species is closely allied to *E. kalinda*, but appears to differ in having the ocellus on the *forewing* on both sides very much smaller, and the underside much more uniform in colouration, the *hindwing* lacking the greyish irrorations, and the *forewing* the dark ferruginons patch which covers almost the whole wing in *E. kalinda*.

Erebia turanica, Erschoff, is figured by Serge Alphéraky, (Hor. Soc. Ent. Ross., vol. xvi, p. 413, pl. xv, fig. 22 (1881), and is of very different aspect. It is a dark brown insect of uniform colouration on both sides; the UPPERSIDE with a discal row of three yellow spots on the *forewing*, the first just beyond the cell large and divided by the lower discoidal nervule, the other two smaller, one on each median interspace; and on the *hindwing* a submarginal row of five smaller yellow spots, one on each interspace from the apex. The UNDERSIDE is similar, but it has in addition on the *hindwing* a prominent pure white discal band outwardly dentate, inwardly even and macular towards the costa; also a small white spot near the end of the cell, and another below it. It is said to be very common everywhere between 3,000 and 10,000 feet altitude during the summer in the Tian-chian mountains.

Erebia kalmuka, Alphéraky, is figured and described in the same work (p. 414, pl. xv, figs. 18 ♂, 19 ♀), and is again of a totally different aspect. DESCRIPTION: "UPPERSIDE brownish-fuscous. *Forewing* with the costa, apex, disco-cellular nervules, and outer margin, and *hindwing* with outer margin, narrowly-irrorated with whitish (less densely in the female).

---

* *E. maracandica*, Erschoff. The male is described and figured in Erschoff's Lepidoptera of Turkestan p. 17, n. 56, pl. i, fig. 13 (1874). DESCRIPTION: "UPPERSIDE fuscous. *Forewing* with a large outer patch marked with a black ocellus with a white pupil. *Hindwing* with an outer patch, fulvous. UNDERSIDE, *both wings* fuscous. *Forewing* fulvescent at the base. *Hindwing* with a transverse outer series of whitish dots." (*Erschoff*, l. c.)

UNDERSIDE of the MALE. *Forewing* chestnut, the costa, the outer margin, and the disco-cellular nervules irrorated with silvery-whitish scales. *Hindwing* powdered with greyish-silvery throughout. Of the FEMALE the *forewing* is paler, the *hindwing* brownish-grey with whitish nervules." (*Alphéraky*, l. c.) Found from 9,000 feet elevation up to the limit where vegetation ceases in the mountains near Kuldja.

Erebia sibo, Alphéraky, is also figured and described in the same work (p. 416, pl. xv, figs. 20 ♂, 21 ♀). It is found in the same mountains, and somewhat resembles *E. kalmuka* in aspect, both species being totally devoid of ocelli or white dots of any sort on either wing on either surface, but is rarer and more local. DESCRIPTION : " Wings rounded, costa arched. MALE much larger, the wings more ample. FEMALE with the wings narrower. UPPERSIDE fuscous, between the nervules chestnut towards the outer margin. UNDERSIDE of the MALE. *Forewing* chestnut, with black nervules. *Hindwing* greyish-fuscous, with ashy nervules, three undulate arched streaks fuscous, one subbasal, one median, and one before the margin, of which the last two unite above the anal angle. Of the FEMALE, very different from the male. *Forewing* dilute brownish-grey, with a submarginal and a median series of dots, and the basal dots, irregular, brown, [in the figure the basal area is darker, defined by a dark lunulate median streak, beyond which is another lunulate dark submarginal streak]. *Hindwing* brownish-ashy, the nervules paler, a broad median fuscescent fascia, everywhere irregularly defined with fuscous, and a submarginal series of angulate marks brownish-fuscous."

In a paper on the Lepidopterous fauna of Transcaucasia* Lederer notes the occurrence of the following species of *Erebia* in the tract dealt with :—*E. tyndarus*, Esper ; *E. pronoë*, Esper ; *E. hewitsonii*, Lederer ; *E. ligea*, Linnæus ; and *E. afra*, Fabricius ; also of *E. melancholica*, Herrich-Schäffer. Of the last we have no figure or description available ; the other five belong to a different section of the genus which is numerously represented in Europe, and in which the characteristic colouring is dark brown with an incomplete rather narrow ferruginous band on each wing bearing a series of ocelli ; of course the extent to which these characters are present and developed varies greatly in the various species. It is very unlikely that any *Erebias* of this section of the genus will be found to occur within our limits.

Genus 25.—CALLEREBIA, Butler. (PLATE XV).

Callerebia, Butler, Ann. and Mag. of Nat. Hist., third series, vol. xx, p. 217 (1867).

" Very similar to *Erebia ;* differs in the form and markings of the wings, the anal angle of the *hindwing* being frequently produced and lobe-shaped ; also in the more slender antennæ less distinctly clavate, and in the more angulate palpi. Otherwise as in *Erebia.*" (*Butler*, l. c.)

Callerebia is apparently almost exclusively confined to the Himalayas and out-lying ranges ; a single species occurs in the Khasi hills, and one species has been described from Moupin in Thibet, all the rest occur in the Western Himalayas, some of them extending to the Eastern Himalayas as far as Nepal. They affect lower elevations than the *Erebias* do, and are common in the outer ranges at 6,000 feet altitude; they differ in colour and markings from the *Erebias*, as pointed out above ; and are sombre brown insects with weak pitching flight and similar habits, but are more frequently found in shady places and among the undergrowth in forests ; they all have a bipupilled ocellus on both sides of the *forewing*, and at least one subanal ocellus with a single pupil on the *hindwing*, except occasionally in *C. scanda* ; on the underside of the *hindwing* also at least one of the submarginal dots, and often several of them, are developed into ocelli, except occasionally in *C. orixa.* Nine species or varieties have been described ; all of them are more or less variable in their markings, and all are closely allied to each other, many of them being very doubtfully distinct. The male insect has no sexual patches or tufts of hair on the wings, and the sexes are but very slightly differentiated in colour and markings ; the females chiefly differ in the somewhat broader and more rounded outline and the slightly paler tone of colouration. When the specimens of this genus are fresh and newly emerged from the chrysalis, they are beautifully glossed with deep blue in some lights.

---

* Annales de la Soc. Ent. de Belgique, Tome xiii, p. 25 (1869-70).

C. scanda is quite distinct, and so also is *C. orixa*, the only species found in the Khasi hills. *C. annada*, *C. hybrida* and *C. nirmala* can typically be easily distinguished, but there are numerous intermediate forms. Typical *C. hybrida* can be distinguished from *C. annada* by the shape of the wings, from typical *C. nirmala* it may be known by the far greater prominence of the discal and submarginal brown lines of the underside, and in having only two ocelli near the anal angle. *C. intermedia* and *C. cashapa* only differ from *C. nirmala* in the ocellation of the *hindwing*, and as neither form is at all constant in this respect, and numerous intermediate variations are found linking all three together, they seem to be inseparable as species. *C. daksha*, the smallest of the group, is also closely allied to *C. nirmala*, but the uniform dark brown colour of the underside and the prominence of the white spots render it sufficiently distinct, though it also shows variations in ocellation.

Key to the Indian species of Callerebia.

A. Upperside dark brown, with one (occasionally two to five, on *hindwing*) ocellus on each wing, that on the *forewing* bipupilled and oval; no ferruginous patches on either wing.

- *a.* Upperside with the margins of both wings broadly and distinctly paler; underside uniform brown; *hindwing* with the inner half only densely irrorated with pure white; two prominent subanal ocelli and four white spots in a submarginal series; but no transverse dark lines.

  235. C. SCANDA, Western Himalayas.

- *b.* Upperside almost uniform brown.
  - *a*¹. The ocellus of the *forewing* widely encircled with bright fulvous on upper and undersides. The underside tinged throughout with fulvous; *hindwing* with the white irrorations interrupted with numerous fulvous-brown undulated striæ; the two subanal ocelli small and blind, or wanting; the white spots also wanting.

    236. C. ORIXA, Khasi Hills.

  - *b*¹. The ocelli all with narrow irides on the upperside.
    - *a*². Underside brown; *hindwing* with grey irrorations throughout, and crossed by more or less distinct submarginal and median sinuate brown lines, between which and on the inner margin the grey irrorations are denser, sometimes also a subbasal line, the white spots often obsolete, the two subanal ocelli prominent but often blind.
      - *a*³. *Forewing* elongate, outer margin nearly straight.

        237. C. ANNADA, Western Himalayas.

      - *b*³. *Forewing* short, outer margin convex.

        238. C. HYBRIDA, Western Hymalayas.

    - *b*². Underside greyish brown, the disc of the *forewing* maroon; *hindwing* with the grey irrorations very fine and indistinct, with little or no trace of brown lines or undulations; the ocelli round, the four white spots present and irregularly developed into ocelli; often more than one ocellus on the upperside of the *hindwing*.

      239. C. NIRMALA, Western Himalayas.
      C. intermedia, Western Himalayas.
      C. cashapa, Western Himalayas.

    - *c*². Underside uniform dark brown, with no white irrorations; *hindwing* with the white spots prominent and irregularly developed into perfect ocelli.

      240. C. DAKSHA, Western Himalayas.

235. Callerebia scanda, Kollar.

Erebia scanda, Kollar, in Hügel's Kaschmir, vol. iv., pt. ii, p. 452, pl. xvii, figs. 3, 4 (1844); *Callerebia scanda*, Butler, Ann. and Mag. of Nat. Hist., third series, vol. xx, p. 217, n. 1 (1867).

HABITAT: Western Himalayas.

EXPANSE: 2·0 to 2·3 inches.

DESCRIPTION: "Wings entire, rounded. UPPERSIDE fuscous-black. *Forewing* with a black ocellus near the apex on both sides, bordered with ferruginous, and with two white pupils. *Hindwing* with one ocellus near the anal angle on the upperside, and two on the underside, pupilled with white. UNDERSIDE. *Both wings* paler, the *hindwing* irrorated with white."

"The upperside is black-brown, a little lighter towards the anterior and exterior margins; the ocellus of the *forewing* is oblong. *Hindwing* with a lighter marginal line. UNDERSIDE with four white dots in an arched line above the ocelli." (*Kollar*, l. c.)

We have never seen the FEMALE of *C. scanda*. Kollar's description of it is appended for reference; * but he seems to have described a female of *C. annada* by mistake. These *Callerebias* were at that time hardly known at all, and the specimens available for examination were few in number: to judge from analogy the female of *C. scanda* will be found to differ but little from the male in colour or style of markings.

C. scanda is a very distinct species and shows little variation. The chief distinguishing features are—on the upperside the paling of the outer margins, and on the underside the absence of the ferruginous tint on the disc of the *forewing*, the concentration of the white irrorations on the inner half of the *hindwing*, and the presence of the four submarginal white dots above the ocelli. The only variation worth noticing is in the occasional disappearance of the single ocellus on the upperside of the *hindwing*. In shape it corresponds with *C. nirmala*, but it has the outer margin of the *forewing* more convex.

"This species appears in the height of the rainy season (July and August) about the hedges and banks in lower Kunawar at 6,000 to 7,000 feet altitude. Good fresh specimens are of a velvety black-brown on the upperside, and on the underside have the *hindwing* very whitely salted, so that as they fly they look distinctly parti-coloured." (*Colonel A. M. Lang, R.E.*, in Proc. Zool. Soc. Lond., 1865, p. 501). *C. scanda* is common throughout the outer ranges of the Western Himalayas, as far east as Mussoorie, and is probably found in Kumaon, but we have no record of its occurrence further east. Our collections contain only specimens from Pangi taken by Mr. Robert Ellis, from Simla and from Mussoorie.

236. **Callerebia orixa**, Moore.

C. orixa, Moore, Proc. Zool. Soc. Lond., 1872, p. 555.

HABITAT: Khasi Hills, Munipur.

EXPANSE: 2·2 to 2·4 inches.

DESCRIPTION: "MALE: UPPERSIDE dark chocolate velvety-brown, with an indistinct narrow submarginal black line. *Forewing* with a large subapical ocellus, composed of a round black spot, encircled by a broad bright ferruginous ring, and centred with two white dots. *Hindwing* with a small similar ocellus near the anal angle. UNDERSIDE brighter brown. *Forewing* mottled at the apex, the ocellus as above, with a posterior dusky border. *Hindwing* with numerous greyish-white transverse short strigæ, which are most numerous from the abdominal margin and less frequent before and below the apex; two very small contiguous anal black spots encircled by a ferruginous ring, each without a central white dot."

"This species may be known from *C. annada* by the ocellus on the *forewing* being twice as large, much more prominent, and brighter-coloured." (*Moore*, l. c.)

C. orixa is also a very distinct species, isolated in its geographical range from the rest of the genus. The FEMALE is unknown, but it probably differs very slightly, if at all, from the male. We have specimens taken by Mr. A. O. Hume in the eastern hills of Munipur in May, and others taken by Dr. E. R. Johnson at Shillong in May and June, and at Terria Ghât below Shillong in the autumn.

237. **Callerebia annada**, Moore.†

Erebia annada, Moore, Horsfield and Moore, Cat. Lep. E. I. C., vol i, p. 226, n. 475 (1857); *C. scanda*, var. *b*, Butler, Ann. and Mag. of Nat. Hist., third series, vol. xx, p. 217, pl. iv, fig. 8.

HABITAT: The Himalayas, from Kashmir to Bhutan.

EXPANSE: 2·4 to 2·8 inches.

---

* *Callerebia scanda*. "The FEMALE is somewhat larger, the *hindwing* perceptibly lobed at the anal angle: the white pupils of the ocelli absent on both sides, or very indistinct. UNDERSIDE. *Hindwing* with the white irrorations less distinct, the four white dots above the ocelli wanting." (*Kollar*, l. c.)

† The figure (plate xv, fig. 44) which is named *C annada* on the plate, really represents *C. hybrida*, the next species, which had not been discriminated when the plate was printed.

DESCRIPTION : "Differs from *Erebia* [*Callerebia*] *scanda* in being larger, and in having the anal angle more falcated. On the UNDERSIDE, the *forewing* is of a bright ferruginous ; the *hindwing* is mottled with white nearly throughout, and from near the anal angle, below the ocelli, extends a curved white line." (*Moore*, l.c.)

C. annada is the largest species of the genus, and has the *forewing* most elongate, the outer margin being oblique and almost straight, sometimes slightly concave ; it most nearly approaches *C. orixa* both in outline and markings, and also geographically in its range.

The ferruginous tint of the UNDERSIDE of the *forewing* is very bright in specimens from the Eastern Himalayas ; in those from the Western Himalayas it is much less pronounced, except on a discal patch which includes the ocellus, and is outwardly more or less distinctly margined with fuscous. On the *hindwing* the white mottlings are not uniformly spread as in *C. scanda*, but are distinctly grouped into undulated striæ, as in *C. orixa* ; and there usually is no trace of the four submarginal white spots ; the "curved white line" mentioned above is nebulous and composed of these same whitish irrorations. In typical specimens there are no distinctly formed transverse dark lines, but at the places they should occupy the whitish irrorations are less dense, showing more of the ground-colour ; in other specimens the lines are distinctly formed, the submarginal one lunulate and ending before the ocelli, the median one highly and irregularly sinuated, the subbasal one scarcely traceable in any. The ocelli at the anal angle are somewhat misshapen and placed obliquely, that at the anal angle being nearest to the margin ; and both are almost always blind, though occasionally with small pupils even in typical specimens. The FEMALE is rather larger and paler coloured, but does not otherwise differ from the male.

C. annada is probably not uncommon, but we have few specimens in our collections. Colonel A. M. Lang, R.E., took it in Lower Kunawar, and Mr. Hocking in the Kangra District ; Major C. H. T. Marshall took it in the Chumba State in May ; and Mr. de Nicéville at Simla ; the type was taken in Bhutan. The Indian Museum has a specimen from Nepal, and it probably is to be found in all the intermediate region, occurring in the rainy season.

238. **Callerebia hybrida**, Butler. (PLATE XV, FIG. 44 ♂.*)

C. hybrida, Butler, Proc. Zool. Soc. Lond., 1880, p. 147, n. 4 ; *C. nada*, Moore, Trans. Ent. Soc. Lond., 1881, p. 306.

HABITAT : North-Western Himalayas.

EXPANSE : ♂, 2·0 to 2·4 ; ♀, 2·5 inches.

DESCRIPTION : "Dr. Watt obtained a series of a *Callerebia* exhibiting intermediate forms between *C. annada* and *C. nirmala*. In the colouration of the UNDERSIDE of the *forewing* they agree almost entirely with *C. nirmala*, but show the submarginal stripe strongly as in *C. annada* ; on the *hindwing* they are coloured like *C. annada*, but have rounded ocelli varying in number from two to five. In expanse they are intermediate, and therefore correspond with *C. scanda* in this respect." (*Butler*, l. c.)

From the above description *C. hybrida* would seem to be nearest allied to *C. nirmala*, but it is really most closely allied to *C. annada*. The original description of *C. nada*, which is appended below for reference,† gives a far more accurate idea of this species than Mr. Butler's description of *C. hybrida* does ; we have never seen any specimen with more than two ocelli on the hindwing that could be separated from *C. nirmala*, and had not Mr. Moore recently admitted (Proc. Zool. Soc. Lond., 1882, p. 237), that his *C. nada* is identical with *C. hybrida*, we should have retained this species under the name of *C. nada*, Moore, and placed *C. hybrida*, Butler, as a variety of *C. nirmala*.

---

* Erroneously named *C. annada* on the plate.

† *Callerebia nada*, Moore. HABITAT : Kunawur. EXPANSE : *male*, 2·00 ; *female*, 2·50 inches. DESCRIPTION : "MALE *and* FEMALE. Nearest to *C. annada*. Exterior margins of *both wings* more convex. UPPERSIDE similar, the ocellus of the *forewing* comparatively more rounded. UNDERSIDE similar ; *forewing* with the reddish patch somewhat broader, and extending to below the lower median nervule ; *hindwing* with less prominent grey strigæ ; the transverse zig-zag brown line distinctly formed and more erect, the two subanal ocelli larger and white-pupilled ; above these there is an indistinct row of white spots." (*Moore*, l. c.)

Typical *C. hybrida* is readily distinguished from *C. annada* by the shape of the forewing, and generally also by the markings of the hindwing, though these latter are variable and show gradations between the two species. There is no discernible difference in the shape of the ocellus of the forewing on the upperside (but the iris is less prominent), nor in the extent of the reddish patch on the underside ; but on the UNDERSIDE of the *hindwing* the whitish irrorations are less distinct and much less prominently grouped into undulated striæ ; the transverse lines are almost always distinct, and the median line is more regularly sinuate and subparallel with the outer margin ; the white submarginal spots are almost always present ; the subanal ocelli are shaped and placed as in *C. annada*, but are almost always distinctly pupilled with whitish. Two very remarkable specimens taken in Kulu by Mr. A. Graham Young have the ocelli quite blind, and the markings altogether almost exactly as in *C. annada*, but the shape of the wings shows conclusively that they belong to this species, *C. hybrida*.

C. hybrida is very common in the Western Himalayas throughout the outer ranges at moderate elevations from May to September ; we have no specimens from further east than Mussoorie, but it probably extends to Kumaon even if not still further eastwards.

239. **Callerebia nirmala,** Moore.

Erebia nirmala, Moore, Proc. Zool. Soc. Lond., 1865, p. 501, n 91 ; *Callerebia intermedia* and *C. cashapa*, Moore, id., 1882, p. 236 ; *C. scanda*, var. *c*, Butler, Ann. and Mag. of Nat. Hist., third series, vol. xx, p 217, pl. iv, fig. 9 (1867).

HABITAT : Western Himalayas.

EXPANSE : 2·0 to 2·4 inches.

DESCRIPTION : " MALE : UPPERSIDE uniform dark brown. *Forewing* with a subapical black ocellus, having two white pupils and a dark ferruginous iris. *Hindwing* with a similar but single-pupilled ocellus near the anal angle. UNDERSIDE greyish brown, discal portion of *forewing* maroon-brown, ocelli of *both wings* as above, but with the irides yellow ; a white dot below the ocellus of the *forewing*, and a discal series of four white dots anterior to the ocellus of the *hindwing*. *Cilia* brown."

" *Remark.*—Allied to *E. scanda*, Kollar, but differs in having a somewhat more elongated forewing. On the underside it may be distinguished by the absence of the numerous white striæ on the hindwing, and by there being a *single ocellus only* near the anal angle." (*Moore*, l. c.) The FEMALE is similar to the male, but a little larger and paler.

Var. *intermedia*, Moore. HABITAT : Kangra district. EXPANSE : ♂, 2·1 ; ♀, 2·4 inches. DESCRIPTION : " Intermediate between *C. nirmala* and *C. cashapa*. UPPERSIDE similar to *C. nirmala*, with *one* ocellus only on each wing. UNDERSIDE with two lower ocelli, a third ocellus between the third median and discoidal nervules, and two small apical spots above." (*Moore*, l. c).

Var. *cashapa*, Moore. HABITAT : Dharmsala, Mussoorie, Simla. EXPANSE : 2·0 to 2·2 inches. DESCRIPTION : " Allied to *C. nirmala*. MALE and FEMALE comparatively larger in size. UPPERSIDE similar, but the *hindwing* having *three* well-formed ocelli, the one between the discoidal and third median nervules sometimes absent. UNDERSIDE : *Forewing* less brightly chestnut-coloured. *Hindwing* with a *complete series* of ocelli, one between each pair of nervules ; some specimens with three anterior and two posterior ocelli ; the upper one and sometimes the lowest being minute." (*Moore*, l. c).

Typical *C. nirmala* most nearly resembles *C. hybrida* on the upperside, being almost uniform dark brown throughout, but the ocelli are smaller and the irides fainter still ; it is also as a rule a smaller insect. On the underside its aspect is very different, the forewing is much more uniform in colour, and usually strongly tinged with maroon brown, the outer zone of the ocellus very indistinct ; on the hindwing the greyish irrorations are very fine and indistinct ; the transverse lines are indistinct or totally wanting, and the ocellus is quite round, with a very distinct iris and outer ring. The variation in the ocelli is inadequately represented in the varieties above described, as there are numerous gradations between each of these forms. The typical arrangement on the underside of the hindwing is one perfect subanal ocellus, and three white submarginal dots from the costa. Next we find a second subanal ocellus developed, and then a fourth white spot completing the series: and of this series, with the single exception of the upper subanal ocellus on the lower median interspace, which is constant, the whole of the spots vary at random; sometimes one, sometimes another, is totally absent, or on the other hand developed into a perfect ocellus; the number of perfect ocelli varies from one to six; where there are two only it is sometimes the third and fifth, sometimes the fifth and sixth; where there are three, it may be the third, fifth and sixth, or the second, third, and fifth, and so on. There are also sometimes one, sometimes two, ocelli below the subapical ocellus on the underside of the forewing. On the upperside of the hindwing there is typically only a single ocellus corresponding to the constant fifth of the underside; often a second is developed corresponding with the third in series, sometimes a third corresponding with the sixth, and occasionally, though rarely, the whole series of six is developed. If there is more than one ocellus on the upperside there are usually (but not always) at least four on the underside; and wherever the series is complete on the underside, more than one is almost invariably developed on the upperside.

C. nirmala in all its forms is very common at moderate elevations throughout the Western Himalayas from May till September. It affects the undergrowth in glades in forests, and may be seen on the wing even on damp and cloudy days.

240. **Callerebia daksha,** Moore.

C. daksha, Moore, Proc. Zool. Soc. Lond., 1874, p. 266, pl. xliii, fig. 1.

HABITAT: Kashmir.

EXPANSE: ♂, 1·75 to 2·15; ♀, 1·87 inches.

DESCRIPTION: "MALE and FEMALE: UPPERSIDE dark brown. *Forewing* with a small subapical black-bipupilled ocellus. *Hindwing* with a smaller subanal black spot, having a single white pupil, a white dot beyond it on the middle of the disc, some specimens showing also an intermediate dot. UNDERSIDE slightly paler, but uniform brown. *Forewing* with a pale ferruginous ring encircling the subapical ocellus, beneath which is a minute white dot. *Hindwing* with a pale ferruginous ring encircling the subanal black spot; a minute anal and a transverse discal series of five prominent white dots, which in some specimens appear on a black spot with a ferruginous ring."

"This is the smallest species of the genus yet described, and may be distinguished on the upperside by the absence of the ferruginous ring round the ocellus, on the underside by being of an uniform colour and without mottlings on the hindwing." (*Moore*, l. c.)

C. daksha is a comparatively rare insect, and appears to be local. The type specimens were taken at Goolmurg, 9,000 to 10,000 feet altitude. Mr. de Nicéville took a single specimen at Gond also in Kashmir; and Mrs. Bazett took a large number at Katabal near Goolmurg, at 8,000 to 9,000 feet altitude in June; but we have no other records of its capture. The development of the ocelli on the underside of the hindwing varies as in *C. nirmala*, but the white spots are generally much more prominent. It is also variable in size.

Genus 26.—ZIPŒTES, Hewitson. (PLATE XVII.*)

Zipætis, Hewitson, Ex. Butt., vol. iii, p. 100 (1863); *Ziboetes* or *Zipætes*, Wood-Mason, Journ. A. S. B., vol. l, pt. ii, p. 86 (1881), *note*.

"BODY small, hairy. *Eyes* small, smooth. *Antennæ* slender, short, slightly thicker from the middle to the tip; the articulations short, easily seen. *Palpi* long, compressed, thickly clothed with long hair; the last joint scarcely seen. FOREWING with the costal margin arched, the apex rounded, the inner margin nearly straight. *Costal* nervure alone swollen at the base, reaching the middle of the wing. *Subcostal* nervure with four branches, equi-distant; two before the end of the discoidal cell. The *discoidal cell* half the length of the wing, closed; *upper disco-cellular* nervule very short, the *middle* one half as long as the

* ZIPŒTES, erroneously spelt ZIPAETIS on the plate.

lower, slightly curved inwards; the *lower* one curved outwards, united to the third branch of the median nervure (which joins at an angle) at a distance from its base. HINDWING with the *costal* nervure joining the margin at the middle of the wing; *subcostal* nervure with its first branch arising at its middle; the *discoidal cell* closed obliquely; the *upper disco-cellular* nervule arising at a short distance below the first branch of the subcostal nervure; the *lower* one twice its length, joining the third median nervule at a short distance from its base." (*Hewitson*, l. c.)

Zipætes is very closely allied to *Callerebia*; structurally indeed they are almost identical, but in style of markings they differ considerably. In *Zipætes* there are no ocelli on the upperside, but on the underside on the hindwing the ocelli are very large, irregular, and enclosed in brilliant silvery bands. The male has no sexual patches or tufts on the wings, and the sexes are similar in colour and style of markings.

Only two species of *Zipætes* are known, both of them Indian—one from North-Eastern India, and the other from the hills of South India. Neither of them appear to be very common.

Key to the species of Zipœtes.

A. Upperside dark brown, with no ocelli; UNDERSIDE, hindwing with the ocelli large irregular, and enclosed by brilliant silvery bands.
- *a.* Both wings with a broad transverse white band; the ocelli of the hindwing enclosed by silvery bands in two groups.
  - 241. Z. SAITIS, South India.
- *b.* Dark brown, paler at the margins, but no white bands; the ocelli of the hindwing enclosed by silvery bands in a single group.
  - 242. Z. SCYLAX, North-East India.

241. Zipœtes saitis, Hewitson. (PLATE XVII, FIG. 58 ♀.)

Zipætis saitis, Hewitson, Ex. Butt., vol. iii, p. 100, pl *Hypocista* and *Zipætis*, fig. 6 (1863), *male*.

HABITAT: Hills of South-India.

EXPANSE: ♂, 2·3 to 2·5; ♀, 2·5 to 2·7 inches.

DESCRIPTION: "MALE: UPPERSIDE dark brown. *Both wings* crossed beyond the middle by a band of white. UNDERSIDE as above, except that the *hindwing* is crossed by a band of five ocelli [within the white band], with white pupils and rufous iris, bordered with silver; the first, fourth, and fifth small, the second large and with two pupils, the third half its size." (*Hewitson*, l. c). The silver border encloses the first and second ocelli in one group, and the third, fourth, and fifth in another. The FEMALE is paler in colouration, larger, the white bands wider, and with the wings somewhat broader.

We have as yet only received *Z. saitis* from Mr. Harold Fergusson, who took it in May and June at Mynall in the Ashamboo hills in Travancore at an altitude of 2,600 feet. It is also found in the Nilgiris and the Wynaad, and probably in the other hill ranges in the south of the Peninsula, but appears to be nowhere common.

The figure shows the upper and undersides of a female specimen from the Ashamboo range in Travancore in Major Marshall's collection.

242. Zipœtes scylax, Hewitson. (PLATE XVII, FIG. 62 ♀.)

Zipætis scylax, Hewitson, Ex. Butt., vol. iii, p. 100, pl. *Hypocista* and *Zipætis*, fig. 7 (1863).

HABITAT: Naga hills, Sylhet, Sikkim.

EXPANSE: 2·3 to 2·4 inches.

DESCRIPTION: "UPPERSIDE dark brown, paler towards the margins; the outer margins rufous, traversed by a submarginal black line. UNDERSIDE as above, except that there are two submarginal lines of black; that the *forewing* has a band of five small ocelli, the pupils blue, the iris rufous; and that the *hindwing* has a band of five ocelli, the pupils blue, the iris rufous; the first, fourth, and fifth small, the fourth oval with two pupils, the third large, all surrounded by a common band of silver." (*Hewitson*, l. c). There is also a less brilliant silver band on the forewing on the inner side only of the series of ocelli. The FEMALE is similarly coloured and marked, but larger, paler, and with broader wings; the submarginal dark lines are also both visible on the upperside in both sexes.

Z. scylax is rather a rare insect; it was originally recorded from Sylhet, but has not since been obtained from that district. Mr. Otto Möller has taken it at moderate elevations in Sikkim, and Mr. de Nicéville met with it in the Great Runjit valley in October, it will probably be found to occur here and there in the lower ranges on the north-eastern frontier of Bengal and Assam.

The figure shows the upper and undersides of a female specimen from the Great Runjit valley, Sikkim, in the Indian Museum, Calcutta.

The remaining genera of this subfamily show an approach to *Elymnias* in the clothing of the palpi, which are provided with a distinct tuft of hairs at the back of the middle joint, where it lies against the face; they are all aberrant, in that the palpi in front are not clothed with long porrect hairs, and in that the nervures of the forewing are not perceptibly dilated at the base. In *Melanitis* and *Hipio* there are no sexual marks on the wings of the male insect; but in both *Cyllogenes* and *Parantirrhœa*, there are very remarkable sexual characters. All of them are tropical or sub-tropical insects.

Genus 27.—MELANITIS, Fabricius. (PLATES I and XII).

Melanitis, Fabricius, Illiger's Mag., vol. vi, p. 282 (1807); *Cyllo*, Boisduval, Voy. Astrol., Lep., p. 140 (1832); id., Westwood, Gen D. L., vol. ii, p. 360 (1851).

"BODY small, weak; wings large; forewing emarginate along the outer margin; hindwing angulated or tailed in the middle of the outer margin. HEAD moderate-sized, hairy, with a broad short tuft in front. *Eyes* prominent, naked. *Palpi* rather short, compressed, broad, obliquely porrected upwards, the tip not reaching to the level of the top of the eyes; thickly clothed with short scaly hairs lying close together; the back of the middle joint with a thick tuft of hairs extending from the middle to the tip. *Antennæ* of variable length, slender, terminated by a gradually formed elongate club, scarcely thicker than the rest of the antenna. *Thorax* rather short, compressed, elevated in its hinder portion. *Abdomen* small, or but moderately robust. FOREWING, subtriangular; costal margin [more or less] strongly arched, apex rounded; outer margin [generally, not always] angulated or rather dilated a little below the apex, below which it is emarginate; inner margin nearly straight. None of the nervures dilated at the base; *costal nervure* extending a little beyond the middle of the costa; *subcostal* nervure with its branches as in *Lethe; upper disco-cellular* nervule very short, oblique, arising near the middle of the wing; *middle* disco-cellular equally short, more transverse; *outer* disco-cellular long, much curved, the curve being towards the base of the wing, the extremity directed outwards, and uniting with the third branch of the median nervure at about the same distance from its base as exists between the origin of its first and second branches, the third branch angulated at the point of junction with the lower disco-cellular, beyond which it is nearly straight. HINDWING broadly subovate; apex rounded; outer margin scalloped, strongly angulated, or tailed in the middle at the extremity of the third branch of the median nervure. *Subcostal* nervure nearly straight; *costal* nervure extending nearly to the apex; *subcostal* nervure branching at a moderate distance from the base (which is rather nearer the body than the præcostal nervule); *upper disco-cellular* nervule short, curved; *lower* disco-cellular considerably longer, nearly straight, oblique, uniting with the third branch of the median nervure at a short distance beyond its origin, closing the discoidal cell in an acute point. FORELEGS very minute, clothed with short hairs, not forming a brush; the *tibia* nearly equal in length to the femur; *tarsus* about two-thirds of the length of the tibia. Forelegs of the FEMALE rather longer, scaly; the femur clothed with short hairs beneath; tibia and tarsus of nearly equal thickness throughout; the latter obliquely truncate at the tip, with a few minute spines visible at or near the tip beneath, indicating the articulations. *Middle* and *hindlegs* of moderate length, slender, scaly; tibiæ with a very few very slender spines beneath; tibial spurs small; tarsus with the articulations very distinct, armed beneath, and at the tips, with rather long fine spines ; *claws* curved, acute ; armed beneath near the tip with a distinct acute tooth, nearly equal in size to the apical tooth of the claw."

"LARVA long, somewhat pisciform, being narrowed behind the head, gradually thickening to the middle of the body, and then gradually acuminated to the tail, which is terminated by two long setose pointed horns ; head somewhat heart-shaped, the upper edge armed with two erect obtuse setose horns. PUPA thick, simple ; head-case terminated in an obtuse point." (*Westwood*, l. c.)

Key to the Indian species of Melanitis.

A. Underside finely striated throughout, and with distinct black ocelli with white pupils.

- *a.* Pale brown ; the striation of the underside uniform, bold and distinct ; the ocelli perfect and prominent ; the costa of forewing usually moderately arched ; the inner margin rather short. Falcation of the forewing usually prominent ; outer margin sometimes straight or slightly concave.

  243. M. LEDA, India, Ceylon, Burma, Malayana, China.

- *b.* Dark brown ; the striation of the underside irregular, and less distinct on the outer half : the ocelli less prominent ; the costa of forewing strongly arched, increasing greatly the breadth of the wing, and the inner margin comparatively longer. Outer margin of forewing entire or only slightly falcated.

  244. M. ASWA, India, Ceylon, Burma.
  M. tristis, India.
  M. suyudana, Ceylon, Java.

B. Underside very variable but without distinct striation ; the ocelli wanting altogether, or where present blurred or irrorated, and indistinct. Falcation of the forewing prominent.

- *a.* With dull indistinct ferruginous marks on the forewing often entirely wanting ; the upperside always dark brown.
  - *a*¹. Upperside very dark brown, ashy at the margins ; a dull ferruginous streak from the costa, always indistinct, often obsolete.

    245. M. BELA, India, Burma.
  - *b*¹. Upperside dusky olive-brown ; the apex suffused with dull ferruginous.

    246. M. TAMBRA, Ceylon.
  - *c*¹. Upperside with no trace of ferruginous markings.
    - *a*². Upperside with two white spots on the forewing ; underside ashy tinged with olive on the basal half ; hindwing with a submarginal series of paler spots.

      247. M. VARAHA, S. India.
    - *b*². Upperside with no white spots on the forewing ; underside glossy olive-brown, tinged or irrorated with ashy white on the basal two-thirds ; hindwing with a white dot near the anal angle, and another at the end of the cell.

      248. M. GOKALA, S. India.
- *b.* With bright ferruginous markings on the upperside of the forewing towards the apex.
  - *a*¹. Upperside brown, scarcely irrorated with ashy at the outer margin ; the ferruginous mark incompletely encircling a blackish patch with two white spots, and not reaching the costa.

    249. M. ISMENE, India, Ceylon, Burma, Andaman Isles, Malayana
  - *b*¹. Upperside brighter brown (much darker in the males), more broadly irrorated with ashy on the margin than in *M. ismene ;* the ferruginous mark consisting of a streak from the costa, and in the females extending round the black patch, and by suffusion to the outer margin.

    250. M. DURYODANA, N. India, Orissa, Burma.
  - *c*¹. Upperside brighter brown (darker in the males), the marginal irrorations less prominent ; the ferruginous mark a broad diffused subapical band interrupted on its inner edge by a blackish patch usually without white spots.

    251. M. ZITENIUS, India, Burma, Andaman Isles.
  - *d*¹. Upperside brown ; the ferruginous mark a broad subapical band as in *M. zitenius*, but without the black patch interrupting it.

    252. M. GNOPHODES, India.

The most striking feature of the genus *Melanitis* is the extent to which the outer margin of the forewing is falcated or produced into a point below the tip of the lower discoidal nervule; this falcation varies much, being scarcely traceable in some specimens of *M. leda* and *aswa*, but in most of the species it is very prominent. The extreme shortness of the middle disco-cellular nervule of the forewing is another well-marked character, the two discoidal nervules originating close together just below the subcostal nervule; the nearest approach to this character being in *Rhaphicera*.

The Butterflies of this genus are of dull colouration, and moderately large size; the usual colour is some shade of brown on the upperside, variegated in many species with black and ferruginous towards the apex of the forewing, with one or two white spots; the underside is in some species extremely variable, showing every variety of autumnal tint, and in all cases beautifully harmonising with the dead leaves among which the insects generally settle. They shun the sunshine, and are found in shady forests or secluded spots in gardens, but always under the shade of trees or bushes; they are almost crepuscular in their habits, being active on the wing only towards sunset. They feed on juices, and numbers may be found crowding round slits in the bark of fruit trees when the sap exudes, and where date palms are found they may often be observed in large numbers imbibing the juice of the trees when cut for toddy.

The genus *Melanitis* is widely distributed in the Indian region, one or two species being found commonly almost everywhere; in the hills they do not ascend to any great elevation, and north of the Himalayas they are unknown, but a few species are found in Africa, and others extend through the Malay Archipelago to Australia and China. The great variation shown by these insects renders it difficult to define the species; great differences of opinion on this point have naturally resulted. Mr. Kirby includes the whole of the Indian species as varieties of *M. leda*; but so far as we can see at present there are several quite distinct forms.

243. **Melanitis leda**, Linnæus. (PLATE I).

Papilio leda, Linnæus, Syst. Nat., vol. i, pt. ii, p. 773, n. 151 (1767); id., Drury, Ex. Ins., vol. i, pl. xv, figs. 5, 6 (1773); id., Cramer, Pap. Exot., vol. iii, pl. cxcvi, figs. C, D (1779); *Oreas marmorata leda*, Hübner, Samml. exot. Schmett., vol. i, pl. xci, figs. 1—4 (1806-1816); *Melanitis leda*, Fabricius, Ill. Mag., vol. vi, p. 282 (1807); id., Moore, Lep. Cey., vol. i, p. 15, pl. x, figs. 1, 1*b*, *male*; 1*a*, *female* (1880); id., Distant, Rhop. Malay., p. 41, pl. iv, fig. 10 (1882), *male*; *Hipio leda*, Hübner, Verz. bek. Schmett., p. 56, n. 538 (1816); *Satyrus leda*, Godart, Enc. Méth., vol. ix, p. 478, n. 4 (1819); *Hipparchia leda*, Horsfield, Cat. Lep. E. I. C., pl. viii, figs. 9, *larva*; 9 *a*, *pupa*; 9 *b—h*, *structure* of *imago* (1829); *Cyllo leda*, Butler, Ann. and Mag. of Nat. Hist., third series, vol. xix, p. 51 (1867); id., Hewitson, Journ. Linn. Soc. Lond., Zoology, vol. viii, p. 144 (1864).

HABITAT: Throughout India, Burma, the Malay Peninsula, Ceylon, Andaman Isles, and the Malay Archipelago to China.

EXPANSE: 2·5 to 3·1 inches.

DESCRIPTION: MALE and FEMALE: UPPERSIDE uniform, somewhat pale brown. *Forewing* with two rounded black spots, the lower the larger, confluent and placed midway between the end of the cell and the outer margin, one on either side of the third median nervule. The lower spot is centred with pure white, the upper one has a somewhat larger white spot on its outer margin. The black spots are very obscurely more or less surrounded with ferruginous, and there is a very diffused black patch between the upper one and the costa, and another similar patch internal to it, extending into the end of the cell, these two patches being divided by a very obscure ferruginous bar. *Hindwing* with a series of submarginal ocelli, varying in number and distinctness coincident with the ocelli on the underside, black with white pupils and ochreous irides. UNDERSIDE much paler, uniformly striated throughout with darker brown. *Forewing* with from three to five submarginal ocelli, the one between the upper median nervules always the largest and further removed from the margin. *Hindwing* with six more or less distinct ocelli, the upper one the largest, the remainder gradually increasing to the fifth which is nearly as large as the first, the sixth at the anal angle smaller, often bipupilled, sometimes geminate; all the ocelli on both wings black with white (sometimes irrorated with blue) pupils, yellow irides, and dark brown outer ring.

Typically there are no fasciæ on the UNDERSIDE, but in some cases the striæ coalesce into dark bands from the costa of the forewing, the first reaching the outer angle, the second continued as a discal band across both wings, and with other abbreviated and less distinct bands between; there is every gradation between the two extremes to be found wherever the species exist, but the fasciæ are more highly developed in some specimens from Mhow in Central India, taken by Colonel C. Swinhoe, than in any others that we have seen. On the UPPERSIDE some specimens have distinct traces of ferruginous marks on the forewing showing in this feature an approximation to *M. ismene*, but in all these cases the markings of the underside are quite sufficient to establish their identity with *M. leda*.

M. leda is extremely common in many parts of the country, and has a very wide range; it is found throughout the plains of India from Travancore to the Punjab, and also in Ceylon, Burma, the Andamans, Malayana and China. It is on the wing more or less throughout the year but is perhaps most common in the autumn. Details of the structure of *M. leda* are given on Plate I, copied from Horsfield's plate.

Var. (a). UNDERSIDE with the fasciæ and a distinct suffused marginal band ochreous or ferruginous, the entire basal area also tinged with ochreous or ferruginous, the striation finer and closer but equally uniform, the ocelli much smaller, and many of them often obsolete. This variety has been found in Kulu in the N.-W. Himalayas, in Burma, at Poona in the Deccan, and at Trevandrum in Travancore. It is distinctly intermediate between *M. leda* and some varieties of *M. aswa*, not only in the style of the fasciæ and marginal band, and in the less distinct and prominent ocellation, but also in outline, for it has the costa more strongly arched, and the forewing consequently broader than in *M. leda*, but never so much so as in *M. aswa*, and this and its paler colouration will always serve to distinguish it from *M. aswa* in any of its forms. It appears to be a fairly constant form.

The LARVA of *M. leda*, figured in Horsfield's Cat. Lep. E. I. C., pl. viii, fig. 9 (1829) is green, covered with short hairs, and has several longitudinal streaks of a deeper green. According to Colonel Lang it feeds on *Saccharum ravennæ*. The PUPA is figured on the same plate (fig. 9*a*) and is green with yellow markings.

244. **Melanitis aswa,** Moore.

Cyllo aswa, Moore, Proc. Zool. Soc Lond., 1865, p. 769; *C. tristis*, Felder, Reise Novara, Lep., vol. iii, p. 464, n. 785 (1867); *Melanitis suyudana*, Moore, Horsfield and Moore, Cat. Lep. E. I C., vol. i, p. 224, n. 466 (1857).

HABITAT: India, Burma, Ceylon.

EXPANSE: 2·2 to 3·0 inches.

DESCRIPTION: "MALE: UPPERSIDE uniform dark brown, without spots or other markings. UNDERSIDE brown, uniformly covered with short grey striæ. *Forewing* with four or five more or less defined apical ocelli, each composed of a black spot, white pupil, pale ferruginous iris and dark brown outer circle, a marginal band ferruginous brown. *Hindwing* with a transverse discal line and broad marginal band ferruginous brown; a submarginal series of six well-defined ocelli, each composed of a black spot, white pupil, ferruginous iris, and dark brown outer circle." (*Moore*, l. c.) The FEMALE is apparently unknown.

M. aswa may always be distinguished from *M. leda* by the very dark brown colour of the UPPERSIDE, and by the peculiar shape of the forewing, the inner margin being long, and the costa highly convex, giving great breadth to the wing; the outer margin is typically even and straight, or but slightly convex, but in some specimens the falcation is as distinct as in some of *M. leda*, and in many a trace of it is perceptible. Typically also both wings are unspotted, but in some cases the *forewing* has one or two, or even three, white spots on a blackish ground, and there is a single white spot indistinctly ringed with blackish on the lower median interspace of the hindwing, and sometimes two others, one on either side of the first spot. The UNDERSIDE also is much darker; the fasciæ are placed as in *M. leda*, var. (*a*), but are less distinct and more ferruginous in tone, and the striation is less uniform, being far less distinct on the outer area.

It inhabits much the same range as the variety of *M. leda* referred to; we have specimens from Kulu, Sikkim, Sibsagar, Shillong, Burma, the Wynaad and Travancore.

Var. *tristis*, Felder, (PLATE XII, FIG. 27, *male*). HABITAT: North India (*Felder*); South India. EXPANSE: 2·6 to 3·0 inches. DESCRIPTION: "MALE: Upperside obscure fuscous, paler at the margins. UNDERSIDE: *Both wings* obscure ferruginous-swarthy, densely and finely variegated with white. *Forewing* with five minute ocelli, arranged as in *C. leda* [=*M. leda*]. *Hindwing* with an obsolete ferruginous discal streak, subangulate externally, with six ocelli much smaller than in *C. leda*. The form of the wings differs proportionally from all the examples of *C. leda* from many localities now before us. The *forewing* is longer in the inner margin; the *hindwing* likewise is broader, but *shorter* within than in *C. leda*." (*Felder*, Reise Novara, Lep., vol. iii, p. 464, n. 785 (1867).

M. tristis is clearly distinct from *M. leda*, but we are unable to find any character which satisfactorily separates it from *M. aswa*, of which it appears to be merely a variety. The paler margins of the upperside, and the extent to which the ferruginous bands of the underside are developed show much variation in different specimens. The figure shows the upper and undersides of a male specimen from the Wynaad, in the Indian Museum, Calcutta.

Var. *suyudana*, Moore. HABITAT: Java (*Moore*), Ceylon. EXPANSE: 2·6 to 2·8 inches. DESCRIPTION: "UPPERSIDE deep dark brown, paler on the margins; a single whitish spot near the apex of the *forewing*, and a minute dot on the *hindwing*. UNDERSIDE deep mottled ferruginous-brown, with indistinct darker usually transverse streaks; a triangular space of mottled greyish-white from the costal margin near the apex. *Hindwing* with six small pale spots centred with a white dot." (*Moore*, Horsfield and Moore, Cat. Lep. E. I. C., vol. i, p. 224, n. 466, 1857.)

We have two specimens from Ceylon which answer very closely to this description. In one of them the upperside is immaculate, but the underside of both agree almost exactly. The outer margin of the forewing is very slightly angled. As a species it appears inseparable from *M. aswa*, but the subapical triangular pale patch on the underside of the forewing is more prominent than in any specimens of *M. aswa* we have seen. It is not included in Moore's "Lepidoptera of Ceylon."

245. **Melanitis bela**, Moore.

M. bela, Moore, Horsfield and Moore, Cat. Lep. E. I. C., vol. i, p. 223, n 465 (1857).

HABITAT: Eastern Himalayas, Assam, Tenasserim, South India.

EXPANSE: 2·9 to 3·3 inches.

DESCRIPTION: "UPPERSIDE deep dusky-brown. *Forewing* with a small indistinct ferruginous streak, below which the space is blackish; the two usual white spots. *Hindwing* with one minute white dot. UNDERSIDE deep mottled ferruginous-brown: triangular patch near the apex of the *forewing* paler. *Hindwing* with six spots." (*Moore*, l. c.) The FEMALE is slightly paler than the male, and the wings broader, but it is identical in markings.

M. bela, as found in North-Eastern India, appears to be less variable than the other species of *Melanitis*; the UPPERSIDE is very dark brown, the margins irrorated with ashy, most broadly about the apex of the forewing; the ferruginous streak from the costa is never very distinct, and often scarcely discernible, the black patch is indistinct; the white spots are almost invariably both present and prominent, the upper one the larger; and there is almost always a single submarginal white dot on the hindwing on the lower median interspace, and sometimes another on the upper median interspace. On the UNDERSIDE too it is comparatively constant, sometimes the ferruginous tint, sometimes an ashy grey tint prevails, but usually the basal half is somewhat darker than the rest; and the ground-colour is variegated by dark brown mottlings tending to coalesce in irregular patches, and with greyish mottlings indistinctly grouped into transverse bars on the forewing; the ocelli are blurred and often indistinct, and the addition of a few ochreous dots completes the resemblance to a dark and withered leaf. The forewing is moderately falcate in all the specimens we have seen.

From South India we have a fairly typical specimen taken by Mr. G. Vidal at Khandalla on the 4th April; and a very curious variety taken by Mr. Rhodes Morgan in the Wynaad in which the ocelli of the underside on the forewing are placed on a series of diffused white patches largest on either side of the upper median nervule. It also seems not unlikely from the descriptions that *M. varaka* and *M. gokala* are merely South Indian varieties of *M. bela*, and from the figures that *M. tambra* is a variety from Ceylon, but on these points we are as yet unable to speak definitely.

M. bela is not uncommon in Sikkim, and at Sibsagar in Upper Assam. Captain C. H. E. Adamson took it at Akyab in October, Captain C. T. Bingham took it in Tenasserim in the Meplay Valley in January and February, and in the upper and lower Thoungyeen forests in March, April and May; and Mr. Harold Fergusson has sent a single specimen from Travancore.

246. **Melanitis tambra,** Moore.

M. tambra, Moore, Lep. Cey., p. 15, pl. ix, figs. 2, 2*b*, *male*; 2*a*, *female*; 2*c*, *larva* and *pupa* (1880).

HABITAT: Ceylon.

EXPANSE: ♂, 2·5; ♀, 2·75 inches.

DESCRIPTION: "MALE: UPPERSIDE dark dusky olive-brown. *Forewing* ferruginous-brown at the apex, with a subapical small white spot (in some specimens an indistinct lower spot), and an indistinct black contiguous spot. *Hindwing* without markings. UNDERSIDE dusky-ferruginous or purple-ferruginous, nervures speckled with pale ochreous, basal area densely covered with dark purple-ferruginous strigæ, forming three confluent irregular fasciæ on the forewing, but more uniformly disposed on the hindwing, which has a narrow discal fascia only. *Forewing* with a pale triangular costal space before the apex, and four small ochreous brown-ringed spots, the penultimate spot with a contiguous inner white spot, posterior margin broadly dull sap-brown. *Hindwing* with a pale ochreous space and a contiguous dusky spot within end of the cell; disc transversely washed with greyish-purple, a submarginal row of small ochreous brown-ringed spots. FEMALE: UPPERSIDE ferruginous olive-brown. *Forewing* with a subapical dusky-black patch extending paler across end of the cell to costal nervure, and suffusedly bordered externally and across the apex with paler ferruginous, and centred with two white spots, the lowest spot small or obsolete. *Hindwing* with three or four lower submarginal small white spots. UNDERSIDE ferruginous; strigæ, transverse fasciæ, and outer border dark ferruginous, subapical spots on *forewing* and submarginal spots on *hindwing* with double rings and whitish centre, the penultimate subapical spot with a contiguous inner larger whitish spot. *Body* brown. *Legs* ferruginous."

"LARVA elongated, thickened in the middle; head with two long pubescent red processes; last segment also with two processes; green with longitudinal and transverse darker lines; face striped with red. PUPA green; head and thorax flattened." (*Moore*, l. c.)

"Found in the western and central provinces of Ceylon. Plains and up to 3,000 feet. June to September. Habits same as *M. leda*." (*Hutchison*).

The figures given by Moore do not at all answer to his description quoted above. The MALE is shown as having the UPPERSIDE dark brown, the margins irrorated with pale ashy brown; the forewing with the usual two white spots and a well-defined oval ochreous patch on the costa, the hindwing unmarked; the FEMALE is dark brown, slightly paler and mottled with blackish on the margin; the forewing with a single indistinct white spot, the middle of the costa suffused with ferruginous and mottled with blackish; the hindwing unmarked. The UNDERSIDE is shown as uniform dark chestnut brown, slightly paler at the margins, and with very indistinct darker striæ; a single ferruginous brown discal streak on each wing; the forewing with a single pure white spot, the hindwing with four submarginal ochreous spots and two similar spots at the end of the cell; a few whitish scales along the nervules at apex of forewing and abdominal half of hindwing. In the figures of the upperside the outer margin of the forewing is falcated, in that of the underside it is straight and nearly even.

We have seen no specimens and can make nothing satisfactory of this species; from the description it appears to be allied to *M. aswa*, var. *suyudana*, which also occurs in Ceylon; but from the figures it would seem to be merely a variety of *M. bela*.

247. **Melanitis varaha,** Moore.

M. varaha, Moore, Horsfield and Moore, Cat. Lep. E. I. C., vol. i, p. 224, n. 467 (1857).

HABITAT: Canara, South India.

EXPANSE: 2·37 inches.

DESCRIPTION: "UPPERSIDE dusky-brown, ashy-brown along exterior margins; subapical patch indistinctly black, with two white spots. UNDERSIDE ashy, tinged with olive from the base to the middle of wing: near apex of *forewing* two small brown dots. *Hindwing* with a submarginal row of indistinct paler spots." (*Moore*, l. c.)

We are unable to identify this species; nothing that we have in our collections answers exactly to the description; the shape of the forewing is not indicated; the very small size is only approached by some specimens of *M. aswa*; but it seems to us that it is nearest to *M. bela*, of which it may probably prove to be merely a small variety.

248. **Melanitis gokala,** Moore.

M. gokala, Moore, Horsfield and Moore, Cat. Lep. E. I. C., p. 224, n. 468 (1857).

HABITAT: Canara, S. India.

EXPANSE: 3 inches.

DESCRIPTION: "UPPERSIDE brown, suffused with ashy about the apex and exterior margins; an indistinct blackish subapical patch (without spots.) UNDERSIDE glossy olive-brown, washed on the basal two-thirds with pulverulescent ashy-white; a small white dot on lower disco-cellular nervule, and another near anal angle of *hindwing*." (*Moore*, l. c.)

This species also we are unable to identify; the outline of the forewing is not indicated; it seems to be closely allied to *M. bela*, but the complete absence of the white spots of the upperside, and of the submarginal series of the underside of the hindwing would, if constant, suffice to distinguish it. In all the specimens of *M. bela* that we have seen the anterior spot on the upperside of the forewing is invariably present, and in almost all cases both are visible.

249. **Melanitis ismene,** Cramer. (PLATE XII, FIG. 28 ♂.)

Papilio ismene, Cramer, Pap. Ex., vol. i, pl. xxvi, figs A, B (1775); *P. mycena*, idem, id., vol. iv, pl. ccxci, fig. F; *P. arcensia*, idem, id., pl. ccxcii, fig. C (1780); *Melanitis ismene*, Moore, Lep. Cey, vol. i, p 14, pl. x, figs. 2, 2a, *male*; 2b, *larva* and *pupa* (1880); idem, id., Distant, Rhop. Malay., p. 42, n. 2, pl. iv, figs. 9, 12, *male*; 11, *female* (1882).

HABITAT: Throughout India, Ceylon, Burma, Andaman Isles, and the Malay Peninsula and Archipelago.

EXPANSE: 2·8 to 3·2 inches.

DESCRIPTION: MALE and FEMALE: UPPERSIDE uniform rather dark brown. *Forewing* with a large black spot pupilled with white, placed between the second and third median nervules, with another somewhat elongated black spot in the interspace above it also with a white spot, but placed upon or near to its exterior margin; sometimes with a third indistinct suffused spot below the second median nervule. These spots are inwardly and beneath, below the second median nervule, bordered with bright ferruginous; there is also a somewhat square patch of this colour above the uppermost black spot. In some specimens there is a suffused black patch merging into the dark ground-colour on either side of the subapical squarish ferruginous patch. *Hindwing* usually with one or two submarginal black spots with white centres near the anal angle; these vary much in size, as also in number, and in some specimens are entirely wanting. The costa near the apex of the forewing, and the outer margin of both wings is in some specimens paler, thickly sprinkled with darker atoms, showing in this respect an approach to *M. duryodana*. UNDERSIDE extremely variable. The ground-colour in some specimens is very pale buff-brown, in others ferruginous, in some gray, and again in others almost black, with innumerable shades between all these colours. In most specimens there is a dark discal band common to both wings, with another similar band, but straighter, across the forewing about midway between the first band and the apex. Many specimens are covered with irregular black or dark brown spots and blotches resembling fungi on dead leaves; some specimens have one or two white spots on the forewing, and a submarginal series of six more or less perfect ocelli on the hindwing, these latter being more usually represented merely by whitish spots, and are always more or less blurred. In all the specimens we have seen the *forewing* is more or less falcate (sometimes almost truncate) at apex, and caudate in the hindwing. The FEMALE is somewhat paler, and the ferruginous markings are rather more diffused.

"LARVA elongated, thickened in the middle, pubescent; head large, surmounted by two short pubescent red processes; last segment also with two processes; pale green with longitudinal rows of whitish dots; dorsal and lateral line darker green; head bluish, face striped with green and black. Feeds on *Gramineæ*. PUPA green, cylindrical; head and thorax obliquely flattened." (*Moore*, l. c.)

M. ismene appears to be everywhere the commonest species of the genus. The upperside is very fairly constant in colouration throughout its range, some specimens, however, having the ground-colour darker than others; but the underside varies strangely even in the same locality; in fact no two specimens can be found exactly alike, and in their markings and tints they harmonise so completely with the autumnal colouration of decaying vegetation that when settled amongst dead leaves and dried up grass it is almost impossible to see them. Its range scarcely extends into the North-West Himalayas. Mr. C. J. Rodgers took it below Dalhousie. In four years collecting in the neighbourhood of Simla Mr. de Nicéville only took two specimens at a low elevation in November. The Indian Museum has a single specimen from Mussoorie, and to the eastward it becomes increasingly commoner. Similarly in the plains it is comparatively rare in the Punjab; in the North-Western Provinces it is much commoner, but throughout Bengal and Central and Peninsular India it is very common, and we have specimens from Assam, Sylhet, Cachar, Burma, Ceylon, and the Andaman Isles.

The figure on PLATE XII shows the upper and undersides of a male specimen from Calcutta in Major Marshall's collection. An outline figure of this species is given on PLATE I.

250. **Melanitis duryodana,** Felder.

Cylo duryodana, Felder, Reise Nov., Lep., vol. iii, p. 464, n. 786 (1867).

HABITAT: Sikkim, Cachar, Upper Assam, Khasi hills, Orissa, Burma and Upper Tenasserim.

EXPANSE: 2·9 to 3·1 inches.

DESCRIPTION: "MALE: UPPERSIDE swarthy, obscurely variegated with swarthy and hoary near the external margin (especially on the hindwing). *Forewing* with the subcostal area increasingly deep fuscous, with an oblique yellow bar-shaped fasciole scarcely reaching beyond the lower discoidal nervule to the hindward, and spreading over the apical third at the costa near the cell; immediately below that two wide black spots, defined externally with fulvous powdering, the upper rather large, the lower much larger, minutely pupilled with ochraceous. *Hindwing* with three hinder ochraceous dots, obscurely circled with fuscous. UNDERSIDE densely variegated with ferruginous-brown, with ochraceous external dots. *Forewing* with three costal fascioles, and the terminal area of the costa variegated with ochraceous. *Hindwing* with a subangulate ferruginous discal streak, the costal border and a streak before the margin ochraceous, variegated. FEMALE: UPPERSIDE paler than in the male. *Forewing* with the yellow fasciole much broader, paler. UNDERSIDE much paler, obsoletely variegated. *Hindwing* with a blackish discal spot near the streak. Larger than *C. banksia*, [Fabricius, an African form of *M. ismene*]; all the wings longer, and more strongly angulated." (*Felder*, l. c.)

The Indian Museum, Calcutta, contains three males from Sibsagar, two from Khurda in Orissa, and one from Kulu. They are easily distinguished from the other species in the genus by their rich deep ferruginous brown uppersides, and in having a distinctly lighter outer border to both wings, thickly powdered (especially in the hindwing) with darker atoms. The straight, sharply inwardly defined ferruginous bar extending from the upper black spot almost to the costa of the forewing, is also a marked feature in this species. There is also a single male from Shillong in Major Marshall's collection. The females are less easy to distinguish; they are as pale as *M. ismene*, but of a brighter brown, the forewing much more falcate; the ferruginous mark extends round the black patch and beyond it to the outer margin, which is broadly suffused with ferruginous, but the distinctive feature is that this ferruginous mark extends to, and is continued along the costa, which it never does in *M. ismene*. The UNDERSIDE of the male greatly resembles that of *M. bela*, to which it is closely allied; that of the female is chiefly remarkable for the bright ochreous tint which prevails, and in both sexes the colouration is comparatively constant. We have specimens of the female from Sikkim, from Shillong taken in November, from Pegu, and from Tenasserim taken in May and October.

251. Melanitis zitenius, Herbst. (PLATE XII, FIG. 29 ♀).

Papilio zitenius, Herbst, Naturs. Schmett., vol. viii, p. 5, pl. clxxxii, figs. 1, 2 (1796); *Melanitis vamana*, Moore, Horsfield and Moore, Cat. Lep. E. I. C , vol. i, p. 223, n. 463 (1857).

HABITAT: Eastern Himalayas, Godavari District, Orissa, Burma, Andaman Isles.

EXPANSE: 3·1 to 3·8 inches.

DESCRIPTION: "Differs from *Melanitis banksia* [an African form of *M. ismene*] in being larger, the subapical ferruginous patch on the *forewing* occupying a larger space; the deep black patch extends to the costal nervure; the upper white spots smaller, the lower being very indistinct; two white dots on the *hindwing*. UNDERSIDE marked as in some specimens of *M. banksia*." (*Moore*, l. c.)

This is the largest species of the genus, excluding *M. constantia*, which has been generically separated under the name of *Hipio*, and is conspicuous from its ochreous tone of colouration, and the large extent of the ferruginous markings near the apex of the forewing. The white spots on the upperside of the forewing are very variable in size, and are sometimes entirely obsolete. The MALE is rather darker than *M. ismene*, specimens from South India and the Andamans being especially dark, and in these latter the ferruginous band is smaller and better defined than in North Indian specimens, and without the white spots. In one specimen the outer margin of the forewing is almost entire; in another the falcation is no more prominent than in typical specimens of *M. leda*. The band usually is interrupted by two black marks, partially or entirely coalesced into a quadrate patch, and above this the band is broadly defined at both edges by diffused black patches, the inner of which coalesces with the quadrate patch on the band; the margins are scarcely paler, and only slightly irrorated with ashy. On the UNDERSIDE it is somewhat variable, but not nearly so much so as *M. ismene*. The prevailing colour is generally grey, more or less variegated with ochreous or fulvous, and irregularly mottled throughout with dark brown dots, here and there clustered into patches; the submarginal spots and the fasciæ usually very indistinct, though sometimes prominent. The FEMALE is larger and paler, with the forewing highly falcate; the outer margins more broadly irrorated with grey and mottled with dusky; the ferruginous band wider and extended narrowly along the costa; it approaches very closely to the female of *M. duryodana*, but it is larger; the white spots of the forewing are indistinct or altogether wanting, and the ferruginous bar above the black patch extends much more obliquely to the costa. The UNDERSIDE is as in the male, but paler and generally much more ochreous or fulvous in tone, and the dark mottlings much less profuse.

M. zitenius is found in the Eastern Himalayas, and the Khasi hills, and through Burma to Tenasserim. We also have specimens from the Upper Godavery taken by Mr. C. B. Morris in September, and from Khurda in Orissa, taken by Mr. W. C. Taylor. In Tenasserim it was taken by Captain C. T. Bingham in the Thoungyeen forests in April; in the South Andamans taken by Mr. F. A. de Roepstorff in August; and there are specimens from the Daffla hills and from Sikkim and Yunan in the Indian Museun, Calcutta.

The figure shows the upper and undersides of a female from Sikkim, in the Indian Museum, Calcutta.

252. Melanitis gnophodes, Butler.

M. gnophodes, Butler, Cat. Lep. B. M., *Satyridæ*, p. 5, pl. ii, fig. 1 (1868).

HABITAT : India.

EXPANSE : 3·2 to 3·3 inches.

DESCRIPTION : "MALE and FEMALE : UPPERSIDE coloured as in *Gnophodes (parmeno)*. UNDERSIDE variegated, the colours as in *phedima* or *banksia*. The male of this species resembles *Gnophodes parmeno** on the upperside; the female has a brighter orange band, and resembles the Natal form of the same insect." (*Butler*, l. c.)

Judging from Butler's figure of *M. gnophodes* the distinctive feature appears to be a fulvous almost straight band across the *forewing* beyond the cell from the costa to the hinder angle, bordered internally throughout its length, and externally near the costa, with dusky; the *hindwing* has two or three submarginal white spots near the anal angle. The forewing is considerably falcated, the outline of the wings being similar to that of *M. zitenius*, but it seems to differ from that species not only by the absence of the two large black patches on the forewing, which is an inconstant character, but also by the shape of the fulvous band, which is narrower, more regular, and more produced toward the hinder angle than in *M. zitenius*; in *M. gnophodes* the outer edge of the band is directed from the costa to the tip of the third median nervule, while in *M. zitenius* it is directed towards the tip of the falcation above the third median nervule. In Mr. de Nicéville's collection are four females of *Melanitis zitenius* from Sikkim which agree fairly well with Butler's figure of *M. gnophodes*, in that the two black spots on the forewing are obsolete in two specimens, very obscure in the other two. The ground-colour of the upperside is also paler than in most examples of *M. zitenius*, but these specimens are clearly only varieties of that species, and they suggest a doubt as to whether *M. gnophodes* is really distinct. At all events we have no specimens precisely agreeing with Butler's figure, and in the absence of specimens it must for the present be retained as distinct.

Genus 28.—HIPIO, Hübner.

Hipio, Hübner, Verz. bek. Schmett., p. 56 (1816).

The next species has been retained by Butler under the subgeneric name *Hipio* of Hübner, and on his authority we adhere to the name, but we are unable to indicate any structural features to distinguish it from *Melanitis*. The subgenus contains several species from the Malayan Archipelago, but only a single one is recorded from India, and that appears to be excessively rare; we have never seen a specimen, and have doubts as to whether it really occurs in India at all. Its principal feature is the yellow transverse band of the forewing; the nearest approach to which is in *M. gnophodes*; and its large size which considerably exceeds that of any of the Indian *Melanitis*. It has large distinct ocelli on the underside of the hindwing as in *M. leda*.

253. Hipio constantia, Cramer.

Papilio constantia, Cramer, Pap. Ex., vol. ii, pl. cxxxiii, figs, A, B (1777); *Satyrus constantia*, Godart, Enc. Méth., vol. ix, p. 477, n. 1 (1819); *Cyllo constantia*, Hewitson, Journ. Linn. Soc. Lond., Zoology, vol. viii, p. 143 (1864).

HABITAT : Darjiling and N. India (*Moore*); Malayana.

EXPANSE : 4·1 inches.

DESCRIPTION : FEMALE : UPPERSIDE deep rich brown. *Forewing* crossed beyond the cell from the costa to the inner angle by a broad band of ochreous, darker at the edges, and bearing in the interspace above the third median nervule a triangular white spot, bordered with black; below which is a black ocellus, pupilled with white and with a rufous iris. The outer dark area bears a single small round black spot above the lower discoidal nervule. *Hindwing* with a black submarginal line and three black spots near the anal angle, the two

* A south and west African species.

outer ones pupilled with white. UNDERSIDE paler brown, thickly striated throughout with deeper brown. *Both wings* with a common dark brown subbasal fascia commencing at the subcostal nervure of the forewing, and ending at the median nervure of the hindwing: also with another wider and more prominent deep brown fascia commencing at the costa of the forewing, cutting the cell just beyond its middle, and crossing the hindwing beyond the cell in an inwardly curved line, and ending at the abdominal margin. This fascia is faintly bordered with pale brown outwardly on the forewing, more broadly and with a paler shade of the same colour on the hindwing. The outer margin of both wings of a deeper brown than the ground-colour, this border terminating on the hindwing at the tail, from thence to the anal angle the margin is but little deeper than the ground. *Forewing* crossed by a straight, transverse, outwardly sharply defined deep brown fascia, commencing at the costa, crossing the wing just beyond the cell, and not reaching the inner angle. This fascia is outwardly bordered with a band of pale brown. A submarginal series of three spots, the lowest in the interspace above the third median nervule somewhat large and white; the one above it black, pupilled with white and with a yellow iris; the third in the next interspace very small and white. *Hindwing* with a submarginal series of seven oval black ocelli, pupilled with white, and with yellow irides; the first the largest, the fourth and fifth also large and nearly equal in size, the sixth and seventh geminated. (Described from Cramer's plate).

"MALE: UPPERSIDE differs from the female only in having the transverse band more rufous and nearer the apex, the UNDERSIDE darker, with the ocelli of the *hindwing* much larger and more distinct." (*Hewitson*, l. c.)

The next species was originally described as a *Melanitis*, but was subsequently separated by Mr. Butler on the grounds stated below. The differences appear to be sufficiently marked to warrant generic separation.

Genus 29.—CYLLOGENES, Butler. (PLATE XIII).

Cyllogenes, Butler, Cat. Lep. B. M., *Satyridæ*, p 6 (1868).

"Differs from *Melanitis* in the violet colouring of the UPPERSIDE; the concave form of the disco-cellulars of the *forewing*; the more wedge-shaped cell of the *hindwing*; and in the presence of a large silky dark patch in the forewing of the male." (*Butler*, l. c.)

Only a single species is known, which inhabits Sikkim; it has a short, curved, yellow band near the apex of the forewing in both sexes.

254. Cyllogenes suradeva, Moore. (PLATE XIII, FIG. 30 ♂ ♀).

Melanitis suradeva, Moore, Horsfield and Moore, Cat. Lep. E. I. C., vol. i, p. 225, n. 469 (1857).

HABITAT: Sikkim.

EXPANSE: 3 inches.

DESCRIPTION: "MALE: UPPERSIDE deep vinaceous-brown, darkest at the apex, and having in some lights a purple gloss. *Forewing* with a large black patch in the middle; a short narrow obliquely-curved yellow subapical streak. UNDERSIDE dull ochreous, suffused with brown, and covered with short, narrow, undulating striæ, as in *Melanitis leda*; a transverse darker streak across the middle of *both wings*; four small whitish submarginal spots on the *forewing*, and two near the anal angle." (*Moore*, l. c.) In the specimen in the Indian Museum, Calcutta, the male has also on the UNDERSIDE a purplish-white cloudy discal band on *both wings* beyond the darker streak. The FEMALE differs from the male in having the wings much broader, the yellow band broader, reaching the costa and extending partially along it, and it lacks the dark silky patch on the *forewing*; on the UNDERSIDE it is paler, and lacks the transverse purplish-white band.

C. suradeva appears to be a very rare insect. Colonel A. M. Lang, R.E., has five males in his collection, all from Sikkim, and Mr. Otto Möller has taken a female specimen also in Sikkim. The figure is taken from a male and a female from Sikkim in the Indian Museum, Calcutta, and shows the uppersides only.

The last genus of the *Satyrinæ* included by us in the Indian fauna contains but one species, and is perhaps one of the most remarkable in the subfamily. Mr. Wood-Mason notes: "No Asiatic genus of *Satyrinæ* presents us with any approach to the remarkable arrangement of the two hindermost veins of the forewing; but, in the South American genus *Antirrhœa*, we meet with identically the same arrangement, the first median nervule in *A. archæa* and its congeners running back to the inner angle, and the submedian nervure ending a considerable distance short of that angle, though not nearly so far short of it as in the Indian form. I propose the name *Parantirrhœa* in allusion to these remarkable points of resemblance. The species of the subfamily *Elymniinæ* alone present the same disposition of the three anterior nervules of the hindwing."

Genus 30.—PARANTIRRHŒA, W.-M.

Parantirrhoea, Wood-Mason, Journ. A. S. B., vol. xlix, pt. ii, p. 248 (1880); *Parantirrhœa*, id., Ann. and Mag. of Nat. Hist., fifth series, vol. vii, p. 333 (1881).

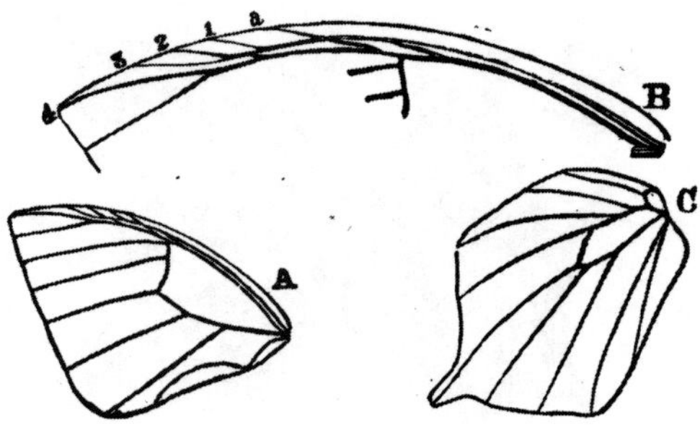

A. Right *forewing* from the underside, natural size, to show the whole venation, and the inflected lobe of the inner margin. B. Anterior portion of the same, much enlarged, to show the relations of the nervules to one another: *a*, costal nervure; 1, 2, 3, 4. terminations of the four branches of the subcostal nervure. C. Right *hindwing*, from the underside, natural size.

"MALE: FOREWING triangular; costal margin moderately and regularly arched; apex acute; outer margin almost straight, being only just perceptibly convex; inner angle rounded; inner margin sinuous, being lobed at the base much as in the males of *Clerome* and *Æmona*, genera of *Morphinæ*; *subcostal* nervure four-branched, the first branch given off before, and the second beyond, the end of the discoidal cell, the first, second, and third coalescing successively and respectively with the costal nervure; the first, and the second, and all three in turn becoming free and running off at a tangent, like the costal nervure, to the anterior margin, the fourth being perfectly free from its origin and running to the apical angle; *lower disco-cellular* nervule long, very slightly concave outwards, almost straight; *middle* one not quite half the length of the lower one, *upper* one rudimentary; *submedian* nervure sinuous, short, terminating near the inner margin at about the level of the junction of the basal and second fourth of the length of that margin, being, in fact, hardly more developed than is the internal nervure of the *Papilioninæ* as compared with that of many Heterocerous Lepidoptera; the *first median* nervule directed straight outwards and backwards, out of its normal course, to the inner angle, and supplying the place of the rudimentary submedian nervure. On turning to the underside, it is seen that a narrow rounded lobe of the functional sutural area [inner margin] about six times as long as it is broad, is folded back upon the under surface, to which it is firmly adherent. This lobe occupies the middle two-fourths of the length of the inner margin, and is thickly clothed on its surface and fringed at its free edge with firmly attached, long, and somewhat raised modified scales, rendered conspicuous by their rich dark brown colour and satiny lustre. The outline of this turned-up lobe is marked out on the upperside by a curvilinear groove. HINDWING tailed, subquadrate, with four distinct margins, *viz.*, a strongly and irregularly arched costal margin, nearly straight external and hind margins, and an inner or abdominal margin, marked out by the obtuse-angled apex, the tail, and the well-rounded anal angle; with a black, oval, sexual mark, divided by the submedian nervure, near the anal angle; *costal* nervure short and straight, terminating before, and the first branch of the subcostal which originates close to the base of its nervure ending beyond, the middle of the length of the costal margin, the second branch being given off before the middle of the discoidal cell, and extending into the apical angle; the *discoidal nervule* in the same straight or slightly curved line with the subcostal; the *disco-cellular* nervule sinuous; the *third median* nervule produced to a conspicuous tail. *Antennæ* fine and distinctly clubbed. FEMALE unknown." (*Wood-Mason*, l. c., in Journ. A. S. B.)

255. Parantirrhœa marshalli, W.-M.

P. marshalli, Wood-Mason, Journ A. S B., vol. xlix, pt ii, p. 250 (1880); idem, id., Ann. and Mag. of Nat. Hist., fifth series, vol. vii, p. 335 (1881).

HABITAT: Trevandrum, Travancore.

EXPANSE: 2·4 inches.

DESCRIPTION: "MALE: UPPERSIDE, *both wings* dark fuscous, suffused with rich deep violet. *Forewing* with an outwardly and forwardly arched, subcrescentic, pale violet or mauve band, commencing beyond the middle of the wing at the costal nervure, terminating at the inner angle, and crossed obliquely by a series of three small white spots disposed in a straight line parallel to the outer margin, and placed upon folds of as many consecutive interspaces, the last being between the second and third median nervules. *Hindwing* relatively longer tailed than in *Melanitis ismene*, Cramer, with the membranous parts of the divergent tail almost wholly formed by the produced wing-membrane of the interspace between the second and third median nervules, a very narrow anterior membranous edging only being contributed by the interspace next in front; and with rather more than the basal two-thirds of its length in front of the discoidal nervule and subcostal nervure ochreous. UNDERSIDE, *both wings* ochreous, obscurely striated with a deeper shade of the same colour, and marked with a submarginal series of inconspicuous brown specks, the probable rudiments of ocelli. The FEMALE will, in all probability, prove to differ from the male not only in the absence of the sexual spot in the hindwing, but also in having the inner margin of the forewing straight, and neither lobed at the base nor turned up in the middle, and the first median nervule and the submedian nervure normally arranged and developed, and directed respectively to the outer margin and to the inner angle after the manner usual among butterflies." (*Wood-Mason*, l. c., in Journ. A. S. B.)

P. marshalli has as yet only been found in Travancore, where it was discovered by Mr. H. S. Fergusson on the Ashamboo Hills in May.

The figure shews the upper and undersides of a male specimen from Trevandrum, South India, in the Indian Museum, Calcutta.

SUBFAMILY III.—ELYMNIINÆ, Herrich-Schäffer. (PLATE XVII).

Elymniina, Herrich-Schäffer, Prodr. Syst. Lep., pt. i, p. 15 (1864); *Eurytelidæ*, in part, Westwood, Gen D. L., vol. ii, p. 403 (1851).

BODY moderately robust. HEAD moderate-sized. *Eyes* naked, prominent. *Antennæ* slender, with a slender gradually-formed indistinct club. *Palpi* elongate, porrect, clothed beneath with short appressed hairy scales and perceptibly tufted above, the tuft lying against the face and following the contour of the eye. WINGS large, weak, generally dentate, and very seldom ocellated. FOREWING with the *costal nervure* always greatly swollen at the base. *Discoidal cell* short and very broad; *upper disco-cellular* nervule very short, just beyond the second subcostal nervule; the upper discoidal nervule originating close to the subcostal nervure; the *middle disco-cellular* much longer, inwardly oblique, the *lower disco-cellular* considerably the longest, highly concave, and closing the cell by junction with the median nervure at the origin of its second branch. *Submedian* nervure undulate, extending to the hinder angle. HINDWING, *male* with a glandular patch in the upper half of the cell, overlaid by two tufts of erectile hairs laid along the atrophied trunk of the discoidal nervure in the middle of the cell; *discoidal cell* short, broad; *upper disco-cellular* originating generally at some distance beyond the first subcostal nervule, moderately long; *lower disco-cellular* considerably longer and uniting with the median nervure at the origin of the second median nervule; *costal* nervure divided at the base, forming a false prædiscoidal cell; abdominal margin slightly channelled to receive the abdomen. FORELEGS small, those of the MALE more or less hairy, cylindrical, blunt at tip; those of the FEMALE also small, cylindrical, and blunt at the tip, but longer and not perceptibly hairy.

"LARVA cylindrical, rather attenuated before and behind. Head armed with two erect spines; abdomen terminated by two more elongated divergent spines. PUPA suspended by the tail, with small tubercles along the back and sides; the middle of the dorsum of the thorax-case elevated into an obtuse point; head terminated by two conical points." (*Westwood*, l. c., p. 404.)

The *Elymniinæ* constitute a small group of Old World butterflies ranging from West Africa to New Guinea, the head quarters of which are in the Malayan Archipelago. Westwood, in the Genera of Diurnal Lepidoptera, grouped them with *Eurytela*, *Ergolis*, *Byblia* (=*Hypanis*) (*Nymphalinæ*), and a few American genera, in a separate family under the name of *Eurytelidæ*, at the same time remarking that he should prefer to rank it as a subfamily only. Mr. Kirby, in his Synonymic Catalogue of the Diurnal Lepidoptera (1871), places it alone as a separate subfamily between the *Satyrinæ* and the *Morphinæ*. Mr. Distant, in his Rhopalocera Malayana (1882), includes it in the *Satyrinæ* with the following remark: "I have included this genus in the *Satyrinæ*, in which subfamily it possesses a somewhat unique position, not only in general colouration and markings, but also by its neuration, the second and third median nervules of the forewing having a common origin;" and he adds that Mr. Kirby has also recently included it among the *Satyrinæ*. In habits and weakness of flight the *Elymniinæ* closely resemble the *Satyrinæ*. In the sexual patch and tuft of the *hindwing* of the male they shew an affinity to some *Morphinæ*, and also to *Mycalesis*. In the dilation of the base of the costal nervure they also show affinity with the *Satyrinæ*, with at least one genus of the *Morphinæ* (*Clerome*), and with the genera *Eurytela*,

Ergolis and *Byblia* of the *Nymphalinæ*. In the clothing of the palpi they resemble *Melanitis*, which in this respect is an aberrant genus of *Satyrinæ*, but the short wide cell in both wings closed at the origin of the *second* median nervule, the brilliant colouring which among the *Satyrinæ* is only approached in *Cœlites*, the almost universal absence of ocellation, the frequency of an irregular dentate outline of the wings, and above all the highly mimetic character of the species, make it a group by itself, and justify its retention as a separate subfamily; it appears to have little in common with the *Morphinæ* except in its habits, and perhaps in the brilliant colours of the upperside.

The subfamily consisted, till comparatively recently, of a single genus—*Elymnias*. In 1869 Mr. A. R. Wallace, in a paper on Eastern Butterflies (Trans. Ent. Soc. Lond., 1869, p. 321) wrote: "It is interesting to observe that the species from the Austro-Malayan islands form a compact group, distinguished by a regular and somewhat rounded outline of wings, and resembling in colouration some of the broad winged *Euplœas*, or the genus *Drusilla* [a peculiar genus of *Morphinæ* which now stands under the name *Tænaris*, confined to the Malayan archipelago]; while the species of India and the Indo-Malayan islands are almost always characterised by a more irregular outline, waved, dentate, or even caudate, and generally coloured like species of *Danais*, or the more elongate forms of *Euplœa*." Following on this in 1871, Mr. A. G. Butler (Proc. Zool. Soc. Lond., 1871, p. 518) in a monograph of the subfamily divided it into two genera, *Elymnias* and *Dyctis*, basing the division mainly on the character of the neuration of the hindwing, and omitting the features of outline indicated by Mr. Wallace, for though the genus *Dyctis* as defined, embraces all the Austro-Malayan species, it also includes several of the Indian and Indo-Malayan species; some of the latter being indistinguishable, so far as outline is concerned, from species which are retained as true *Elymnias*. In a highly mimetic subfamily such as this, outline is a feature on which little reliance can be placed as a generic character, and style of colouration is of little use even for the determination of minor groups within a genus; even the style of neuration is not always a safe guide, but as there is a well-marked difference in the shape of the disco-cellular nervules of the hindwing to separate *Dyctis* from *Elymnias*, we retain them as distinct.

The *Elymniinæ* are forest-loving insects, with a weak flight, frequenting dense undergrowth or bush jungle, and usually avoiding the open sunshine; they are all tropical or sub-tropical insects, and within our limits are only found in the region of heavy rainfall, in Ceylon, the hills of South India and along the East Coast to Bengal; thence they stretch westwards along the warm valleys of the outer Himalayas as far east as Mussoorie, and eastwards through Assam, Sylhet and Burma into the Malay peninsula.

Genus 31.—ELYMNIAS, Hübner. (PLATE XVII.)

Elymnias, Hübner, Verz. bek. Schmett., p. 37 (1816); *Melanitis* (part), Fabricius, Ill. Mag., vol. vi, p. 282 (1807); id., Westwood, Gen. D. L., vol. ii. p. 403 (1851); *Biblis* (part), Latreille, Enc. Méth., vol. ix, p. 10 (1819); *Elymnias* (restricted), Butler, Proc. Zool. Soc. Lond., 1871, p. 519.

CHARACTERS of the subfamily, but with the lower disco-cellular nervule of the *hindwing* highly concave from the origin of the discoidal nervule.

The butterflies of this genus vary much in outline, but with the single exception of *E. penanga* all the Indian species have the outer margin of the forewing perceptibly dentate, the hindwing is dentate in all, and in many of them strongly caudate. *E. penanga* has three black ocellular dots on the underside of the hindwing; *E. obnubila* has a complete submarginal series of small ocellular spots, and *E. mimus* has them largely developed; in *E. undularis* and some of its allies the only trace of the series is a silvery subcostal spot; the magnified pupil of an obsolete ocellus, and sometimes as many as four smaller spots, one in each interspace, from the anal angle, but in no other Indian species of the restricted genus is there any trace of ocellation whatever. Of the species which have blue markings on the upperside, *E. undularis* and its allies are distinguished by having the outer margin of the hindwing ferruginous or fulvous, the blue markings being confined to a submarginal series of spots on the forewing; *E. penanga* has a large blue patch on both wings, with paler blue streaks in it on the forewing only; *E. saüeri* and *E. leucocyma* both have the large blue patch, with paler blue spots on it on the forewing only, but the outline of the wings differs, and the underside is quite distinct, being in *E. saüeri* beautifully marbled throughout with shades of brown and yellow and a little grey, while in *E. leucocyma* it is an uniform shade of brown, with numerous yellowish or ochreous transverse striæ.

Key to the Indian species of Elymnias.

A. Hindwing with the lower disco-cellular nervule highly concave.

a. Males with a patch of loosely attached scales* at the base of the interspace between the median and submedian nervures on the upperside of the forewing. Hindwing with the upper disco-cellular nervule suberect, or inwardly oblique, the outer margin dentate or slightly caudate.

a^1. Male blackish-brown, with a submarginal series of blue spots on the upperside of the forewing; outer margin of hindwing broadly ferruginous. Female marked somewhat as in *Danais chrysippus* or *D. alcippus*.

256. E. UNDULARIS, North and East India, Burma.

257. E. TINCTORIA, Tenasserim.

b^1. Male with the blue spots on the upperside of the forewing obsolete; the outer margin of hindwing fulvous. Female similar to *E. undularis*.

258. E. FRATERNA, Ceylon.

c^1. Male and female dark brown, with a submarginal band of dull ferruginous on the upperside of both wings. No blue spots on the forewing.

259. E. COTTONIS, South Andamans.

b. Males with no patch of loosely attached scales* at the base of the interspace between the median and submedian nervures on the upperside of the forewing.

a^1. Hindwing with the upper disco-cellular nervule suberect.

a^2. Hindwing almost entire, not caudate. Male, upperside purplish-brown, with a large blue patch on both wings. Female bluish-brown, with a large whitish patch on the forewing.

260. E. PENANGA, Tenasserim, Malay Peninsula.

b^2. Hindwing distinctly caudate.

a^3. Male, upperside blackish-brown; forewing with a series of white spots. Female marked like *Danais genutia*.

261. E. CAUDATA, South India.

b^3. Male and female, upperside brown, with a pale brown submarginal band to both wings. Underside, hindwing with prominent ocelli.

262. E. MIMUS, Nicobars.

c^3. Male and female, upperside fuscous, with a pale ferruginous band to both wings. Underside, hindwing with the ocelli small.

263. E. OBNUBILA, Tenasserim.

b^1. Hindwing with the upper disco-cellular nervule obliquely directed outward.

a^2. Outer margin very slightly dentate, almost entire, hindwing not caudate. Male and female, upperside coloured and marked almost as in *Euplœa midamus*. Underside marked with pale ochreous striæ, more prominent in the female.

264. E. LEUCOCYMA, North-East India, Burma.

b^2. Outer margin dentate, hindwing slightly caudate. Upperside dark chestnut-brown, forewing shot with violet, with a violet patch on the disc, and pale violet discal spots. Underside thickly marbled with dark chocolate-brown strigæ. Female unknown.

265. E. SAÜERI, Tenasserim.

c^2. Outer margin more dentate. Forewing somewhat falcate, hindwing distinctly caudate. Upperside marked with pale greenish or yellowish or bluish streaks between the nervules.

266. E. TIMANDRA, North-East India, Burma.

---

* These scales are precisely similar in form and structure to those of the rest of the wing, but they are slightly larger and less densely packed, allowing the wing-membrane to show in tiny points and giving a slight sheen to the patch in certain lights. They come off easily with a slight rub leaving the patch bare.

E. timandra is quite distinct from every other Indian *Elymnias*, so far as its markings are concerned, but in outline of the wings it is identical with *D. peali* (see next genus *Dyctis*). Of those species without blue markings on the upperside, *E. caudata* may be distinguished by its submarginal series of white spots on the forewing, and *E. cottonis* by its less dentate and caudate outline, and the complete absence of markings on the upperside and of ocelli on the underside. Males of *E. undularis*, *E. fraterna* and *E. cottonis* have a patch of scales on the upperside of the forewing at the base of the interspace between the median and submedian nervures, which are loosely attached to the wing membrane, and easily removed by a camel's hair paint brush. Mr. Butler pointed out this feature (Proc. Zool. Soc. Lond., 1871, p. 519), calling it a "patch of thickened scales," but did not state in what species it occurred: it is not a very conspicuous feature, nor is its morphological value clear, but so far as we know it is confined to *E. undularis* and its allies, being much more marked in the typical species than in the others.

The habits of the species of *Elymnias* are as in the subfamily.

256. **Elymnias undularis**, Drury. (PLATE XVII, FIG. 59 ♂ ♀).

Papilio undularis, Drury, Ill. Ex. Ent., vol. ii, pl. x, figs. 1, 2 (1773), *male*; id., Cramer, Pap. Ex., vol. iii, pl. cclvi, figs. A, B (1779), *male*; *Biblis undularis*, Godart, Enc. Méth., vol. ix, p. 326, n. 2 (1819); *Melanitis undularis*, Horsfield, Cat. Lep. E. I. C., pl. viii, figs. 8, *larva*; 8a, *pupa*; 8b–8h, *structure* of *imago* (1829); *Elymnias undularis*, Wallace, Trans. Ent. Soc. Lond., 1869, p. 322, n. 1; *E. jynx*, Hübner, Ex-Schmett., figs. 37, 38 (1818), *male*; *Papilio protogenia*, Cramer, Pap. Ex., vol. ii, pl. clxxxix, figs. F, G (1777), *female*; *Biblis protogenia*, Godart, Enc. Méth., vol. ix, p. 327, n. 5 (1819).

HABITAT: North-Eastern and Central India, Burma, Java.

EXPANSE: 2·3 to 3·4 inches.

DESCRIPTION: MALE: UPPERSIDE dark velvety blackish brown. *Forewing* with bluish irrorated striæ along the costal margin, and a curved submarginal series of bluish irrorated spots one on each interspace, elongate near the apex, rounded below the lower discoidal nervule. *Hindwing* with the outer margin broadly suffused with dark ferruginous. *Cilia* short, whitish. UNDERSIDE brown, slightly paler on the outer half, especially on the hindwing, and covered with coarse confluent chestnut-brown undulations; some greyish-white irrorations on the outer half of the costa of the forewing; and others forming an indistinct and incomplete submarginal nebulous band on the hindwing. A prominent whitish subcostal spot on the hindwing.

This species is subject to considerable variation; the typical form described above occurs most frequently in North-East Bengal and Burma, but neither this nor any of the variations from it in the male insect which occur in India, appear to be peculiar to any locality or range. On the upperside the violet blue spots of the forewing vary in intensity, in some specimens those near the apex are coalesced into a subapical band, while in others the spots are all separate and distinct; on the hindwing the outer border varies from dull dark furruginous to bright pale ferruginous, sometimes quite unmarked, rarely divided by dark nervules, sometimes with a paler spot on each interspace; these spots are in some specimens very pale ferruginous, in others they are irrorated with pure white, and in some the spot nearest the costa is blue, like those on the forewing. On the UNDERSIDE the most frequent variation is in the whitish irrorations of the costa of the forewing being coalesced into a prominent sharply-defined triangular patch with its apex near the lower discoidal nervule; and the outer half of the wings is often also distinctly paler, tinged with grey and sparingly marked with fine chestnut undulations; rarely there is a submarginal series of whitish spots on the hindwing.

The FEMALE is coloured something after the style of *Danais chrysippus*; on the UPPERSIDE the *forewing* is blackish-brown, with a large tawny patch on the lower half, occupying the lower half of the cell, the interno-median interspace almost to the margin, the lower median interspace to not quite so far, and the basal area of the two next interspaces above it; some white transverse striæ on the costa, a broad subapical white transverse band, followed by three decreasing white spots one below each median nervule. The *hindwing* is tawny, broadly bordered with blackish-brown, on which are three or four large round white submarginal spots. UNDERSIDE coloured as on the upperside, but paler and more suffused, the white markings represented by a nebulous band on both wings expanding at the apex of the forewing more or less distinctly into a triangular patch as in the male; the whole area of both wings being coarsely undulated with chestnut-brown most densely on the darker portions. The FEMALE too is subject to variation; in Burman specimens the *hindwing* is often suffused more or less, (sometimes entirely, the tawny colour being wholly displaced), as in *Danais alcippus* with white on both sides over the whole tawny area; on the underside the subcostal whitish spot is sometimes prominent, often totally absent; in some specimens from Calcutta the underside is more like that of the male; the basal area is darker; beyond this there is a distinct paler band, and then the dark border on the margin; the whitish triangular patch near apex of forewing is distinct, and the spots near the outer margin of both wings are distinct and well separated.

E. undularis is the common *Elymnias* of Northern India; and is the most wide-spread of all the species; it is common in the warm valleys of the outer Himalayas, as far east as Mussoorie at all events. In Bengal, where the rainfall is heavy, it extends into the plains, and is found in Assam, Sylhet, Eastern Bengal and along the East Coast as far south as Rajahmundry on the Godavari at all events; and it also occurs in the Deccan; to the south and south-west it is replaced by another species, *E. caudata*; on the east it extends through Arakan and Tenessarim. In the Malay Peninsula it appears to be replaced by *E. discrepans* and *E. nigrescens*, as it is not included in Distant's Rhopalocera Malayana, but it re-appears in Java with but little modification from the original type. Like all other species of the genus it affects bush jungle and shady undergrowth.

The figure shows the upperside of both sexes from specimens taken at Calcutta. A structural figure of the imago of this species is also given on PLATE I, copied from Horsfield's plate.

257. **Elymnias tinctoria**, Moore.

E. tinctoria, Moore, Proc. Zool. Soc. Lond., 1878, p. 826.

HABITAT: Meetan, 3,000 feet, April; Moolai, 3,000 to 6,000 feet; Upper Tenasserim.

EXPANSE: 3 inches.

DESCRIPTION: "Allied to *E. undularis* of India. MALE: UPPERSIDE dark blue-black, the marginal blue spots on the *forewing* larger; the border of the *hindwing* dusky purple, with a series of small white spots. FEMALE with prominent blue-black borders and white markings." (*Moore*, l. c.)

We have never seen this species; of all the numerous specimens of *E. undularis* we have received from Tenasserim none have the border of the hindwing "dusky purple;" in all it is some shade of ferruginous, and none of them are separable from *E. undularis*.

Two more varieties of this species have been separated under the names of *E. discrepans*, Distant*; and *E. nigrescens*, Butler†, both of them occur in the Malay Peninsula; the males

* *Elymnias discrepans*, Distant, Ann. and Mag. of Nat Hist., fifth series, vol. ix, p. 397 (1882). HABITAT: Penang, Province Wellesley. EXPANSE: 2·70 to 2·95 inches. DESCRIPTION: "MALE: UPPERSIDE, *forewing* blackish, with the following bright bluish markings:—a short portion of the costal area about apex of the cell continued in a subapical oblique fascia to the lower discoidal nervule, and followed by four submarginal spots, placed between the nervules; the outer margin shaded with castaneous-brown. *Hindwing* blackish, but somewhat paler than the forewing, and with a broad castaneous-brown marginal band. UNDERSIDE, *both wings* castaneous-brown, thickly mottled with pale strigæ. *Forewing* with a more or less distinct pale apical area, which is continued along the outer margin. *Hindwing* with a more or less distinct, pale, broad, and irregular submarginal fascia, and with a very pale bright bluish spot near the costa, situated between the subcostal nervules (this spot is sometimes absent). *Body* and *legs* more or less concolorous with the wings. *Antennæ* variable in hue, sometimes stramineous, mottled with brown above and pale stramineous beneath; or fuscous above and stramineous mottled with brown beneath, with the apex pale stramineous. FEMALE: UPPERSIDE, *forewing* as in the male. but with a large ochraceous basal area, which occupies the lower portion of the cell, the greater part of the space between the second median nervule and the submedian nervure, and terminates near the end of the cell and the bases of the third and second median nervules; the subapical fascia and submarginal spots larger and paler blue in colour. *Hindwing* pale fuscous, becoming paler and shaded with dull ochraceous towards the outer margin, and with a more or less distinct pale submarginal spot, situated between the discoidal and third median nervules. UNDERSIDE much paler than in the male. *Forewing* ochraceous near the inner margin. *Hindwing* with a very broad and well-defined pale marginal fascia, and with a very pale bluish spot, situated as in the male. *Body* and *legs* more or less concolorous with the wings." (*Distant*, Rhop. Malay., p. 60, pl. vi, figs. 2, *male*; 3, *female* (1882), l. c)

† *Elymnias nigrescens*, Butler, Proc Zool. Soc. Lond., 1871, p. 520, n. 2, pl. xlii, fig. 1. HABITAT: Malay Peninsula, Billiton, Borneo. EXPANSE: *Male*, 2·9; *Female*, 2·9 to 3·1 inches DESCRIPTION: "MALE: UPPER and UNDERSIDE, *both wings* resembling those of the male of *E. discrepans*, but with the bluish subapical fascia and submarginal spots considerably larger. (In some specimens, and notably a Bornean one in the collection of the British Museum, the hindwing has the pale submarginal spots, as found in most females; these

are scarcely distinguishable from some Indian examples of *E. undularis*, but the females are in both cases widely different from that sex of *E. undularis;* whereas in the variety from Ceylon, *E. fraterna*, it is the male sex that is differentiated, the female being scarcely distinguishable from that sex of *E. undularis*. In *E. discrepans* the female is only partially differentiated from the male insect, while in *E. nigrescens* the female closely resembles the male in general style of colour.

258. **Elymnias fraterna,** Butler.

E. fraterna, Butler, Proc. Zool. Soc. Lond., 1871, p. 520, pl. xlii, fig. 3, *male;* id., Moore, Lep. Ceylon, vol. i, p. 25, pl. xiii, figs. 1, *male;* 1*a*, female; 1*b*, *larva* and *pupa* (1880).

HABITAT: Ceylon.

EXPANSE: ♂, 2·65 to 3·1; ♀, 3·0 to 3·4 inches.

DESCRIPTION: "MALE: UPPERSIDE dark purple-brown. *Forewing* with the exterior margin slightly fulvous; an oblique subapical indistinct blue maculated fascia. *Hindwing* with a broad fulvous marginal band having paler centres between the nervules. UNDERSIDE dark purplish-ferruginous, a triangular apical space and outer borders broadly covered with numerous grey-brown strigæ, the basal areas also with more regularly disposed strigæ, a distinct bluish-white spot on the anterior border of the *hindwing*. FEMALE: UPPERSIDE blackish purple-brown. *Forewing* with the basal and discal areas fulvous, a subapical oblique purple-white fascia and three lower marginal spots. *Hindwing* with the basal and discal area fulvous, the median nervules and abdominal area grey-speckled, a marginal row of four bluish-white spots. UNDERSIDE as in the male, but paler, the basal area slightly fulvous, and the strigæ on the borders more prominent." (*Moore*, l. c.)

"LARVA elongated, slightly thickened in the middle, pubescent; head small, yellow, surmounted by two pink pubescent processes, last segment also with two processes; green, with three lateral yellow lines, the upper line ornamented with chrome-yellow spots, and the fifth to eighth segments with a red or blue spot. Feeds on *Palmaceæ*. PUPA green, with longitudinal yellow streaks bordered by red streaks or spots; head and thorax flattened, with three short tubercles." (*Moore*, l. c.)

E. fraterna is nothing more than a local variety of *E. undularis;* the females are indistinguishable, but the males have the ferruginous border of the hindwing narrower and brighter, and scarcely any trace of the bluish marks on the forewing; the underside is also paler. A specimen of *E. undularis* from Akyab in British Burma, taken by Captain C. H. E. Adamson, approaches more nearly to *E. fraterna* than any continental specimen we have seen.

259. **Elymnias cottonis,** Hewitson.

Melanitis cottonis, Hewitson, Ann. and Mag. of Nat. Hist., fourth series, vol. xiv, p. 358 (1874): *Elymnias cottonis*, Wood-Mason and de Nicéville, Journ. A. S. B., vol. l, pt. ii, p. 245 (1881).

HABITAT: South Andamans.

EXPANSE: ♂, 2·5; ♀, 3·1 inches (*Hewitson*); 3·00 to 3·35 inches.

DESCRIPTION: "MALE. UPPERSIDE dark red-brown. *Both wings* with the outer margins rufous. *Forewing* with the costal margin lilac-blue. UNDERSIDE as above, undulate with

are very faintly visible in Malaccan male specimens in the same collection). FEMALE: UPPERSIDE, *forewing* dark glossy fuscous, with the basal area more or less suffused with castaneous-red, with the bluish subapical fascia and submarginal spots as in the male, but which are much larger and paler in colour. *Hindwing* fuscous, becoming paler towards the outer margin (the outer margin is sometimes dull ochraceous), and with a submarginal row of four white spots placed between the nervules, of which the first and smallest is placed above the discoidal nervule, and the fourth is situate between the second and third median nervules (a fifth small and faintly marked spot is found in some specimens between the third median nervule and submedian nervure). These spots are very inconstant, being practically obsolete in some specimens. UNDERSIDE similar in pattern and colouration to that of the same sex of *E. discrepans*."

"This species or race is one which affords much difficulty and doubt as to its distinctive position. I have neither seen nor received any male specimens from Province Wellesley, though females are not uncommon from that district. The British Museum, however, posseses several male specimens which were collected by Captain Pinwill in Malacca, but these do not altogether agree with the Bornean typical specimen described by Butler. The difference is principally that of faintness or partial obliteration of the submarginal white spots to the hindwing, but as this is a variable character in female specimens, collected in such a limited area as Province Wellesley, I naturally predicate the same amount of variability in the other sex. Another peculiarity of *E. nigrescens* is the considerable similarity of the sexes. Are *E. discrepans* and *E. nigrescens* but seasonable varieties of one species? This is neither impossible nor improbable." (*Distant*, Rhop. Malay., p. 61, pl. vi, fig. 1, *male;* pl. ix, fig. 1, *female* (1882). There is a single specimen of a female of this species in the Indian Museum, Calcutta, from Sinkip Island, which agrees very closely with Distant's description and figure.

grey, the outer margins broadly undulate with grey and brown. *Forewing* with a large triangular grey spot, undulate with brown near the apex. *Hindwing* with a white spot near the middle of the costal margin. FEMALE like the male, except that it is much larger and paler, and that the *forewing* has, on the UPPERSIDE, some grey spots on the costal margin. I prefer to consider this a distinct species rather than to place it as a variety of *M.* [*E.*] *undularis*. Both sexes are alike, are without spots, and have a broad rufous margin. (*Hewitson*, l. c.) This species evidently belongs to the *undularis* group, as it has, like that species and *E. fraterna*, a patch of loosely attached scales at the base of the interspace between the median and submedian nervures on the upperside of the forewing of the male.

"Hewitson states that the sexes are alike in this species, but the three FEMALES before us have the outer margins on the UPPERSIDE of *both wings* lighter, with a more or less distinct submarginal rounded-angulate macular band in the *forewing*, corresponding to the band of blue spots in the male of *E. undularis*, and in two specimens two, and in the other four, distinct whitey-brown spots, the blurred pupils of the obsolete ocelli of the underside showing through, on the *hindwing*. UNDERSIDE much lighter than in the male, the subapical triangular patch of lilacine ground-colour in the *forewing*, and the submarginal lilacine ground of *both wings*, but especially in the *hindwing*, being whiter, and consequently more distinct than in the male; there are also six pupils of ocelli instead of one distinctly traceable, and the anastamosing chestnut striation besides being lighter is less confluent. The female, in fact, much resembles the male of *E. undularis*. Hewitson makes no mention of the beautiful rich deep plum-colour which suffuses the dark parts of the upperside in *both sexes* almost equally, nor of the faint red-violet reflections emitted by the light borders. *Danais chrysippus*, the model of the females of the allied continental form, has not yet been detected at Port Blair." (*Wood-Mason* and *de Nicéville*, l. c.)

This species is apparently common at Port Blair, but it does not occur at the Nicobar Islands. Mr. de Roepstorff has sent us numerous specimens taken in all the months between April and August.

260. **Elymnias penanga,** Westwood.

Melanitis penanga, Westwood, Gen. D. L., p 405, n. 9, *note* (1851); *Melanitis mehida*, Hewitson, Ex. Butt, vol. iii, pl. *Melanitis*, figs. 2 and 3 (1863), *male*; *Elymnias mehida*, Wallace, Trans. Ent. Soc. Lond., 1869, p. 323, n. 5; id., Butler, Proc. Zool. Soc. Lond., 1871, p. 523, n. 16; *Elymnias penanga*, Wallace, l. c., p. 325, n. 9; id., Butler, l. c., p. 521, n. 8; id., Distant, Rhop. Malay., p. 63, pl. vii, fig. 6, *male*; pl. vi, fig. 11, *female* (1882).

HABITAT: Upper Tenasserim; Province Wellesley; Malacca; Singapore.

EXPANSE: ♂, 2·7; ♀, 2·8 inches.

DESCRIPTION: " MALE. UPPERSIDE, *forewing* purplish brown, with very strong bright blue reflections, which become more fixed and distinct on the apical half, and with five pale blue elongate spots, of which the upper two are longest, and are situated on each side of the lower discoidal nervule; the remaining three being much smaller, and divided by the median nervules. The bluish reflection does not extend to the outer margin, which is distinctly purplish brown. *Hindwing* purplish brown, with bright bluish reflections, but less intense than on the forewing. UNDERSIDE castaneous-brown, much mottled with paler strigæ, which on the *forewing* forms a more or less distinct subapical space, widest at the costa, and narrowing downwards beneath the cell; the space beneath the third median nervule much paler. *Hindwing* with the basal portion to a little beyond the apex of the cell dark castaneous, the remainder much paler and thickly irrorated with the pale strigæ, and with two or three small but distinct dark submarginal spots situated between the median nervules; a somewhat large pale stramineous* spot, near the costa, placed between the subcostal nervules. *Body* and *legs* more or less concolourous with the wings. FEMALE. UPPERSIDE, *both wings* obscure bluish brown in some specimens, or with brighter indigo shadings in other specimens. *Forewing* crossed by a broad subapical white fascia, commencing at the costa, and terminating about the second

---

* STRAMINEOUS, straw coloured (*strāminĕus*, made of straw).

median nervule. *Hindwing* slightly darker on the disc. UNDERSIDE marked generally as in the male, but with the ground-colour much darker (this is somewhat variable, being little paler than above in some specimens, or more shaded with castaneous, in other specimens), and with the subapical whitish fascia of the forewing above, more diffused towards the apex beneath. The pale subcostal spot on the underside of the hindwing of the male is generally absent in the female, though present in the typical form of the species contained in the British Museum."

"The male form here described and figured was described by Mr. Hewitson under the name of *M. mehida*, whilst the female form is the typical *M. penanga* of Professor Westwood. Mr. Hewitson appended to his description of *M. mehida* the remark :—"This and *M. penanga* are very probably the sexes of one species." The form, however, which he figured as *M. penanga* was a closely allied but distinct Sumatran race, which Mr. Wallace has very properly separated under a distinctive name [*E. sumatrana**]. The two forms, however, are sufficiently similar to show that Hewitson exhibited acumen in making that remark. Having found all the specimens I have examined to exhibit sexual constancy with the different colouration, and as the undersides of the two forms are so very similar, I have felt constrained to consider the descriptions of both Westwood and Hewitson as referring to the sexes of one species, and Westwood's name has therefore priority. This race or species appears to be confined to the Malay peninsula." (*Distant*, l. c.).

A single male specimen of *E. penanga* was taken by Capt. C. H. E. Adamson in Upper Tenasserim in April, 1880; this is the only record of its occurrence beyond the limits of the Malay peninsula. Capt. Adamson remarks that the comparatively great length of the forewing is not noticed by Mr. Distant, though his figure does show a slightly pointed apex. We have never seen a specimen of this butterfly, the even outer margin of the forewing without dentations is a very marked feature.

261. **Elymnias caudata,** Butler.

E. caudata, Butler, Proc. Zool. Soc. Lond., 1871, p. 520, n. 5, pl. xlii, fig. 4, *male*.

HABITAT : South India.

EXPANSE : 3·15 to 3·60 inches.

DESCRIPTION : MALE : UPPERSIDE, *forewing* velvety purplish black, the basal area and outer margin tinged with ferruginous brown ; an oblique subapical band divided by the dark nervules, and three submarginal spots, one below each median nervule, white, irrorated at the edges with lilac. *Hindwing* ferruginous-brown, darkest at the base, a broad fulvous band on the outer half, and the margin beyond broadly brown ; this colour extending up the nervules, widest towards the margin. UNDERSIDE chestnut-brown, covered with darker chestnut coarse confluent striæ. *Forewing* with pure white and greyish partly confluent striæ disposed in a triangular apical patch, and an irregular submarginal band. *Hindwing* with a broad band on the outer half of similar partly confluent white and greyish striæ, corresponding with the fulvous band on the upperside, but reaching both costal and inner margins ; occasionally a few greyish striæ on the basal half ; but the silvery whitish subcostal spot so prominent in *E. undularis* and other species is wanting. FEMALE as in *E. undularis*, female, but the *forewing* with the subapical white band broader. *Hindwing* with the nervules broadly defined with brown, the fulvous patch extending in streaks between them much nearer to the margin, and coalescing with the whitish submarginal spots, which are obsolete, tinted with fulvous and merged

* *Elymnias sumatrana*, Wallace. Trans. Ent. Soc. Lond., 1869, p. 325, n. 10; *Melanitis penanga*, Hewitson, Ex. Butt., vol. iii, pl. *Melanitis*, figs. 1, 4 (1863), *female*) HABITAT: Sumatra. EXPANSE: 3·1 inches. DESCRIPTION: "FEMALE, UPPERSIDE, *both wings* dark brown, blue-green from the base to the middle. *Forewing* crossed near the apex by a broad band of white. *Hindwing* with a large white spot beyond the middle. UNDERSIDE with the basal half red-brown; the outer half grey, undulated throughout with brown. *Forewing* with a large white triangular spot on the costal margin from its middle to the apex. *Hindwing* with an indistinct pale spot near the base." (*Hewitson*, l. c.)

"This species is remarkably like *M. penanga*, but as the conspicuous golden-yellow spot on the costal margin of the underside of the hindwing is entirely absent, and as it also differs in the white patch on the upperside of the hindwing, and in its somewhat more angular outline, I feel compelled to separate it." (*Wallace*, l. c.)

into the streaks. UNDERSIDE much as in the male, but paler and very similar in both sexes to the underside of *E. undularis*, female, but the white striation, especially on the hindwing, is far bolder. Mimics *Danais (Salatura) genutia*. The tail is also longer than in *E. undularis*, and the outer margin of the forewing more scalloped. It appears to belong to a different group, as there is no patch of loosely attached scales on the upperside of the forewing in the male.

E. caudata is a very handsome and distinct species; it has only been found in the south of peninsular India; the male was originally recorded from Canara; the female has never been previously described. Mr. H. S. Fergusson has taken both sexes in Travancore on the Ashamboo hills, where it is fairly common in April and May. The Indian Museum has specimens from Calicut, the Wynaad, and the Kadur district in Mysore.

The next two species belong to the group of which *E. panthera* is the type, and are distinguished by having a more or less distinct submarginal series of ocelli on the underside of the hindwing. This feature is found to a certain extent in *Dyctis singhala*, and to a very much lesser degree in *E. penanga*; while *Dyctis patna* has a submarginal series of white spots representing the ocelli, but in all other Indian species of the subfamily, the series is entirely wanting or only represented by a silvery subcostal spot.

262. **Elymnias mimus**, W.-M. and de N.

E. mimus, Wood-Mason and de Nicéville, Journ. A. S. B., vol. l, pt. ii, p. 230 (1881).

HABITAT: Nicobar Islands.

EXPANSE: ♂, 2·7; ♀, 2·9 inches.

DESCRIPTION: "MALE: UPPERSIDE, black fuscous of a fuliginous tint, somewhat paler on the costal margin of the forewing, still paler at the apex of the same wing, and on the outer margins of both wings, the extreme edges and the points of the lobes of which margins are again darker; with the *cilia* whitish on the interspaces. UNDERSIDE, *both wings* brownish, coarsely and confluently striated with rich dark chestnut for their basal two-thirds, whence they become suddenly lighter, owing to the striation being more rare as well as lighter coloured. *Forewing* with the outer margin of the closely striated portion sharply defined, and angulated outwards between the first and second discoidal nervules; and with the ground-colour immediately beyond the anterior and shorter of the two lines forming the angulated outline of the basal portion whitish. *Hindwing* with the ground beyond the chestnut base pale sepia, passing to whitish around the outer-marginal ocelli, obscurely and rarely striated before, but more richly and closely at the outer margin beyond the ocelli with vandyke-brown; and with seven suboval submarginal black ocelli, of which the second is the largest of all but only slightly larger than the fifth, the first is subequal to the sixth, and the third, fourth, and seventh (which touches the sixth in the same interspace) are subequal and much smaller than the rest, the first and second have a white pupil (which in the latter is eccentric) irrorated at the edges with light metallic greenish-blue scales, and the rest have the pupil almond-shaped, with some mauve-coloured irrorations on and around its inner end. FEMALE: UPPERSIDE much lighter, with a submarginal whitey-brown common band which passes straight across *both wings* from near the anal angle of the *hindwing* to the third branch of the median nervure of the *forewing*, at which point it turns sharply off at a right angle to the costal margin; with the light intervals between the striations of the underside visible as light bars on the anterior margin, and the apical dark portion lighter than the basal, of the *forewing*; and with two infuscations (less perceptible in the darker male) on the *hindwing* corresponding to the fifth and sixth ocelli of the underside. UNDERSIDE lighter, with the chestnut striæ less confluent permitting more of the ground-colour to be seen; and with the anterior ocellus larger and much diffused circumferentially, the second with the pupil rudimentary, and the third larger than the fourth."

"One male from Kar Nicobar and one female from Pulo Kondul."

"Closely allied to *E. dusara* (*panthera*, Fabricius), Horsfield, Cat. Lep. E. I. C., pl v, figs. 7, 7a (1829), *female* (no description), from which it would appear to differ in having the light band of the *forewing* distinctly angulated, and the costal margin of the same barred with lighter, in its more highly developed and unequal ocelli, in the more abrupt definition of the basal chestnut from the rest of the underside, and apparently also in its more strongly lobed wing-margins and finer tails. It in all probability mimics *Euplœa camorta*, a species which abounds on all the islands of the Nicobar group." (*Wood-Mason* and *de Nicéville*, l. c.)

Since the above was written, one male from Great Nicobar, two males and a female from Kamorta, two males from Trinkutt, and two females from Teressa, have been received by the Indian Museum, Calcutta, from Mr. de Roepstorff. The males are all very constant, but the Kamorta female differs from the Pulo Kondul female in having the apex of the forewing more produced, and the submarginal band on the upperside of both wings hardly lighter than in the males. On the underside the ocelli are also much smaller than in the type specimen.

263. **Elymnias obnubila,** Marshall, n. sp.

HABITAT : Upper Tenasserim ; Mergui.

EXPANSE : ♂, 2·4 ; ♀, 3·0 inches.

DESCRIPTION : MALE : UPPERSIDE dark velvety chestnut-brown glossed with violet in certain lights, with a much paler outer band from beyond the middle of the costa of the forewing to the inner margin of the hindwing, inwardly diffused, outwardly extending to the margin, except at the apex of the forewing, which is suffused with dusky. UNDERSIDE dark grey, closely undulated with broad chestnut-brown striæ except upon the area corresponding with the pale band of the upperside, on which the undulations are much finer and wider apart. *Forewing* with a conspicuous whitish triangular costal patch near the apex ; the hinder angle tinged with yellow. *Hindwing* with a submarginal series of six black spots with silvery pupils ; the first near the costa having the silvery pupil very large, scarcely ringed with black. FEMALE larger, paler. UPPERSIDE with the pale band much wider, occupying on the hindwing the whole of the outer half. A submarginal series of four dark brown obsolete dots, corresponding to the ocelli on the underside. UNDERSIDE also paler. *Hindwing* with the silvery subcostal spot larger, the rest of the ocelli smaller and imperfect, being reduced to blackish dots with faint white irrorations on the inner edge. Shape, as in *E. undularis*, but the inner margin of the forewing longer, the outer margin more erect, straight, more prominently dentate, and the hindwing more prominently tailed. This is the continental representative of *E. panthera*, Fabricius, from Java; it differs from *E. panthera* in shape, in having the outer margin straight, not convex, and the inner margin longer ; and in markings, in that on the upperside the pale band is broader and continued to the margin, and of a rich bright chestnut colour, and bears no spots on the hindwing in the male, though the female has a series of four very obscure spots ; whereas in *E. panthera* the outer margin is broadly clouded with dusky brown, and the hindwing has three small submarginal ocellular spots ; and on the underside similarly the pale band formed by the partial absence of striæ is narrow and submarginal in *E. panthera*, broad and marginal in *E. obnubila* ; in *E. panthera* also the white triangular patch of the forewing is obsolete, and the ocelli of the hindwing are larger, the first near the costa being like the others instead of having the silvery pupil greatly predominating.

Only two specimens of this rare species have as yet been taken so far as we know; a single male now in the Indian Museum, Calcutta, was taken by Dr. J. Anderson in the Mergui Archipelago in January ; and a single female, now in Major Marshall's collection, was taken by Captain C. T. Bingham in the Thoungyeen forests in Upper Tenasserim in December.

E. panthera, Fabricius, is figured by Horsfield in his Cat. Lep. E. I. C., pl. v, figs. 7, 7*a* (1828), *female*, under the name of *Melanitis dusara*. Mr. Wallace remarks of it that "the female is like the male, but the pale bands are broader and somewhat yellower, and contain three or four pale spots on the hindwing ; the species varies but little, and seems to be very constant in both sexes, with but little difference between them." (Trans. Ent. Soc. Lond., 1869, pp. 322, 323).

E. lutescens * also belongs to this group. It is very closely allied to *E. mimus*, and differs from that species on the upperside in the *forewing* being but slightly paler on the margins, and having no submarginal paler band; the band on the hindwing is, however, much more prominent, and bears a submarginal row of spots. Underside very similar, the ocelli rather smaller.

264. **Elymnias leucocyma,** Godart. (PLATE XVII, FIG. 60 ♂ ♀).

Biblis leucocyma, Godart, Enc. Méth., vol. ix, p. 326, n. 3 (1819); *Dyctis leucocyma*, Moore, Proc. Zool. Soc. Lond., 1878, p. 826; *Melanitis malelas*, Hewitson, Ex. Butt., vol. iii, pl. *Melanitis*, figs. 6, 7 (1863), *male*.

HABITAT: North-Eastern India, Arakan, Tenasserim.

EXPANSE: 3·2 to 4·2 inches.

DESCRIPTION: MALE: UPPERSIDE velvety blackish brown, the outer two-thirds beautifully shot with violet in certain lights; a submarginal series of paler violet irrorated spots, and four similar spots on the disc, two beyond the cell below the lower discoidal nervule, and one between each pair of median nervules. *Hindwing* brighter brown, paler externally, and with or without a submarginal series of small ashy dots. UNDERSIDE pale brown, closely undulated with greyish yellow striæ, most densely on the outer two-thirds. FEMALE as in the male, but with the violet shot confined to the outer half of the forewing, the spots white, partially irrorated with violet towards the apex; the whole of the interspaces on the hindwing and below the median nervule in the forewing marked with numerous transverse yellowish-grey striæ more or less confluent into longitudinal streaks. UNDERSIDE as in the male, but with the pale striæ much wider and whiter. Mr. Wallace (Trans. Ent. Soc. Lond., 1869, p. 327) considered *E. malelas* distinct from *E. leucocyma*, and remarked, "allied to *E. leucocyma*, but differing in the smooth outline of the wings, and the produced outer angle of the hindwing." There can be but little doubt, however, that they are one and the same species.

E. leucocyma in both sexes is an excellent mimic of *Euplœa midamus;* its highly elongate forewing distinguishes it from all other species of the subfamily. It is common in the submontane districts of Northern and Eastern Bengal, extending through Burma as far south as Tavoy, but not apparently into the Malay peninsula proper. Mr. T. C. Hill took it in Tavoy in March; Captain C. T. Bingham found it commonly in the Thoungyeen forests in the autumn and again in April; Captain C. H. E. Adamson found it commonly in Moulmein in September, and again at Akyab. Mr. Wood-Mason took it in Cachar in June and July. The Indian Museum, Calcutta, contains specimens from Sylhet and Upper Assam; Mr. de Nicéville has taken it round villages in Sikkim at about 2,000 feet elevation in October; and Mr. E. T. Atkinson records it from Kāli Kumaon on the western border of Nepal.

The figure shows the upperside of a male specimen from Sylhet, and of a female from Sibsagar, Upper Assam, both in the Indian Museum, Calcutta.

The next species, *E. saüeri*, differs from all the foregoing in the pattern of the underside, which is marbled throughout, with no definite pattern and no defined spots on either wing, and no paler nebulous outer band.

---

* *Elymnias lutescens*, Butler, Ann. and Mag. of Nat. Hist., third series, vol. xx, p. 404, pl ix, fig. 10 (1867), *female;* id., Wallace, Trans. Ent. Soc. Lond., 1869, p. 323, n. 4; id., Butler, Proc. Zool. Soc. Lond., 1871, p. 521, n. 6; id., Distant, Rhop. Malay., p. 62, pl. vi, figs. 4. *male;* 5. *female* (1882). HABITAT: Penang; Province Wellesley; Malacca; Ayerpanas; Singapore; Sumatra; Borneo. EXPANSE: 3·0 to 3·2 inches. DESCRIPTION: "MALE: UPPERSIDE, *both wings* dark glossy fuscous. *Forewing* with the outer margin somewhat broadly and slightly paler. *Hindwing* with a broad, pale greyish submarginal fascia, the inner margin of which is somewhat scalloped between the nervules; this is broadest near the anal angle and narrowest at the apex, and contains a series of prominent fuscous spots placed between the nervules, two between first median nervule and submedian nervure, the others placed singly (these spots are variable in number, not being found above the third median nervule in some specimens, but in other specimens continued towards the apex). UNDERSIDE, *both wings* pale castaneous, mottled with numerous greyish striæ, and with a more or less well-defined broad submarginal fascia, which is broadest and most clearly defined on the *hindwing*, and there possesses six dark blue rounded spots, with pale blue centres, which are continued in streaks beyond their inner margins; these spots are placed between the nervules, the first above the discoidal nervule, and the fifth and sixth together between the first median nervule and the submedian nervure; a pale and bright bluish spot between the subcostal nervules. *Body* and *legs* more or less concolourous with the wings. FEMALE larger than the male. UPPERSIDE paler and more ferruginous. *Forewing* with a broad and well-defined outer ferruginous fascia. *Hindwing* with the pale submarginal fascia broader and less scalloped inwardly than in the male, and with five or six fuscous spots with paler centres placed between the nervules. UNDERSIDE paler than in the male, but with the *hindwing* spotted as in that sex. The tail-like prolongation of the *hindwing* at the apex of the third median nervule is longest in the female." (*Distant*, l.c.)

265. **Elymnias saüeri,** Distant.

E. saüeri, Distant, Rhop. Malay., p. 65, pl. ix, fig. 3 (1882), *male*.

HABITAT : Tenasserim ; Malay Peninsula.

EXPANSE : ♂, 3·55 inches.

DESCRIPTION : "MALE : UPPERSIDE, *forewing* dark violaceous, with paler suffusions on the apical area, and with the following very pale violaceous spots :—Three discal ; one large, placed between the third and second median nervules, the others exceedingly small and indistinct, and situated between the discoidal nervules, and between the second and first median nervules ; five large submarginal spots divided by the nervules, of which the two upper, inner, and largest are contiguous and separated by the lower discoidal nervule, the fifth being situated between the first median nervule and the submedian nervure ; there is also a very faint indication of a spot at the end of the cell. Costal area with the basal third minutely spotted with greyish, the remaining portion with three or four pale bluish spots. *Hindwing* castaneous, with the basal area fuscous. The extreme margins of *both wings* are alternately fuscous and white. UNDERSIDE pale ferruginous, thickly mottled with dark chocolate-brown strigæ, irregular in shape and size. *Forewing* with a number of pale greyish spots on the costal area ; the upper portion of the cell and the apical area somewhat paler in hue, and with indications of a dark waved fascia near the end of the cell. *Hindwing* somewhat darker, the strigæ being more numerous and contiguous, with indications of a much-waved and irregular dark fascia crossing the wing about the end of the cell, and a more or less distinct, broad, submarginal fascia, followed by several waved, broken, and indistinct lines. *Body* and *legs* more or less concolourous with the wings."

"This fine species is somewhat intermediate between *E. casiphone** and *E. leucocyma*, agreeing best with the latter above, and with the first beneath. It appears to be a mimic of a species of *Euplæa* belonging to the *midamus* group, though the female still remains to be discovered. Since this description was written, a specimen collected by Captain Bingham in Tenasserim has been presented to the British Museum." (*Distant*, l. c.)

We have never seen this species, and the above record is the only one of its occurrence within our limits.

The next species, *E. timandra*, is of very different style of colouration and outline. The type of the group is *E. lais*, Cramer, from Java, Sumatra and Borneo, and also from the Malay Peninsula. The upperside has on both wings the nervures and the outer margin broadly defined with blackish brown, and the interspaces white tinged with creamy or yellowish or grey or verditer blue. They mimic species of *Danais* of the *Limniace* group. *E. timandra* chiefly differs from *E. lais* in the more dentate outline of the outer margin of the forewing, and the basal area of both wings on the underside is much darker.

---

* *Elymnias casiphone*, Hübner, Samml. Ex. Schmett., vol. iii, pl. xviii ? (1816-1824) ; id., Butler, Trans. Ent. Soc. Lond , 1870, p. 488; idem, id , Proc. Zool Soc Lond , 1871, p. 522, n. 14; idem, id . Distant, Rhop. Malay , p. 64, pl. vi, fig. 10 (1882), *male*. HABITAT : Singapore ; Java. EXPANSE : *male*, 3·00 ; *female*, 3·25 inches. DESCRIPTION : "MALE : UPPERSIDE, *both wings* pale chocolate-brown. *Forewing* with the apical area much suffused with violaceous, and with the following pale greyish macular markings ; a number of irregularly-sized and shaped spots on the costal area, gradually increasing in size from the base ; a rounded spot just beyond the end of the cell ; two discal spots divided by the second median nervule, and a submarginal series of six spots, divided by the nervules, the first and innermost of which is placed above the upper discoidal nervule, and the sixth between the first median nervule and the submedian nervure. *Hindwing* with a submarginal series of obscure greyish spots, preceded by a few discal spots of the same colour. UNDERSIDE pale ferruginous, mottled with numerous and irregularly-sized chocolate strigæ. *Forewing* with a costal series of pale greyish spots ; four larger pale discal spots situate one beyond the end of the cell, two divided by the second median nervule, and the fourth placed between the discoidal nervules ; there are also faint indications of a submarginal series of spots placed between the nervules, of which the two most prominent are placed above and beneath the first median nervule. *Hindwing* with some dark and confluent strigæ principally distributed on the basal half, and with a prominent dark submarginal fascia, which is preceded by pale greyish, and followed by several narrower, waved, and somewhat fused dark marginal fasciæ. *Body* and *legs* more or less concolorous with the wings." (*Distant*, l. c.) "FEMALE : UPPERSIDE, same pattern as *E. timandra*, female, Wallace, but the whole apical area pale violet, and the rest of the ground-colour of a browner tint than in that species. UNDERSIDE, markings the same as in the male, but ill-defined, the *hindwing* whitish." (*Butler*, l. c., in Trans. Ent. Soc. Lond.)

266. **Elymnias timandra,** Wallace.

E. timandra, Wallace, Trans. Ent. Soc. Lond., 1869, p. 326, n. 13.

HABITAT: Sylhet; Tenasserim.

EXPANSE: 3·0 to 3·7 inches.

DESCRIPTION: "Like *E. lais**; outline of the wings more dentate, especially on the hindwing. MALE. UPPERSIDE like *E. lais*, but the markings broader, and of a rich verditer blue on the *forewing*. UNDERSIDE, the base of the wings is much darker. FEMALE. Wings more elongate; markings pale ochre, tinged with bluish on the *forewing*, the tooth at the outer angle of the *hindwing* forming a short tail."

"Very closely allied to *E. lais*, but the different outline of the wings, and distinct colouring, render it neccessary to separate it." (*Wallace*, l. c.)

The Indian Museum, Calcutta, contains specimens from Sylhet, and Captain Bingham took a single male in the Donat range in Tennasserim in April, and one female was taken at Kanhlete by Captain Adamson in September. Wallace also records it from Moulmein, but it is apparently a rare species. On the upperside the Sylhet males are decidedly marked with green, while the Tenasserim males are equally decidedly blue, and the forewing is somewhat longer proportionally than the Sylhet males.

E. casiphone has been recorded from Singapore. On the underside it is marked very similarly to *E. lais*, but the general tone of the ground-colour is more rufous; on the upperside, however, it is very different. It is intermediate between *E. saüeri* and *E. lais*.

Genus 32.—DYCTIS, Boisduval. (PLATE XVII.)

Dyctis, Boisduval, Voy. de l'Astrolabe, p. 138 (1832); id., Westwood, Gen. D. L., p. 353 (1851); id., Butler, Proc. Zool. Soc. Lond., 1871, p. 523.

Differs from *Elymnias* (restricted) in having the *lower disco-cellular* nervule of the *hindwing* straight or feebly concave in continuation of the upper disco-cellular nervule.

The full diagnosis of *Dyctis* as given by Mr. Butler is appended below;† but the sole reliable feature on which the distinction can be maintained is the shape of the discoidal cell in the hindwing as indicated above. The hindwing in *Elymnias* restricted also has a false prædiscoidal cell; the position of the origin of the first subcostal nervule is inconstant, in most species of *Elymnias* it is nearer to the base of the wing than to the apex of the cell, and in most species of *Dyctis* it is nearer to the apex of the cell than to the base of the wing, but no tangible line of separation can be drawn; the distance between the origin

* *Elymnias lais*, Cramer, Pap. Ex., vol. ii, pl. cx, figs. A, B (1777), *male*; *Biblis lais*, Godart, Enc. Méth., vol. ix, p. 326, n. 4 (1819); *Elymnias lais*, Wallace, Trans. Ent. Soc. Lond., 1869, p. 325, n. 11; id., Distant, Rhop. Malay., p. 62, pl. ix, fig. 2 (1882), *male*. HABITAT: Province Wellesley; Siam; Malay Archipelago. EXPANSE: 3 inches. DESCRIPTION: "MALE: UPPERSIDE, *both wings* dark chocolate-brown, variegated with greenish markings. *Forewing* with the costal area (particularly the basal portion) irrorated with numerous greyish spots and strigæ; a large greenish fascia in the cell, narrowest at the base, and widened and somewhat truncate near the apex, and with the following longitudinal fasciæ of the same colour placed between the nervules:— The upper two are placed above and below the first discoidal nervule, and are very faint and slender, with their apices broad and macular; the third above the third median nervule is slender, but macular at both ends, and inwardly approaches the disco-cellular fascia; the following three separated by the median nervules are broadest at base, narrowing at apical portion, but macular at apex, and the last runs along the inner margin. *Hindwing* with similar longitudinal fasciæ as on the forewing, and which are also placed between the nervules, but are broken near their apices, which thus appear as a submarginal series of spots; of these fasciæ the inner two (placed on each side of the submedian nervure) are longest, and the upper two (placed on each side of the discoidal nervule) are the faintest; there is also a very faint disco-cellular streak. UNDERSIDE dull greyish, suffused with fuscous, and mottled with dark strigæ; on the *forewing* these become more or less confluent and dark chocolate in colour, forming an irregular spot in the cell, a larger irregular spot or fascia at the end of the cell, and appearing very prominently towards the outer margin; on the *hindwing* these darker shadings do not extend beyond the basal half of the wing, but again appear as a more or less well-defined outer submarginal fascia. *Body* and *legs* more or less concolourous with the wings. FEMALE, somewhat larger than the male, the fasciæ and spots of the UPPERSIDE being creamy in hue, and with the outer margins of *both wings* distinctly and somewhat brightly castaneous. UNDERSIDE, *both wings* much paler, and the numerous shadings are of like pattern but fainter impression." (*Distant*, l. c.)

† *Dyctis*, Butler. "Forewing as in *Elymnias*; hindwing with a false prædiscoidal cell; the first subcostal nervule emitted towards the end of the cell, nearer to the end in the females than in the males; second and discoidal nervules emitted somewhat near together; upper disco-cellular nervule more or less oblique, slanting outwards; lower disco-cellular feebly concave or angulated, and about twice the length of the upper one; second and third median nervules emitted near together." (*Butler*, l. c.)

of the second branch and that of the discoidal nervule scarcely differs at all throughout the subfamily; and throughout the subfamily also the second and third median nervules are emitted close together at the apex of the cell.

Of the five Indian species placed in this genus, three (*D. esaka*, *D. patna* and *D. vasudeva*) were included in it by Mr. Butler; one, *D. singhala*, subsequently described, was classed by Mr. Moore as an *Elymnias*, and one, *D. peali*, has only just been discovered. The two latter would seem from their outline and markings to belong to *Elymnias*; *D. singhala* is identical in outline with *E. lutescens*, and only differs from it in having the pale band on the upperside composed of partially confluent striæ and without black submarginal spots, and the underside with the ocelli minute and obsolescent; and *D. peali* is identical in outline with *E. timandra*; but both *D. singhala* and *D. peali* have the cell of the hindwing formed as in *Dyctis*. The remaining three species have the outline much more even, as in the typical species from the Austro-Malayan region. *D. esaka* is the most typical; *D. vasudeva* somewhat less so, but remarkable from its colouration which mimics some species of *Delias* or other dark *Pieris* with a large patch of white on the hindwing; *D. patna* has the outer margin distinctly, though feebly, dentate, and mimics an *Euplœa* of the *superba* type in colouration.

As far as the females are known they are but little differentiated, whereas in many of the species of *Elymnias* the females differ very considerably in colour and markings from the males.

Key to the Indian species of Dyctis.

B. Hindwing with the lower disco-cellular nervule straight or feebly concave.

- *a*. The upper disco-cellular suberect or outwardly oblique, almost in the same line as the lower.
  - *a*¹. Forewing elongate; outer margin irregularly dentate and distinctly falcate; hindwing distinctly caudate; (outline exactly as in *E. timandra*).
    - *a*². Male, upperside dark violet-black, with a diffused submarginal lavender band on both wings; female unknown.

      267. D. PEALI, Assam.
  - *b*¹. Forewing short broad, outer margin dentate, but not falcate; hindwing dentate and distinctly caudate; (outline much as in *E. caudata*).
    - *b*². Male and female, upperside blackish-brown, with a submarginal band of partially coalescent creamy-white or buff striæ on both wings.

      268. D. SINGHALA, Ceylon.
  - *c*¹. Forewing elongate, but broad; outer margin of both wings even, regularly but not very prominently dentate; (outline as in *E. leucocyma*, but the wings much broader and inner margin longer).
    - *c*². Male and female chestnut brown, dark and shot with violet on the forewing. Forewing with longitudinal violet streaks on the disc; hindwing with white submarginal spots.

      269. D. PATNA, Sikkim, Cachar, Sylhet.
  - *d*¹. Forewing short broad; outer margin of both wings very slightly dentate; (outline as in *E. cottonis*, but the apex of forewing rounded, not acute).
    - *d*². Male and female dark brown, forewing with grey streaks, hindwing with a large white patch on inner half.

      270. D. VASUDEVA, Sikkim, Tenasserim.
  - *e*¹. Forewing short, very broad; outer margin of both wings even; outline an arc of a circle with the base of the wings as a centre; the inner margin of forewing and costa of hindwing being both equal to the costa of forewing.

    271. D. ESAKA, Mergui.

267. Dyctis peali, W.-M.

Elymnias peali, Wood-Mason, Ann. and Mag. of Nat. Hist., fifth series, vol. xi, p. 62, pl. ii, figs. A, B (1883), *male*.

HABITAT: Aideo, Sibsagar district, Assam.

EXPANSE: ♂, 3·15 inches.

DESCRIPTION: "MALE: UPPERSIDE, *both wings* violescent black-blue, gradually darkening from the outer margin to the bases, with the markings deep lavender-blue, and the *cilia* between the nervules greyish white. *Forewing* with an oblique subapical band placed nearly at right angles to the complete submarginal series of rather faint and diffused blotches, and the apical subcostal interspace, all lavender-blue, and with the costal and subcostal areas transversely striated with the same colour. *Hindwing* with a corresponding submarginal band, which is very prominent and broken up into coarse striæ between the third median nervule and the abdominal margin, towards which it passes from blue into red-violet. UNDERSIDE much as in *E. undularis* and its allies, but more richly coloured than in any species of that group."

The type specimen, the only one known, is in the Indian Museum, Calcutta.

268. **Dyctis singhala,** Moore.

Elymnias singhala, Moore, Proc. Zool. Soc. Lond., 1874, p. 568; idem, id., Lep. Cey., p. 26, pl. xiii, figs. 2, *male*; 2a, *female* (1880).

HABITAT : Ceylon.

EXPANSE : 3·0 to 3·5 inches.

DESCRIPTION : " MALE : UPPERSIDE dark purple-brown. *Forewing* with a marginal macular band formed of pale greenish-grey quadrate patches, a few ochreous strigæ on the costal margin. *Hindwing* with a broad marginal band of pale greenish-ochreous longitudinally-confluent strigæ. UNDERSIDE, basal areas purple-brown, outer areas pinkish-grey, covered with numerous black strigæ, most dense on basal areas and along extreme outer margins; an indistinct purple-white apical spot, and a submarginal row of black dots on the *hindwing*. FEMALE brighter coloured, the marginal bands more prominent." (*Moore*, l.c., in Lep. Cey.). "Occurs at Kandy." (*Wade*). The type specimen was described from Colombo. The Indian Museum, Calcutta, contains a single pair.

269. **Dyctis patna,** Westwood.

Melanitis patna, Westwood, Gen. D. L., p. 405, *note*, pl. lxviii, fig. 2 (1851), *Elymnias patna*, Wallace, Trans. Ent. Soc. Lond., 1879, p. 327, n. 17; *Dyctis patna*, Butler, Proc. Zool. Soc. Lond., 1871, p. 525, n. 13.

HABITAT : Cachar; Sylhet; Sikkim.

EXPANSE : 3·35 to 3·95 inches.

DESCRIPTION : "UPPERSIDE fuscous. *Forewing* and the outer angle of the *hindwing* with a slight violaceous sheen, with elongate purple streaks beyond the middle and another in the middle. *Hindwing* with four whitish submarginal dots. UNDERSIDE pale fuscous. *Forewing* with three, *hindwing* with seven white dots; the outer margin of the *hindwing* irrorated with white." (*Westwood*, l.c.) There are two FEMALE specimens of this species from Sikkim in the Indian Museum, Calcutta. They differ from the male in being paler on both upper and undersides, the elongate purple streaks on the upperside of the *forewing* larger and more diffused, and in one specimen there is a submarginal series of five white spots, one in each interspace, except the lower discoidal. They of course lack the sexual glandular patch of scales and tufts of hair on the upperside of the hindwing near the costal margin which is present in all the males of this subfamily.

"A fine species, somewhat resembling *Elymnias leucocyma*, but with the spots beneath as in *E. hewitsoni* from Macassar and Celebes." (*Wallace*, l.c.)

"Mimics *Euplœa callithoë*, a species allied to *E. splendens* and *E. superba*; it bears a superficial resemblance to *Elymnias leucocyma.*" (*Butler*, l.c.)

D. patna bears a general resemblance to *Euplœas* of the *superba* type both in form and colour; the *forewing* is tinged with violet, and the *hindwing* with chestnut-brown; the purple streaks on the *forewing* are longest at the costa and extend in a curved regularly decreasing series to the submedian nervure, one in each interspace, except that the streak above the third median nervule is abbreviated or altogether wanting; the patch in the middle is situated at the end of the cell, and is often indistinct; the whitish irrorations of the underside of the *hindwing* are grouped into irregular undulated striæ on the outer and abdominal margins of the *hindwing*, and continued less prominently on to the disc of the *forewing*; in some specimens they are obsolete. It most nearly resembles *E. leucocyma*, but differs in having the wings shorter and broader; on the upperside the discal series of purple spots on the *forewing* far more elongate, the inner series absent; and on the *hindwing* in the presence of the white submarginal spots: and on the underside it has white submarginal spots and the outer margin only variegated, whereas *E. leucocyma* has no white spots, and almost the entire undersurface variegated with pale striæ.

It is not a common species, and we have as yet only seen it from Sikkim, Cachar and Sylhet. Mr. de Nicéville took it in the valley of the Great Runjit, Sikkim, in October; and Mr. Wood-Mason took a single specimen on Nemotha, Cachar, in September. It most probably mimics *Euplœa (Stictoplœa) hopei*, which Mr. de Nicéville has taken in Sikkim at the same time and in the same locality.

270. **Dyctis vasudeva,** Moore. (PLATE XVII, FIG. 61 ♂).

Elymnias vasudeva, Moore, Horsfield and Moore, Cat. Lep. E. I. C., vol. i, p. 238, n. 513; *Dyctis vasudeva*, Butler, Proc. Zool. Soc. Lond., 1871, p. 525, n. 16; *Elymnias thycana*, Wallace, Trans. Ent. Soc. Lond., 1869, p. 323, n. 7.

HABITAT: Sikkim, Upper Tenasserim.

EXPANSE: 2·75 to 3·20 inches.

DESCRIPTION: "MALE: UPPERSIDE, *forewing* black, glossed with slaty-blue; costal margin with small bluish-white dots; longitudinal spots in the middle of the wing, and spots from near the apex to the posterior angle bluish-white. *Hindwing*, from the abdominal margin to the middle of the wing, white; anterior and posterior border black, the latter with some marginal white spots. UNDERSIDE white, nervures black. *Forewing* covered throughout with deep black striæ [or as Wallace describes it, black, irregularly blotched and irrorated with white]. *Hindwing* with the exterior margin covered with deep black striæ; the base of the wing black, with numerous small white spots, and a large red spot below the cell; abdominal margin broadly suffused with yellow." (*Moore*, l. c.) "FEMALE: UPPERSIDE paler, with the bluish and white portions more diffused. UNDERSIDE very much whiter, with finer irrorations, and the yellow patch more diffused." (*Wallace*, l. c.) The secondary sexual characters of the male differ from those of all other Indian species of the subfamily, as not only are the usual tufts of hair on the upperside of the hindwing present, but the inner margin of the forewing is folded upwards, and encloses a tuft of long ochreous-brown probably erectile hairs.

"Mimics either *Delias descombesi* or *D. indica*." (*Butler*, l. c.) "*Pieridæ* of the genus *Thyca*." (*Wallace*, l. c.)

D. vasudeva is not very common, but will probably be found in all the hill ranges between Sikkim and Tenasserim.

The figure shows the upper and undersides of a male specimen from Sikkim, in the Indian Museum, Calcutta.

271. **Dyctis esaca,** Westwood.

Melanitis esaca, Westwood, Gen. D. L., vol. ii, p. 405, n. 10 (1851), *note*; id., Hewitson, Ex. Butt., vol. iii, pl. *Melanitis*, fig. 5 (1863): *Elymnias esaca*, Wallace, Trans. Ent. Soc. Lond., 1869, p. 322, n. 2; *Dyctis esaca*, Butler, Proc. Zool. Soc. Lond., 1871, p. 523, n. 4.

HABITAT: Assam, Mergui, Borneo.

EXPANSE: 2·3 to 2·5 inches.

DESCRIPTION: "Wings entire. UPPERSIDE blackish, with a slight olivaceous gloss. *Forewing* very broad, almost perpendicularly truncated, with an oblique pale lilascine subapical fascia continued by three spots of the same colour along the outer margin. *Hindwing* with a slight purple gloss, the *outer margin grey*. UNDERSIDE fuscous, much irrorated with grey. *Forewing* paler about the apex, with two black dots. *Hindwing* with a series of *minute black dots*." (*Westwood*, l. c.)

The only other recorded notice of this species is by Hewitson who figures the underside in his "Exotic Butterflies," and adds the following short description, which somewhat differs from Westwood's quoted above. "UPPERSIDE: dark brown; crossed near the outer margin by a curved band of six large ill-defined lilac spots. *Hindwing* with a marginal *band of five indistinct grey spots.* UNDERSIDE red-brown, closely undulated throughout with grey. *Forewing* with the apex nearly white, marked with two black spots. *Hindwing* with a black spot dotted with white near the costal margin before the middle, and a submarginal band of five *black spots indistinctly dotted with white.*" (*Hewitson*, l. c.)

The Indian Museum, Calcutta, contains a single male specimen of this rare species, which was taken by Dr. J. Anderson in the Mergui Archipelago on the 20th December, 1881. It is smaller than the types, being 2·3 inches in expanse; the forewing is, as in Hewitson's description, "crossed near the outer margin by a curved band of six large ill-defined lilac spots," the spots near the apex being elongate, almost coalescent, and separated only by the dark nervules; all the spots more or less irrorated with white in the centre; but the hindwing is as in Westwood's description, the outer margin broadly grey, outwardly almost pure white, inwardly diffused and irrorated with lilac; the extreme outer margin is narrowly blackish.

The shape of the wings of *D. esaca* is very peculiar, and sufficient to distinguish it at a glance from all other Indian *Elymniinæ*, indeed from almost every other Indian Butterfly; the costal and inner margins of both wings are all of nearly equal length, so that the outline between the apex of the forewing and the anal angle of the hindwing is an arc of a circle with its centre at the base of the wings.

SUBFAMILY IV.—MORPHINÆ, Butler.

Morphinæ, Butler, Cist. Ent., vol. i, p. 3 (1869); id., Kirby, Syn. Cat. D. L., p. 115 (1871); *Morphidæ* and *Nymphadidæ (part)*, Westwood, Gen. D. L., vol. ii, p. 332 (1851); *Morphina*, Distant, Rhop. Malay, p. 67 (1882).

BODY robust, seldom elongate. HEAD usually small, tufted; *eyes* large, prominent, naked; *antennæ* long, slender, with a slender very gradually formed club; *palpi* slender, somewhat elongate, erect (or sometimes porrect), the front edge not dilated, clothed in front with dense appressed scaly hairs, at the back with longer hairs grouped in a tuft against the face. WINGS broad, ample, but varying in outline; generally ocellated on the underside. FOREWING with the nervures usually simple, the costal nervure sometimes slightly and gradually dilated at the base: *discoidal cell* short, very broad, completely closed by perfect nervules; the apex always beyond the origin of the second median nervule; the first branch of the subcostal nervure long, originating near the end of the cell and often anastomosing with the costal nervure; the remaining branches originating far beyond the cell close together near the apex (except in *Xanthotænia* in which they are widely separated); the *upper* and *middle disco-cellular* nervules short, the *lower* very long, outwardly oblique and generally concave. HINDWING with the *discoidal cell* partially or entirely open, except in *Xanthotænia*, where it is completely closed by a very slender lower disco-cellular nervule: no prædiscoidal cell; the *discoidal nervule* appearing as a third subcostal branch; the anal margin broadly channelled and enclosing the entire abdomen. In the male furnished with glands or patches of raised scales or tufts of hair in various positions. FORELEGS of the MALE small, brush-like; those of the FEMALE larger, longer, and less hairy.

"LARVA: with a more or less developed bifid tail." (*Distant*, l. c.) "PUPA: short, thick, cylindrical, or slightly carinated down the back." (*Westwood*, Gen. D. L., vol. ii, p. 332 (1851).

The *Morphinæ* are confined to South America and the Malayan region, extending in India as far as the Indo-Malayan fauna penetrates. The typical genus *Morpho* is entirely South American, and contains some of the largest and most brilliantly coloured butterflies in the world; all the other genera are Asiatic.

Great differences of opinion have prevailed as to the propriety of separating this group into a subfamily; the original separation was suggested by Doubleday and adopted by Westwood in the Genera of Diurnal Lepidoptera, but with much hesitation; the group as there defined excludes *Amathusia*, *Zeuxidia*, and *Discophora*, which were left with *Kallima* among the *Nymphalinæ*, and includes many American genera now classed as *Brassolinæ* in a distinct subfamily. In 1864, Mr. H. W. Bates, in a review (Journal of Entomology, vol. ii, p. 177) of the primary and secondary divisions of the suborder, united the *Morphinæ* with the true *Nymphalinæ*, with the remark that "they exhibit no good character whereby they may be distinguished from the *Nymphalinæ*," and the combined group he defined as having the "lower disco-cellular nervule, at least of the hindwing, more or less atrophied." In 1869, Mr. A. G. Butler established the group as it now stands, merely remarking that it "includes the genera *Morpho*, *Clerome*, *Drusilla*, *Discophora*, *Amathusia*, *Bia*, and comes between the *Brassolinæ* and *Nymphalinæ*" (Cistula Entomologica, vol. i, p. 3), but giving no distinctive features. In this he was followed by Mr. Kirby in 1871 in his Synonymic Catalogue of Diurnal Lepidoptera. And in 1882, Mr. W. L. Distant, in his Rhopolocera Malayana, reverts to Mr. Bates' arrangement and unites them with the *Nymphalinæ*, but makes them a separate group, basing the groups on the dilation of the anterior edge of the palpi.

It is true that a strict definition of the subfamily is very difficult, if not impossible, to lay down, but since they do possess features to a large extent distinctive, and as their affinities with the *Satyrinæ* are apparently as great as their affinities with the *Nymphalinæ*, Mr. Butler's arrangement appears to us the most convenient to adopt until their life history becomes more fully known.

The *Morphinæ* resemble the *Satyrinæ* in having large wings and weak flight; they also love the shade, are chiefly found in undergrowth in forests, and some at least are crepuscular in their habits; the underside of the wings is almost always ocellated; the hindwing of the male always bears more or less pronounced secondary sexual characters; the antennæ are long and very slender, never abruptly clubbed, and the discoidal cell of the forewing is always closed. They resemble the *Elymniinæ* in habits and in the brilliant colouring of the upperside; they resemble the *Nymphalinæ* in having the cell of the hindwing open, except in *Xanthotænia*, but the palpi are not dilated at the base; and lastly the larvæ, so far as they are known, approximate to a type which is dominant among the *Satyrinæ*, but aberrant among the *Nymphalinæ*. Their distinctive structural features are chiefly in the neuration of the forewing in which the cell is short (it is long in *Morpho*, but short in all the Asiatic genera) and very broad; the second branch of the subcostal nervure is either wanting altogether or originates far beyond the apex of the cell, and the first and second branches often anastomose with each other, and the costal nervure for a short distance, and then run free to the costa. These with the structure of the palpi separate them from the *Nymphalinæ*; the open cell in the hindwing separates them from *Satyrinæ* and *Elymniinæ;* and the want of a prædiscoidal cell in the hindwing separates them from *Elymniinæ* and *Brassolinæ* (an American subfamily).

The *Morphinæ* are connected on the one hand with the *Nymphalinæ* through the genera in which the cell of the hindwing is completely open; and on the other hand with the *Satyrinæ* through *Xanthotænia*, in which the special characters are least developed, it having the cell of the hindwing completely closed. *Amathusia* and *Zeuxidia*, especially the latter, greatly resemble *Kallima* (a genus of *Nymphalinæ*) in outline; but the arrangement of the subcostal nervules in the forewing, the presence of ocelli, and of the secondary sexual characters on the hindwing of the males at once distinguish them from it.

Key to the Indian Genera of MORPHINÆ.

A. Antennæ long, slender, with long gradually-formed slender club: palpi slender, the anterior edge not widely dilated. *Forewing* with the costal nervure slightly and gradually dilated at base; the first subcostal branch emitted near the end of the cell, the second (if present) beyond it; the apex of the cell far beyond the origin of the second median nervule. *Hindwing* with no prædiscoidal cell.

- *a*. Hindwing with the discoidal cell closed by a very slender lower disco-cellular nervule near the origin of the second median nervule.
  - *a*¹. Forewing, subcostal nervure with its four branches all free.
    - *a*². Forewing with the apex round, outer margin convex. Hindwing with the anal angle rounded, outer margin convex.

      XXXIII.—XANTHOTÆNIA.
- *b*. Hindwing with the discoidal cell partially closed by an atrophied lower disco-cellular nervule.
  - *a*¹. Forewing, subcostal nervure with four branches, the first anastomosing with the costal nervure.
    - *a*². Forewing with the apex acute; the inner margin convex throughout; the median nervure with the commencement of a fourth branch beyond the apex of the cell. Hindwing with a narrow somewhat acute tail at anal angle.

      XXXIV.—ZEUXIDIA.
- *c*. Hindwing with the discoidal cell completely open, but apparently partially closed by a transverse fold in the wing membrane some distance beyond the origin of the second median nervule.
  - *a*¹. Forewing with the apex slightly rounded, outer margin concave, inner margin slightly convex at base, then straight. Hindwing with either a short broad, or somewhat long narrow tail at anal angle.

    XXXV.—AMATHUSIA.

d. **Hindwing with the discoidal cell completely open.**

a[1]. Forewing with the apex acute, the outer margin straight or slightly concave. Hindwing with the anal angle square or acute.

a[2]. Hindwing with the outer margin angled at tip of third median nervule ; forewing, subcostal nervure with four branches of which the first two anastomose. Male with an oval patch of plush-like scales on hindwing upperside.

XXXVI.—DISCOPHORA.

b[2]. Hindwing with the outer margin more regularly convex ; forewing, subcostal nervure with three branches only, the first anastomosing, second obliterated. Male without the oval patch of plush-like scales.

XXXVII.—ENISPE.

b[1]. Forewing with the apex acute ; the outer margin straight, or slightly sinuous. Hindwing with the anal angle evenly rounded.

a[2]. Hindwing with the outer margin somewhat angled at tip of third median nervule ; forewing, subcostal nervure with four branches, as in *Discophora*. Male with no patch of plush-like scales, but with a slender pouch and tuft near end of *submedian* nervure.

XXXVIII.—ÆMONA.

c[1]. Forewing with the apex rounded, the outer margin convex ; hindwing with the anal angle rounded, the outer margin regularly convex.

a[2]. Forewing, subcostal nervure with four branches, the first two anastomosed as in *Discophora*. Male with a tuft of erectile hairs at base of *subcostal* nervure on upperside of hindwing.

XXXIX.—THAUMANTIS.

b[2]. Forewing, subcostal nervure with three branches only, all free, the second being obliterated. Male with a tuft as in *Thaumantis*.

XL.—STICHOPHTHALMA.

c[2]. Forewing, subcostal nervure with four branches, all free. Male with a tuft of hairs near base of *median* nervure folded upwards over the nervure.

XLI.—CLEROME.

Genus 33.—XANTHOTÆNIA, Westwood.

Clerome subgenus *Xanthotænia*, Westwood, Trans. Ent. Soc. Lond., new series, vol. iv, p. 187 (1856).

Separated from *Clerome* with the following remarks : "In the shortness and roundness of the forewing, and in the upperside being destitute of ocelli, this insect agrees with the genus *Clerome;* but differs in the broad oblique yellow fascia and subapical white spot of the forewing, as well as the more elongated form [in breadth] of the hindwing ; and the insertion of the second branch of the subcostal nervure [of the forewing] at a [comparatively] short distance beyond the extremity of the discoidal cell, (opposite to the extremity of the costal nervure, which only reaches to the middle of the costa,) the third and fourth branches of the subcostal nervure of the forewing rise a moderate distance apart ; the lower disco-cellular nervule of the forewing (closing the discoidal cell), although oblique, is nearly straight. The palpi are much compressed, of moderate size, thickly clothed with close appressed hairs, the terminal joint distinct, slender, acute at the tip, and raised to the level of the top of the crown of the head. The antennæ are long, gradually but slightly clavate, the tip a little curved and acute ; they are brown, the outer half ferruginous. From all these characters I have no hesitation in regarding this insect as a distinct subgenus, to which I have applied the name *Xanthotænia*, in allusion to the yellow fascia of the forewing." (*Westwood*, l. c.)

Xanthotænia in reality bears only a superficial resemblance to *Clerome*; the following are its chief distinctive characters: FOREWING, *subcostal* nervure with all its branches free, the second originating not far beyond the end of the cell; *middle disco-cellular* nervule comparatively long and oblique; *lower* disco-cellular about twice as long as the middle one, and nearly straight, oblique. HINDWING with the cell closed by a very slender concave nervule joining the median nervure near the origin of its second branch; the origin of the subcostal branches and of the discoidal nervule well separated, and some distance from the base of the wing; the latter arising at the junction of the disco-cellulars. The secondary sexual characters of the MALE consist of a raised fold along the inner edge of the submedian nervure, scantily fringed with long hairs, and terminating rather beyond the middle in a denser tuft of erect hairs. No tufts near the base of the median or subcostal nervures, nor on the abdomen of the insect.

Mr. W. L. Distant (Rhop. Malay., p. 82), states that the cell of the hindwing has the apex entirely open, but according to Westwood's, original diagnosis it is closed, and this is also the case in all the specimens from Tenasserim which we have examined. Only a single species is known.

272. **Xanthotænia busiris**, Westwood.

Clerome (Xanthotænia) busiris, Westwood, Trans. Ent. Soc. Lond., new series, vol. iv, p. 187, n. 6 (1856); *Xanthotænia busiris*, Moore, Proc. Zool. Soc. Lond., 1878, p. 827; id., Distant, Rhop. Malay., p. 82, pl. v, fig. 7 (1882).

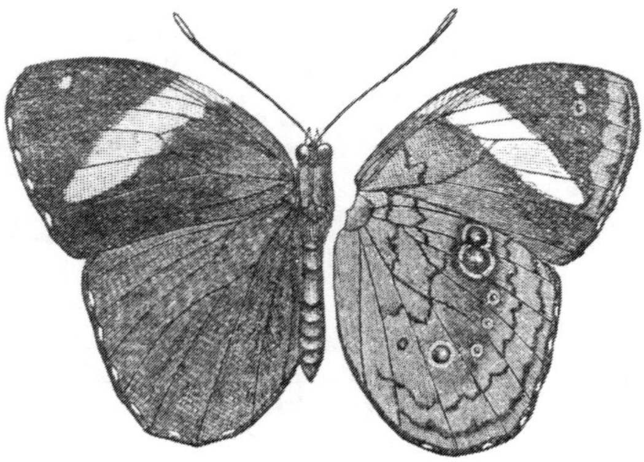

HABITAT: Upper Tenasserim, Malacca, Sumatra, Java, Borneo.

EXPANSE; ♂, 2·6 to 2·85 inches.

DESCRIPTION: "UPPERSIDE chestnut-fuscous. *Forewing* with the apical half fuscous, a straight oblique yellow fascia, and a white subapical dot. UNDERSIDE paler. *Hindwing* with four very wavy fuscous streaks, and eight ocelli irregular in size. The general colour of the UPPERSIDE is rich but dull chestnut-brown; the *hindwing* immaculate; the *forewing* with the outer half dark brown, with a moderately broad, nearly straight yellow fascia, extending from the middle of the costa nearly to the outer margin (below the middle), and with a subapical white dot. UNDERSIDE pale brown (without any chestnut tinge), the *hindwing* with four deeply scalloped, slender brown strigæ; the space between the second and third being the widest, enclosing eight ocelli of unequal size, the second and sixth from the costa being the largest; they are thickly powdered with grey scales, and are surrounded by a very narrow yellow ring; the space between the third and fourth strigæ is paler than the rest of the wing, and between the first and second strigæ is a short transverse dark line, being the nervule closing the discoidal cell. In the *forewing* the discoidal cell is marked in the middle with a very strong angulated brown slender line, and between the white subapical dot and the extremity of the yellow oblique fascia are two small nearly rudimentary ocelli similar to those of the hindwing." (*Westwood*, l.c.) "The FEMALE resembles the male." (*Distant*, l. c.)

X. busiris is found in the Malay Peninsula, extending northwards as far as Upper Tenasserim, where Limborg took it near Moolai at 3,000 to 6,000 feet altitude; and Captain C. T. Bingham also took it in the Donat range and the lower Thoungyeen forests in April. All the specimens we have seen are males.

The figure shows the upper and undersides of a male specimen in Major Marshall's collection taken in Upper Tenasserim.

Genus 34.—ZEUXIDIA, Hübner.

Zeuxidia, Hübner, Samml. Ex. Schmett. (1816-1824); id., Westwood, Gen. D. L., p. 327 (1851).

BODY very hairy. HEAD moderately large, hairy; *eyes* large, prominent, naked; *palpi* elongate, compressed, erect, the third joint rising above the level of the top of the head, thickly clothed with appressed scales in front, slightly hairy at the back of the middle joint; terminal joint slender, well-defined, and rather long; *antennæ* rather less than half the length of the forewing, slender, the articulations rather long, distinct; the club very slender, elongate, gradually formed and slender at the tip. FOREWING large, triangular, the *costa* convex; the *apex* acute; the *outer margin* oblique, slightly concave; the *hinder angle* rounded, the *inner margin* convex in the male. The *first subcostal* nervule given off before the end of the cell, about three-fourths its distance from the base, and anastomosed with the costal nervure; the second emitted before the end of the costal nervure; the third and fourth close together towards the apex; the *upper disco-cellular* obliquely directed outwards, the *second* twice as long and in a straight line with the upper portion of the *lower*, which is very long and slightly concave, joining the median nervure midway between the points where the second and third median nervules are given off; the median nervure continued beyond the point where the third median nervule is given off in a short outwardly curved spur not reaching the lower discoidal nervule, which spur is merged in the fold of the wing, giving the appearance of a fourth median nervule; the *submedian* nervure straight for a short distance from its base, then angled, and following the contour of the convex inner margin. HINDWING large, the *costa* convex, the *apex* rounded, the *outer margin* convex, and produced at the anal angle into a distinct narrow but not acute tail; the *inner margin* highly convex and channelled to receive the abdomen; the *discoidal* nervule almost straight in continuation of the subcostal; an incomplete *lower disco-cellular* nervule originating at the point on the median nervure where the third median nervule is given off, and not reaching the discoidal nervule, but becoming merged in the wing membrane which is discoloured with yellow at its termination, thus only partially closing the discoidal cell. FORELEGS of the *male* very slender, scarcely hairy; *tarsus* about half the length of the tibia, and equally slender; *femur* about as long as the tibia but not so slender. Of the *female* rather longer and more robust, *tibia* rather shorter then the femur, *tarsus* two-thirds of the length of and rather thicker than the tibia, spiny along the whole length beneath.

. About eight species of the genus *Zeuxidia* are known, all from the Indo-Malayan region. The outline of the wings is very similar indeed to that of *Kallima* (*Nymphalinæ*, a genus comprising the great "Oak-leaf" Butterflies of India), but the outer margin of the forewing is less convex and angled near the hinder angle, and the pattern of the underside is different; in *Kallima* the discal line extends from the apex of the forewing to the anal angle of the hindwing like the midrib of a leaf; and there are no ocelli; in *Zeuxidia* the discal line commences from the middle of the costa of the forewing, and the hindwing has two ocelli. The upperside of the males is somewhat similar in colouring to the *amythaon* group of *Amathusia*, but the hindwing has usually also a patch of bright blue. But in addition to the structural characters noted above perhaps the most remarkable features of the genus are the secondary sexual characters of the male insect. There are no lateral tufts on the abdomen as in *Amathusia phidippus*, but the *hindwing* bears no less than three. The submedian nervure is sunk in a fold and angled at a short distance from its base where it bears a thick tuft of long bright brown coarse hairs, and the edge of the fold above is thickly covered with finer wooly hairs; in the discoidal cell there is an oval shining bare patch denuded of scales in the centre, on which lies a thick tuft of long brown hairs; and above the subcostal nervure before the base of its first branch is a similar but smaller tuft on a black patch in the centre of a similar patch denuded of scales.

Only a single species is certainly known to occur within our limits, where it is found in Upper Tenasserim. Another species is recorded from India, but the authority is somewhat doubtful. All the species are rare, and a single male of *Z. masoni* in Major Marshall's collection is the only specimen of the genus in the collections in this country so far as we know.

Key to the Indian Species of Zeuxidia.

A. Males. Upperside dark brown, forewing crossed by a broad band of purplish-blue or blue; hindwing, with a similar band on the outer margin.

a. The patch on the hindwing from the anal angle almost to the discoidal nervule.

273. Z. MASONI, Upper Tenasserim.

b. The patch extending from the outer to the anal angle.

274. Z. DOUBLEDAII, India (?)

273. Zeuxidia masoni, Moore.

Z. masoni, Moore, Proc. Zool. Soc. Lond., 1878, p. 826; id., Marshall, Journ. A. S. B., vol. li, pt. ii, p. 39, n. 4 (1882).

HABITAT: Upper Tenasserim.

EXPANSE: ♂, 4·1; ♀, 4·5 inches.

DESCRIPTION: MALE: UPPERSIDE velvety blackish-brown, paler at the margins. *Forewing* crossed by a purplish-blue subapical decreasing band extending from the costa just beyond the cell to the hinder angle. *Hindwing* with a broad purplish-blue patch from the anal margin extending on the outer border to the fold below the discoidal nervule. UNDERSIDE brown, with violet-whitish markings; the basal half of *both wings* darker, and defined by a dark brown median line from the middle of the costa of the forewing to the anal angle of the hindwing. *Forewing* with three whitish bands in the cell, and one just beyond it, the costal half beyond the median line being clouded with whitish to the apex. *Hindwing* with three nebulous whitish bands on the basal half, that nearest the base the broadest and most distinct; the median line edged exteriorly with whitish irrorations; two moderate-sized ocelli, one between the subcostal nervules, brown, with diffused yellowish pupil, narrow yellowish iris, and outer dark brown line; the other on the lowest median interspace yellowish with eccentric brown pupil and dark outer line. Described from the male in Major Marshall's collection. "FEMALE differs from *Z. amethystus*, female, in the paler colour of the wings, and in the greater breadth of the yellow oblique band, the band entire, and terminating at the middle median nervule, below which are two similarly-coloured spots; a small pale patch before the apex of the wing. *Hindwing* pale cinnamon-brown broadly along outer border." (*Moore*, l. c.)

Closely allied to *Z. amethystus** from the Malay Peninsula, Sumatra and Borneo. The female of *Z. masoni* was taken by Limborg in Upper Tenasserim at Meetan 3,000 feet altitude in April; the male was taken by Captain C. T. Bingham in the Lower Thoungyeen forests in the same district at the same season. It is a very rare insect.

---

* *Zeuxidia amethystus*, Butler, Proc. Zool. Soc. Lond., 1865, p. 485, n. 5; idem, id., Trans. Linn. Soc., Zoology, second series, vol. i, p. 538, n. 1 (1876); id., Distant, Rhop. Malay., p. 72, pl. vii, figs. 1, *male*; 2, *female* (1882); *Z. wallacei*, Felder, Reise Novara, Lep., vol. iii, p. 461, n. 777, pl lxii, fig. 3 (1866), *male*. HABITAT: Province Wellesley; Malacca; Sumatra; Borneo. EXPANSE: *Male*, 3·6 to 3·8; *Female*, 4·35 to 4·75 inches. DESCRIPTION: MALE: "UPPERSIDE. *forewing* deep brown, glossed with purple; a broad lilac band glossed with purple near the apex, extending from the anterior margin, just beyond the cell, to the third median nervule, wider above than below; outer margin pale. *Hindwing*, anal angle caudate; rich brown, lower portion glossed with purple; a broad lilac patch, glossed with purple, bisinuate on its inner edge, at the anal angle, extending from just below the body to the fold between the second and third median nervules; cell hirsute, hair ochreous; outer margin pale. UNDERSIDE, *forewing*, golden-brown, dusky towards the inner margin; a narrow, irregular, oblique, deeper brown band crossing the middle of the wing; three irregular paler brown bands crossing the cell at equal distances; a pale brown spot on the anterior margin, just beyond the central band; two similar spots near the apex. *Hindwing*, golden brown; a deeper, oblique, narrow, irregular, brown band crossing the wing at the end of the cell, from near the end of the costal nervure to beyond the middle of the third median nervule; two indistinct, pale brown, irregular bands near the base, the inner one extending to the median nervure, the outer one to the middle of the cell; a large, oval, ochreous ocellus, pupilled with white, between the first and second subcostal nervules, and a circular ochreous ocellus pupilled with white, between the

274. **Zeuxidia doubledaii,** Westwood.

Z. doubledaii, Westwood, Gen. D. L., p. 329, n. 2, *note*, pl. lii, fig. i (1851), *female*.

HABITAT : India (?)

EXPANSE : 4·25 to 4·75 inches.

DESCRIPTION : "The British Museum also contains both sexes of an allied species [to *Z. luxerii**] from India, the MALE of which is distinguished by its more acuminated *forewing*, destitute of the pale spot near the tip ; the broad lilac bar of *Z. luxerii* is replaced by a much narrower and more curved blue bar ; the *hindwing* has the tail much less acuminated ; the lilac patch of this wing is replaced by a very broad blue fascia, which extends to the anal angle ; the middle of the discoidal cell has an elongate-ovate smooth spot destitute of hairs (which may, however, have been abraded). [UNDERSIDE] the dark brown streak across both wings is curved towards the tip at its junction with the costa, and the second and third median nervules" (*Butler*, l. c in Proc. Zool. Soc. Lond.) "FEMALE : UPPERSIDE, *both wings* pale brownish. *Forewing* becoming chocolate-brown beyond the apex of the cell, and there possessing the following pale stramineous markings :—A waved fascia commencing on the costal margin a little beyond the cell, and terminating above the first median nervule, where it is outwardly followed by a small spot ; beneath are six spots placed three above and three beneath the second median nervule ; and near the apex there is also an indication of a pale spot. *Hindwing* with the outer marginal area more or less ochraceous, on which is a submarginal waved and broken dark chocolate fascia, becoming in some specimens obsolete towards the anal angle ; on the inner side of this ochraceous area is an ill-defined darker apical patch or suffusion, on which are three pale ochraceous spots, two above and one beneath the discoidal nervule ; there is also a similar but much fainter spot beneath the first median nervule (in one Malaccan specimen these spots are nearly obsolete) ; anal caudate prolongation marked with white on each side. UNDERSIDE generally as in the male, but the smaller ocellated spot on the hindwing in the male is absent, and the whitish suffusion more distinct. Considerable variation in depth of colouration is observable both above and beneath amongst male specimens." (*Distant*, l. c.)

* *Zeuxidia luxerii*, Hübner, Samml. Ex. Schmett. (1816-1824) ; id., Westwood, Cab. Or. Ent., p. 40, pl. xix, fig. 5 (1848), *neuration of forewing* HABITAT : Java. EXPANSE : 3·1 inches. DESCRIPTION : In the Genera of Diurnal Lepidoptera (p. 329) Professor Westwood records the following note ; "A MALE specimen of the type of this genus, *Z. luxerii* from Java, in the British Museum has the *forewing* marked with a very broad lilac bar, extending in a somewhat curved direction from the middle of the costa to the anal angle ; the outer angle of the *hindwing* marked with a broad patch of lilac, and the middle of the discoidal cell with an elongate-oval patch of brown hairs ; the tail of the hindwing is also considerably acuminate. The UNDERSIDE is purplish-brown, with dark clouds, and with the dark streak across *both wings* slightly bent towards the base of the forewing, at its junction with the costa, and the ocellus on the disc of the hindwing next the costa is very much smaller than the one towards the anal angle ; the extremity of the forewing is also marked with a small pale oval patch Dr. Boisduval possesses the FEMALE of this species, the wings of which on the UPPERSIDE are brown, darker in the middle of the *forewing*, beyond which is an oblique bluish-white fascia, obliterated towards the anal angle, where are three obscure fulvous spots, the hind one occupying the anal angle the *hindwing* is brown, with an internally subdentate dull fulvous margin. On the UNDERSIDE it agrees with the male, but is more uniform in its colours." (*Westwood*, l. c.)

ocellus next the costa is very much larger and more distinct than that near the anal angle. The FEMALE of this species (represented in the Gen. D. L., plate lii, fig. 1, as the female of *Z. luxerii*) has the outer half of both wings tinged with a blue gloss, with an oblique bluish-white broad bar extending from the middle of the costa to the third branch of the median nervure, where it is broken up into three rows of spots; the interior conical, the middle row nearly rounded, and the outer ones semicircular. There is a slight trace of these spots continued along the outer half of the hindwing." (*Westwood*, l. c.)

The woodcut which accompanies represents the female of *Z. doubledaii*, and is copied from the figure in the Gen. D. L. It is doubtful whether this species does really occur in India, in any case it is extremely rare; we have never seen a specimen.

The four species of this genus referred to above are all very closely allied, and appear to differ mainly in the tone and character of the blue markings on the upperside in the males.

Z. masoni has the blue patch on the hindwing extending from the anal margin nearly up to the discoidal nervule.

Z. amethystus has the patch extending from the anal margin to the fold in the second median interspace only.

Z. luxerii has the patch lilac, and at the outer angle only.

Z. doubledaii has the patch blue, and extending from the outer angle to the anal angle.

Genus 35.—AMATHUSIA, Fabricius.

Amathusia, Fabricius, Illiger's Mag., vol. vi, p. 279 (1807); id., Westwood, Gen. D. L., vol. ii, p. 326 (1851); *Mitocerus*, Billb., Enum. Ins., p. 79 (1820).

" BODY rather small, very hairy. HEAD rather small [in *A. phidippus*, large in *A. portheus*], hairy, with a small, frontal, conical tuft of hairs; *neck* short. *Palpi* rather slender and compressed, porrected obliquely to about the length of the head, and raised at the tip nearly to the level of the top of the eyes, not united into a conical beak, scaly beneath; the back of the second and third joints hairy, the hairs of the middle joint being erect, and resting on the front of the face and side of the frontal tuft; terminal joint ovate-conic. [In *A. portheus*, the palpi are erect, and rise in front considerably above the level of the top of the eyes.] *Antennæ* about three-sevenths of the length of the forewing, slender, not straight; the joints very distinct; club long, very gradually formed, and very slender, finely carinated beneath, articulations distinct, the terminal ones gradually acuminate. THORAX ovate, very hairy, neither large nor robust. WINGS large, hindwing with two ocelli wide apart on the underside. FOREWING large, elongate-triangular, *costa* very much arched, *apex* rather rounded, *outer margin* about two-thirds of the length of the costa, entire, slightly concave; *hinder angle* rounded, *inner margin* nearly straight, rather narrowed towards the base. *Subcostal* nervure slender, the first branch nearly at the distance of one-third of the wing from the base, extending to the costa at about three-fourths of its length; second, third and fourth branches arising close together at about three-fourths of the length of the wing; the second and third very short, joining the costa; the fourth longer, extending to the tip; the remainder of the nervure extending to the apex below the tip. *Upper disco-cellular* nervule arising from the subcostal at about two-fifths of the length of the wing, extremely short and oblique; *middle* disco-cellular twice its length, and transverse; *lower* disco-cellular very long, strongly angulated in the middle, the anterior part continuing in the same line as the middle disco-cellular, the posterior part very oblique, uniting with the median nervure at a distance from its base equal to half the distance between the bases of the first and second branches of the median nervure, thus closing the discoidal cell in an acute point at nearly half the length of the wing; the third median nervule beyond the junction much arched, or rather angulated, at about the same distance beyond the junction as exists between the first and second median nervules. HINDWING subtriangular, *costa* arched, *apex* rounded, *outer margin* with wide but not deep scallops, *anal angle* produced into a broad short tail [in *A. phidippus*, but into a much longer and narrower one in *A. portheus*], extending between the extremity of the first branch of the median nervure and the submedian nervure. The *præcostal* nervure is curved at its tip towards the body.

Costal nervure curved, but extending only to two-thirds of the length of the costa. *Subcostal* nervure branching very near its base, its first branch extending to the outer angle of the wing. *Discoidal cell* very narrow, open. *Median* nervure branching far from the base, with a considerable distance between its first and second branches ; at about the same distance from the base of its third branch as exists between the first and second branches is a thickening or swelling of the disc of the wing between this branch and the discoidal nervule, forming, as it were, an incomplete termination of the discoidal cell. FORELEGS of the MALE small, slender ; *tarsus* hairy, forming a slender brush of nearly equal thickness throughout. Of the FEMALE considerably longer than those of the male, scaly ; *femur* much longer than the tibia ; *tibia* and *tarsus* gradually but slenderly dilated to the tip, where it is obliquely truncate."

"LARVA long, hairy, especially about the head ; *head* with two short broad dentated horns, with two dark transverse bars between the first and second, and second and third thoracic segments ; extremity of the body forked. PUPA long, boat-shaped, entire, *head* acuminated and bifid." (*Extracted from Westwood's Gen. D. L.*)

The genus *Amathusia* comprises a few very handsome tropical Asiatic species of large size, chiefly inhabiting the Malay Archipelago; like the rest of the subfamily they affect shady places, and the typical species is crepuscular ; they have somewhat the appearance of the genus *Kallima* on the upperside and in outline, but the tail of the hindwing is shorter, and the underside has not the appearance of a leaf, it has numerous transverse stripes, with ocelli on the hindwing. Within our limits the genus is only found in Burma, and through the north-east corner of Bengal to Sikkim, and again in the South Andamans.

There are two distinct types of colouration, and the secondary sexual characters of the male insect appear to differ.

Key to the Indian species of Amathusia.

A. Upperside brown, the apex and outer margin tinged with yellowish, with no broad transverse fascia on the forewing in either sex. Hindwing with a broad short tail at the anal angle.
- *a.* Male with lateral sexual tufts of hair along the abdomen, and with a tuft of hair below the submedian nervure of the hindwing, and another placed in a pouch above it.
  - 275. A. PHIDIPPUS, Burma ; Tenasserim ; Andaman Isles ; Malayana.

B. Upperside blackish, forewing with a broad transverse fascia, blue in the male, yellow in the female. Hindwing with a narrower tail at the anal angle.
- *a.* Males generally, perhaps always, with a large dense tuft of hairs below the submedian nervure opposite the middle of the abdomen on the upperside of the hindwing*.
  - *a*[1]. Male with the transverse fascia very broad, extending near the outer margin from the second discoidal nervure to the submedian nervure.
    - 276. A. AMYTHAON, Sylhet.
  - *b*[1]. Male with the transverse fascia almost straight, regularly decreasing in width towards the hinder angle, and extending near the outer margin from the second median nervule to the hinder angle.
    - 277. A. WESTWOODII, Sylhet.
  - *c*[1]. Male with the transverse fascia curved, scarcely decreasing in width till it terminates near the outer margin, where it extends from the fold above the second median nervule to just below the submedian nervure.
    - 278. A. PORTHEUS, N.-E. India ; Tenasserim.

275. Amathusia phidippus, Linnæus.

Papilio phidippus, Linnæus, Syst. Nat., vol. i, pt. ii, p. 752, n. 37 (1767) ; id., Cramer, Pap. Ex., vol. i, pl. lxix, figs. A, B (1775), *female* ; *Morpho phidippus*, Godart, Enc. Méth., vol. ix, 439, n. 2 (1819) ; *Amathusia phidippus*, Horsfield, Cat. Lep. E. I. C., pl. vii, figs. 10, *larva* ; 10*a*, pupa ; 10*b*—*h*, *structure of imago* (1829) ; id., Doubleday, Hewitson, Gen. D. L., vol. ii, p. 327, pl., liv*, fig. 2 (1850) *male* ; id., Horsfield and Moore, Cat. Lep. E. I. C., vol. i, p. 209, n. 428, pl. vi, figs. 4, *larva* ; 4*a*, *pupa* (1857) ; id., Distant, Rhop. Malay., p. 70, pl. vi, figs. 6, *male* ; 7, *female* (1882).

HABITAT : Burma ; Upper Tenasserim ; Andaman Isles ; Malay Peninsula and Archipelago.

EXPANSE : 4·0 to 4·4 inches.

DESCRIPTION : "MALE : UPPERSIDE : *Both wings* dark fuliginous-brown. *Forewing* with the costal and outer margins somewhat paler, and with a distinctly paler submarginal fascia.

* See remarks on this group, p. 290.

Hindwing with the outer margin paler, and with a distinctly paler submarginal fascia, the marginal fringe ochraceous, the broad tail at the anal angle somewhat paler, and bearing two sublunulate black spots, outwardly margined with white; these spots are placed near the apices of the first median nervule and submedian nervure. UNDERSIDE greyish, crossed by numerous fuscous fasciæ of varying width and hue; the first commences near the costal base of the forewing, and is continued on the hindwing, narrowing and becoming somewhat evanescent a little beyond the middle of the submedian nervure; the second crosses the cells of both wings about their centres, and terminates on the innerside of the first median nervule at about half its length; the third is short, crossing the cell, but not passing the median nervure of the forewing; the fourth is pale, with its margins darker, waved, and deflected beneath the third fascia on the forewing, passing a little beyond the second on the hindwing, and becoming confluent and terminating with that fascia beneath the median nervure; the fifth is wide and darkest, crossing both wings at the apices of the discoidal cells and terminating a little beneath the second median nervule; the sixth is widest, somewhat paler, with darker margins, outwardly sinuate and placed a little beyond the fifth; this sixth fascia is followed by three narrow fasciæ, which terminate on the abdominal margin of the hindwing, one being marginal and two submarginal, the middle one darkest and the inner one palest. The *hindwing* bears two large submarginal ocellated spots, which are ochraceous, speckled with fuscous, with white centres and black outer margins, the inner borders of which are narrowly ochraceous; the lower and larger spot has the white centre somewhat lunulate, and is followed posteriorly by a broad blackish suffusion; the upper of these spots is situated between the subcostal nervules, and the lower one between the first and second median nervules. The anal tail of the hindwing is spotted as on the upperside, and has a large central castaneous suffusion. *Body* and *legs* more or less concolorous with the wings. The male has four long, curved tufts of hair on each side of the terminal segments of the abdomen. A somewhat similar tuft is situated about the middle of the abdominal margin of the hindwing, on the inner side of the submedian nervure; and between the submedian nervure and first median nervule within a fold of the wing are also a few long hairs. Both of these, judging by analogous reasoning, are probably the coverings of scent-glands or pouches. FEMALE, larger than the male. UPPERSIDE, *both wings* paler, with an ochraceous discal fascia crossing both wings, widest near the costa of the forewing, and very narrow on the hindwing; the submarginal fasciæ as in the male, but concolourous with the ochraceous margins. UNDERSIDE as in the male, but much paler. This species varies in the depth and intensity of hue of the fuscous fasciæ on the underside." (*Distant*, l. c.)

LARVA cylindrical, of nearly equal thickness throughout, covered with long hairs placed in tufts on tubercles placed in rows along the body: colour pale brown, marked with a dorsal and two subdorsal longitudinal paler lines, with darker marks on each side of the dorsal line two on each segment: head dark brown, anal segment furnished with a somewhat short bifid tubercular tail. PUPA boat-shaped, acuminated to a long and somewhat sharp point at the head, and marked with streaks of a deeper green than the ground-colour. (Described from Horsfield and Moore's figures). Dr. Horsfield states that in Java it "feeds on the young leaves of *Coccos nucifera*, from December to April."

Several writers have noted the crepuscular habits of *A. phidippus*, and it is often found in cocoanut palm groves. We have specimens from Upper Tennasserim, and the Andaman Islands, and Dr. Anderson took a single male in the Mergui Archipelago in January, and Captain Adamson took it at Akyab in November.

Of the next group, in which the forewing bears a broad transverse fascia, blue in the males and yellow in the females, three species have been described from India. The first was described, but not figured, by Doubleday in 1847 as *A. amythaon*; in 1848 Westwood figured and described a species under the name of *A. amythaon*, Doubleday, but which does not at all correspond to Doubleday's original description; and in 1851 Westwood in the Gen. D. L. recorded some notes on *A. amythaon* which seem to refer to the species figured by him and not to that described by Doubleday. In 1865 Dr. Felder described another species, *A. portheus;* and in 1869 Mr. A. G. Butler pointed out the differences between the *A. amythaon* as described by Doubleday, and as figured by Westwood, and gave to Westwood's figure the name of *A. westwoodii*, remarking at the same time that *A. portheus*, Felder, was probably the true *A. amythaon*, male, of Doubleday.

So far as recent experience goes, but a single species of this group is positively known to occur in Indian limits, and this species, of which we possess several specimens of both sexes, corresponds exactly with the description of *A. portheus*, Felder. We have seen no specimens of either of the other species, and we have no certain knowledge as to where specimens exist. Judging from the descriptions and figures only, the distinctions between the three species are of two kinds : (1) the sexual tufts and patches in the male ; (2) the shape and extent of the transverse blue fascia of the forewing. As regards the first point, the evidence is chiefly negative and cannot be relied on ; all that we can say is that for *A. amythaon*, Doubleday makes no mention whatever of any tufts or patches. Westwood says : "The internal basal portion of the hindwing is clothed with long jet black velvety scales, and there is a tuft of elongate brown hairs opposite the middle of the abdomen" ; (Gen. D. L., vol. ii, p. 327), but his remarks probably apply to *A. westwoodii* and not to the true *A. amythaon*. For *A. westwoodii*, Westwood makes no special mention of the tufts in the description, while in the figure he shows the tuft below the submedian nervure greatly developed, but no discal patch of velvety scales. For *A. portheus*, Felder correctly describes the tuft and velvety patch of the known Indian species. As regards the second point, the shape and extent of the blue fascia, there appear to be sufficient differences to separate all three species, and on this we have based our key.

276. **Amathusia amythaon,** Doubleday.

A. amythaon, Doubleday, Ann and Mag. of Nat. Hist., vol. xix, p. 175 (1847).

HABITAT : Sylhet.

EXPANSE : 5 inches.

DESCRIPTION : "UPPERSIDE, *both wings* fuscous-black, darker, especially the hindwing, near the base. *Forewing* traversed by a broad oblique band of a beautiful light blue, with purplish reflections, commencing on the costa above opposite to the middle of the cell, and occupying in width about one-third of the costa, extending obliquely across to the submedian nervure, and terminating near the outer margin, where its upper boundary is the second discoidal nervule. UNDERSIDE, *both wings* pale chocolate, with lavender reflections, traversed by seven transverse lines ; the first commencing on the costa of the forewing near the base, continued along the præcostal and first median nervules of the hindwing ; the second continued across both wings to the origin of the second median nervule of the hindwing ; the third short, just crossing the cell [of the forewing] a little beyond the middle ; the fourth beyond the cell, continued nearly to the anal angle [of the hindwing] ; the fifth more oblique, only reaching the first median nervule of the hindwing ; the sixth arising near the apex, meeting the fourth at its termination ; the seventh submarginal, common. *Hindwing*, slightly produced into a short round tail or palette at the anal angle, having, besides the markings already described, two ocelli composed of an oval black ring with a white pupil, the larger one near the costa between the first and second subcostal nervules ; the second between the first and second median nervules at the point of junction of the fourth and sixth strigæ ; the anal palette with two black dots edged with white. The *cilia* all white. HEAD, thorax, and abdomen brown. FEMALE paler, with the band of the forewing much narrower, not occupying any part of the cell, fulvous, marked near the outer margin with a brown waved striga. Much resembling *A. phidippus* in form, but known at once by the blue band above, and different markings of the under surface." (*Doubleday*, l.c.)

We have never seen this insect ; no mention is made in the description of the very remarkable tufts borne by the male insect in the two following species ; and it is strange that if present they should have escaped the attention of so profound an entomologist as Mr. Doubleday.

277. **Amathusia westwoodii**, Butler.

A. amythaon, Westwood, Cab. Or. Ent., p. 39, pl. xix, figs. 1, 2, *male*; 3, *female* (1848); *A. westwoodii*, Butler, Ent. Month. Mag., vol. vi, p. 55 (1869).

HABITAT: Sylhet.

EXPANSE: ♂, 5·2; ♀, 5·5 inches.

DESCRIPTION: "UPPERSIDE fuscous. *Forewing*, with an oblique broad fascia, light blue in the male, fulvous in the female. UNDERSIDE, pale chocolate, with seven transverse, unequal, darker streaks. *Hindwing* with two oval ocelli, having white pupils, and the short tails with two black dots. MALE. UPPERSIDE, *both wings* blackish brown, the basal portions being the darkest; the *forewing* traversed by a broad oblique band of a beautiful light blue, with purplish reflections, commencing close to the costa, a little beyond the middle of the cell, and occupying in width about one-third of the costa, extending obliquely across to the inner [hinder] angle of the wing, terminating near the outer margin, where its upper boundary is the second branch of the median nervure. *Hindwing* with the anal margin of a delicate pale lavender grey, fringed with a very thick row of long pale brown hairs; the anal angle is produced into a rather broad short tail, in which are two small black dots. UNDERSIDE, *both wings* pale chocolate coloured, with lavender reflections, the forewing traversed by seven, and the hindwing by four richer brown transverse lines, the first crossing both wings near the base; the second extending from the costa across the discoidal cell of the forewing, and terminating near the middle of the discoidal cell of the hindwing; the third very slender, crossing the discoidal cell of the forewing beyond the middle; the fourth extending from the costa of the forewing, and terminating just above the inner [lower] of the ocelli of the hindwing; the fifth paler and more oblique, extending only across the forewing, crossing the third branch of the median nervure where it is angulated; the sixth extending from near the apex of the forewing to the outside of the inner [lower] ocellus of the hindwing, beyond which it again reappears for a short distance; and the seventh very slight and submarginal, extending into the anal tail, and again ascending along the anal margin of the hindwing. The *hindwing* is, moreover, marked with two oval ocelli, consisting of a very slender dark brown ring with a white pupil, the remaining space filled with minute irrorations, one near the costal margin, beyond the middle, the other towards the tail, which is marked as above. The *body* and *antennæ* are brown. The FEMALE differs in having the wings paler brown, with the oblique fascia of the forewing much narrower, commencing outside of the discoidal cell, and of a fulvous colour, marked across within the outer margin by a brown waved striga. This species nearly resembles *A. phidippus* from Java, but differs in the blue band and the markings of the underside of the wings. It also resembles [superficially] the Javanese *Zeuxidia luxerii*, but this latter species has the outer portion of the hindwing glossed with blue, a patch of hairs in the middle of the discoidal cell of the same wing; the underside is also quite different, and the arrangement of the nervures of the forewing places it in a different genus." (*Westwood*, l. c.)

This is Westwood's description of the insect, which he also figures under the name o *A. amythaon*, Doubleday. In 1869 Mr. A. G. Butler pointed out that it was distinct from *A. amythaon*, and proposed the name *A. westwoodii* for it with the following remarks: "The figure in the 'Oriental Entomology' represents a species with a much narrower and duller violet band on the forewing, leaving a large brown space at the apex; the brushes on either side of the body seem also to be unusually developed. There can be little doubt that this is a distinct species." (*Butler*, l. c.) We have never seen a specimen; the shape of the blue fascia is quite different from that of *A. portheus*; it is much widest at the costa, its outer margin is nearly straight, and it narrows backward to the hinder angle. Westwood in the Gen. D. L. in writing about *A. amythaon*, though more probably he referred to the species afterwards separated as *A. westwoodii*, says:—"The internal basal portion of the hindwing [in the male] is clothed with long, jet black, velvety hairs, and there is a tuft of elongate brown hairs opposite the middle of the abdomen." It is possible that the secondary sexual characters are the same in the males of all the species of this group, though Mr. Doubleday omitted to mention them as regards *A. amythaon*.

278. **Amathusia portheus**, Felder.

A. portheus, Felder, Reise Novara, Lep., vol. iii, p. 461, n. 780 (1865); id., Butler, Ent. Month. Mag., vol. vi, p. 55 (1869).

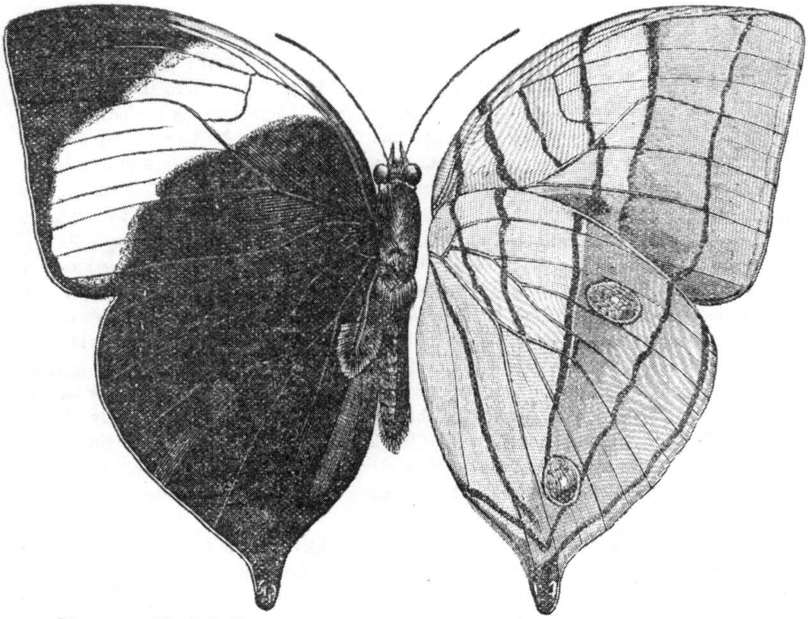

HABITAT: North India.

EXPANSE: ♂, 4·8 to 5·0; ♀, 5·3 inches.

DESCRIPTION: "MALE: UPPERSIDE as in *A. amythaon*, but the *forewing* with the fascia narrower towards the costa, and much wider hindward than in that species [evidently *A. westwoodii* is here referred to]. *Hindwing* with a patch of raised blackish scales filling almost the entire cell as in *Discophora*, and with similar scales below the median nervure and a tuft of brown hairs. UNDERSIDE as in *A. porthaon** [from Java], but with the streaks of the hindwing including the ocelli more divergent. FEMALE: UPPERSIDE as in *A. amythaon*, but the yellow fascia of the forewing less excised, not at all interrupted, the hinder end divided by a streak of the ground-colour; a yellowish spot below it between the first and second median nervules. UNDERSIDE as in the male, but with the streaks a little wider." (*Felder*, l. c.)

Butler remarks (l. c.):—"Felder's Indian species is probably the true male *A. amythaon* of Doubleday." It is impossible for us to settle the point without seeing the type of the latter species, but the descriptions apparently apply to different insects.

The underside is almost exactly similar in all these species; we have one male specimen of *A. portheus* however from Sikkim which entirely lacks the upper ocellus on the underside of the hindwing. *A. portheus* is a rare insect: Captain C. T. Bingham took a few specimens of both sexes in the autumn and winter months in the Thoungyeen forests in Upper Tenasserim, and the Indian Museum, Calcutta, has specimens from Sibsagar in Assam, from Sikkim, and from Cachar taken by Mr. Wood-Mason in August.

The figure shows the upper and undersides of a male specimen in the Indian Museum, Calcutta, from Sibsagar in Upper Assam.

* *A. porthaon*, Felder. HABITAT: Java. EXPANSE: not given. DESCRIPTION: "MALE: UPPERSIDE as in *A. amythaon*, but the *forewing* with the fascia pale plumbeous-blue, a little wider, but much less dilated at the costa. *Hindwing* with the internal gutter whitish, the interno-anal margin beyond the first median nervule irrorated with violet. UNDERSIDE as in *A. amythaon*, but the *forewing* with the two discal strigæ more divergent. *Hindwing* with the outer one directed to higher up the inner margin, the ocelli larger." (*Felder*, Reise Novara, Lep., vol. iii, p. 461, n. 779, 1867).

Genus 36.—DISCOPHORA, Boisduval.

Discophora, Boisduval, Spec. Gén., vol. i, pl. xii, fig. 3 (1836); id., Westwood, Gen. D. L., vol. ii, p. 329 (1851).

BODY robust, very woolly. HEAD rather small, woolly, with a small woolly frontal tuft [between the tips of the *palpi*]; *eyes* large, prominent, broadly oval; *palpi* compressed, directed obliquely upwards and reaching as high as the level of the top of the eyes, almost erect; basal joint hairy beneath, middle joint scaly in front, but very hairy behind, the hairs resting on the sides of the frontal tuft, terminal joint very short; *antennæ* not quite half the length of the forewing, slender, terminated by a long and gradually formed but slender club, finely carinated beneath, the seven terminal joints gradually acuminated. THORAX very robust and woolly; *abdomen* of moderate size. FOREWING large, triangular; *costa* much arched; apex acute; *outer margin* straight, oblique or slightly concave; *hinder angle* scarcely rounded; *inner margin* straight, nearly equal in length to the outer margin; *costal* nervure and first and second *subcostal* nervules anastomosing for part of their length; *upper* and *middle* disco-cellulars both very short, the *discoidal* nervules originating close together near the subcostal; *lower disco-cellular* long, but much shorter than is usual in this subfamily, concave and closing the cell considerably beyond the origin of the second median nervule; *submedian* nervure nearly straight. HINDWING with the *costa* slightly arched; the *outer margin* convex, sometimes angled at the extremity of the third median nervule, and slightly sinuate throughout; *discoidal cell* entirely open; *anal* angle acuminate; the *anal* margin convex and highly channelled to receive the abdomen, and straight beyond the body. FORELEGS of the MALE small, very hairy; those of the FEMALE rather longer, scaly, almost destitute of hairs.

"LARVA long, cylindrical, with hairy tubercles; extremity of the body armed with two small conical spines. PUPA broadly boat-shaped, simple, widest across the wing-cases; head-piece acuminated into two long points." (*Westwood*, l.c.)

The species of *Discophora* are very closely allied, and the markings of the underside are of the same general pattern throughout the genus; they are entirely Indo-Malayan, but extend to North-East India, South India and Ceylon in the region of heavy rainfall. Nine species are recognised, of which five are included in the Indian list, the other four inhabit the islands of the Malay Archipelago. The upperside is typically brown of various shades, marked on the forewing with three series of spots on the outer half, sometimes continued on the hindwing; and the variations consist in the more or less complete obsolescence of the spots on the one hand, and in the development of a subapical fascia on the forewing on the other band; the colour of the spots also differs in the different species. In all the species the male insect has a prominent oval patch of raised plush-like scales on the upperside of the hindwing at the lower end of the cell.

Key to the Indian species of Discophora.

A. Males, upperside brown, with deep indigo-blue reflections, the spots ochreous. Females brown, with a broad subapical fulvous fascia on the forewing.

a. Males, forewing with the submarginal series of spots usually complete, sometimes obsolescent, the discal and median series obsolete, except near the costa.

a[1]. All the spots small and well separated.

279. D. CELINDE, N.-E. India, Burma, Andaman Isles, Malay Peninsula, Java, Borneo.

b[1]. The spots of the discal and median series near the costa large and tending to coalesce into a subapical bar.

280. D. NECHO, Tenasserim, Java.

B. Male, upperside purplish brown, forewing with the spots large bluish-white, three (sometimes four) in number, the uppermost in the median, the rest in the discal series, but all arranged in a curved series beyond the cell. Female, forewing with the three series of spots large bluish-white, the uppermost of the median and discal series merged in a broad whitish fascia.

281. D. LEPIDA, S. India, Ceylon.

C. Male, with the upperside pure velvety brown, with three series of small spots, usually all bluish-white, sometimes irregularly tinged with fulvous; female with three series of large spots, white, the inner tinged with blue.

282. D. TULLIA, N.-E. India, Burma, Upper Tenasserim.

D. Male, with the upperside pure velvety brown unspotted. Female with three series of large spots, the median bluish-white, the discal fulvous below, bluish above, the outer pure fulvous.

283. D. ZAL, Burma, Malay Peninsula.

In all the males the hindwing is unmarked or with barely a trace of obsolete spots. In the females of *D. celinde* and *D. necko* there are more or less obsolete traces of fulvous lunular spots; in those of *D. lepida* there are three series of prominent fulvous lunules or marks, and in those of *D. tullia* and *D. zal* there are three complete series of fulvous spots in continuation of those of the forewing.

The habits of *D. tullia* and *D. celinde* very much resemble those of the species of the genus *Melanitis*. In Calcutta Mr. de Nicéville has found the former not uncommonly throughout the year under bamboo clumps and bushes amongst dry leaves, starting up when disturbed, flying a short distance, and then settling again amongst the leaves; they not unfrequently enter houses. In Sikkim, at low elevations, he found males of *D. celinde* commonly sucking up moisture from damp spots with their wings folded: when disturbed they fly off into the jungle. The rich indigo blue of the upperside of the male of this species when fresh makes it a very handsome insect on the wing.

279. Discophora celinde, Stoll.

Papilio celinde, Stoll, Suppl. Cramer, Pap. Ex., pl. xxxvii, figs. i, iA (1790), *male*; *P. menetho*, Fabricius, Ent. Syst., vol. iii, pt. i, p. 83, n. 260 (1793); id., Donovan, Ins. India, pl. xxx, fig. 1 (1800); *P. aristides*, Fabricius, Ent. Syst., vol. iii, pt. i, p. 86, n. 268 (1793); *Morpho celinde*, Godart, Enc. Méth., vol. ix, p. 446, n. 18 (1819); *M. menetho*, idem, id., n. 20 (1819); *Discophora celinde*, Herrich-Schaffer, Ex. Schmett., figs. 5, 6 (1850), *male*; id., Distant, Rhop. Malay., p. 75, pl. v, figs. 10, *male*; 11, *female* (1882).

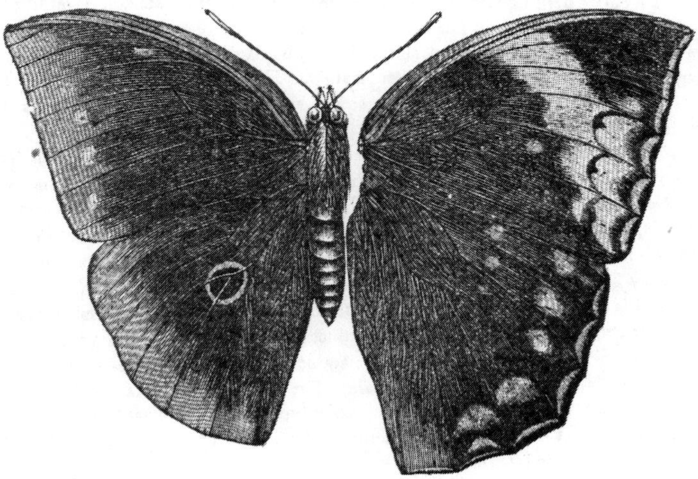

HABITAT: North-East India, Burma, Andaman Isles, Malayana.

EXPANSE: ♂, 3·4 to 3·8; ♀, 4·0 to 4·5 inches.

DESCRIPTION: MALE: UPPERSIDE dark olivaceous, with deep indigo-blue reflections. *Forewing* with a linear discal spot below the first discoidal nervule (in the median series), another beyond it below the second discoidal nervule (in the discal series), and a submarginal series of five spots, all ochraceous. *Hindwing*, with the usual patch of raised plush-like scales. UNDERSIDE reddish ochraceous, with dark brown transverse striæ, most numerous on the outer half, a dark brown median fascia across the middle of *both wings*, and two submarginal lunulate lines, the outer indistinct; the ground-colour between the two irrorated with whitish on the forewing and near the anal angle of the hindwing; the colour between these and the median fascia suffused with brown in the middle, forming a broad indistinct transverse band; a subbasal highly irregular dark zigzag line crossing the middle of the cell on both wings, within which are on the forewing three dark spots in a row across the cell, and on the hindwing two dark dots below the cell; between it and the median fascia the dark brown striæ are longer and more pronounced. *Hindwing*, with two ocelli just beyond the median fascia, one between the subcostal nervules, the other smaller between the lower median nervules, reddish brown, with diffused white pupil, narrow yellowish and black rings, and a yellowish outer lunule along the inner edge. FEMALE: UPPERSIDE vinaceous brown, lacking the bluish reflections and darkest on the outer half, where it is suffused with fuscous, especially about the apex of the forewing. *Forewing* with a broad fulvous fascia from the middle of the costa beyond the cell to near the outer margin between the third median nervule and submedian nervure, divided at its outer end by a submarginal, highly lunulate dark line into three submarginal lunulate patches. *Hindwing*, with a more or less prominent continuation of the dark lunulate submarginal line inwardly defined with fulvous lunules, sometimes reduced to a row of small fulvous submarginal spots, the outer margin of both wings tinged with fulvous. No discal patch of raised scales on the hindwing. UNDERSIDE, as in the male but much paler, and the dark markings ill-defined; the brown striæ pale, but almost uniformly distributed, especially on the basal half.

The ochreous spots on the forewing of the MALE are not constant; in a specimen from the South Andamans all of them are obsolete, except the linear one between the discoidal nervules; in many specimens from Sikkim and some from Malacca there are two spots in the discal series, and in most specimens from Malacca there are three; the constant spot being in all cases the lowest of the series. The markings of the FEMALE also vary to a certain degree; the form above described, in which the outer end of the fulvous fascia is divided by a lunulate dark line into three submarginal spots is the common form in Sikkim; in a specimen from the Andaman Islands the dark line is obsolete at its upper end, and in the form figured by Mr. Distant from Malacca the line is altogether absent, the fulvous fascia extending uninterruptedly to near the outer margin. There are also traces of the median series of spots below the fascia; generally a single spot on the forewing, sometimes two or more on the hindwing.

D. celinde has rather a wide range; it is recorded from Nepal in the British Museum. In Sikkim it is not uncommon; the Indian Museum, Calcutta, has specimens from Sibsagar in Upper Assam, but we have as yet no record of its occurrence between Assam and Tenasserim; in Upper Tenasserim it appears to be more closely allied to *D. necho*, Felder, from Java, and was identified as such by Mr. Moore from Limborg's specimens; the only specimen, a male, sent by Captain C. T. Bingham is apparently intermediate between the forms *celinde* and *necho*, and is referred to below under the latter name; in the Malay peninsula it is common, but the Malayan race appears to be nearly as distinct from the typical Sikkim race as *D. necho* is; and those from the Andamans are again separable as an insular race from the obsolete character of the fulvous markings in the male. Dr. Anderson took a single male in the Mergui Archipelago in March. It is of the *necho* type, but the spots are smaller than in our specimen of this species from Upper Tenasserim, and it is an even more decided connecting link between *D. celinde* and *D. necho*.

The figure shows the uppersides of a male and a female both from Sikkim in the Indian Museum, Calcutta.

280. **Discophora necho**, Felder.

Discophora necho, Felder, Reise Novara, Lep., vol. iii, p. 462, n. 782 (1867); id., Moore, Proc. Zool. Soc. Lond., 1878, p. 827; *Morpho? celinde*, Horsfield, Cat. Lep. E. I. C., pl. vi, fig. 6, *female*; pl. vii, fig. 11, *larva*; 11*a*, *pupa*; 11*b*—*k*, *structure* of *imago* (1829).

HABITAT: Upper Tenasserim, Java.

EXPANSE: ♂, 4·0; ♀, 4·2 inches.

DESCRIPTION: "MALE: UPPERSIDE paler than in *D. celinde*. *Forewing* with an oblique abbreviated fascia immediately beyond the middle, deeply and angulately cut through between the median nervules, and outwardly above below the lower discoidal nervule, and three outer lunular spots closely approximating to it, whitish. *Hindwing* with the velvety patch broader than in *D. celinde.* UNDERSIDE as in *D. celinde*, but the *forewing* with the discal striga arched and slightly drawn back, and the powdery whitish border streak very macular and slightly arched. *Hindwing* with the discal striga more directed inwardly at the hinder end, the upper ocellus much smaller, the lower minute, the whitish border spots evanescent. FEMALE: UPPERSIDE as in *D. celinde*, but the *forewing* with the fascia rather broad, extending a little beyond the first median nervule immediately beyond the cell, and three outer spots, large, adherent, pale ochraceous. *Hindwing* with spots almost all as in *D. celinde*, but more obscure, much smaller, and more obsolete. UNDERSIDE as in the male, but very pale, the strigæ scarcely visible. Larger than *D. celinde*." (*Felder*, l. c.)

LARVA cylindrical, slightly tapering at each end, pale purplish brown; with a dorsal whitish line marked on each side on each segment with a black dash, a lateral darker line defined on both sides with still darker brown. On either side of this line is a series of tubercles one on each segment furnished with long pale brown hairs. The lower portion of the insect bearing the legs paler brown than the rest of the body, this pale portion sharply defined; the anal segment furnished with a bifid tubercular process. PUPA boat-shaped, reddish-brown, streaked with darker brown, tapering to a point at either end. (Described from Horsfield's figures).

The single male specimen we have received from Upper Tenasserim has the submarginal series of spots on the forewing larger, the constant spot of the discal series much larger and another below it, the spot of the median series also much larger, with a short streak above and a spot below, all paler ochraceous than in *D. celinde*, but not whitish; the five last mentioned spots are almost coalescent into a subapical fascia, and the specimen is clearly intermediate between *D. necho* and *D. celinde*; on the underside the lower ocellus of the hindwing is obsolete, but has a prominent white pupil; it is a good deal larger than our largest male specimen of *D. celinde*. It was taken by Captain C. T. Bingham, at Houndraw, on the 18th December. Limborg's specimens, which came from the same locality, were identified by Mr. Moore as *D. necho*.

281. **Discophora lepida**, Moore.

Enispe lepida, Moore, Horsfield and Moore, Cat. Lep. E. I. C., vol. i, p. 213, n. 435 (1857); *Discophora lepida*, id., Lep. Ceylon, p. 36, pl. xviii, figs. 1, *male*; 1a, 1b, *female* (1880).

HABITAT: Hills of South India, Ceylon.

EXPANSE: ♂, 3·6 to 4·3; ♀, 4·0 inches.

DESCRIPTION: MALE: UPPERSIDE, velvety brown, slightly purplish, darkest in the middle, paler at the base and outer margin of *both wings*. *Forewing* with an oblique band beyond the cell of three coalescent bluish-white spots, sometimes a fourth separate below, and some faint marginal dots near the hinder angle. *Hindwing* unmarked, except for the oval patch of plush-like scales on the disc, though sometimes with a discal and submarginal series of obscure ochreous spots. UNDERSIDE almost exactly as in *D. celinde*, but darker and the dark markings less distinct. FEMALE paler brown. *Forewing* with a bluish-white band from the costa beyond the cell to the third median nervule, below which are three series of three bluish-white spots, the first marginal linear, the second submarginal lunulate, the third discal irregular. *Hindwing* paler brown, with three series of fulvous spots in continuation of the series on the forewing, the first reaching the anal angle, the second reaching the first median nervule, and the third only extending to the end of the cell; outer margin of both wings fulvous, divided by a brown line. UNDERSIDE pale ochreous, indistinctly covered with numerous slender brown strigæ; other markings as in the male, but less distinct.

D. lepida is found in Ceylon and in the hills of South India. We have as yet only received it from Travancore, where both sexes have been taken by Mr. H. S. Fergusson in the Ashamboo Hills; it is a rare butterfly everywhere. In Ceylon it has been "taken in forest land near Galle in July; very rare." (*Hutchison.*) Mr. Moore in his 'Lepidoptera of Ceylon' includes this genus among the *Nymphalinæ*.

282. **Discophora tullia,** Cramer.

Papilio tullia, Cramer, Pap. Ex., vol. i, pl. lxxxi. figs. A, B (1775), *female; Morpho tullia*, Godart, Enc. Méth., vol. ix, p. 446. n. 19 (1819); *Discophora tullia*, Moore, Horsfield and Moore, Cat. Lep. E. I. C., vol. i, p. 211, n. 431, pl. xii, figs. 15, *larva*; 15*a*, *pupa* (1857).

HABITAT: North-East India, Burma.

EXPANSE: ♂, 3·3 to 3·8; ♀, 3 5 to 3·9 inches.

DESCRIPTION: MALE: UPPERSIDE velvety fuliginous brown. *Forewing* with three nearly complete series of bluish, fulvous, or white spots, one submarginal, one near to it discal, and one more remote median. *Hindwing* with the usual patch of plush-like scales, two obsolete submarginal series of ochraceous spots. UNDERSIDE paler than in *D. celinde*, but more uniform in tone, the dark markings not so prominent. FEMALE paler brown, sometimes with a fulvous tinge. *Forewing* with the three series of spots larger, white, the discal ones only irrorated with bluish, the median and discal spots between the discoidal nervules coalesced. *Hindwing* with three corresponding series of bright fulvous spots, and a series of indistinct fulvous spots on the outer margin. UNDERSIDE as in the male, but much paler and duller in colour.

LARVA brown, thickly covered with brown hairs, with a paler dorsal line, and a dark brown spot on each side of it on each segment; the first three segments with a yellow ring. "Feeds on *Bambusa*." (l. c.) PUPA pale brown, smooth, boat-shaped, tapering to a fine point at the head. (Described from Moore's figures.)

D. tullia is commoner than *D. celinde*, and has been taken in more localities, but the geographical range is the same within Indian limits, excepting that *D. tullia* is known to occur in the plains of Bengal as far south as Calcutta at all events. In the MALE the blue spots on the *forewing* are generally small, sometimes partially obsolete; all three series are usually clearly traceable; in some specimens the submarginal series is obsolete, in others the median series has disappeared, with the exception of the spot between the discoidal nervules. In the Malay race figured by Mr. Distant in his Rhopalocera Malayana all three series have disappeared, and the upperside is unspotted, but this latter is probably the male of the next species, *D. zal.* The FEMALE varies much in tone, and in some all three series of spots on the *forewing* are white as in Cramer's type figure without any trace of bluish irrorations. *D. tullia* is common in Sikkim and in Tenasserim from September to April. In the neighbourhood of Calcutta Mr. de Nicéville has taken it throughout the year. They rest under the shade of large trees among the dead leaves on the ground, taking short flights when disturbed, and are easily captured. Mr. Wood-Mason took it commonly in Cachar from May to August; and there are specimens in the Indian Museum, Calcutta, from Sibsagar, and Sylhet.

The figure shows the upperside of both male and female, and is taken from specimens from Sibsagar in the Indian Museum, Calcutta.

283. Discophora zal, Westwood.

D. zal, Westwood, Gen. D. L., vol. ii, p. 331, n. 5 (1851), *note*; idem, id., Trans. Ent. Soc. Lond., new series, vol. iv, p. 188, pl. xxi, figs. 5, 6 (1856), *female*; id., Moore, Proc. Zool. Soc. Lond., 1878, p. 826; *D. tullia*, Distant, Rhop. Malay., p. 74, pl. vii, figs. 8, *male*; 9, *female* (1882).

HABITAT: Pegu, Tenasserim, Malay Peninsula.

EXPANSE: ♂, 2·8 to 3·3; ♀, 3·55 to 4·10 inches.

DESCRIPTION: FEMALE: "*Forewing* with the apex subfalcate. *Hindwing* angulated in the middle of the outer margin and at the anal angle. UPPERSIDE fulvous. *Forewing* with the costa pale, and with the outer half fuscous, bearing a triple series of spots; the inner series white, the rest fulvous. *Hindwing* fulvous, with a triple series of fuscous lunules and a cloudy fuscous submarginal line. UNDERSIDE whitish-yellow, with a narrow line and spots near the base fuscous, an obscure not very distinct median fascia, and two small ocelli placed beyond the middle."

"This species is remarkable for the somewhat falcate form of the forewing, and the angulated hindwing; the white colour also of the innermost row of spots on the forewing is characteristic. In this wing the ground-colour is brown, the spots being pale coloured, but in the hindwing the spots are so much increased in size as to constitute the ground-colour of the wing, reducing the separating dark parts to rows of obscure lunules. The oblique nervule which closes the discoidal cell [in the *forewing*] is curved at its base, and marked by a dark brown spot, with a dark dot beneath it. There is also a corresponding dark dot on the discoidal cell of the hindwing, which is not closed by a disco-cellular transverse nervule. The very pale buff colour of the underside of the wings, with the markings nearly obsolete, is also very characteristic." (*Westwood*, l. c. in Trans. Ent. Soc. Lond.) Expanse of Westwood's figure, 3·85 inches.

The above description evidently refers to a FEMALE specimen, and the male has not as yet been discriminated. The fulvous colour of the two outer rows of spots on the forewing renders it notably distinct from the female of *D. tullia* independently of other minor differences. We have a female specimen from Rangoon which answers exactly to the description of *D. zal*, except that the basal half of the upperside is fulvous brown rather than fulvous, and bears an incomplete but prominent fourth series of spots (shewn in Westwood's figure), the median series is pure white, and the two upper discal spots are tinted bluish-white; all the rest are pure fulvous: and Limborg took others in Upper Tenasserim, but among all the numerous males that we have received from Tenasserim none are separable from *D. tullia*. From Mr. Distant's figure and description the females in the Malay Peninsula are all of the *D. zal* type, but differing as in the Rangoon specimen noted above only more prominently; the basal area is more decidedly brown, and the upper three spots of the discal series are tinted with blue; the fourth series of spots is, however, only represented by a spot in the cell of the forewing and one beyond it; and they are clearly the *D. zal* of Westwood. The MALE of the Malayan race, as described and figured by Mr. Distant, differs from *D. tullia* in having the upper surface entirely unspotted, all three series of spots being obsolete; and the conclusion we come to is that *D. zal* is a well defined local race of *D. tullia*.

Genus 37.—ENISPE, Westwood.

Enispe, Westwood, Gen. D. L., vol. ii, p. 292 (1850); idem, id., p. 330 (1851).

BODY robust, woolly. FOREWING with three branches only to the *subcostal* nervure, the second branch being obliterated, the first anastomosing with the costal nervure. HINDWING with the outer margin evenly convex, not angled at the tip of the third median nervule. MALE without the discal patch of raised plush-like scales, but having the discoidal cell and the fold below the median nervure clothed with long hairs; otherwise not differing from *Discophora*. FORELEGS in both sexes slightly longer than in *Discophora*, those of the FEMALE more distinctly hairy, but not nearly so hairy as in the male. Transformations unknown.

The genus *Enispe* comprises as yet only two species, both of which inhabit the north-eastern corner of India not extending to the Malay peninsula. The typical species has the wings bright orange-red, with several series of blackish markings; but the other species has very much the colouring of a *Discophora*. Little or nothing is known of their habits, which are probably similar to those of the closely-allied *Discophoras*.

Key to the species of Enispe.

A. Forewing with the outer margin straight and the apex acute; hindwing with the outer margin regularly convex, and the anal angle acute.

a. Both sexes bright orange with black markings.

284. E. EUTHYMIUS, N.-E. India, Tenasserim.

b. Both sexes brown, with a lilac band and spots on the forewing; female with ochreous yellow spots on both wings.

285. E. CYCNUS, N.-E. India.

284. Enispe euthymius, Doubleday.

Adolias euthymius, Doubleday, Ann. and Mag. of Nat. Hist., vol. xvi, p. 179 (1845); *Enispe euthymius* Doubleday, Hewitson, Gen. D. L., vol. ii, p. 292, pl. xl, fig. 2 (1850), *male*.

HABITAT: Sikkim, Naga and Khasi Hills, Assam, Cachar, Upper Tenasserim.

EXPANSE: 3·4 to 3·9 inches.

DESCRIPTION: "MALE: UPPERSIDE, *both wings* bright orange-red. *Forewing* with a large [fuscous] spot on the disco-cellular nervules, followed by two small ill-defined ones on [either side of] the lower discoidal nervule; the outer margin broadly fuscous black, with faint indications of four or five reddish lunules; this black border dilated towards the apex, much dentate internally, preceded by a broad zigzag [fuscous] striga, commencing near the anterior and extending nearly to the inner margin; the median nervules each with a round fuscous spot before their middle [and similar spots on the discoidal nervules completing the series]. *Hindwing* clothed at the base with long hairs; a discoidal spot, two lunulated bands, and the outer margin slightly fuscous. UNDERSIDE paler. *Both wings* marked at the base with some indistinct fuscescent spots, beyond which is an undulating striga crossing the middle of the discoidal cell of the forewing, and reaching the inner margin of the hindwing near the middle. Beyond this is a less curved band commencing on the costa beyond the middle and reaching nearly to the anal angle, followed by a space rather paler than the rest of the wing. Beyond the middle are four black dots [on the hindwing], the first and fourth largest, the latter pupilled with white [these dots are sometimes obsolete]. Faint indications of the bands above are visible below. HEAD rufous. *Antennæ* brown, darker towards the apex. *Palpi* red. *Thorax* and *abdomen* brick-red." (*Doubleday*, l. c.) FEMALE similar to the male, but with the fuscous marks more defined and extended. *Forewing* with the reddish marginal lunules prominent and dividing the fuscous margin as on the hindwing. *Hindwing* with a discal series of fuscous lunules in continuation of the macular series on the forewing; *both wings* with a prominent fuscous median line, corresponding with the median band of the underside, thus making five complete series of dusky markings on both wings in addition to the patch at the end of the cell of the forewing. UNDERSIDE as in the male.

The markings of the male insect vary, approximating more or less from the form described above to the markings of the female. The tone of the ground-colour also varies a good deal, a male specimen taken by Mr. Wood-Mason on Nemotha in Cachar in September being of a far deeper and richer orange-red than any other specimens we have seen.

E. euthymius is found in the mountains to the north and east of Bengal, extending southward as far as Tenasserim. It is not uncommon in Sikkim; the Indian Museum, Calcutta, has specimens from the Naga Hills; it was not met with by Limborg, but Captain C. T. Bingham has taken it in the lower Thoungyeen forests in Upper Tenasserim in March and April.

The figure shows the upper and undersides of a male speciemen from Sikkim in the Indian Museum, Calcutta.

285. **Enispe cycnus**, Westwood.

E. cycnus, Westwood, Gen. D. L., vol. ii, p. 330 (1851), *note*; id., Moore, Horsfield and Moore, Cat. Lep. E. I. C., vol. i. p. 212, n. 434 (1857).

HABITAT: Sikkim, Upper Assam, Sylhet.

EXPANSE: ♂, 3·12; ♀, 3·62 to 4·00 inches.

DESCRIPTION: "MALE: UPPERSIDE blackish-brown; base and exterior margins paler. *Forewing* with an oblique band from the middle of the anterior margin terminating in a transverse series of lunular spots, and a parallel outer row of four quadrate spots, lilac-white. *Hindwing* with very indistinct marginal and submarginal pale spots. UNDERSIDE with a transverse brown dentate band from middle of costal margin to anal angle [outwardly distinctly and inwardly indistinctly edged with a darker line]; the base of the wings orange-yellow, with narrow irregular transverse markings [arranged as in *E. euthymius*, but much more prominent]; exterior half of wings light brown [darkest inwardly], with [three] indistinct transverse [lunular] lines. *Hindwing* with a small anterior black dot and a posterior white dot. FEMALE: UPPERSIDE: *Forewing* with the base obliquely dull chocolate-brown, the rest brownish-black; the lilac-white oblique band and spots as in male, but larger, with two inner rows and terminal spots ochreous-yellow. *Hindwing* with the basal half to abdominal angle dull chocolate-brown, with a marginal, submarginal, an inner third and a short fourth row of ochreous-yellow spots, the spaces between blackish. UNDERSIDE yellow throughout, with a slight greenish tinge; transverse dentate band and markings as in male." (*Moore*, l. c.) The discal band and markings of the basal area are very prominent, those on the outer half obsolescent.

E. cycnus is a rare and very interesting species; the MALE has the colouring of a *Discophora*, and it has the hairy clothing of the *hindwing* far more extended than in *E. euthymius*, the long hairs covering the whole discoidal cell and as far beyond as the curve in the third median nervule. The FEMALE also has the *forewing* marked as in *Discophora* and the *hindwing* as in *Enispe*, and on the whole most nearly resembling the same sex of *D. lepida*, but in structure it is a true *Enispe*. The type specimen was received from Sylhet; the Indian Museum, Calcutta, has a male specimen from Sibsagar in Upper Assam; another with no record of locality, and a female from Sikkim. We know of no other specimens in collections in this country.

Genus 38.—ÆMONA, Hewitson. (FRONTISPIECE.)

Aemona, Hewitson, Ex. Butt , vol. iv, pl. *Zeuxidia* and *Aemona* (1868); *Æmona*, Wood-Mason, Journ. A. S. B., vol. xlix, pt. ii, p. 175 (1880).

"HEAD small. *Antennæ* rather short. FOREWING acutely pointed and produced, or sharply angulated, at the apex; its inner margin straight in both sexes, not being lobed at the base in the male as it is in *Clerome* and less distinctly in *Thaumantis;* the *costal* nervure reaching to the end of the fifth seventh of the length of the anterior margin; the subcostal four-branched, the first branch given off just before the end of the cell, and, after running free for nearly the same distance beyond that point as it originates before it, completely coalescing with the costal, but again becoming free just before this last named nervure turns off to the anterior margin; the three remaining branches free. HINDWING more elongated than, and not quite so rounded as, in *Clerome;* without the pencil of erectile setæ which, in the males of *Thaumantis*, arises from the wing-membrane of the discoidal cell close to the subcostal nervure, and lies obliquely across a patch of elevated and crowded scales on the other side of this nervure, the male scent-fans, if such are really present in this genus, being situated in a different part of the wing, *viz.*, in the anal region, where a line of setæ running along the anterior side of the submedian nervure ends in a curled whisp which, when at rest, lies in a slight groove or fold of the wing-membrane. In the form of the hindwing and in the position of the male scent-fans *Æmona* agrees best with *Xanthotænia*, and in its pointed fore-wing with *Zeuxidia*, *Enispe*, and *Discophora*, but it differs from these and from all the other Indian genera of *Morphinæ* in the relations of the costal and subcostal nervures to one another, and in other respects." (*Wood-Mason*, l. c.)

The genus *Æmona* is confined to the north-east corner of India extending into Upper Tenasserim. It contains three species only; they are "plain and delicate butterflies of a pale fulvous colour, inconspicuously or obsoletely ocellated on the underside." (*Wood-Mason*, l. c., p. 176). *Æ. lena* is a very distinct species; *Æ. amathusia* and *Æ. pealii* are very closely allied, differing chiefly in the apex of the forewing, which in the former species is sharply produced; in the latter more rounded. Nothing is known of the habits of any of the species, and all of them are very rare. We have not seen a female specimen of any of the species.

Key to the species of Æmona.

A. Forewing produced and pointed at the apex, with its outer margin concave-sinuous.
- *a.* Forewing marked with a series of five pale lanceolate blotches on the upperside.
  - 286. Æ. LENA, Upper Tenasserim.
- *b.* Forewing with no pale blotches on the upperside.
  - 287. Æ. AMATHUSIA, Northern India, Naga Hills.

B. Forewing sharply angulated at the apex, with its outer margin convex.
- *a.* Upperside marked almost exactly as in *Æ. amathusia.*
  - 288. Æ. PEALII, Upper Assam.

286. Æmona lena, Atkinson.

Æ. lena, Atkinson, Proc. Zool. Soc. Lond., 1871, p. 215, pl. xii, fig. 1, *male;* id., Moore, Anderson's Researches, vol. i, p. 924, vol. ii, pl. lxxxi, fig. 1 (1878); id., Wood-Mason, Journ. A. S. B., vol. xlix, pt. ii, p. 177, n. 2 (1880).

HABITAT: Upper Tenasserim.

EXPANSE: ♂, 3·25 inches.

DESCRIPTION: MALE: "UPPERSIDE: *Forewing* pale brownish grey, crossed by a dark brown band, interrupted by the nervures from before the apex to near the posterior margin at two-thirds of its length from the base; beyond the band darker, with a slightly marked and incomplete submarginal line, before which is a series of five pale lanceolate blotches between the nervules directed towards the outer margin. All the nervures tinged with yellow, and more or less dark-bordered. *Hindwing:* Anterior portion from base to outer margin pale, posterior portion bright yellow, crossed by a submarginal series of three dark-bordered white blotches, and a fourth fainter blotch between the nervures, forming a short interrupted band from near the apex to the second median nervule. The submedian nervure fringed from its origin to near its extremity with long yellowish hairs, longest and most conspicuous towards its extremity. UNDERSIDE : *Both wings* crossed by a dark ferruginous band with sharply defined outer edge from the costa of the forewing near the apex to near the extremity of the submedian nervure of the hindwing, and having a faintly traced submarginal line, before which is a series of blind white-centred ocelli. The cell of the forewing crossed near its middle by a curved ferruginous band. *Hindwing* crossed by a ferruginous band near the base. *Antennæ* ferruginous ; *palpi* and *legs* tawny yellow." (*Atkinson*, l. c.)

"Atkinson does not give the sex of the specimen described and figured by him, but, as the two specimens in the Indian Museum obtained at the same time are males and agree perfectly in size and markings with his figure, he may be presumed to have described a male. In a specimen of the male recently received from the Upper Thoungyeen forests, British Burmah, by Major G. F. L. Marshall, [where it was taken in April], the three white spots on the anterior half of the hindwing are larger, forming a band divided by the veins." (*Wood-Mason*, l. c.)

This species was also taken by Limborg in Upper Tenasserim at Moolai, 3,000 to 6,000 feet elevation.

287. **Æmona amathusia,** Hewitson. (FRONTISPIECE, FIGS. 2, 2*a* ♂.)

Clerome amathusia, Hewitson, Trans Ent. Soc. Lond., third series, vol. v, p. 566 (1867) ; *Aemona amathusia*, id., Ex. Butt., vol. iv, pl. *Zeuxidia* and *Aemona*, figs. 3, 4 (1868), *female*; id., Wood-Mason, Journ. A. S. B , vol. xlix, pt. ii, p. 176, n. 1, pl. vi, figs. 2, 2*a* (1880), *male*.

HABITAT : Northern India, Naga Hills.

EXPANSE ; ♂, 2·9 ; ♀, 3·2 inches.

DESCRIPTION : "FEMALE : UPPERSIDE rufous-brown, the bands of the underside seen through. *Forewing* crossed beyond the middle by a band of orange-yellow : the apex dark brown. *Hindwing* with some arcuate spots near the apex. UNDERSIDE rufous, tinted with darker colour. *Both wings* crossed at the middle by a common rufous-brown band : both with a band of minute rufous ocelli, some of which are pupilled with white : both with a submarginal rufous band. *Forewing* with a pale rufous band near the base, and a spot of the same colour at the end of the cell. *Hindwing* with a dark rufous band near the base." (*Hewitson*, l. c.) "MALE : Lighter-coloured than the female. UPPERSIDE pale fulvous, the strigæ or bands of the underside showing through. *Forewing* darker at the base and at the tip, between which darker parts the colour is very pale yellowish-fulvous. *Hindwing* of the same shade as the base of the forewing to within a short distance of the margin, whence it is paler, and with an indistinct submarginal series of arcuate marks extending from the apical to the anal angle. UNDERSIDE uniform pale fulvous ; the strigæ as in the female ; the ocelli (one, the second and largest, perfect, the remaining five rudimentary) of the *hindwing* also as in the female, but in the *forewing* only the one between the first and second median nervules and faint traces of that between the first median nervule and the submedian nervure are present ; the thin submarginal brown line more obviously engrailed than in the female." (*Wood-Mason*, l. c.)

The male specimen described above is unique in the collection of the Indian Museum, Calcutta.

288. **Æmona pealii,** Wood-Mason. (FRONTISPIECE, FIGS. 3, 3*a* ♂.)

Æ. pealii, Wood-Mason, Journ. A. S. B., vol. xlix, pt. ii, p. 177, n. 3, pl. vi, figs. 3, 3*a* (1880), *male*.

HABITAT : Sibsagar, Upper Assam.

EXPANSE : 2·8 inches.

DESCRIPTION : "MALE : Closely allied to *Æ. amathusia*. UPPERSIDE coloured and marked in the same manner, but with the ocelli as well as the strigæ of the underside showing through. *Forewing* with the apex angulated, but not produced, the outer margin arched instead of concave-sinuous, and the inner angle not so broadly rounded. *Hindwing* darker-coloured and also paling towards the outer margin, but with the submarginal series of arcuate marks smaller and less distinct. UNDERSIDE coloured and marked in much the same manner, but with more perfectly formed and more numerous ocelli ; the forewing having three (the first between the submedian nervure and the first median nervule, the second the largest and best defined) perfect ocelli and two or three rudimentary ones following them, and the hindwing, one rudimentary (close to the submedian nervure) and six (the first in the same interspace with the rudimentary one, and the second the largest of all) perfect ones; each ocellus dark brown encircled by a very fine line of the colour of the strigæ and pupilled with iridescent silvery-white; the thin submarginal brown line rather more deeply engrailed." (*Wood-Mason*, l. c.) The FEMALE is unknown.

There are two male specimens of this species, including the type, in the Indian Museum, Calcutta.

Genus 39.—THAUMANTIS, Hübner.

Thaumantis, Hübner, Samml. Ex. Schmett. (1816-1824); id., Westwood, Gen. D. L., vol ii, p. 335 (1851), *in part*; idem, id., Trans. Ent. Soc. Lond., new series, vol. iv, p. 170 (1856), *Monograph*.

BODY somewhat robust, hairy. HEAD large, hairy, with a small frontal tuft. *Eyes* large, prominent, naked; *palpi* slender, compressed, nearly erect, scarcely rising above the level of the eyes, densely clothed in front with short scaly appressed hairs, a tuft of longer hairs at the back of the middle joint against the face, terminal joint short, slender. WINGS large, rounded, ample. FOREWING with the *apex* more or less rounded, the *hinder angle* much rounded; *subcostal* nervure with four branches, the first anastomosing with the costal nervure for part of its length, the second anastomosing with the first, the third and fourth free; *upper* and *middle disco-cellular* nervules short, the middle usually longer than the upper; the *lower* disco-cellular long, feebly concave or nearly straight. HINDWING with the costa, apex, outer margin and anal angle all rounded; the *third median* nervule much bent and approximating closely at the bend to the discoidal nervule. The *internal* nervure long, nearly straight. FORELEGS of the MALE slender and very slightly hairy; of the FEMALE much longer, more slender, scaly, and somewhat truncate at tip.

The genus *Thaumantis* contains some of the most beautiful and largest Butterflies of the Eastern world; in the size of its wings it is exceeded by the allied genus *Stichophthalma* and by the *Amathusias* of the *portheus* group, but in brilliancy of colouring it is surpassed by neither.

Only seven species are known, all from the Indo-Malayan region. Even as restricted by the exclusion of *Stichophthalma* (which some authors still unite with it) the genus presents two distinct groups, differing both in style of colour and in structural features.

Key to the Indian species of Thaumantis.

A. Wings black, with brilliant metallic purple reflections; the forewing with the apex much rounded; males with a distinct tuft of erectile hairs on the hindwing along the subcostal nervure, the rest of the base of the wing scarcely hairy.

  a. The brilliant metallic purple reflections confined on the forewing to a broad curved band.

    289. T. DIORES, N.-E. India.

  b. The brilliant metallic purple reflections much spread inwardly, and occupying on the forewing nearly the entire disc.

    290. T. RAMDEO, N.-E. India.

    T. ODANA, Singapore, Java.

    T. LUCIPOR, Malay Peninsula, Borneo.

    T. NOUREDDIN, Malay Peninsula, Borneo.

B. Wings brown, with a pale yellowish or white oblique fascia on the forewing; the apex and outer portion of the hindwing bright fulvous. Forewing with the apex less rounded, the outer margin straight. Males with the entire base of the hindwing clothed with long hairs, longest and partially erectile below the subcostal nervure.

    291. T. PSEUDALIRIS, Tenasserim, Malay Peninsula.

    T. ALIRIS, Malacca, Borneo.

289. Thaumantis diores, Doubleday.

T. diores, Doubleday, Ann. and Mag. of Nat. Hist., vol. xvi, p. 234 (1845); id., Westwood, Trans. Ent. Soc. Lond., new series, vol. iv, p. 171 (1856).

HABITAT: Sikkim, Assam, Naga Hills, Sylhet.

EXPANSE: 4·0 to 4·7 inches.

DESCRIPTION: Sexes alike. "UPPERSIDE: *Both wings* fuscous black, the *forewing* with a broad band-like spot, commencing near the costa beyond the middle, and extending towards the anal angle as far as the lowest median nervule. This spot is of a brilliant metallic, changeable blue, much paler and less changeable externally. On the *hindwing* is a large patch of the same rich blue, paler in the centre, occupying the whole disc of the wing. UNDERSIDE, *both wings* less black than above, the outer margin paler; this pale portion bounded internally by an undulated pale or whitish striga, becoming brown towards its termination at the anal angle of the hindwing; between this and the margin is another less distinct similar striga. The *forewing* has besides two fuscous strigæ in the discoidal cell inclosing a paler space, and a third striga commencing on the costa beyond the cell, and extending obliquely nearly to the anal angle, slightly bordered internally with whitish. The *hindwing* has a transverse fuscous striga near the base, and another commencing near the middle of the costa, and reaching nearly to the anal angle. Just within the pale submarginal striga near the costa is a round yellowish spot, enclosing a brown one placed towards its outer margin, and between the first and second median nervules a round black spot sprinkled with blue atoms anteriorly, and surrounded by a yellowish and a black iris. Anal angle with a geminate spot, composed of black and white atoms. *Head*, thorax and abdomen fuscous." (*Doubleday*, l. c.)

"The MALE has a patch of brown hairs capable of erection at the base of the *hindwing* on the UPPERSIDE. The apical angle of the forewing and the anal angle of the hindwing is much more rounded than in *T. odana*; the body is also much less robust. The branches of the subcostal nervure of the forewing in this species are of the same number and almost identical in their arrangement with those of *T. odana*." (*Westwood*, l. c.)

The metallic blue band on the forewing of this species seldom extends to below the first median nervule; in a single specimen in the Indian Museum, Calcutta, it extends to the inner margin, but even in this one the inner edge of the band is parallel to the outer margin, and scarcely extends into the cell; on the hindwing the metallic blue patch only reaches the first median nervule and scarcely tinges the cell. It is not uncommon in Sikkim, and is confined to the north-east corner of Bengal, not extending so far as is known into British Burma. Mr. Wood-Mason took it on Nemotha in Cachar in September and October.

290. **Thaumantis ramdeo**, Moore.

T. ramdeo, Moore, Horsfield and Moore, Cat. Lep. E. I. C., vol. i. p. 215, n. 441; id., Westwood, Trans. Ent. Soc. Lond., new series, vol. iv, p. 172 (1856).

HABITAT: Sikkim; Assam.

EXPANSE: 4·0 to 4·75 inches.

DESCRIPTION: "Differs from *Thaumantis diores* in being larger, and in having the brilliant blue patch very large, it being an inch in diameter either way, and extends over the whole of the middle of the wings. The UNDERSIDE is paler than in *T. diores*, and the wavy line running near the exterior margins of *T. diores* is nearly obsolete in *T. ramdeo;* the two ocelli on the *hindwing* are very small." (*Moore*, l. c.) FEMALE like the male, but larger, and lacking the erectile tuft of hairs on the hindwing.

Thaumantis ramdeo is found over the same ground as *T. diores;* the Indian Museum has specimens from Sikkim, from Sibsagar in Assam, and from the Dafla hills. It is a very beautiful species; the metallic blue patch is paler with an even more brilliant metallic sheen: on the forewing it extends to the inner margin and well into the discoidal cell, and on the *hindwing* it extends well below the first median nervule and covers the entire cell to the base.

The figure shows the upper and undersides of a male specimen from Sibsagar, Upper Assam, in the Indian Museum, Calcutta.

T. odana,* the typical species of this section, inhabits Singapore and Java; it differs from the Indian species in lacking the metallic blue patch on the hindwing. Two other species of the group, *T. lucipor* and *T. noureddin*, occur in the Malay Peninsula,† descriptions of them are appended for reference. They have the anal angle less rounded and more produced than in the Indian species.

---

* *Morpho* [*Thaumantis*] *odana*, Godart, Enc. Méth., vol. ix, p. 445, n. 16 (1819); id., Horsfield, Cat. Lep. E. I. C., pl. vi, figs. 5, 5*a* (1829); *Thaumantis odana*, Boisduval, Spec. Gén., Lép.. vol. i, pl. xii (viii B.) fig. 1, (1836). HABITAT: Singapore, Java. EXPANSE: 4 inches. DESCRIPTION: "Sexes alike in colour. UPPERSIDE, *both wings* blackish-fuscous. *Forewing* with a broad oblique purplish blue discal fascia, shining paler in the middle, and a white subapical dot. UNDERSIDE with discal strigæ and outer margin greyish or lilac-white. *Hindwing*, with a small costal marginal dot, and a large ocellus towards the anal angle circled with yellow above. The underside varies considerably in the intensity of the markings, especially in specimens from Singapore, from whence it has been sent by Mr. Wallace. The male has a patch of hairs at the base of the hindwing on the upperside" (*Westwood*, Trans. Ent. Soc. Lond., new series, vol. iv, p. 170 (1856). Mr. Distant does not include this species in his Rhopalocera Malayana.

† *Thaumantis lucipor*, Westwood, Gen. D. L., vol. ii, p. 337, n. 5 (1851), *note*; idem, id., Trans. Ent Soc. Lond., new series, vol. iv, p. 173, n. 5, pl. xix (1856); id, Distant, Rhop. Malay., p. 77, pl. ix, figs. 8, *male;* 9, *female* (1882). HABITAT: Province Wellesley, Borneo. EXPANSE: *Male*, 3·5 to 3·7; *Female*, 3·8 inches. DESCRIPTION: "MALE, UPPERSIDE, *both wings* pale chocolate-brown, the discs darker, and with dark and resplendent bluish reflections, which do not extend to the costal area and wide outer margin (diminishing from the apex) of the forewing, nor to the abdominal or outer margin of the hindwing. UNDERSIDE, *both wings* chocolate-brown, with the outer margins broadly and distinctly paler. *Forewing* with three very indistinct and irregular pale fasciæ crossing the cell; an oblique distinct pale fascia commencing about the costal nervure a little beyond the apex of the cell, and terminating about the first median nervule near the pale outer margin, which possesses a submedial and much waved darker line, on the innerside of which the colour is much suffused with greyish; beneath the first median nervule the colour is pale brownish. *Hindwing* with the basal area much suffused with greyish, on which is a large, irregular and curved fascia, which is broadest on the costal margin and narrowest at its termination near the submedian nervure. At the boundary of the pale outer margin the colour is much darker, and between the first median nervule and the submedian nervure appears as a suddenly bent and reflexed fascia; this area contains two ocellated spots, the first and uppermost of which, situated between the subcostal nervules, is dark with a slightly paler margin, and its inner third white; the lower is situated between the second and first median nervules, and has its inner margin white. The outer pale margin possesses a submedial and much-waved darker line, on the innerside of which the colour is much suffused with greyish, and between the first median nervule and the submedian nervure is an oblong black spot with an outer white continuation. *Body* and *legs* more or less concolorous with the wings. The male possesess two basal patches of pale (described as black by Professor Westwood in the typical specimen, so probably variable in hue) hairs near the costal base of the upperside of the hindwing, which probably denote scent-secretory organs. FEMALE larger, and with the wings on the upperside slightly paler than in the male, with similar blue reflections as in that sex, but which do not extend beyond the basal halves of both wings. *Forewing* with the blue reflection outwardly bounded by a more or less distinct pale oblique but broken fascia, commencing above the first discoidal nervule and terminating near the first median nervule; two small subapical ochraceous spots on each side of the fifth subcostal nervule, followed by a much-waved and sinuated submarginal ochraceous fascia, commencing near the first discoidal nervule and terminating near the outer angle. *Hindwing* with a much-waved and sinuated fuscous submarginal fascia, commencing near the apex of the first subcostal nervule and terminating near the anal angle; between the subcostal nervules this fascia is outwardly bordered by a pale ochraceous marginal spot. UNDERSIDE somewhat paler and brighter than in the male, excepting the dark shadings, which are as intense as in that sex. *Hindwing* crossed by a narrow undulating dark fascia, commencing near the costa, crossing near the apex of the cell, and terminating at the first median nervule (this is faintly discernible in the male); the submedial waved fasciæ to the pale outer margins of both wings are also very distinct." (*Distant*, l. c.)

Thaumantis noureddin, Westwood, Gen. D L., vol. ii, p. 337, n. 6 (1851), *note*; idem, id., Trans. Ent. Soc. Lond., new series, vol. iv, p. 175, n 6, pl. xx (1856); id., Distant, Rhop. Malay., p. 78, pl. vii, fig. 3, *male;* pl. ix, fig. 7, *female* (1882). HABITAT: Province Wellesley, Malacca, Borneo. EXPANSE: *Male*, 3·7; *Female*, 3·7 to 3·9 inches. DESCRIPTION: "MALE: UPPERSIDE, *both wings* dark fuscous-brown; the outer margins broadly paler. *Forewing* with the pale outer margin much waved inwardly, and there denoted by a row of more or less distinct whitish spots placed upon the nervules; the costal area and basal portion of the cell also somewhat paler. *Hindwing* has the paler outer portion much less well defined, broadest at the anal angle, and terminating

The apices of the forewing in the females of both species are also somewhat truncated, not rounded, as in *T. diores* and *ramdeo*; the male of *T. lucipor* has the apex of the forewing acute. *T. lucipor*, male, has the upperside almost entirely suffused with blue; in the female this colour is confined to the basal areas of both wings, but it has a deeply dentate submarginal line, ochreous in the forewing, fuscous in the hindwing. In *T. noureddin* the blue colour is obsolete on the upperside in the male, but present at the base of both wings in the female, which latter has a submarginal and discal series of five ochreous spots, the inner series bent inwards anteriorly.

291. Thaumantis pseudaliris, Butler.

T. pseudaliris, Butler, Journ. Linn. Soc. Lond., Zoology, vol. xiii, p. 115 (1876); id., Trans. Linn Soc. Lond., Zoology, second series, vol. i, p. 538, pl lxviii, fig. 1 (1876), *male*; *Thaumantis aliris*, Westwood, Trans. Ent. Soc. Lond., new series, vol. iv. p. 176 (1856), *male*; *Thaumantis pseudaliris*, Distant, Rhop. Malay., p. 79, pl. viii, fig. 3 (1882), *male*; id., Butler, Ann. and Mag. of Nat. Hist., fifth series, vol. x, p. 372 (1882).

HABITAT: Tenasserim, Malay Peninsula.

EXPANSE: ♂, 4·4 to 4·7; ♀, 4·5 to 5·4 inches.

DESCRIPTION: MALE: UPPERSIDE, *forewing* velvety blackish-brown, the outer margin slightly paler, the base suffused with dull ferruginous; a pale ochreous transverse fascia from the costa just beyond the cell to the first median nervule and continued to near the hinder angle by a coalescent spot of the same colour below the first median nervule; two white spots near the apex. *Hindwing* velvety blackish-brown, the base suffused with dull ferruginous; the apex and the anal third from discoidal nervule to abdominal margin bright orange fulvous. UNDERSIDE, *forewing* with the basal area greyish ochreous, densely clothed with short hairs, a chestnut line across the cell, within which is a large chestnut spot and a smaller one above it on the costa, the pale fascia of the upperside but whiter and continuous, the space between it and the basal area chestnut shading into deep brownish-black near the hinder angle, and into greyish-ochraceous along the inner margin; beyond the fascia the outer margin is broadly ferruginous, inwardly sharply defined by a fuscous line; the triangular space left between this border, the costa, and the pale transverse fascia also ferruginous, irrorated with dusky, darkest near the fascia, palest outwardly and suffused with white at the extremity. *Hindwing* with the basal area greyish-ochraceous as in the forewing, extending almost to the anal angle, and bearing a large chestnut spot near the costa, a small one just below it, one near the base of the cell and a few indistinct ones below; defined outwardly by a rich chestnut band broadest at the costa, narrowing to a point at the anal angle; the inner edge even, the outer highly irregular, greatly constricted just below the discoidal nervule, where and above which it is decreasingly bordered with whitish; outer half pale ferruginous bearing an indistinct dusky submarginal lunular line and two large reddish ocelli ringed narrowly with black and pale ochreous, the upper one between the subcostal nervules irrorated with a few white atoms in the centre, the lower one between the first and second median nervules bearing a black patch at its inner end, beyond which is a whitish linear mark and numerous whitish dots; between these two ocelli are three white dots, placed one in each interspace; an elongated black spot on the margin between the first median nervule and

---

on the abdominal margin. UNDERSIDE, *both wings* pale castaneous; crossed by an almost straight submarginal dark castaneous fascia, bordered outwardly with greyish. *Forewing* with a pale waved fascia crossing the cell near its centre; a narrow oblique greyish fascia beyond the cell, commencing near the costal nervure, and terminating at the third median nervule, beyond which it is continued and indicated by a narrow dark line only; between these pale fasciæ the colour is somewhat darker, and is thus continued in a waved and narrower form on the hindwing, where it terminates in a faint and indistinct manner about the middle of the abdominal margin. *Hindwing* with two ocellated spots on the innerside of the submarginal fascia; these spots are inwardly margined with white, and are situated one between the subcostal nervules, and one between the second and first median nervules; the apical angle with a fuscous spot, bordered on each side with greyish The male is provided with two tufts of long dark hairs near the base of the upperside of the hindwing, covering the discs of two distinct pseudo scent-glands or pouches FEMALE larger than the male UPPERSIDE, *both wings* with distinct basal resplendent bluish reflections. *Forewing* with a discal, curved, and outwardly convex series of five ochraceous spots placed between the nervules, commencing above the first discoidal nervule, and terminating near the first median nervule, and a straight submarginal series of five ochraceous spots also placed between the nervules. *Hindwing* with a waved fuscous marginal fascia. UNDERSIDE slightly paler than in the male, the oblique greyish fascia beyond the cell of the *forewing* much more distinct, broader, and continuous, the straight submarginal fascia to *both wings* outwardly much more widely bordered with greyish; ocellated spots larger, and anal angle less produced than in the male The males of this species vary in the amount of melanism. In some specimens the submarginal series of pale spots on the upperside are scarcely visible." (*Distant*, l. c)

the submedian nervure. FEMALE identical in colour and markings with the male, but much larger, and the base of the hindwing much less hairy on the upperside.

The above description is from specimens in Major Marshall's collection, which were taken by Captain C. T. Bingham in Upper Tenasserim. They differ from the figure of the male in Mr. Distant's Rhopalocera Malayana, which was taken from the specimen in the British Museum. On the UPPERSIDE Mr. Distant's figure shows the wings tinted with ferruginous throughout the dark portion instead of only at the base; the pale fascia of the forewing is narrower, much attenuated outwardly, coming to a point at the first median nervule and not nearly reaching the outer margin; whereas in our Tenasserim specimens it touches nearly one-third of the length of the first median nervule. On the *hindwing* in Mr. Distant's figure the anal fulvous patch extends broadly up to the base of the wing, whereas in our specimens it stops short beyond the extremity of the abdomen, where it shades into the dark brown ferruginous-tinted basal area. On the UNDERSIDE the differences are less striking, the triangular costal patch on the *forewing* is outwardly much suffused with violet in Mr. Distant's figure, and on the *hindwing* the basal area is much paler, the upper ocellus is yellow, and the lower is densely irrorated with violet-white. Further, Mr. Distant remarks that the "male has two large basal tufts of hair on the upperside of the hindwing, the smaller near the costa, the larger at the base of the cell." In the Tenasserim specimens there is no trace of the smaller tuft near the costa, but the male has in addition to the large tuft in the cell the whole basal area below the subcostal nervure very hairy, and large lateral tufts of hair on the abdomen as in *Amathusia phidippus*, but curved upwards not downwards. It seems very probable that the Tenasserim species is distinct, but without comparing them with specimens from Malacca it is impossible to say.

Captain C. T. Bingham has taken this rare and beautiful butterfly in the Thoungyeen forests and in the Donat range in October and in April; it was not met with by Limborg who collected over the same ground from December to April.

Westwood's original description of *T. aliris** from Borneo, and Butler's original description of *T. pseudaliris*† are appended for reference.

Genus 40.—STICHOPHTHALMA, Felder.

Stichophthalma,‡ Felder, Wien. Ent. Monatsch., vol. vi, p. 27 (1862); *Thaumantis*, Westwood, Gen. D. L., vol, ii, p. 335 (1851), *in part*; id., Trans. Ent. Soc. Lond., new series, vol. iv, p. 170 (1856), *in part*.

"Differs from *Thaumantis*, Hübner, in the following points: HEAD smaller; *antennæ* shorter; *palpi* much longer, differing in the sexes. FOREWING with the *subcostal nervure*

---

* *Thaumantis aliris*, Westwood, Trans. Ent. Soc. Lond., new series, vol. iv, p. 176, pl. xvii (1856), *female*. HABITAT: Borneo. EXPANSE: *Female*, 6·25 inches. DESCRIPTION: "UPPERSIDE, *forewing* fuscous, the base more ferruginous, an oblique median fascia, and two subapical spots, white. *Hindwing* fuscous, the outer half more or less fulvous. UNDERSIDE, *both wings* grey at the base, with brown irregular spots; a broad oblique irregular brown fascia. *Forewing* with the oblique white fascia of the upperside, joining a pale line parallel with the outer margin. *Hindwing* with two large equal ocelli beyond the middle, and the apex broadly fulvous." (*Westwood*, l. c.) Westwood's figure of the female of this species differs from our female specimen of *T. pseudaliris* from the Donat range, on the upperside being entirely dark brown, not tinted at the base with ferruginous; the white band on the forewing is much wider and of nearly equal width throughout, and almost reaches the inner margin, where it is tinted with lilac. On the underside the white band is developed into a large triangular patch, broken at the costa beyond its middle by a patch of brown, covered with numerous darker striæ. On the hindwing the ocelli are many times larger than in our specimen, and the markings throughout are darker and bolder.

† *Thaumantis pseudaliris*, Butler, Trans. Linn. Soc. Lond., Zoology, second series, vol. i, p. 538, n. 2, pl. lxviii, fig. 1 (1876), *male*; *T. aliris*, Westwood, Trans. Ent. Soc. Lond., new series, vol. iv, p. 176, n. 7 (1856), *male*. HABITAT: Malacca. EXPANSE: 4·6 to 5·0 inches. DESCRIPTION: "This species differs from the male of *T. aliris*, from Borneo, in having the band of the *forewing* above half the width, not notched, and yellower in tint; the basal area of *both wings* ferruginous. UNDERSIDE, the area beyond the band is not striated, and is of the same rusty red colour as the broad outer border; the latter is also paler at the edge, and is cut much shorter by the obliquity of the transverse band; the basal spots are rusty red instead of red-brown and black; the irregular band of the *hindwing* is paler and much more constricted in the middle, the external and discal areas are altogether paler and more uniform in tint; the ocelli are considerably smaller and paler, the spots between the ocelli and the yellow submarginal spots are obsolete. As Professor Westwood figures the Bornean female, I am obliged to rename the Malacca male." (*Butler*, l. c.)

"The MALE is considerably smaller [than *T. aliris*, female, from Borneo], with the oblique fascia of the UPPERSIDE of the *forewing* about half the width of that of the female, and with two white spots near the tip, which is considerably suffused with ferruginous at the base; such is also the colour of the base of the *hindwing*, which is gradually shaded off to a rich fulvous colour; there is, however, a broad dark longitudinal patch extending to the outer margin of the wing, occupying the space between the second and third branches of the subcostal nervure. On the UNDERSIDE the markings agree in the two sexes, except that the oblique bar of the *forewing* is even rather narrower than on the upperside, and the great ocelli are also much less conspicuous than in the female. The middle of both *fore* and *hindwing* is occupied with a broad irregular chocolate-ferruginous bar." (*Westwood*, l. c.)

‡ Στικος, series; ὀφθαλμὸς, ocellus.

having four branches [including the terminal portion], all the branches free; the *upper discoidal* nervule more remote from the subcostal than from the lower discoidal nervule; the *lower disco-cellular* nervule highly convex in the middle. HINDWING with the upper trunk of the nervules more deflexed; the *third median* nervule not at all bent; the *internal nervure* lower, shorter, and more bent." (*Felder*, l. c.)

This genus contains the largest and handsomest butterflies of the subfamily; indeed *S. camadeva* and *S. louisa* are amongst the most splendid of the butterflies occurring in India. Only five species are known, of which three are included in the Indian list, but the authority for one of them, *S. nourmahal*, is doubtful; the other two are found one in China, *S. howqua*, and the other in Cambodia, *S. cambodia*. They all have in a more or less defined degree a curiously arranged series of spots on the outer margin of the forewing, consisting of a triangular or diamond shaped submarginal series, the outer corner of each produced and coalescing with a marginal series of concave lunules. The secondary sexual characters of the male insect consist only of a small erectile tuft of hairs on the hindwing near the base of the subcostal nervure; in colour and pattern the sexes are similar so far as is known.

Key to the Indian species of Stichophthalma.

A. Upperside, basal area of both wings rich brown, outer area of forewing purplish-white.

292. S. CAMADEVA, N.-E. India.

B. Upperside, basal area of both wings pale bright fulvous; outer area of forewing nearly pure white.

293. S. LOUISA, Upper Tenasserim.

C. Upperside, basal area of both wings rich chestnut brown; outer area of forewing fulvous, the extreme apex fuscous.

294. S. NOURMAHAL, Sikkim (?) Borneo.

292. Stichophthalma camadeva, Westwood.

Morpho (Thaumantis) camadeva, Westwood, Cab. Or. Ent., p. 9, pl. iv (1848); *Thaumantis camadeva*, id., Trans. Ent. Soc. Lond., new series, vol. iv, p. 177, n. 8 (1856); id., Doubleday, Hewitson, Gen. D. L., vol. ii, p. 337, pl. lv, fig. 2 (1851).

HABITAT: Eastern Himalayas, Assam, Cachar, Sylhet.

EXPANSE: 5·1 to 6·3 inches.

DESCRIPTION: "UPPERSIDE: *Forewing* white, tinged with a delicate purplish leaden colour, the base of a rich brown; with a row of lozenge-shaped spots, and another of brown continuous lunules near the outer margin. *Hindwing* brown, the base of a richer colour; considerably beyond the middle is a row of large leaden-white lunules, and a smaller row close to the margin of the wing. UNDERSIDE: The basal portion of *both wings* is of a delicate buff with a slight greenish tinge, and the apical portion fulvous; a broad irregular fulvous fascia runs across both wings before the middle, edged on each side by a black line, and beyond the middle, each wing has a row of five red ocelli, with black irides, beyond which are two pale brown continuous fasciæ. The three or four round brown spots on the upperside preceding the rows of lozenge-shaped marks near the extremity of the forewing occupy the place of the ocelli of the underside; and the broad row of white lunules on the hindwing is the continuation of the pale space between the lozenge-shaped spots and row of lunules of the forewing; since, in a strong light, the dark ground-colour of the hindwing also exhibits a row of still darker-coloured lozenge-shaped spots, preceding the pale lunules. On the underside of the forewing the broad fascia is dilated on the anterior half of the wing, so as to include half of the discoidal cell and the like distance beyond it, inclosing a black lunule which marks the nervule which closes the cell; the ocelli are preceded by a longitudinal darker cloud; the larger ocelli bear a slender white central lunule, and the red pupil is separated from the black iris by a fulvous ring; the anal angle is marked with a black spot, outwardly edged with white. The upperside of the body is brown, but the underside, with the palpi, legs, and anal area of the hindwing, are fulvous." (*Westwood*, l. c. in Cab. Or. Ent.)

"The general appearance of the two sexes is nearly identical; the male has a tuft of hairs at the base of the hindwing, on the upperside." (*Westwood*, l. c. in Trans. Ent. Soc. Lond.)

STICOPHTHALMA CAMADEVA, Moore.

Mr. Wood-Mason met with this species in profusion in May in the forests around Silcuri, Cachar; other specimens were taken in July. Mr. A. O. Hume found it commonly in the forests of Eastern Munipur in the spring, and Mr. Otto Möller has taken numerous specimens in the neighbourhood of Darjiling in June.

The figure on the opposite page shows the upper and undersides of a female specimen from Sikkim in the Indian Museum, Calcutta.

293. **Stichophthalma louisa,** W.-M.

Thaumantis louisa, Wood-Mason, Proc. A. S. B., p. 163 (1877); id., Journ. A. S. B., vol. xlvii, pt. ii, p. 175, pl. xii (1878), *male*; id., Moore, Proc. Zool. Soc. Lond., 1878, p. 827; id., Marshall, Journ. A. S. B., vol. li, pt. ii, p. 40, n. 5 (1882), *female*.

HABITAT: Upper Tenasserim.

EXPANSE: ♂, 5·25; ♀, 5·8 inches.

DESCRIPTION: "MALE: UPPERSIDE whitish. *Forewing* with the basal half, and *hindwing* with the basal two-thirds deep and pure fulvous; each wing, as in *S. howqua*, with a submarginal lunular fascia with spear-shaped spots coalescing, deep violaceous-fuscous; the lunules and spots of the hindwing much larger. UNDERSIDE luteous-fulvous. *Forewing* with the median part only whitish, scarcely tinted with luteous; with four sinuate lines, two basal deep brown, two others submarginal, obsolete, and only near the anal angle brown coloured. *Forewing* with five ocelli all obsolete; *hindwing* with two, rufous, with whitish pupil and slender black iris, and three intermediate obsolete." (*Wood-Mason*, l. c. in Journ. A. S. B.). "FEMALE differs from the figure of the male in the following particulars: UPPERSIDE with the fulvous ground-colour on the *hindwing* extending completely up to, and embracing the heads of, the hastate border spots, the ground-colour of the outer portion of *both wings* being not white but pure French grey, the only traces of pure white being on the *forewing*, at the middle of the costal margin and outside the median transverse line and decreasing from its costal end. The dusky tipping at the apex also extends below the subcostal nervure. UNDERSIDE with the fulvous portions not luteous, but strongly suffused with grey, and altogether of a far colder tone; the hastate border spots of the upperside pale, but perfectly distinct and complete. *Hindwing* with the outer submarginal lunular line obsolete, the inner one slender and incomplete, whereas in the figure of the male both these lunular lines are complete and prominent. It of course lacks the tuft of erectile hairs on the hindwing which is present in the male." (*Marshall*, l. c.)

"This fine and distinct species belongs to the same division of the genus as *S. camadeva*, *S. nourmahal*, *S. cambodia*, and *S. howqua*,* to the last of which it is most nearly related, but from which it differs in having the upperside of the wings white and fulvous, instead of fulvous throughout, and in having five spots, the red rings of the ocelli, on the underside of the forewing, and only two well-developed ocelli on the hindwing, instead of three and five ocelli respectively." (*Wood-Mason*, l. c. in Journ. A. S. B.)

The type specimen was taken at Taoo, 3,000 to 6,000 feet altitude, by Limborg in the cold weather. Capt. C. T. Bingham took the female above described between March and May in the Lower Thoungyeen forests, and Mr. Butler records it (Ann. and Mag. of Nat. Hist., fifth series, vol. x, p. 372, 1882) from the Thoungyeen valley, from specimens also collected by Capt. Bingham.

---

* *Thaumantis howqua*, Westwood, Trans. Ent. Soc. Lond., new series, vol. i, p. 174 (1851); idem, id., vol. iv, p. 178, n. 9, pl. xviii, figs 2, 2a (1856); *Stichophthalma howqua*, Felder, Wien Ent. Monatsch., vol. vi, p. 28, n. 23 (1862). HABITAT: Shanghai, China. EXPANSE: 5 inches. DESCRIPTION: MALE and FEMALE: UPPERSIDE, *both wings* fulvous, with a submarginal series of much curved black lunules, and inwardly with black spear-shaped spots coalescing with them, which are larger on the hindwing. UNDERSIDE, *both wings* luteous fulvous, paler than above, crossed by two oblique, irregularly sinuate black lines, the inner one crossing both cells but not reaching the abdominal margin of the hindwing, the outer one beyond the middle of the forewing about the middle of the hindwing recurved just before the anal angle of the hindwing, below which is an irrorated fuscous and grey spot. The two black lines are very wide at the costa of the forewing, decreasing irregularly towards the anal angle of the hindwing, the space between them darker than the rest of the ground. A discal series of five ocelli on both wings, red with whitish pupil and slender black iris, the first and fourth on the forewing and the fourth on the hindwing not quite perfect. Within the series of ocelli the ground is somewhat darker, becoming paler before reaching the outer fuscous line. A submarginal somewhat lunulate fuscous line. (Described from Westwood's figure).

294. Stichophthalma nourmahal, Westwood.

Thaumantis nourmahal, Westwood, Gen. D. L., vol. ii, p. 337, n. 8 (1851), *note*; idem, id., Trans. Ent. Soc. Lond., new series, vol. iv, p. 178, pl. xviii. figs. 1, 1*a* (1856); id., Moore, Horsfield and Moore, Cat. Lep. E. I. C., vol. i, p. 215, n. 442 (1857).

HABITAT: India (*Westwood*); Sikkim (*Moore*); Sikkim ? ? (*Kirby*); Borneo.

EXPANSE: ♂, 3·75; ♀, 4·25 (*Westwood*); 4·8 Sikkim (?) specimen in Indian Museum, Calcutta.

DESCRIPTION: "FEMALE: UPPERSIDE chestnut-fuscous. *Forewing* with a very broad oblique fulvous fascia beyond the middle, extending to the outer margin and anal angle, a common submarginal series of fuscous V-shaped marks, and another lunular of the same colour; a whitish subapical dot on the forewing. UNDERSIDE brownish fulvous, with two narrow oblique almost straight greenish silvery bands, the first passing through the middle of the discoidal cell, the second almost from the middle of the costa to the anal angle, each margined inwardly with a black line; the outer margin broadly paler, in which on the forewing are two ferruginous-fulvous ocelli, on the hindwing three, each marked in the middle with a whitish lunular dot; two black submarginal lines very flexuous and dentate, and a black spot at the anal angle slightly irrorated with lilascent."

"The description published by me in the Genera of Diurnal Lepidoptera, was made from a female at that time unique in the collection of W. W. Saunders, Esq., F.R.S. The East India Company has, however, subsequently received both sexes from India. The MALE differs from the female, as I am informed by Mr. F. Moore, merely in wanting the white subapical spot near the extremity of the forewing."

"On the upperside the wings are of a rich chestnut brown colour, the forewing having a very broad oblique fulvous fascia, extending from the costa to the outer margin and anal angle; the tip of the wing being dark brown, with a small white subapical spot in the female. There is also a series of submarginal brown V-shaped marks, and another of brown lunules in both wings. [and the hindwing is outwardly bordered with fulvous in continuation of the fascia of the forewing]. Underside, the colour is paler, with a broad oblique subcentral fascia, edged with a slender black slightly irregular line on each side, the one nearest the base being internally, and the outer one externally edged with a line of pale silvery greyish green scales. The discoidal cell in the forewing is closed by black veins, but in the hindwing the outer black striga forms its termination. The forewing has also five ocelli [the first, third and fourth obsolete, replaced by pale spots], and the hindwing three, in the alternate spaces between the nervules, the intervening spaces being marked by paler dots, indicating obsolete ocelli. Near the apex of both wings are two slender dentated black lines, ending at the anal angle [of the hindwing] in a black dot, slightly suffused with lilac scales." (*Westwood*, l. c. in Trans. Ent. Soc. Lond.)

There is a single female specimen in the Indian Museum, Calcutta, obtained from the old East India Company's Museum, which is marked "Darjeeling," and which is the only specimen we have seen. In spite of the authorities given above for its occurrence in India, we very much doubt the fact; of late years, at any rate as far as we know, no specimens have been obtained within our limits.

Genus 41.—CLEROME, Westwood.

Clerome, Westwood, Gen. D. L., vol ii, p. 333 (1851); idem, id., Trans. Ent. Soc. Lond., new series, vol. iv, p. 182 (1856), *Monograph*; *Faunis*, Hübner, Verz. Bek. Schmett., p. 55 (1816).

"BODY moderately robust; wings large, plainly coloured, with a row of small spots between the middle and the outer margin on the underside. *Head* rather broad. *Antennæ* long (two-thirds the length of the forewing), nearly straight, composed of rather long joints, terminated by a long, but very slender, scarcely distinct club formed of short joints. *Palpi* compressed, ascending obliquely to about the height of two-thirds of the eye, porrected in front nearly to the length of the head, not convergent, scaly; middle joint clothed behind with hairs applied to the face. *Thorax* oval, very hairy. *Abdomen* rather small and slender.

FOREWING large, oval-triangular. *Costa* very much arched; apex rounded; outer margin about two-thirds of the length of the costa, entire, slightly convex; inner angle rounded; inner margin rather longer than the outer, slightly dilated at the base in the male. *Costal* nervure extending to about two-thirds of the length of the costa; *subcostal* nervure with its first branch arising at about two-sevenths of the length of the wing; second branch arising at about three-fifths of the length of the wing; third and fourth arising at short distances beyond the second; all these branches free, the fourth extending to the tip of the wing; *upper disco-cellular* nervule very short, arising nearly at one-third of the length of the wing; *middle* disco-cellular equally short, nearly transverse; *lower* disco-cellular very long and curved, somewhat like the letter ഗ, the extremity reaching nearly to the middle of the wing, where it joins the third branch of the median nervure at a short distance beyond its base, terminating the closed discoidal cell nearly in a point. HINDWING broadly ovate; costa scarcely curved; outer margin rounded; anal angle rounded. The disc above, near the extremity of the thorax, is furnished with a tuft of fine hairs in the male. *Præcostal* nervure short, curved towards the body; *costal* nervure extending to about two-thirds of the length of the costa; *subcostal* nervure with its branches arising quite close to the base of the wing, the outer branch extending to the outer angle; *discoidal cell* very narrow and open; *median* nervure with its branches wide apart. FORELEGS of the MALE very small and brush-like, very woolly; of the FEMALE longer than those of the male, slender, scaly; tarsus not half the length of the tibia; articulations indistinct, except when denuded of scales; obliquely truncate at the tip; armed with very small spines. Four HINDLEGS long, strong, scarcely spined beneath; tibial spurs minute." (*Westwood*, l. c. in Gen. D. L.)

Clerome is a genus of plain-looking Butterflies, the upperside fulvous, marked only in some species with darker or lighter shades of the ground-colour towards the margins, but spotted and sometimes ocellated on the underside, and marked with fuscous lines. About fourteen species are at present known, inhabiting N.-E. India, Burma, the Malay peninsula and islands, and extending to China.

Key to the Indian species of Clerome.

A. Male and female, upperside fulvous. Underside with three fuscous strigæ, and a series of ochreous spots across both wings.

a. Male and female alike. Of moderate size (under three inches).

295. C. ARCESILAUS, Sikkim, Sylhet, Burma, Malay Peninsula, Java.

b. Male, upperside, forewing uniform fulvous; female with a discal paler band. Of large size (3·5 inches and above).

296. C. ASSAMA, Assam, Khasi Hills.

Except in size there is little difference between the males of the two Indian species, but as that difference is considerable, it will at once be found sufficient to separate them. The females are very distinct.

295. Clerome arcesilaus, Fabricius.

Papilio arcesilaus, Fabricius, Mant. Ins., vol. ii, p 28, n. 305 (1787); id., Donovan, Ins. India, pl. xxx, fig. 2 (1800); *Clerome arcesilaus*, Doubleday, Hewitson, Gen. D. L., vol. ii, p. 334, n. i, pl. liv*, fig. 5 (1851), *female*; id., Westwood, Trans Ent. Soc. Lond., new series, vol. iv, p. 183 (1856); *Faunis canens*, Hübner, Samml. Ex. Schmett. (1816-24); *Morpho leonteus*, Zinken, Nova Acta Acad. Nat. Cur., vol. xv, p. 170 pl. xvi, figs. 14, 15 (1831).

HABITAT: Sikkim, Sylhet, Upper Tenasserim, Siam, Malacca, Singapore, Java.

EXPANSE: 2·1 to 2·75 (*Westwood*); 2·7 to 2·9 inches.

DESCRIPTION: "Wings entire. UPPERSIDE fuscous-ochraceous, unmarked. UNDERSIDE fuscous or brownish-fuscous; *both wings* crossed by three obscure strigæ (the first sometimes subobsolete), and a series of yellowish dots."

"The uniform colour of the upperside of both wings, united to the minute and uniform size of the row of pale dots on the underside, will suffice to distinguish this species from *C. eumeus* [from China]. Specimens sent from Malacca by Mr. Wallace (about 2·5 inches in expanse) differ in the richer red-brown colour of the upperside, and in having the outer dark strigæ obsolete [on the underside] of the forewing. A specimen from Singapore, in the British

Museum, about 2·75 inches in expanse, does not differ from Javanese individuals in the same collection; whilst specimens from India and Sylhet, in the same collection, and of the same size, have the upperside richer and redder fulvous than the Java specimens, and on the underside the middle striga is more distinct, and much more angulated, and the series of white dots small." (*Westwood*, l. c.)

Mr. Distant does not give *C. arcesilaus* in his "Rhopalocera Malayana," but there is a female specimen in the Indian Museum, Calcutta, acquired from the old India Museum, London, from Singapore, and Westwood mentions *(ante)* a specimen in the British Museum from the same locality. We have specimens from Sikkim from the collection of the late L. Mandelli; from the Donat range in Upper Tenasserim taken by Captain C. Bingham in January, and others taken by him in the Thoungyeen forests in March and December. All these specimens are males and are very constant. Our female specimen from Singapore differs from the male in being a very little larger, and the inner margin of the forewing straight, and no tuft of hair on the upperside of the hindwing; it differs in tone of colouration from Indian examples as mentioned by Westwood. The Javan specimen in the India Museum is identical with Indian ones on the underside, but on the upperside the forewing especially is a darker fulvous. Limborg also met with this species above Ahsown in Upper Tenasserim in the cold weather.

An allied species has been recorded from Malacca.* It differs from *C. arcesilaus* in being smaller, the upperside ferruginous rather than fulvous, and with an ocellus on the hindwing. The underside is also ferruginous, the fifth lower spot on the forewing is developed into an ocellus, as also are the first and fifth on the hindwing.

296. **Clerome assama,** Westwood.

C. assama, Westwood, Trans. Ent. Soc. Lond., new series, vol. iv, p. 184 (1856).

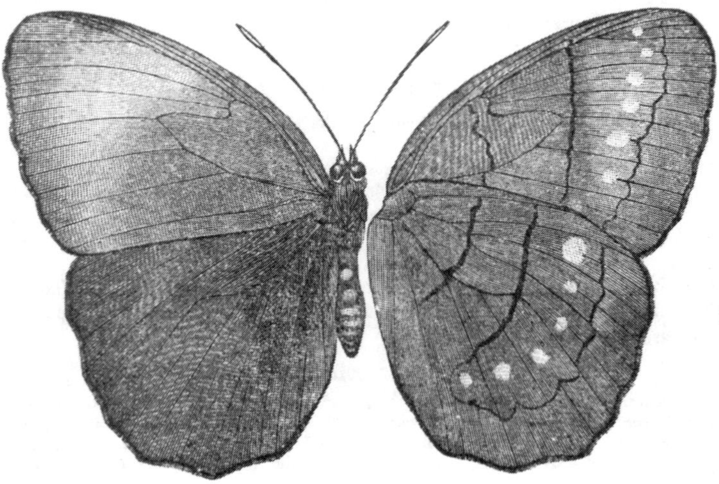

* *Clerome gracilis*, Butler, Ann. and Mag. of Nat. Hist., third series, vol xx, p. 401, pl. viii, fig. 7 (1867), *male*; id., Distant, Rhop. Malay., p. 81, pl. viii, fig. 1 (1882), *male*. HABITAT: Malacca, Singapore, Borneo. EXPANSE: *Male*, 2·3 inches. DESCRIPTION: "MALE: UPPERSIDE, *both wings* brownish ochraceous. *Hindwing* with a somewhat faint discal ocellated spot, situated between the second and first median nervules. UNDERSIDE somewhat paler, and crossed by two waved narrow fuscous fasciæ; the first passing through the middle of both cells, and the second commencing about the costal margin of the forewing, passing beyond the cellular apices and terminating near the middle of the abdominal margin of the hindwing; a submarginal and strongly sinuated narrow fuscous fascia to both wings. Between the middle and submarginal fasciæ are placed the following spots: on the forewing a series of four small whitish spots placed between the nervules, the first above the upper discoidal nervule, and the fourth beneath the first median nervule, followed between the second and first median nervules by an ocellated spot, black, with a pale centre and ochraceous and black margins. *Hindwing* with an ocellated spot between the subcostal nervules, followed by three whitish spots between the nervules, and an ocellated spot between the second and first median nervules *Body* and *legs* more or less concolorous with the wings. I have not seen the female of this species. It is one of the smallest species of the genus, and appears to be seldom found by collectors." (*Distant*, l. c.)

Habitat: India, Assam, Khasi Hills.

Expanse: 4·0 (*Westwood*); ♂, 3·4; ♀, 4·0 inches.

Description: **Male**: **Upperside** uniform fulvous. **Underside** darker fulvous, crossed by three fuscous lines, the first subbasal, the second beyond the middle of the wings, the third submarginal, very sinuous. Between the two outer lines in the *forewing* is a series of six small ochreous rounded spots from the costa to the first median interspace, the penultimate one the largest; on the *hindwing* there are six similar spots, the first much the largest. **Female** larger. **Upperside**, *both wings* a deeper fulvous, especially at the apex of the *forewing*, which is crossed by a broad curved lighter fulvous band, broadest at the costa, obsolete at the hinder angle; this band is outwardly somewhat distinctly defined by the darker ground-colour, inwardly it is diffused. **Underside** marked as in the male, but all the strigæ and the spots better defined, the latter being much larger.

This species is perhaps only a geographical variety of the *C. eumeus*, Drury, from China. It is larger, and has "the broad, oblique, fulvous fascia of the forewing [on the upperside of the female] but ill-defined, and gradually shaded off to the darker ground-colour of the wing. The three strigæ of the underside are distinct, the outer one more angulated; the white spots are of unequal size; the fifth in the forewing, and the first in the hindwing, being the largest." (*Westwood*, l. c.) These remarks evidently refer to the female, which is the sex of *C. eumeus* figured by Drury. The MALE apparently has not previously been described, unless the following remarks of Westwood (l.c.) refer to a male specimen: in no case does he state the sex of the specimens of this species described by him: "A specimen from Northern India, measuring 3·5 inches in expanse, has the wings on the upperside of an uniform fulvous brown colour, whilst on the underside they are similar to the above described individuals from Northern India."

The Indian Museum, Calcutta, has a male from the Khasi hills taken by Colonel Godwin-Austen, and another without history, but probably taken at the same time; and two females from the same locality, one of which is figured above, and shows the upper and undersides.

Another species, formerly included in the genus *Clerome*, occurs in the Malay Peninsula. It is a very remarkable butterfly, the wings are semi-transparent, upperside pale fuscous, hindwing with the abdominal half below the cell bright yellow, and the underside with two conspicuous lunulate discal fuscous strigæ, and other fuscous markings at the base of the wings. It has been placed under a separate subgeneric title, **Melanocyma**,* and forms the type and only species of the subgenus.

---

* Subgenus **Melanocyma**, *Westwood*.

Melanocyma, Westwood, Trans. Ent. Soc. Lond., new series, vol. iv., p. 186 (1856).

"In the 'Genera of Diurnal Lepidoptera' I arranged this singular insect in the genus *Thaumantis*. The arrangement of the branches of the nervures of the forewing is, however, unlike that of any of the species of that genus, agreeing in the circumstance of the second branch of the subcostal nervure of the forewing arising far beyond the extremity of the discoidal cell, as well as in the shortness of the wings, with *Clerome*, in which latter respect also it differs from *Drusilla*. The fact, however, of its being entirely destitute of ocelli is perhaps of sufficient importance to warrant its subgeneric separation, in which case it may receive the name of *Melanocyma*. The second branch of the subcostal nervure of the forewing arises at about three-fourths of the length of the wing from the base opposite to the junction of the costal nervure with the costa, and the fourth branch opposite to the junction of the extremity of the first branch with the costa. The lower disco-cellular nervule closing the discoidal cell is singularly angulated, and the costal nervure of the hindwing also extends to the middle of the costal margin. Another peculiarity of the species consists of the slight clothing of the wings, which enables the black undulated markings of the underside to be partially seen from above. The specimen which I have examined is a female." (*Westwood*, l. c.)

Melanocyma faunula, *Westwood*.

Thaumantis faunula, Westwood, Gen. D. L., vol. ii, pl. liv, fig. 1 (1851), *female*; *Clerome faunula*, idem, id., p. 334, *note*; *Clerome (Melanocyma) faunula*, Westwood, Trans. Ent. Soc. Lond., new series, vol. iv, p 186, pl. xxi, fig. 2 (1856), *female*; *Clerome faunula*, Distant, Rhop. Malay., p. 81, pl. viii, fig. 2 (1882), *female*. **Habitat**: Malacca, Mount Ophir, Singapore, Cambodia. **Expanse**: *Female*, 3·9 inches. **Description**: "**Female**: **Upperside**, *both wings*, pale fuscous. *Hindwing* with the abdominal half beneath the cell, and to about the second median nervule bright shining yellow. *Forewing* with the upper disco-cellular nervule very darkly infuscated, and with the following dark markings: a transverse streak across the cell near the apex, preceded by a rounded spot, beneath which are two other spots situated between the base of the first median nervule and the submedian nervure; two discal, transverse, strongly waved and sinuated fasciæ, the first crossing the wing a little beyond the apex of the cell, and the second being somewhat submarginal; and a very faint, waved, narrow, marginal fascia, which is obsolete towards the apex. *Hindwing* with the following dark markings: an oblique fascia near the base terminating about the internal nervure; two very strongly waved and sinuated discal fasciæ, which become united at the lower subcostal nervule, the inner one then crossing the wing at the apex of the cell, and terminating near the middle of the submedian nervure, the outer one somewhat submarginal, and much less strongly waved and sinuated after passing the first median nervule, till it terminates at the submedian nervure; and a waved marginal fascia becoming obsolete towards the anal angle. UNDERSIDE pale greyish, marked as above, but with the yellow colouration of the *hindwing* richer and darker, and with all the fasciæ and spots very dark fuscous; costal area of the *forewing* pale fuscous. *Body* and *legs* more or less concolorous with the wings. This is not only a beautiful but also an aberrant species, it being quite destitute of ocellated spots—a character which Professor Westwood was reasonably of opinion should warrant its subgeneric separation. The wings are also semi-diaphanous, thus allowing the fasciæ beneath to be visible above." (*Distant*, l. c.)

SUBFAMILY V.—ACRÆINÆ, Bates.

Acræinæ, Bates, Journ. Ent., vol. ii, p. 176 (1864); *Acræidæ*, Doubleday, Gen. D. L., vol. i, p. 137 (1848).

"HEAD rather small, scaly, but little if at all hairy. *Eyes* oval or rounded, prominent. *Palpi* divergent, ascending, rising considerably above the forehead; basal joint short, hairy; second joint elongate, mostly much swollen, hairy. the hairs often very thinly scattered; third joint very short, especially in those species which have the second joint most swollen. *Antennæ* scarcely more than half the whole length of the body, rather abruptly clavate; the club compact, obtuse at the apex, the joints composing it not more distinct than those of the other portion of the antennæ. *Thorax* oval, generally rather elongate; the prothorax very distinct. *Abdomen* elongate, clavate, much arched; the last segment in the female often furnished with a corneous appendage. FOREWING opaque, or partially or wholly diaphanous, subtriangular, elongate; the apex more or less rounded; the costa but little arched; outer margin seldom more than half the length of the costa, sometimes nearly straight, except towards the apex, sometimes rounded; inner margin nearly straight. *Costal* nervure extending considerably beyond the middle of the costa; *subcostal* nervure invariably five-branched [if the termination of the subcostal nervure is counted as a branch, if not, it is only four-branched]; its first branch thrown off at or near to the end of the cell; the second always considerably beyond the cell; *discoidal cell* seldom more than half the length of the wing; *upper disco-cellular* nervule very short, or entirely wanting; *internal* nervure wanting. HINDWING obovate; the costa nearly straight; the outer margin much rounded; the inner margin about equal in length to the outer, slightly embracing the base of the abdomen. *Discoidal cell* always closed, narrow, sometimes very short, rarely half the length of the wing; *discoidal nervule* sometimes appearing to be a third subcostal nervule; sometimes united to the subcostal nervure, or to its second branch by a distinct upper disco-cellular; *lower disco-cellular* always united to the third median nervule, often very close to its origin. FORELEGS of the MALE with the femur mostly longer than the tibiæ; tibiæ nearly cylindric, smooth or very slightly spiny, longer than the tarsus; tarsus cylindrical or slightly fusiform, sometimes one-jointed, sometimes showing indications of four or five joints. Of the FEMALE with the tarsus four or five-jointed; each joint, except the fifth when present, armed at the apex with a short pair of spines, sometimes covered by a bunch of stiff hairs arising from the base of the following joints: first joint generally about as long as the rest combined; the second, third and fourth progressively shorter, generally very obliquely truncate at the apex; fifth, when present, always very minute, barely distinguishable. MIDDLE and HINDLEGS rather short, with the tibiæ and femora about equal in length; tarsi rather shorter; tibiæ spiny, especially towards the apex, nearly cylindrical; tarsi spiny, the spines much longest at the sides; the first joint more than equal to the two following combined, nearly cylindric; second and third rather flattened, elongate ovate; the second slightly longer than the third; fourth joint shorter than the third; fifth rather longer than the second; claws without paronychia or pulvilli, broad at the base, where there is a large lobe, then suddenly narrowed, tapering to a very acute point, often much bent, especially the outer claw in the males, which is much shorter than the inner in many species."

"LARVA cylindric, spiny. PUPA suspended, slender, angulate." (*Doubleday*, l. c.)

The head-quarters of this subfamily is in Africa, but numerous species have been described from the New World, a few from Australia, and only two species from India, one of which occurs again in Java. Where they occur these two species are numerous in individuals, though in the North-West Himalayas one species, *A. vesta*, is decidedly local. Their flight is slow and sailing, they frequently settle, often at the end of a branch, stick, leaf or other conspicuous position, and appear to be quite unmolested by birds. Mr. de Nicéville has experimented with the carnivorous *Mantis* on many of the Butterflies believed to be offensive to birds, and he has found *A. violæ* is the only Butterfly which all the species of *Mantis* he has experimented with refuse to eat. The abdominal plate or pouch with which the females of both the Indian species are provided, is also found in the genus *Parnassius*, a genus of the subfamily *Papilioninæ*.

The *Acræinæ* are distinguished by their elongate wings, the hindwing being free from the abdomen along its inner margin and not channelled to enclose it. They are closely related to the *Heliconinæ* of America. The subfamily originally contained but a single genus, *Acræa*, which Doubleday in the Genera of Diurnal Lepidoptera divided into six well-marked sections, and these, so far as the Indian species go, appear to be worthy of generic separation. The general characters of the genus *Acræa* are those of the subfamily; the special characters of the sections represented in India are given in the following key.

Besides the six sections of *Acræa* only one other genus of the subfamily has been recognized (*Alæna*, Boisduval), which contains a single species (*A. amazoula*) from South Africa.

Neither of the Indian species have any sexual tufts or patches on the wings of the male insect.

Key to the Indian Genera of ACRÆINÆ.

A. Palpi very small, compressed, not rising to the level of the top of the eyes. Antennæ with a gradually formed club. Hindwing with the first subcostal nervule given off from the subcostal nervure some distance beyond the cell.

XLII.—PAREBA.

B. Palpi long, porrected forwards, rising to the level of the top of the eyes. Antennæ with an abruptly clavate flattened club. Hindwing with the first subcostal nervule given off from the subcostal nervure before the end of the cell.

XLIII.—TELCHINIA.

Genus 42.—PAREBA, Doubleday.

Acræa, section v, *Pareba*, Doubleday, Gen. D. L., vol. i, p. 142 (1848).

"PALPI small, the second joint but little swollen, scaly and hairy. First subcostal nervule of the forewing thrown off at [just before] the end of the cell. Discoidal nervure of the hindwing thrown off from the subcostal nervure considerably before it divides." (*Doubleday*, l. c.)

This genus contains but a single species, which occurs all along the Himalayas, and from Assam to Burma, and again in Java. As far as we know, it is only to be found in or very near to hills.

297. Pareba vesta, Fabricius.

Papilio vesta, Fabricius, Mant. Ins., vol. ii, p. 14, n. 130 (1787); id., Donovan, Insects China, pl. xxx, fig. 1 (1799); *Acræa vesta*, Godart, Enc. Méth., vol. ix, p. 233, n. 9 (1819); id., Horsfield, Cat. Lep. E. I. C., pl. iii, fig. 21, *larva* (1829); *Papilio terpsichore*, Cramer, Pap. Ex., vol. iv, pl. ccxcviii, figs. A—C (1780); *Telchinia issoria*, Hübner, Verz. bek. Schmett., p. 27, n. 220 (1816); *Acræa anomala*, Kollar in Hügel's Kaschmir, vol. iv, pt. ii, p. 425, pl. iii, figs. 3, 4 (1848).

HABITAT: Himalayas, Assam, Upper Burma, Java.

EXPANSE: 2·0 to 3·5 inches.

DESCRIPTION: MALE and FEMALE: UPPERSIDE, *both wings* fulvous, with the veins black, and more or less broadly bordered with black irrorations. *Forewing* with the costa and outer margin black, the latter bearing a marginal series of eight fulvous oblong spots, one in each interspace, except the last, which has two. A hook-shaped black mark in the cell, the disco-cellulars broadly defined with black, beyond which is a black streak from the costa to the second median nervule, angulated inwards at the third median nervule; a black mark near the base of the first median interspace, and another in continuation below the first median nervule. *Hindwing* with a series of four blackish spots, one in each interspace outside the cell from the first median nervule; a marginal highly dentate line leaving a series of yellow spots on the margin, one in each interspace, this line more or less coalescing with a submarginal series of diffused spots, the space between them being richer ochreous. UNDERSIDE, paler. *Forewing* marked as above, but the space between the angulated discal streak and a submarginal ochreous band whitish; the margin ochreous, bearing a highly dentate blackish line, obsolete at the apex. *Hindwing* with two submarginal black lines, the outer lunulate, the points of each lunule resting on the margin at the ends of the nervules, and the inner irregular, the space between them rich ochreous. Between the inner black line and the end of the cell is a broad band of whitish extending from the costa to the abdominal margin. Collar and costal base of the forewing rich ochreous, body black, marked with two series of round whitish spots. The markings of the female are usually darker than in the male.

A. vesta is a very variable species; in some specimens the black markings coalesce everywhere leaving only spots of ochreous on the forewing, which on that wing vary in tone from deep ochreous to pale whitish buff; in others again the black markings are confined to a narrow band on the costa of the forewing, and on the outer margin of both wings bearing a complete series of large ochreous spots; the disco-cellulars of the forewing are broadly black, and all the rest of the nervures of both wings are narrowly pencilled black. Between these two extremes every gradation is found. The size of the insect too varies greatly.

"LARVA feeds on the willow-leaved nettle (*Bohœmeria salicifolia*). Imago, July to September. Eggs deposited in September, and hatch in about twenty days. Length of young larva three to four lines, entirely black. When about three weeks old they moult and then hibernate, re-appearing in the following April. They moult again early in May, when they assume the red head. The larvæ generally feed on the upper branches of the plant, are gregarious, and drop to the ground when disturbed. Third moult early in June, about the middle of which month they suspend themselves by the tail near the bottom of the stems of the bushes, and there change to the pupa state. The imago appears in about fifteen days, in the first or second week in July. A few come out in August and September, but not in sufficient numbers to constitute a succession of broods. The imago is seldom found far from the food-plant, which grows near running water." (*A. Graham Young*, Proc. Zool. Soc. Lond., 1882, p. 243).

A. vesta is found, locally, throughout the Himalayas from the Chenab to Sikkim and extending through the Khasi hills to Upper Burma. Major C. H. T. Marshall has taken it in Chumba in May and June. Mr. A. Graham Young records the following note of its occurrence in Kulu:—

"It is a very local insect, but, where occurring, abundant. It is to be found in wet ravines at from 3,000 to 4,000 feet elevation in Kulu. It is not a rapid flier and is easily captured; when at rest it may be taken with the fingers. It is very constant in its appearance, frequenting the same localities year after year. The imago does not hibernate." (Note by *Mr. A. Graham Young*, Proc. Zool. Soc. Lond., 1882, p. 243.)

Freiherrn v. Hügel took it at Mussoorie; Mr. E. T. Atkinson records it from the submontane tracts of Kumaon. In Sikkim Mr. de Nicéville met with it in profusion at from 2,000 to 7,000 feet elevation in October, the larvæ covering the weeds all along the cart-road between Chunabati and Darjiling; in Simla he only met with it in a limited area of about 200 yards in the bed of a stream; and the Indian Museum has specimens from Bhutan, Sibsagar, the Dafla and Khasi hills, and from Upper Burma.

Genus 43.—TELCHINIA, Hübner.

Telchinia, Hübner, Verz. bek. Schmett., p. 27 (1816); id., Moore, Lep. Cey., p. 65 (1881); *Acræa*, section iv, *Telchinia*, Doubleday, Gen. D. L., vol. i, p. 141 (1848).

"FOREWING narrow, triangular; costa slightly arched towards the end, apex scarcely rounded; exterior margin oblique, slightly convex; inner margin short. *Costal* nervure extending to two-thirds of the margin: first subcostal nervule emitted at a short distance before the end of the cell; second, third and fourth at about equal distances apart beyond the end of the cell; *discoidal cell* long; *disco-cellulars* very oblique, *upper* bent near the subcostal nervure, concave below, *lower* straight; *discoidal* nervules from the angle and end of the upper disco-cellular; *second median* nervule emitted at a short distance before the end of the cell, *first* at one-half the length of the cell; *submedian* nervure slightly recurved. HINDWING small, short, broadly ovate; costa straight, outer margin convex; *costal* nervure extending to the apex, *præcostal* nervure slightly bent outward at its end; *first subcostal* nervule emitted at four-fifths from the base; *discoidal cell* long; *disco-cellulars* very oblique, the *upper* concave, the *lower* straight, *discoidal* nervule from their middle; *second median* nervule emitted at a short distance before the end of the cell; *third median* nervule from more than one-half the length of the cell; *submedian* and *internal* nervures slightly recurved. BODY slender, abdomen long, last segment of the female furnished with a corneous appendage; *palpi* ascending, stout, finely pilose, second joint projecting slightly beyond the head, third joint very short; *legs* slender; anterior tarsi of the male clothed with short spiny scales, fore tarsi of the female armed with a pair of spines on each joint; *antennæ* abruptly clavate." (*Moore*, l. c.)

This genus is represented by but a single species in India, which seems chiefly confined to the plains, seldom ascending into the mountains. It occurs in the moister tracts of eastern continental, and throughout peninsular India and in Ceylon, where it has been taken up to 4,000 feet elevation. There are numerous species of this group in Africa and Madagascar.

298. **Telchinia violæ**, Fabricius.

Papilio violæ, Fabricius, Syst. Ent., p. 460, n. 74 (1775); *Acræa violæ*, Horsfield, Cat. Lep. E. I. C., pl. viii, figs. 2, *larva*; 2 *a*, *pupa* (1829); *Telchinia violæ*, Moore, Horsfield and Moore, Cat. Lep. E. I. C., vol i, p. 135, n. 272, pl. v, figs. 1, *larva*; 1*a*, *pupa* (1857); idem, id., Lep. Cey, p. 66, pl. xxxiii, figs. 1, *male*; 1*a*, *female*; 1*b*, *larva* and *pupa* (1881); *Papilio cephea*, Cramer, Pap. Ex., vol. iv, pl. ccxcviii, figs. D, E (1780); *Telchinia cephea*, Hübner, Verz. bek. Schmett., p. 27, n. 213 (1816).

HABITAT: India, Ceylon.

EXPANSE: 1·8 to 2·5 inches.

DESCRIPTION: "MALE: UPPERSIDE, *both wings* ochreous-red. *Forewing* with a small black spot and an oblique streak within the cell, a large disco-cellular streak, an upper discal oblique series of four small spots, a single spot below these, and another between the median and submedian nervures; costal margin black speckled, exterior margin and up the veins for a short distance, black. *Hindwing* with a small black spot at the end of the cell, another on the costal border, and a black marginal band traversed by a series of pale yellow spots. FEMALE paler, with the markings and marginal band broader, the *hindwing* also having two black spots in the cell, two on the disco-cellular nervule, and a curved discal series beyond. UNDERSIDE: MALE glossy red; black spots and marginal border of the *forewing* as on the upperside, the latter bordered inwardly with yellowish-white. *Hindwing* with a basal cluster of five black-ringed white spots, two costal black spots, three discoidal and a discal outer series of smaller spots; the marginal band with larger yellowish-white spots and inner border. FEMALE duller coloured. *Hindwing* pale yellowish-ochreous, marked as above, also with a basal cluster of ochreous-white black-ringed spots, and the marginal band with larger spots."

"LARVA pale purple-brown; the segments armed with six rows of lengthened branched spines. Feeds on *Cucurbitaceæ*. PUPA reddish-white, streaked with black; the abdominal streaks spotted with red." (*Moore*, l. c. in Lep. Cey.)

This species is less variable than *P. vesta*, but in some specimens many of the black spots are obsolete. Mr. de Nicéville has taken it commonly in Calcutta throughout the year. It is not uncommon in Sikkim, and Mr. E. T. Atkinson records it from the submontane districts of Kumaon; which is probably its westerly limit in the north. It is found in the moister parts of the Peninsula on both coasts; we have specimens from Malwan on the west coast, and from Rajamundry on the East; and there are specimens in the Indian Museum, Calcutta, from Badrachallum, Madras City, Bangalore and Trevandrum. "Found generally in Ceylon in the plains and up to about 4,000 feet throughout the year." (*Mackwood*). "Common at Kandy." (*Wade*).

The figure shows the upper and undersides of a male specimen from Calcutta, in the Indian Museum, Calcutta.

INDEX TO VOL. I.

[Specific names are printed in small type (actæa); specific synonyms and varieties in italics *(adamsoni)*; generic names in small capitals (ACRÆA); generic synonyms in small capital italics (*AEMONA*); subfamily and family names in large capitals (ACRÆINÆ); and subfamily and family synonyms in large capital italics (*ACRÆIDÆ*.)]

NOTE.—Part I, containing the title page, dedication, list of illustrations of Vol. I, glossary of technical terms, preface, introduction, and pp. 21—94, with Frontispiece and Plates I—IX, was published in August, 1882. Part II, containing pp. 95—327, with Plates X—XVI, was published in August, 1883.

END OF VOL. I.

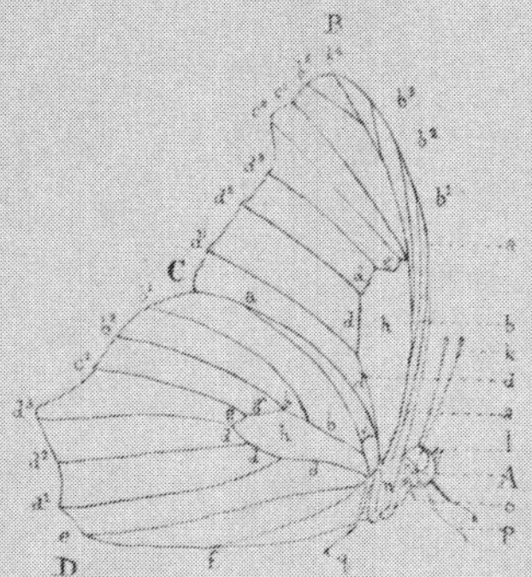

MELANITIS ISMENE

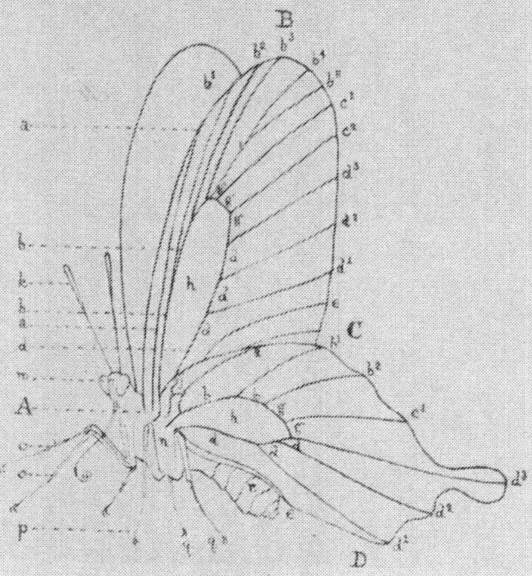

PAPILIO ARISTOLOCHIÆ

OUTLINE FIGURES.

a, costal nervure. b, subcostal nervure. b, b, b, b, b, subcostal nervules. c, c, discoidal nervules. d, median nervure. d, d, d, median nervules. e, submedian nervure. f, internal nervure. g, discocellular nervules. h, discoidal cell. j, præcostal nervure. k, antennæ. l, labial palpi. m, eye. n, thorax. o, forelegs (minute in Melanitis). p, midlegs. q, hindlegs. A, base of wings. B, apex of forewing. C, hinder angle of forewing and apex of hindwing. D, anal angle of hindwing. A, B, costal margin of forewing, or, costa. B, C, outer margin of forewing. A, C, inner margin of forewing, or, costa of hindwing. C, D, outer margin of hindwing. D, A, inner margin of hindwing, or, abdominal margin.

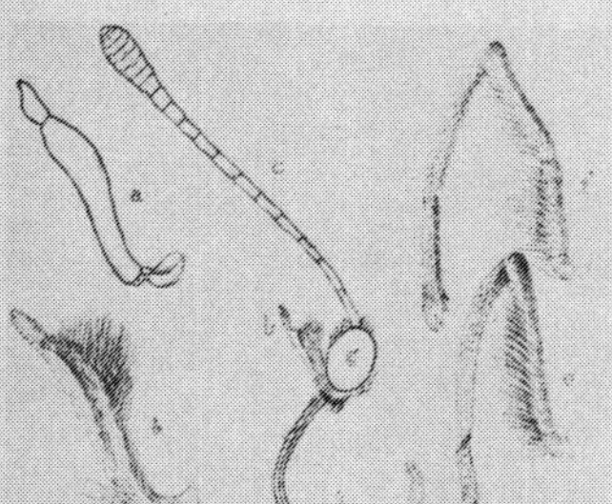

JUNONIA ASTERIE.

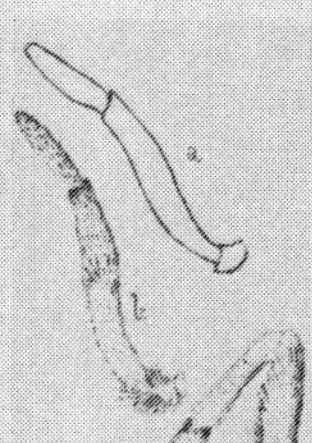

MYRINA JAFRA.

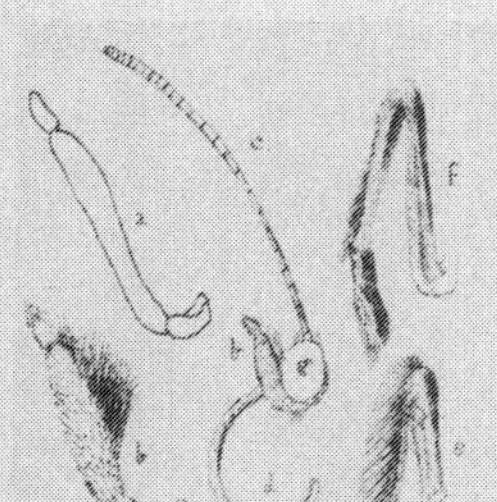

ELYMNIAS UNDULARIS.

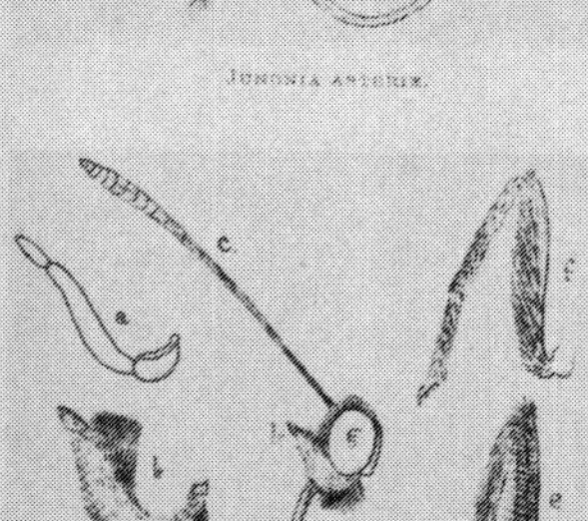

MELANITIS LEDA.

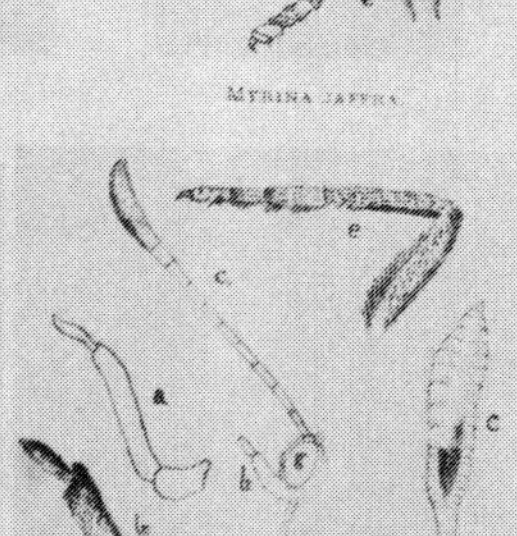

LAMPIDES ÆLIANUS.

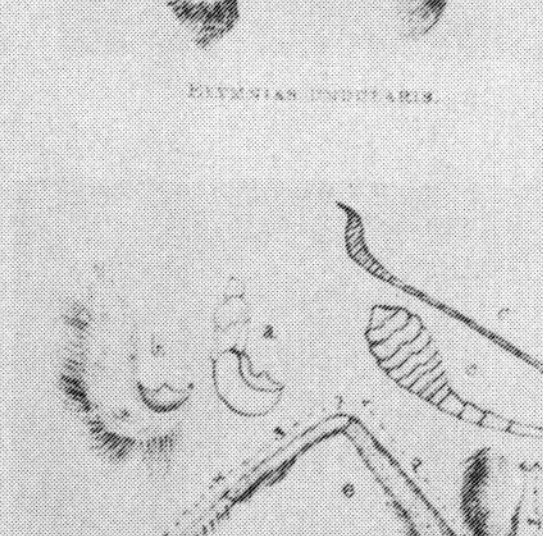

PAPILIO AGAMEMNON.

DISSECTIONS. a, palpi denuded of scales. b, palpi. c, antennæ. d, proboscis. e, foreleg of male. f, foreleg of female. g, eye. 1, coxa. 2, femur. 3, tibia. 4, tarsus. 5, ungues, or, claws (highly magnified).

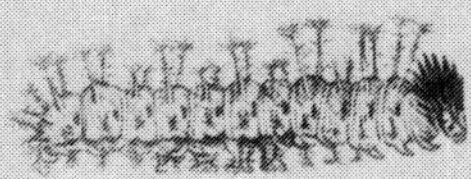

Athyma leucothoe

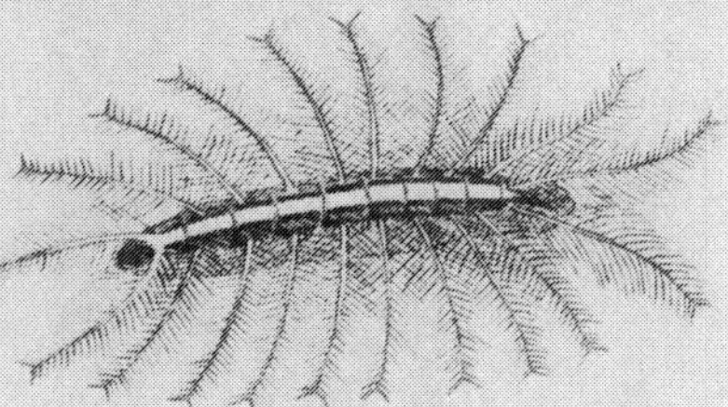

Adolias garuda

Amblypodia timoleon

Hebomoia glaucippe

Papilio polytes

Ismene œdipodia

TYPICAL CATERPILLARS.

Athyma leucothoe

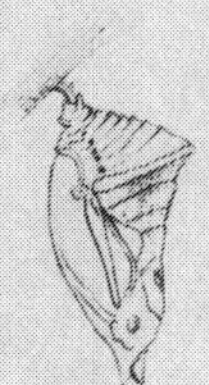

Adolias lubentina.

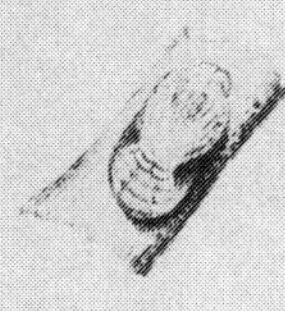

Amblypodia timoleon.

Hebomoia glaucippe

Papilio polytes

Ismene œdipodia

TYPICAL CHRYSALISES.

PLATE III

Fig. 1. HESTIA JASONIA, Westwood. ♂

PLATE II

Fig. 2. HESTIA CADELLI. W-M. & de N. ♂

Fig. 3. HESTIA CADELLI. W-M. & de N. ♀

B. L. Das del. J. Schaumburg part. del. et Lith. Calc. Cent. Press

PLATE V.

Fig. 4. IDEOPSIS DAOS, Boisduval. ♂

♀ ♂

Fig. 5. DANAIS MELANEUS, Cramer.

Fig. 6. DANAIS CROCEA, Butler. ♂

PLATE VI.

♂ ♀

Fig. 7. DANAIS AGLEA, Cramer

♂ ♀

Fig. 8. DANAIS SEPTENTRIONIS, Butler.

Fig. 9. DANAIS NILGIRIENSIS, Moore. ♂

PLATE VII.

Fig. 10. DANAIS CHRYSIPPUS, Linnæus.

♂ ♀

Fig. 11. EUPLŒA (SALPINX) RHADAMANTHUS, Fabricius.

Fig. 12. EUPLŒA (SALPINX) SINHALA, Moore.

PLATE VIII.

♂ ♀

Fig. 13. Euplœa (Trepsichrois) midamus, Linnæus

Fig. 14. Euplœa (Macroplœa) elisa, Butler ♂

Fig. 15. Euplœa (Crastia) crameri, Lucas. ♂

PLATE IX.

♂ ♀

Fig. 16. Euplœa core, Cramer.

♂ ♀

Fig. 17. Euplœa alcathoe, Godart.

♂ ♀

Fig. 18. Euplœa (Stictoplœa) hopei, Felder.

PLATE X.

Fig. 19. Zophoessa jalaurida, de Nicéville. ♂

Fig. 20. Lethe maitrya, de Nicéville. ♂

Fig. 21. [illegible] yama, Moore. ♂

♂ ♀

Fig. 22. Lethe dyrta, Felder.

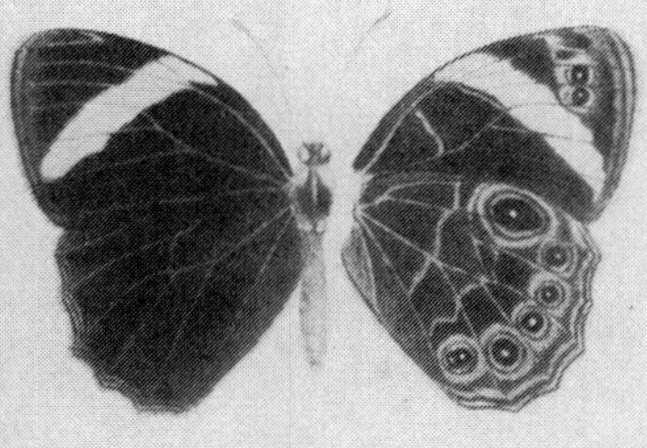

Fig. 23. Lethe verma, Kollar. ♂

PLATE XI

♂ ♀

Fig. 26 Lethe [illegible] Moore

Fig. 27 Neope pulaha Moore ♀

Fig. 28 Neope bhima Marshall ♀

PLATE XII.

Fig. 27. MELANITIS TRISTIS, Felder. ♂

Fig. 28. MELANITIS ISMENE, Cramer. ♂

Fig. 29. MELANITIS ZITENIUS, Herbst. ♀

♂ ♀

Fig. 30. [illegible], Moore.

Fig. 31. [illegible] ♂

Fig. 32. [illegible] damaris, Gray. ♂

PLATE XIV.

Fig. 33. Zethera diademoides, Moore. ♂

Fig. 34. Neorina crishna, Westwood. ♀

Fig. 35. Anadebis himachala, Moore. ♀

Fig. 36. RAGADIA CRISILDA, Hewitson. ♀

Fig. 37. ŒNEIS PUMILUS, Felder. ♂

Fig. 38. RHAPHICERA MOOREI, Butler. ♂

Fig. 39. EPINEPHILE DAVENDRA, Moore. ♀

♂ ♀

Fig. 40. EPINEPHILE PULCHELLA, Felder.

Fig. 41. EPINEPHILE MAIZA, Lang. ♀

Fig. 42. EREBIA SHALLADA, Lang. ♂

Fig. 43. EREBIA MANI, de Nicéville. ♂

Fig. 44. CALLEREBIA ANNADA, Moore. ♂

Fig. 45. AMECERA SCHAKRA, Kollar. ♂

Fig. 46. AMECERA SCHAKRA, Kollar. ♀

PLATE XVI
Hipparchia parisatis, Kollar
Hipparchia lehana, Moore
Aulocera werranga, Lang
Erites angularis, Moore
Mycalesis visala, Moore
Mycalesis oculus, Marshall
Mycalesis anaxias, Hewitson
Mycalesis blasius, Fabricius
Mycalesis junonia, Butler

PLATE XVII.

Fig. 67. Ypthima sakra, Moore. ♂